Multimedia Information Hiding Technologies and Methodologies for Controlling Data

Kazuhiro Kondo
Yamagata University, Japan

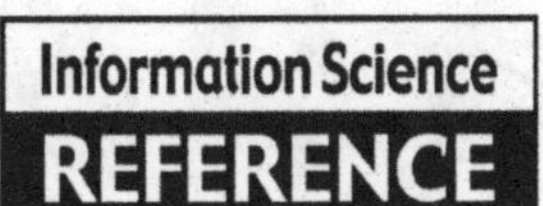

Managing Director: Lindsay Johnston
Editorial Director: Joel Gamon
Book Production Manager: Jennifer Romanchak
Publishing Systems Analyst: Adrienne Freeland
Development Editor: Christine Smith
Assistant Acquisitions Editor: Kayla Wolfe
Typesetter: Alyson Zerbe
Cover Design: Nick Newcomer

Published in the United States of America by
Information Science Reference (an imprint of IGI Global)
701 E. Chocolate Avenue
Hershey PA 17033
Tel: 717-533-8845
Fax: 717-533-8661
E-mail: cust@igi-global.com
Web site: http://www.igi-global.com

Library of Congress Cataloging-in-Publication Data

Multimedia information hiding technologies and methodologies for controlling data / Kazuhiro Kondo, editor.
p. cm.
Includes bibliographical references and index.
Summary: "This book presents the latest methods and research results in the emerging field of Multimedia Information Hiding (MIH)"--Provided by publisher.
ISBN 978-1-4666-2217-3 (hardcover) -- ISBN 978-1-4666-2218-0 (ebook) -- ISBN 978-1-4666-2219-7 (print & perpetual access) 1. Multimedia systems--Security measures. 2. Data encryption (Computer science) 3. Digital rights management 4. Digital watermarking. I. Kondo, Kazuhiro.
QA76.575.M83295 2012
006.7--dc23

2012019289

British Cataloguing in Publication Data
A Cataloguing in Publication record for this book is available from the British Library.

All work contributed to this book is new, previously-unpublished material. The views expressed in this book are those of the authors, but not necessarily of the publisher.

Editorial Advisory Board

List of Reviewers

Table of Contents

Chapter 15
A Benchmark Tool for Digital Watermarking 335
Keiichi Iwamura, Tokyo University of Science, Japan

Section 3
Information Hiding for Text and Binary Data

Chapter 16
Data Hiding for Text and Binary Files 351
Hirohisa Hioki, Kyoto University, Japan

Chapter 17
Data Embedding Methods Not Based on Content Modification 372
Hirohisa Hioki, Kyoto University, Japan

Section 4
New Directions in Multimedia Information Hiding

Chapter 18
Data-Embedding Pen 396
Seiichi Uchida, Kyushu University, Japan
Marcus Liwicki, German Research Center for Artificial Intelligence (DFKI), Germany
Masakazu Iwamura, Osaka Prefecture University, Japan
Shinichiro Omachi, Tohoku University, Japan
Koichi Kise, Osaka Prefecture University, Japan

Chapter 19
Multimedia Copyright Protection Scheme Based on the Direct Feature-Based Method 412
Rimba Whidiana Ciptasari, Kyushu University, Japan & Telkom Institute of Technology, Indonesia
Kouichi Sakurai, Kyushu University, Japan

Compilation of References 440

About the Contributors 464

Index 470

Detailed Table of Contents

Foreword xiv

Preface xvi

Acknowledgment xxii

Section 1
Information Hiding for Audio and Speech

Chapter 1
Information Hiding for Audio Signals 1
Akira Nishimura, Tokyo University of Information Sciences, Japan
Kazuhiro Kondo, Yamagata University, Japan

This chapter provides a general overview of audio data hiding. The general issues are discussed first, followed by the basic techniques used to hide data in audio signals, including bit stealing, spread spectrum methods, echo methods, and quantization index modulation. This is followed by a brief description of the recent proposals presented at the Institute of Electronics, Information, and Communication Engineers of Japan (IEICE) Multimedia Information Hiding (MIH) Technical Group Meetings.

Chapter 2
Reversible Audio Data Hiding in Spectral and Time Domains 19
Akira Nishimura, Tokyo University of Information Sciences, Japan

Reversible data hiding is a technique whereby hidden data are embedded in host data in such a way that the host data consistency is perfectly preserved and the host data are restored when extracting the hidden data. This chapter introduces basic algorithms for reversible data hiding, histogram shifting, histogram expansion, and compression. This chapter also proposes and evaluates two reversible data hiding methods, i.e., hiding data in the frequency-domain using integer Discrete Cosine Transform (DCT) and modified DCT and hiding in the time domain using linear prediction and error expansion. As no location map is required to prevent amplitude overflow, the proposed method in the time domain achieves a storage capacity of nearly 1 bit per sample of payload data. The proposed methods are evaluated by the payload amount, objective quality degradation of stego signal, and payload concealment.

This chapter introduces a state-of-the-art scheme of non-blind digital-audio watermarking, based on the properties of the human cochlear. It is based on the concept of embedding inaudible watermarks into an original sound by controlling its phase characteristics in relation to the characteristics of Cochlear Delay (CD). Inaudible watermarks are embedded into original signals by applying Infinite Impulse Response (IIR) all-pass filters with CDs and they are then extracted from the phase difference between the original and watermarked sounds. The results obtained from objective and subjective evaluations and robustness tests revealed that the CD-based approach is considerably more effective in satisfying the requirements for non-blind inaudible watermarking. Embedding limitations with the CD-based approach were investigated with various evaluations. These results also revealed that embedding limitations with the CD-based approach could be improved by using parallel, cascade, and composite architectures for the CD filters.

In this chapter, a time-domain high-bit-rate information hiding method using interpolation techniques, which can extract embedded data in both informed (non-blind) and non-informed (blind) ways, is proposed. Three interpolation techniques are introduced for the information hiding method, i.e., spline interpolation, Fourier-series interpolation, and linear-prediction interpolation. In performance evaluation, spline interpolation was mainly examined as an example implementation. According to the simulation of information hiding in music signals, the spline interpolation-based method achieved audio-information hiding for CD-audio signals at bit rate of about 2.9 kbps, and about 1.1 kbps under MP3 compression (160 kbps). The objective sound quality measured by the Perceptual Evaluation of Audio Quality (PEAQ) was maintained if the length of interpolation data increased. The objective sound quality was also evaluated for the Fourier series-based implementation and the linear prediction-based one. Fourier series interpolation achieved the same sound quality as spline interpolation did. Linear prediction interpolation required longer interpolation signals to get good sound quality.

This chapter presents a method of aerial acoustic communication in which data is modulated using OFDM (Orthogonal Frequency Division Multiplexing) and embedded in regular audio material without significantly degrading the quality of the original sound. It can provide data transmission of several hundred bps, which is much higher than is possible with other audio data hiding techniques. The proposed method replaces the high frequency band of the audio signal with OFDM carriers, each of which is power-controlled according to the spectrum envelope of the original audio signal. The implemented system enables the transmission of short text messages from loudspeakers to mobile handheld devices at a distance of around 3m. This chapter also provides the subjective assessment results of audio clips embedded with OFDM signals.

This chapter proposes two data-hiding algorithms for stereo audio signals. The first algorithm embeds data into a stereo audio signal by adding data-dependent mutual delays to the host stereo audio signal. The second algorithm adds fixed delay echoes with polarities that are data dependent and amplitudes that are adjusted such that the interchannel correlation matches the original signal. The robustness and the quality of the data-embedded audio will be given and compared for both algorithms. Both algorithms were shown to be fairly robust against common distortions, such as added noise, audio coding, and sample rate conversion. The embedded audio quality was shown to be "fair" to "good" for the first algorithm and "good" to "excellent" for the second algorithm, depending on the input source.

G.711 is the most popular speech codec for Voice over IP (VoIP). This chapter proposes a method for embedding data into G.711-coded speech for conveying side information for enhancing speech quality such as bandwidth extension or packet loss concealment. The proposed method refers to a low-bit rate encoder to determine how many bits are embedded into each sample. First, a variable-bit rate data hiding method is proposed as a basic framework of the proposed method. Then, the proposed method is extended to achieve fixed bit rate data hiding. According to comparison experiments, the proposed method is proved to achieve higher speech quality compared with the conventional method. Moreover, the authors developed a low-complexity speech bandwidth extension method that uses the proposed data hiding method.

Steganography can transmit supplementary data without changing conventional data formats. The concept of high value-added communications is drawn from this advantage of steganography. As a specific application of the concept, this chapter describes two topics about the enhancement of the speech quality in telephony communications by steganography. A packet loss concealment technique and a band extension technique are explained. These techniques employ steganography for transmitting side information for improving the performance of signal processing. In addition, this chapter describes an efficient steganography technique devised for G.711, the most common codec for telephony speech standardized by ITU-T. The proposed technique, named selective LSB replacement technique, outperforms the conventional one in order to decrease the degradation caused by embedding side information into speech data by steganography.

These authors are developing audio watermarking techniques that enable the extraction of embedded data by mobile phones. They applied acoustic interpolation of human auditory organs to embed data in full phone-line frequency ranges, where human auditory response is important for facilitating data extraction, using 3G mobile phones. They are interested in applying this technique to a mobile guide system for use in museums. In particular, they are considering applying audio watermarking techniques for synchronizing the stored contents of mobile terminals based on the spatial positions of the terminal and the temporal positions of playback contents in surrounding media. For this purpose, they are developing five linear spatial location identification codes that transfer to mobile terminals via two-channel stereo audio media that have embedded watermarks. They are also developing time codes that continuously transfer to mobile terminals via audio media. In this chapter, the authors initially describe their proposed audio watermarking algorithm and then present the main topic of novel audio watermarking applications for position information delivery to mobile terminals.

This chapter reviews information hiding methods, with a focus on steganography and steganalysis. First, the authors summarize image data structures and image formats required by computers and the Internet. They then introduce several information hiding methods based on image formats including lossless (non-compression based), limited color-based image data, JPEG, and JPEG2000. The authors describe a steganographic method in detail, which is based on image segmentation using a complexity measure. They also introduce a method for applying this to palette-based image formats, reversible information hiding for grayscale images, and JPEG2000 steganography. The steganographic methods for JPEG and JPEG2000 described in this chapter give particular consideration to the naturalness of cover data. In the steganalysis section, the authors introduce two methods, i.e., a specific steganalysis method for LSB steganography and Bit-Plane Complexity Segmentation (BPCS) stegnography.

This chapter addresses a new class of Reversible Information Hiding (RIH) and its application to verifying the integrity of images. The method of RIH distorts an image once to hide information in the image itself, and it not only extracts embedded information but also recovers the original image from the distorted image. The well-known class of RIH is based on the expansion of prediction error in which a location map, which indicates the pixel block positions of a certain block category, is required to recover the original image. In contrast, the method described in this chapter is free from having to memorize

Chapter 15
A Benchmark Tool for Digital Watermarking...335
Keiichi Iwamura, Tokyo University of Science, Japan

This chapter presents an overview of benchmark tools for digital watermarking and describes a new benchmark tool that supports various attacks and has a graphical user interface. Digital watermarks are used to prevent unauthorized use of digital content such as illegal copying, unauthorized distribution, and falsification. Benchmark tools are required to measure the strength of digital watermarks. Stirmark and JEWELS are well-known benchmark tools. However, the functionality of existing tools is insufficient because they lack evaluation functions for multiple image attacks. In addition, users need to memorize each attack command and check results on another viewer because almost all the existing tools are implemented as command-line-based software without image viewers. Therefore, the authors classify attacks on digital watermarks and develop a new benchmark tool that includes attacking functions using multiple as well as single images. In addition, the tool has a graphical user interface that makes it easy to perform combinations of two or more attacks.

Section 3
Information Hiding for Text and Binary Data

Chapter 16
Data Hiding for Text and Binary Files...351
Hirohisa Hioki, Kyoto University, Japan

This chapter presents an overview of text-based and binary-based data hiding methods. Text methods, through which secret information is embedded into innocent-looking textual data, are mostly used for steganography. Binary methods are applied to program binary codes: executables and libraries. In binary methods, information is embedded into a binary code so that its functionality is preserved. Data hiding methods for binary codes have been studied intensively to perform watermarking for protecting software from piracy acts. A message can also be embedded into a binary code in a steganographic manner. Another method is also introduced, which is proposed for enhancing the performance of an executable file.

Chapter 17
Data Embedding Methods Not Based on Content Modification 372
Hirohisa Hioki, Kyoto University, Japan

Creation of a stego object by embedding information in a cover object often distorts the cover object. As more information is embedded, more annoying noise is introduced in stego objects. Although reversible embedding methods enable us to restore the original cover object even after embedding, stego objects are not free from distortions. Embedding information does not, however, always result in damaging the contents of the cover object. This chapter introduces data embedding methods that are not based on modification of the contents of cover objects: permutation steganography, metadata steganography, and cover generation methods. This chapter focuses on elaborating the basic principles of these techniques.

Section 4
New Directions in Multimedia Information Hiding

Chapter 18
Data-Embedding Pen 396
Seiichi Uchida, Kyushu University, Japan
Marcus Liwicki, German Research Center for Artificial Intelligence (DFKI), Germany
Masakazu Iwamura, Osaka Prefecture University, Japan
Shinichiro Omachi, Tohoku University, Japan
Koichi Kise, Osaka Prefecture University, Japan

In this chapter, the authors present a new writing device called data-embedding pen, where a single inkjet nozzle is attached to its pen tip. When writing a stroke, the nozzle produces an additional ink-dot sequence along the stroke. The ink-dot sequence can represent various meta-information, such as the writer's ID, the writing date, and a certain URL. Since the embedded meta-information is placed on the paper, it can be extracted by scanning or photographing the paper. Accordingly, by the data-embedding pen, a physical paper conveys any digital information. In other words, handwriting by the data-embedding pen can be a new medium connecting the physical and cyber worlds.

Chapter 19
Multimedia Copyright Protection Scheme Based on the Direct Feature-Based Method 412
Rimba Whidiana Ciptasari, Kyushu University, Japan & Telkom Institute of Technology, Indonesia
Kouichi Sakurai, Kyushu University, Japan

This chapter discusses the direct feature-based method as an alternative approach to digital watermarking. Fundamentally, the direct feature-based method is an extension of the digital signature scheme, which aims at multimedia authentication. The method covers several copyright protection properties, i.e. robustness to content manipulations and sensitivity to content modification. In addition, this method provides solutions to inherent problems that arise in traditional watermarking, such as quality degradation, the trade-off between data payload, and imperceptibility or robustness.

Compilation of References 440

About the Contributors 464

Index 470

Foreword

"Information Hiding" sounds a bit like a bad practice among people who are not always trusted by others. If you are asked by a friend "Are you hiding something from me?" you would instantly deny it, saying "No! No! I have nothing to hide. I'm a very honest man and trusted by all." However, that isn't really true, because you have a lot of information which you don't like to have known, even by your loved ones.

Yes, everyone has several types of confidential information. Therefore, everyone wants to have some good means to hide it securely. Information hiding technology in general came from such a natural desire.

The information age directed people's eyes toward new digital technologies called "watermarking" and "steganography." These two are different in usage, but belong to the same category of information technology, namely, information hiding. They are not evil tricks, but are beneficial solutions for your digital life today.

"Multimedia information hiding" indicates that you are making use of some multimedia data, such as photos, music, videos, and text, to hide your secret data. In most cases, you are replacing parts of a multimedia data file with your confidential data in an imperceptible manner. Such an operation is referred to as "data embedding." If needed, you can easily extract the embedded data by using a special program with a relevant key. Such an operation is termed "data extracting."

This book is neither an easy read on information hiding, nor a collection of survey papers. Instead, it is intended to provide a wide range of hot topics in Multimedia Information Hiding.

The contents of each chapter are summarized in the Preface by the editor, and the respective chapters are written by different authors. All are original writings. Some authors are intending to give a general introduction to the chapter topic, but others are either proposing a new technical scheme for solving difficult problems on the topic, or reporting their new research framework with remarkable outcomes. This book is good for graduate-level students and also very instructive for senior IT engineers now working in industry.

As you read through the chapters, you will often encounter such terms as "hiding," "watermarking," "steganography," "original data," "stego data," "cover," "payload," "robustness," "degradation," and so on. They are all important concepts in information hiding, but they are rather application-oriented terminologies. For example, the idea of "robustness" is necessary for watermarking applications, while "payload" comes in with some steganographic applications. "Degradation" is a concept that should be kept very small in score in order for the embedding operation to not be noticed by third parties.

I myself think "multimedia information hiding" can be rephrased as "multi-layered information data-structure for multimedia contents," because there are some applications where you don't need to hide anything. A typical number of layers in such a structure is just two, consisting of the internal and the external layers.

Let us take an example in a "Content Delivery System over the Internet," where you want to transmit one of your copyrighted photo works only to a designated recipient without it being intercepted when it travels through the transmission line. This type of system can be implemented by using a large-capacity oriented embedding algorithm. An experimental program of such algorithm is already available on the Internet.

The content delivery system here is like the following:

A. You use some "cover" to carry the copyrighted photo.
B. You need to make the cover "translucent" in order for anyone to see what is inside by just looking from the outside.
C. The photo work has no value as long as it stays in the cover.
D. Opening the cover is only possible by using a special extracting program and a key. The key is handed from you to the recipient in a very safe way.
E. More specifically, an example photo work is an "artistic portrait file" of a lady, and the cover is its degraded image file, which was created by a noise-adding operation. The noise-added image looks like it is contained in some translucent material. The file format of both images may be BMP.

According to the information hiding terminology, the portrait embedded cover image, originally the degraded portrait, is a "stego image." While, in my rephrased expression, it is a "double layered portrait image" where the original data is in the internal layer and the degraded data is on the external layer. The most important point in this structure is that the external layer is "translucent," in other words, the internal layer is not hidden. I have never heard of any "translucent stego image" in the traditional multimedia information-hiding framework. I feel my terminology is a little better in this type of application.

I suggest all the readers of this book pay attention to realize which data, cover, or payload is more important than the other when they are reading through the chapters. In my wording, you should know which layer is more focused than the other in each topic.

Eiji Kawaguchi
Kyushu Institute of Technology, Japan
Summer 2012

Eiji Kawaguchi *received the Dr. Eng. Degree from the Department of Electronics Engineering, Kyushu University, Japan, in 1971. He worked for Kyushu Sangyo University, Kyushu University, Kyushu Institute of Technology, and Keio University from 1969 through 2006. Currently, he is a Professor Emeritus at Kyushu Institute of Technology. His research interests include speech recognition, pattern recognition, image processing, information hiding, content access control, and natural language semantics. He is a co-inventor of BPCS-Steganogrpahy.*

Preface

Since ultra-high-speed networks have become ubiquitous, handling of digital media over these networks has become very easy and very common. Perfect copies of these media are quite easy, and these copies now can be distributed globally in an instant. Thus, control of copyrighted material through some measures is necessary. Data hiding originally came about for this purpose. Copyright information such as the author ID, the distributor, or some other information that can be used to verify or track digital media can be embedded into media signals unperceivably by some signal processing.

Recently, however, copyright management is not the only objective of data hiding. Meta data is often hidden into media signals, which can be used to provide additional functions to the media signals.

Since the requirements of the uses of data hiding described above is quite different, new proposals for data hiding methods, which meet the different requirements, are emerging constantly. Thus, this area is still an emerging one. There is still plenty of room for new methods and applications. We should be able to expect new discoveries and innovations for years to come.

Accordingly, a small group of researchers working on data hiding started a research group in the Information and Systems Society (ISS, 2011) within the Institute of Electronics, Information, and Communication Engineers (IEICE) in early 2007. The main focus of the group was on Multimedia Information Hiding (MIH) technology, and so it was called the MIH research group (MIH, 2010). Without funding, the group organized 12 intense workshops within the next 3 years, and many data hiding methods and applications have come out of these workshops. The group has also grown to over 30 active members.

The MIH research group evolved into a permanent IEICE fully funded research group, with a broader scope. The group was renamed as the Enriched Multi-Media (EMM) technical group to emphasize its broadened scope (EMM, 2011). We felt that this was the perfect timing to look back and compile all of the results that came from these fruitful workshops into one comprehensive book. Some results obviously have appeared in full papers, but we felt that an in-depth thorough description of the technology, all in one piece, was needed. The collection of recent results of this emerging field into one source should be of benefit to all researchers and engineers working in this field globally. We also would like the book to inspire new graduate-level students to start working in this exciting field.

The MIH also has been organizing invited sessions for the IEEE International Conference on Intelligent Information Hiding and Multimedia Signal Processing (IIHMSP), one of a few conferences with focus on this field, for many years (IIHMSP, 2011). Although the majority of the presented papers were from within the MIH research group, many were from outside the group especially from Taiwan, China, and South Korea, which all have a significant number of researchers working in this field. Accordingly, we selected a number of research efforts from these presentations to contribute to this book. This should provide a valuable and broader spectrum to the book.

This book aims to provide relevant theoretical frameworks, the latest empirical research results, as well as new applications in multimedia data hiding. It is written for professionals who are thriving to devise new hiding methods, for newcomers who would like some basic background material in this field before starting to conduct their own research, and for media content manufacturers who would like to apply this technology into their products.

CONTENTS OF THE BOOK

This book is organized as follows.

Chapter 1 provides a general overview of the technology involved in speech and audio watermarking. General issues of the topic are first discussed, including definitions and classification of audio data hiding, as well as its benchmarking. This is followed by the basic techniques used to hide data in audio signals, including bit replacement, spread spectrum methods, echo methods, quantization index modulation, patchwork method, and frequency hopping. This is followed by a brief description of the recent proposals presented at the IEICE Multimedia Information Hiding Technical Group meetings. Some of these are embedding methods, including amplitude modulation embedding and modified patchwork algorithm, as well as exploration into the application of audio data embedding, including universal data display systems for the visually impaired, motion picture pirating position tracking in theatres, and data hiding into sirens. Some perspectives for future directions of the audio data-hiding field are also given.

Chapter 2 gives a description of the reversible data hiding technique to embed hidden data into host data while preserving perfect consistency of the restored host data as a result of the extraction process. Reversible data hiding is being considered for authentication, meta-data recording, tampering detection, covert communication, and so forth. Although reversible audio data hiding technique is fragile and inferior in sound quality compared with the conventional steganography technique, its perfect reconstruction of the host signal opens new possibilities and possibilities of new applications.

Chapter 3 introduces a state-of-the-art scheme of digital-audio watermarking, based on the properties of the human cochlear. Data is embedded as inaudible watermarks into the original sound by controlling its phase characteristics in relation to the characteristics of Cochlear Delay (CD). Inaudible watermarks are embedded into original signals by applying Infinite Impulse Response (IIR) all-pass filters with CDs, and are then extracted from the phase difference between the original and watermarked sounds. The results obtained from subjective evaluations and robustness tests revealed that the proposed approach can satisfy the requirements for inaudible watermarking, and is superior in inaudibility and robustness to typical watermarking methods such as least significant bit replacement, direct spread-spectrum, echo hiding, and periodical phase modulation approaches. Embedding limitations with the proposed approach was investigated with various evaluations. These results also revealed that embedding limitations with the method could be improved by using parallel, cascade, and composite architectures for the CD filters.

Chapter 4 proposes a time-domain high-bit-rate information hiding method using an interpolation technique, which can extract embedded data in both informed (non-blind, using the original host signal) and blind (without the use of the original signal) manner. Three interpolation techniques are introduced for the information hiding method, i.e., spline interpolation, Fourier-series interpolation, and linear-prediction interpolation. As an example, spline interpolation was applied in the proposed method. According to the simulation of information hiding in music signals, the spline interpolation-based method achieved audio-information hiding for CD-audio signals at bit rate of about 2.9kbps, and about 1.1kbps under MP3 compression (160kbps). The objective sound quality measured by the Perceptual Evaluation of Audio Quality (PEAQ) was improved if the length of the interpolation data increased. Other interpolation methods were evaluated, including the Fourier series and the linear prediction. Fourier series interpolation achieved the same sound quality as the spline interpolation. Linear prediction interpolation required longer interpolation signals to achieve good sound quality.

Chapter 5 presents a method of aerial acoustic communication in which the data is modulated using OFDM (Orthogonal Frequency Division Multiplexing), and data is embedded in regular audio material without significantly degrading the quality of the embedded sound. The proposed method can provide data transmission of several hundred bps, which is much higher than is possible with other conventional audio data hiding techniques. The proposed method replaces the high frequency band of the audio signal with OFDM carriers, each of which is power-controlled according to the spectrum envelope of the original audio signal. The resultant signal is extremely robust, even with analog aerial transmission. The implemented system enables the transmission of short text messages from loudspeakers to mobile handheld devices at a distance of around 3m. This chapter also provides the subjective assessment results of audio clips embedded with OFDM signal.

Chapter 6 proposes two data hiding schemes for stereo audio signals. The first proposal tries to embed data into stereo audio signals by adding data-dependent mutual delay to the host stereo audio signals. The second proposal adds fixed delay echoes whose polarity will be data-dependent, and whose amplitude will be adjusted so that the inter-channel correlation will match the original signal. The robustness as well as the quality of the data embedded audio will be given and compared for both schemes. Both proposals were shown to be fairly robust to common distortions, including added noise, audio coding, and sample rate conversion. The embedded audio quality was shown to be "very good" with the former method, while it was shown to be almost transparent with the latter.

Chapter 7 proposes a method for embedding data into ITU-T G.711-coded speech for conveying side information for enhancing speech quality, such as bandwidth extension or packet loss concealment. The proposed method uses a low-bitrate encoder to determine how many bits are embedded into each sample. First, a variable-bitrate data hiding method is proposed as a basic framework of the proposed method. Then, the proposed method is extended to achieve fixed bitrate data hiding. Comparison experiments proved that the proposed method can achieve higher speech quality compared with conventional hiding methods. A low-complexity speech bandwidth extension method that uses the proposed data hiding method was also developed.

Chapter 8 describes two topics for the enhancement of the speech quality in telephony communications by steganography. A packet loss concealment technique and a band extension technique are described. These techniques employ steganography for transmitting side information for improving the performance of signal processing. In addition, this chapter describes an efficient steganography technique for the ITU-T standard G.711 codec, the most common codec for telephony speech. The proposed technique, referred to as selective LSB replacement technique, was shown to be able to embed side information with much less degradation compared to conventional methods.

In Chapter 9, audio watermarking techniques that enable the extraction of embedded data by mobile phones are described. Acoustic interpolation of the human auditory system is used to embed data in full phone-line frequency ranges of 3G mobile phones. This technique is being considered for application to a mobile guide system for use in museums. In particular, application to audio watermarking techniques for synchronizing the stored contents of mobile terminals based on the spatial positions of the terminal and the temporal positions of playback contents in surrounding media. For this purpose, five linear spatial location identification codes that transfer the position to mobile terminals via two-channel stereo audio media with embedded watermarks were developed. Time codes that continuously transfer to mobile terminals via audio media were also developed. In this chapter, the proposed audio watermarking algorithm is described, and then a novel audio watermarking application for position information delivery to mobile terminals is also described.

Chapter 10 provides a general overview of the technology involved in image and video watermarking, with a focus on steganography and steganalysis. First, image data structures and image formats required by computers and the Internet are quickly summarized. Then, a brief introduction of several information hiding methods based on image formats including lossless (non-compression based), limited color-based image data, JPEG, and JPEG2000 is given. A steganographic method, which is based on image segmentation using a complexity measure, is described in detail. This is followed by an introduction of a method for applying the steganographic method to palette-based image formats, reversible information hiding for grayscale images, and JPEG2000 steganography. The steganographic methods for JPEG and JPEG2000 described in this chapter focuses on the naturalness of the cover data. In the steganalysis section, two methods are described, *i.e.*, a specific steganalysis method for Bit-Plane Complexity Segmentation (BPCS) and a universal method based on sparse code shrinkage.

Chapter 11 addresses a new class of Reversible Information Hiding (RIH) and its application to the verification of image integrity. The RIH method distorts an image once to hide information in the image itself, and in the detection process, it not only extracts embedded information but also recovers the original image from the distorted image. The A well-known class of RIH is based on prediction error expansion in which a location map, which indicates the pixel block positions of a certain block category, is required to recover the original image. In contrast, the method described in this chapter is free from having to memorize any parameters, including location maps. This feature suits the applications of image authentication application in which the extracted information guarantees the integrity of a suspected image. If image dependent parameters such as location maps are required, the suspected images need to be first identified from among a large database of all possible images. The method described in this chapter reduces such costly processes.

Chapter 12 proposes two types of new approaches using a single dot pattern and an Artificial Fiber (AF) pattern in order to solve disadvantages of conventional information hiding technologies for paper media. In this chapter, each scheme is described in detail, followed by its characteristics and how to improve their robustness. As the result, more than 80% extraction rate with 91kbits information capacity when using a single dot pattern and 100% extraction rate with color characters as a foreground when using an artificial fiber pattern, was achieved.

Chapter 13 proposes a Discrete Cosine Transform (DCT)-based watermarking method using the calculation of the watermark weighting factor and the Human Visual System (HVS) for the given peak signal to noise ratio of a still image as well as the specified length of watermarks to be inserted. Using the energy relationship of the DCT, an equation that directly computes the watermark weighting factor in the DCT domain is derived. In addition, a digital watermarking method for still images, in which the HVS is used in the DCT domain, is proposed. The modulation transfer function of the HVS model is employed to increase the invisibility of the inserted watermark in images. Experimental results with objective evaluation show that the proposed watermarking method is an effective method compared to other conventional watermarking algorithms.

Chapter 14 gives a survey about self-embedding watermarking, which enables not only detection of tampered regions but also the recovery of the damaged information. An introduction of the pioneering method as well as the representative schemes, including adjacent-block detection, hierarchical detection and self-recovery, dual watermarks, reference sharing, and flexible self-recovery, is given. Their distinguishing features and loopholes are analyzed by considering four key techniques, namely the secure block-mapping function, the unambiguous authentication, the reference information extraction, and the watermark embedding approaches.

Chapter 15 discusses benchmarking tools for digital watermarking of still pictures. To prevent unauthorized use of digital content using digital watermarking, the robustness of the watermarking should be evaluated in detail. Benchmark tools, such as JEWELS and Stirmark, have been developed for this purpose. These tools can show which attacks will break embedded digital watermarks. However, such conventional tools are difficult to use because they operate on a command-line basis without an image viewer. Furthermore, their functions for evaluating robustness are inadequate, as they work only for attacks using a single image. Therefore, most current digital watermarking technology aims to be robust to single-image attack. However, attacks using multiple images are very powerful compared to those using a single image, and they can be performed very easily. In addition, they do not degrade the images significantly. Therefore, evaluation of robustness against such attacks is essential and has practical use in benchmark tools for digital watermarking. A new benchmark tool that overcomes these limitations has been developed. This tool has attacking functions using a single image and plural images, and it can evaluate attacks using plural images easily. In addition, a Graphical User Interface (GUI) enables easy manipulation by untrained users.

Chapter 16 gives a brief overview of text-based and binary-based data hiding methods. Text-based methods are mostly used for steganography. Secret information is embedded into innocent-looking textual data. Binary-based methods are applied to program binary codes: executable files and libraries. Examples of both of these methods are also given.

Chapter 17 introduces embedding methods that do not distort the contents of cover objects: permutation steganography, metadata steganography, and cover generation method. Creation of a stego object by embedding information in a cover object often distorts the cover object. As more information is embedded, more annoying noise is introduced in these objects. Although reversible embedding methods enable us to restore the original cover object even after embedding, stego objects are not free from distortions. However, embedding information does not always result in damaging the contents of the cover object. This chapter gives such a solution.

Chapter 18 present a new writing device called a data-embedding pen, where a single inkjet nozzle is attached to its pen tip. When writing a stroke, the nozzle produces additional ink-dot sequences along the stroke. The ink-dot sequence can represent various meta-information, such as the writer's ID, the writing date, and a related URL. Since the embedded meta-information is placed on the paper, it can be extracted by scanning or photographing the paper. Accordingly, using the data-embedding pen, a physical paper can convey any digital information. In other words, handwriting by the data-embedding pen can be a new medium connecting physical and cyber worlds. Numerous new applications should be possible with this pen.

Finally, Chapter 19 discusses a direct feature-based method as another approach in digital watermarking. The direct feature-based method is an extension of the digital signature scheme, which aims at multimedia authentication. The method covers several copyright protection properties, i.e., robustness to content manipulations and sensitivity to content modification. In addition, this method provides a solution to inherent problems in traditional watermarking, such as quality degradation and trade-off between imperceptibility and robustness. A discussion on various multimedia copyright protection schemes based on the direct feature-based method is given, e.g., image, audio, text document, geospatial data, and relational databases. A good copyright protection scheme should be not only robust enough to acceptable manipulations but also secure enough against malicious attacks. In addition, the direct feature-based method can be considered as a possible solution for trade-off problems among data payload, fidelity, and robustness.

Kazukiro Kondo
Yamagata University, Japan

REFERENCES

EMM. (2011). *The IEICE ISS enriched multi-media technical group page*. Retrieved from http://www.ieice.org/iss/emm/

IIHMSP. (2011). *The IEEE international conference on intelligent information hiding and multimedia signal processing*. Retrieved from http://bit.kuas.edu.tw/~iihmsp11/

ISS. (2011). *The institute of electronics, information and communication engineers of japan (IEICE) information and systems society (ISS) page*. Retrieved from http://www.ieice.org/iss/

MIH. (2010). *The IEICE ISS multi-media information hiding technical group page*. Retrieved from http://www.ieice.org/iss/mih/index.html.en

Acknowledgment

I would like to thank all of the authors, most of whom also contributed as reviewers, for their contributions to this book. I would also like to thank the editorial advisory board. The board was especially helpful in compiling a list of prominent authors in the field. All of the board members are also founding members of the IEICE Multimedia Information Hiding Technical group. The book is focused on the major contributions made by that group. I would also like to express my gratitude to the publishing team at IGI Global, who made the realization of this book possible. The editing process of this book was a first for me, and it was both a challenging and stimulating experience. It gave me an excellent chance to view this field from a different perspective. It also gave me the chance to review the technology involved in different media, especially its similarities and differences.

Kazuhiro Kondo
Yamagata University, Japan
March 2012

Section 1
Information Hiding for Audio and Speech

Chapter 1
Information Hiding for Audio Signals

Akira Nishimura
Tokyo University of Information Sciences, Japan

Kazuhiro Kondo
Yamagata University, Japan

ABSTRACT

This chapter provides a general overview of audio data hiding. The general issues are discussed first, followed by the basic techniques used to hide data in audio signals, including bit stealing, spread spectrum methods, echo methods, and quantization index modulation. This is followed by a brief description of the recent proposals presented at the Institute of Electronics, Information, and Communication Engineers of Japan (IEICE) Multimedia Information Hiding (MIH) Technical Group Meetings.

INTRODUCTION

The concept of information hiding was first studied rigorously in the context of images and videos. Similar methods were then applied to audio signals. With the explosive growth in digital audio and speech data and the available communication bandwidth, the necessity of controlling the distribution of such data has contributed to the interest in research on audio watermarks, which is another form of data hiding for audio signals. Many of the methods of audio data hiding use the perceptual properties of the Human Auditory System (HAS) to hide the data without the possibility of detection. However, the amount of data that can be hidden remained quite small compared to the capacity of images and video. This is quickly changing, and high data rate hiding schemes have recently been introduced, including methods that are considerably robust against attacks. All of these factors contribute to the actual application of audio data hiding in practical audio systems.

DOI: 10.4018/978-1-4666-2217-3.ch001

This chapter intends to provide a brief description of audio data hiding, followed by a brief description of the methods of data hiding proposed at the IEICE Multimedia Information Hiding Meetings. It is not intended to present a full description of the topic, but the reader will be provided with a comprehensive list of references for further detail.

DEFINITION OF INFORMATION-HIDING FOR AUDIO

Information-hiding applications are typically classified into two categories: watermarking and steganography. Figure 1 shows an outline of information-hiding technology for audio data. In Figure 1 the technology is classified by payload data and application type. As an introduction, the keywords that are usually applied in information hiding and their definitions are briefly introduced.

The data that are embedded are referred to as the watermark or payload data. The data to be embedded are referred to as the host data or cover data. As a consequence, the watermark is embedded in the host data. The majority of the embedding and extraction algorithms require a common key. This key is essentially different from the cryptography key. It defines where to embed or the order of embedding, which is intended to conceal the payload data in the embedding algorithm by altering the amount of physical variables used in the embedding. The data generated as a result of embedding are referred to as the stego data. The stego data are expressed as quantized waveform data or encoded bit-stream data. It is generally necessary to decode the latter data to the stego waveform data using the conventional decoder of the same codec used in the encoding process. The degradation in the quality of the stego waveform must be low enough to still serve the user's appreciation or listening purposes. The payload data is extracted by the appropriate users and is utilized for the intended purpose.

Watermark or watermarking is a term used in information hiding that is mainly applied to copy-control or digital rights management. A typical watermarking application embeds a content ID and/or a consumer ID into the host audio signal

Figure 1. An outline of audio information-hiding technologies

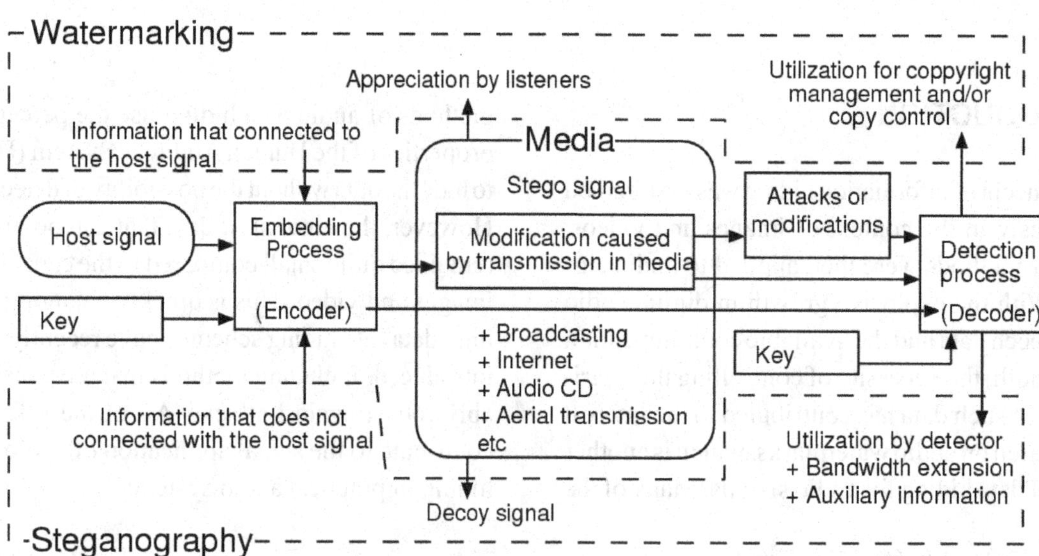

that is delivered from commercial Internet sites or conventional audio media, such as television or radio programs, compact discs, etc. If the stego signal is distributed over the Internet illegally, the crawler program in the music's contents is able to detect the identity of the watermarked content automatically and determine where it was distributed and who purchased it.

In such an application, the extraction process of the payload data should be robust against any modifications of the stego signal as a result of the distribution of the contents. Perceptual coding for Internet distribution and digital broadcasting, bandwidth limitations, analog-to-digital and digital-to-analog conversions, and additive noise for analog broadcasting should be considered as modifications. In addition, malicious attacks such as pitch conversion and time expansion or contraction have to be considered in the context of intended illegal distribution.

In the field of image watermarking, Stirmark is a well-known tool for robustness evaluation (Petitcolas, Anderson, & Kuhn, 1998). A similar approach, Stirmark for Audio (Steinebach, et al., 2001), has also been proposed for audio watermarking. However, it is currently not popular, and it has not been applied in many studies.

Steganography is also referred to as covert communication. In contrast to watermarking, the payload data of steganography is generally not concerned with the contents of the host signal. In other words, the payload data is usually worth transmitting or utilizing, rather than the host signal. Therefore, the stego signal in which the payload data is embedded is called the decoy signal. The advantage of steganography is that it conceals both the data and the communication itself using communication via decoy, whereas communication via cipher cannot conceal the fact of the communication. For example, who would guess that a photograph on a blog page might contain information vital to national security?

The application of information-hiding technology to audio signals is not restricted to the typical uses described above, watermarking and steganography. For example, payload data can be used in the bandwidth extension of a narrow band speech signal (Aoki, 2006) or to monitor the commercial messages broadcast on a radio network.

Data hiding technology is additionally classified into the blind detection method, which does not require a host signal in the detection process, and the non-blind detection method, which requires a host signal to be present. It is clear that blind detection is widely applicable in various situations that require extraction of a payload.

The following section, which describes algorithms of audio data hiding, is an overview of the information-hiding technologies that achieve blind detection of audio signals. It focuses on the methods and features of various types of technologies of audio data hiding.

PERFORMANCE EVALUATION

The factors considered in the evaluation of information-hiding technologies depend somewhat on their application. Watermarking requires a great payload, higher robustness against various modifications on the stego signal, and the low-quality degradation of the stego signal. These three factors are usually thought to require a trade-off. For example, a higher sound quality in the stego signal causes a smaller payload or lower robustness. Therefore, the evaluation of watermarking technology generally fixes one factor as the priority, such as the amount of the payload. The evaluation is conducted in terms of the other two factors, such as the robustness and sound quality degradation. However, there are no standards or criteria for the evaluation of robustness against various modifications and attacks.

The assessment of the subjective quality degradation of the audio signal must be conducted with caution to avoid the development of artifacts related to the experimental procedure. International Telecommunication Union Radio

Communications Sector (ITU-R) recommendation BS.1116-1 defines the method of the subjective assessment of small impairments in audio systems to assess this subjective degradation of quality. The experimental procedure defined by BS.1116-1 is the "double-blind triple-stimulus with hidden reference" method, which has been found to be especially sensitive and stable and to permit the accurate detection of small impairments. The degraded music and the reference music are randomly assigned to buttons labeled "A" and "B" on the computer screen. A button labeled "X" is also displayed on the screen and assigned to the reference. The subject is able to listen to each piece of music arbitrarily by pressing one of the three buttons during the course of a trial. The reproduced sound cannot be interrupted by pressing the buttons until the music ends because the three sounds are synchronized in a time scale. The listener is able to listen repeatedly and is asked to assess the impairments on "A" or "B" compared to "X" using a five-grade impairment scale with a resolution of one decimal place. The Subjective Difference Grades (SDGs), the difference between the grades given to the hidden reference and the degraded object, are corrected and analyzed statistically. BS.1116-1 also recommends the selection and training of the listeners, program materials, reproduction devices, listening conditions, statistical analysis, and so forth. Therefore, the subjective measurement of the sound quality degradation of the stego signal is a difficult task.

An objective measurement of the sound quality degradation may be substituted for the subjective measurement. However, there is no appropriate objective measure for the sound quality degradation because physical indexes, such as the Signal to Noise Ratio (SNR), do not correspond to subjective evaluation. The Perceptual Evaluation of Audio Quality (PEAQ) algorithm recommended by ITU-R BS.1387, which is intended to measure the subjective quality of the perceptual audio codes, may be a reasonable choice. PEAQ uses a number of psycho-acoustical measures that are combined to provide a measure of the difference in quality between two instances of a signal (a reference and a test signal). The outputs of PEAQ, also known as the Objective Difference Grades (ODGs), are tuned to show a high correlation to the SDG obtained from the audio signals degraded by the perceptual audio codecs. There are insufficient studies on relationship between subjective and objective quality degradation induced by audio data hiding. Much more effort should be applied to the evaluation of quality degradation induced by audio data hiding (Nishimura, 2007a; Yiqing & Abdulla, 2008).

Steganography usually presumes that no modification will be applied to the stego signal because it should be considered a normal audio signal. Therefore, the stego signal of steganography has no robustness against modifications, but it must achieve a high level of concealment against statistical tests that reveal the existence of hidden material. The concealment of the payload—that is, the difficulty an outsider experiences in detecting the existence of the payload or extracting the payload—is important in both watermarking and steganography. A practical application also requires a small computational load for embedding and extraction.

AUDIO DATA HIDING ALGORITHM

This section will briefly describe some commonly used data hiding algorithms for audio signals. These algorithms are classified into two categories: hiding in audio signals that only pass through digital channels and those that can pass through analog channels. The former algorithm is so fragile that no modification to the stego signal is allowed. It is generally used in steganography. The latter algorithm is designed to be robust against attacks on the stego signal. This type of algorithm is generally used in watermarking.

Most of the following algorithms originated in visual data hiding, since data structure of the time-frequency domain of audio data resembles visual data in the two-dimensional structure. In addition, the technique of conversion and analysis to the frequency-domain of audio data resembles that of visual data. However, modulation and echo hiding methods, which utilize characteristics of the time-domain data, are unique to audio data hiding. It is important to bear in mind that if the visual data-hiding algorithm is applied to audio data, the perceptual detectability of the modifications to visual data and audio data will be quite different. A common characteristic is less perceptual importance in the high-frequency region. The characteristics specific to the auditory perception are that the frequency analysis of the human auditory system is based on logarithmic frequency axis, and also that the masking effects along the temporal as well as the frequency axes are induced by the intense signal components.

Hiding in Audio Signals that do not pass through Analog Channels

Data hiding in the digital-domain presumes that the stego signal is distributed over media such as the Internet, broadcasting, telephone, or disk media without modification, and that the payload is extracted successfully. In other words, modification of the stego signal generally results in disabling the extraction of the payload data. The maximum payload reaches several tens of percent in the amount of the host data without severe degradation in the quality of the stego signal.

Bit Replacement Methods

A bit replacement method is a process that replaces the Least Significant Bits (LSB) in the coded bit-stream of the audio signal with the payload bits. The simplest method is to replace the lowest bit of 8-bit or 16-bit quantized amplitude with the payload bit. This method is so fragile to the modification of the stego signal that it is used to detect any modifications of the stego signal (Löytynoja, Cvejic, Lähetkangas, & Seppänen, 2005).

To maintain the perceptual quality of the stego signal, it is important to find perceptually insignificant bits. A practical example is proposed by Geiger, Yokotani, and Schuller (2006). It transforms host waveform data into integer spectral data using the integer Modified Discrete Cosine Transform (intMDCT). It then locates the imperceptible spectral bits that are below the masked threshold using the psychoacoustic model and replaces them into the payload bits. The stego waveform is obtained by applying the inverse intMDCT to the modified MDCT spectrum.

Data Hiding along with Coding

Modern digital audio media is often stored or transmitted after lossy coding such as mu-law, Code-Excited Linear Prediction (CELP), or perceptual audio codec, also known as MP3 or AAC. This coding process eliminates the redundant information of the stego waveform so that the embedded payload data in the waveform domain is difficult to extract after encoding. Therefore, embedding, along with encoding of the codec or embedding into the coded bit-stream data is an effective way to survive codec transformation. The extraction of the payload data is processed to the encoded bit-stream or during the decoding process. If the conventional decoder is used for decoding the stego bit-stream, the output signal is somewhat degraded.

Bit replacement can be applied to the coded data. However, a special feature of data hiding with coding is the use of the coding algorithm or the characteristics of the coded data. For example, a data hiding method for the CELP codec that partitions the codebook optimally into several subsets that correspond to the payload information has been proposed (Geiser & Vary, 2007). Another method embeds the payload data into the scale factor of the MP3 coded data (Koukopoulos &

Stamatiou, 2001). Generally, it is not possible to detect the payload data from the decoded stego waveform data.

Hiding in Audio Signals that pass through Analog Channels

The embedding and extraction of payload data are generally conducted in the digital domain. However, the stego signal can be transformed into the analog domain via Digital-to-Analog (DA) and Analog-to-Digital (AD) conversion. Data hiding technologies intended for watermarking should be robust against these conversions. Because they do not affect the sound quality of the stego signal, the illegal copies created by such operations must be detected via watermarking. Additional modifications of the stego signal that result in small degradations of the sound quality are as follows: a small (below 0.1%) sampling rate conversion, the addition of quantization noise, a small total harmonic distortion below 0.1% (-60 dB) accompanied by DA and AD conversion, and the perceptual coding and decoding of a high bit-rate (above 64 kbps/ch). The target amount of the payload for such a technology can range from several tens to several hundreds of bits per second without severe degradation of the sound quality. If the stego signal is required to provide more robustness against modifications, such as air transmission by reproduction via a loudspeaker then reception via a microphone or malicious attacks such as pitch conversion or time-stretching and shrinking conversions, the amount of the payload generally drops to several tens of bits or several bits per second.

The data domain to be embedded is classified into the time domain, the frequency domain, and the time-frequency domain. Time-domain embedding directly modifies the waveform of the host audio signal. Frequency-domain embedding modifies the short-term power spectrum or phase spectrum of the host audio signal. Time-frequency domain embedding regularly modifies the two-dimensional data plane composed of the time and frequency axes and obtained by successive short-term frequency analysis applied to the short segments of the host audio signal. The following subsections are arranged according to the embedding data domain: that is, the time domain, the frequency domain, the time-frequency domain, and all the domains.

Modulation Method

A regular modulation in phase (Takahashi, Nishimura, & Suzuki, 2005) or in amplitude (Nishimura, 2006) is applied to the waveform of the host signal. The payload information is expressed as the change in this regularity: that is, phase difference (phase-shift keying) or amplitude difference (amplitude-shift keying), in the sinusoidal modulation. In other words, the host signal is considered a carrier of the modulation and the payload data is a modulator of the modulation. The advantage of these methods is that slow modulations are difficult to perceive with the human auditory system.

Echo Hiding

Echo hiding is a method that adds an echo whose delay time is approximately shorter than 10 ms to the waveform of the host signal. The payload information is assigned to the delay time (Gruhl & Bender, 1996). Figure 2 shows impulse responses applied to the host signal of a constant time segment. For example, an echo of a solid line represents bit "0" and an echo of a dotted line represents bit "1" in Figure 2; these echoes are switched according to the bit values. Switching several echoes and using positive and negative echoes increases the amount of payload data. The characteristics of echo hiding are its low computational costs and the addition of short time echoes, which do not seriously degrade the sound quality of the stego signal.

Figure 2. Impulse responses used for echo hiding

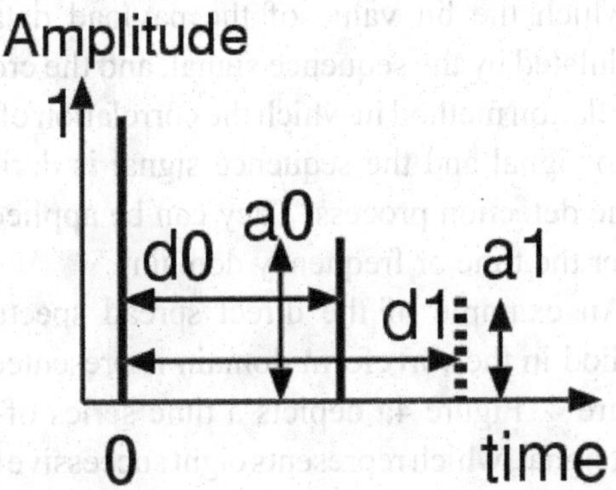

Figure 3. An example of an impulse response used for the spread echo hiding method

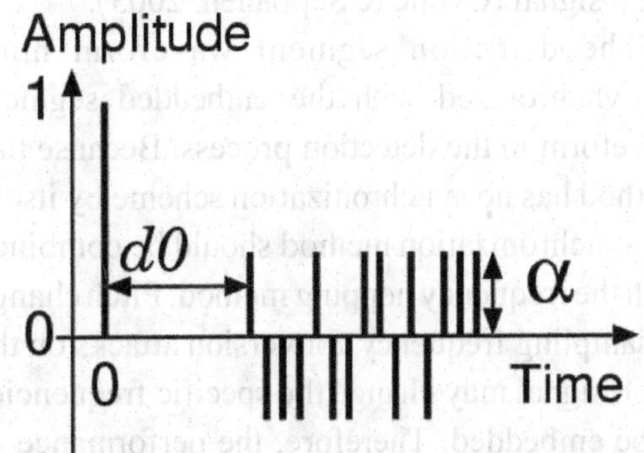

Detection of the echo hiding requires detection of the time segments that has an echo component with the constant delay in the stego waveform. The Discrete Fourier Transform (DFT) is applied to the segmented stego waveform to convert it to the spectral data. Inverse DFT is applied to the logarithmic amplitude of the spectral data to convert to the complex cepstrum. The absolute values of the complex cepstrum exhibit periodic peaks at multiples of the delay time of the echo, and the embedded data is detected using the corresponding peaks. However, this detection process reveals the poor concealment of the existence of data hiding.

To be robust against modifications of the stego signal, longer segments and/or higher amplitude of the echoes are required. However, the former diminish the amount of the payload data, and the latter induces degradation in the quality of the stego signal.

A highly secured concealment of the payload data and lower audibility of the existence of hiding are accomplished via a method of spread echo hiding. This method uses an impulse response consisting of n echoes whose amplitude is $-a$ or $+a$, according to a binary PN sequence instead of a single echo (Ko, Nishimura, & Suzuki, 2004). Figure 3 presents an example of the impulse response of $n = 15$. Multiple echoes reduce their amplitudes to $1/\sqrt{n}$ compared with a single echo. A single echo produces periodic peaks and dips in the transfer function; however, multiple echoes produce peaks and dips at apparently random frequencies, similar to an actual room response. Therefore, the impairment of the sound caused by multiple echoes is smaller than that caused by a large single echo. In general, the multiple echoes consist of the PN sequence of $n = 1023$, which are separated by the sampling periods.

The detection process calculates the complex cepstrum of the embedded region in the same way as in the echo-hiding method. A cross-correlation between the real part of the complex cepstrum and the PN sequence used in the embedding process reveals a peak that corresponds to the delay time *d0* of the impulse response. The payload data can be expressed by the delay time in the same way as in the echo-hiding method. It can be expressed in the same way as in the cross-correlation method of the spread spectrum method.

Frequency Hopping

The intensity of the specific frequency components of the host signal is modified according to a secret key or the feature values of the host signal. The host signal is segmented to the short time frame and converted into spectral data using the Fourier transform or the wavelet transform.

The amplitude spectra are then modified and an inverse transformation is applied to obtain the stego signal (Cvejic & Seppänen, 2003).

The detection segment waveform must be synchronized with the embedded segment waveform in the detection process. Because this method has no synchronization scheme by itself, the synchronization method should be combined with the frequency hopping method. Pitch change or sampling frequency conversion attacks on the stego signal may change the specific frequencies to be embedded. Therefore, the performance of payload detection depends on the frame synchronization algorithm and the decision algorithm of the frequency position.

Spread Spectrum

The spread spectrum method embeds payload data into a wide spectral region using the M-sequence signal or a pseudo-random noise sequence signal consisting of an amplitude value of -1 or 1. It is classified into the direct spread spectrum method in which the bit value of the payload data is modulated by the sequence signal, and the cross-correlation method in which the correlation of the stego signal and the sequence signal is derived in the detection process. They can be applied to either the time or frequency domain.

An example of the direct spread spectrum method in the waveform domain is presented in Figure 4. Figure 4a depicts a time series of the data signal, which represents eight successive bits corresponding to a payload bit of 1 or -1. The ratio of the number of the successive bits of the data signal to the sampling rate is defined as the data rate. Figure 4b presents part of a pseudo random sequence. Figure 4c shows a spread signal, which is derived by multiplying the pseudo random sequence and the data signal. Figure 4d compares the spectra of the data signal and the spread signal. A periodic spectrum of the data signal is spread by the multiplication of the pseudo-random sequence of the white spectrum.

Figure 4. Signal representation of the direct spread spectrum method

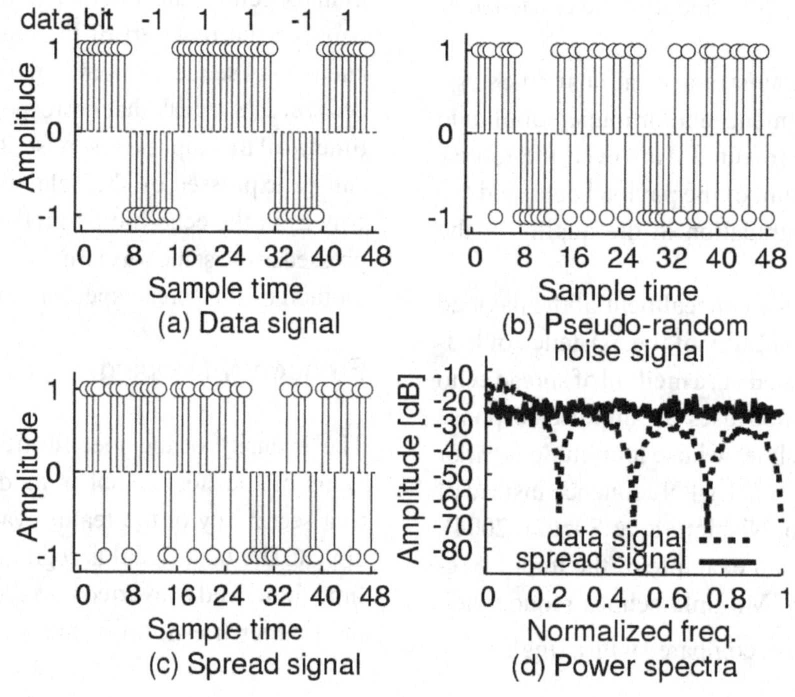

The embedding of the payload data is accomplished by adding the spread signal to the host signal by adjusting the spectrum and amplitude of the spread signal in accordance with their levels of detectability and/or the audibility of the spread signal. To ensure the inaudibility caused by embedding and high-detection performance through various modifications, the data rate should be between 0.05 and 0.2 seconds, and the amplitude of the spread signal should be small, as a longer data rate results in a higher detection rate. Figure 5a shows the host signal waveform and the stego signal waveform.

In the beginning of the detection process, the signal frame that added the spread signal is detected: that is, the frame synchronization is conducted. Generally, it is realized using the cross correlation method described below. The framed stego signal that is multiplied by the sequence signal used in the embedding process spreads the host signal component, while the data signal component is despread by the disappearing sign of the sequence signal, which is multiplied twice, in the embedded and extraction processes. Next, the sign (1, -1) of the averaged data signal in the data frame rate represents the embedded data value (1, 0) (See Figure 5b).

The cross-correlation method adds the sequence signal iteratively by adjusting its amplitude to the host signal. Detection of the embedded data segment, also known as the synchronization of the cross-correlation method, is accomplished by finding peaks in the cross-correlation function between the sequence signal and the stego signal. The segment between the successive peaks corresponds to the data segment because the peaks appear at every length of the sequence signal. The payload information is expressed as the negative or positive addition of the sequence signal or as the width of the cyclic shift of the sequence signal (Cvejic & Seppänen, 2001). If one keeps the amplitude of the sequence signal small to diminish the audibility of the embedding, the sequence should be long or a synchronous addition of the sequence signals should be made to retain the detectability of the data segments.

The characteristics of the spread-spectrum method are its robust detection against frequency band elimination or filtering of the stego signal, as well as against the additive noises at the low Signal to Noise Ratio (SNR). In addition, the sequence signal used in the embedding process is required as the key data in detecting the payload information. The above descriptions are based on the

Figure 5. A stego signal waveform and the detection process of the direct spread spectrum method

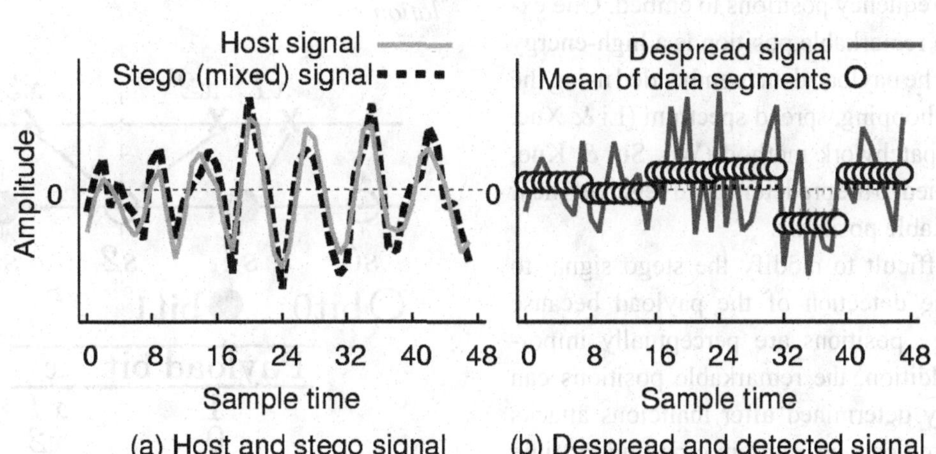

embedding in the time domain; however, the same method can be applied to audio data expressed in the spectral domain or in the cepstrum domain.

Patchwork Method

A patchwork method is a typical data hiding method for image data. For audio data, two specific regions in the spectral or temporal domain are selected based on a secret key. For example, if the intensity of one region is emphasized and that of the other region is diminished, it expresses payload data bit "0." Opposite-intensity modifications correspond to payload data bit "1." The two data regions can be selected from the vast regions of the data domain. The detection of the payload data is achieved by a statistical test that determines which region has the greater intensity. This emphasis and diminution in intensity are achieved in the smooth regions, which are usually adjacent regions. Payload detection after the modifications of filtering or the addition of noise on the stego signal is generally robust because the payload data is spread over wide frequencies and temporal regions (Tachibana, Shimizu, Kobayashi, & Nakamura, 2002)

Content Analysis

The host signal is analyzed to find remarkable time and frequency positions to embed. One example of a remarkable position is a high-energy segment. The payload data is embedded using the frequency hopping, spread spectrum (Li & Xue, 2004), or patchwork method (Wu, Su, & Kuo, 1999) applied to the predetermined segments near the remarkable positions.

It is difficult to modify the stego signal to prevent the detection of the payload because high-energy positions are perceptually important. In addition, the remarkable positions can be robustly determined after malicious attacks such as pitch change, random cropping, or time scale modifications. However, embedding only the remarkable positions leaves the majority of segments that are not embedded, resulting in a small amount of payload.

Quantization Index Modulation

The Quantization Index Modulation (QIM) method modifies the quantized physical property or feature value x to the quantized value s, which is assigned payload data (Chen & Wornell, 1998). The upper scale of Figure 6 represents x of the host signal, assuming a value of $x1$, $x2$, and $x3$. The lower scale of Figure 6 represents the quantized value after embedding, which is scaled from $s0$ to $s3$. The quantized values $s0$, $s1$, $s2$, and $s3$ are assigned to bits "0" and "1" alternatively. If the payload bits are 1, 0, and 0, $x1$, $x2$, and $x3$ are quantized to the nearest values $s1$, $s2$, and $s2$, which are assigned to the payload bit values, respectively.

In the detection process, $s1$ and $s2$ can be different from the quantized value due to some types of attack or modification. However, if this deviation from the quantized value is less than one-half of the quantization interval, rounding the modified value off to the quantized value extracts the cor-

Figure 6. A concept of quantization index modulation

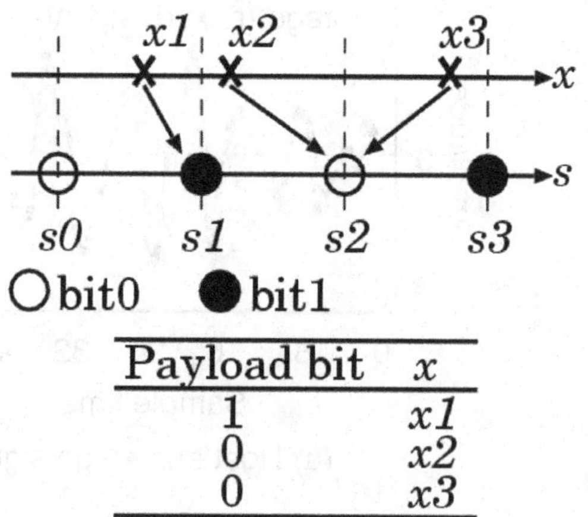

Payload bit	x
1	$x1$
0	$x2$
0	$x3$

rect embedded payload bits. This can be applied to either time or frequency-domain data.

The simplest physical property of the host signal x is the amplitude of the waveform. The practical physical property of the host signal is the frequency of the specific component or the energy of the octave bandwidth. If the physical property of the host signal is the energy of the host waveform segment that corresponds to the amplitude, it is fragile to attacks that apply an emphasis to or diminution of the overall amplitude and the addition of noise. Providing a reference to the quantization, such as the energy of the specific frequency band or the energy of the pilot signal, overcomes the fragility of the amplitude modification.

Supplementary Technology to Data Hiding

Several supplementary technologies have been proposed to combine with the basic embedding algorithms described in the previous section. Two typical technologies that improve robustness and sound quality are presented in this section.

Psychoacoustic Modeling

A signal that only contains a watermark can be calculated by subtracting the host signal from the stego signal and be considered as a noise signal that is added to the host signal. If the power of the added noise is below the psychoacoustic threshold of the human auditory system—the absolute threshold and the masked thresholds of the temporal and frequency domains—it is difficult for human listeners to perceive.

Many studies dating back to the early years of such research utilize the psychoacoustic threshold to determine the intensity of embedding for every short time segment according to this idea. For example, the spread spectrum (Cvejic & Seppänen, 2001), spread echo (Ko, Nishimura, & Suzuki, 2004), and patchwork methods (Tachibana, Shimizu, Kobayashi, & Nakamura, 2002) determine the intensity of the watermarking based on the power spectrum of each frequency band of the host signal.

Attack Characterization

Attack characterization is a scheme that characterizes the distortions induced by typical attacks and selects the regions that are less distorted for the embedding of the payload data (Cvejic & Seppänen, 2004). Figure 7 presents a simplified schematic diagram of the attack characterization (lower part) and psychoacoustic modeling (upper part). The psychoacoustic model determines which frequency region is appropriate to embed in terms of its inaudibility, and the attack characterization process shows which frequency region is appropriate to embed in terms of detectability.

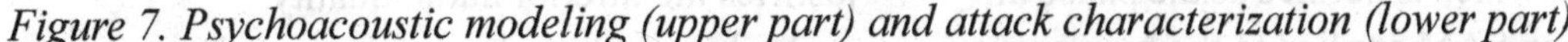

Figure 7. Psychoacoustic modeling (upper part) and attack characterization (lower part)

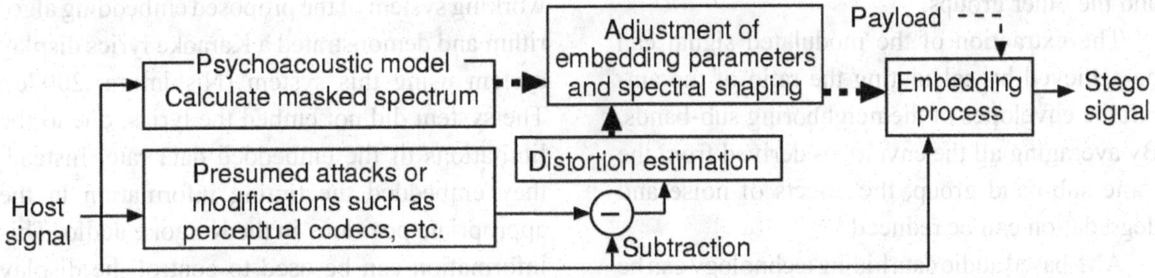

DATA HIDING METHODS PROPOSED AT THE MIH RESEARCH GROUP MEETINGS

This section will introduce some novel algorithms and applications presented at the MIH research group meetings. Some of these algorithms are based on the fundamental audio data hiding algorithms described in this chapter, but they have been vastly improved for better performance. Many of the novel algorithms are described in the following chapters and are not listed here. We include only a brief description of the proposed algorithms that are not described elsewhere in this book.

Algorithm Proposals

Audio Data Hiding using Amplitude Modulation

Nishimura (2006, 2007b, 2007c, 2010) proposed a data hiding method for audio based on sub-band amplitude modulation that is highly robust to analog transmission. To embed the data, the host signal is split into sub-bands with equal bandwidths. Sinusoidal Amplitude Modulation (SAM) at a relatively low modulation frequency, applied to neighboring sub-band signals at opposite phases, is used as a carrier of the embedded information. The sub-bands are grouped into a predetermined number of groups according to a key defined by a known pseudo-random number generator. The embedded information is encoded via Phase Shift Keying (PSK), which is defined as the phase difference between SAM applied to the base group and the other groups.

The extraction of the modulated signal can be achieved by calculating the ratio of the amplitude envelopes of the neighboring sub-bands. By averaging all the envelopes derived from the same sub-band group, the effects of noise and degradation can be reduced.

AM-based audio data hiding technology can be applied in watermarking for copyright protection (Nishimura, 2006) with sufficiently small sound quality degradation and high robustness against various modifications. However, one special feature of this technology is its application in aerial transmission.

Nishimura was able to embed data at 8 bps into speech and audio signals at 8 kHz sampling. The embedded data were proven robust to additive noise, reverberation, and Adaptive Multi-Rate (AMR) speech coding at 12.2 kbps, which is intended to simulate aerial transmission and transmission through the cellular phone network, with a detection rate of approximately 80%. The robustness was also demonstrated in signals played from a loudspeaker and recorded through a cellular phone in a lecture room, although at a somewhat lower detection rate.

The average embedded speech quality was shown to be approximately 2.87 using the ITU standard P. 862 Perceptual Evaluation of Speech Quality (PESQ) algorithm (ITU-T P.862, 2001). This quality score can be classified to be between "poor" and "fair." However, the average audio quality was calculated to be −2.3 on the Objective Difference Grade using the ITU standard BS.1387-1 Perceptual Evaluation of Audio Quality (PEAQ) algorithm (ITU-R BS.1387-1, 2001). This score can be classified to be slightly lower than the "slightly annoying" classification, and in the "annoying" class.

Therefore, the embedded audio quality requires further improvement. However, the robustness of this embedding algorithm for aerial transmission justifies the inferior audio quality.

Nishimura has also implemented a real-time working system of the proposed embedding algorithm and demonstrated a Karaoke lyrics display system using this system (Nishimura, 2007c). The system did not embed the lyrics, due to the limitations of the embedded data rate. Instead, they embedded the timing information in the appropriate positions in the Karaoke audio. This information can be used to control the display timing of a segment of the lyrics, which are assumed to be pre-stored on the system, along with the timing information. The timing information can be extracted from the audio signals played from loudspeakers.

Audio Data Hiding Using the Modified Patchwork Algorithm

Hiratsuka, Kondo, and Nakagawa (2007, 2008) proposed a data hiding method using the Modified Patchwork Algorithm (MPA), which is a minor modification to the patchwork algorithm described briefly in the previous section.

In the conventional patchwork algorithm (Bender, Gruhl, Morimoto, & Lu, 1996), two sets of samples (patches) are selected from a range of host signals, referred to here as sets A and B. The embedding of data in these patches simply adds a small fixed value d to the samples in A and subtracts d from B. This creates a bias between the patches, which can be used to detect the existence of embedded data. In other words, the expectation of the difference between the samples in patch A and patch B can be calculated. If the expectation is close enough to the expected difference, $2d$, we can assume that data have been embedded.

The patchwork method was intended for still images, and it worked relatively well. However, some modifications were needed to apply it to audio signals, which have a much smaller number of samples to work with. Arnold (2000) applied the patchwork algorithm to speech signals in the frequency domain transformed using the Discrete Cosine Transform (DCT). Yeo and Kim (2001) further improved the patchwork algorithm by modifying the small bias to be proportional to the pooled mean of sets A and B and switching the sign of the bias by the sign of the difference between the means of the samples in set A and set B, respectively. In other words, the bias is added to set A and subtracted from set B when the mean of the samples in A is larger than the mean in B, and vice versa. These modifications were shown to improve the robustness of this algorithm in audio signals significantly.

The work developed by Hiratsuka intended to improve the robustness of this algorithm for transmission through analog channels, focusing on synchronization because the correct synchronization of the DCT frames is crucial for watermark detection using this algorithm.

M-sequence synchronization patterns were embedded as synchronization headers with the MPA watermark. The synchronization at the decoder was accomplished by detecting the maximum correlation between the detected sync pattern and the correct sync pattern. This synchronization was shown to be possible with an Embed Frame Length (EFL) of 32 samples and higher with no perturbations. The accuracy degraded considerably in the presence of analog loopback. In addition, with modest levels of additive Gaussian noise and sample rate conversion in addition to analog loopback, robustness was demonstrated in some samples, while in other samples, the synchronization was not detectable in all of the trials.

Frame synchronization is an essential issue in the robustness of analog transmission in frame-based algorithms. This work is an ongoing issue, and it is still being pursued actively.

Applications

A number of interesting applications of data hiding for audio were also proposed. We will briefly describe a few examples here.

Universal Data Display Systems for the Visually Handicapped Using Audio Data Hiding

Munekata et al. attempted to embed data into audio from PA systems to transmit an audio message as text data to visually handicapped users (Handa, Nishimura, Munekata, & Suzuki, 2007; Munekata, Yamaguch, Nishimura, & Suzuki, 2011). The embedded message contained essentially the same content as the audio. The researchers' intention was to convey the same information to visually impaired users in the same range at which the audio from PA systems convey information to users with normal hearing.

The data were embedded into the audio signals using the time-spread echo method (Ko, Nishimura, & Suzuki, 2005), which spreads the echo impulses temporally using pseudo-noise signals. The relative delay of the echo was altered according to the embedded data. The time-spread echo method is known to be significantly more robust than conventional echo data hiding methods. They implemented this system onto an ultra-portable PC (Sony VGN-UX90S) and attempted a field trial in an actual indoor environment. They found that they could detect data from an analog-transmitted audio signal from 77 meters away in a corridor inside a building. They were also able to detect data from audio recorded outside the building 32 meters away from the source. Therefore, the system seems to demonstrate applicable performance in a real environment. They are currently investigating the system's performance under more realistic situations, e.g., with simultaneous playback from multiple speakers, in corridors with corners, etc.

Movie Pirate Position Tracking Using Multi-Channel Audio Watermark Detection

Babaguchi et al. have been applying audio watermarks to movies' audio tracks to detect the camera positions of camcorders being used to make illegal copies of films in movie theaters (Nakashima, Kaneto, Tachibana, & Babaguchi, 2007; Nakashima, Tachibana, & Babaguchi, 2009; Babaguchi, 2011). They attempted to embed data into multiple audio channels in a theater. The embedded data included the theater ID and the time stamp that can be detected and used to track the exact date and location of the recording. Moreover, the relative delay of the embedded data from each of the channels can be detected to estimate the approximate location of the camcorder within the theater. These data can be used with the theater ID and time stamp to identify the purchaser of the seat if the seating is reserved (although in reality, this was found to be impossible to pursue for various reasons).

The data were embedded using the two-dimensional pseudo array code (Tachibana, Shimizu, Kobayashi, & Nakamura, 2002). This method adds pseudo-random data, which are spread-spectrum embedded data, to the frequency-temporal host data obtained using the short-term FFT. This embedding method is known to be very robust to analog transmission.

The position of the recording is estimated using likelihood estimation of the relative delay of the audio from each of the speaker channels. The estimated delays can be used to calculate the position of the recording using the estimated relative distance from each of the loudspeakers in the theater. The researchers attempted a field test in an actual theater (round seating, 250 seats, radius of 8.8 meters) with three speaker channels using actual soundtracks of several movies (*Pretty Woman*, *Bourne Identity*, *Harry Potter and the Goblet of Fire*, and *Rent*). They found that the estimation of the recording position is possible with an error of less than 0.5 meters.

Data Hiding in Siren Signals

Sonoda et al. have attempted to embed information in sirens in emergency vehicles (Sonoda, Suzuki, & Takizawa, 2008; Sonoda, Yoshioka, & Takizawa, 2007). Their intention was to convey simultaneous supplemental information to users in the audible range of the siren. They embedded the data by adding a higher harmonic signal to the host data. The embedded data can be extracted from the signal by detecting the harmonic signal of the received signal. Therefore, siren signals, which are known to be affected by Doppler shifts in frequency, can be detected reliably with this method. Additionally, the strong tonal structure of the siren signals makes the detection more feasible with this method. A spread spectrum was applied to the embedded data for robustness, and forward error correction codes (BCH codes) were added. They were able to embed the data at a rate of 4 bps. They were also able to detect data at error rates below 10%, even with a Doppler shift of 10% and additive white noise at SNR −5 dB.

FUTURE RESEARCH DIRECTIONS

As previously described in this chapter, many audio data hiding methods were intended for use in digital form only without taking the analog channels that might be present in data transmission or storage into account. This means that the hidden data must be robust against analog-to-digital conversions or digital-to-analog conversions and to the noise that might be introduced in analog form. This also means that some of the frame-based algorithms must incorporate a means of recovering the original frame positions. These issues pose problems that are difficult to solve. However, it is becoming clear that many practical applications do require analog conversions. Some methods, such as the modulation-based method proposed by Nishimura (2007b, 2010), are designed to be robust in these situations, and others appear likely to follow.

In addition, most of the data hiding methods for audio were intended for watermarking, i.e., to protect copyrighted material by marking the ownership information transparently in audio signals. These watermarks are required to be robust, undetectable, and able to resist attempts to "erase" them. However, many recent data hiding methods are now targeted toward embedding meta-data in which additional information about the audio might be "hidden" and later used to provide additional information about its content. For instance, the URL of the artist who created an audio clip might be hidden in order to automatically display the artist's website. The research by Sonoda (Sonoda, Suzuki, & Takizawa, 2008; Sonoda, Yoshioka, & Takizawa, 2007) and Munekata (Handa, Nishimura, Munekata, & Suzuki, 2007; Munekata, Yamaguch, Nishimura, & Suzuki, 2011) can also be classified in this category. These types of hidden data may not need to be as robust as the watermarking application, but they may require a higher hidden data rate to be useful.

CONCLUSION

This chapter provided an overview of the current status of the audio data hiding technology. The basic issues involved, as well as their requirements, were outlined. The basic technology involved in hiding data in audio signals was described. We did not attempt an exhaustive description of the state of the art. Rather, we tried to present a snapshot of the many presentations made at the IEICE Multimedia Information Hiding research group meetings, which should offer a comprehensive sample of the current work on audio data hiding, especially in Japan. The readers are encouraged to read the following chapters in this book for other research in the MIH group. They are also encouraged to refer to the references listed in the additional reading section for other research in this field.

REFERENCES

Aoki, N. (2006). A band extension technique for G.711 speech using steganography. *IEICE Transactions on Communications, 89*(B), 1896-1898.

Arnold, M. (2000). *Audio watermarking: Features, applications, and algorithms.* Paper presented at the IEEE International Conference on Multimedia and Expo. New York, NY.

Babaguchi, N. (2011). *Multimedia processing for rights protection*. Paper presented at the 1st Meeting of the IEICE Technical Group on Enriched Multimedia. Tokyo, Japan.

Bender, W., Gruhl, D., Morimoto, N., & Lu, A. (1996). Techniques for data hiding. *IBM Systems Journal*, *35*(3-4), 313–336. doi:10.1147/sj.353.0313

Chen, B., & Wornell, G. W. (1998). *Digital watermarking and information embedding using dither modulation*. Paper presented at the IEEE Second Workshop on Multimedia Signal Processing. Santa Clara, CA.

Cvejic, N., & Seppänen, T. (2001). *Improving audio watermarking scheme using psychoacoustic watermark filtering*. Paper presented at the 1st IEEE International Symposium on Signal Processing and Information Technology. Cairo, Egypt.

Cvejic, N., & Seppänen, T. (2003). *Robust audio watermarking in wavelet domain using frequency hopping and patchwork method*. Paper presented at the third International Symposium on Image and Signal Processing and Analysis. Rome, Italy.

Cvejic, N., & Seppänen, T. (2004). Spread spectrum audio watermarking using frequency hopping and attack characterization. *Signal Processing*, *84*, 207–213. doi:10.1016/j.sigpro.2003.10.016

Geiger, R., Yokotani, Y., & Schuller, G. (2006). *Audio data hiding with high data rates based on Int-MDCT*. Paper presented at IEEE International Conference on Acoustics, Speech and Signal Processing. Toulouse, France.

Geiser, B., & Vary, P. (2007). *Backwards compatible wideband telephony in mobile networks: CELP watermarking and bandwidth extension*. Paper presented at IEEE International Conference on Acoustics, Speech and Signal Processing. Honolulu, HI.

Gruhl, D., Lu, A., & Bender, W. (1996). Echo hiding. *Lecture Notes in Computer Science*, *1174*, 295–315. doi:10.1007/3-540-61996-8_48

Handa, H., Nishimura, R., Munekata, T., & Suzuki, Y. (2007). *Prototype of universal information system using audio watermarking*. Paper presented at the 2nd Meeting of the IEICE Technical Group on Multimedia Information Hiding. Miyagi Zao, Japan.

Hiratsuka, K., Kondo, K., & Nakagawa, K. (2008). *On the accuracy of estimated synchronization positions for audio digital watermarks using the modified patchwork algorithm on analog channels*. Paper presented at the IEEE International Conference on Intelligent Information Hiding and Multimedia Signal Processing. Harbin, China.

Hiratsuka, K., Nakagawa, K., & Kondo, K. (2007). *The tolerance of digital watermarking using patchwork method on analog channels*. Paper presented at the 2nd Meeting of the IEICE Technical Group on Multimedia Information Hiding. Miyagi Zao, Japan.

ITU-R BS. 1387-1. (2001). *Method for objective measurements of perceived audio quality*. Retrieved from http://www.itu.int

ITU-T P.862. (2001). *Perceptual evaluation of speech quality (PESQ): An objective method for end-to-end speech quality assessment of narrow-band telephone networks and speech codecs*. Retrieved from http://www.itu.int

Ko, B.-S., Nishimura, R., & Suzuki, Y. (2004). Robust watermarking based on time-spread echo method with subband decomposition. *IEICE Transactions on Fundamentals*, *87*, 1647–1650.

Ko, B.-S., Nishimura, R., & Suzuki, Y. (2005). Time-spread echo method for digital audio watermarking. *IEEE Transactions on Multimedia*, *7*(2), 212–221. doi:10.1109/TMM.2005.843366

Koukopoulos, D., & Stamatiou, Y. C. (2001). *A compressed-domain watermarking algorithm for mpeg layer 3*. Paper presented at the workshop on Multimedia and security: New Challenges. Ottawa, Canada.

Li, W., & Xue, X. (2004). Audio watermarking based on music content analysis: Robust against time scale modification. *Lecture Notes in Computer Science*, *2939*, 289–300. doi:10.1007/978-3-540-24624-4_22

Löytynoja, N., Cvejic, N. E., Lähetkangas, E., & Seppänen, T. (2005). *Audio encryption using fragile watermarking*. Paper presented at the Fifth International Conference on Information, Communications and Signal Processing. Bangkok, Thailand.

Munekata, T., Yamaguchi, T., Nishimura, R., & Suzuki, Y. (2011). *Information hiding technologies for establishing a barrier-free environment in sound space.* Paper presented at the 12th Meeting of the IEICE Technical Group on Multimedia Information Hiding. Sendai, Japan.

Nakashima, Y., Kaneto, R., Tachibana, R., & Babaguchi, N. (2007). *Maximum-likelihood estimation of recording position based on synchronization position of audio watermarking.* Paper presented at the 2nd Meeting of the IEICE Technical Group on Multimedia Information Hiding. Miyagi Zao, Japan.

Nakashima, Y., Tachibana, R., & Babaguchi, N. (2009). Watermarked movie soundtrack finds the position of the camcorder in a theater. *IEEE Transactions on Multimedia*, *11*(3), 443–454. doi:10.1109/TMM.2009.2012938

Nishimura, A. (2006). *Audio watermarking based on sinusoidal amplitude modulation*. Paper presented at IEEE International Conference on Acoustics, Speech and Signal Processing. Toulouse, France.

Nishimura, A. (2007a). *Subjective and objective quality evaluation for audio watermarking based on sinusoidal amplitude modulation*. Paper presented at the 19th International Congress on Acoustics. Madrid, Spain.

Nishimura, A. (2007b). *Robustness against speech codecs on an audio data hiding based on amplitude modulation.* Paper presented at the 2nd Meeting of the IEICE Technical Group on Multimedia Information Hiding. Miyagi Zao, Japan.

Nishimura, A. (2007c). *Presentation of information synchronized with the audio signal reproduced by loudspeakers using an AM-based watermark.* Paper presented at the 3rd International Conference on Intelligent Information Hiding and Multimedia Signal Processing. Kaohsiung, Taiwan.

Nishimura, A. (2010). Audio data hiding that is robust with respect to aerial transmission and speech codecs. *International Journal of Innovative Computing, Information, & Control*, *6*(3B), 1389–1400.

Petitcolas, F. A. P., Anderson, R. J., & Kuhn, M. G. (1998). Attacks on copyright marking systems. *Lecture Notes in Computer Science*, *1525*, 219–239. doi:10.1007/3-540-49380-8_16

Sonoda, K., Suzuki, J., & Takizawa, O. (2008). *Information hiding for moving public address audio signal.* Paper presented at the 5th Meeting of the IEICE Technical Group on Multimedia Information Hiding. Sendai, Japan.

Sonoda, K., Yoshioka, K., & Takizawa, O. (2007). *Information hiding for public address audio signals using FH/FSK spread-spectrum scheme.* Paper presented at the 3rd IEEE International Conference on Intelligent Information Hiding and Multimedia Signal Processing. Splendor Kaohsiung, Taiwan.

Steinebach, M., Petitcolas, F. A. P., Raynal, F., Dittmann, J., Fontaine, C., & Seibel, S. ... Ferri, L. C. (2001). *StirMark benchmark: Audio watermarking attacks*. Paper presented at the International Conference on Information Technology: Coding and Computing. Las Vegas, NV.

Tachibana, R., Shimizu, S., Kobayashi, S., & Nakamura, T. (2002). An audio watermarking method using a two-dimensional pseudo-random array. *Signal Processing, 82*(10), 1455–1469. doi:10.1016/S0165-1684(02)00284-0

Wu, C.-P., Su, P.-C., & Kuo, C.-C. J. (1999). Robust audio watermarking for copyright protection. *Proceedings of the Society for Photo-Instrumentation Engineers, 3807*, 387–397. doi:10.1117/12.367655

Yeo, I.-K., & Kim, H. J. (2001). *Modified patchwork algorithm: A novel audio watermarking scheme*. Paper presented at the International Conference on Information Technology: Coding and Computing. Las Vegas, NV.

Yiqing, L., & Abdulla, M. H. (2008). *Perceptual evaluation of audio watermarking using objective quality measures*. Paper presented at IEEE International Conference on Acoustics, Speech and Signal Processing. Las Vegas, NV.

ADDITIONAL READING

Cvejic, N. (2004). *Algorithms for audio watermarking and steganography*. (Ph.D. dissertation). University of Oulu. Oulu, Finland.

Cvejic, N., & Seppänen, T. (Eds.). (2008). *Digital audio watermarking techniques and technologies*. Hershey, PA: IGI Global.

Mintzer, F., & Braudaway, G. W. (1999). *If one watermark is good, are more better?* Paper presented at the IEEE International Conference on Acoustics, Speech, and Signal Processing. Phoenix, AZ.

Moore, B. C. J. (2012). *An introduction to the psychology of hearing* (6th ed.). Bradford, UK: Emerald Group Publishing.

Nakayama, A. (2007). *Design and application of compound audio media that embed information imperceptibly.* (Ph.D. dissertation). Nara Institute of Science and Technology. Ikoma, Japan.

Nishimura, A. (2011). *Audio data hiding based on amplitude modulation and its application.* (Ph.D. dissertation). Kyushu University. Fukuoka, Japan.

Chapter 2
Reversible Audio Data Hiding in Spectral and Time Domains

Akira Nishimura
Tokyo University of Information Sciences, Japan

ABSTRACT

Reversible data hiding is a technique whereby hidden data are embedded in host data in such a way that the host data consistency is perfectly preserved and the host data are restored when extracting the hidden data. This chapter introduces basic algorithms for reversible data hiding, histogram shifting, histogram expansion, and compression. This chapter also proposes and evaluates two reversible data hiding methods, i.e., hiding data in the frequency-domain using integer Discrete Cosine Transform (DCT) and modified DCT and hiding in the time domain using linear prediction and error expansion. As no location map is required to prevent amplitude overflow, the proposed method in the time domain achieves a storage capacity of nearly 1 bit per sample of payload data. The proposed methods are evaluated by the payload amount, objective quality degradation of stego signal, and payload concealment.

INTRODUCTION

Reversible data hiding is a technique that allows embedding hidden data in host data, such that the host data consistency is perfectly preserved. The host data are restored to their original form after the extraction process retrieves the hidden data. This is also referred as lossless data hiding. Semi-reversible data hiding implies that the host data are not recovered perfectly but that the recovered data are more similar to the host data than the stego data. Reversible data hiding is considered useful for authentication, metadata recording, tampering detection, covert communication, and quality enhancement, and so forth. The technological requirements are minimal stego signal quality degradation, large payload, and undetectable hidden data concealment. This chapter introduces basic reversible data hiding methods. It then introduces recent progress in reversible audio data hiding techniques in the spectral and time domains. The proposed methods are evaluated using the payload amount, the objective quality degradation of stego signals, and payload data concealment.

DOI: 10.4018/978-1-4666-2217-3.ch002

BACKGROUND

Previous Works

Researchers have proposed several methods for reversible audio data hiding. These methods can be classified into three categories based on the embedding data domain: time (waveform) domain (van der Veen, et al., 2003, Yan & Wang, 2008), spectral domain (Huang, et al., 2010), and compressed data domain (Li, et al., 2008).

Reversible audio data hiding techniques in the time domain are usually simple and require a smaller computational load. van der Veen et al. (2003) proposed an amplitude expansion method that applies a bit-shift of the amplitude data to the Most Significant Bit (MSB). This operation enables the insertion of payload data into the Least Significant Bit (LSB) position. To prevent amplitude overflow induced by the bit-shift operation, amplitude compression is applied before the bit-shift operation. Compounding errors induced by amplitude compression are losslessly compressed and embedded into the LSB position as overhead data.

Yan and Wang (2008) proposed a prediction error expansion method for reversible audio data hiding using linear prediction. One to three previous host waveform samples and integer coefficients are multiplied and added to predict the current sample. The difference between the current and predicted amplitudes is multiplied by two, and the payload bit is added to the result. These processes form the "prediction error expansion." The expanded difference is added to the predicted amplitude to obtain the stego sample. A "no expansion" flag for that sample avoids amplitude overflow caused by the difference expansion. A location map that indicates which samples are not expanded is losslessly compressed and replaced in the LSBs of the last segment of the stego data.

Techniques for reversible audio data hiding in the frequency domain first convert segmented waveform signals into spectral data using an integer conversion, such as an integer Discrete Cosine Transform (DCT) (Huang, et al., 2010). Amplitude spectra in the high-frequency region are shifted by one bit towards the MSB to add payload data to the LSB position. An inverse transform of the embedded spectral data generates the stego waveform data. Amplitude overflows in the waveform domain are prevented by a non-embedding processing of the frequency regions that exhibit high amplitudes. A location map that indicates which frequency regions are not processed is also embedded within the payload data.

A major limitation in previous studies is that they require overhead data, such as the location map. These overheads shrink the available payload data area, especially when the audio data are short and/or have large amplitudes. In addition, payload data concealment is imperfect, as the LSB data in the stego waveform (van der Veen, et al., 2003) or in the DCT spectrum (Huang, et al., 2010) always represent the payload data. Furthermore, the number of secret keys representing the prediction coefficients is small; there are typically only 64 patterns (Yan & Wang, 2008).

Basic Reversible Data Hiding Techniques

Three basic reversible hiding techniques are histogram shifting, histogram expansion, and compression. They can be applied to both image and audio data hiding. Histogram shifting and expansion methods are applied to integer-type data. As these techniques slightly modify their histogram shapes, the nature of the stego data is not so different from that of the host data. The stego data are audible but somewhat degraded. A compression technique (Li, et al., 2008) losslessly compresses the host data and adds payload data to the compressed host data. The nature of the resultant stego data is quite different from that of the host data. The stego data in the compression technique are thus not audible without appropriate decompression.

The following sections introduce the basic histogram shifting and expansion techniques. These techniques can be applied to any data domain: the time and spectral domains or some types of transformed domains. The advanced reversible audio data hiding methods in the time and spectral domains, which are discussed below, adopt the histogram expansion technique. The following subsections are thus worth understanding for the purposes of extending the fundamental reversible data hiding technique.

Histogram Shifting

Histogram shifting is also referred to as histogram modification. It shifts the host data towards large values and adds payload data to the shifted space. Assume that the host data are represented by X, the shifting boundary is s, payload data fall in the set $b \in \{0, 1, \ldots, a\text{-}1\}$, and Y represents the stego data. The embedding process is expressed as follows:

$$Y = \begin{cases} X + a & (s < X) \\ X + b & (X = s) \\ X & (X < s) \end{cases} \tag{1}$$

The recovering process is expressed as follows:

$$X = \begin{cases} Y - a & (s + a \le Y) \\ s & (s \le Y < s + a) \\ \mathrm{Y} & (\mathrm{Y} < s) \end{cases} \tag{2}$$

The payload extraction process is expressed as follows:

$$b = \begin{cases} Y - s & (s \le Y < s + a) \\ null & (\text{otherwise}) \end{cases} \tag{3}$$

The payload amount depends on the appearance frequency of s in Y. To increase the payload amount, the multiple border value s can be applied recursively. However, as the modified histogram is easily detected by investigating the statistical irregularity of the histogram, the hiding concealment is relatively poor. The payload data should be embedded in some transformed data domain for which a histogram cannot be easily obtained.

Histogram Expansion

The histogram expansion technique multiplies the host data by a (a is an integer and greater than 2) and adds the payload data. Multiplying by a enables the embedding of the payload data. Assume that X represents the host data, payload data fall in the set $b \in \{0, 1, \ldots, a\text{-}1\}$, and Y represents the stego data. The embedding process is expressed as follows:

$$Y = X \times a + b \tag{4}$$

The recovering process is expressed as follows:

$$X = \lfloor Y / a \rfloor \tag{5}$$

The payload extraction process is expressed as follows:

$$B = Y \bmod a \tag{6}$$

The number of payload bits is $\log_2 a$ bits per sample. Combining other rules, the payload capacity can be controlled (Yan & Wang, 2008). The histogram expansion technique can be considered an extension of the histogram shifting technique. Both techniques cause overflow and underflow in the host data quantization limits. Researchers have proposed several solutions for the under/overflow problem (van der Veen, et al., 2003; Yan & Wang, 2008; Huang, et al., 2010). Overhead data, i.e., a location map that indicates which samples are not expanded, must be stored to avoid this problem in these studies.

REVERSIBLE DATA HIDING IN THE SPECTRAL DOMAIN

We have proposed a technique for reversible audio data hiding in the spectral domain (Huang, et al., 2010). This method first converts segmented waveform signals into spectral data by using an integer Discrete Cosine Transform (intDCT). Amplitude spectra in the high-frequency region are shifted by one bit towards the MSB to add payload data to the LSB position. An inverse transform of the embedded spectral data generates the stego waveform data. Amplitude overflow in the waveform domain is prevented by a non-embedding processing of the frequency regions that exhibit high amplitudes. A location map that indicates which frequency regions are not processed is also embedded alongside the payload data.

This section explains and evaluates a method for reversible data hiding using the integer DCT (Huang, et al., 2010). The method has some disadvantages associated with quality degradation and payload data concealment. An improved method using an integer Modified DCT (intMDCT) is then proposed, which exhibits better sound quality and payload data concealment.

Reversible Data Hiding Using Integer DCT

The embedding phase occurs in the spectral domain and is calculated using the host signal intDCT (Hai Bin, et al., 2004). The high-frequency DCT coefficients are doubled before the embedding process to accommodate the embedding data, as the embedding data replace the LSB of the modified high-frequency coefficient. The data to be embedded contains the location data for embedding, stored LSB data for amplitude adjustment, and payload. The inverse intDCT converts the frequency spectrum to the waveform data to yield the stego signal. If amplitude overflow or underflow in the stego signal occurs, the amplitude adjustment process before the inverse intDCT is

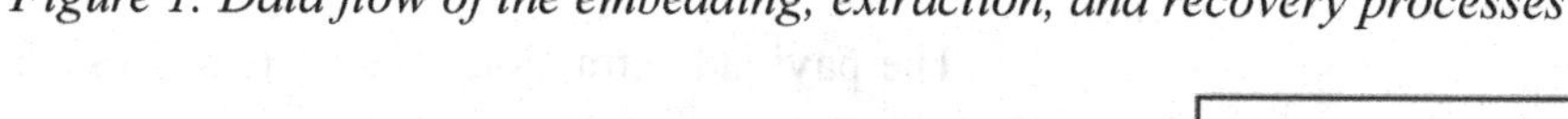

Figure 1. Data flow of the embedding, extraction, and recovery processes

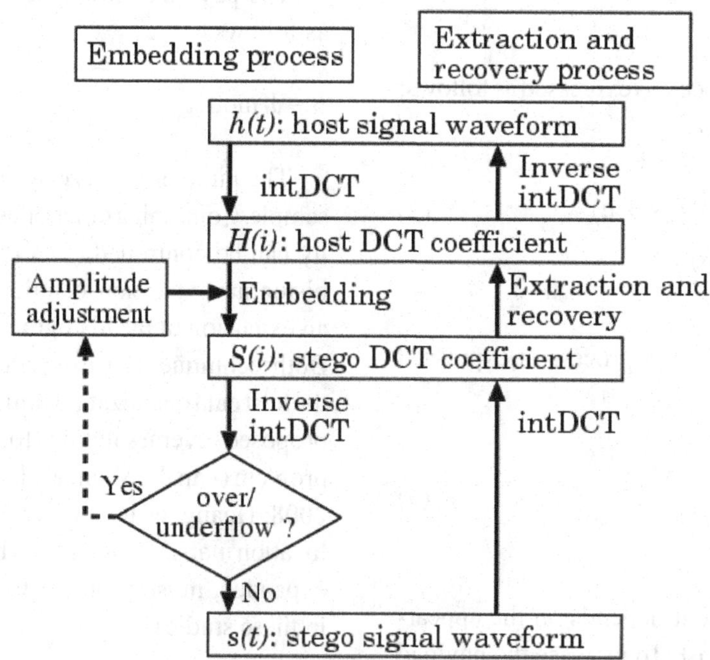

repeated until the overflow or underflow is not observed. Figure 1 shows the data flow of the embedding, extraction, and recovery processes.

Embedding Process

At first, the intDCT coefficients $H(i)$ (i=1, 2, …, N) are divided into M (M=16 in the current implementation) frequency regions. The power levels for each frequency region $p(m)(1 \leq m \leq M)$ are also calculated. Location data L with a length of M bits correspond to the frequency region location, i.e., the value $L(m)$ points to the intDCT coefficients $H(i)(i = (m\text{-}1)N/M+1,\ldots,mN/M)$. Each bit value of L classifies the frequency regions to be used for embedding. The first $M/2$-bit indicates low-frequency regions for amplitude adjustment, and the last $M/2$-bit indicates high-frequency regions for data hiding. If M=16 and the initial values of L are {0, 0, 0, 0, 0, 0, 0, 0, 0, 0, 0, 0, 1, 1, 1, 1}, the highest $N/4$ coefficients in the DCT spectra are used for embedding. The border between the low-frequency no-modification and the high-frequency embedding regions is an embedding parameter. The current evaluation is conducted using the highest $N/4$ coefficients for embedding.

The high-frequency intDCT coefficients, indicated by $L(m)$ = 1, are expanded by doubling to reserve embedding space. The embedding data replace the LSB of the intDCT coefficients of the expanded regions. Figure 2 shows a schematic embedding process when no overflow/underflow occurs by expansion.

By applying the inverse intDCT to the expanded intDCT coefficients $S(i)$, the stego waveform amplitude $s(t)$ may cause overflow or underflow in the intense signal segment, which means that an amplitude of the waveform exceeds the upper or lower bounds. We propose an adaptive amplitude adjustment technique in the intDCT domain. If the overflow or underflow occurs in $s(t)$, the LSB data of $H(i)$ that exhibit maximum power levels in the $L(m)$ = 0 frequency regions are stored. Simultaneously, 1 is subtracted from $L(m)$. The stored LSB data are embedded in the lowest expanded frequency region, indicated by $L(m)$ = 1. The frequency region indicated by $L(m)$ = -1 is divided by $\sqrt{2}$ (-3dB), and the inverse intDCT is applied to $S(i)$. These processes are repeated until no overflow or underflow is observed in $s(t)$. Figure 3 shows overflow/overflow/underflow prevention in the embedding process by attenuating the DCT coefficients of the low-frequency region.

The highest DCT coefficients, indicated by m = M, are reserved to embed the location (|L|; M bits) and payload data. An embedding key should cipher and scramble these data to hide informa-

Figure 2. Schematic diagram of the embedding process with no overflow/ overflow/ underflow

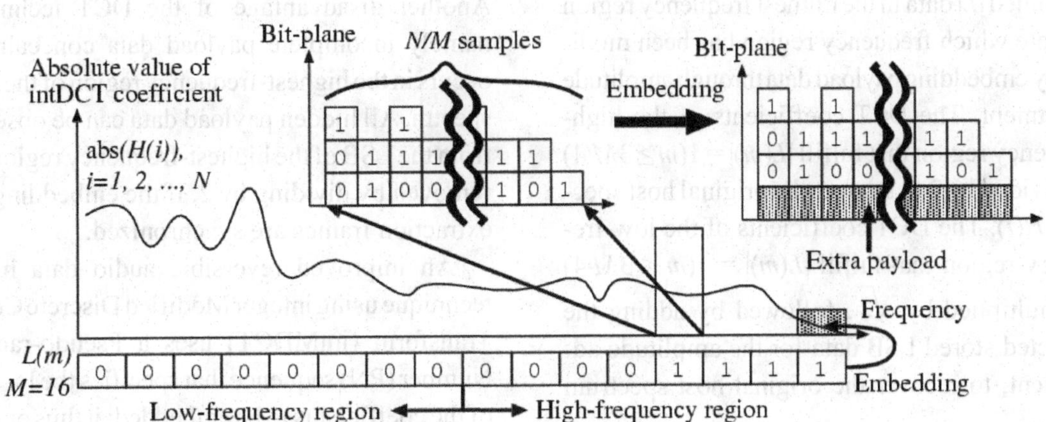

Figure 3. Preventing overflow/ overflow/ underflow in the embedding process

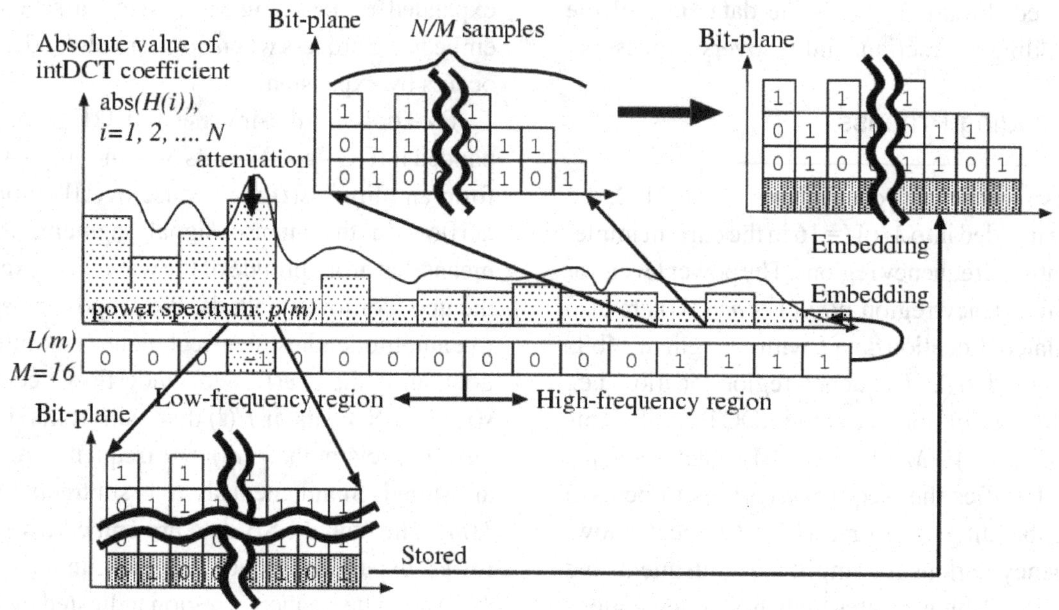

tion. Other frequency regions, indicated by $L(m) = 1$, are used for the stored LSB and payload data. The total amount of the payload can be obtained by ((number of $L(m) = 1$) - (number of $L(m) = -1$)) $\times N/M - M$.

Payload Extraction and Host Data Reconstruction

At the beginning of the extraction process, the embedded data are extracted by applying module 2 to $S(i)$. The extracted, deciphered, and descrambled $|L|$ data in the highest frequency region indicate which frequency region has been modified by embedding payload data through amplitude adjustment. The DCT coefficients of the high-frequency region that fulfill $|L(m)| = 1 (m \geq 3M/4)$ are divided by 2 to recover the original host spectrum $H(i)$. The DCT coefficients of the low-frequency region that fulfill $|L(m)| = 1 (m < 3M/4)$ are multiplied by $\sqrt{2}$, followed by adding the extracted stored LSB data for the amplitude adjustment, to recover the original host spectrum $H(i)$. The reconstructed $h(t)$ is obtained by the inverse intDCT. The host signal is thus recovered perfectly from the stego signal.

Reversible Audio Data Hiding Using Integer MDCT

The reversible audio data hiding technique using integer DCT (Huang, et al., 2010) has several limitations. Converting data to the framed audio waveform using the inverse DCT causes discontinuities at the border of the framed waveform. Another disadvantage of the DCT technique, namely incomplete payload data concealment, occurs in the highest-frequency region of the DCT spectra. All hidden payload data can be observed from the LSB of the highest-frequency region and removed by dividing by 2, if the embedding and extraction frames are synchronized.

An improved reversible audio data hiding technique using integer Modified Discrete Cosine Transform (intMDCT) uses a Pseudo-random Number (PN) sequence that specifies the location of the coefficients to be embedded; it thus ensures the concealment of the data hiding evidence. Sinusoidally overlapped windows combined with MDCT yield smooth connections between the waveforms of adjacent frames.

Encoding: Basic Process

The host signal waveform is segmented and fed into the *N*-point intMDCT. IntMDCT is implemented with the intDCT type IV (Hai Bin, et al., 2004) and the lifting scheme using a half-overlapped sine-window (Geiger, et al., 2001). The PN sequence randomly contains +1 and -1 in equal probabilities. It is generated by the known secret key and defines the discrete frequency positions in the high-frequency embedding region, indicated by +1. The border between the low-frequency no-modification and high-frequency embedding regions is an embedding parameter. The current implementation defines it as half of the Nyquist frequency. The intMDCT transforms the *N*-sample waveform into *N*/2-sample frequency data. The PN sequence length is therefore *N*/4.

IntMDCT coefficients of the embedding position are amplified by two before the embedding process to accommodate the embedding data, as the embedding data replace the LSB of the amplified high-frequency coefficients. The inverse intMDCT converts the resultant frequency spectrum to waveform data to yield the stego signal. If amplitude overflow or underflow occurs in the stego signal, the amplitude adjustment process before the inverse intMDCT is repeatedly applied until the overflow/overflow/underflow is not observed. The left part of Figure 4 shows a schematic diagram of the embedding process.

Controlling Amplitude Overflow/Overflow/Underflow

The embedding frequency region is segmented into *M* regions. The amplitude adjustment process selects the frequency region that exhibits

Figure 4. Schematic diagram of the embedding process and overflow/ overflow/ underflow prevention

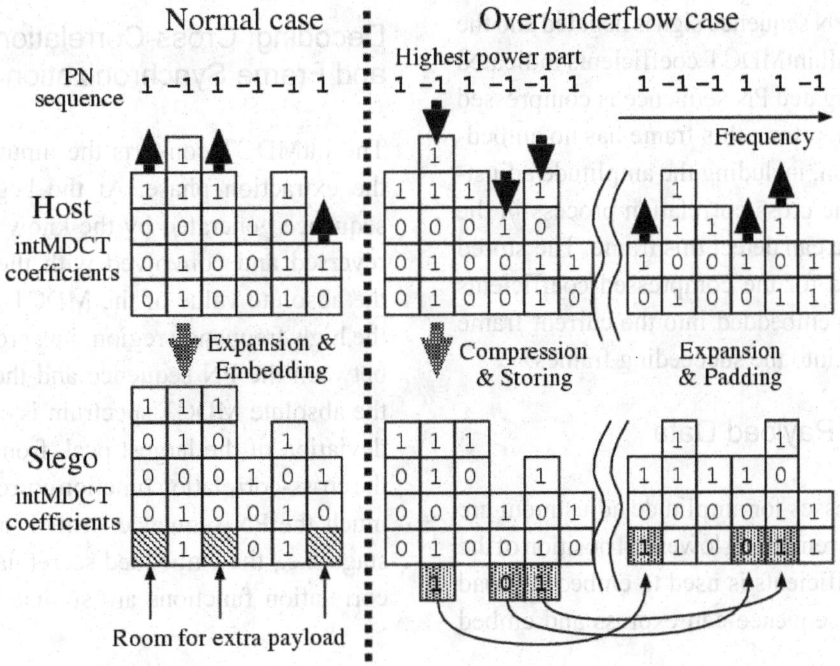

Normal case
Over/underflow case
Highest power part
PN sequence
1 -1 1 -1 -1 1
1 -1 1 -1 -1 1
1 -1 -1 1 1 -1
Frequency
Host intMDCT coefficients
Expansion & Embedding
Compression & Storing
Expansion & Padding
Stego intMDCT coefficients
Room for extra payload

the highest power level among the M-1 regions, excluding the highest region. The highest region is reserved to embed the amplitude adjustment table described below. The embedding coefficients' amplitudes, indicated by +1 in the PN sequence in the selected regions, are not modified. The coefficients' amplitudes, indicated by -1 in the PN sequence in the selected regions, are compressed by half. The compressing process includes storing the LSBs and embedding them into the MDCT coefficients in the adjacent frequency region. The M-bit table, indicating the compressed regions of the coefficients, is embedded into the coefficients of the highest-frequency region. The right part of Figure 4 shows a schematic overflow/overflow/underflow prevention diagram.

These amplitude adjustment selection, compressing, and embedding processes are iterated to expand their selected regions by, at most, M-1 times until no overflow/underflow occurs. However, the overflow/underflow still occurs after M-1 iterations in the loud waveform frame because the previous frame also has a large amplitude. In that case, the amplitude compressing process is applied to the MDCT coefficients of the previous frame. If the resultant stego waveform still has underflow/overflow, the PN sequence sign is negated and the amplitude of all intMDCT coefficients indicated by -1 of the negated PN sequence is compressed by half, and therefore, this frame has no embedded information, including the amplitude adjustment table. The cross-correlation process in the decoding stage can detect this frame. The stored lowest bit data for the compressed coefficients that cannot be embedded into the current frame are embedded into the succeeding frames.

Embedding Payload Data

After all processes for amplitude adjustment are completed, the remaining lowest bit position of the amplified coefficients is used to embed payload data. The PN sequence can express and embed more secret data. The PN sequence is circular shifted by the number of integer values representing the secret data in every K frames and utilized to indicate the embedding frequency location. Consequently, the embedding frequency location is concealed and cannot be observed from the stego signal and its spectrum. If the size of MDCT is $N(= 2^n)$-point and the sampling frequency is f Hz, the embedding bit-rate of the secret data is

$$\frac{(n-1)f}{NK} \text{ bps}$$

The current implementation adopted two parameter sets: $N = 2048$, $K = 8$, and $N = 1024$, $K = 16$, where $f = 44100$ and $M = 8$ are kept constant.

The above method fails for audio data with little high-frequency energy, for example, when many zeros are distributed among the high-frequency intMDCT coefficients. In that case, positive PN sequence values are added to the MDCT coefficient before amplitude expansion. Adding the PN sequence is recorded as another bit value attached to the amplitude adjustment table, i.e., the size of the table practically amounts to $M + 1$ bits.

Decoding: Cross-Correlation and Frame Synchronization

The intMDCT converts the input stego data in the extraction phase. At the beginning, a PN sequence generated by the known secret key is reversed and convolved with the logarithm of the absolute value of the MDCT coefficients in the high-frequency region, i.e., cross-correlation between the PN sequence and the logarithm of the absolute MDCT spectrum is calculated. The deviation of the largest peak from the center of the cross-correlation function corresponds to how much the PN sequence shifted in the encoding stage, i.e., the embedded secret data. The cross-correlation functions are summed up among K

successive frames, and the location of the largest peak corresponds to the embedded secret data.

Attempting to locate the exact frame location in the decoding process is critical, as a small gap between frame locations invalidates the data extraction. Geiger et al. (2006) used a synchronization code to embed into the integer MDCT coefficients to determine the exact position of the embedded frame with step-by-step searching. The current approach involves step-by-step searching by shifting the initial frame sample to find the largest peak in the cross-correlation function for frame synchronization without any synchronization codes. Figure 5 shows a schematic representation of the calculation of the cross-correlation functions and extraction of the embedded secret data in the decoding process. If no data are embedded into the MDCT coefficient of the frame, the PN sequence sign is negated. There is no amplitude adjustment table in such a table. This frame can be found because the peak amplitude of the cross-correlation function is negative, compared to the peak amplitude of the other K-1 frames.

Data Extraction and Recovery

The embedded data are extracted by applying modulo two to the intMDCT coefficients indicated by the PN sequence. The extracted data from the highest-frequency region are assigned to the amplitude adjustment table. According to the table data, the M-1 regions of the MDCT coefficients indicated by the positive PN sequence are classified into expanded and compressed regions. The embedded data are extracted from the intMDCT coefficients of the expanded regions. The extracted data are classified into the stored LSBs of the compressed intMDCT coefficients of the host and payload data. The recovered intMDCT coefficients of the compressed region are obtained by multiplying the compressed coefficients by $\sqrt{2}$ and adding the stored LSBs to them.

Figure 5. Schematic representation of the calculation of the cross-correlation functions and extraction of the embedded secret data in the decoding process

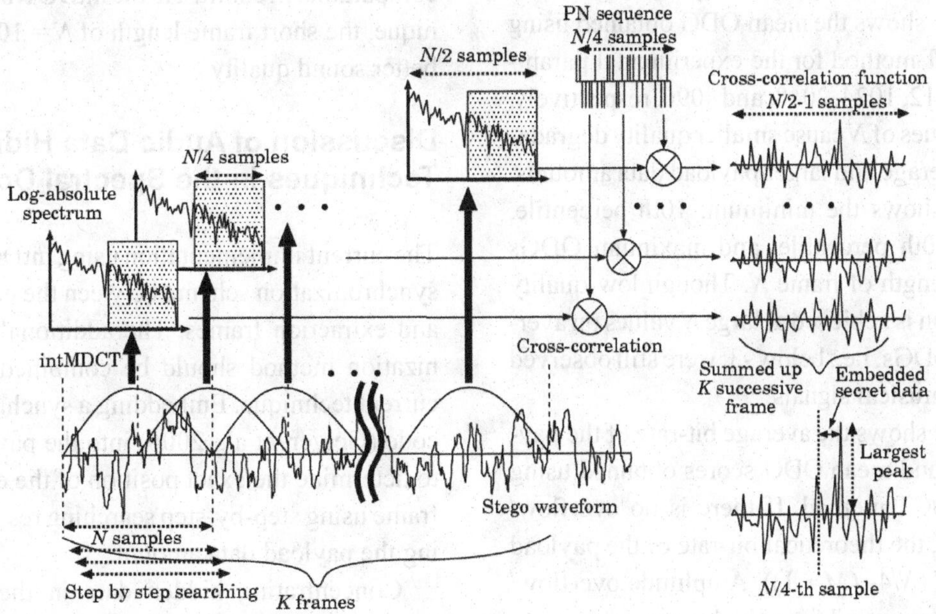

The intMDCT coefficients recovered from the expanded region are obtained by dividing by two. The recovered host signal is obtained by applying the inverse intMDCT to the recovered intMDCT coefficients.

Evaluation

The host audio data included 100 total pieces of music from a database containing various types of music (RWC-MDB-G-2001) (Goto, et al., 2003). The 20 s between the initial 40 and 60 s left-channel signal of each piece was used. To model the payload data, random-bit data were embedded into the host signal. The Perceptual Audio Quality Evaluation (PEAQ) was used to evaluate the objective stego audio quality degradation, as recommended by ITU-R BS.1387. An Objective Difference Grade (ODG), which corresponds to the degree of subjective quality degradation of the impaired stego audio signal compared to the original audio signal, was obtained using PEAQ software (Kabal, 2002). For subjective quality, an ODG value of 0 corresponds to no difference, -1 corresponds to perceptible but not annoying, and -2 corresponds to slightly annoying.

Table 1 shows the mean ODG obtained using the intDCT method for the experimental parameters N=512, 1024, 2048, and 4096, respectively. Larger values of N cause smaller quality degradation on average and larger payload data amounts. Figure 6 shows the minimum, 10th percentile, median, 90th percentile, and maximum ODGs for each length of frame N. Though low-quality degradation is achieved at large N values on average, low ODGs, i.e., below -3, were still observed for some musical signals.

Table 2 shows the average bit-rate of the payload data and mean ODG scores obtained using the intMDCT method. If there is no overflow/underflow, the theoretical bit-rate of the payload data is f/N (N/4- (M+ 1)). Amplitude overflow/underflow occurred for only 4 tunes.

Table 1. Mean ODG obtained using the intDCT method and the payload amount in kilobits per second

N	Mean ODG	Mean Payload [kbps]
512	-1.95	9.65
1024	-1.50	10.3
2048	-1.19	10.7
4096	-0.770	10.9

The resulting average ODG for the stego music signals was -0.72 for N = 1024, which corresponds to better than the perceptual evaluation of "perceptible, but not annoying". The average ODG score for 128-kbps MP3-compressed music for the same tune was -0.89. This indicates that the stego music sound quality is slightly better than 128-kbps MP3 music.

Figure 7 shows the minimum, 10th percentile, median, 90th percentile, and maximum ODGs for each length of frame N using the intMDCT method. This method achieves better sound quality compared to the intDCT-based technique shown in Figure 6, while the payload data amounts are comparable. In contrast to the intDCT-based technique, the short frame length of N = 1024 shows better sound quality.

Discussion of Audio Data Hiding Techniques in the Spectral Domain

The current implementation using intDCT has no synchronization scheme between the embedding and extraction frames. The additional synchronization method should be combined with the current technique. Embedding a synchronization code (Geiger, et al., 2006) into the payload data to determine the exact position of the embedded frame using step-by-step searching results in losing the payload data amount.

Concentrating hidden data in the highest-frequency region of DCT coefficients is associ-

Figure 6. Minimum, 10th percentile, median, 90th percentile, and maximum ODGs for each length of frame N using the intDCT method

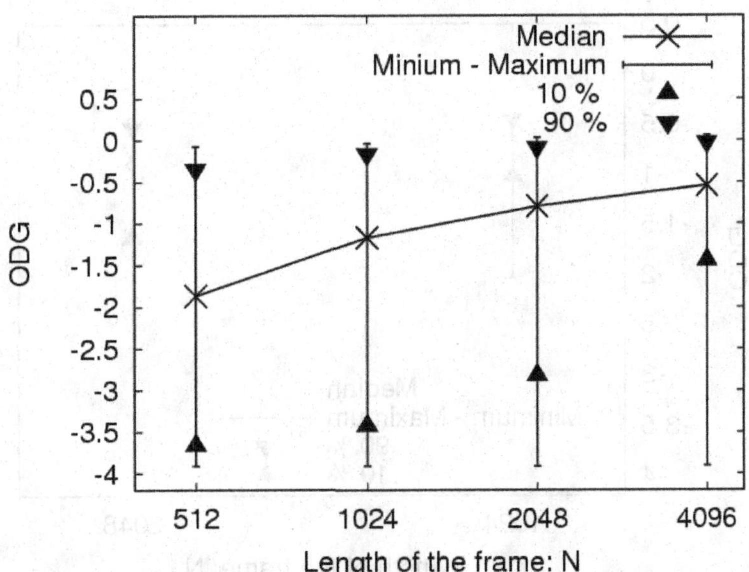

Table 2. Bit-rates of embedding data and mean ODG obtained using the intMDCT method for 20 s of 100 tunes from RWC-MDB-G-2001

Embedding Data	Minimum	Mean	Maximum	ODG
	$N = 1024, M = 8, K = 16$			-0.715
Payload data [kbps]	10.66	10.68	10.68	
Secret data [bps]		26.5		
Total [kbps]	10.69	10.71	10.71	
	$N = 2048, M = 8, K = 8$			-1.00
Payload data [kbps]	10.84	10.84	10.91	
Secret data [bps]		26.5		
Total [kbps]	10.87	10.87	10.94	

ated with several disadvantages in hidden data concealment and sound quality degradation. Incomplete payload data concealment occurs in the highest-frequency region of the DCT spectra. All hidden payload data can be observed from the LSB of the highest-frequency region and removed by dividing by two if embedding and extraction frame synchronization is achieved.

Conversely, an improved reversible audio data hiding technique using intMDCT applies a PN sequence to specify the location of coefficients to be embedded such that the data hiding evidence is guaranteed to be concealed. In addition, the cross-correlation between the MDCT coefficients in the embedded region and PN sequence achieves synchronization between the embedding and extraction waveform frames.

However, frame synchronization and hidden data concealment can also be achieved by applying a PN sequence to specify the location of the DCT

Figure 7. Minimum, 10th percentile, median, 90th percentile, and maximum ODGs for each length of frame N using the intMDCT method

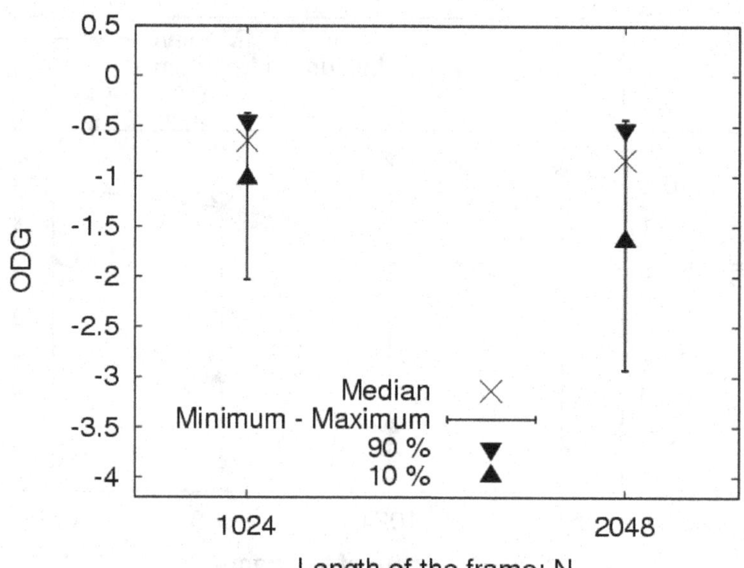

coefficients to be embedded in the same manner. The most important advantage of the technique using intMDCT is low sound-quality degradation of the stego signal, as shown in Figures 6 and 7.

Using DCT, stego signal sound quality degradation is significant for piano music, which has many pulse-like onsets and line spectra. Conversion to the framed audio waveform using the inverse DCT causes discontinuities at the framed waveform border. Figure 8 shows waveforms from track 62, which exhibit an ODG of -3.91. The upper waveform is the host signal, the middle waveform is the stego signal, and the lower waveform is the difference between the host and stego waveforms, expanded by a factor of 10. The stego waveform discontinuity is clearly observed.

The current computer simulation identified the prominent peak in the cross-correlation function between the high-frequency MDCT coefficients and PN sequence for all frames. However, a large deviation in the high-frequency MDCT coefficients may interfere with the embedded PN sequence such that no correct peak position is found in the cross-correlation function. The detectability of the secret data can be checked by examining the cross-correlation function at the encoding process. An additional amplitude adjustment process to ensure secret data detection may be required with additional amplitude adjustment table data for some host signals.

REVERSIBLE DATA HIDING IN THE TIME DOMAIN

This section proposes three means of improving the conventional prediction error expansion techniques for reversible audio waveform data hiding of audio waveforms (Yan & Wang, 2008). First, errors in deriving the predicted amplitudes are reduced using floating-point multiplication and rounding the resulting output to minimize the stego audio quality degradation. Second, no location map is used to prevent amplitude overflow, allowing the method to achieve a storage capacity of nearly 1 bit per host data sample.

Figure 8. Waveforms from track 62: upper, host signal; middle: stego signal; lower: difference between the host and stego waveforms, expanded 10 times

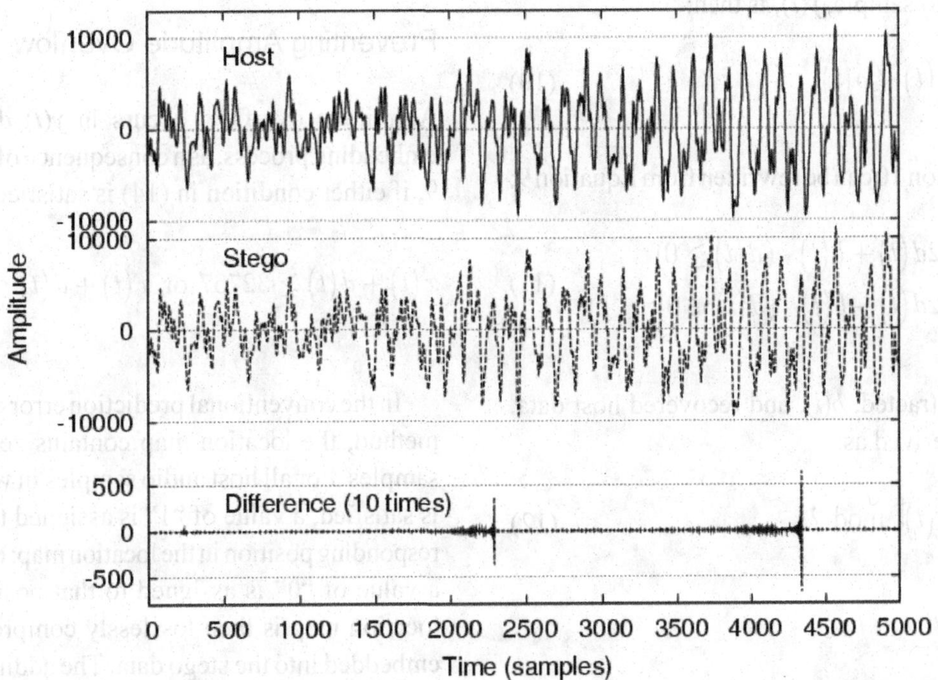

Finally, payload data concealment is realized by autoregressive coefficients and/or an exclusive or (XOR) operation on the secret key of the LSB of the initial stego samples.

Prediction Error Expansion

Basic Embedding and Extraction

We define an n-th order autoregressive linear prediction, $p(t)$, as:

$$p(t) = \sum_{i=1}^{n} \text{round}\left(a(i) \times (t-i)\right) \quad (7)$$

for time series host data $x(t)$, where $t = 0, 1, 2, \ldots, N - 1$ and N is the amount of host data. The difference between general linear prediction and Equation 7 is the rounding function. It is introduced to obtain an integer value for $p(t)$. $a(i)$, which can be derived by applying the Burg method (Burg, 1975) to all $x(t)$, are the prediction coefficients for $x(t)$. Each set of n-th order $a(i)$ is considered a host-specific secret key, to which the extraction process must refer.

Embedding using prediction error expansion outputs stego data, $y(t)$, according to the following rules:

$$d(t) = x(t) - p(t) \quad (8)$$

$$y(t) = \begin{cases} x(t) + d(t) + b(t) & (t > 0 \text{ and } d(t) \geq 0) \\ x(t) + d(t) - b(t) & (t > 0 \text{ and } d(t) < 0) \\ x(t) & (t = 0) \end{cases} \quad (9)$$

where $b(t) \in \{0, 1\}$ is the payload data.

During the extraction process, the predicted amplitude value, $p(t)$ $(t > 0)$, for the current sample is derived from Equation 7 using both $y(0)$ and the recovered host data, $x(t)$ ($t > 0$), in sequence. The difference, $d'(t)$, between $p(t)$ and the amplitude of the stego sample, $y(t)$, is then:

$$d'(t) = y(t) - p(t) \tag{10}$$

and Equation 10 can be rewritten from Equation 9:

$$d'(t) = \begin{cases} 2d(t) + b(t) & (d(t) \geq 0) \\ 2d(t) - b(t) & (d(t) < 0) \end{cases} \tag{11}$$

The extracted, $b(t)$, and recovered host data, $x(t)$, are derived as:

$$b(t) = |d'(t)| \bmod 2 \tag{12}$$

and

$$x(t) = \begin{cases} p(t) + \lfloor |d'(t)|/2 \rfloor & (d(t) \geq 0) \\ p(t) - \lfloor |d'(t)|/2 \rfloor & (d(t) < 0) \end{cases} \tag{13}$$

Figure 9. Basic embedding and extraction process

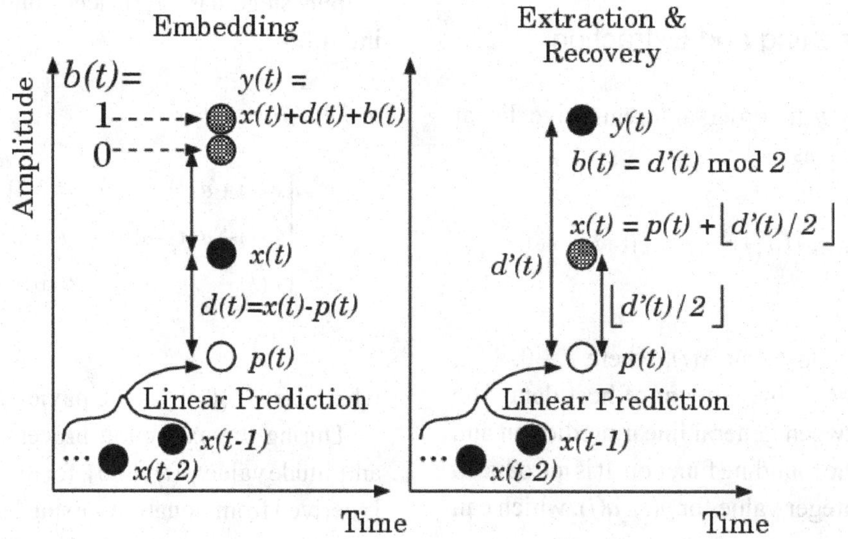

Figure 9 schematically shows the basic embedding and extraction processes.

Preventing Amplitude Overflow

Amplitude overflow occurs in $y(t)$ during the embedding process, as a consequence of Equation 9, if either condition in (14) is satisfied:

$$x(t) + d(t) \geq 32767 \text{ or } x(t) + d(t) \leq -32768 \tag{14}$$

In the conventional prediction error expansion method, the location map contains zero-valued samples. For all host audio samples in which (14) is satisfied, a value of "1" is assigned to the corresponding position in the location map; otherwise, a value of "0" is assigned to that position. The location map is then losslessly compressed and embedded into the stego data. The additional embedding of the location map can cause a large loss in the amount of payload data that can be stored, especially when amplitude overflow often occurs.

The key idea of the proposed method is to embed the marking bit before the current sample to indicate which stego sample is not embedded. If (14) is satisfied for the host sample, the embedding process should be canceled, i.e., $y(t) = x(t)$ at that sample. In this case, the stego sample satisfies one of the following conditions:

$$y(t) + d'(t) \geq 32767 \text{ or } y(t) + d'(t) \leq -32768 \quad (15)$$

However, if the host sample satisfies either of the conditions:

$$32767 - 3d(t) \leq x(t) \leq 32768 - d(t)$$
$$\text{or } -32768 - d(t) \leq x(t) \leq -32768 - 3d(t) \quad (16)$$

and Equation 9 is used to embed and obtain the stego data, the stego sample also satisfies one of the conditions in (15). Therefore, the conditions (15) cannot use to identify whether the stego sample $y(t)$ is embedded or not in the detection process.

During the embedding process, marking variables, $m(t)$, all of which are initially zero, are introduced to mark which posterior sample causes overflow. Let k be an index of the marking offset, with an initial value of 1. To find an available sample for marking (as successive overflow may have occurred) if (14) is satisfied, k is incremented from 1 until we find the k value where $m(t - k) = 0$. At this point, $b(t)$ is set to *null*, $b(t - k)$ is set to 0, and $m(t - k)$ and $m(t)$ are set to 1, which correspond to no embedding in $x(t)$ and embedding data marking bit in the prior sample $x(t - k)$. Additionally, if (16) is satisfied during the embedding process, stego data produced from Equation 9 do not cause overflow, but (15) is satisfied. Therefore, if (16) is satisfied, $m(t - k)$ is set to 1 and $b(t - k)$ is set to 1. The left part of Figure 10 shows the no-embedding condition that satisfies (14) in the embedding process. The right part of Figure 10 shows the recovery and no-embedding detection,

Figure 10. Left: no-embedding condition that satisfies (14); right: detecting the no-embedding condition

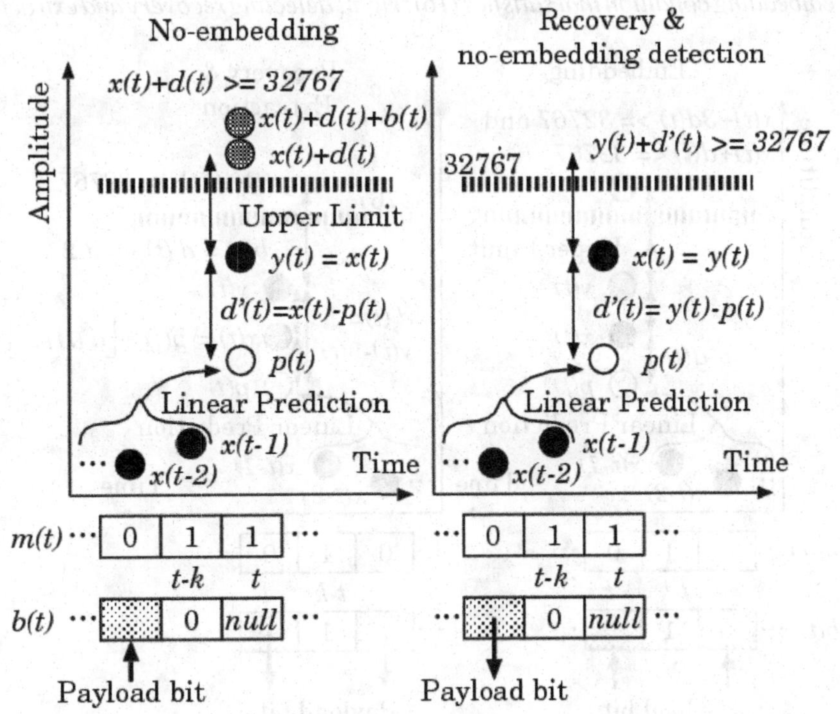

which satisfies (15) in the extraction process. The left part of Figure 11 shows the embedding condition, which satisfies (16) in the embedding process. The right part of Figure 11 shows the recovery and extraction processes that satisfy (15). The left parts of Figures 10 and 11 satisfy (15) in the extraction process; they can, however, be discriminated using the extracted $b(t\text{-}k)$ data. Actually, the index value of k is 1 in most cases, as shown in examples in Figures 10 and 11; the marking bit is embedded into the previous sample. However, the segments with large amplitude often satisfy (14), and therefore, the marking bit cannot be embedded into the previous sample. Therefore, k is incremented from 1 until $m(t - k) = 0$ to determine which sample is available for embedding the marking bit.

In practice, the embedding process first scans $x(t)$ and finds samples that satisfy (14) or (16) to generate $m(t)$ and $b(t)$. Payload data are then embedded into the samples indicated by each t for which $m(t) = 0$. Otherwise, $b(t)$ is a marking bit that has already been selected for embedding.

The practical extraction and recovery processes are as follows. Marking variables, $m(t)$, and the marking offset index, k, are also introduced into the extraction process. Their values are decided as in the embedding process. If (15) is satisfied and $b(t - k) = 1$, then $y(t)$ is embedded; otherwise $y(t)$ is not embedded.

It is important to note that $m(t - k)$ and $b(t - k)$ can be generated prior to the time series data, $x(t)$ or $y(t)$, indicating that the embedding and extraction processes are causal.

Concealment of Payload Data and Overhead Data

Prediction coefficients, $a(i)$, depend on the host signal and are usually considered to be the host-dependent secret key required for embedding and extraction. $a(i)$ are expressed as 16-bit IEEE754 half-precision floating point numbers and can

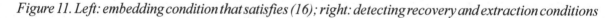

Figure 11. Left: embedding condition that satisfies (16); right: detecting recovery and extraction conditions

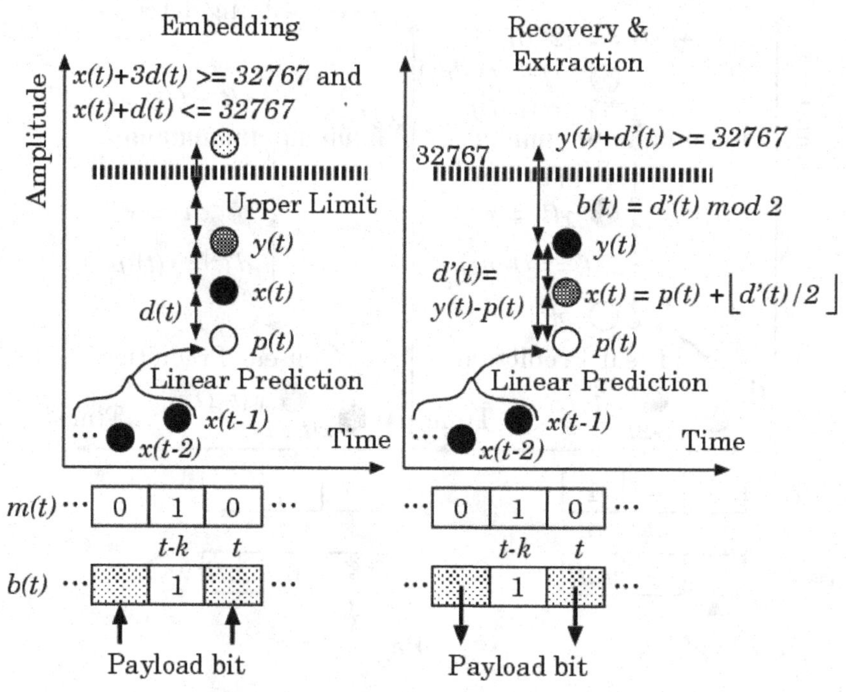

be transmitted independent of the stego data or embedded into the stego data. For the latter case, the LSBs of the last $16n$ samples are embedded into the samples before the last $16n$ samples with $m(t) = 0$. The bit-stream of the $a(i)$ is scrambled and placed into the LSB of the last $16n$ samples. As a result, $16n$-bits of overhead data are stored in the stego data. In practical situations, a common secret key can be required for certain host signal forms. An XOR operation of the constant-length L-bit secret key on the LSB of the first L samples of the stego signal ($y(t)$, $0 \leq t < L$) generates the modified stego signal. The extraction procedure then requires the XOR operation of the secret key a priori. It is impossible to recover the host data and extract the payload data without this key, as the exact $p(t)$ cannot be obtained from the modified $y(t)$.

Evaluation

The performance of the proposed and conventional methods (Yan & Wang, 2008) were evaluated using two simulated host conditions: 100 pieces of 20 s CD-quality audio signals and 100 pieces of 1.6 s large amplitude signals. The intention in using the CD-quality data was to demonstrate the advantage gained by using the proposed method to reduce the stego audio sound quality degradation. The large-amplitude and short-duration conditions in the second datasets were intended to simulate the types of audio signals that frequently overflow. This second situation allowed for smaller payloads to be embedded due to the larger amount of overhead data and non-embedding samples. To model the hidden data, random-bit data were embedded into the host signal.

Objective quality degradation of the stego audio was evaluated by the segmental Signal-to-Noise Ratio (SNR) and Perceptual Audio Quality Evaluation (PEAQ), as recommended by ITU-R BS.1387. A large SNR implies a small difference between the stego and host signals. An Objective Difference Grade (ODG), which corresponds to the degree of subjective quality degradation of the impaired stego audio signal when compared to the original audio signal, was obtained using PEAQ software (Kabal, 2002). For subjective quality, an ODG value of 0 corresponds to no difference, -1 corresponds to perceptible but not annoying, and -2 corresponds to slightly annoying.

The conventional method requires selecting one of 64 prediction coefficient sets, C1: $a(i) = \{0, 0, 0\}$, C2: $a(i) = \{0, 0, 1\}$, …, C5: $a(i) = \{0, -1, 0\}$, …, C64: $a(i) = \{3, -3, 3\}$, that exhibited the best objective stego audio quality when measured by SNR (Yan & Wang, 2008) or ODG. The conventional study, however, does not propose the best ODG condition. The location map was packed every 16 bits into unsigned integer data and compressed using the Gzip compression tool. The compressed location map and selected coefficient set, expressed by 6 bits, were combined and embedded as overhead data.

The maximum order of the prediction coefficient, $a(i)$, for the proposed method was $n = 8$. The overhead size was therefore 8 16 = 128 bits.

The methods were evaluated by comparing the storage amount lost for the stego audio payload data, SNR, and ODG. Here, the amount of payload data loss is the sum of the non-embedding samples, marking samples, and overhead data for each method.

CD-Quality Data Condition

The host audio data included 100 total pieces of music from a database containing various types of music (RWC-MDB-G-2001) (Goto, et al., 2003). The 20 s between the initial 40 and 60 s left-channel signal of each piece was used.

Table 3 shows the payload loss amount, SNR, and ODG for both methods. The payload loss for the proposed method was lower for all pieces of music. The results show that the proposed method is superior in the average amount of lost payload and objective quality degradation. While the proposed method achieved a larger payload

Table 3. Comparison of the payload loss, SNR, and ODG performances of the conventional and proposed methods for 100 pieces of 20 s CD-quality audio signals

Condition	Conventional		Proposed
	Best SNR	Best ODG	
Mean loss of payload [bits]	1391.1	1346.2	209.4
Mean SNR [dB]	18.2	15.1	21.0
Std. Dev. SNR [dB]	6.1	3.6	6.2
Mean ODG	-1.97	-1.58	-1.33
Std. Dev. ODG	0.50	0.19	0.50

amount, the advantage is negligible compared with the theoretical maximum payload of 1 bit per sample. The payload bit-rate for the proposed method is 44.09 kbps.

Figure 12 shows the minimum, 10th percentile, median, 90th percentile, and maximum ODGs for the conventional and proposed methods. Though a large ODG deviation for the proposed method is found compared to the best ODG method, the proposed method achieves the best sound quality on average.

Large Amplitude Condition

The host audio data included 100 total pieces of 1.6 s music taken from the RWC-MDB-G-2001 database. The 1.6 s between the initial 40 and 41.6 s left-channel signal of each piece was used. To simulate large-amplitude segments apt to overflow, the host signal amplitude was doubled and clipped at the maximum and minimum of the 16-bit resolution.

Table 4 shows the results for payload data loss, SNR, and ODG for both methods. The payload data loss for the proposed method was again lower than that for the conventional method for all pieces. The results show that the proposed method is superior in the average payload data loss and objective quality degradation. The bit-rate of the payload amount is 43.78 kbps, which still roughly corresponds to 1 bit per sample. The improvement in payload storage using the proposed method is 777.3 bits on average. The

Figure 12. Minimum, 10th percentile, median, 90th percentile, and maximum ODGs for the conventional and proposed methods

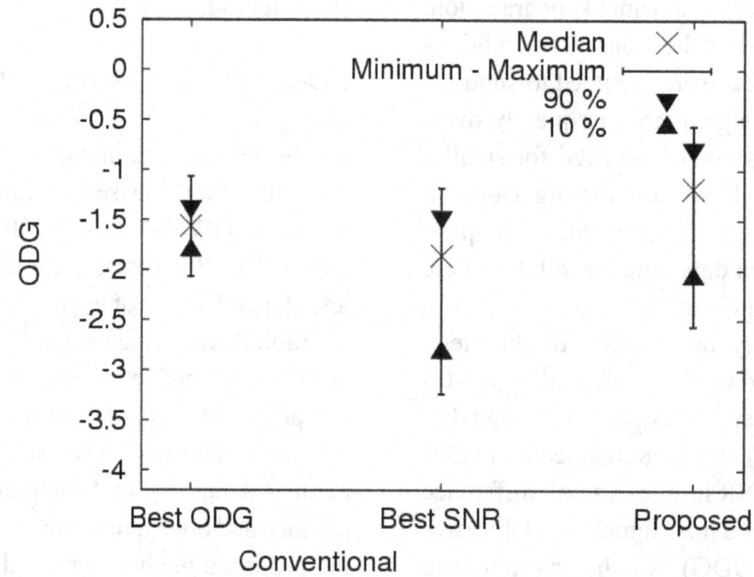

Table 4. Comparison of payload loss, SNR, and ODG performances of the conventional and proposed methods for 100 pieces of 1.6-s large-amplitude audio signals

Condition	Conventional		Proposed
	Best SNR	Best ODG	
Mean loss of payload [bits]	1289.9	1314.3	512.6
Mean SNR [dB]	18.7	15.4	21.4
Std. Dev. SNR [dB]	5.8	4.9	5.7
Mean ODG	-1.97	-1.56	-1.40
Std. Dev. ODG	0.55	0.22	0.56

payload improvement is 1.1% of the maximum payload of 44100 × 1.6 bits. Figure 13 shows the relationship between the number of non-embedded samples as a result of Equation 9 and the amount of payload loss for each piece of music. This figure shows that the amount of payload loss is proportional to the number of non-embedded samples and that the amount of payload loss for the proposed method is less than half that of the conventional method.

Figure 14 shows the minimum, 10th percentile, median, 90th percentile, and maximum ODGs for the conventional and proposed methods. The pattern observed is quite similar to that of Figure 12. Though a large ODG deviation for the proposed method is found compared to the best ODG method, the proposed method achieves the best sound quality on average.

Discussion of Data Hiding in the Time Domain

Selecting one of the coefficient sets (C1 to C64) in the conventional method is based on the least objective quality degradation. As a result, only five coefficient sets were actually chosen for each 100 host audio pieces. This suggests that almost all host data recovery and payload data extraction can be achieved using only five decoding trials of coefficient set changes without knowing the true coefficient sets. Therefore, payload data concealment is poor for the conventional method.

Figure 13. Relationship between the number of non-embedded samples and payload loss amount for each 1.6 s audio signal

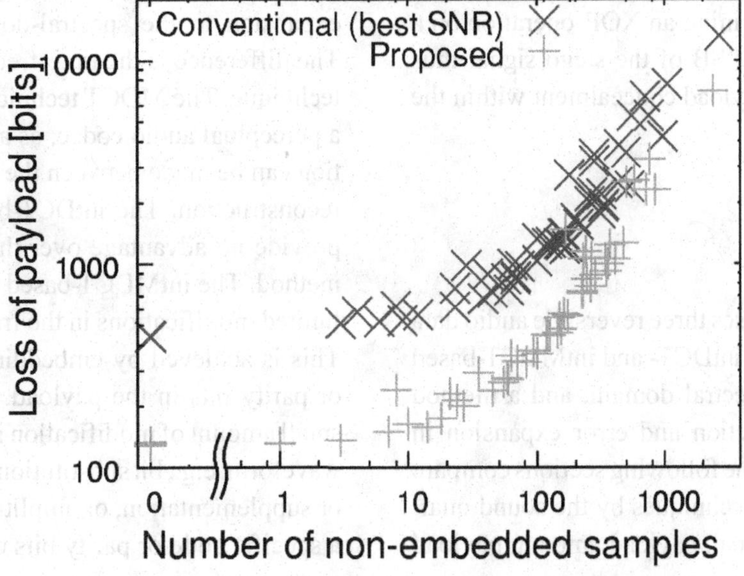

Figure 14. Minimum, 10th percentile, median, 90th percentile, and maximum ODGs for the conventional and proposed methods

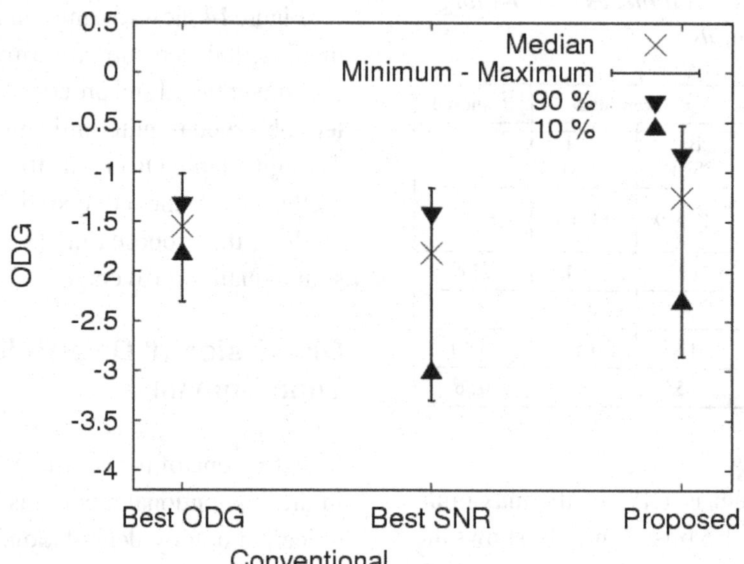

Even if we intend to find the best coefficient set among the limited five sets, and not among the 64 sets, the conventional method clearly requires a high computational load compared to the proposed method.

The proposed method utilizes prediction coefficient sets represented by the 128-bit secret data; however, close values in the coefficient sets can be obtained by applying the Burg method to the stego audio. Performing an XOR operation on a secret key for the LSB of the stego signal thus achieves higher payload concealment within the stego data.

DISCUSSION

This chapter proposes three reversible audio data hiding techniques, intDCT- and intMDCT-based methods in the spectral domain, and a method using linear prediction and error expansion in the time domain. The following sections compare and discuss these techniques by the sound quality of the stego signal, payload amount, payload concealment, and promising applications. Further research directions are also given for the reversible audio data hiding technique and its efficiency for possible applications.

The intMDCT-based method is superior to the intDCT-based method in stego signal sound quality and frame synchronization in the extraction processes. These methods are based on essentially the same idea, namely amplitude expansion to the spectral-domain coefficients. The difference is the time-frequency conversion technique. The MDCT technique is also used for a perceptual audio codec, as a seamless connection can be made between the framed signals for reconstruction. The intDCT-based method may provide no advantage over the intMDCT-based method. The intMDCT-based method can detect limited modifications in the framed stego signal. This is achieved by embedding a specific code or parity bits in the payload. If there is even a small amount of modification in the framed stego waveform, e.g., bit substitution, sample cropping, or supplementation, or amplitude modifications, a specific code or parity bits cannot be detected from the extracted payload. Copying and pasting the waveform can be detected by embedding sequential numbers in the frame signals, and the framed host signal can also be recovered from the non-modified stego signal frames. Conversely, the linear prediction-based method currently has no scheme to segment the host signal into frames. It is so fragile that modifying a single stego sample causes host signal recovery and payload data extraction to fail.

The linear prediction-based method achieves the largest payload data amount. It is four times larger than the other methods, while its sound quality degradation is larger than that in the other methods. If the payload data amount is controlled using the previously proposed technique (Yan & Wang, 2008), the stego signal sound might be improved.

Payload concealment in the linear prediction-based method is comparable to that of the MDCT-based method. Both methods require the key used in the embedding process to extract a payload.

In summary, the linear prediction-based method is superior to the current reversible data hiding methods applied to the spectral domain.

Promising Applications of Reversible Audio Data Hiding

The most useful advantage of reversible data hiding when compared with conventional steganography technology is that the host signal can be recovered from the stego signal. Steganography has been considered useful for recording of meta-data (Kunisa, 2007), covert communication (Mason, 1999), and quality enhancement such as bandwidth extension (Aoki, 2006). Reversible data hiding can be applied not only to these applications but also to applications that require high-quality audio, including commercial music and music recording.

Audio content used in broadcasting and recording is generally transmitted and saved as waveform data or losslessly compressed waveform data, as audio quality is indispensable. Such audio data require metadata, e.g., time stamp, recording target, copyright information, editing processes and their parameters, and their histories. These metadata can be recorded in the header area of the waveform file or other files accompanying the waveform file. However, data in the header area are not guaranteed to be preserved through the file format conversion. Reversibly embedding these metadata into the originally recorded waveform file results in non-destructive editing, which can be used to trace the editing history, copyright management, and transmission, regardless of the waveform file and lossless compression formats. Audio editing software that supports the reversible data-hiding format can be used to read, edit, and rewrite the metadata as payload only for authenticated users. Therefore, reversible audio data hiding technology will be useful in high quality, non-destructive, secured audio editing and recording environments.

FUTURE RESEARCH DIRECTIONS

The reversible data hiding technique is generally fragile in terms of modified stego data, i.e., host data cannot be recovered and the payload data cannot be extracted after modification.

One future research direction involves detecting tampering in the framed host signals. The scheme to detect modified stego signal frames while recovering other frames is required. It may be possible to detect a cut and paste operations to the stego signal. It is useful for probative recording in the investigation process, where editing and modifying are strictly prohibited. However, the step-by-step searching to synchronize signal frames involves a high computational load, as MDCT calculations are iterated many times. Synchronization algorithms with low computational loads are to be developed. The linear prediction-based method must also be improved to be applied to the segmented host signals. Another future research direction in reversible data hiding involves providing robustness against modifications to the stego signal and semi-reversibility for the modified stego signal while maintaining perfect recovery from the non-modified stego signal. To implement this idea, robust and fragile payload data should be embedded into the host data. The amount of robust payload data must be small, while the amount of fragile payload data must be large. The advantages of this technique over the conventional robust watermarking technique include perfect reversibility for the non-modified stego signal and semi-reversibility for the modified stego signal. A possible application that involves robust, reversible, and semi-reversible audio data hiding at the same time is copyright management for high-quality audio content. The host signal reconstructed from the reversible feature allows authenticated users to listen and edit original-quality audio. The purpose of the extracted payload includes value-added information, e.g., bandwidth extension and expanded sampling resolution of the audio waveform, and metadata, e.g., recording conditions and editing histories. If the stego signal is modified or lossily compressed, the semi-reversible feature is used to recover the semi-reconstructed signal, excluding the effect of hiding payload from the modified stego signal. Moreover, modification of stego signal may not remove the robust payload, which is utilized for copyright management.

CONCLUSION

This chapter introduces recent progress in reversible audio data hiding techniques in the spectral and time domains. The reversible audio data hiding techniques are evaluated by the payload amount, objective sound quality degradation of the stego signals, and payload data concealment.

The integer DCT-based method simply expands and adds payload data to the DCT coefficients at higher frequencies. However, concentrating hidden data in the highest-frequency region has several disadvantages in sound quality degradation and hidden data concealment. The improved method utilizes the integer MDCT to convert a host waveform into the spectral domain. The host waveform is segmented into half-overlapped frames, and the sinusoidal window is applied to the framed waveform. The MDCT coefficients to be embedded are selected according to a PN sequence, which serves as a secret key. The objective stego signal sound quality degradation and payload data concealment are considerably improved.

Finally, this chapter proposes improvements to the conventional prediction error expansion method for reversible audio waveform data hiding. These improvements do not require a location map to prevent amplitude overflow, and the proposed method achieves a storage capacity of nearly 1 bit per sample of host data. The proposed method is shown to be superior, as it involves smaller payload data loss and less objective quality degradation on average for 100 CD-quality and 100 large-amplitude, short-duration pieces of music. Additionally, payload concealment within the stego data is better than for the conventional method.

REFERENCES

Aoki, N. (2006). A band extension technique for G.711 speech using steganography. *IEICE Transactions on Communications*, *89*, 1896–1898. doi:10.1093/ietcom/e89-b.6.1896

Burg, J. P. (1975). *Maximum entropy spectral analysis*. (Doctoral dissertation). Stanford University. Palo Alto, CA. Retrieved from http://sepwww.stanford.edu/theses/sep06/

Geiger, R., Sporer, T., Koller, J., & Brandenburg, K. (2001). *Audio coding based on integer transforms*. Paper presented at the 111th Audio Engineering Society Convention. New York, NY.

Geiger, R., Yokotani, Y., & Schuller, G. (2006). *Audio data hiding with high data rates based on intMDCT*. Paper presented IEEE International Conference on Acoustics, Speech and Signal Processing. Toulouse, France.

Goto, M., Hashiguchi, H., Nishimura, T., & Oka, R. (2003). *RWC music database: Music genre database and musical instrument sound database*. Paper presented at the 4th International Conference on Music Information Retrieval. Baltimore, MD.

Hai Bin, H., Susanto, R., Rongshan, Y., & Xiao, L. (2004). *A fast algorithm of integer MDCT for lossless audio coding*. Paper presented at IEEE International Conference on Acoustics, Speech and Signal Processing. Quebec, Canada.

Huang, X., Echizen, I., & Nishimura, A. (2010). *A new approach of reversible acoustic steganography for tampering detection*. Paper presented at International Conference on Intelligent Information Hiding and Multimedia Signal Processing. Darmstadt, Germany.

Kabal, P. (2002). *An examination and interpretation of ITU-R BS.1387: Perceptual evaluation of audio quality*. TSP Lab Technical Report. Montreal, Canada: McGill University. Retieved from http://www-mmsp.ece.mcgill.ca/Documents/Reports/2002/KabalR2002v2.pdf

Kuisa, A. (2007). *Host-cooperative metadata embedding framework*. Paper presented at International Conference on Intelligent Information Hiding and Multimedia Signal Processing. Kaohsiung, Taiwan.

Li, M., Jiao, Y., & Niu, X. (2008). *Reversible watermarking for compressed speech*. Paper presented at International Conference on Intelligent Information Hiding and Multimedia Signal Processing. Harbin, China.

Mason, M., Sridharan, S., & Prandolini, R. (1999). *Digital coding of covert audio for monitoring and storage*. Paper presented at the Fifth International Symposium on Signal Processing and its Applications. Queensland, Australia.

van der Veen, M., van Leest, A., & Bruekers, F. (2003). *Reversible audio watermarking*. Paper presented at the 114th Audio Engineering Society Convention. Amsterdam, The Netherlands.

Yan, D., & Wang, R. (2008). *Reversible data hiding for audio based on prediction error expansion*. Paper presented at International Conference on Intelligent Information Hiding and Multimedia Signal Processing. Harbin, China.

ADDITIONAL READING

Yan, C.-Y., Lin, C.-H., & Hu, W.-C. (2010). *Reversible watermarking by coefficient adjustment method*. Paper presented at International Conference on Intelligent Information Hiding and Multimedia Signal Processing. Darmstadt, Germany. Tian, J. (2003). *High capacity reversible data embedding and content authentication*. Paper presented at IEEE International Conference on Acoustics, Speech and Signal Processing. Hong Kong, China.

Chapter 3
Method of Digital-Audio Watermarking Based on Cochlear Delay Characteristics

Masashi Unoki
Japan Advanced Institute of Science and Technology, Japan

Ryota Miyauchi
Japan Advanced Institute of Science and Technology, Japan

ABSTRACT

This chapter introduces a state-of-the-art scheme of non-blind digital-audio watermarking, based on the properties of the human cochlear. It is based on the concept of embedding inaudible watermarks into an original sound by controlling its phase characteristics in relation to the characteristics of Cochlear Delay (CD). Inaudible watermarks are embedded into original signals by applying Infinite Impulse Response (IIR) all-pass filters with CDs and they are then extracted from the phase difference between the original and watermarked sounds. The results obtained from objective and subjective evaluations and robustness tests revealed that the CD-based approach is considerably more effective in satisfying the requirements for non-blind inaudible watermarking. Embedding limitations with the CD-based approach were investigated with various evaluations. These results also revealed that embedding limitations with the CD-based approach could be improved by using parallel, cascade, and composite architectures for the CD filters.

INTRODUCTION

There have recently been serious social issues involved in protecting the copyrights of all digital-audio content by preventing it from being illegally copied and distributed on the Internet. Digital-audio watermarking has been focused on as a state-of-the-art technique enabling copyrights to be protected and defended against malicious attacks and tampering (e.g., Digital-Right Management, DRM). This technique has aimed to embed codes to protect the copyright in audio content, which are inaudible to and inseparable by users, and to precisely and robustly detect embedded codes from watermarked signals.

DOI: 10.4018/978-1-4666-2217-3.ch003

Image/video watermarking algorithms were initially developed (Bender, Gruhl, & Morimoto, 1996; Cox & Miller, 2001) and audio watermarking algorithms were introduced slightly later (Petitcolas, et al., 1999; Hartung & Kutter, 1999; Swanson, Zhu, & Tewfik, 1999). Many algorithms for embedding and detecting watermarks in audio signals have also been developed in the past several years. All these algorithms have been in the time or frequency domain and in the amplitude or phase domain, and they have been based on the advantages of the perceptual properties of the human auditory system (psychoacoustical model) to enable watermarking to be embedded into the audio signal.

Based on their requirement for watermark detection, all these algorithms may also be classified under one of three schemes: the non-blind watermarking scheme, and blind watermarking schemes with and without synchronization information (Foo, 2008). For the non-blind watermarking scheme, the original signal is required to extract the embedded watermarks from the watermarked signal and only the owner of the original signal can control the copyright information. In contrast, for the blind watermarking scheme, the embedded watermarks can be extracted from the watermarked signal even if the owner does not have the original signal. Therefore, the blind watermarking scheme is the most useful and practical for use in real situations, since it does not require double storage capacity or double communication channels for watermarking to be detected.

Methods of digital-audio watermarking must, therefore, generally satisfy four requirements to provide useful and reliable forms of copyright protection (Cvejic & Seppänen, 2007): (a) inaudibility (inaudible to humans with no sound distortion caused by embedded data), (b) robustness (not affected when subjected to techniques such as data compression), (c) blindness (high possibility of detecting the embedded codes without the original signal), and (d) confidentiality (secure and undetectable concealment of embedded data).

The first requirement for inaudibility is the most important in the method of audio watermarking because it must not affect the sound quality of the original audio. The original content may lose its commercial value if the sound quality of the original is degraded. The second requirement for robustness is important to ensure that watermarking methods are tamper-proof so that they can resist any manipulations carried out by illegal users. The third requirement for blindness is important to detect watermarks from the watermarked signal. This is used to check whether we can blindly detect embedded codes from watermarked signals. The last requirement for confidentiality is important to protect copyright by concealing watermarks, and it is important that users do not know whether the audio content contains watermarking or not. Therefore, watermarking algorithms are generally unpublished to satisfy the last requirement. Thus, the first three requirements are generally discussed as to whether they can be satisfied as useful techniques in digital-audio watermarking schemes, as the trend is to evaluate the performance of these digital-audio watermarking schemes.

Typical methods of watermarking have been based on manipulations of signals in quantization/coding levels or in the time domain. There are, for example, methods based on Least Significant Bit (LSB) replacement in quantization (e.g., Bassia & Pitas, 1998; Cvejic & Seppännen, 2005; and embedding in the Adaptive Differential Pulse Code Modulation (ADPCM) quantizer, e.g., Iwakiri & Matsui, 1997). These methods have been used to directly embed watermarks such as copyright data into quantization/coding levels and directly detect embedded data from watermarked signals without using the original signal. Although methods of bit-replacement/manipulation such as LSB are relatively less audible than other conventional techniques of watermarking, they are not robust against various manipulations such as down-sampling/up-sampling or compression (Foo, 2008). Thus, these do not completely satisfy the four requirements, especially with regard to robustness.

There have been simpler approaches in the amplitude domain. Straightforward methods of watermarking based on the properties of human-auditory perception such as various masking phenomena have been proposed. The most well known method is based on the psychoacoustical model (e.g., Zwicker & Fastl, 1990; Zwicker & Zwicker, 1991), which can account for simultaneous masking and/or temporal masking. Another method based on the effect of masking for Amplitude Modulation (AM) has been proposed by Nishimura (2010). These psychoacoustically embed watermarks into the amplitude of digital-audio signals, based on human auditory perception. Although this embedding generally seems to successfully produce inaudible watermarks, the sound quality of the watermarked signal is reduced when these averaged characteristics of masking are unconsciously perceived by users. Even if the watermarks are embedded into the amplitude of signals as well, one can easily detect small differences in the amplitudes of the signal due to the fundamental properties of the human-auditory system. It is therefore difficult to embed inaudible watermarks into amplitudes by using various masking phenomena. In particular, audio/speech coding techniques have the same advantage in compressing redundant information to reduce the total bit rates of digital sound so that these methods have drawbacks in robustness.

There have been other typical methods of watermarking based on manipulations of signals in amplitude (or the amplitude spectrum). There are, for example, the spread spectrum approach (e.g., the Direct Spread Spectrum [DSS] proposed by Boney *et al.* [1996] and the secure spread spectrum proposed by Cox *et al.* [1995]), and other methods (e.g., Kirovski & Malvar, 2003; Malik, et al., 2008; He & Scordilis, 2008) that have improved on these. These methods have been used to directly embed watermarks such as copyright data into the amplitude of digital-audio signals and detect the embedded data from the watermarked signals without using the original signal, i.e., the blind watermarking scheme. Spread spectrum methods such as DSS are relatively more robust than the others because watermarks are spread throughout whole frequencies that are preserved. However, this does not completely satisfy the four requirements, especially with regard to inaudibility (e.g., Şehirli *et al.* [2004], Table 1 in this chapter, and future research direction of He and Scordilis [2008]). Because most methods based on the spread spectrum must incorporate the frequency and/or temporal masking model (psychoacoustical model) to mask artifacts such as expanded noise due to the spread spectrum, these may pose the same problems that were described above. They especially have to preserve unmasked parts that may be audible to retain watermarks that are robust to audio/speech coding or compression in the watermarked signals. It is therefore difficult to embed inaudible watermarks into amplitude information.

Other typical methods of watermarking that show promise have been based on phase spectra (or group delay characteristics). There have been, for example, the echo-hiding approach proposed by Gruhl *et al.* (1996) and the method based on periodical phase modulation (PPM) proposed by Nishimura *et al.* (2001; 2004). These can be regarded as watermarking based on phase modulation. Echo-hiding approaches have been used to directly embed watermarks into audio signals as time shifts. Thus, the two main advantages of using these approaches have been to embed watermarks into the original signal with less distortion and at lower computational cost. Although

Table 1. Results from objective evaluations: (a) PEAQ, (b) LSD, and (c) bit-detection rate

Evaluations / Methods	LSB	DSS	ECHO	PPM	CD
(a) PEAQ (ODG)	0.07	-3.40	0.17	-2.11	0.09
(b) LSD (dB)	0.14	1.34	0.02	0.49	0.35
(c) Bit detection rate (%)	100.0	100.0	96.7	84.7	99.3

they satisfy the inaudibility requirement, the former has a drawback in confidentiality because it is less secure (anyone can easily detect the echo information via autocorrelation techniques even if the algorithm is not published) and neither method is as robust as the other established methods.

The PPM approach was based on aural capabilities in that it is relatively inaudible to humans. This approach can detect embedded watermarks with and without the original signal, i.e., non-blind and blind watermarking schemes. Ozawa *et al.* (1993) and Nishimura *et al.* (2001) found these phenomena when they conducted psychoacoustical experiments. However, as phase modulation randomly disrupts the phase spectra of components at higher frequencies, these modulated components (embedded data) may be able to be detected by humans in watermarked pulse-like sounds, especially around rapid onsets in musical sounds such as onsets in piano pieces. This is because humans can perceive rapid phase variations related to long and rapid group delays in sounds (Plack, 2005; Moore, 2003; Akagi & Yasutake, 1998).

In summary, the typical watermarking methods used in LSB, DSS, ECHO, and PPM approaches could partially satisfy the four requirements. PPM was especially found to be the best of these methods. These methods can also be categorized as watermarking processes in the amplitude or phase (time-delay) domains. The first two methods are in the amplitude domain, while the last two are in the phase domain. As previously mentioned, it is very difficult to achieve digital-audio watermarking that can satisfy all four requirements, especially inaudibility and robustness simultaneously, while confidentiality is satisfied by keeping algorithms unpublished. It is also important to satisfy the requirement for blindness to achieve practical inaudible watermarking. Although the non-blind watermarking scheme is not useful in practice due to double capacity and double communication channels, this scheme is theoretically interesting and very important for investigating the properties of digital-audio watermarking.

This chapter discusses our aims to find an inaudible watermarking scheme based on human auditory perception (without using amplitude manipulations or various masking phenomena) to satisfy the (a) inaudibility and (b) robustness criteria. With regard to the last two requirements of (c) blindness and (d) confidentiality, we assumed that the watermarks could be detected from the watermarked signal with the original signal, i.e., non-blind inaudible watermarking, and also can be kept confidential by keeping the algorithm for this inaudible watermarking unpublished. This chapter introduces a novel approach to an inaudible method of non-blind watermarking based on the properties of the human cochlear, that is, the characteristics of cochlear delay. This chapter explains embedding limitations with non-blind digital-audio watermarking based on the cochlear delay and then introduces methods of watermarking to reduce these embedding limitations by using cascade, parallel, and composite architectures for cochlear-delay filters.

CONCEPT UNDERLYING INAUDIBLE WATERMARKING

Cochlear Delay

The cochlea is a fluid-filled cavity that is within the same compartment as the scala vestibuli, scala media, and scala tympani, and has a thin-tube that has been coiled up to save space, as shown in the top left of Figure 1. The whole structure of the cochlea forms a spiral like a snail's shell, which is not a straight tube. The cochlea can be represented by the shape at the bottom left of Figure 1 by stretching out this form and uncoiling the spiral (note that this cannot actually be done). The tube is divided along its length by two membranes, i.e., Reissner's membrane and the Basilar Membrane (BM), which create three fluid-filled compartments: the scala vestibuli, scala media, and scala tympani. A traveling wave of sound enters the cochlea through an opening (the oval window) covered by a membrane. As the fluid in the cochlea is almost incompressible, if the oval window suddenly moves inward, due to pressure from the stapes, Reissner's membrane and the BM are pushed down, and the round window moves outward. It follows that the vibration of the stapes leads to vibration of the BM. As the properties of the BM vary continuously between these extremes along its length, each location on the BM has a particular frequency of sound, i.e., a characteristic frequency. These patterns of vibrations are called a "traveling wave," as shown at the bottom and center of Figure 1. The characteristic motion of the traveling wave occurs because there is progressive phase delay from the base to the apex. That is, the vibration of the BM at the apex lags behind that at the base.

Based on the above properties of the human cochlea, let us consider a pulse-like sound that is perceived by humans as synchronous. However, this is not synchronous to the BM motion of the cochlea even if the sound components physically begin synchronously. The reason for this is as follows.

A transient sound wave progresses along the BM in the cochlea (from the basal to the apical side), passing through the outer ear as spectral modifications (air-pressure variations) and the middle ear as an impedance-matching transformer (mechanical vibrations). The BM motions are then converted into neural firings to be transmitted to the brain passing through the cochlear nucleus, superior olive, lateral lemniscus, inferior colliculus, medical geniculate, and auditory cortex. Since the vibrations of the BM result in the frequency components of an acoustic signal becoming spatially separated, a pulse-like sound must be represented as white-like spectra (having all frequencies) throughout the entire frequencies. The low-frequency components of pulse-like sound require more time to reach the area of maximum displacement in the BM, near the apex of the cochlea, while the higher frequency components of the sound elicit a maximum closer to the base. The time course of pulse-like sound is, therefore, represented as asynchronous components in the BM. This time course is referred to as "cochlear delay" (Dau, et al., 2000).

Related Studies on Perception

In a physiological study, the Auditory Brainstem Response (ABR) was shown to be salient by a time-shifted pulse in which the phase relation was modified to compensate for the cochlear delay (Dau, et al., 2000). In Dau *et al.*'s study, simultaneous displacement maxima by compensating for travel-time differences along the cochlear partition were theoretically produced by using the time course of frequency change for the chirp. They used a rising frequency chirp to investigate the inclusion of activity from lower frequency regions with regard to ABR. Since the ABR components they considered presumably reflect neural response from the brainstem, they found that the effect of optimized synchronization with regard to cochlear delay at the peripheral level can also be observed at the brainstem level. If this physiological saliency is directly correlated to the perceptual accuracy of onset detection, the judgment of perceptual synchrony could become more accurate by compensating rather than by enhancing cochlear delay.

In a psychoacoustical study, Aiba *et al.* (2007, 2008) investigated whether cochlear delay significantly affected the perceptual judgment of the synchronization of two sounds or not. They used three types of chirp sounds: (1) a pulse sound (intrinsic cochlear delay), (2) a compensatory delay chirp (i.e., group delay was compensated to be zero at the BM. This was just a corresponding rising chirp frequency that was used in Dau *et al.* [2000]), and (3) an enhanced delay chirp (i.e., group delay was longer than the previous

Figure 1. Schematic of cochlea with unwound spiral and cochlear delay observed in basilar membrane motion. Vertical dimension has been exaggerated relative to horizontal. Reissner's membrane and scala media have not been illustrated. Bottom right panel indicates compensation of delay pattern for simulated cochlear delay following Dau et al. (2000). Waveforms of part of sinusoidal components (A-C) follow bold line of cochlear delay pattern.

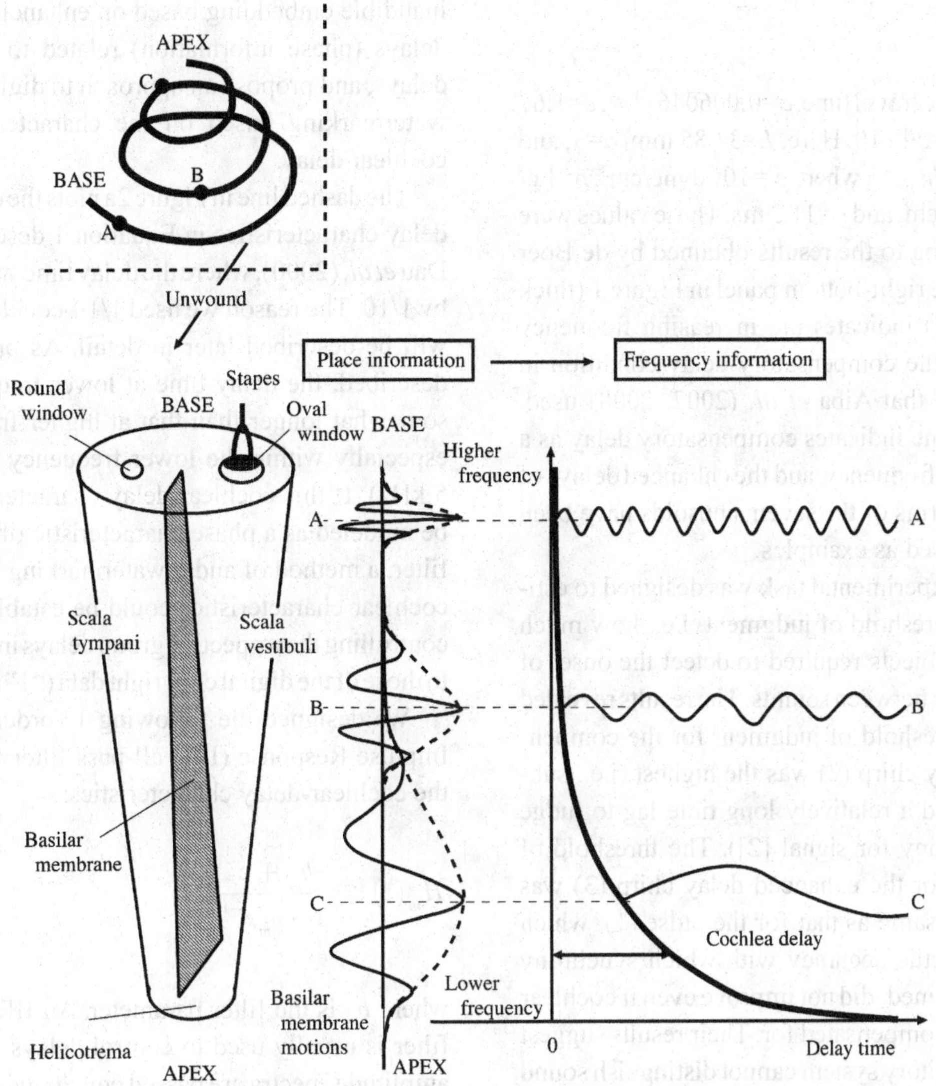

one according to cochlear delay), by following the procedure that Dau *et al.* (2000) used.

The increasing chirp-frequency pattern originally calculated by Dau *et al.* (2000) was based on the one-dimensional linear cochlear model of de Boer (1980). The stiffness of an object is largely responsible for the speed of propagation of a traveling wave. Therefore, the basic assumption underlying this increasing frequency pattern is that the physical stiffness of the human BM decreases exponentially along the cochlear partition from the base to the apex. According to de Boer (1980), the instantaneous frequency, derived from the BM stiffness and the frequency-place transformation with regard to BM length, can approximately be represented as:

$$f = \frac{1}{a}\left(\left[e^{-(\alpha/2)/L}\left(1 + \frac{t_0 - t}{\beta}\right)\right]^{-2/\alpha c} - 1\right) \quad (1)$$

where t is the travel time, a=0.006046 Hz^{-1}, $\hat{c}$=1.67 mm, and $c=\hat{c}/\ln 10$. Here, L=34.85 mm, α=3, and $\beta=2/\alpha\{2\rho/hc_0\}^{1/2}$, where $c_0=10^{-9}$ dyne/cm^3, ρ=1 g/cm^3, h=0.1 cm, and t_0=11.2 ms. These values were set according to the results obtained by de Boer (1980). The right-bottom panel in Figure 1 (thick solid curve) indicates the increasing frequency pattern of the compensatory-delay condition in Equation 1 that Aiba *et al.* (2007, 2008) used. The bold line indicates compensatory delay as a function of frequency, and the enhanced delays of the waveforms of the seven sinusoids have been superimposed as examples.

Their experimental task was designed to estimate the threshold of judgment, i.e., how much time the subjects required to detect the onset of asynchrony between sounds. The results revealed that the threshold of judgment for the compensatory delay chirp (2) was the highest (i.e., subjects needed a relatively long time lag to judge the synchrony for signal [2]). The threshold of judgment for the enhanced delay chirp (3) was almost the same as that for the pulse (1), which meant that the accuracy with which synchrony was determined, did not improve even if cochlear delay was compensated for. Their results suggest that the auditory system cannot distinguish sound with enhanced delay and non-processing sound.

Inaudible Watermarking Scheme

Based on the results obtained by Aiba *et al.* (2007, 2008), we found that it was very difficult for us to discriminate an enhanced delay chirp with the original (intrinsic sound) while it was very easy to discriminate a compensatory delay chirp with the original. We considered that these characteristics could be used to effectively embed inaudible watermarks (copyright data) into an original signal. We thus investigated the feasibility of a method of inaudible embedding based on enhancing group delays (phase information) related to cochlear delays, and propose an approach to digital-audio watermarking based on the characteristics of cochlear delay.

The dashed line in Figure 2a plots the cochlear-delay characteristics in Equation 1 described by Dau *et al.* (2000), where the delay time was scaled by 1/10. The reason we used 1/10-cochlear delay will be described later in detail. As previously described, the delay time at lower frequency is somewhat longer than that at higher frequency, especially within the lower frequency range (≤ 5 kHz). If this cochlear-delay characteristic can be modeled as a phase characteristic of a digital filter, a method of audio watermarking based on cochlear characteristics could be established by controlling the respective group delays in the filter to those of the digital copyright data ("1" and "0").

We designed the following 1st order Infinite Impulse Response (IIR) all-pass filter to model the cochlear-delay characteristics:

$$H_m(z) = \frac{-b_m + z^{-1}}{1 - b_m z^{-1}} \quad (2)$$

where b_m is the filter parameter. An IIR all-pass filter is usually used to control delays in which amplitude spectra are passed equally without any loss. Although a higher order IIR filter could be considered to incorporate the characteristics of cochlear delay in Equation 1, we used the simplest 1st order IIR filter in Equation 2.

To determine the optimal value of filter parameter b_m in Equation 2, we fitted the group delay characteristics of $H_m(z)$ to the cochlear-delay characteristics (scaled by 1/10 as indicated

Figure 2. Cochlear delay and group-delay characteristics of IIR all-pass filter in Equation 2. Cochlear delays are scaled by 1/10

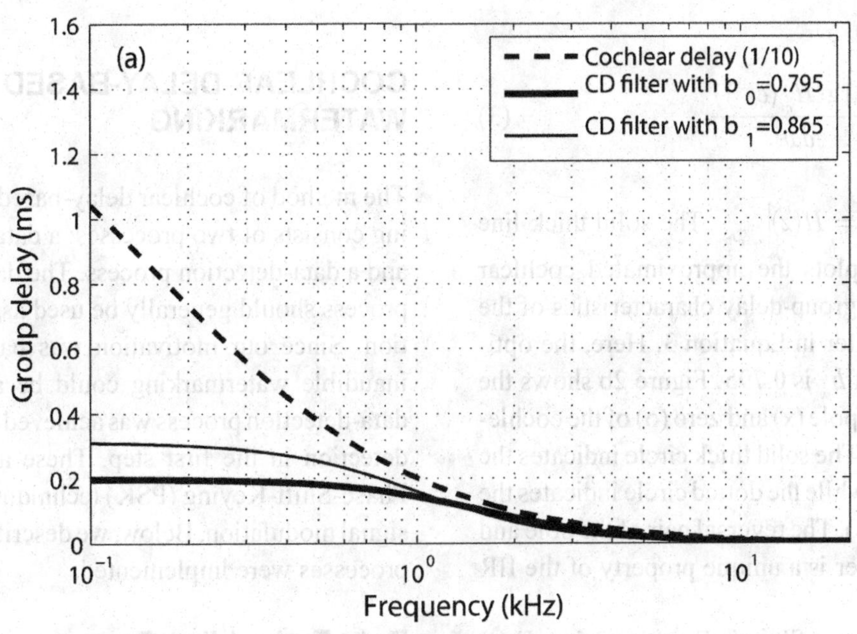

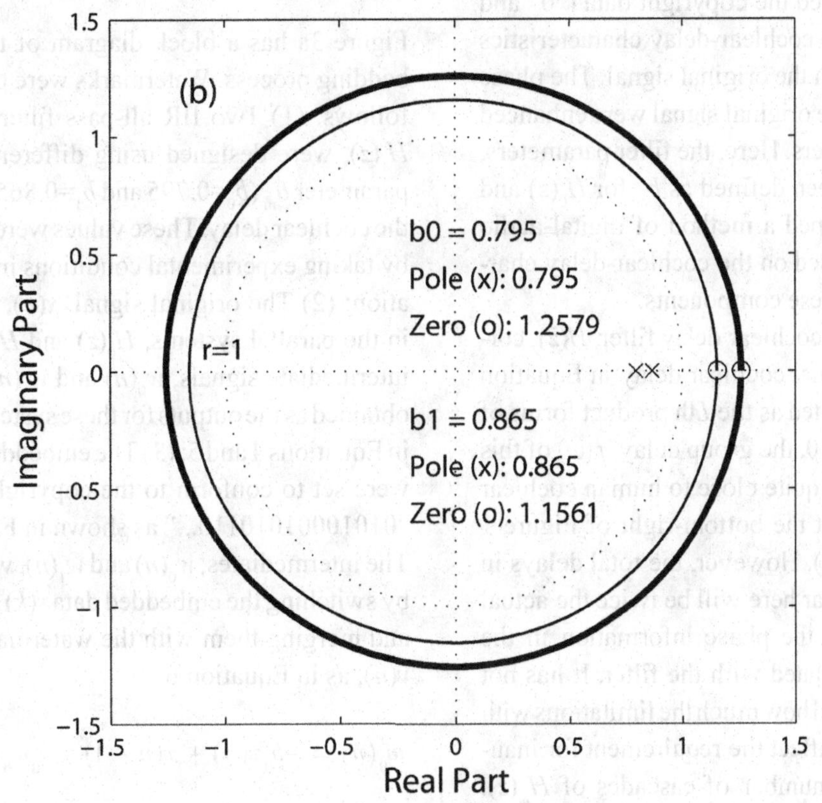

by the dashed line in Figure 2a) by utilizing LMS optimization. Group delay $\tau_m(\omega)$ in the fit can be obtained as:

$$\tau_m(\omega) = -\frac{d \arg(H_m(e^{j\omega}))}{d\omega} \quad (3)$$

where $H(e^{j\omega}) = H(z)\big|_{z=e^{j\omega}}$. The solid thick line in Figure 2a plots the approximated cochlear delay, i.e., the group-delay characteristics of the IIR all-pass filter in Equation 3. Here, the optimized value of b_m is 0.795. Figure 2b shows the location of the pole (x) and zero (o) of the cochlear-delay filter. The solid thick circle indicates the circle on zero while the dotted circle indicates the unit circle (r=1). The reversal pair of the pole and zero of the filter is a unique property of the IIR all-pass filter.

We used the two filters in Equation 2, i.e., $H_0(z)$ and $H_1(z)$, to embed the copyright data ("0" and "1") based on the cochlear-delay characteristics (scaled by 1/10) in the original signal. The phase components of the original signal were enhanced by using these filters. Here, the filter parameters, b_0 and b_1, have been defined as b_m for $H_0(z)$ and $H_1(z)$. We developed a method of digital-audio watermarking based on the cochlear-delay characteristics with these components.

Generally, the cochlear delay filter, $H(z)$, corresponding to actual cochlear delay in Equation 1, can be represented as the Lth product forms of $H_m(z)$. Where L=10, the group delay $\tau(\omega)$ of this $H(z)$ filter can be quite close to human cochlear delay as shown at the bottom-right of Figure 1 (thick solid curve). However, the total delays in the human cochlear here will be twice the actual cochlear delay if the phase information in the signals is manipulated with the filter. It has not yet been confirmed how much the limitations with group delay will affect the requirement for inaudibility, i.e., the number of cascades of $H_m(z)$. Thus, in this case, a simplest 1st-order IIR all-pass filter was employed as the standard CD-based watermarking technique.

COCHLEAR DELAY-BASED WATERMARKING

The method of cochlear delay-based watermarking consists of two processes: a data embedding and a data-detection process. The data-detection process should generally be used as blind detection. Since our motivation was based on how inaudible watermarking could be attained, the data-detection process was achieved as non-blind detection in the first step. These are based on Phase-Shift-Keying (PSK) techniques for digital signal modulation. Below, we describe how these processes were implemented.

Data Embedding Process

Figure 3a has a block diagram of the data-embedding process. Watermarks were embedded as follows: (1) Two IIR all-pass filters, $H_0(z)$ and $H_1(z)$, were designed using different values for parameter b_m (b_0=0.795 and b_1=0.865) to enhance the cochlear delay. These values were determined by taking experimental conditions into consideration; (2) The original signal, $x(n)$, was filtered in the parallel systems, $H_0(z)$ and $H_1(z)$, and the intermediate signals, $w_0(n)$ and $w_1(n)$, were then obtained as the outputs for these systems as shown in Equations 4 and 5; (3) The embedded data, $s(k)$, were set to conform to the copyright data, e.g., "01010001010110..." as shown in Figure 3a; (4) The intermediates, $w_0(n)$ and $w_1(n)$, were selected by switching the embedded data $s(k)$ ("0" or "1"), and merging them with the watermarked signal, $y(n)$, as in Equation 6.

$$w_0(n) = -b_0 x(n) + x(n-1) + b_0 w_0(n-1) \quad (4)$$

Figure 3. Block diagram for (a) data embedding and (b) data detection in inaudible watermarking based on cochlear delay characteristics

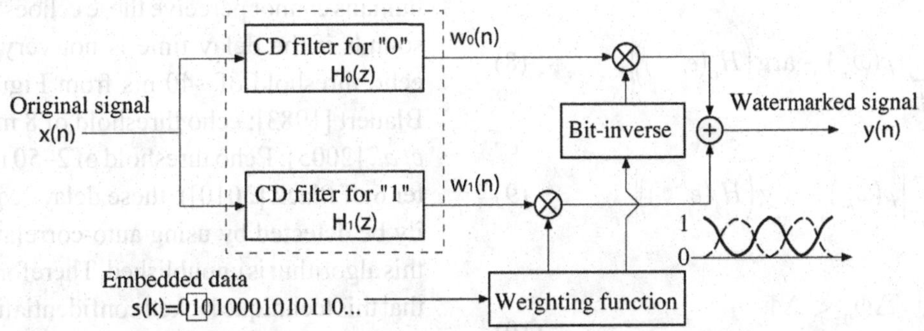

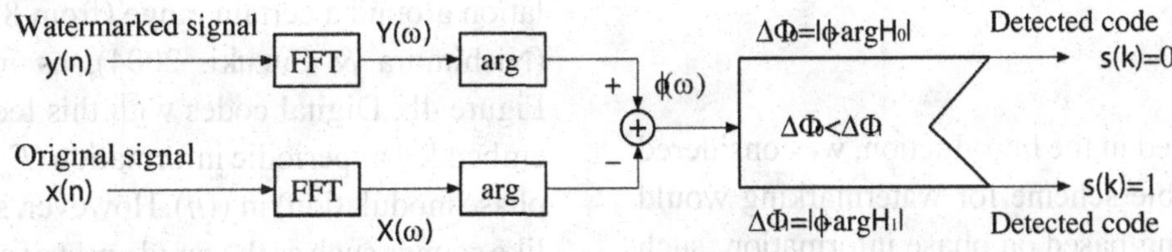

$$w_1(n) = -b_1 x(n) + x(n-1) + b_1 w_1(n-1) \tag{5}$$

$$y(n) = \begin{cases} w_0(n), & s(k) = 0 \\ w_1(n), & s(k) = 1 \end{cases} \tag{6}$$

where $(k\text{-}1)\Delta W \leq n < k\Delta W$. Here, n is the sample index, k is the frame index, and $\Delta W = f_s / N_{bit}$ is the frame length. In addition, f_s is the sampling frequency of the original signal and N_{bit} is the bit rate per second (bps).

To avoid discontinuity in this method between the marked segment in the watermarked signal ($w_0(n)$ and $w_1(n)$), a weighting ramped cosine function was used. In this case, the frame overlap was half of one frame. This processing is usually used as the Overlap-Add (OLA) method in the Short-Term Fourier Transformation (STFT) for signal representations.

Data Detecting Process

Figure 3b outlines the flow for the data-detection process we used. Watermarks are detected as follows: (1) We assume that both $x(n)$ and $y(n)$ are available with this watermarking method; (2) The original, $x(n)$, and the watermarked signal, $y(n)$, are decomposed to become overlapping segments using the same window function used in embedding the data; (3) The phase difference, $\varphi(\omega)$, is calculated in each segment, using Equation 7; FFT[.] is the Fast Fourier Transform (FFT); (4) To estimate the group delay characteristics of $H_0(z)$ or $H_1(z)$ used in embedding the data, the summed phase differences of $\varphi(\omega)$ to the respective phase spectrum of the filters ($H_0(z)$ and $H_1(z)$), $\Delta\Phi_0$ and $\Delta\Phi_1$, are calculated as in Equations 8 and 9; (5) The embedded data, $\hat{s}(k)$, are detected using Equation 10.

$$\varphi(\omega_m) = \arg\left(\mathrm{FFT}\left[y(n)\right]\right) - \arg\left(\mathrm{FFT}\left[x(n)\right]\right) \tag{7}$$

$$\Delta\Phi_0 = \sum_m \left|\varphi(\omega_m) - \arg\left(H_0(e^{j\omega_m})\right)\right| \tag{8}$$

$$\Delta\Phi_1 = \sum_m \left|\varphi(\omega_m) - \arg\left(H_1(e^{j\omega_m})\right)\right| \tag{9}$$

$$\hat{s}(k) = \begin{cases} 0, & \Delta\Phi_0 < \Delta\Phi_1 \\ 1, & \text{otherwise} \end{cases} \tag{10}$$

Key Point

As mentioned in the Introduction, we considered that a suitable scheme for watermarking would be processing based on phase information, such as echo-hiding and periodic-phase modulation. These methods are similar to the processing domain in the Cochlear-Delay (CD) approach. Figure 4 is a schematic of the key point used in these watermarking methods.

The echo-hiding approach controls echo delay (T_0 and T_1) corresponding to digital codes ("0" and "1") in $y(n)$, using an echo-impulse response (relative amplitude A and echo delay (T_0 and T_1)) (Gruhl, et al., 1996), as seen in Figure 4a. Although humans cannot perceive these echoes as different sounds if the delay time is not very long (e.g., echo threshold of ~40 ms from Figure 3. 12 in Blauert [1983]; echo threshold of 8 ms in Tahara *et al.* [2005]; Echo threshold of 2–50 ms in Chapter 6 of Plack [2010]), these delays can very easily be detected by using auto-correlation even if this algorithm is unpublished. Therefore, we found that this technique lacked confidentiality (requirement [d]).

The PMM approach periodically controls certain group delays derived from phase modulation around a certain range (from 8 to 20 kHz) (Nishimura & Suzuki, 2004), as indicated in Figure 4b. Digital codes with this technique are embedded as periodic information (F_{m0} and F_{m1} in phase modulation) in $y(n)$. However, since pulse-like sounds such as the rapid onset of sounds have wide frequency components, this kind of phase modulation disrupts the phase spectra of components at higher frequencies and these may be able to be detected by humans. The reason for this may be able to be accounted for by the related studies of Aiba *et al.* (2007, 2008) with regard to the judgment of perceptual synchrony. Therefore, we

Figure 4. Schematic of key point in watermarking methods

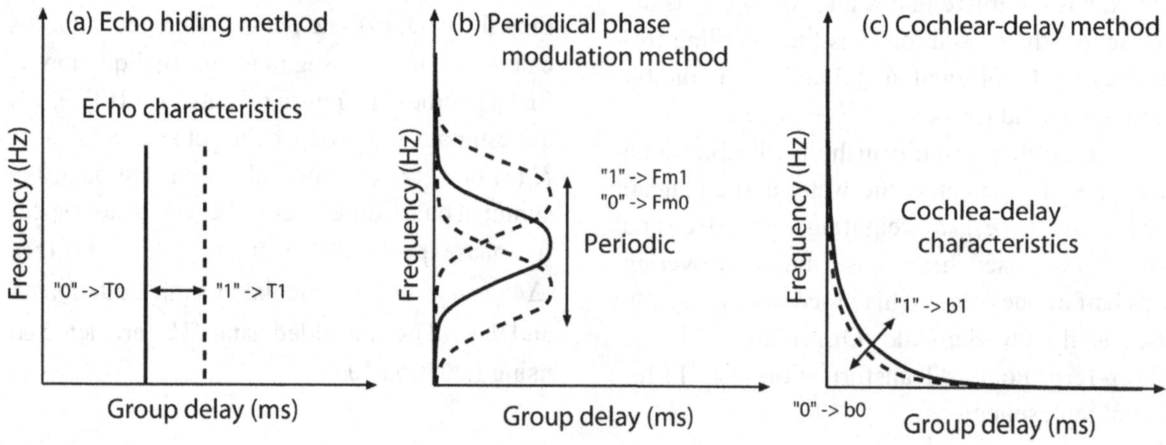

discovered that this technique occasionally suffers from slight problems with regard to inaudibility (requirement [a]).

These two drawbacks motivated us to consider the possibility of inaudible watermarking based on human auditory perception. As introduced in the previous section, cochlear-delay characteristics can be relied on as Figure 4c indicates. Digital codes ("0" and "1") are embedded with the CD-based approach corresponding to the CD (the dashed or solid curve: b_0 for $H_0(z)$ or b_1 for $H_1(z)$) in the watermarked signal, $y(n)$. Although the origin of the idea for inaudible watermarking with the CD-based approach is different in PPM, manipulations of group delay are very similar with both methods, as shown in Figures 4b and 4c. Based on the results of psychoacoustical studies (Aiba, et al., 2007, 2008) and our experiments, humans cannot perceive these delays in the watermarked signal if the delay curve is plotted on the curves of CD. From the results of evaluations in the next section, we found that the CD-based technique satisfied the requirements for inaudibility and robustness. These are significant advantages of the new technique.

EVALUATIONS

Objective and subjective evaluations and robustness tests were carried out to find how effective the Cochlear-Delay (CD) method was, accounting for inaudibility and robustness. These evaluations and tests were also done for the other methods so that they could be comparatively studied with the CD-based approach.

Database and Conditions

All 102 tracks of the RWC music genre database (Goto, et al., 2003) were used as the original signals in the evaluation. The original tracks had a sampling frequency of 44.1 kHz, were 16 bits, and had two channels (stereo). The same watermarks with eight characters ("AIS-lab") were embedded into both R-L channels using the CD method. The STEP2001 (STEP2001, 2001) project suggested that 72 bits per 30 seconds was required to ensure a reasonable bit-detection rate with the method of audio watermarking. Thus, we used N_{bit}=4 bps as this critical condition.

We evaluated the CD-based method of watermarking by comparing it with four others (LSB, DSS, ECHO, and PPM) and carrying out two objective tests: Perceptual Evaluation of Sound Quality (PEAQ) (Kabel, 2002) and Log Spectrum Distortion (LSD). These measures were used to perceptually evaluate the digital-audio watermarking in Lin and Abdulla (2008). There have been some performance evaluations of digital-audio watermarking (e.g., Gordy & Bruton, 2000; Şehirli, et al., 2004; Yu, et al., 2011). They usually used SNR-types of measures to objectively discuss inaudibility. In this chapter, SNR-types of measures were not used because these measures were known to be uncorrelated with subjective evaluations (e.g., Lin & Abdulla, 2008). Bit-detection tests were also carried out. The N_{bit} in these tests was fixed at 4 bps. The tip rate and data rate in the DSS method were set to 4 and 8192. A carrier frequency of 0 Hz and the key of a pseudo-random sequence of 1374 were used. The delay times for the echoes, T_0 and T_1, were 2.3 and 3.4 ms with the ECHO method (Gruhl, et al., 1996), as shown in Figure 4a. The relative amplitude of the echoes was set to A=0.6. The F_{m0} and F_{m1} in PPM were set to 8 and 10 Hz (Nishimura & Suzuki, 2004), as shown in Figure 4b. Here, data with LSB, DSS, and ECHO were detected as being blind watermarking while data with PPM were detected as being non-blind watermarking. None of the algorithms were run on original source codes, but were simulated with codes determined from their publication, so that these can be improved to increase performance.

All these signals were watermarked under the above conditions and they were then tested to detect the embedded data from all the watermarked signals. An evaluation criterion for each objective measure was used to find whether the CD-based approach could satisfy inaudibility and robustness requirements. This criterion will be defined step-by-step later.

Objective Evaluations

We carried out an objective experiment (simulation) to evaluate the PEAQ measurements (Kabel, 2002) between the original and embedded signals. PEAQ measurements, recommended by ITU-R BS.1387, were used to output the Objective Difference Grade (ODG), which corresponded to the Subjective Difference Grade (SDG) obtained from the procedure to evaluate subjective quality. The ODGs were graded as 0 (imperceptible), -1 (perceptible but not annoying), -2 (slightly annoying), -3 (annoying), and -4 (very annoying). The basic version of PEAQ (Kabel, 2002) was used to assess the ODGs of the stimuli. An evaluation criterion of PEAQ (ODG) over -1 was chosen as the embedding limitation to evaluate the PEAQs in this experiment.

Table 1a summarizes the averaged ODGs of the PEAQs for the watermarked signals. The PEAQs for the CD, LSB, and ECHO-methods were over the evaluation criterion (ODG > -1) in which the bit rate, N_{bit}, was fixed at 4 bps.

We also carried out LSD measurements to evaluate the sound quality of the watermarked signals.

$$\text{LSD} = \sqrt{\frac{1}{K}\sum_{k=1}^{K}\left[10\log_{10}\frac{\left|Y(\omega,k)\right|^2}{\left|X(\omega,k)\right|^2}\right]^2} \tag{11}$$

where k is the frame index, K is the number of frames, and $X(\omega,k)$ and $Y(\omega,k)$ are the Fourier amplitude spectra for original signal $x(n)$ and watermarked signal $y(n)$ at the k-th frame. A frame length of 25 ms and 60% overlap (15 ms) were used in this research. An evaluation criterion of LSD under 1 dB was chosen as the embedding limitation to evaluate the LSDs in this experiment. In general, LSD of 1 dB is usually used to evaluate sound quality for speech synthesis and speech coding.

Table 1b lists the averaged LSD for the watermarked signals at 4 bps. These results ensure that the CD method with an N_{bit} of 4 bps could be used to embed the watermarks into the original signals to satisfy requirement (a). The LSDs in the CD, LSB, ECHO, and PPM methods were under the evaluation criterion of 1 dB.

We carried out a bit-detection test to evaluate how well the CD method could accurately detect embedded data from the watermarked audio signals. The same original signals were used in this experiment. The bit-detection rates for all signals were evaluated as a function of the bit rate. The evaluation criterion for a detection rate of over 75% was chosen as the limitation for embedding to evaluate the bit-detection rate in this experiment. 75% detection was usually used as the threshold for signal detection (two alternative forced choice tasks of "0" or "1" while the chance level was 50%). In this case, various techniques for error detection and correction were not used for all methods.

Table 1c lists the averaged bit-detection rate for the watermarked signals without any attacks. The detection rates were over the evaluation criterion (>75%) in which the bit rate was 4 bps. This ensured that the method could be used to detect the watermarks from the watermarked signals to satisfy requirement (b). The bit-detection rate with the other methods (DSS, LSB, ECHO, and PPM) were also over the evaluation criterion (>75%).

Subjective Evaluations

We conducted a subjective experiment to determine the inaudibility of sound distortion caused by embedded data based on CD. Twenty tracks in the RWC music-genre database (Goto, et al., 2003) were used in the subjective evaluation. The tracks were chosen according to the PEAQ (ODG) score for all 102 tracks in the database. Track Nos. 14, 5, 9, 23, 26, 10, 12, and 29 from RWC-MDB-G-2001 were objectively evaluated, and the distortion caused by embedding was small (maximum value of ODGs at 4 bps was 0.18 and that of minimum was 0.15). Track Nos. 63, 58–2, 97, 99, 86, 95, 21, 90, 98, 27, and 22 from RWC-MDB-G-2001 were evaluated, and the distortion was large (maximum value of ODGs was 0.16 and that of minimum was -0.27). The same watermarks with eight characters ("AIS-lab.") were embedded into the L channel of the tracks by using CD, PPM, and DSS methods. The bit rate, N_{bit}, was 4 bps.

Six naive paid volunteers with normal hearing took part in the experiment. Two tracks, the first of which was an original track (Org) and the second of which was the same original track (Org) or an embedded track (CD, PPM, or DSS), were sequentially presented to the participants in a trial. Each participant's task was to judge the similarity between the two tracks by using a subjective scale that consisted of four scores of 0: completely the same, 1: probably the same, 2: probably different, and 3: completely different. Each participant performed 20 trials for 80 track combinations (20 tracks × 4 combinations [Org-Org, Org-CD, Org-PPM, and Org-DSS]).

We calculated the mean scores of judgments by each of the six participants (the mean scores for all participants are in Figure 5) and performed two-way (20 tracks × 4 combinations) analysis of variance (ANOVA) on the mean scores of each (n=6). The results for ANOVA revealed significant interaction between the two factors ($F_{57,285}$=17.4, $p<$ .001). Post hoc multiple comparison tests revealed that there were no significant differences between the mean scores of 20 tracks in the Org-Org and Org-CD combinations, whereas the main effect of tracks was significant in the Org-PPM and Org-DSS combinations. Furthermore, the differences between the mean scores for the Org-Org and Org-CD combinations in all tracks were not significant. These results indicate that the sound distortion caused by embedded data based on CD was inaudible, and inaudibility was not

Figure 5. Results from subjective evaluations

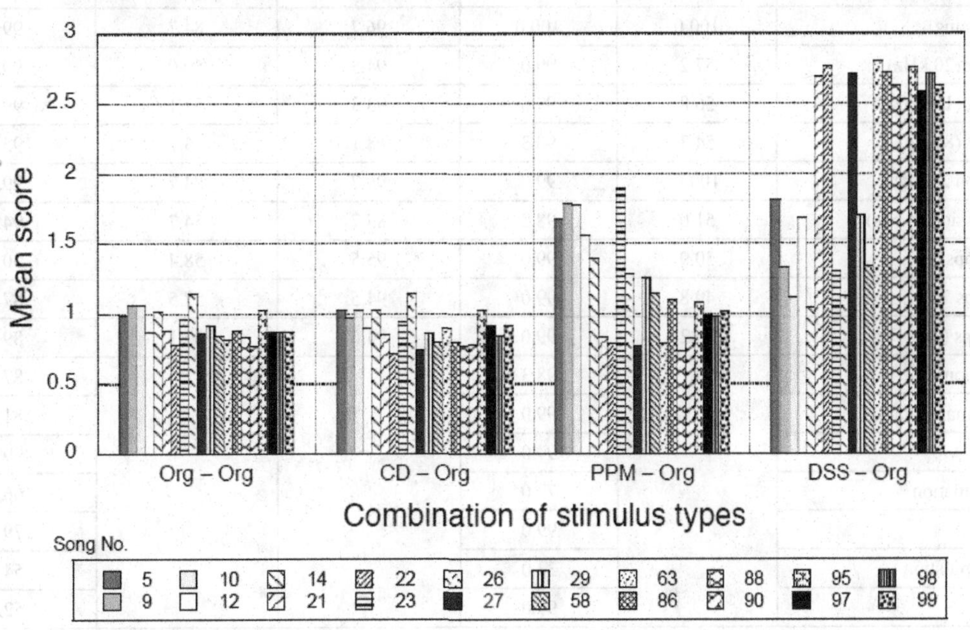

affected by the characteristics of the tracks. The same demonstrations that we used in subjective evaluations are available on our Web site (see URL: http://www.jaist.ac.jp/~unoki/02_demo/).

Robustness

We carried out three types of robustness tests to evaluate how well the methods could accurately and robustly detect embedded data from the watermarked-audio signals. Based on suggestions from STEP2001 (STEP2011, 2001), the main manipulation conditions used were: (1) down sampling (44.1 kHz → 20, 16, and 8 kHz), (2) quantization manipulation (16 bits → 24-bit extension and 8-bit compression), and (3) data compression (mp3: 128 kbps, 96 kbps, and 64 kbps-mono). In these tests, the bit rate, N_{bit}, was 4 bps. All 102 tracks of the RWC music genre database were used in the same way as in the objective evaluations.

The first nine rows in Table 2 list the results of evaluations for the CD method and the other methods (DSS, LSB, ECHO, and PPM). From the first row of Table 2, bit detection with the CD method was 99.3% where there were no attacks (default case). From the second to ninth rows, the bit-detection rates under strong manipulation conditions (down sampling from 44.1 kHz to 8 kHz, bit compression from 16 bits to 8 bits, and data compression of 96 kbps) corresponded to 95.3%, 94.2%, and 87.3%. Hence, these results indicate that the CD-based approach could accurately and robustly detect inaudible watermarks that copyrighted data in the original digital-audio content from the manipulated watermarked-signals. In contrast, we found that LSB and PPM were fragile against manipulation in watermarking while DSS and ECHO could satisfy the robustness requirement. As mentioned in the Introduction, we confirmed that LSB has drawbacks in robustness in watermarking. The PPM method may make it possible to improve these results, by fine-tuning the processing since we have not done any optimizations here.

Table 2. Results of robustness tests: bit-detection rates (bps) for LSB, DSS, ECHO, PPM, and CD methods

Manipulations / Method	LSB	DSS	ECHO	PPM	CD
Non-processing	100.0	100.0	96.7	84.7	99.3
Resampling (20 kHz)	57.2	99.0	94.3	59.0	99.2
Resampling (16 kHz)	56.8	99.0	93.3	57.1	99.1
Resampling (8 kHz)	54.3	98.3	88.1	53.1	95.3
Bit extension 24 bits	100.0	99.0	96.7	84.7	99.3
Bit compression (8 bits)	51.0	98.2	85.7	54.7	94.2
Mp3 128 kbps	50.9	99.0	95.5	58.4	90.6
Mp3 96 kbps	49.8	99.0	94.5	57.5	87.3
Mp3 64-kbps (mono)	50.2	99.0	94.6	57.1	89.8
Noise addition		98.3			87.9
Amplitude manipulation		99.0			81.5
Bit change		99.0			99.3
Data manipulation		73.0			66.0
Filtering		99.0			79.6
Phase manipulation		33.0			54.4
Echo		99.0			52.3

We finally carried out other robustness tests by using actual attacks to evaluate how well the methods could accurately and robustly detect embedded data from the watermarked-audio signals. Here, only CD and DSS methods were evaluated because the others did not seem to be robust from the previous tests. The reason the DSS method was used was to do a comparatively study with the CD method, as DSS is known to be too robust, as was mentioned in the Introduction. The attack tool employed in these robustness tests was the StirMark Benchmark for Audio (Steinebach, et al., 2001) version 1.3.2 (SMBA). Thirty-five SMBA attacks were used in these tests. The parameter in each attack was a default value. We categorized the 35 attacks into seven groups of (1) Noise: noise addition (AddBrumm, AddDynNoise, AddFFTNoise, AddNoise, AddSinus, and NoiseMax), (2) Amplitude: amplitude operation (Amplify, Compressor, Normalizer1, and Normalizer2), (3) Bits: bit handling (BitChanger and LSBzero), (4) Data: data substitution operation (CopySample, CutSample, Exchange, FlipSample, ReplaceSamples, ZeroCross, ZeroLength1, ZeroLength2, and ZeroRemove), (5) Filtering: filtering process (BassBoost, ExtraStereo, FFT_HLPassQuick, RC_LowPass, RC_HighPass, Smooth1, Smooth2, State1, State2, and VoiceRemove), (6) Phase: phase manipulation (FFT_Invert, FFT_RealReverse, and Invert), and (7) Echo: reverberation process (Echo). The main competitor with the CD method in these tests was the DSS method, which was the strongest in the robustness test against signal modifications.

The last seven rows in Table 2 summarize the results obtained from the benchmark tests with the CD method. These rows indicate the attack categories. The results indicate that the bit-detection rates for (1) Noise, (2) Amplitude, (3) Bits, and (5) Filtering are 75% or more. They revealed that the CD method is robust against (1) Noise, (2) Amplitude, (3) Bits, and (5) Filtering. The results indicate that the bit-detection rates for (4) Data, (6) Phase, and (7) Echo are less than 75%. The attacks on (4) Data, (6) Phase, and (7) Echo involve signal processing that distorts the phase of the watermarked signal. Therefore, the CD method that was used to embed a watermark in the phase domain is not robust to (4) Data, (6) Phase, or (7) Echo attacks. In contrast, the last seven rows in Table 2 list the results from the benchmark tests on the DSS method that indicate that it is predictably robust against many attacks. The accuracy for (6) Phase is, however, less than 33%. These indicate that the DSS method is not robust to (6) Phase attacks. These results suggest that the CD-based approach has similar robustness to that of the DSS method.

Discussion

The features from four typical methods we obtained were reconfirmed with the predicted features mentioned in the Introduction from the results of the objective/subjective evaluations and robustness tests. As mentioned in the Introduction, the LSB method is generally fragile to signal manipulation and attacks while it has an advantage in inaudibility. The DSS method has a drawback in inaudibility while it has an advantage in robustness. The ECHO method was pointed out to have a weakness in confidentiality because it can easily detect watermarks even if they are unpublished, while it has an advantage in inaudibility.

We reconfirmed that LSB had a drawback in robust watermarking although it could satisfy the (a) inaudibility and (c) blindness requirements. We also reconfirmed that DSS and ECHO could satisfy (b) robustness and (c) blindness, but DSS had a drawback with (a) inaudibility and ECHO with (d) confidentiality. Although PPM, especially, was predicted to be the best of these methods, the present results indicated that it had slight problems with (a) inaudibility and (b) robustness. In these tests, since the DSS method might seem to have low inaudibility to retain a high degree of robustness, this method offers the possibility of improving inaudibility by fine-tuning it to reduce robustness. Since we did not have the original code for PPM, these two problems may be able to be resolved if PPM is precisely tuned.

In summary, the typical watermarking methods used in LSB, DSS, ECHO, and PPM approaches could partially satisfy the four requirements of (a) inaudibility, (b) robustness, (c) blindness, and (d) confidentiality. These reconsiderations suggest that it is very difficult to achieve inaudible watermarking that can satisfy all four requirements, particularly both the requirements for (a) inaudibility and (b) robustness, simultaneously. In contrast, we found from the results of these evaluations that the CD-based technique adequately satisfied both the requirements for (a) inaudibility and (b) robustness, simultaneously. Since we assumed that the data-detection process was achieved as non-blind detection in the first step, further studies still remain to be done with regard to (c) blindness, i.e., carrying out blind detection of watermarks and investigations into collusive attacks in the next step. All algorithms including the CD-based approach were unpublished to satisfy the requirement for (d) confidentially. Although these are the next steps we intend to do in future work, the CD-based approach can be regarded to adequately satisfy all requirements by resolving the remaining issues. The results we obtained from all evaluations indicate significant advantages of the new technique and these suggest that the CD-based approach can provide a useful way of protecting copyrights in non-blind digital-audio watermarking.

EXTENDED METHOD

The previous section discussed our aims in finding an inaudible watermarking scheme based on the human auditory perception (cochlear delay characteristics) to satisfy the (a) inaudibility and (b) robustness criteria. This previous section also discussed our evaluations of the CD-based approach to non-blind inaudible digital-audio watermarking done by comparing it with four other methods (LSB, DSS, ECHO, and PPM) and carrying out objective and subjective evaluations, a bit-detection test, and robustness tests. These results revealed significant advantages of the new technique and these suggest that the CD-based approach can provide a useful way of protecting copyrights in non-blind digital-audio watermarking. This section discusses our investigations into how effective this method was in embedding watermarks into digital-audio signals to clarify its limitations with embedding.

Embedding Limitations with CD Method

We evaluated the CD method by comparing it with four others (LSB, DSS, ECHO, and PPM) in the same way by carrying out three tests: PEAQ, LSD, and bit-detection rates, where the N_{bit} was 4, 8, 16, 32, 64, 128, 256, 512, 1024, 2048, 4096, and 8192 bps to investigate embedding limitations with the CD method.

Figure 6 shows the results obtained from the comparative evaluations. All plots and values were averaged for all stimuli. The criteria to evaluate PEAQ (ODG) of -1, LSD of 1 dB, and bit-detection of 75% were the same as those we used in the previous section. We reconfirmed that LSB had a drawback in (b) robustness against watermarking although it could satisfy the (a) inaudibility and (c) blindness requirements even if the bit rate per second, N_{bit}, increased from 4 to 8192 bps. Although embedding limitations with the LSB method seem to be very high, these limitations will definitely be restricted by the issue with (b) robustness. We also reconfirmed that DSS and ECHO could satisfy (b) robustness, but DSS had a drawback with (a) inaudibility and ECHO with (d) confidentiality. In particular, we reconfirmed that the results with the ECHO method, PEAQ, and bit-detection rate decreased as N_{bit} increased, and that LSD with the ECHO method increased as N_{bit} increased. Embedding limitations with the

ECHO method were regarded to have very low bit rates. PPM had a reasonable LSD measure except with PEAQ; however, these may be able to be resolved if PPM is precisely tuned.

In contrast, objective evaluations of the CD-based approach indicated that PEAQs were over the evaluation criterion (> -1) in which N_{bit} ranged from 4 to 1024 bps while the PEAQs were gradually reduced as N_{bit} increased over 128 bps. We also found that LSDs increased as N_{bit} increased and that they were under this evaluation criterion (< 1 dB) under all conditions. In addition, we found that the bit detection rates were greater than the evaluation criterion (75%) in which N_{bit} ranged from 4 to 1024 bps. We found that the CD method with N_{bit} =1024 bps could be used to detect the watermarks from the watermarked signals. In all cases, these considerations ensured that the CD method with N_{bit} =1024 bps could be used as non-blind inaudible watermarking, which can satisfy

Figure 6. Results from evaluation of watermarking methods: standard CD and composite CD method with composite architecture (L=2 and N=2) for (a) PEAQ, (b) LSD, and (c) bit-detection rate

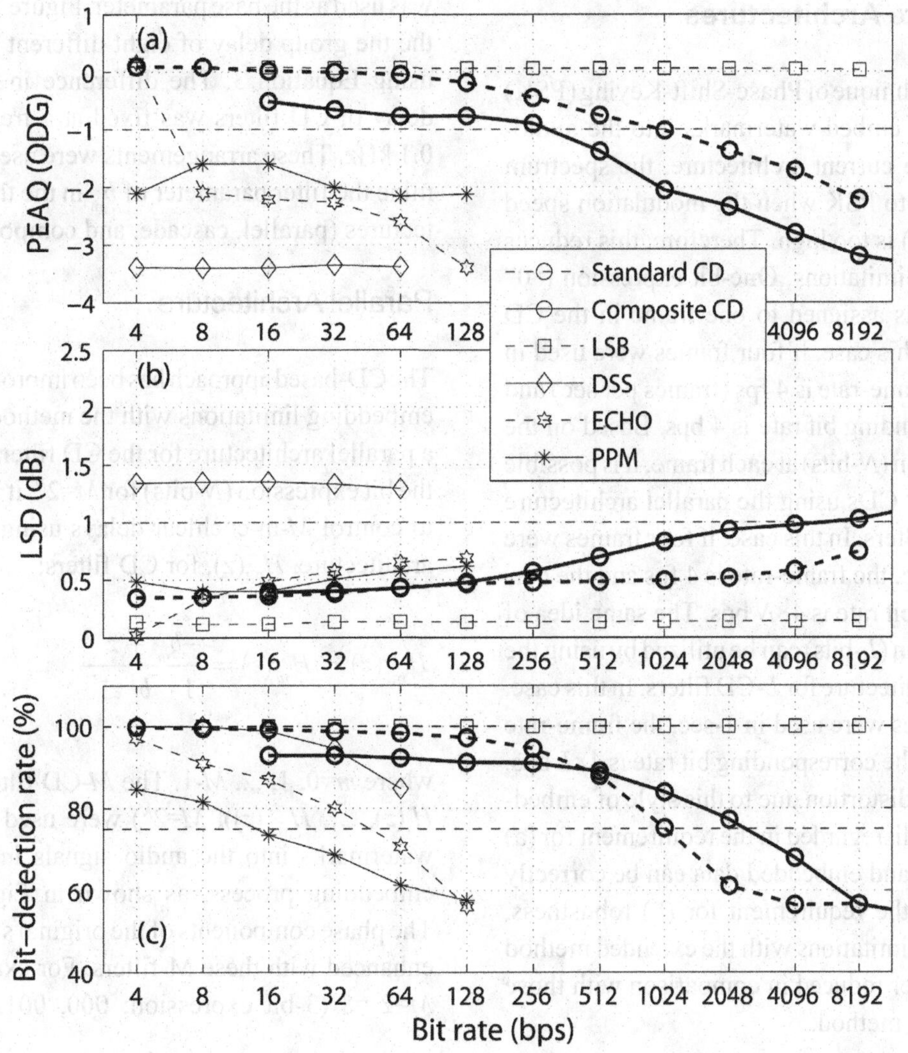

all evaluation criteria. However, we easily predicted that N_{bit} (1024 bps in this case) would be restricted from the results of robustness tests.

These considerations enabled us to predict that embedding limitations with the CD method amounted to around 1024 bps and that these limitations would be restricted even more from the results of robustness tests. We found that there was a trade-off between embedding limitations derived from the (a) inaudibility and (b) robustness requirements. Thus, we will reconsider the filter architecture for the CD filters to reduce embedding limitations with the CD method.

Parallel, Cascade, and Composite Architectures

Since the technique of Phase-Shift-Keying (PSK) was used to embed watermarks into the audio-signal in the current architecture, the spectrum spreads due to PSK when the modulation speed (i.e., bit rate) is too high. Therefore, this reduces embedding limitations. One-bit expression ("0" and "1") was assigned to one frame in the CD method. In this case, if four frames were used in 1-sec, the frame-rate is 4 fps (frames per sec) and the corresponding bit rate is 4 bps. Based on the bit expression (N-bits) at each frame, it is possible to control 2^N CDs using the parallel architecture for 2^N-CD filters. In this case, if four frames were used in 1-sec, the frame-rate is 4 fps and the corresponding bit rate is $4 \times N$ bps. The same idea of bit expression (L-bits) can be utilized by using the cascade architecture for L-CD filters. In this case, if four frames were used in 1-sec, the frame-rate is 4 fps and the corresponding bit rate is $4 \times L$ bps.

If signal distortion due to this style of embedding can be disregarded in the requirement for (a) inaudibility and embedded data can be correctly detected in the requirement for (b) robustness, embedding limitations with the extended method can be further reduced in comparison with those with the CD method.

The arrangement of parameter b_m for the CD filter in this case should be carefully reconsidered to have uniform differences in the group delay of CD filters. By substituting $|H(z)| = 1$ and $\varphi(z) = \frac{1}{j}\left(\ln(1 - bz) - \ln(b - z)\right)$ into Equation 3, the relationship between b_m and $\tau_m(\omega)$ can be derived as:

$$b_m = \frac{\tau_m(\omega)\cos(\omega T) \pm \sqrt{-\sin^2(\omega T)\tau_m^2(\omega) + 1}}{\tau_m(\omega) + 1} \tag{12}$$

where $0 < b_m < 1$. In the CD method, b_0=0.795 was used as the base parameter. Figure 7 indicates the the group delay of eight different CD filters using Equation 3. The difference in the group delay of CD filters was fixed at a frequency of 0.1 kHz. These arrangements were used to determine the filter parameter of b_m in the three architectures (parallel, cascade, and composite).

Parallel Architecture

The CD-based approach has been improved to ease embedding limitations with the method by using a parallel architecture for the CD filter. Based on the bit expression (N-bits) for M=2^N, it is possible to control M-th cochlear delays using a parallel architecture, $H_{Prl}(z)$, for CD filters:

$$H_{prl}(z) = H_m(z) = \frac{-b_m + z^{-1}}{1 - b_m z^{-1}} \tag{13}$$

where m=0, 1, ..., M-1. The M-CD filters ($H_0(z)$, $H_1(z)$, ..., $H_{M-1}(z)$), M=2^N) were used to embed watermarks into the audio signals in the data-embedding process, as shown in Figure 8a-1. The phase components of the original signal were enhanced with these M-filters. For example, for M=2^3=8 (3-bit expression: 000, 001, ..., 111),

Figure 7. Group-delay characteristics of cochlear delay filter

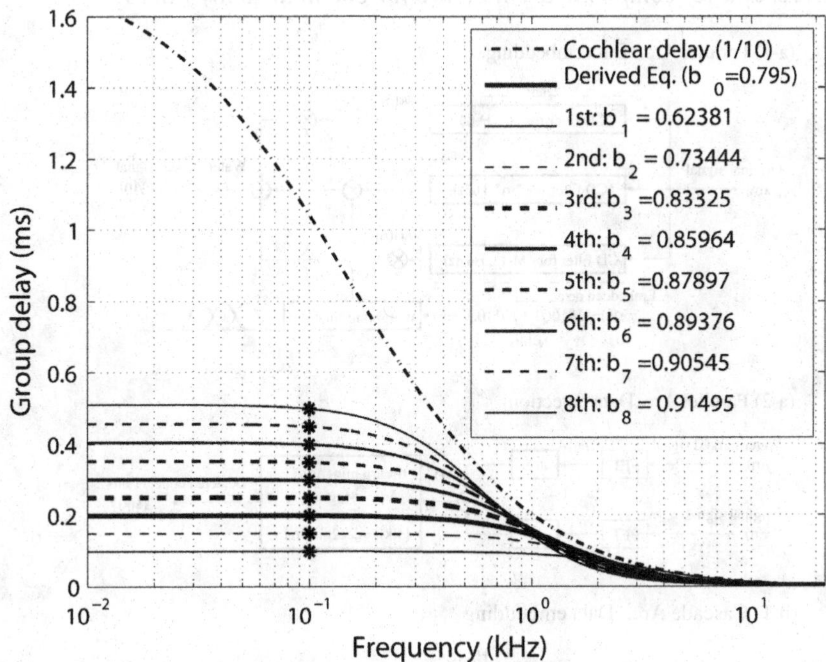

eight types (M=8) of cochlear delays, according to the b_0, b_1, ..., b_7 shown in Figure 7, were used.

The data-detection process, seen in Figure 8a-2, involves estimating the group delays ($\arg H_0(z)$, $\arg H_1(z)$, ..., $\arg H_{M-1}(z)$) from the phase difference between the original and the watermarked sounds $\left(\varphi(\omega)\right)$ to the respective phase spectrum of the filter $\left(\Delta\Phi_m = \left|\varphi(\omega) - \arg H_m(\omega)\right|\right)$ to detect the embedded signal, $s(k)$. The selected filter number, m, corresponds to the bit expression (e.g., m=7 and "111" for watermarks).

Cascade Architecture

The CD method of easing embedding limitations has also been improved with a different approach to using the cascade architecture for CD filters. Based on the expression of L-bits, it is also possible to control L-th CDs using the cascade architecture. A total of L-th-order-CD filters, $H_{\mathrm{Cas}}(z)$, were used to embed watermarks into audio signals in the data-embedding process shown in Figure 8b-1. The $H_{\mathrm{Cas}}(z)$ is represented as:

$$H_{\mathrm{Cas}}(z) = \prod_{\ell=1}^{L} H_\ell(z) = \prod_{\ell=1}^{L} \frac{-b_\ell + z^{-1}}{1 - b_\ell z^{-1}} \qquad (14)$$

For example, for $R=2^L=8$ (L=3, expression of 3 bits: 000, 001, ..., and 111), eight types of cascaded CD filters were used, as seen in Figure 8b-1. Thus, if $s(k)$=000, the total group delay of the cascaded CD filters is a third of the group delay of the CD filter.

The data-detection process in the cascade architecture, shown in Figure 8b-2, involves estimating the group delays from the phase difference between $x(n)$ and $y(n)$ to detect the embedded signal, $s(k)$. The matched group delay, p, corresponds to the representation of L-bits of $s(k)$, k=1, ..., L. As a result, this process is the same as that with the parallel architecture. Note that for $R=2^L$, the CD filters in the cascade architecture can be expressed

Figure 8. Block diagram for (1) data embedding and (2) data detection in (a) parallel architecture, (b) cascade architecture, and (c) composite architecture for cochlear delay filters

(a-1) Parallel Arc. Data embedding

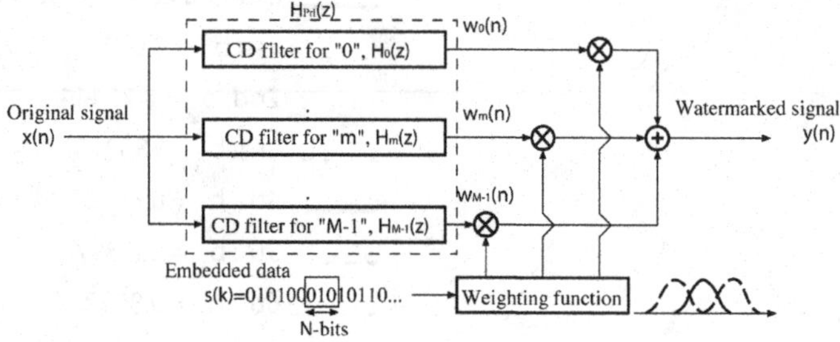

(a-2) Parallel Arc. Data detection

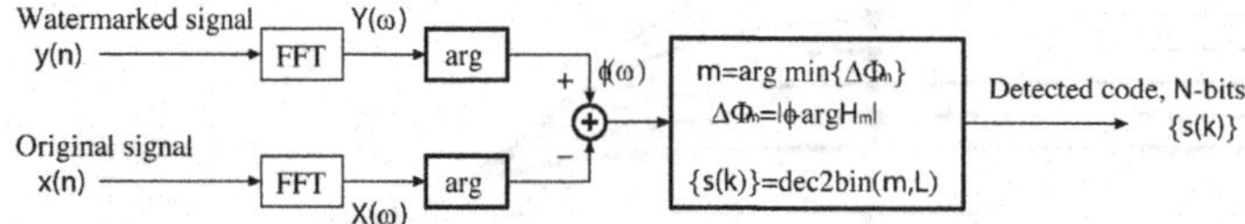

(b-1) Cascade Arc. Data embedding

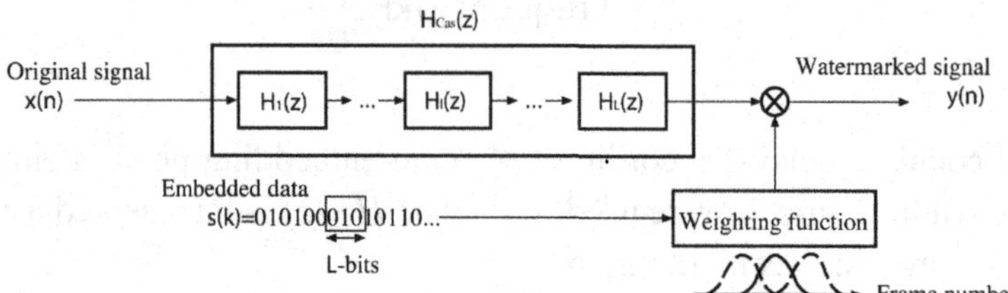

(b-2) Cascade Arc. Data detection

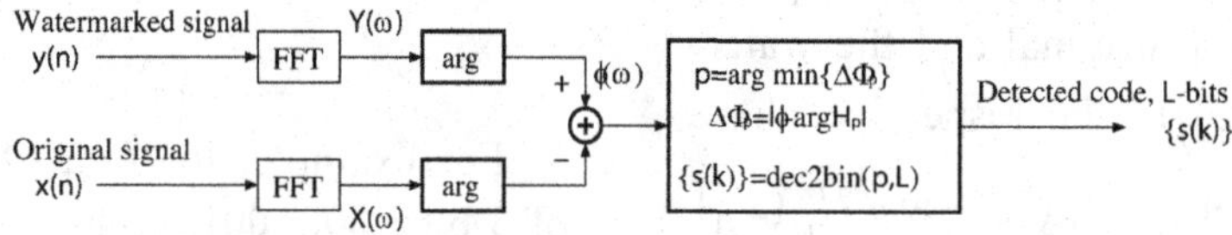

(c-1) Composite Arc. Data embedding

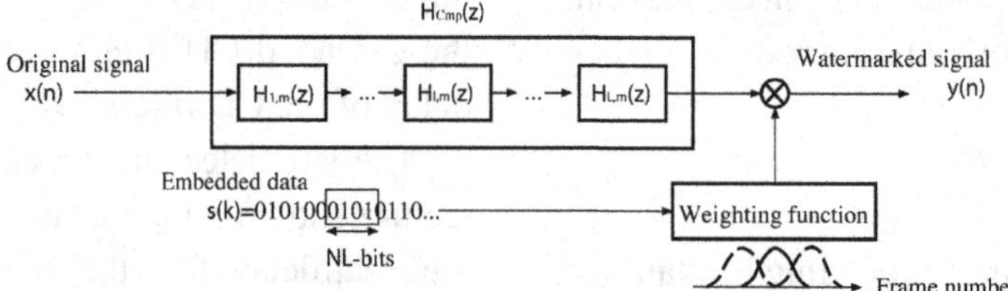

(c-2) Composite Arc. Data detection

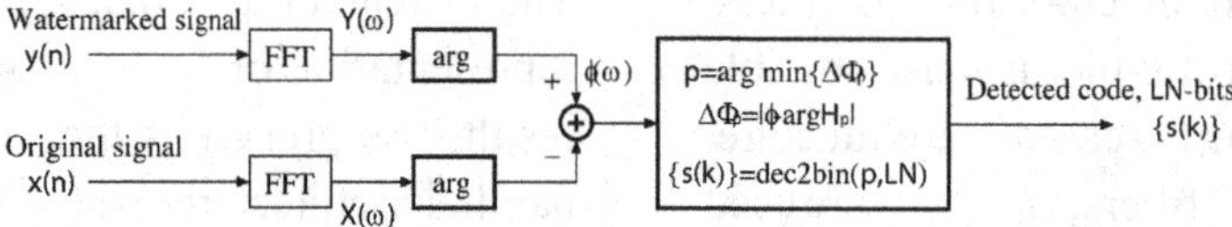

in the L-order IIR filters, while the M=2^L-th CD filters in the parallel architecture can be expressed in the first order III filter; the essential difference between these architectures is they have a different dynamic range to be expressed as M-th CD filters.

Composite Architecture

Based on the expression of N-bits, it is possible to control M(=2^N)-th CDs using the parallel architecture. However, M-th CDs must not be beyond the CD that was scaled by 1/10. Based on the expression of L-bits, it is possible to control R(=2^L)-th CDs using the cascade architecture. However, inaudibility will be affected due to PSK spreading the spectrum when the number of R-th CDs is increased. Thus, a composite architecture can be proposed by reasonably incorporating parallel and cascade architectures. Based on the expression of $N\times L$-bits, it is also possible to control 2^{NL}-th CDs using the composite architecture.

Figure 8c-1 has a block diagram of the data-embedding process. The composite architecture for the CD filter is designed as:

$$H_{\mathrm{Cmp}}(z) = \prod_{\ell=1}^{L} H_{\ell,m}(z) = \prod_{\ell=1}^{L} \frac{-b_{\ell,m} + z^{-1}}{1 - b_{\ell,m} z^{-1}} \tag{15}$$

where $\ell = 1, 2, \ldots, L$ and m=0, 1, …, M-1. Here, the group delay, $\tau_{\mathrm{Cmp}}(\omega)$, can be obtained as:

$$\tau_{\mathrm{Cmp}}(\omega) = \sum_{\ell=1}^{L} \tau_{\ell,m}(\omega) \tag{16}$$

$$\tau_{\ell,m}(\omega) = -\frac{d \arg(H_{\ell,m}(e^{j\omega}))}{d\omega} \tag{17}$$

For example, the group delays in the composite architecture with N=2 and L=2 are represented as 16-types of $\tau_{\mathrm{Cmp}}(\omega)$ in Equation 16. Therefore, the composite architecture can embed 4 bits per frame into the original signal.

Figure 8c-2 shows the flow for the data-detection process. Watermarks were detected as follows: (1) it was assumed that both $x(n)$ and $y(n)$ were available with this watermarking method; (2) The original, $x(n)$, and the watermarked signal, $y(n)$, were decomposed to become overlapping segments using the same window function used for embedding the data; (3) The phase difference of $\varphi(\omega)$ to the respective phase spectrum of the filters $\left(\Delta\Phi_p = \left|\varphi(\omega) - \arg H_p(\omega)\right|\right)$ was calculated to estimate the group delay characteristics of ($H_{\mathrm{cmp}}(z)$=$H_p(z)$) used for embedding the data; (4) The embedded data, $\hat{s}(k)$, were detected using the k-th CD filter.

Evaluations of Embedding Limitations

We evaluated the CD-based and extended methods (the parallel (N=1, 2, 3, and 4), the cascaded (L=1, 2, 3, and 4), and the composite architectures (N=2 and L=2) by carrying out three objective evaluations, PEAQ, LSD, and bit-detection rate and robustness tests to investigate the extent of embedding limitations with the extended methods. In general, although (N, L) = (3, 3) and (4, 4) were candidates for the composite architecture in the evaluations, these conditions were not used from the results of preliminary studies. All stimuli that were used in these evaluations were the same (all 102 tracks in the RWC music-genre database). The frame rates (bit rates per frame) in these experiments were 4, 8, 16, 32, 64, 128, 256, 512, 1024, 2048, 4096, and 8192 fps. Note that the frame rates can be commonly controlled in these evaluations for the extended methods because the bit rates in these methods depend on the filter architecture. The same watermarks with eight characters ("AIS-lab") were embedded into both channels by using the methods.

The first three rows in Table 3 summarize the embedding limitations with three evaluation criteria (PEAQ (ODG) > -1, LSD ≤ 1 dB, and bit-detection rate > 75%) for the methods. The units for the limitations were bits per second (bps) in which they were first calculated from frames per second (fps) in this case. In this table, the fps have been indicated in parentheses. As the results for the composite architecture were quite effective, these have been indicated in Figure 6 by the thick solid line with the circles. The results for the others have not been plotted there. Note that the PEAQs in this figure are plotted as a function of the bit rates so that the starting point is 16 bps (=4 fps×4) not 4 bps.

The PEAQs in the composite architecture (N, L) = (2, 2) were over the evaluation criterion (> -1) in this case in which the frame rates ranged from 16 to 256 bps (= 4 to 64 fps×4). The LSDs in the composite architecture (N, L) = (2, 2) were under the evaluation criterion (≤ 1 dB) in which the bit rates ranged from 16 to 4096 bps (= 4 to 1024 fps×4). The detection rates in the composite architecture (N, L) = (2, 2) were over the evaluation criterion (> 75%) in which the bit-rate rates ranged from 16 to 2048 bps (4 to 512 fps×4). In comparison with the CD method (standard CD), the results in Figure 6 revealed that the range of bit rates with regard to the bit-detection rate in the extended method with the composite architecture has been about doubled while these

Table 3. Results of objective evaluations and robustness tests on embedding limitations (bps)

Methods Measures	Standard	Parallel			Cascade			Composite
	L=1, N=1	L=1, N=2	L=1, N=3	L=1, N=4	L=2, N=1	L=3, N=1	L=4, N=1	L=2, N=2
PEAQ	**1,024**	**1,024** (512)	**768** (256)	512 (128)	1,024 (512)	**768** (256)	256 (64)	**256** (64)
LSD	8,192	8,192 (4,096)	12,288 (4,096)	16,384 (4,096)	8,192 (4,096)	12,288 (4,096)	8,192 (2048)	4,096 (1,024)
Detection Rate	**1,024**	**1024** (512)	1,536 (512)	1,024 (256)	512 (256)	**768** (256)	512 (128)	2,048 (512)
DS 20 kHz	256	512 (256)	768 (256)	512 (128)	256 (128)	384 (128)	128 (64)	512 (128)
DS 16 kHz	256	512 (256)	768 (256)	512 (128)	256 (128)	384 (128)	128 (64)	512 (128)
DS 8 kHz	128	256 (128)	384 (128)	256 (64)	256 (128)	192 (64)	128 (64)	**256** (64)
BC 24 bits	256	512 (256)	768 (256)	512 (128)	256 (128)	384 (128)	512 (128)	512 (128)
BC 8 bits	256	512 (256)	768 (256)	512 (128)	256 (128)	384 (128)	128 (64)	**256** (64)
mp3 128 kbps	128	256 (128)	384 (128)	256 (64)	256 (128)	192 (64)	128 (32)	**256** (64)
mp3 96 kbps	**64**	**128** (64)	192 (64)	128 (32)	**128** (64)	***96*** *(32)*	---	**256** (64)
mp3 64 kbpt	128	256 (128)	192 (64)	256 (64)	**128** (64)	192 (64)	128 (32)	**256** (64)

Note that embedding limitations in parallel, cascade, and composite architectures were calculated as bit-representations in one frame multiples with fps. Fps has been indicated in parentheses.

ranges for the PEAQs and LSD have been narrowed to about a quarter.

The results from Table 3 also revealed that the most optimal parallel, cascade, and composite architectures corresponded to (*N*, *L*) = (2, 1), (1, 3), and (2, 2). In this case, the minimum detection rates for the parallel, cascade, and composite architectures in the first three rows in Table 3 were 512 fps at (*N*, *L*) = (1, 2), 256 fps at (*N*, *L*)= (1, 3), and 64 fps at (*N*, *L*) = (2, 2). Therefore, the embedding limitations with the most optimal parallel (*N*, *L*) = (2, 1), cascade (*N*, *L*) = (1, 3), and composite (*N*, *L*) = (2, 2) architectures corresponded to 1024 (512 fps×2), 768 (= 256 fps×3), and 256 (= 64 fps×4) bps. Their values are indicated by the bold font in the first three rows of Table 3. As has already been summarized, the embedding limitation with the CD method (standard CD) is 1024 bps.

Three robustness tests were also carried out. The main manipulation conditions used were: (1) down sampling (44.1 kHz → 20, 16, and 8 kHz), (2) amplitude manipulation (16 bits →24-bit extension and 8-bit compression), and (3) data compression (mp3: 128 kbps, 96 kbps, and 64 kbps mono). These results have been given in the last eight rows of Table 3, which summarizes the maximum bits per second over the evaluation criterion (> 75%) of bit detection. The maximum detection rate with all architectures decreased when the signals were compressed by mp3 with 96 kbps. This means that the embedding limitations, corresponding to detection rates in parallel, cascade, and composite architectures, were restricted under the condition of mp3 with 96 kbps (10th row in Table 3). Here, the minimum detection rates under all conditions, i.e., the embedding limitations, were 128 bps (= 64 fps×2) with the parallel (*N*, *L*) = (2, 1) architecture, 128 bps (= 64 fps×2) with the parallel (*N*, *L*) = (1, 2) architecture, and 256 bps (= 64 fps×4) with the composite architecture (*N*, *L*) = (2, 2). These values are denoted by the bold font in the last eight rows of Table 3. The bit detection rate with the cascade architecture (*L*=4) did not exceed the evaluation criterion at any frame rate (denoted as "---") in Table 3.

Finally, a robustness test for the StirMark benchmark was carried out to clarify the robustness of the parallel, cascade, and composite architectures, (*N*, *L*) = (2, 1), (1, 2), and (2, 2), for the CD filters against the watermark being cracked. The results for both the parallel and cascade architectures, (*N*, *L*) = (2, 1) and (1, 2), are the same as those for the CD method (standard CD) as listed in the last seven rows of Table 3. In contrast, the results for the composite architecture, (*N*, *L*) = (2, 2), indicate that the bit-detection rates for (1) Noise, (2) Amplitude, (3) Bits, (4) Data, (5) Filtering, (6) Phase, and (7) Echo are 81.9%, 77.0%, 91.7%, 63.6%, 76.5%, 53.7%, and 52.4%, respectively. Although there is a slight reduction from those of the CD method, composite CD has the same trend in robustness compared with the CD method (standard CD) as well as the DSS method. In summary, these results revealed that the composite architecture with the CD method is robust against (1) Noise, (2) Amplitude, (3) Bits, and (5) Filtering while it is not generally robust to (4) Data, (6) Phase, or (7) Echo.

Embedding limitations with CD and extended CD methods were derived from the results of objective evaluations and robustness tests to satisfy all the requirements for (a) inaudibility and (b) robustness. The embedding limitations with the CD method (standard CD), derived from the first evaluations in the three rows (objective evaluations (PEAQ and LSD), bit-detection tests) in Table 3 and the second evaluations (robustness tests) in the last seven rows in Table 3, corresponded to 1024 and 64 bps. Hence, the overall embedding limitation with the standard CD was 64 bps.

In contrast, embedding limitations with the extended CD method (composite CD) depended on the number of CD filters in the parallel, cascade, and composite architectures. From the results of robustness tests, the CD methods with a composite architecture (*N*, *L*) = (2, 2) can be regarded as reasonable. Embedding limitations with the extended method (composite CD), derived from the first evaluations (the objective evaluations and bit-detection tests) in the first three rows of Table 3 and the second evaluations (robustness tests) in the last seven rows of Table 3, correspond to 256 and 256 bps. Hence, the overall embedding limitation with the composite CD was 256 bps.

Hence, the best overall embedding limitation was 256 bps and its architecture was the composite CD with $(N, L) = (2, 2)$.

FUTURE RESEARCH DIRECTIONS

The next step in future work with the CD-based approach is to (1) consider blind digital-audio watermarking, i.e., the blind detection of embedded data from watermarked signals to satisfy requirement (c) of blindness and (2) extend the CD method as reversible watermarking to rewritable watermarking in digital-audio signals to enable reasonable control of copyrights.

The blind watermarking based on PPM in the study done by Sonoda *et al.* (2004) may provide a very useful way in future work with regard to the (1) blind detection of embedded data from watermarked signals. This is because the CD-based approach can be regarded as a simple means of PPM such as static phase modulation. Two CD filters, $H_0(z)$ and $H_1(z)$, were used in the inaudible watermarking shown in Figure 4c, to embed the codes ("0" and "1") in the original signal, $x(n)$. In this case, the filter properties of poles/zeros were also embedded in the watermarked signal, y(n). If the values of b_m, related to the poles/zeros of $H_m(z)$ could be correctly estimated from $y(n)$, the embedded code, $s(k)$, could be correctly detected using b_m. Therefore, one of the solutions may be to use the chirp z-transform.

With regard to the future work of (2) extending the CD method as reversible watermarking to rewritable watermarking in digital-audio signals, we have been able to consider the possibility of removing watermarks $s(k)$ from watermarked signal y(n) in reversible processing. The complex-conjugate time-reversal filtering of $H_0(z)$ and $H_1(z)$ may be able to be applied to all segments to obtain restored signal $x(n)$ by removing the group delay related to CD from $y(n)$ according to the detected $s(k)$.

CONCLUSION

This chapter described a novel non-blind digital-audio watermarking method based on cochlear delay characteristics. CD methods were evaluated with regard to the requirements for inaudibility and robustness to find how effective the CD-based approach was. Four typical methods (LSB, DSS, ECHO, and PPM) were also comparatively evaluated with the CD method through objective and subjective evaluations and robustness tests. The results obtained from objective and subjective evaluations revealed that the CD method could be used to embed inaudible watermarks into the original signals, and that subjects could not detect the embedded data in any of the watermarked signals we used. Evaluations of robustness demonstrated that it could precisely and robustly detect embedded data such as those copyrighted with a watermarked signal to protect them against various signal modifications. Hence, these results indicated that the CD-based approach is considerably more effective in satisfying the requirements for non-blind inaudible watermarking. The comparative results also suggest that the CD-based approach could provide a useful way of protecting copyrights.

Embedding limitations with CD (standard, parallel, cascade, and composite) methods of digital-audio watermarking were systematically investigated by carrying out five tests on PEAQ, LSD, bit-detection, and robustness (signal modifications and the StirMark benchmark). The results to satisfy the requirements of inaudibility and robustness revealed that the CD method with parallel, cascade, and composite architectures could be used to embed watermarks into the original signals and to accurately and robustly detect the embedded data from the watermarked signals. This also meant that the best results were achieved with the composite architecture. Hence, the overall embedding limitation with the extended CD method (composite architecture of L=2 and N=2) was 256 bps, while that with the CD method (standard CD) was 64 bps.

REFERENCES

Aiba, E., & Tsuzaki, M. (2007). Perceptual judgement in synchronization of two complex tones: Relation to the cochlear delays. *Acoustical Science and Technology*, *28*(5), 357–359. doi:10.1250/ast.28.357

Aiba, E., Tsuzaki, M., Tanaka, S., & Unoki, M. (2008). Judgment of perceptual synchrony between two pulses and verification of its relation to cochlear delay by an auditory model. *The Japanese Psychological Research*, *50*(4), 204–213. doi:10.1111/j.1468-5884.2008.00376.x

Akagi, M., & Yasutake, K. (1998). *Perception of time-related information: Influence of phase variation on timbre. Technical report of IEICE*. IEICE.

Bassia, P., & Pitas, I. P. (1998). Robust audio watermarking in the time domain. In *Proceedings of EUSIPCO 1998, European Signal Processing Conference*, (pp. 25-28). EUSIPCO.

Bender, W., Gruhl, D., & Morimoto, N. (1996). Techniques for data hiding. *IBM Systems Journal*, *35*(3/4), 131–336.

Blauert, J. (1983). *Spatial hearing: The psychophysics of human sound localization*. Cambridge, MA: MIT Press. doi:10.1121/1.392109

Boney, L., Tewfik, H. H., & Hamdy, K. H. (1996). Digital watermarks for audio signals. In *Proceedings of International Conference on Multimedia Computing and Systems,* (pp. 473-480). IEEE.

Cox, I., Kilian, J., Leighton, T., & Shamoon, T. (1995). *Secure spread spectrum watermarking for multimedia.* Technical Report 95-10. Princeton, NJ: NEX Research Institute.

Cox, I., & Miller, M. (2001). Electronic watermarking: The first 50 years. In *Proceedings of the IEEE Workshop on Multimedia Signal Processing,* (pp. 225-230). Cannes, France: IEEE Press.

Cvejic, N., & Seppänen, T. (2005). Increasing robustness of LSB audio steganography by reduced distortion LSD coding. *Journal of Universal Computer Science, 11*(1), 56–65.

Cvejic, N., & Seppänen, T. (Eds.). (2008). *Digital audio watermarking techniques and technologies*. Hershey, PA: IGI Global.

Dau, T., Wegner, O., Mallert, V., & Kollmeier, B. (2000). Auditory brainstem responses (ABR) with optimized chirp signals compensating basilar membrane dispersion. *The Journal of the Acoustical Society of America, 107*, 1530–1540. doi:10.1121/1.428438

de Boer, E. (1980). Auditory physics, physical principles in hearing theory I. *Physics Reports*, *62*, 87–187. doi:10.1016/0370-1573(80)90100-3

Foo, S. W. (2008). Three techniques of digital audio watermarking. In Cvejic, N., & Seppanen, T. (Eds.), *Digital Audio Watermarking Techniques and Technologies* (pp. 104–122). Hershey, PA: IGI Global.

Gordy, J. D., & Bruton, L. T. (2000). Performance evaluation of digital audio watermarking algorithms. In *Proceedings of IEEE Midwest Symposium on Circuits and Systems*, (pp. 456-459). IEEE Press.

Goto, M., Hashiguchi, H., Nishimura, T., & Oka, R. (2003). RWC music database: Music genre database and musical instrument sound database. *Proceedings of ISMIR*, *2003*, 229–230.

Gruhl, D., Lu, A., & Bender, W. (1996). Echo hiding. In *Proceedings of Information Hiding 1st Workshop*, (pp. 295-315). IEEE.

Hartung, F., & Kutter, M. (1999). Multimedia watermarking techniques. *Proceedings of the IEEE*, *8*(7), 1709–1107.

He, X., & Scordilis, M. (2008). Spread spectrum for digital audio watermarking. In Cvejic, N., & Seppanen, T. (Eds.), *Digital Audio Watermarking Techniques and Technologies* (pp. 11–49). Hershey, PA: IGI Global.

Iwakiri, N., & Matsui, K. (1997). Embedding a text into audo codes under ADPCM quantizer. *Journal Information Processing Society of Japan*, *38*(10), 2053–2061.

Kabal, P. (2002). *An examination and interpretation of ITU-RBS.1387: Perceptual evaluation of audio quality. TSP Lab Technical Report*. Montreal, Canada: McGill University.

Kirovski, D., & Malvar, H. S. (2003). Spread-spectrum watermarking of audio signals. *IEEE Transactions on Signal Processing*, *51*(4), 1020–1033. doi:10.1109/TSP.2003.809384

Lin, Y., & Abdulla, W. H. (2008). Perceptual evaluation of audio watermarking using objective quality measure. *Proceedings of ICASSP*, *2008*, 1745–1748.

Malik, H., Ansari, R., & Khokhar, A. (2008). Robust audio watermarking using frequency-selective spread spectrum. *IET Information Security*, *2*(4), 129–150. doi:10.1049/iet-ifs:20070145

Moore, J. C. B. (2003). *An introduction to the psychology of hearing* (5th ed.). New York, NY: Academic Press.

Nishimura, A. (2010). Audio watermarking based on subband amplitude modulation. *Acoustical Science and Technology*, *31*(5), 328–336. doi:10.1250/ast.31.328

Nishimura, R., Suzuki, M., & Suzuki, Y. (2001). Detection threshold of a periodic phase shift in music sound. In *Proceedings of the 17th International Congress on Acoustics*. IEEE.

Nishimura, R., & Suzuki, Y. (2004). Audio watermark based on periodical phase shift. *Journal of Acoustical Society of Japan*, *60*(5), 269–272.

Ozawa, K., Suzuki, Y., & Sone, T. (1993). Monaural phase effects on timbre of two-tone signals. *The Journal of the Acoustical Society of America*, *93*, 1007–1011. doi:10.1121/1.405548

Paliwal, K. K., & Alsteris, L. (2003). Usefulness of phase spectrum human speech perception. *Proceedings of Eurospeech*, *2003*, 2117–2120.

Petitcolas, F. A. P., Anderson, R. J., & Kuhn, M. G. (1999). Information hiding -- A survey. *Proceedings of the IEEE*, *87*(7), 1062–1078. doi:10.1109/5.771065

Plack, C. J. (2005). *The sense of hearing*. London, UK: Lawrence Erlbaum Association.

Plack, C. J. (2010). *The Oxford handbook of auditory science*. Oxford, UK: Oxford University Press.

Şehirli, M., Gűrgen, F., & Ikizoğlu, S. (2004). Performance evaluation of digital audio watermarking techniques designed in time, frequency and cepstrum domains. *Lecture Notes in Computer Science*, *3261*, 430–440. doi:10.1007/978-3-540-30198-1_44

Sonoda, K., Nishimura, R., & Suzuki, Y. (2004). Blind detection of watermarks embedded by periodical phase shifts. *Acoustical Science and Technology*, *25*(1), 103–105. doi:10.1250/ast.25.103

STEP2001. (2001). News release: Final selection of technology toward the global spread of digital audio watermarks. *Japanese Society for Rights of Authors, Composers and Publishers*. Retrieved from http://www.jasrac.or.jp/ejhp/release/2001/0629.html

Steinebach, M., Petitcolas, F. A. P., Raynal, F., Dittmann, J., Fontaine, C., & Seibel, C. … Ferri, L. C. (2001). StirMark benchmark: Audio watermarking attacks. In *Proceedings of Coding and Computing 2001*, (pp. 49-54). IEEE.

Swanson, M., Zhu, B., & Tewfik, A. (1999). Current state-of-the-art, challenges and future directions for audio watermarking. In *Proceedings of the IEEE International Conference on Multimedia Computing and Systems,* (pp. 19-24). Florence, Italy: IEEE Press.

Tahara, Y., Sato, H., & Nishiwaki, S. (2005). A study on auditory integration characteristics based on critical time delay for distinct perception of echo. *Journal of the Acoustical Society of Japan, 61*(11), 14–23.

Yu, G., Zuo, J., & Cui, D. (2011). Performance evaluation of digital audio watermarking algorithm under low bits rates. *Lecture Notes in Computer Science, 6987*, 336–343. doi:10.1007/978-3-642-23971-7_42

Zwicker, E., & Fastl, H. (1990). *Psychoacoustics facts and models*. Berlin, Germany: Springer-Verlag.

Zwicker, E., & Zwicker, U. T. (1991). Audio engineering and psychoacoustics: Matching signals to the final receiver, the human auditory system. *Journal of the Audio Engineering Society. Audio Engineering Society, 39*, 115–126.

ADDITIONAL READING

Aoki, N. (2006). A band extension technique for G.711 speech using steganography. *IEICE Transactions on Communications, 8*(6), 1896–1898. doi:10.1093/ietcom/e89-b.6.1896

Arnold, M., Baum, P. G., & Voeßing, W. (2009). A phase modulation audio watermarking technique. *Lecture Notes in Computer Science, 5806*, 102–116. doi:10.1007/978-3-642-04431-1_8

Bassia, R., Pitas, I., & Mikolaidis, N. (2001). Robust audio watermarking in time domain. *IEEE Transactions on Multimedia, 3*(2), 232–241. doi:10.1109/6046.923822

Cvejic, N., Keskinarkaus, A., & Seppänen, T. (2001). Audio watermarking using m-sequences and temporal masking. *Proceedings of WASPAA, 2001*, 227–230.

Huang, X., Abe, Y., & Echizen, I. (2010). Capacity adaptive synchronized acoustic steganography scheme. *Journal of Information Hiding and Multimedia Signal Processing, 1*(2), 72–90.

Ji, B., Yan, F., & Zhang, D. (2003). A robust audio watermarking scheme using wavelet modulation. *IEICE Transactions on Fundamentals, 86*(12), 3303–3305.

Karabat, C., & Keskinoz, M. (2008). Robust non-blind detection for spread spectrum watermarking system. *Proceedings of IIHMSP, 2008*, 1221–1224.

Kim, H. J., Choi, Y. H., Seok, J., & Hong, J. (2004). Audio watermarking techniques, intelligent watermarking techniques. In Pan, J.-S., Huang, H.-C., & Jain, L. C. (Eds.), *Intelligent Watermarking Techniques* (pp. 185–217). Singapore: World Scientific Publishing. doi:10.1142/9789812562524_0008

Ko, B.-S., Nishimura, R., & Suzuki, Y. (2004). Robust watermarking based on time-spread echo method with subband decomposition. *IEICE Transaction on Fundamentals, 87*(6), 1647–1650.

Ko, B.-S., Nishimura, R., & Suzuki, Y. (2005). Time-spread echo method for digital audio watermarking. *IEEE Transactions on Multimedia, 7*(2), 212–221. doi:10.1109/TMM.2005.843366

Lee, S.-K., & Ho, Y.-S. (2000). Digital audio watermarking in the ceptsrum domain. *IEEE Transactions on Consumer Electronics*, *46*(3), 744–750. doi:10.1109/30.883441

Lemma, A. K., Aprea, J., Oomen, W., & Kerkhof, L. (2003). A temporal domain audio watermarking technique. *IEEE Transactions on Signal Processing*, *51*(4), 1088–1097. doi:10.1109/TSP.2003.809372

Lie, W.-N., & Chang, L.-C. (2006). Robust and high-quality time-domain audio watermarking based on low-frequency amplitude modification. *IEEE Transactions on Multimedia*, *8*(1), 46–59. doi:10.1109/TMM.2005.861292

Muramatsu, I., & Arakawa, K. (2004). Digital watermark for audio signals based on octave similarity. *IEICE Transaction A*, *87*(6), 797-796.

Nishimura, A. (2007). Information hiding in audio signals: Digital watermarking and steganography. *Journal of Acoustical Society of Japan*, *63*(11), 660–667.

Nishimura, R., Abe, S., Fujita, N., Suzuki, Y., Enomoto, N., Kitamura, T., & Iwata, A. (2010). Reinforcement of VoIP security with multipath routing and secret sharing scheme. *Journal of Information Hiding and Multimedia Signal Processing*, *1*(3), 204–219.

Salma, M., Maha, C., & Chokri, B. A. (2011). A robust audio watermarking technique based on the perceptual evaluation of audio quality algorithm in the multiresolution domain. In *Proceedings of IEEE International Symposium on Signal Processing and Information Technology (ISSPIT)*, (pp. 326-331). IEEE Press.

Takahashi, A., Nishimura, R., & Suzuki, Y. (2005). Multiple watermarking for stereo audio signals using phase-modulation techniques. *IEEE Transactions on Signal Processing*, *53*(2), 806–815. doi:10.1109/TSP.2004.839901

Wey, H., Ito, A., Okamoto, T., & Suzuki, Y. (2010). Multiple description coding using time domain division for mp3 coded sound signal. *Journal of Information Hiding and Multimedia Signal Processing*, *1*(4), 269–285.

Chapter 4
Information Hiding Using Interpolation for Audio and Speech Signals

Mamoru Iwaki
Niigata University, Japan

ABSTRACT

In this chapter, a time-domain high-bit-rate information hiding method using interpolation techniques, which can extract embedded data in both informed (non-blind) and non-informed (blind) ways, is proposed. Three interpolation techniques are introduced for the information hiding method, i.e., spline interpolation, Fourier-series interpolation, and linear-prediction interpolation. In performance evaluation, spline interpolation was mainly examined as an example implementation. According to the simulation of information hiding in music signals, the spline interpolation-based method achieved audio-information hiding for CD-audio signals at bit rate of about 2.9 kbps, and about 1.1 kbps under MP3 compression (160 kbps). The objective sound quality measured by the Perceptual Evaluation of Audio Quality (PEAQ) was maintained if the length of interpolation data increased. The objective sound quality was also evaluated for the Fourier series-based implementation and the linear prediction-based one. Fourier series interpolation achieved the same sound quality as spline interpolation did. Linear prediction interpolation required longer interpolation signals to get good sound quality.

DOI: 10.4018/978-1-4666-2217-3.ch004

INTRODUCTION

There are many application fields of information hiding. For example, digital watermarking is applied for copyright protection, fingerprinting, authentication, copy control, owner identification, broadcast monitoring, security control, and tamper proofing (Cox, 2002; Seadle, 2002; Voloshynovskiy, 2001; Wu, 2004; Cano, 2002; Ruiz, 2000; Anand, 1998; Miaou, 2000; Kalker, 1999). As for the human audio system, louder sounds usually tend to mask weaker sounds in the time and frequency domains. Audio-watermarking methods are classified according to choice of hiding domain as time-domain ones or frequency-domain (transformation-domain) ones. Under the premise that human audio system cannot detect small changes in certain temporal portions (Bassia, 1998; Bender, 1996; Deller, 2000; Lee, 2005), time-domain methods embed watermarks by modifying audio-signal samples according to amplitude (Van Schyndel, 1994; Foote, 2003; Ozer, 2005). Compared to frequency-domain methods, time-domain methods generally have an advantage in terms of high bit rate. However, time-domain methods are usually not robust against modification of stego signals (Johnson, 2000) because the process they use for detecting hidden information supposes that stego signals can be received cleanly without deformation in the transmission channel like noise (Linnartz, 1998; Miller, 1999). In contrast, frequency-domain (and transformed-domain) methods embed watermarks in the frequency domain; for example, spread-spectrum watermarking hides a narrow-band watermark signal in a wide-band host signal (Cox, 1997; Ruiz, 2000). Frequency-domain methods are robust against modification of stego signal; however, their maximum bit rate is not that large. Some watermarking techniques exploit both temporal and frequency information in the embedding process (Boney, 1996; Petitcolas, 1998). Other techniques utilize insensitivity of human hearing to acoustical echoes or phase difference (Voloshynovskiy, 2001; Chen, 2001; Cheng, 2001; Gurijala, 2003; Deller, 2000; Celik, 2005). A suitable information-hiding method should provide high bit rate and achieve high robustness without producing noticeable auditory distortion. However, bit rates of most digital-watermarking methods for audio signals are about 10 to 100 bps, and they cannot handle high bit rate.

Although time-domain methods generally provide good sound quality and high bit rate, they have a weakness in terms of robustness against signal modification. When a signal value is modified, embedded information is simultaneously destroyed, because the hidden information is coded directly in the signal value of the original audio signal. Aiming to address this issue, here, we introduce the idea that a set of signal values should stand for one bit of embedded information. This condition will improve the robustness of time-domain methods against signal modification because most signal values recall the embedded information correctly even if some signal values have been varied. This can be understood by an improvement in the LSB modification method (Schyndel, 1994) and in the quantization index modulation (Chen, 2001; Liu, 2003, 2004).

In this chapter, a new information-hiding method for audio and speech signals with interpolation technique is proposed, and some examples are given. This method can detect and extract hidden information from a stego signal independently of the availability of the original host signal (i.e., the information is blindly detectable). Additionally, it can provide high bit rate. Using spline interpolations of degrees two and three, it achieved bit rate of about 2.9 kbps per channel for CD-audio music signals, and about 1.2 kbps even if watermarked signals were degraded by MP3 128-kbps compression while maintaining high sound quality.

INFORMATION-HIDING METHOD WITH INTERPOLATION

Outline of Information Hiding Method with Interpolation

Portions of an audio signal can be estimated with an interpolation function applied to its surrounding audio signal. By replacing the portion with the interpolation data, a slightly different auditory signal from the original one is created. Appropriate interpolation methods make the interpolated audio signal difficult to distinguish from the original one by hearing. Accordingly, it is possible to create a stego signal by embedding binary information in an audio signal by making use of the difference between the original signal and the interpolation signal. The embedded information in the stego signal can be detected by checking which sound data is detected in the embedded portion, i.e., the original audio data or the interpolation data. Such detection is easily carried out by checking if there is difference between the stego signal and the original signal (cover signal). Additionally, this information-hiding method is still applicable even when the original audio signal is not available.

Information-Embedding Algorithm

The watermarking method using interpolation is shown schematically in Figure 1. First, the original audio signal $s(k)$ is divided into distinct frames of length N. The data of the i-th frame is expressed by $x_i(n) = s(Ni + n), (n = 0, 1, \ldots, N-1)$. Next, the data in each frame is divided into two groups, G_1 and G_2, then the interpolation of the frame, $\hat{x}_i(n)$, is calculated using the data in G_1. According to the binary information m_i, the watermarked frame $x_i'(n)$ is constructed as follows:

$$x_i'(n) = \begin{cases} x_i(n), & \text{if } m_i = 0 \\ \hat{x}_i(n), & \text{if } m_i = 1 \end{cases} \tag{1}$$

Figure 1. Information embedding process with interpolation

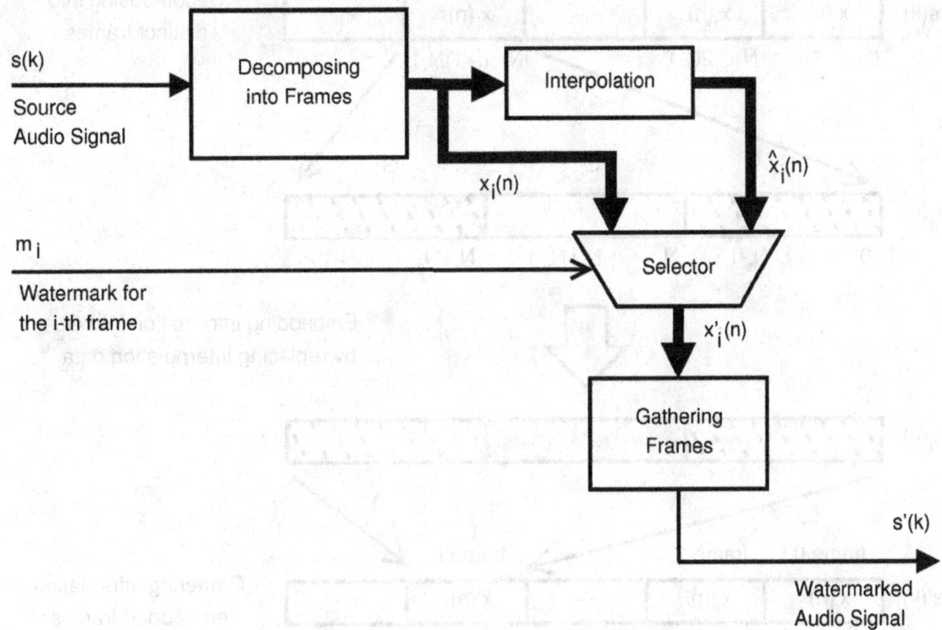

The watermarked signal, $s'(k)$, is obtained by gathering the above watermarked frames $x'_i(n)$. An example of the frame division and data-group allocation in a frame is shown in Figure 2. For example, group G_1 is set $\{ x_i(n) \mid n = 0, 1, \ldots, N_1-1, N_1+N_2, N_1+N_2+1, \ldots, N-1\}$, and G_2 is set $\{ x_i(n) \mid n = N_1, N_1+1, \ldots, N_1+N_2-1\}$. Here, N_2 is the number of samples in G_2, and $N-N_2$ is the number of samples in G_1. If $N_1 = (N-N_2)/2$, the first and the last halves of G_1 have the same size.

Information Extraction Algorithm

The embedded information can be extracted by checking whether the data frame is replaced with interpolation signal or the original signal. In this section, firstly, an extraction method with difference from the original signal, which is feasible when the original signal is available (i.e., non-blind or informed condition), is described. Next, an extraction method with recalculation of interpolation, which works even when original signal is not available (i.e. blind condition), is described.

Extraction Method Using Difference of Stego Signal from Original Signal for Non-Blind Watermarking

When a cover signal (original signal), as well as a stego signal (watermarked signal), is available (that is, a non-blind or informed condition), an intuitive extraction method for the embedded information is available. An extraction process using the difference between the original signal and the stego signal is shown schematically in Figure 3. First, the difference signal $z(n)$ between the stego signal $s'(k)$ and the original signal $s(k)$ is calculated, and $z(n)$ is divided into distinct frames $z_i(n)$, in the same way as the embedding process. According to the magnitude of $z_i(n)$ the embedded information is extracted as follows:

Figure 2. Example of frame structure (data-group allocation in a frame)

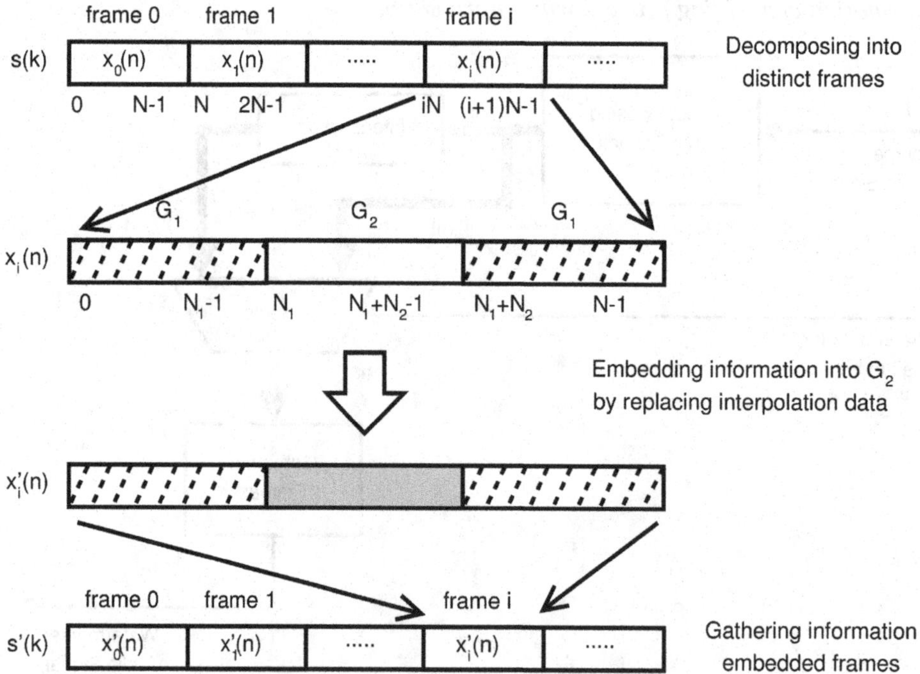

Figure 3. Information extraction process using the difference from the original signal

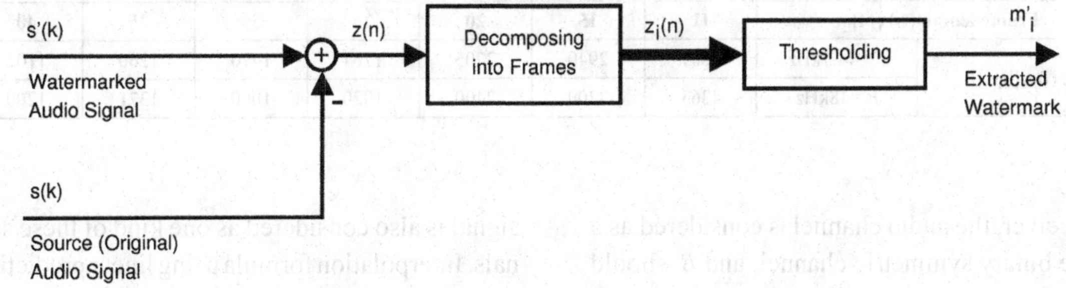

$$m_i' = \begin{cases} 1, & \text{if } d(z_i) > a_1 \\ 0, & \text{if } d(z_i) \le a_1 \end{cases} \quad (2)$$

where $d(v)$ is the Euclidean norm of *v*, and a_1 is a threshold previously determined. For example, a_1 is set so that the probability of extracting zeros in the case of a watermarked signal embedded with the same number of zeros and ones randomly is almost equal to 0.5.

Extraction Method Using Recalculation of Interpolation for Blind Watermarking

When a cover signal is not available (that is, a blind condition), extraction methods for the embedded information can still be constructed from the stego signal. An extraction method with recalculation of interpolation is shown schematically in Figure 4. With this method, watermarked signal $s'(k)$ is divided into frames $y_i(n)$. Each frame is separated into two sample groups in the same way as in embedding process. On the basis of the difference between $y_i(n)$ and $\hat{y}_i(n)$, the embedded information is extracted as follows:

$$m_i' = \begin{cases} 1, & \text{if } d(y_i - \hat{y}_i) \le a_2 \\ 0, & \text{if } d(y_i - \hat{y}_i) > a_2 \end{cases} \quad (3)$$

where a_2 is a threshold previously determined like a_1 in Equation 2.

Bit Rate

Theoretically, maximum bit-rate is evaluated as follows:

$$B_r = \frac{bF_s}{N} \quad (4)$$

Here, *b* is the number of hidden information bits in a frame, *N* is the number of samples in a frame, and F_s is the sampling frequency. Table 1 lists examples of the theoretical limits of bit rate. When error exists between the transmitter and

Figure 4. Information extraction process with recalculation of interpolation

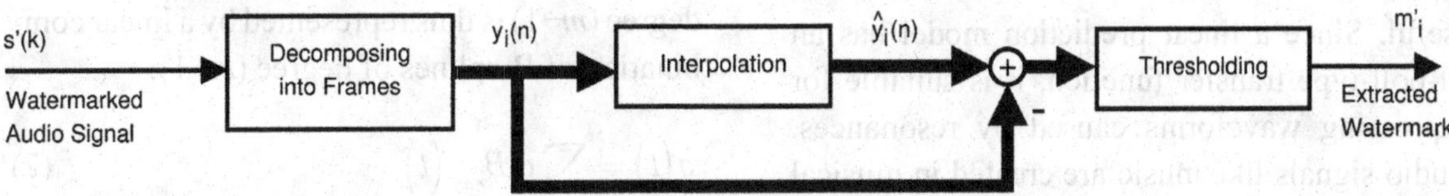

Table 1. Examples of theoretical maximum bit-rate (b=1)

Frame length (N) [pt]		11	15	20	25	30	35	40
Bit rate (B_r) [bps]	F_s=44.1kHz	4009	2940	2205	1764	1470	1260	1102
	F_s=48kHz	4363	3200	2400	1920	1600	1371	1200

the receiver, the audio channel is considered as a simple binary symmetric channel, and B_r should be multiplied by the channel capacity of a binary symmetric channel, which is determined by error rate (crossover probability).

Interpolation Methods for Information Hiding

There are many interpolation methods available for information hiding. Polynomial interpolation is one traditional interpolation method. However, a polynomial of higher degree generally tends to oscillate easily, so polynomial interpolation is not suitable for many data points because the degree of the interpolation polynomial is proportional to the number of data points. Spline interpolation is an improved polynomial-based interpolation method (de Boor, 1978). It is a set of piecewise polynomials with minimum curvature. It is expected that this property of smoothness should work well for audio signals. A Fourier series is another way to express waveforms. Since the expression is a linear combination of sinusoidal functions, the expansion coefficients are another expression of the original waveform in the frequency domain. The expansion coefficients naturally absorb the frequency component of the original waveform. It is thus expected that the natural expression in the frequency domain will contribute significantly to audio-signal interpolation. As another way to express waveforms, a linear prediction model is useful. Since a linear prediction model has an all-poll-type transfer function, it is suitable for expressing waveforms caused by resonances. Audio signals like music are created in musical instruments with specific resonances. A speech signal is also considered as one kind of these signals. Interpolation formula using linear prediction model is introduced.

Spline Interpolation for Information Hiding

As spline functions are a set of piecewise polynomials, it can make smooth interpolation with fewer unexpected oscillations. This interpolation technique has been applied to DA-converters of sound systems, and it should be suitable for short interval interpolation of an audio signal.

If $B_{r,m}\left(t\right)$ denotes the r-th B-spline of degree $(m-1)$, the following recurrent relation holds:

$$B_{r,m}\left(t\right) = \frac{t - t_r}{t_{r+m-1} - t_r} B_{r,m-1}\left(t\right) + \frac{t_{r+m} - t}{t_{r+m} - t_{r+1}} B_{r+1,m-1}\left(t\right) \tag{5}$$

$$B_{r,1}\left(t\right) = \begin{cases} 1, & \xi_r \le t < \xi_{r+1} \\ 0, & \text{otherwise} \end{cases} \tag{6}$$

where ξ_r is the knot point where polynomials are changed while keeping $(m-2)$ continuous differentiability. Here, $\xi_r < \xi_{r+1}$ is simply assumed. B-spline function $B_{r,m}\left(t\right)$ is not negative and has a local support (ξ_r, ξ_{r+m}). Spline function $g(t)$ of degree $(m-1)$ is thus represented by a linear combination of B-splines of degree $(m-1)$:

$$g\left(t\right) = \sum_r c_r B_{r,m}\left(t\right) \tag{7}$$

Spline functions construct function space with B-splines as basis. Spline interpolation for data set $(t_n gn)$, $n = 0, 1, \ldots, N_s-1$ is formulated as follows:

$$g\left(t_n\right) = \sum_{r=0}^{N_s-1} c_r B_{r,m}\left(t_n\right) = g_n, \quad (8)$$
$$n = 0, 1, \ldots, N_s - 1$$

Solving the linear equations for spline coefficients c_r with an appropriate boundary condition gives spline interpolation of the given data set. Since the obtained spline function approximately minimizes the sum of curvature, spline interpolation is the smoothest piecewise polynomial of degree $(m-1)$. This smoothest property should work better for representing audio waveforms.

Fourier Series Interpolation for Information Hiding

A Fourier series is a linear combination of trigonometric functions, so it can naturally express frequency components in oscillating waveforms. Differences of frequency characteristics are important for distinguishing sounds. A Fourier series, which can directly describe an audio signal in the frequency domain, should be suitable for our information hiding. Here, a Fourier-series interpolation method is introduced as a candidate for the information-hiding method.

Fourier series $g\left(t\right)$ is expressed by the following partial sum of complex exponential functions:

$$g\left(t\right) = \sum_{q=-Q}^{Q} c_q e^{j\frac{2\pi qt}{T}} \quad (9)$$

where j is the imaginary unit, and T is the period of $g\left(t\right)$. For a given data set (t_n, g_n), $n = 0, 1, \ldots, N_s-1$, Fourier series interpolation is formulated as follows:

$$g\left(t_n\right) = \sum_{q=-Q}^{Q} c_q e^{j\frac{2\pi qt_n}{T}} = g_n, \quad (10)$$
$$n = 0, 1, \ldots, N_s - 1$$

By solving the linear equations for Fourier coefficients c_q, we can obtain Fourier series interpolation of the given data set. However, the number of equations N_s is not equal to the number of data $(2Q+1)$. Since sound signals are usually expressed as mixture of many harmonics, $(2Q+1) > N_s$ is assumed in our usage. The equations are not well defined. Now, we introduce a smoothness criterion to $g\left(t\right)$ like cubic spline interpolation. If $g\left(t\right)$ represents the shape of an elastic string which is bent to pass through the data points, the stress in the string is represented by the sum of squared curvature of the locus. For simplicity, the curvature is replaced by the second derivative of the locus, which is a good approximation for the curvature when the gradient of the locus is not large. So the stress for passing through the data is estimated as follows:

$$A = \int_D \left|g''\left(t\right)\right|^2 dt \quad (11)$$

where D is the domain of $g\left(t\right)$. Then, the equations become solvable with restriction to minimize the value of A. This makes $g\left(t\right)$ the Fourier series interpolation for the given data with maximal smoothness.

Here, if D is a closed region $[T_1\ T_2]$, such that $T_1 \leq t_k \leq T_2$ and $T = T_2 - T_1$, then the Fourier coefficients c_q, $q = 0, \pm1, \pm2, \ldots, \pm Q$, of the above Fourier series interpolation are obtained by solving the following linear equation.

$$\begin{pmatrix} 2\mathbf{G} & \mathbf{L} \\ \mathbf{L}^{\mathrm{H}} & \mathbf{O} \end{pmatrix} \begin{pmatrix} c_{-Q} \\ \vdots \\ c_Q \\ \lambda_1 \\ \vdots \\ \lambda_{N_{ss}} \end{pmatrix} = \begin{pmatrix} 0 \\ \vdots \\ 0 \\ g_1 \\ \vdots \\ g_{N_{ss}} \end{pmatrix} \quad (12)$$

where $\mathbf{L}^{\mathrm{H}}$ is the complex conjugate transpose of $\mathbf{L}$, and $\mathbf{G}$ and $\mathbf{L}$ are matrices defined as follows:

$$\mathbf{G} = \left(\frac{2\pi}{T}\right)^4 \begin{pmatrix} (-Q)^4 & & 0 \\ & \ddots & \\ 0 & & Q^4 \end{pmatrix} \quad (13)$$

$$\mathbf{L} = \begin{pmatrix} e^{-j\frac{2\pi(-Q)t_1}{T}} & \cdots & e^{-j\frac{2\pi(-Q)t_{N_s}}{T}} \\ \vdots & \ddots & \vdots \\ e^{-j\frac{2\pi Q t_1}{T}} & \cdots & e^{-j\frac{2\pi Q t_{N_s}}{T}} \end{pmatrix} \quad (14)$$

The obtained Fourier series approximately minimizes the sum of curvature like spline interpolation; however, Fourier series is not polynomials but trigonometric functions. Therefore, the obtained Fourier coefficients can represent frequency structure of audio signal directly rather than spline coefficients. This property should work better for representing audio waveforms.

Linear Prediction Interpolation for Information Hiding

Acoustical waveforms are generated by vibration of sound sources. Such signals (in a short time) are considered to be output of resonators. A linear prediction model is suitable for expressing such signals. Here an interpolation method using a linear prediction model is introduced as another candidate for the information-hiding method.

Linear prediction is an estimation method for future values of a discrete-time signal by a linear function of previous samples. For a discrete-time signal v_n, linear prediction of v_n is represented by a linear combination of the previous values as follows:

$$\hat{v}_n = -\sum_{p=1}^{P} \alpha_p v_{n-p} \quad (15)$$

where α_p are the prediction coefficients and P is an autoregressive model order. Specifically, this type of prediction is called forward linear prediction. The residual generated by the difference between v_n and $\hat{v}_n$ is:

$$\varepsilon_n = v_n - \hat{v}_n \quad (16)$$

The coefficients α_p are usually determined based on the root mean square criterion. Here we minimize the expected value of the squared error $E[\varepsilon_n^2]$. For discrete-time signal $\{v_1, v_2, \ldots, v_K\}$, the coefficients α_p are calculated by solving the following equation:

$$\mathbf{V}\boldsymbol{\alpha} = \mathbf{e}_1 \quad (17)$$

where matrix $\mathbf{V}$ and vectors $\boldsymbol{\alpha}$ and $\mathbf{e}_1$ are defined as follows:

$$\mathbf{V} = \begin{pmatrix} v_1 & 0 & \cdots & 0 \\ v_2 & v_1 & \ddots & \vdots \\ \vdots & v_2 & \ddots & 0 \\ v_K & \vdots & \ddots & v_1 \\ 0 & v_K & & v_2 \\ \vdots & \ddots & \ddots & \vdots \\ 0 & \cdots & 0 & v_K \end{pmatrix} \boldsymbol{\alpha} = \begin{pmatrix} 1 \\ \alpha_1 \\ \vdots \\ \alpha_P \end{pmatrix} \mathbf{e}_1 = \begin{pmatrix} 1 \\ 0 \\ \vdots \\ 0 \end{pmatrix} \quad (18)$$

This yields the Yule-Walker equation:

$$\begin{pmatrix} R_0 & R_1 & \cdots & R_{P-1} \\ R_1 & R_0 & \ddots & \vdots \\ \vdots & \ddots & R_0 & R_1 \\ R_{P-1} & \cdots & R_1 & R_0 \end{pmatrix} \begin{pmatrix} \alpha_1 \\ \alpha_2 \\ \vdots \\ \alpha_P \end{pmatrix} = \begin{pmatrix} -R_1 \\ -R_2 \\ \vdots \\ -R_P \end{pmatrix} \quad (19)$$

where R_k are autocorrelation of v_n. It is known that this equation is efficiently solvable by the Levinson-Durbin algorithm. Similarly, backward linear prediction is expressed as follows:

$$\tilde{v}_n = -\sum_{p=1}^{P} \beta_p v_{n+P+1-p} \quad (20)$$

where β_p are the prediction coefficients. The coefficients β_p and α_p satisfies:

$$\beta_p = \alpha_{P+1-p} \quad (p = 1, 2, \ldots, P) \quad (21)$$

Now, we consider the interpolation problem for a given data set $\{(t_1, g_1), \ldots, (t_L, g_L), (t_{N-L+1}, g_{N-L+1}), \ldots, (t_N, g_N)\}$. Here, $2L$ is the number of data points given. The interpolated values h_n on t_n, $n = L+1, L+2, \ldots, N-L$, are obtained by the weighted sum of forward prediction $\hat{g}_n$ from $\{(t_1, g_1), \ldots, (t_L, g_L)\}$ and backward prediction $\tilde{g}_n$ from $\{(t_{N-L+1}, g_{N-L+1}), \ldots, (t_N, g_N)\}$ as follows:

$$h_n = \left(1 - w_{n-L-1}\right) \hat{g}_n + w_{n-L-1} \tilde{g}_n, \quad n = L+1, L+2, \ldots N-L \quad (22)$$

$$w_n = \frac{n}{N - 2L - 1} \quad (23)$$

Since linear prediction absorbs information about resonances in the signal, the interpolation values h_n are also interpreted as representing the variation of resonances in time. Therefore, we can expect that the obtained interpolation represents frequency structure of audio signal naturally and efficiently, and it is available for our information hiding method.

IMPLEMENTATION EXAMPLES AND THEIR PERFORMANCE

To demonstrate the feasibility and evaluate the performance of the proposed information-hiding method, computer programs for implementing the method were written with MATLAB. First, the performance of the spline interpolation based method was evaluated subjectively and objectively. Next, the three interpolation methods were compared in terms of objective sound quality.

Performance Evaluation of Information Hiding with Spline Interpolation

The performance of information hiding by using spline interpolation was evaluated. First, sound quality of the stego signals was evaluated with respect to the degree of spline functions and the frame length of the spline interpolation. Next, the detection ratio of the embedded information was evaluated for spline interpolation of degree three ($m = 4$).

Experiment Conditions

A piece of classical music was used as the sound signal to be watermarked. It was a 10-second-long monaural signal with sampling frequency of 44.1 kHz and quantization of 16 bits. Frame length N in Figure 2 was 11, 15, 20, 25, 30, 35, or 40, where the lengths of the first half and last halves of G_1 were fixed to five and the frame length N_2 of G_2 was variable. The embedded binary information consisted of randomly permutated zeros and ones. The degree of spline interpolation was zero, one, two, or three ($m = 1, 2, 3$, and 4). MP3 compression was set to 160 kbps, 128 kbps, 112 kbps, 96 kbps, or 80 kbps.

Subjective Evaluation of Sound Quality vs. Frame Length and Degree of Spline Function

Sound quality of several watermarked sounds was evaluated subjectively by the ABX method. Each sound was presented through headphones. The subjects were two males and three females (22 to 24 years old) with normal hearing ability. Each subject adjusted the sound volume to their usual listening level before the experiment. Sounds A and B were either the original sound or a watermarked one, and sound X was a watermarked sound. Using a two-alternative-forced-choice paradigm, the subjects judged whether sound X was closer to A or B. A perceptibility index (based on the recognition ratio of the judgment) and an imperceptibility index (based on the subtraction of the perceptibility from one) are introduced in the following paragraph. The chance level for these indices is 0.5 and the 95% confidence level of perceptibility for 8 trials is 0.75 for each subject. Hereafter, the difference is considered perceptible if the perceptibility index is greater than 0.75. Similarly, the difference is considered imperceptible if the imperceptibility index is greater than 0.25.

The imperceptibility indices for the above subjective judgment were measured under 16 conditions (frame length: 11, 15, 20, and 25; degree of spline: 0, 1, 2, and 3) for each sound and averaged for each condition. A contour plot of the imperceptibility indices is shown in Figure 5. For a frame length longer than 20, the index was almost zero and independent of the degree of spline functions. For a frame length less than 15 and a degree greater than two, the ratio increased to 0.25. This result means that the watermarked sounds with the above-stated parameters were difficult to distinguish from the original sounds.

Figure 5. Imperceptibility index (imperceptibility index was 0.5 for higher degree of spline in shorter frame)

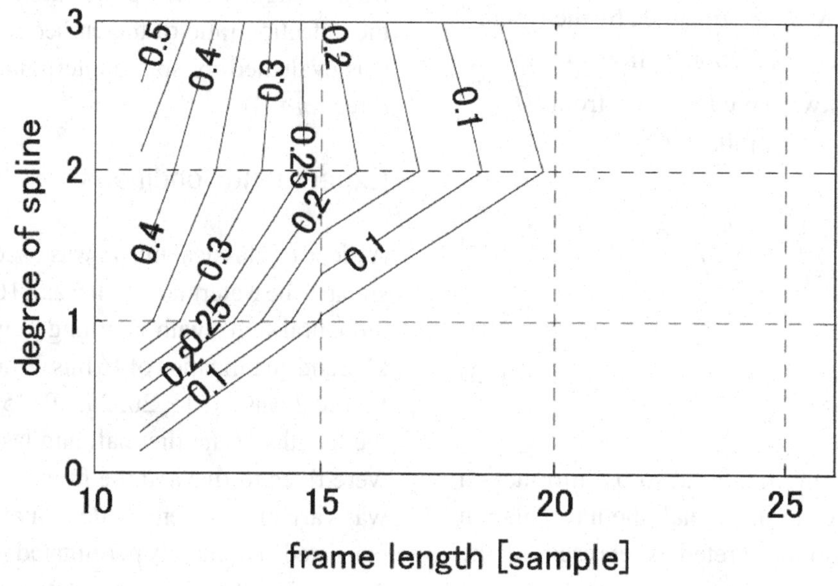

The perceptibility index for a degree three (m = 4) is shown in Figure 6. It was calculated as the complement of the above imperceptibility index.

Objective Evaluation of Sound Quality vs. Frame Length and Degree of Spline Function

Sound quality of a watermarked sound was evaluated objectively in terms of segmental SNR (SNRseg) as follows:

$$\mathrm{SNR}\left(i\right) = 10\log_{10}\frac{\sum_{n}\left\{s_i\left(n\right)\right\}^2}{\sum_{n}\left\{s_i\left(n\right) - s_i'\left(n\right)\right\}^2}\left[\mathrm{dB}\right] \quad (24)$$

$$\mathrm{SNR}_{seg} = \frac{1}{I}\sum_{i=1}^{I}\mathrm{SNR}\left(i\right)\left[\mathrm{dB}\right] \quad (25)$$

Here, $s_i\left(n\right)$ is the original sound in the i-th segment, $s_i'\left(n\right)$ is the watermarked sound in the i-th segment, and I is the number of segments in the measured sound (Deller, 2000; Wang, 1992). SNR_{seg} is evaluated as the arithmetic mean of SNR in the i-th segment $\mathrm{SNR}\left(i\right)$. In this experiment, segment length was 1410 samples (about 32 ms) long, and segment shift was half of the segment length. The SNR_{seg} values for the above subjective judgment were measured under 16 conditions (frame length: 11, 15, 20, and 25; degree of spline: 0, 1, 2, and 3) for each sound and averaged for each condition. A contour plot of the SNR_{seg} values is shown in Figure 7. The SNR_{seg} for degree of three (m = 4) is plotted in Figure 8. It is clear that as the frame length increases, SNR_{seg} monotonically decreases. On the contrary, as the degree of spline functions increases, SNR_{seg} increases, and saturates at degrees

Figure 6. Perceptibility index of the difference between watermarked signals and the original ones for spline interpolation of degree three (m = 4), with standard-deviation bars shown

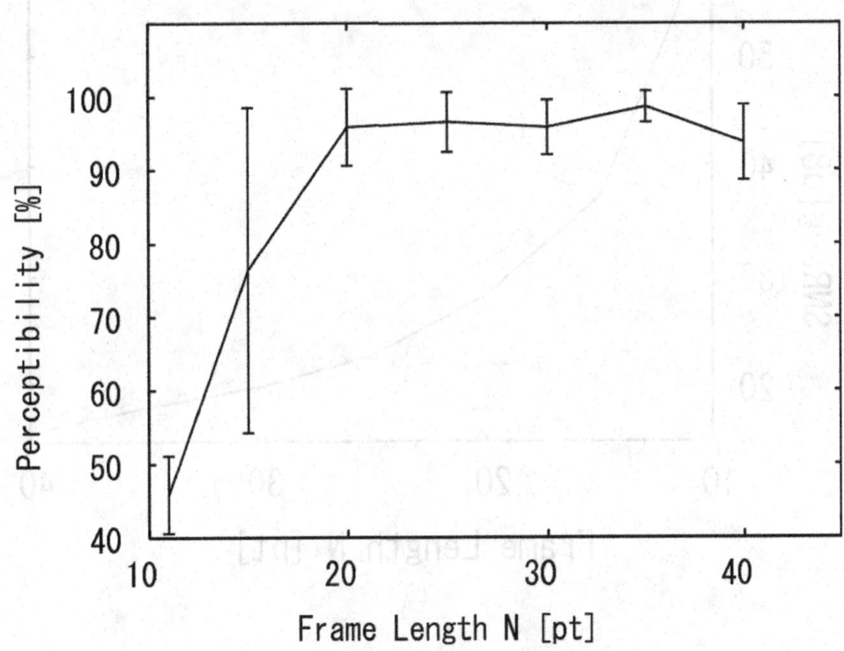

Figure 7. Segmental SNR (SNR_{seg} *was larger for higher degree of spline in shorter frames)*

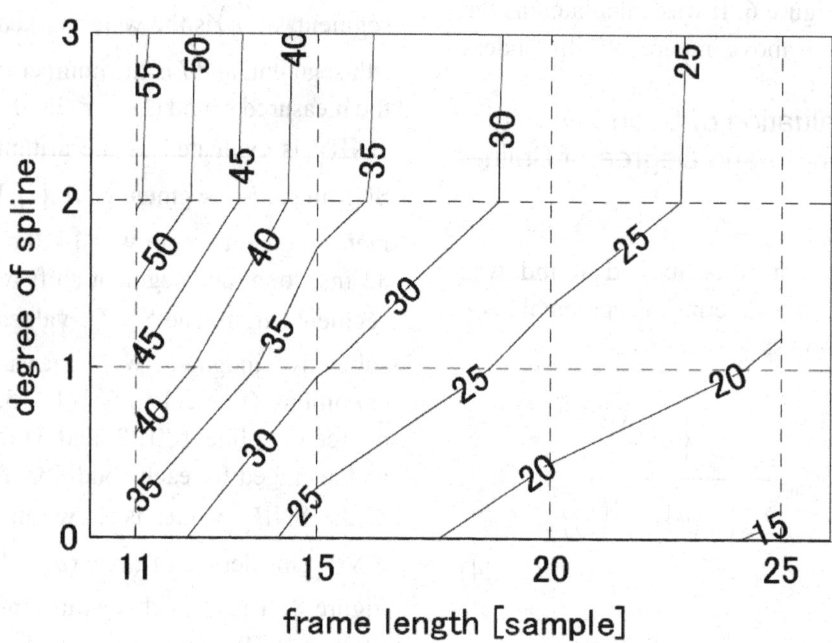

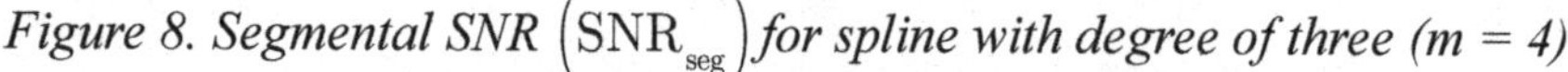

Figure 8. Segmental SNR $\left(\mathrm{SNR}_{seg}\right)$ *for spline with degree of three (m = 4)*

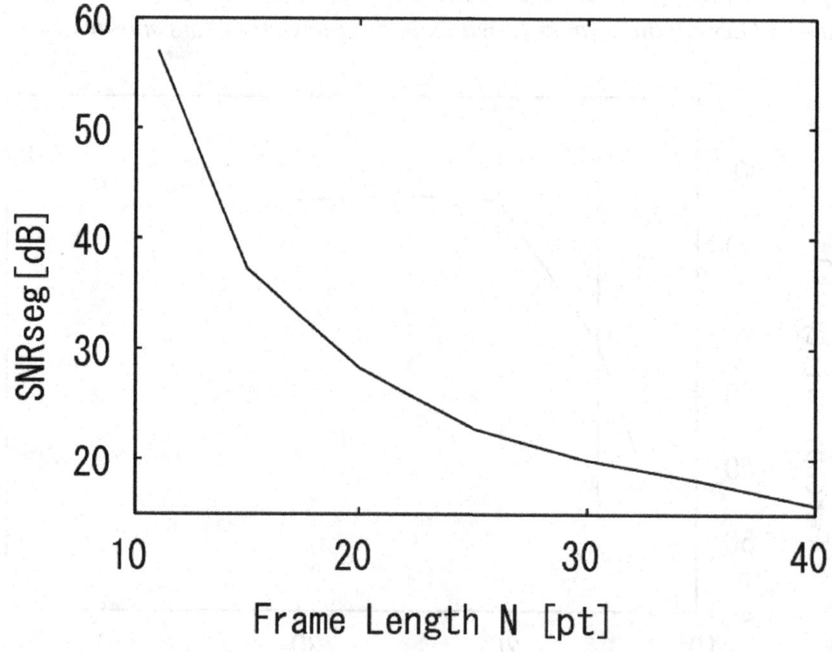

of two and three ($m = 3$ and 4). For watermarked sounds with perceptibility less than 75%, average SNR_{seg} is greater than 25dB. Accordingly, $SNR_{seg} > 25$dB can be considered a simple measure for imperceptibility. When the frame length is less than 20 and the degree of spline functions is greater than one ($m = 2$), the average SNR_{seg} is kept above 25 dB.

Extraction Ratio (with Spline Interpolation of Degree Three, m = 4)

Extraction ratio of embedded information from a stego signal was evaluated. To check the robustness of the information-hiding method, it was also evaluated for stego signals modified by MP3 compression. The average extraction ratios for five trials of the recalculation-based extraction method are plotted in Figure 9 (blind case). Longer frames indicate better extraction ratios. The average extraction ratios for five trials of the difference-based extraction method are plotted in Figure 10 (non-blind case). This figure shows a similar trend; that is, extraction ratio increased as frame length increased. When a stego signal was not modified by MP3-encoder/decoder system, extraction ratios were 100% (or 99% for the shortest frame). For frame length of 11, the length of the interpolated data portion stands for only one sample. Because only one sample value stands for one bit of embedded information, information hiding by the interpolation method could not maintain robustness even for a small modification of signal values. When a stego signal was modified by MP3-encoder/decoder, extraction ratio decreased as compression ratio increased. Shorter frames indicate smaller extraction ratios, and the difference-based extraction method (non-blind case) achieved higher extraction ratio than the recalculation-based extraction method (blind case). The bit rate obtained by spline interpolation of degree three ($m=4$) and frame length of 15 was about 2.9 kbps for noise-free channels, while the bit rate was about 1.1 kbps for MP3 (160 kbps).

Performance Evaluation of Information Hiding among Interpolation Methods

The performances of the three interpolation methods were compared in terms of information hiding. The Objective Difference Grade (ODG)

Figure 9. Average extraction accuracy of the spline recalculation method (degree three, m = 4)

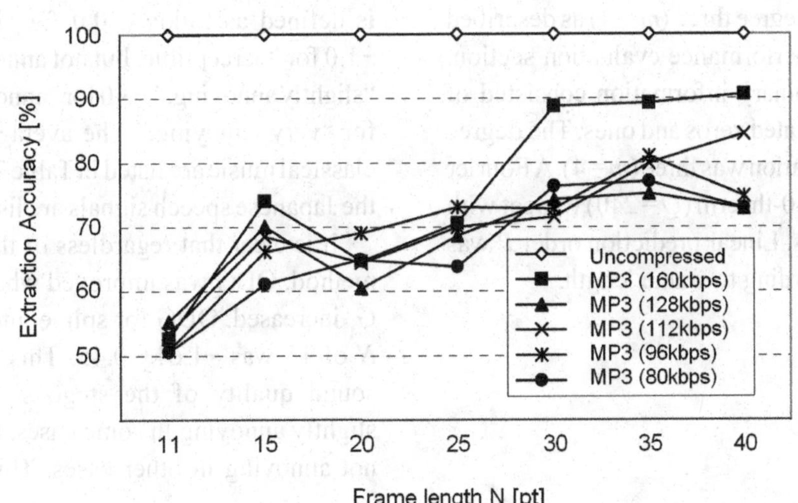

Figure 10. Average extraction accuracy of the differentiating method (degree three, m = 4)

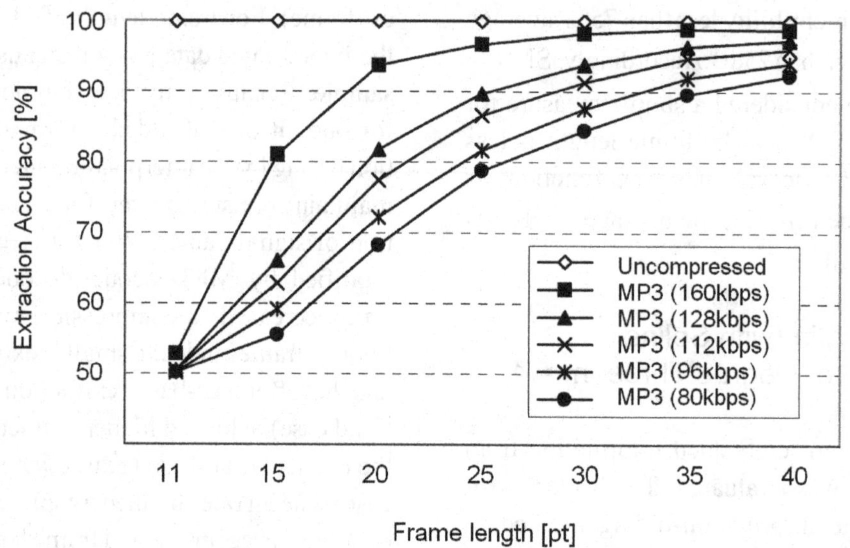

for three frame lengths was evaluated. The cover signals were classical music and speech signals.

The sound signals to be watermarked in this evaluation were the beginning parts of 12 pieces of classical music and 12 pieces of Japanese speech. They were 60-second-long monaural signal with sampling frequency of 48 kHz and quantization of 16 bits. Frame length (N, see Figure 2) was 15, 45, or 389, where the frame length N_2 of G_2 was fixed to five, and the length of the last half of G_1 was N_1 (the length of the first half of G_1). This frame structure performed well for spline interpolation of degree three ($m = 4$) as described in the previous performance evaluation section. The embedded binary information consisted of randomly permutated zeros and ones. The degree of spline interpolation was three ($m = 4$). A Fourier series up to the 240-th term ($Q = 240$) was set with period T of 10 ms. Linear prediction order P was 5, 19, or 41 according to frame length.

Objective Evaluation with the Difference Grade

Sound quality of stego signal was evaluated on the basis of the "Perceptual Evaluation of Audio Quality (PEAQ)" (Kabal, 2002) of ITU-R BS.1387. PEAQ is available for subjective sound-quality prediction by simulation of the human auditory system. The Objective Difference Grade (ODG) was evaluated. ODG is intended to correspond to the subjective difference grade used in human-based audio tests. It has a range from 0 to −4 and is defined as follows: 0.0 for "imperceptible," −1.0 for "perceptible, but not annoying," −2.0 for "slightly annoying," −3.0 for "annoying," and −4.0 for "very annoying." The averages of ODG for classical music are listed in Table 2a, and those for the Japanese speech signals are listed in Table 2b.

It is clear that regardless of the interpolation method, ODG was improved when the length of G_1 increased. ODG for spline interpolation with N of 15 was −1.61± 0.45. This means that the sound quality of the stego signals might be slightly annoying in some cases, but it is usually not annoying in other cases. This result agrees

Table 2. The objective difference grade (ODG) achieved by combination of data-group allocation in a frame and the interpolation method

(a) Classical Music as Cover Signal						
				Objective Difference Grade (ODG)		
Frame length (N)	Length of G_1 (N–N_2)	Length of G_2 (N_2)	Bit-rate (B)	Spline (Degree three, m=4)	Fourier series (T=10 ms, Q=240)	Linear prediction
15	5+5	5	3200	−1.61±0.45	−1.58±0.60	−3.87±0.04 (P=5)
45	20+20	5	1066	−0.53±0.22	−0.58±0.27	−3.84±0.07 (P=19)
389	192+192	5	123	−0.50±0.14	−0.51±0.14	−1.91±1.16 (P=41)
(b) Speech Signal as Cover Signal						
				Objective Difference Grade (ODG)		
Frame length (N)	Length of G_1 (N–N_2)	Length of G_2 (N_2)	Bit-rate (B)	Spline (Degree three, m=4)	Fourier series (T=10 ms, Q=240)	Linear prediction
15	5+5	5	3200	−3.48±0.30	−3.33±0.37	−3.90±0.01 (P=5)
45	20+20	5	1066	−1.87±0.77	−1.79±0.75	−3.57±0.26 (P=19)
389	192+192	5	123	−0.58±0.38	−0.57±0.36	−0.43±0.20 (P=41)

with that of the subjective evaluation described in the previous section. According to Table 2a, spline interpolation and Fourier series interpolation were evaluated as "imperceptible" up to a bit-rate of 1066 bit/s for classical music, although the linear prediction interpolation was judged "annoying." Meanwhile, according to Table 2b, the proposed three interpolation methods were evaluated as "imperceptible" only at a low bit-rate (123 bit/s) for the Japanese speech. In this case, linear prediction interpolation achieved better ODG than other two methods.

DISCUSSION

The spline interpolation-based time-domain audio watermarking method was evaluated as depicted in Figures 5 through 10. Spline interpolation of degrees two and three (m = 3 and 4) worked better than those of the other degrees (m = 1 and 2). Since spline functions of degree two and three (m = 3 and 4) are continuously differentiable, they should be suitable for representing smooth waveforms like sound. Higher-degree spline interpolation is no longer required to attain high performance because the sound quality already looks saturated at degree two (m = 3) in Figure 5. This characteristic has an advantage in the sense of computational complexity. In general, lower-degree spline interpolation can be calculated locally in time with small computational complexity. The spline interpolations of degrees two and three (m = 3 and 4) are thus feasible enough for real-time processing.

It was also indicated that the information hiding using spline interpolation should be used with shorter frame length in order to keep the sound quality high. This characteristic is basically a result of the frame structure described in Figure 2. Shorter frame length is preferable for keeping computational complexity low, and the proposed information-hiding method can be easily implemented in a streaming manner. When the frame length N is short, G_2, which is the spline-interpolated portion in a frame is also short for fixed N_1. This means that a shorter frame cannot be deformed easily or significantly from the original signal, therefore, the perceptibility of the difference becomes low at the expense of degradation of extraction accuracy. The minimum detection ratio under the uncompressed condition in Figures 9 and 10 was 99% for the shortest frame length N (11). Although spline interpolation usually keeps the sound quality of the watermarked signal, the difference between the information hidden signal by spline interpolation and the original signal can be too small to detect, especially for shorter frames. There is therefore a trade-off between sound quality and extraction accuracy with respect to frame length. Another formation of data-group allocation in a frame can improve this property. For example, signal values of G_2 given by interpolation process depend on the first and the last parts of G_1 in the same frame. If the last part of G_1 in the present frame is shared with the first part of G_1 in the next frame, the dependency is relaxed and bit rate can be improved.

The extraction ratio for embedded information decreased as compression ratio of MP3 increased, and the extraction ratio increased as frame length got longer. The extraction ratio of the difference-based extraction method (non-blind case) was better than that of the recalculation-based extraction method (blind case). This is because signal values in both interpolation and interpolated data were varied through the compression/decompression processing of MP3. The information hiding with interpolation is possible with both extraction methods when signal deformation or noise in a channel is small. Otherwise, the difference-based method is better. Redesign of the inner structure of a frame, selection of the appropriate interpolation method, and adaptive determination of thresholds will address the above issue. Improving the robustness of stego signals is a key remaining problem.

SUMMARY

The idea of information hiding by using an interpolation technique was described in this chapter. It can be combined with many kinds of interpolation techniques. In this information-hiding method, each bit of the embedded information is supported by a set of signal values; hence, robustness against signal deformation on a communication channel is expected to be improved. This information-hiding method has an advantage that the embedded information can be extracted by both non-blind and blind manners. In the blind manner, the information-extraction process is constructed by a similar process to embedding. If the adopted interpolation technique can calculate interpolation values locally, both the information embedding and extracting processes are executable in a streaming manner. Spline interpolation was applied for this information-hiding method (Fujimoto, 2006), and its performance was evaluated with respect to processing frame length and degree of spline function. According to the results of computer simulations, the frame length should be shorter than 20 samples, and the degree of spline function should be greater than or equal to two (for keeping acceptable sound quality for CD-audio signals). When this parameter was used, a high bit rate (more than 2.9 kbps) was achieved when no degradation was imposed on the stego signals in the communication channel. With deformation by MP3 (160 kbps), embedded bit rates of about 1.1 kbps was achieved. However, there still remains a tradeoff between sound quality of a stego signal and robustness against deformation of a stego signal, depending on frame length and inner structure of a frame. Interpolations using Fourier series and linear prediction were formulated and applied to the interpolation-based information hiding. Their sound quality increased when the signal length used for interpolation got longer. The sound quality of the Fourier series interpolation-based method was almost the same as that of the spline interpolation-based one.

However, linear prediction interpolation-based method requires longer frame length to achieve the similar sound quality. The information hiding method using interpolation in the time domain is simple and available for high bit-rate applications. However, this work is still in progress. A similar approach was tried for information hiding in an image too (Martin, 2008). Some improvements in robustness for information hiding by spline interpolation (Deshpande, 2009) and developments of interpolation-based information hiding in the frequency domain (Fallahpour, 2009) were reported. Issues in sound quality, robustness, computational cost, and so forth remain, which are all very challenging.

REFERENCES

Anand, D., & Niranjan, U. C. (1998). Watermarking medical images with patient information. In *Proceedings of the 20th Annual International Conference of the IEEE Engineering in Medicine and Biology Society*, (pp. 703-706). Hong Kong, China: IEEE Press.

Bassia, P., & Pitas, I. (2001). Robust audio watermarking in the time domain. *IEEE Transactions on Multimedia*, *3*(2), 232–241. doi:10.1109/6046.923822

Bender, W., Gruhl, D., Morimoto, N., & Lu, A. (1996). Techniques for data hiding. *IBM System Journey*, *35*(3), 313–336. doi:10.1147/sj.353.0313

Boney, L., Tewfik, A., & Hamdy, K. N. (1996). Digital watermarks for audio signals. In *Proceedings of the Third IEEE International Conference on Multimedia Computing and Systems*, (pp. 473-480). Hiroshima, Japan: IEEE Press.

Cano, P., Batlle, E., Kalker, T., & Haitsma, J. (2002). A review of algorithms for audio fingerprinting. In *Proceedings of the 2002 IEEE Workshop on Multimedia Signal Processing*, (169-173). IEEE Press.

Celik, M., Sharma, G., & Tekalp, A. M. (2005). Pitch and duration modification for speech watermarking. In *Proceedings of IEEE International Conference on Acoustics, Speech, and Signal Processing*, (pp. 17-20). Philadelphia, PA: IEEE Press.

Chen, B., & Wornell, G. W. (2001). Quantization index modulation: A class of provably good methods for digital watermarking and information embedding. *IEEE Transactions on Information Theory*, *47*(4), 1423–1443. doi:10.1109/18.923725

Cheng, Q., & Sorensen, J. (2001). Spread spectrum signaling for speech watermarking. In *Proceedings of IEEE International Conference on Acoustics, Speech, and Signal Processing*, (pp. 1337-1349). Salt Lake City, UT: IEEE Press.

Cox, I. J., Kilian, J., Leighton, F. T., & Shanmoon, T. (1997). Secure spread spectrum watermarking for multimedia. *IEEE Transactions on Image Processing*, *6*(12), 1673–1687. doi:10.1109/83.650120

Cox, I. J., Kilian, J., Leighton, T., & Shamoon, T. (1997). Secure spread spectrum watermarking for multimedia. *IEEE Transactions on Image Processing*, *6*(3), 1673–1687. doi:10.1109/83.650120

Cox, I. J., Miller, M. L., & Bloom, J. A. (2002). *Digital watermarking*. San Diego, CA: Academic Press.

de Boor, C. (1978). *A practical guide to splines*. New York, NY: Springer-Verlag. doi:10.1007/978-1-4612-6333-3

Deller, J. R. Jr, Hansen, J. H. L., & Proakis, J. G. (2000). *Discrete time processing of speech signals* (2nd ed.). New York, NY: IEEE Press.

Deshpande, A., & Prabhu, K. M. M. (2009). A substitution-by-interpolation algorithm for watermarking audio. *Signal Processing*, *89*, 218–225. doi:10.1016/j.sigpro.2008.07.015

Fallahpour, M., & Megias, D. (2009). High capacity audio watermarking using FFT amplitude interpolation. *IEICE Electronics Express*, *6*(14), 1057–1063. doi:10.1587/elex.6.1057

Foote, J., Adcock, J., & Girgensohn, A. (2003). Time base modulation: A new approach to watermarking audio. In *Proceedings of International Conference on Multimedia and Expo*, (pp. 221-224). Baltimore, MD: IEEE.

Fujimoto, R., Iwaki, M., & Kiryu, T. (2006). A method of high bit-rate data hiding in music using spline interpolation. In *Proceedings of the 2006 International Conference on Intelligent Information Hiding and Multimedia*, (pp. 11-14). Pasadena, CA: IEEE.

Gurijala, A. R., & Deller, J. R., Jr. (2003). Speech watermarking by parametric embedding with an l_∞ fidelity criterion. In *Proceedings of EUROSPEECH-2003/INTERSPEECH-2003*, (pp. 2933-2936). Geneva, Switzerland: EUROSPEECH.

Johnson, K. F., Duric, Z., & Jajodia, S. (2000). *Information hiding: Steganography and watermarking – Attacks and countermeasures*. Reading, MA: Kluwer Academic Publishers. doi:10.1007/978-1-4615-4375-6

Kabal, P. (2002). *An examination and interpretation of ITU-R BS.1387: Perceptual evaluation of audio quality. TSP Lab Technical Report*. Montreal, Canada: McGill University.

Kalker, T., Depovere, G., Haitsma, J., & Maes, M. (1999). A video watermarking system for broadcast monitoring. *Proceedings of the Society for Photo-Instrumentation Engineers*, *3657*, 103–112. doi:10.1117/12.344661

Lee, H. S., & Lee, W. S. (2005). Audio watermarking through modification of tonal maskers. *ETRI Journal*, *27*(5), 608–616. doi:10.4218/etrij.05.0105.0037

Linnartz, J. P. M. G., Kalker, A. C. C., & Depovere, G. F. (1998). Modelling the false-alarm and missed detection rate for electronic watermarks. In Aucsmith, L. D. (Ed.), *Notes in Computer Science* (*Vol. 1525*, pp. 329–343). Berlin, Germany: Springer-Verlag. doi:10.1007/3-540-49380-8_23

Liu, Y. W., & Smith, J. O. (2003). Watermarking parametric representations for synthetic audio. In *Proceedings of IEEE International Conference on Acoustics Speech and Signal Processing*, (pp. 660-663). Hong Kong, China: IEEE Press.

Liu, Y. W., & Smith, J. O. (2004). Watermarking sinusoidal audio representations by quantization index modulation in multiple frequencies. In *Proceedings of IEEE International Conference on Acoustics, Speech, and Signal Processing*, (pp. 373-376). Montreal, Canada: IEEE Press.

Martin, V., Chabert, M., & Lacaze, B. (2008). An interpolation-based watermarking scheme. *Signal Processing*, *88*, 539–557. doi:10.1016/j.sigpro.2007.08.016

Miaou, S. G., Hsu, C. H., Tsai, Y. S., & Chao, H. M. (2000). A secure data hiding technique with heterogeneous data-combining capability for electronic patient records. In *Proceedings of the 22nd Annual International Conference of the IEEE Engineering in Medicine and Biology Society*, (pp. 280-283). Chicago, IL: IEEE Press.

Miller, M. L., & Bloom, M. A. (1999). Computing the probability of false watermark detection. In *Proceedings of the Third International Workshop on Information Hiding*, (pp. 146-158). Dresden, Germany: IEEE.

Ozer, H., Sankur, B., & Memon, N. (2005). An SVD-based audio watermarking technique. In *Proceedings of the 7th Workshop on Multimedia and Security*, (pp. 51-56). New York, NY: IEEE.

Petitcolas, F. A. P., Anderson, R. J., & Kuhn, M. G. (1998). Attacks on copyright marking systems. In *Proceedings of the Second International Workshop on Information Hiding*, (pp. 218-238). IEEE Press.

Ruiz, F. J., & Deller, J. R., Jr. (2000). Digital watermarking of speech signals for the national gallery of the spoken word. In *Proceedings. of IEEE International Conference on Acoustics, Speech, and Signal Processing*, (pp. 1499-1502). Istanbul, Turkey: IEEE Press.

Seadle, M. S., Deller, J. R., Jr., & Gurijala, A. (2002). Why watermark? The copyright need for an engineering solution. In *Proceedings of the 2nd ACM/IEEE-CS Joint Conference on Digital Libraries*, (pp. 324-325). Portland, OR: ACM/IEEE.

Van Schyndel, R. G., & Osborne, C. F. (1994). A digital watermark. In *Proceedings of IEEE International Conference Image Processing*, (pp. 86-90). Austin, TX: IEEE Press.

Voloshynovskiy, S., Pereira, S., Pun, T., Su, J. K., & Eggers, J. J. (2001). Attacks and benchmarking. *IEEE Communications Magazine*, *39*(8).

Wang, S., Sekey, A., & Gersho, A. (1992). An objective measure for predicting subjective quality of speech coders. *IEEE Journal on Selected Areas in Communications*, *10*(5), 819–829. doi:10.1109/49.138987

Wu, M., & Liu, B. (2004). Data hiding in binary image for authentication and annotation. *IEEE Transactions on Multimedia*, *6*(4), 528–538. doi:10.1109/TMM.2004.830814

KEY TERMS AND DEFINITIONS

Degree of Spline Function: The degree of piecewise polynomials of spline function.

Linear Prediction: An operation for estimating future values of a discrete-time signal by a linear function of previous samples; often called Linear Predictive Coding (LPC).

Order of Spline Function: The number of coefficients of each piecewise polynomials of spline function, which is bigger than the degree of spline function by one.

Spline Function: A polynomial function that consists of piecewise polynomials, keeping some degree of smoothness.

Support of a Function: The closure of the set of points where the function is not zero-valued, $\{x \mid f(x) \neq 0\}$.

Chapter 5
Acoustic OFDM Technology and System

Hosei Matsuoka
NTT DOCOMO, Japan

ABSTRACT

This chapter presents a method of aerial acoustic communication in which data is modulated using OFDM (Orthogonal Frequency Division Multiplexing) and embedded in regular audio material without significantly degrading the quality of the original sound. It can provide data transmission of several hundred bps, which is much higher than is possible with other audio data hiding techniques. The proposed method replaces the high frequency band of the audio signal with OFDM carriers, each of which is power-controlled according to the spectrum envelope of the original audio signal. The implemented system enables the transmission of short text messages from loudspeakers to mobile handheld devices at a distance of around 3m. This chapter also provides the subjective assessment results of audio clips embedded with OFDM signals.

INTRODUCTION

Because of the increasing popularity of mobile handheld devices that offer high-level audio functions, there is a strong possibility of using sound for data transmission from ordinary loudspeakers to the handheld devices. Given wireless short-range communications such as Bluetooth, etc., mobile handheld devices can easily share some data with laptop computers without wires. While the data rates for sound are relatively low compared to media such as radio, sound links can establish an attractive interface for service access. That is, a commercial on the TV or radio can be used to load the URL of the company selling the item into the user's mobile device. Sound is attractive for such applications since no additional hardware infrastructure is needed.

For transmitting a simple URL or e-mail address in a reasonable time (a few seconds), data rates more than hundreds of bps are necessary. Audio data hiding techniques enable the data transmission over aerial links in parallel with regular audio materials, but they can offer only very low data rates less than a hundred bps. Most of them are designed for watermarks and so the

DOI: 10.4018/978-1-4666-2217-3.ch005

data rates for aerial acoustic communications are even lower, because when a signal is broadcast into the air and re-sampled with a microphone, the signal will be subjected to possibly unknown nonlinear modification resulting in phase change, echo, frequency drift, etc. Different approaches for aerial acoustic communications have been proposed. They use the same modulation techniques as radio communications such as ASK and FSK. They send the modulated signal en clair. While these methods can provide higher data rates, from hundreds of bps to more than 1kbps, their sound can be annoying and they cannot be transmitted in parallel with pre-existing sounds such as voice or music. Ultrasound acoustic communication can achieve even higher data rates and is imperceptible to human ears, but ordinary low cost loudspeakers and microphones do not support ultrasound, which prevents the use of ordinary audio devices. Given these considerations, the goals of Acoustic OFDM system are:

1. To transmit at data rates around hundreds of bps.
2. To use the audible audio band so that ordinary low cost loudspeakers and microphones can be used.
3. To embed information in pre-existing sound almost in a perceptually transparent fashion.

Acoustic OFDM system is designed to satisfy the above requirements. The main feature of the Acoustic OFDM is replacing the high frequency band of the audio signal with OFDM modulated data signal where each carrier is power-controlled according to the spectrum envelope of the original audio signal. It can suppress the original audio quality degradation and transmit high bit-rate data.

BACKGROUND

Several audio data hiding techniques have been proposed in recent years. Most of them are designed for watermarks and so offer robustness to D/A-A/D conversion. When an audio source is transmitted as an analog signal across a clean analog line and re-sampled, the absolute signal magnitude and sample quantization change. However, acoustic communication over aerial links is more challenging, because when a signal is broadcast into the air and re-sampled with a microphone, the signal will be subjected to possibly unknown nonlinear modification resulting in phase change, amplitude change, echo, frequency drift, etc. Therefore, most existing data hiding techniques cannot be applied to aerial acoustic communications. The typical data hiding techniques for audio and their problems are described below.

Echo Hiding

Motivated by the fact that the HAS (Human Auditory System) cannot distinguish an echo from the original when delay and amplitude of the echo are appropriately controlled, this method employs two different delay times to carry binary information (Gruhl, 1996). Unfortunately, the signal experiences damping oscillation in the loudspeaker and environmental reflection both of which result in a variety of echoes, which lowers the data rate; its actual data rate becomes insufficient for practical applications.

Phase Coding

To a certain extent, modifications of the phase of a signal cannot be perceived by the HAS. By taking advantage of this fact, data can be embedded by altering the phase in a predefined manner. This can be done by using all-pass filters to modify the phase without changing the magnitude response (Yardimei, 1997). Similar to echo hiding, this method does not suit aerial communications, because the loudspeakers used and the aerial links may cause nonlinear phase distortion, which complicates signal detection and lowers the overall data rate.

Spread Spectrum

The basic spread spectrum technique is designed to encode information by spreading the signal across a wide frequency spectrum (Pickholtz, 1982). By using the masking effect, a faint sound becomes inaudible if overlaid by a louder sounds, a spread signal can be imperceptibly embedded in audio (Boney, 1996; Cox, 1998). This technique spreads the signal by multiplying it by a PN (Pseudo-random Noise) code, which is usually a maximum length sequence called M-sequence. The decoder can retrieve the embedded information by despreading the received signal with the PN code.

The spread spectrum technique is more robust to aerial communication than the other two techniques described above. However, the spreading rate has to be high in order to offset the various distortion and noise sources common in aerial links, and consequently the data transmission rate is less than 40bps.

As described above, existing data hiding techniques fall well short of being able to transmit a short message, such as a simple URL or e-mail address, in a reasonable time.

Acoustic OFDM, described in this chapter, offers data rates more than hundreds of bps and can coexist with pre-existing sound streams. The method uses the audible audio band and so is supported by ordinary audio devices.

ACOUSTIC OFDM TECHNOLOGY

Acoustic OFDM employs OFDM as its modulation scheme. OFDM is a multi-carrier modulation method that distributes the data over a large number of narrow frequency carriers. By selecting a special set of orthogonal carrier frequencies, high spectral efficiency is obtained (Weinstein, 1971). OFDM signal is modulated with IFFT (Inverse Fast Fourier Transform), and demodulated with FFT. The signal is set on the phase of each FFT frequency. One of the main characteristics of OFDM is flat fading of the individual carrier. Conventional single carrier transmission systems suffer spectrum distortion due to frequency selective fading. In multi-carrier transmission systems, however, the individual carrier experiences flat fading as depicted in Figure 1, since each carrier has a narrow bandwidth.

This simplifies the equalization process and improves the signal detection accuracy. Acoustic OFDM takes advantage of these characteristics to transform the OFDM modulated signal into non-annoying sound.

Acoustic OFDM Encoding

The main advance of Acoustic OFDM is that it controls the power of the carriers to mimic the spectrum envelope of the original audio stream. Figure 2 shows the encode step of the Acoustic OFDM signal in the frequency domain. First, the high frequency band of the original audio is eliminated by a Low-Pass Filter (LPF). Next, an OFDM modulated signal is generated in the equivalent high frequency band where each carrier is modulated with PSK, and each carrier is power-controlled to match the frequency spectrum of the original audio signal. The low-band audio signal and the power-controlled OFDM signal are then combined. The resulting synthetic audio

Figure 1. Frequency selective fading

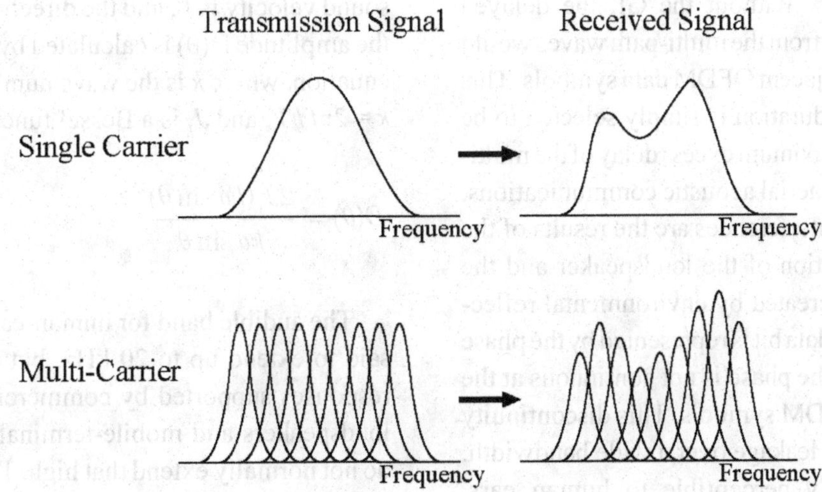

Figure 2. Acoustic OFDM encoding

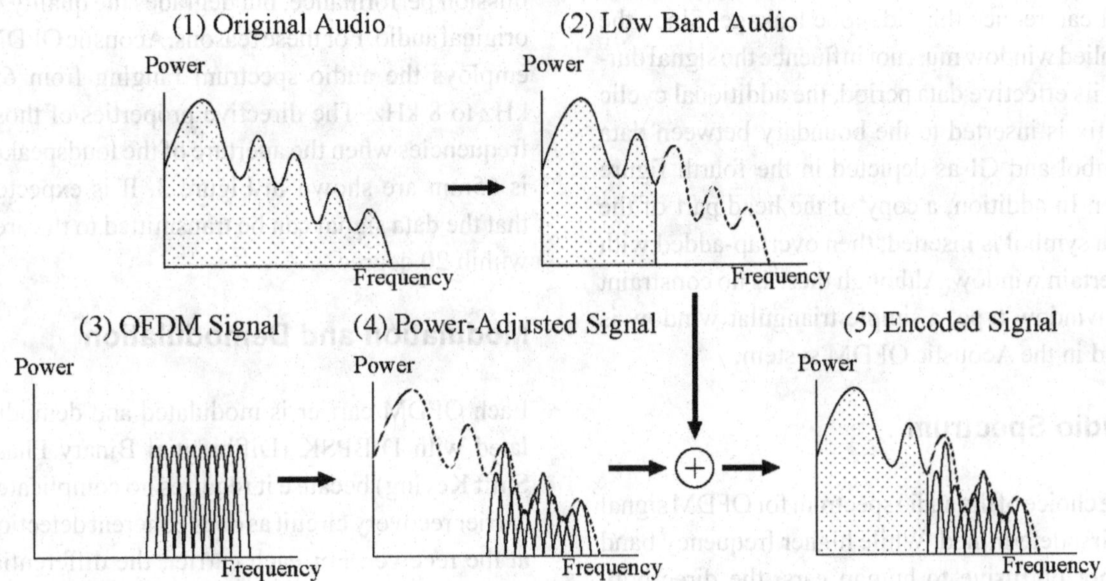

signal can then be played back by conventional loudspeakers.

The sound of the native OFDM modulated signal is simply noisy just like a White Gaussian Noise. However, after power modification, the OFDM signal sounds similar to the high-band signal of the original audio, so the OFDM signal is not so obtrusive or annoying.

Guard Interval

The second key principle of OFDM is the introduction of a GI (Guard Interval) to minimize inter-frame interference under multi-path conditions (Speth, 1988). Each OFDM symbol has a GI and a data symbol. The GI, a copy of the last part of the data symbol, preserves the orthogonality of carriers and the independence of subsequent OFDM symbols. Without the GI, the delayed signals resulting from the multi-path waves would interfere with adjacent OFDM data symbols. This implies that GI duration is simply selected to be larger than the maximum excess delay of the multi-path channel. In aerial acoustic communications, the multi-path interferences are the results of the damping oscillation of the loudspeaker and the delayed waves created by environmental reflection. Since each data bit is represented by the phase of each carrier, the phase is not continuous at the boundary of OFDM symbols. This discontinuity causes side lobe leakage over a wide bandwidth, which is readily perceptible to human ears. Moreover, a radical phase change at the boundary of OFDM symbols also degrades the quality of audio. Windowing is a well-known technique that can reduce this side lobe leakage. Since the applied window must not influence the signal during its effective data period, the additional cyclic prefix is inserted to the boundary between data symbol and GI as depicted in the fourth figure later. In addition, a copy of the head part of the data symbol is inserted, then overlap-added with a certain window. Although there is no constraint on window type, a simple triangular window is used in the Acoustic OFDM system.

Audio Spectrum

The choice of the audio spectrum for OFDM signal is first determined. While higher frequency band is not obtrusive to human ears, the directivity of sound waves becomes sharper. The directive property depends on the frequency and the aperture of loudspeakers. A useful technique for the analysis of the radiation of sound from loudspeaker diaphragms is to replace the vibrating parts with a distribution of equivalent point monopole sound sources. It is possible to estimate the sound field radiated by a vibrating surface by summing up the contribution of all of the equivalent monopoles (Holland, 2001).

When the aperture is a, the frequency is f, the sound velocity is V, and the directivity angle is θ, the amplitude $D(\theta)$ is calculated by the following equation, where k is the wave number referred as $k = 2\pi f / V$, and J_1 is a Bessel function.

$$D(\theta) = \frac{2J_1(ka \sin \theta)}{ka \sin \theta}$$

The audible band for human-ears is generally said to extend up to 20 kHz, but the frequency responses supported by commercially available loudspeakers and mobile-terminal microphones do not normally extend that high. There are many microphones, for example, that can only pick up sound to about 10 kHz. In addition, using wide frequency for OFDM signal improves data transmission performance, but degrades the quality of original audio. For these reasons, Acoustic OFDM employs the audio spectrum ranging from 6.4 kHz to 8 kHz. The directive properties of those frequencies when the aperture of the loudspeaker is 65mm are shown in Figure 3. It is expected that the data signal can be transmitted to the area within 20 degree.

Modulation and Demodulation

Each OFDM carrier is modulated and demodulated with D-BPSK (Differential Binary Phase Shift Keying) because it requires no complicated carrier recovery circuit as does coherent detection at the receiver. For each carrier, the differential phase from the previous symbol is modulated by the binary state of the input signal. When the symbol is 1, there is no change from the phase of the previous symbol, and when the symbol is 0, there is a change of half a cycle.

As described in Figure 2, the power of each carrier is adjusted according to the spectrum envelope of the original audio stream. Since some carriers might not have enough power to transmit data, the powers of those carriers are set to a minimum

Figure 3. Directivity

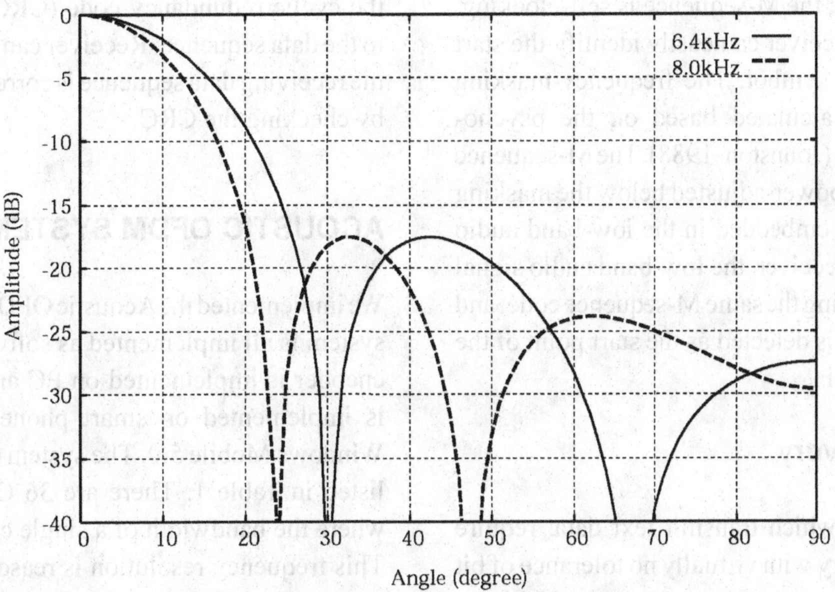

threshold. The minimum threshold should be set to around -65dB from the maximum power of the original audio signal.

Symbol Synchronization

Symbol synchronization is essential if the receiver is to identify the start of the OFDM symbol. Acoustic OFDM embeds a synchronization signal in the low-band audio signal in the same way as the Spread Spectrum data hiding technique. It uses the frequency masking effect by which a faint sound cannot be heard if it exists at the same time as a loud sound at a nearby frequency.

The signal is spread by an M-sequence code and the spread signal is embedded below the frequency-masking threshold of the low-band audio as shown in Figure 4. M-sequences have good autocorrelation properties where the autocorrelation function has peaks equal to 1 at 0, N, 2N

Figure 4. Symbol synchronization signal

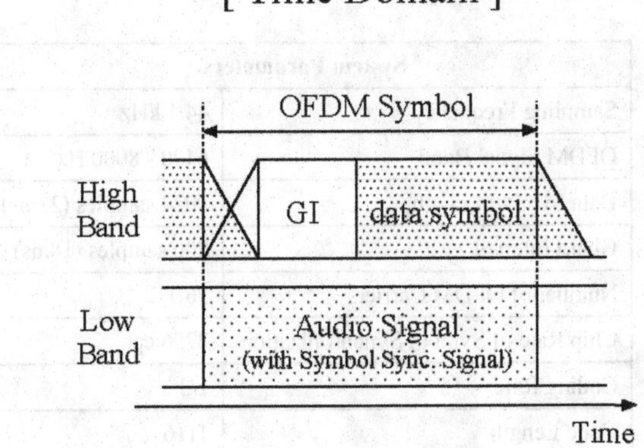

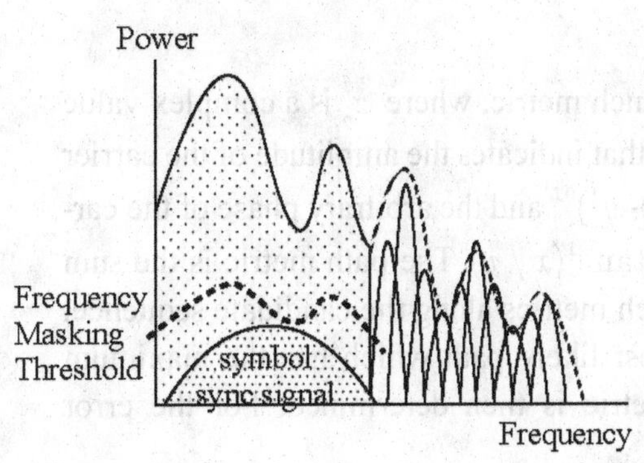

(approximately 1/N elsewhere). Because of these periodic peaks, the M-sequence is self-clocking, and thus the receiver can easily identify the start of the OFDM symbol. The frequency-masking threshold is calculated based on the psycho-acoustic model (Johnston, 1988). The M-sequence code signal is power-adjusted below the masking threshold, and embedded in the low-band audio signal. At the receiver, the low-band audio signal is de-spread using the same M-sequence code, and the peak point is detected as the start point of the OFDM symbol.

Error Recovery

Applications, which transmit text data, require reliable delivery with virtually no tolerance of bit errors. Since some bit errors are unavoidable on aerial acoustic links, it is essential to implement an error recovery scheme. FEC (Forward Error Correction) is an effective error recovery method that works without any feedback channel. Acoustic OFDM employs convolution codes, which have good error recovery performance and work best if the errors of the incoming data are random. Therefore, to randomize the bit errors of the received data sequence, the transmission data is interleaved in both frequency and time. At the receiver, the received data sequence is de-interleaved and applied to the soft-decision Viterbi decoding. The decoding in Acoustic OFDM uses:

$$\lambda(1) = \mathrm{Re}[z_n \cdot z_{n-1}]$$
$$\lambda(-1) = -\mathrm{Re}[z_n \cdot z_{n-1}]$$

as a branch metric, where z_n is a complex value $x + jy$ that indicates the amplitude of the carrier as $(x^2 + y^2)^{0.5}$ and the arbitrary phase of the carrier as $\tan^{-1}(x / y)$. The path metric is the sum of branch metrics along the candidate sequence. The most likely path which has the maximum path metric is then determined. For the error detection in the case that the error recovery fails, the cyclic redundancy code (CRC) is appended to the data sequence. Receiver can make sure that the receiving data sequence is correctly recovered by checking the CRC.

ACOUSTIC OFDM SYSTEM

We implemented the Acoustic OFDM system. The system is all implemented as software where the encoder is implemented on PC and the decoder is implemented on smart phone devices with Windows Mobile 5.0. The system parameters are listed in Table 1. There are 36 OFDM carriers where the bandwidth of a single carrier is 43Hz. This frequency resolution is reasonable because some typical audio codecs such as MP3 and AAC use the approximate equivalent resolutions. The length of a data symbol is 23ms with this frequency resolution. The duration of the GI is determined by the maximum excess delay of the reflected wave in the environment of TV viewing. The duration is set to 18ms, which is enough duration to suppress the multi-pass interference.

Data Frame Structure

The acoustic OFDM system makes use of carousel transmission. The same data signal of the fixed data frame size is transmitted repeatedly. The user can

Table 1. Acoustic OFDM

System Parameters	
Sampling Frequency	44.1 kHz
OFDM Signal Band	6400 - 8000 Hz
Data Symbol Length	1024 samples (23ms)
Guard Interval	800 samples (18ms)
Number of OFDM Carriers	36 + 1
Chip Rate of Symbol Synchronization	2756 cps
Coding Rate	1/3
Code Length	1116

then detect the data signal by picking up the sound for the duration of a single data frame size during any interval in which this signal is transmitted.

A single data frame is composed of 1116 bits, which are allocated in 36 carriers and 31 time slots. Given the coding rate of 1/3, the effective information is 45 bytes. A single data frame is transmitted in 1.5 seconds, so the data transmission rate is approximately 240 bps.

The control signal is used for identifying the start of the data frame. An M-sequence of 31 bits is allocated in the lowest carrier and 31 time slots. The start of the data frame can be determined from the peak of the self-correlation of the M-sequence.

Figure 5 shows the data frame structure of Acoustic OFDM system. The 31st OFDM symbol is followed by the 1st OFDM symbol of the same data frame. The receiver can decode the data frame, from whichever symbol it starts to receive, by receiving 31 consecutive OFDM symbols.

Figure 5. Acoustic OFDM data frame structure

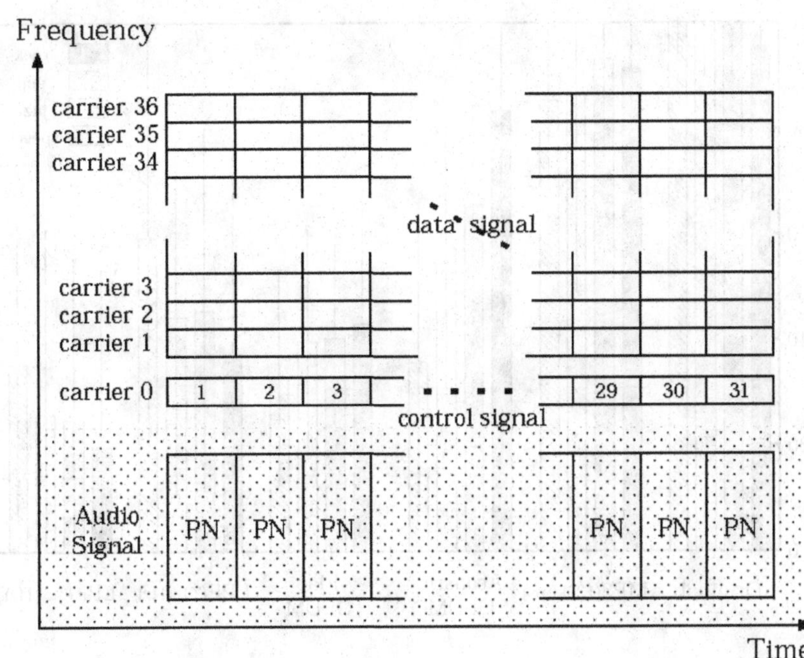

SUBJECTIVE QUALITY TEST

Subjective listening tests were performed in order to evaluate the impact of Acoustic OFDM encoding. The MUSHRA method was used for the subjective quality test of audio clips in which OFDM signal is embedded. This is a method which compares audio clips with a hidden reference, and bandwidth limited anchor signals. It has been recommended at the ITU-R under the name BS.1534 (ITU-R 2001).

For this test, we chose two band-limited anchor signals; one is limited to 3.5 kHz and the other is limited to 7.0 kHz. We also use MP3 encoded signal just for reference. The encoding bit rate is set to 128 kbps for monaural signal. We tested two configurations; one is Acoustic OFDM encoded signal, and the other is flat OFDM encoded signal where the OFDM signal is added in the same way as Acoustic OFDM but the power controlling for the spectrum envelope is not performed. The average OFDM signal power is same as that of the Acoustic OFDM encoding.

For each configuration and reference, 4 audio clips described in Table 2 are tested. "Rock music" has strong power in the OFDM signal band while the "pop music" and "jazz music" has moderate power and "speech only" has little power in the OFDM signal band. "speech only" has only a voice of female. These audio clips are all 44.1 kHz sampled signals.

Figure 6 shows the results obtained for each tested configuration and audio clip. The different configurations and audio clips are spread along the X-axis while the quality scale is along the Y-axis. The average over the 18 listeners and the confidence interval at 95% are displayed.

As expected, the hidden references are rated the highest with a small confidence interval. It is noticeable that the scores given to the Acoustic OFDM configuration considerably depend on the audio clips. For "rock music," the score is relatively high and almost same as that of the MP3 encoding configuration. For "pop music" and "jazz music," the scores are lower than the scores of MP3 encoding configuration, but still higher than the scores of the anchors. The score of "speech only" is low and almost same as the score of the 3.5 kHz band-limited anchor. This is because the OFDM signal is embedded almost without power-adjustment to the spectrum envelope of the original audio. For the same reason, the flat OFDM encoding configuration has low scores for all the audio clips.

To conclude, we can say that on the average, the quality of Acoustic OFDM encoded signal is not significantly degraded for music materials which has large enough power in OFDM signal band.

Table 2. Subjective quality test

Audio Samples
Rock Music
Pop Music
Jazz Music
Speech Only

Figure 6. Subjective assessment results

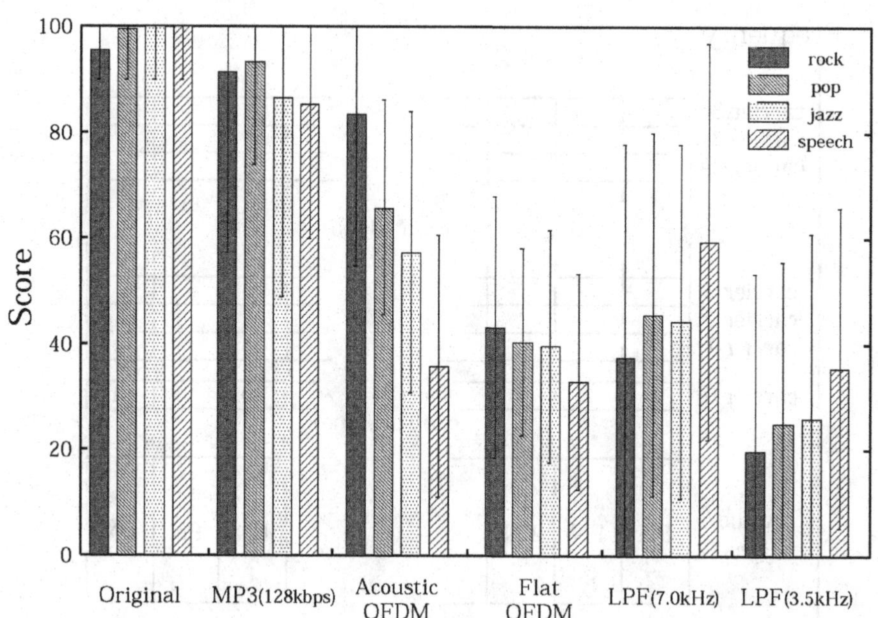

PERFORMANCE MEASUREMENTS

We tested the transmission performance of the Acoustic OFDM encoded signal and the flat OFDM encoding signal. Acoustic OFDM encoded signal is created by encoding the same "rock music" used in the subjective quality testing. The minimum carrier power threshold for the Acoustic OFDM encoding is set to -65dB from the maximum power of the original audio signal.

For the flat OFDM encoding, the carrier power is set where the average OFDM signal power is same as that of Acoustic OFDM encoding. Both signals are played at ordinary volume level of TV viewing, which is approximately 65 dB(A). In this condition, the average power of a carrier is 21dBSPL at a transmission distance of 1m. The power of the background noise is approximately 35 dB(A) and the noise for each carrier frequency was approximately 11dBSPL in the experimental room. Therefore, the signal to noise ratio is 10dB at a transmission distance of 1m.

In the experiments, we used an ordinary low-cost loudspeaker and microphone whose frequency responses ran from 100Hz to more than 10kHz. We evaluated the transmission distance, the directivity performance, and the robustness for audio codec. The tests were made by transmitting 1000 data frames, where each data frame is individually decoded at the receiver. The success rate of the data decoding is measured. If the rate is more than 80%, the receiver can decode the data in a reasonable time by a few trials of data receiving.

Transmission Distance

In the idealized case of the sound radiated by a point monopole under ideal free-field acoustic conditions, the acoustic pressure reduces by 6dB as the acoustic energy becomes spread over double distance. Therefore, the SNR is expected to decrease approximately by 6dB at double transmission distance. Figure 7 shows the relation between the transmission distance and success

Figure 7. Transmission distance

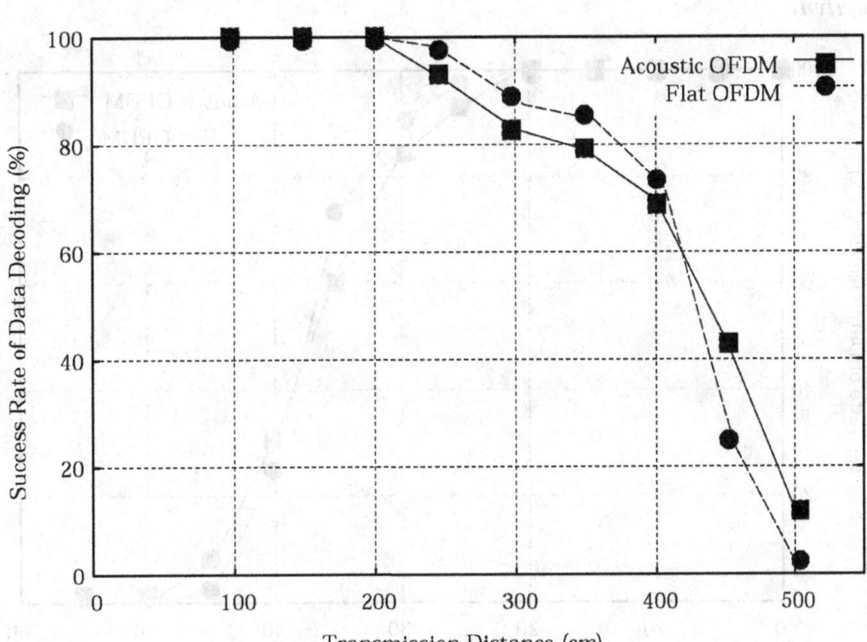

rate of data decoding. The sound radiated from the loudspeaker is recorded at the directivity of 0 degree. For both encoded signals, the success rates of data decoding are 100% up to 2m. From 2m to 3.5m, the success rates are decreased, but still high enough to decode the data by a few trials of data receiving. At the distance of more than 4m, the success rates become low and the decoding becomes more difficult. The performance of the Acoustic OFDM encoded signal is almost same as that of the flat OFDM encoded signal, but it is in a gradual decline compared to the flat OFDM encoding.

Directivity

In the Acoustic OFDM system, the transmission region may be narrow because the data signal is transmitted over relatively high frequency carriers as shown in Figure 3. The actual measurements were made and Figure 8 shows the relation between the directivity angle and the success rate of data decoding. The directivity angle defines the region for the transmission distance of 2m. For both encoded signals, the success rates are 100% up to 20 degree, and they are high up to 30 degree. At the angle of more than 30 degree, they decrease precipitously, and the decoding becomes difficult.

In the same way as the transmission distance, the performances for both signals are almost the same.

Robustness to Audio Codec

Audio compression is widely used in a variety of applications. It reduces sounds that are very hard to hear, for example, sounds of high frequencies or sounds that occur at the same time as other louder sounds. Therefore, the signal of Acoustic OFDM may deteriorate with low bit-rate audio compressions. A typical audio compression is AAC (Advanced Audio Coding), which is used for digital television, DVDs, streaming media on the Internet, etc. We used the AAC coding for evaluating the robustness to audio codecs.

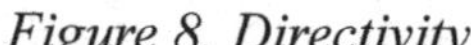
Figure 8. Directivity

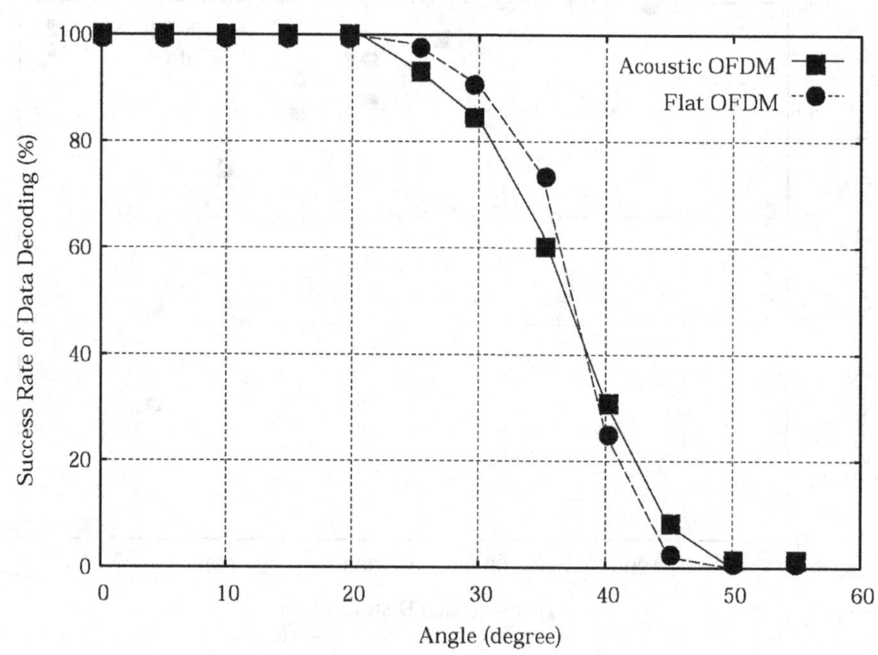

The AAC encoding and decoding processes are inserted between the Acoustic OFDM encoder and decoder. Acoustic OFDM encoded signal is AAC-encoded with some compressed bit-rate and then AAC-decoded. Acoustic OFDM decoding is tried for the AAC-decoded signal without aerial transmission.

Figure 9 shows the relation between the compressed bit-rate for MPEG-4 AAC and the success rate of data decoding. For both encoded signals, the success rates increase as the bit-rates increase, and they become 100% at more than 80kbps. However, it is recommended that the bit-rate be kept more than 96kbps to keep high S/N rate in the OFDM signal for aerial transmission.

ROBUST ACOUSTIC OFDM

Acoustic OFDM embeds an M-sequence code signal into the low-frequency sound, but it may degrade the transmission performance degradation due to the symbol synchronization error. The symbol synchronization determines the start point of the FFT period in the OFDM frame for the demodulation. If the start point is misaligned, the FFT demodulation cannot be executed for the consecutive data symbol. In order to provide more robust transmission, Acoustic OFDM has a robust transmission method with one-half data transmission rate. It does not need the symbol synchronization signal in the sound and does not synchronize OFDM symbols. Instead, it can definitely execute the FFT demodulation for the consecutive data symbol. Figure 10 shows the symbol structure of the robust Acoustic OFDM. Compared to the normal OFDM symbol structure, the robust Acoustic OFDM symbol expands the data part by GI + data length. Receiver decodes from two different points, which are separated by GI + data length. In this case, one of these two points can definitely decode data symbol without symbol synchronization. While transmission data rates become half as normal OFDM, the robustness of the air transmission becomes higher. The other part of the robust Acoustic OFDM scheme is the same as the normal Acoustic OFDM described above. The robust Acoustic OFDM should be used for transmitting an ID or a very short message smaller than URL or e-mail address.

CONCLUSION

In this chapter, we introduce the Acoustic OFDM system that achieves data transmission of about 240bps simultaneously with the playback of conventional audio streams. By adjusting the power of the OFDM carriers so that they match the spectrum envelope of the high-band component of the audio signal, the modulated data signal become unobtrusive.

From the subjective quality testing, the audio quality degradation is much less than that of the flat OFDM encoding when the audio stream has a certain power in the OFDM signal band. The power controlling to the spectrum envelope is effective to suppress the quality degradation. However, for audio streams, which have little power in the OFDM signal band such as speech only, the quality may be significantly degraded. For that case, it might be better to add BGM to the speech before Acoustic OFDM encoding.

From the transmission performance analysis, the performances of the Acoustic OFDM encoding and the flat OFDM encoding are almost same for transmission distance, directivity, and robustness to audio codec. Therefore, the Acoustic OFDM encoding provides higher audio quality and the same transmission performance compared to the flat OFDM encoding.

The Acoustic OFDM system enables applications to transmit short text messages to mobile handheld devices over aerial audio links. A typical application is embedding an URL into the audio stream of a TV or radio program. Users of mobile handsets can access the website via the URL without inputting the URL manually. Experiments showed that the data transmission region is large enough for TV viewing in the home. Since many audio devices are located in public places, aerial acoustic communication, realized by Acoustic OFDM, is considered to be an effective way of establishing ubiquitous communications.

Figure 9. Robustness to codec

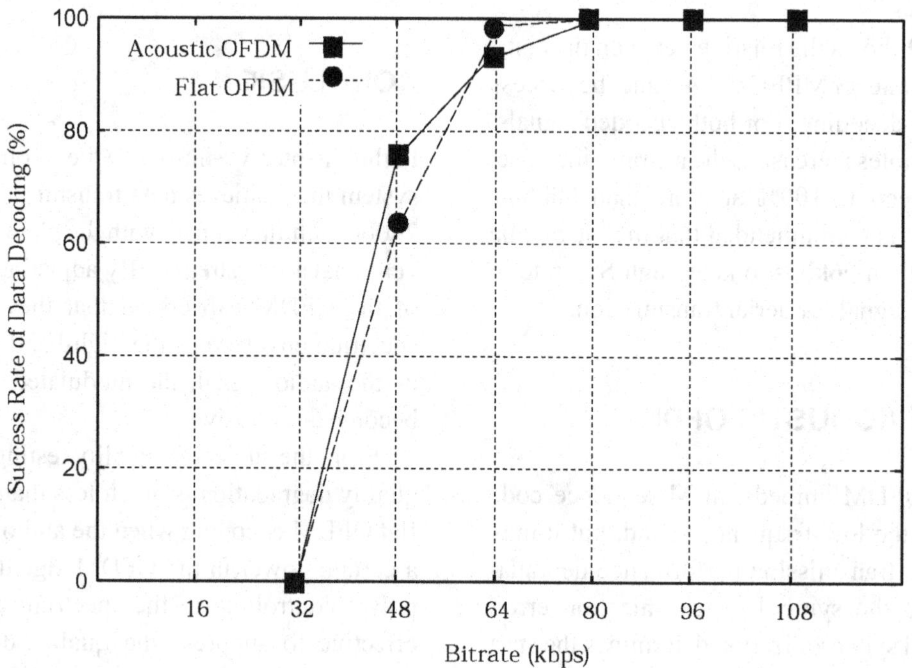

Figure 10. Non-symbol synchronization scheme

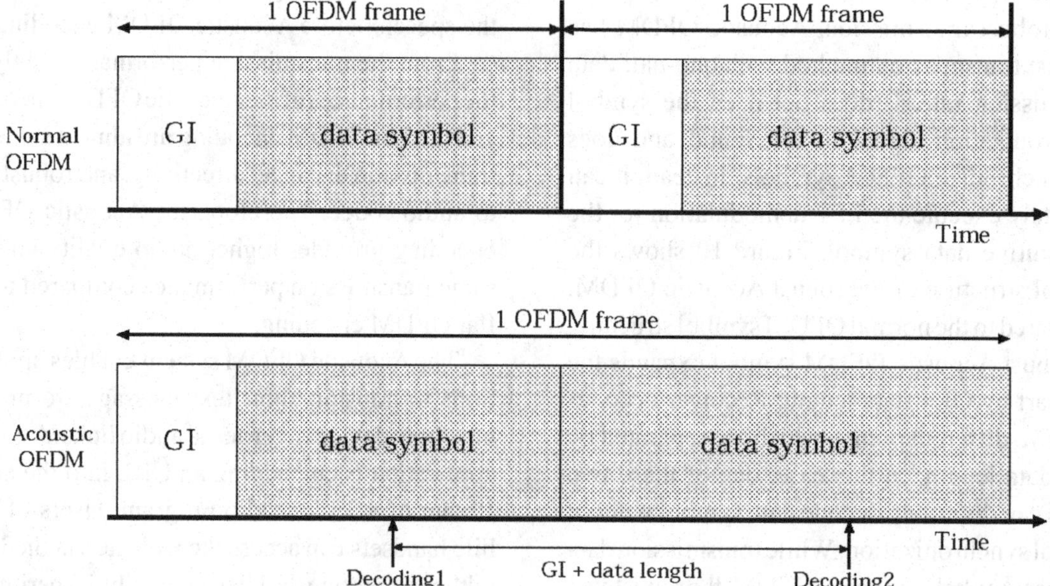

REFERENCES

Boney, L., Tewfik, A., & Hamdy, K. N. (1996). Digital watermarks for audio signals. In *Proceedings of the IEEE International Conference on Multimedia Computing and Systems*, (pp. 473-480). IEEE Press.

Cox, I. J. (1998). *Spread spectrum watermark for embedded signaling*. United States Patent 5,848,155. Washington, DC: US Patent Office.

Gruhl, D., Lu, A., & Bender, W. (1996). Echo hiding. *Proceedings of Information Hiding, 1996*, 295–315. doi:10.1007/3-540-61996-8_48

Holland, K. R. (2001). Chapter in Borwick, J. (Ed.), *Loudspeaker and Headphone Handbook* (pp. 11–13). London, UK: Focal Press.

ITU-R Recommendation BS. 1534. (2001). *Method for the subjective assessment of intermediate quality level of coding systems*. Retrieved from http://www.itu.int

Johnston, J. (1988). Transform coding of audio signals using perceptual noise criteria. *IEEE Journal on Selected Areas in Communications*, *6*, 314–323. doi:10.1109/49.608

Pickholtz, R. L., Schilling, D. L., & Milstein, L. B. (1982). Theory of spread-spectrum communications - A tutorial. *IEEE Transactions on Communications*, *30*, 855–884. doi:10.1109/TCOM.1982.1095533

Speth, M. (1988). Optimum receiver design for wireless broadband systems using OFDM-part 1. *IEEE Transactions on Communications*, *47*, 1668–1677. doi:10.1109/26.803501

Weinstein, S. B., & Ebert, P. M. (1971). Data transmission by frequency-division multiplexing using the discrete fourier transform. *IEEE Transactions on Communications*, *19*, 628–634. doi:10.1109/TCOM.1971.1090705

Yardimei, Y., Cetin, A. E., & Ansari, R. (1997). Data hiding in speech using phase coding. *Proceedings of EUROSPEECH, 1997*, 1679–1682.

ADDITIONAL READING

Borwick, J. (Ed.). (2001). *Loudspeaker and headphone handbook*. London, UK: Focal Press.

Matsuoka, H., Nakashima, Y., & Yoshimura, T. (2008). Acoustic OFDM system and its extensions. *The Visual Computer*, *25*(1), 3–12. doi:10.1007/s00371-008-0281-5

KEY TERMS AND DEFINITIONS

Audible Band: The range of acoustic frequencies that a human being with normal sense of hearing can hear. Generally, from 20 Hz to 20 kHz.

BPSK: A digital modulation method that allows transmission of 1 bit of information at the same time by assigning one value to each of two phases.

Frequency Masking: Using the effect whereby the sound of neighboring frequencies can create disturbance, this technique prevents the perception of quiet sounds at frequencies near those of loud sounds.

Guard Interval: An interval of fixed duration inserted between symbols to prevent interference between symbols caused by delayed waves.

Psychoacoustic Model: Human hearing characteristics modeling aural sensitivity, masking effects, etc.

PN Code: The bit string constituting pseudo-random noise. Because PN periodically repeats a previously determined bit string, a PN code can be easily self-synchronized.

Chapter 6
Data Hiding for Stereo Audio Signals

Kazuhiro Kondo
Yamagata University, Japan

ABSTRACT

This chapter proposes two data-hiding algorithms for stereo audio signals. The first algorithm embeds data into a stereo audio signal by adding data-dependent mutual delays to the host stereo audio signal. The second algorithm adds fixed delay echoes with polarities that are data dependent and amplitudes that are adjusted such that the interchannel correlation matches the original signal. The robustness and the quality of the data-embedded audio will be given and compared for both algorithms. Both algorithms were shown to be fairly robust against common distortions, such as added noise, audio coding, and sample rate conversion. The embedded audio quality was shown to be "fair" to "good" for the first algorithm and "good" to "excellent" for the second algorithm, depending on the input source.

INTRODUCTION

Recent advances in high-speed digital communication networks, most notably the Internet, have caused significant changes in how we address digital media. It has become quite practical to use these networks to access digital media on demand. We can also easily store, copy, edit, and distribute these media. Because digital processing of digital content is possible with virtually no degradation, flawless copies of copyrighted content can be distributed to a large number of users instantly through these networks. This situation has called for the protection of intellectual ownership and prevention of unauthorized tampering of digital media content. One solution is to digitally hide copyright information within digital content without altering its quality, i.e., digital contents are "marked" with copyright information transparently.

Historically, the volume of research on data hiding (commonly known as "watermarking," which refers to copyright data hiding in host signals) has been for images and videos (Bender, Gruhl, Morimoto, & Lu, 1996). However, we have also recently developed new algorithms for information hiding in speech and audio (Cvejic &

DOI: 10.4018/978-1-4666-2217-3.ch006

Seppänen, 2008). Most of these new algorithms take advantage of the Human Auditory System (HAS) to hide information into host speech or audio signals without causing significant perceptual disturbances. Two properties of HAS that are frequently utilized in information hiding for audio are temporal masking (Elliot, 1969) and spectral masking (Zwicker, 1982). These properties are also used in many MPEG audio coding standards (Gibson, Berger, Lookabaugh, Lindberg, & Baker, 1998; ISO/IEC JTC1/SC29/WG11 11172-3, 1999; ISO/IEC JTC1/SC29 13818-7, 2006).

Although there are numerous audio data-hiding algorithms, few are geared toward stereo host audio signals. The redundancy in stereo channels may be exploited to hide data transparently. In this chapter, we will show that it is indeed possible to exploit this redundancy and embed data without significant degradation of the host signal.

In the first part of this chapter, we propose a stereo audio data-hiding algorithm that hides data in a host signal by introducing data-dependent delays to the host signal's high-frequency stereo channels. Because the HAS is known to be relatively insensitive to fine structures in the high-frequency region, the high-frequency portion is replaced with a single mid-channel. The relative delay between the left and right channel is controlled by the hidden data. Although blind detection (detection without the original signal) is shown to be possible, and robustness to common disturbances is experimentally shown, the audio quality degradation of the embedded audio is shown to be significant for many of the sources tested.

In the latter part of this chapter, we propose a data-hiding algorithm that uses the property of the HAS mentioned above to code embedded data in the relative polarity of the added echo between two stereo channels. We add this echo to control the correlation between channels and match this correlation to the original signal, making the alteration more difficult to perceive. This interchannel correlation is known to influence the stereo image "width" of stationary auditory objects. We show that blind detection is also possible. We also show that this algorithm is robust to most of the disturbances tested, and the data-embedded host audio is "good" to "excellent" in terms of quality.

BACKGROUND

Some Examples of Data Hiding for Audio Signals

There are a number of popular methods for embedding data into a host audio signal, e.g., bit stealing, the patchwork algorithm, and the spread-spectrum algorithm. Some of these methods are presented in the overview chapter of this book. The relevant methods for this chapter are briefly described below.

Phase coding has been regarded as an effective method to embed data with minimum impact on perceived quality (Bender, et al., 1996; Nishimura & Suzuki, 2004; He, Iliev, & Scordilis, 2004). The phase of the original audio is replaced with a reference phase based on the data to be embedded. Because HAS is known to be relatively insensitive to small phase distortions (Malik, Ansari, & Khokhar, 2007; Nishimura, Suzuki, & Suzuki, 2001; Lipshitz, Pocock, & Vanderkooy, 1982), this method can potentially embed data without significantly affecting the host signal quality.

Echo data hiding has also been regarded as an effective method to embed data with minimum impact on perceived quality (Bender, et al., 1996; Nishimura, Suzuki, & Ko, 2007; Wu & Chen, 2007). The echo-data-hiding method embeds data by introducing a small amount of echo into the audio signal. Data are hidden by varying the initial amplitude, the decay rate, and the offset of the echo. If the delay is small enough, the human ear cannot distinguish the original signal from the echo, and "fusion" of the original signal and the echo occurs. Although this fusion appears to be signal dependent, in most cases fusion occurs at delays of approximately a few milliseconds (Breebaart & Faller, 2007; Zurek, 1987). The reasons for the HAS being relatively insensitive to small amounts of echo are related to both temporal and spectral masking.

Some data-hiding methods embed data by applying phase modulation to the Bark-scale frequency bands (Kuo, Johnston, Turin, & Quackenbush, 2002). Although their method was for monaural signals and non-blind detection was necessary, they showed that if the amount of modulation is carefully controlled, data can be embedded with no noticeable degradation in quality. They also showed that embedded data error can be eliminated for the Advanced Audio Coding (AAC) standard encoding at 64 kbps if Viterbi decoding and the Bose-Chaudhuri-Hocquenghem (BCH) error correction codes are employed.

Some Examples of Data Hiding for Stereo Audio Signals

There have been some prior attempts to embed data into stereo signals as well. Megias, Herrera-Joancomarti, and Migullon (2004) have attempted to propose a robust watermark for stereo audio signals using the well-known patchwork algorithm. Their goal was to make the watermark resistant to stereo attacks defined in the audio Stirmark benchmark (Dittman, Megias, Lang, & Herrera-Joancomarti, 2006). They first mixed down the stereo signals into a mono signal and then applied the patchwork algorithm to this mono signal. The patchwork algorithm first divides a set of data into randomly selected data subsets. Next, the algorithm either adds or subtracts a small bias from each subset, based on the hidden data, to alter the histogram by subsets. Then, they added the stereo components back to the embedded mono signal. Their algorithm did prove to be robust to audio Stirmark stereo attacks, but it does not fully exploit stereo redundancy.

Takahashi, Nishimura, and Suzuki (2005) have defined a family of data-embedding methods using phase modulation. They defined different embedding methods for fingerprints (FP, unique digital media ID codes), Copyright Management Information (CMI), and Copy Control Information (CCI), depending on the need for robustness and blind detection. The first two require the original signal for detection, that is, they can be classified as non-blind detection. CCI was designed for blind detection. Takashi et al. modulated the phase of stereo signals in sinusoids. The interchannel offset of the sinusoids was used to embed the data. They found that if the frequency ranges used to detect phase were adaptively chosen, then the embedded CCI would be robust.

Modegi (2006) proposed an extremely robust data-embedding algorithm for stereo signals that can be detected from stereo signals recorded by a cell-phone-integrated microphone. He totally or partially suppressed one channel of the low-frequency-band stereo signal according to the embedded data and found that the embedded data can be mostly recovered even with crude microphones. He also claims that the audio quality does not suffer serious degradation, although he has not shown any formal subjective quality test results.

He, Iliev, and Scordilis (2004) proposed a high-capacity watermark for stereo audio using the phase of one of the channels. The phase of one channel (the left channel in the paper) is either copied from the other channel (the right channel) or set to a fixed value, depending on the watermark data. Obviously, this completely destroys the stereo image. The data were embedded at 20 kbps, which can be regarded as very high for audio signals. However, the authors have stated that this watermark is fragile and cannot survive audio compression, which is currently ubiquitous.

Spatial Hearing of the Human Auditory System

When sound is generated from a sound source at an arbitrary location around the listener, the sound travels through space to both ears. If the angle between the line connecting the source and the center of the head and the line connecting both ears is not equal to 90° (i.e., the source is not on the median plane), the path length between the source and the two ears will differ. This difference will create differences in both the level and the delay of the sound observed at each ear. The former is called the Interaural Level Difference (ILD), and the latter is called the Interaural Time Difference (ITD). The HAS uses both as cues to the location of the source. If the level is different, the sound will be perceived closer to the ear that has the larger level. Additionally, if the delay is different, the sound will be perceived as being closer to the ear with the shorter delay (Blauert, 1997). However, there is a difference in the frequency ranges of sound in which each cue plays a dominant role. ITD cues play a dominant role in low-frequency sounds (typically below approximately 1 kHz), and ILD cues play a dominant role above this frequency (Breebaart & Faller, 2007; Zurek, 1987). This difference is known as the duplex theory and was proposed by Lord Rayleigh in 1907.

There is also another property of sound that plays a role in how a sound image is perceived. The Inter-aural Coherence (IC) is the degree of similarity between sound signals observed at both ears. IC can be defined as the maximum value of the normalized cross-correlation between sounds at both ears. If $IC = 1$, the sounds are completely coherent, i.e., the waveforms match except for scale and delay, while if $IC = 0$, the sounds are statistically independent. Sounds with large coherence are perceived as compact auditory objects, i.e., small, sharp sound images. Sounds with small coherence are perceived as broad objects until the coherence is so small that they are eventually perceived as two separate objects (Breebaart & Faller, 2007).

DATA HIDING FOR STEREO AUDIO USING DATA-DEPENDENT INTERCHANNEL DELAY

This section will propose the stereo audio data-hiding method that adds data-dependent interchannel delay to a host signal (Kondo & Nakagawa, 2010). We shall call this first proposed method the interchannel delay stereo method.

It has been known that at least for stationary signals, spatial localization of sound sources in the HAS depends on both amplitude and phase characteristics for low frequencies, but mostly on amplitude characteristics for high frequencies (Gibson, et al., 1998; Breebaart & Faller, 2007). This property of the HAS is exploited in the intensity stereo coding used by select audio codecs, e.g., MPEG 1 Layer 3 (MP3) coders (Herre, Brandenburg, & Lederer, 1994). We will also take advantage of this property and alter the phase of the high-frequency band in the stereo channels according to the embedded data (Kondo & Nakagawa, 2010). The amplitude envelope of these signals will be preserved to keep this alteration unperceivable.

The Data-Embedding Algorithm

This subsection will describe the first data-embedding algorithm for stereo signals, the interchannel delay stereo method. Figure 1 shows the watermark-embedding algorithm. In this algorithm, the high-frequency stereo channels are delayed so that they show relative delays by a fixed number of samples according to the embedded data. The input signal is first split into two sub-bands using the sub-band split filter. The cut-off frequency was set to approximately one-tenth of the full bandwidth, i.e., approximately 2 kHz for the CD-quality 44.1 kHz sampled signal. We used a 128-tap FIR filter designed using the FFT windowing method (Digital Signal Processing Committee, 1979). The left- and right-channel high-band signal powers, P_{LH} and P_{RH}, are calculated on a frame-by-frame basis. Then, the high-band signals are averaged to give one middle high-frequency channel. This signal will be copied for both left- and right-channels and will be delayed on a frame-by-frame basis according to the embedded data. We arbitrarily chose to delay the left-channel to mark a "0" and delay the right-channel to mark a "1." A frame was divided into two equal parts, and only the latter half of the frame was delayed according to the data. This is illustrated in Figure 2. Thus, the first half of the frame is never delayed. We chose this arrangement to enable frame synchronization. For instance, if we embed a known data pattern regularly, e.g., consecutive zeros, there will always be a transition in the left-channel delay at the middle and end of a frame that should easily be detectable using correlation functions.

The amplitudes of each channel were then adjusted to match the power of the original signals, P_{LH} and P_{RH}. These signals are then added back to the low-frequency components to obtain full-bandwidth stereo audio signals.

During preliminary experiments, we found that some of the frames did not contain enough high-frequency components. Obviously, we are not able to encode data into these frames. We simply chose not to embed data in these frames, and no delay was introduced in these frames. An example is shown in the third frame in Figure 2. The added delay should be small enough to be unperceivable. We empirically chose a maximum delay D of 3 samples. Even with this small amount of delay, abrupt changes are noticeable. Therefore, we smoothed the delay changes according to a raised cosine-like pulse pattern. Noninteger delays were introduced using a *sinc* delay filter with an impulse response $h(n)$ that is defined as follows.

$$h(n) = \frac{\sin\left\{\pi \bullet (n-1-\tau)\right\}}{\left\{\pi \bullet (n-1-\tau)\right\}} \qquad (1)$$

Here, n is the sample number, and τ is the delay in samples, which can be fractional. In addition, as described in the next subsection, we will use the interchannel correlation to detect the delay between channel signals. In other words, we compare the cross-correlation between channels with delay and without delay. If the former is larger than the latter, then we can detect the existence of embedded data. However, in some frames, the host signal itself showed relatively flat

Figure 1. Embedding schematic for the interchannel delay stereo method

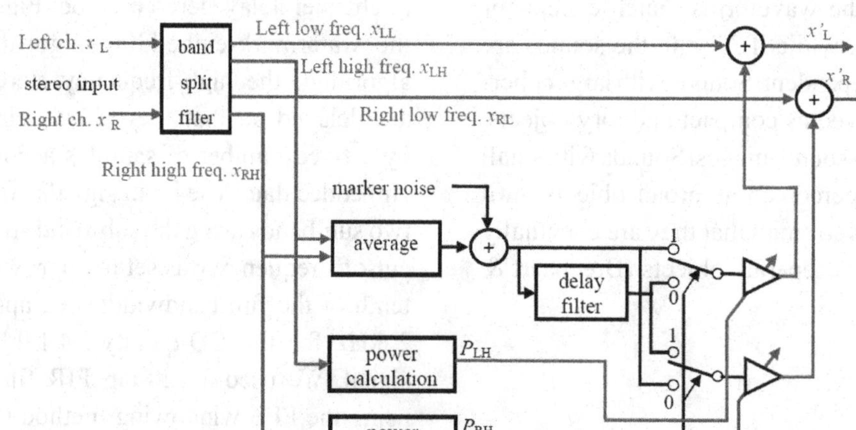

Figure 2. An example of embedded data and the corresponding channel delay

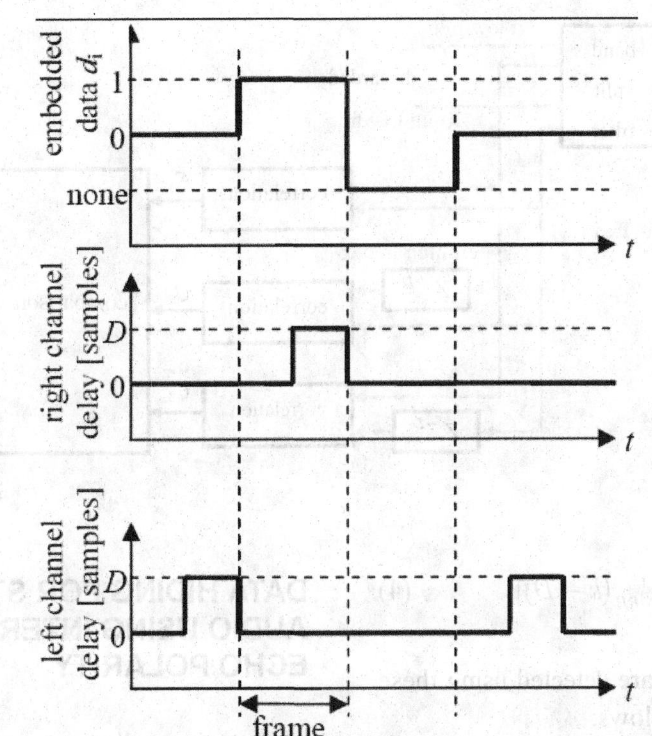

correlation, even for long lags. In these frames, we will not be able to detect delays reliably using correlation. Thus, we added a small amount of band-pass filtered noise as markers to enhance the difference between correlation without delay and with delay. The amount of added noise was empirically chosen to be 10% of the original frame power. However, even with the addition of these markers, some frames still did not display enough correlation difference. Data were not embedded in these rare frames.

The Data Decoding Algorithm

This subsection will describe the embedded data extraction of the interchannel delay stereo method. Figure 3 shows the proposed watermark detection algorithm. This algorithm can be classified as blind detection; it does not require the original source as a reference. The input stereo audio signal with embedded data is first split into subbands using the same band split filter as in the embedding process. The low-frequency components are discarded. The high-frequency components, x'_{LH} and x'_{RH}, are delayed by D samples. Frame boundaries are synchronized. Three normalized correlation values for the latter half of the frame are calculated:

1. Correlation between the left- and right-channel, both with no delay (C_1)

$$C_1 = E[x'_{LH}(k) \bullet x'_{RH}(k)] \quad (2)$$

2. Correlation between the delayed left-channel and right-channel with no delay (C_2)

$$C_2 = E[x'_{LH}(k-D) \bullet x'_{RH}(k)] \quad (3)$$

3. Correlation between the delayed right-channel and left-channel with no delay (C_3)

Figure 3. Detection schematic for the interchannel delay stereo method

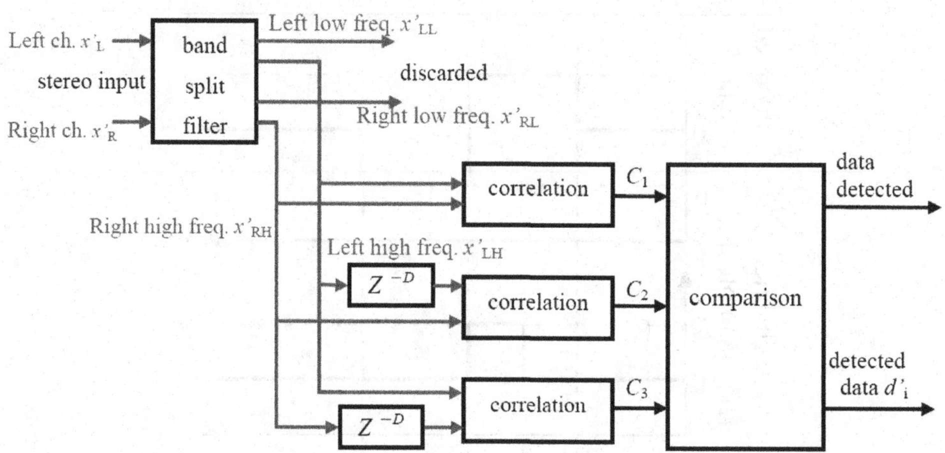

$$C_3 = E[x'_{LH}(k) \bullet x'_{RH}(k-D)] \qquad (4)$$

The embedded data are detected using these correlation values as follows:

1. If the high-frequency energy is below the threshold, we assume that no data has been embedded.
2. If the first correlation (C_1) is the largest of the three, we assume that no data has been embedded.
3. If the second correlation (C_2) is the largest, we detect that a "1" has been embedded.
4. If the third correlation (C_3) is the largest, we detect a "0."

Thus, the detection process is a relatively simple procedure. Frame synchronization may be somewhat expensive, but this process is required only once and does not need to be repeated. Frame synchronization can be established by calculating a sample-by-sample correlation analysis near the embedded sync pattern.

DATA HIDING FOR STEREO AUDIO USING INTERCHANNEL ECHO POLARITY

This section will propose a second stereo audio data-hiding algorithm that adds data-dependent interchannel polarity echoes to the host signal (Kondo, 2011). We shall call this method the reverse-polarity stereo echo method. Similar to the interchannel delay stereo method, the amplitude envelope of the host stereo signals will again be preserved to keep this alteration unperceivable. Our goal is to exploit the characteristics of the HAS and the redundancy of stereo audio signals so that the embedding process is unperceivable while the embedded data are kept relatively robust. Compared to the interchannel delay stereo method, the polarity of the additive echo is altered according to the embedded data. The original signal phase itself is not altered (Kondo, 2011). This improves the embedded audio quality considerably compared to the first method, which showed relatively large degradation due to the alteration of the host signal (shown later in this chapter).

The Data-Embedding Algorithm

This subsection will describe the data-embedding algorithm of the reverse-polarity stereo echo method. In this method, we add fixed-delay echoes with reverse polarity to the stereo channels. The data are embedded as the polarity of the added echoes. Data will be embedded only in the mid- to high-frequency region. Low-frequency signals are kept intact because alterations in this region will have a large impact on audio quality compared to higher-frequency regions. We will calculate the average of both left and right high-frequency channels and use this signal as the mid-channel signal. The interchannel cross-correlation is also adjusted to match the original signal. This is accomplished by adding controlled amounts of echo to the signal. The interchannel cross-correlation is known to influence the stereo image "width" of stationary auditory objects (Breebaart & Faller, 2007). Thus, by preserving the correlation, the stereo image width will also be preserved. The echoes are added to each channel at reverse polarity. The absolute polarity itself is not critical here. Thus, the instantaneous relative polarity of the added echo in both channels can be used to embed data.

Figure 4 shows the proposed data-embedding algorithm. The input stereo signal is first split into two sub-bands using band-split filters. The cut-off of this filter was set at approximately 7% of the full bandwidth. This cut-off frequency roughly equals the threshold at which the Interchannel Level Difference (ILD) dominates the sound localization cue (Breebaart & Faller, 2007). Above this threshold, the level difference tends to control the stereo image and not the phase difference. In all of our experiments, we used CD-quality audio sampled at 44.1 kHz. Thus, the cutoff was approximately 1.5 kHz. We used a 128-tap FIR filter designed using the Hamming window-based FIR filter design method.

The low-frequency band of each channel is not processed. For the high-frequency channels, the interchannel correlation C_{LR} between the high-band left channel signal x_{LH} and the high-band right signal x_{RH} is calculated. C_{LR} is defined as the expectation of the product between x_{LH} and x_{RH}, normalized by the square root of the product of the expectation of x_{LH} and the expectation of x_{RH}. Unlike the interchannel coherence, the phase difference between channels was ignored for simplicity.

Figure 4. Embedding schematic for the reverse-polarity stereo echo method

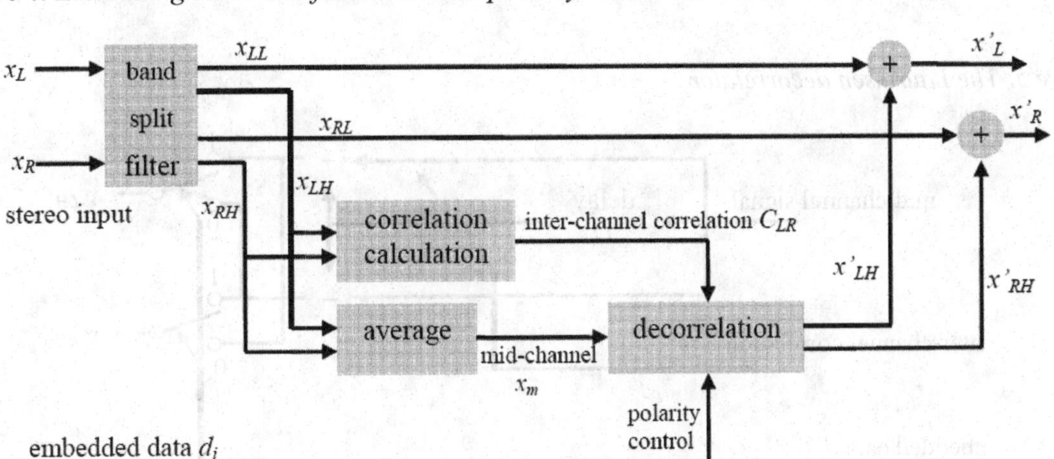

$$C_{LR} = \frac{E\left[x_{LH}x_{RH}\right]}{\sqrt{E\left[x_{LH}x_{LH}\right]E\left[x_{RH}x_{RH}\right]}} = \frac{\sum_{k=1}^{N} x_{LH}(k)x_{RH}(k)}{\sqrt{\left[\sum_{k=1}^{N} x_{LH}(k)x_{LH}(k)\right]\left[\sum_{k=1}^{N} x_{RH}(k)x_{RH}(k)\right]}} \tag{5}$$

Here, N is the number of samples in a frame.

The two high-frequency-band channels are averaged and down-mixed into a single mid-channel signal x_m.

$$x_m(k) = \frac{x_{LH}(k) + x_{RH}(k)}{2} \tag{6}$$

This single mid-channel signal will be decorrelated to match the original interchannel correlation.

Figure 5 shows the Lauridsen decorrelator used to manipulate the interchannel correlation (Breebaart & Faller, 2007). The input signal, i.e., the single mid-channel signal $x_m(k)$, is delayed (D), attenuated (G), and added or subtracted to $x_m(k)$ to obtain the two approximated channel signals x'_{LH} and x'_{RH}.

$$\begin{aligned} x'_{LH}(k) &= x_m(k) \pm G x_m(k-D) \\ x'_{RH}(k) &= x_m(k) \mp G x_m(k-D) \end{aligned} \tag{7}$$

The correlation between x'_{LH} and x'_{RH}, C'_{LR} can be approximated as

$$C'_{LR} = \frac{E\left[x'_{LH}x'_{RH}\right]}{\sqrt{E\left[x'_{LH}x'_{LH}\right]E\left[x'_{RH}x'_{RH}\right]}} = \frac{\sigma_x^2 - G^2\sigma_x^2}{\sqrt{\left\{\sigma_x^2 \pm 2GR_x(D) + G^2\sigma_x^2\right\}\left\{\sigma_x^2 \mp 2GR_x(D) + G^2\sigma_x^2\right\}}} = \frac{\sigma_x^2(1-G^2)}{\sqrt{\left\{\sigma_x^2(1+G^2)\right\}^2 \mp \left\{2GR_x(D)\right\}^2}} \approx \frac{1-G^2}{1+G^2} \tag{8}$$

where σ_x^2 is the variance of the mid-channel signal, and $Rx(D)$ is its autocorrelation estimate of x_m with lag time of D. Thus, the gain G can be used to control C'_{LR}. We can adjust the gain G so that this correlation, $C'_{LR,}$ will match the interchannel correlation of the original signal, C_{LR}. G should be set to the following value in this case:

$$G = \sqrt{\frac{1 - C_{LR}}{1 + C_{LR}}} \tag{9}$$

The polarity of the added/subtracted echo is not present in the definition of the gain factor G or the resulting correlation C'_{LR}. Thus, the echo polarity itself is arbitrary. This obviously means that the polarity can be utilized to embed data into

Figure 5. The Lauridsen decorrelator

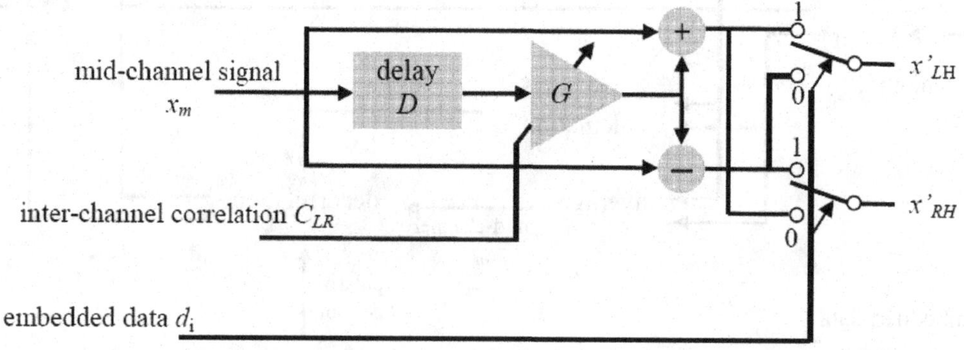

the host audio signal. Arbitrarily, in all experiments, the delayed and attenuated signal will be added to the right channel, and will be subtracted from the left channel when the embedded data d_i is 0, and the polarity will be reversed when the embedded data d_i is 1. That is,

$$x'_{LH}(k) = x_m(k) - Gx_m(k - D) \\ x'_{RH}(k) = x_m(k) + Gx_m(k - D) \tag{10}$$

when $d_i = 0$ and

$$x'_{LH}(k) = x_m(k) + Gx_m(k - D) \\ x'_{RH}(k) = x_m(k) - Gx_m(k - D) \tag{11}$$

when $d_i = 1$.

The delay D of the added echo signal needs to be sufficiently long. The addition/subtraction of delayed samples results in complementary filter characteristics. The longer the delay, the more closely spaced the spectral valleys and peaks of the filter; the peaks and valleys become less noticeable. However, the longer the delay, the more noticeable the echoes become, especially at higher frequencies. Thus, the delay needs to be kept reasonably short. As described in the next subsection, the cross-correlation between the channels will be used in the detection. Thus, the delay needs to be long enough for robust detection because cross-correlation with short lags tends to be significantly large and distinction between the correlation of the original signal and the added echo becomes difficult. However, we found through preliminary experimentation that as long as the delay is within a reasonable range (100 to 1000 samples), the robustness is not critically affected.

The reverse-polarity stereo echo method works well for most of the frames that contain audible sounds. However, some frames did not contain enough high-frequency components to add reliably significant levels of delayed signals. Accordingly, we chose not to embed data in notably low-power frames.

The power threshold was empirically chosen so that the sum-difference correlation $c_{\text{sum,diff}}$ (see Equation 15 in the next subsection) calculated at the decoder for frames above this threshold will be reliable for the majority of frames. For frames below the threshold for which data will not be embedded, the polarities of the added signals were reversed on a sample-by-sample basis to keep the interchannel correlation sufficiently low. For frames with embedded data, the polarity of the added signals was determined frame-by-frame. These polarity conventions will help distinguish frames that do not have data embedded from frames that do because the magnitude of the cross-correlation can be used in these frames with intermediate power levels.

As mentioned before, when the embedded data changes, either from "0" to "1" or vice-versa, the polarity of the added echo changes. Although a short-delay echo fuses with the original signal, thus making the polarity reversal mostly unperceivable, we smoothed the polarity change at the frame boundaries with a linearly varying window just to be safe. The gain value G of the echo also changes from frame to frame according to the interchannel coherence. Thus, changes in the gain were also varied along with the polarity change using a linear window. For example, assuming that the gain value changes from G_i for frame i to G_{i+1} for frame i+1, and the polarity of the added echo changes from addition (positive) for frame i to a subtraction (negative) for frame i+1, the scaling factor of the echo at the frame boundary changes from $+G_i$ to $-G_{i+1}$ linearly. The duration of this smoothing window was experimentally set to 5/16 of the frame length (typically 2000 samples, which amounts to approximately 45 ms at 44.1 kHz sampling).

The Data-Decoding Algorithm

This subsection will describe the embedded data extraction process of the reverse-polarity stereo echo method.

The detection of embedded data is accomplished by first calculating the cross-correlation between the delayed mid-channel component and the added echo signal in each channel. The mid-channel component can be extracted by calculating the sum of both channels, while the added echo component can be calculated by differentiating the channel signals. The sum signal, $\hat{x}_{sum}(k)$ can be given as

$$\begin{aligned}\hat{x}_{sum}(k) &= \hat{x}'_{RH}(k) + \hat{x}'_{LH}(k) \\ &= 2x_{m}(k) + n(k)\end{aligned} \tag{12}$$

where $\hat{x}'_{LH}$ and $\hat{x}'_{RH}$ are the received left and right high frequency channels, and $n(k)$ is the channel noise that may be added during transmission, storage, or even by attacks. The difference signal, $\hat{x}_{diff}(k)$, can be given as

$$\hat{x}_{diff}(k) = \hat{x}'_{RH}(k) - \hat{x}'_{LH}(k) \tag{13}$$

$$= \begin{cases} 2Gx_{m}(k-D) + n(k) & (\text{when } d_i = 0) \\ -2Gx_{m}(k-D) + n(k) & (\text{when } d_i = 1) \end{cases} \tag{14}$$

The sum of the channels can be used as an estimate of the mid-channel, and the difference can be used as an estimate of the added echo. The cross-correlation of the delayed sum and the difference signal, $c_{\text{sum,diff}}$, can be used to extract the polarity of the added echo signal.

$$c_{sum,diff} = E\left[\hat{x}_{sum}(k-D)\cdot\hat{x}_{diff}(k)\right] \tag{15}$$

$$= \begin{cases} 4G{\sigma_x}^2 & (when\, d_i = 0) \\ -4G{\sigma_x}^2 & (when\, d_i = 1) \end{cases} \tag{16}$$

Here we assume that $x_m(k)$ and $n(k)$ are uncorrelated. Thus,

$$E\left[x_m(k)n(k)\right] = 0 \tag{17}$$

The polarity of the cross-correlation can be used directly to detect the embedded data bit. The configuration of this detection process is illustrated in Figure 6.

First, the same band-split filter that was used in the embedding phase splits the incoming stereo signal into low- and high-frequency bands. The low-frequency bands are not used in the detector. From the two high-frequency channels, the sum $\hat{x}_{sum}(k)$ is calculated and delayed by the value used at the decorrelator in the embedding phase. The difference signal, $\hat{x}_{diff}(k)$, is also calculated. Then, the frame-wise cross-correlation of the sum and difference signal, $c_{\text{sum,diff}}$, is calculated. The sign of the correlation is the indicator of the estimated embedded data. If the correlation value is positive, embedded data variable d_i can be assumed to be "0"; if the correlation is negative, d_i can be assumed to be "1."

As stated in the previous subsection, some frames did not have enough power in the high-frequency band to embed data reliably. Thus, for frames with significantly low energy at the detector, we assumed that the frames did not contain embedded data. For frames with slightly larger power, we detected the absolute value of the cross-correlation $c_{\text{sum,diff}}$. If data were not embedded in these frames, the polarity of the added signal is inverted on a sample-by-sample basis and should show significantly lower correlation values. For frames with large enough power, we assumed that data were embedded in these frames. This detection algorithm does not require the original signal and thus is blind detection.

Figure 6. Data detection schematic for the reverse-polarity stereo echo method

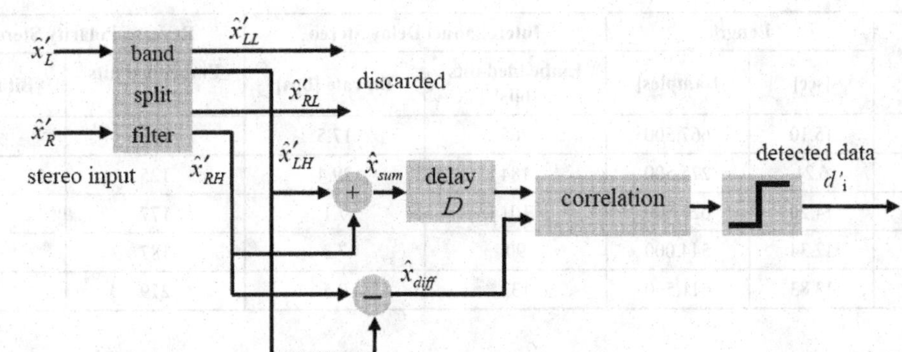

EMBEDDED DATA BIT RATE

We evaluated the two proposed algorithms using the five short stereo audio samples listed in Table 1: one rock instrumental (ABBA) and four classical pieces (Beethoven, Mozart, piano, and trumpet). All sources were CD quality, sampled at 44.1 kHz, stereo, 16 bits/sample. Most sources were selected from the European Broadcasting Union (EBU) Sound Quality Assessment Material (SQAM) audio quality evaluation source CD.

The embedding frame rate was set to 1000 samples, or approximately 23 ms for the interchannel delay stereo method. On the other hand, the frame rate was 2000 samples, or approximately 45 ms, for the reverse-polarity stereo echo method. These frame rates were chosen empirically for robustness.

The embedded number of bits for each source is shown in Table 2. The bit rate is apparently source dependent. It appears possible to embed more data into audio signals with higher energy.

Table 1. Evaluated sound sources

Notation	Description
ABBA	The Visitors (rock instrumental)
Beethoven	Ode to Joy (classics, orchestra & chorus)
Mozart	K. 270 (classics, wind instruments)
piano	Schubert (classics, piano solo)
trumpet	Haydn (classics, orchestra & trumpet solo)

This is most likely because we do not embed data in frames with low amounts of high-frequency energy. In most cases, it was possible to embed more bits with the reverse-polarity stereo echo method compared to the interchannel delay stereo method. The only exception was Beethoven, in which it was possible to embed at almost 30 bps with the interchannel delay stereo method. This embedding rate was by far the highest rate in any of the sources tested using either method. This may be because the selected portion of this clip had high energy, and it was possible to embed bits in almost all frames. On average, it was possible to embed approximately 30% more bits with the reverse-polarity stereo echo method compared to the interchannel delay stereo method over all audio clips tested.

Because the interchannel delay stereo method uses a shorter frame than the reverse-polarity stereo echo method, normally, one would expect that the former would show a higher embedded bit rate. However, this was not the case. This difference in expectation is because a higher energy threshold was necessary for the interchannel delay stereo method to maintain robustness. Many of the frames fell short of this threshold and were not used to embed data. On the other hand, it was possible to use a lower threshold with the reverse-polarity stereo echo method, and the majority of frames were available to embed data.

Table 2. Number of embedded bits and bit rate

Source	Length		Interchannel Delay Stereo		Reverse-Polarity Stereo Echo	
	[sec]	[samples]	Embedded bits [bits]	Bit rate [bps]	Embedded bits [bits]	Bit rate [bps]
ABBA	15.10	667,500	265	17.5	322	21.32
Beethoven	6.21	275,500	184	29.4	125	20.13
Mozart	14.20	627,500	101	7.1	177	12.46
piano	12.34	544,000	90	7.3	187	15.15
trumpet	13.83	611,500	132	9.5	279	20.17

ROBUSTNESS EVALUATION

We first evaluated the robustness of our algorithm against three types of disturbances: additive white Gaussian noise, audio compression, and sample rate conversion. We embedded two bit patterns in our host signals: pattern 1 (**p1**) was a random bit pattern with the same average number of "0s" and "1s," and pattern 2 (**p2**) was an alternating "0" and "1" bit pattern.

Note that for all methods tested, the error rates are for raw embedded data. No error correction or repetition was employed. If a more robust data hiding is required, such as with watermarks that embed copyright data that require the data to be recoverable even after a significant level of attacks, forward error correction (FEC) codes such as the BCH or the Reed-Solomon may be employed.

Because the proposed algorithm can show three error modes (substitution errors, where "0" is replaced with "1" and vice versa; deletion errors, where a data bit is completely dropped; and insertion errors, where a bit is wrongly detected in frames in which data were not embedded), we evaluated bit errors after aligning the detected bit pattern by dynamic programming. We used the *sclite* scoring program from NIST's scoring package, freely available on the net.

We also included two conventional data hiding methods for comparison. The first method uses direct sequence spread-spectrum techniques to spread the data to the entire available frequency range and adds this to the host audio signal after the power of the spread-spectrum data is adjusted to be -20 dB relative to the host signal (to be referred to as *dss* for direct spread spectrum) (He & Scordilis, 2007). Because the *dss* method was not designed to be used on stereo signals, we embedded two separate data streams to each channel signal. The total data rate was set to approximately the same rate as the proposed method (approximately 20 bps).

The second method uses the addition of two different delay echoes to mark the host signal with hidden data (to be referred to as *echo* for echo hiding) (Gruhl, Lu, & Bender, 1996). The echo delays were set to 100 and 150 samples (approximately 2.3 and 3.4 ms at 44.1 kHz). The relative amplitude of the echoes was set at 60% of the original signal. The use of echoes to embed data is similar to both of our proposed methods. However, this method does not exploit stereo redundancy (interchannel correlation) as the proposed methods do. Two separate streams of data were embedded in each channel separately. Still, we were only able to embed data with this method at half the rate of the proposed method because faster rates led to bit errors, even without disturbance.

Robustness to Additive Gaussian White Noise

Figure 7 shows the signal-to-added-noise ratio and the Bit Error Rate (BER) of all sources for the interchannel delay stereo (a), the reverse-polarity stereo echo method (b), the *dss* method (c), and the *echo* method (d) when bit pattern 1 (**p1**) was embedded. For most cases, the BER was relatively low. For the interchannel delay stereo method, there were differences in the BER below 15 dB SNR, but all sources show a BER close to 0% above 20 dB. For the reverse-polarity stereo echo method, the BER was lower than 10% regardless of the SNR except for Mozart and piano. These two clips were the only clips that showed high BERs below 20 dB SNR. Note that added noise larger than 20 dB is quite audible and makes the audio data virtually worthless. The *dss* method is extremely robust to additive noise, and no error was observed. The echo method appears to be affected by additive noise at all SNR levels. In all cases, no significant difference was observed with the embedded bit pattern (pattern 1, **p1**, or pattern 2, **p2**). This result is illustrated in Table 3a for the interchannel delay stereo method and Table 3b for the reverse-polarity stereo echo method.

Figure 7. Bit error rates for random bit pattern (pattern 1) with additive noise

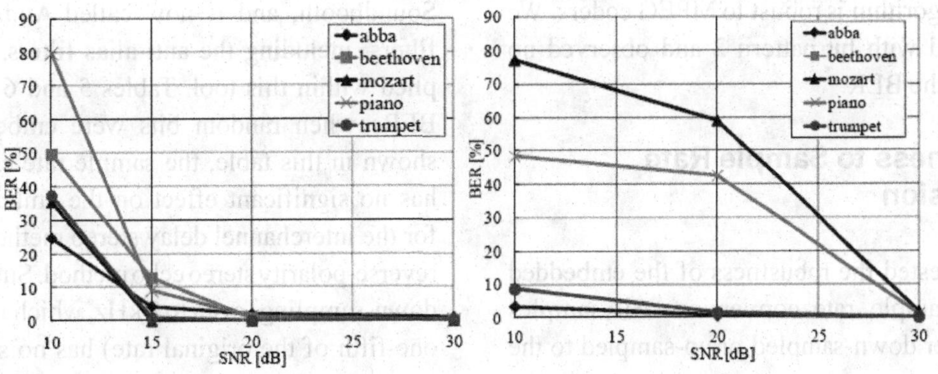

(a) The interchannel delay stereo method

(b) The reverse-polarity stereo echo method

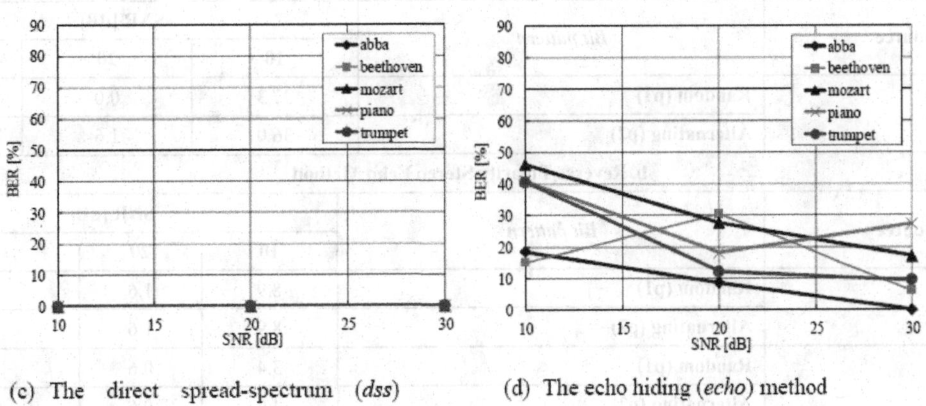

(c) The direct spread-spectrum (*dss*) method

(d) The echo hiding (*echo*) method

Robustness to Audio Coding

We also tested the robustness of the embedded data when coded with MPEG audio codecs. We encoded each source with MPEG 1 Layer 3 (MP3) coding (ISO/IEC JTC1/SC29/WG11 11172-3, 1999) and MPEG 4 AAC codecs (ISO/IEC JTC1/SC29 13818-7, 2006). Lame version 3.98 beta 5 with fixed rates of 96 and 128 kbps with joint stereo coding was used to code sources to MP3 and back to PCM (The LAME Project, 2008). Apple Computer's iTunes version 7.4.3.1 was used to code sources to AAC and back (Apple Inc., 2008). The AAC codec uses the low complexity profile AAC to code sources to fixed bit rates of 96 and 128 kbps. Table 4 shows the BERs when random bits were embedded (pattern 1). In the majority of cases, no bit errors were observed, suggesting that the algorithm is robust to MPEG coders. We also tested with bit pattern 2 and observed no effect on the BER.

Robustness to Sample Rate Conversion

We also tested the robustness of the embedded data to sample rate conversion. All samples were either down-sampled or up-sampled to the specified sample rate f_s and converted back to the original 44.1 kHz. The two selected rates for down-sampling for the interchannel delay stereo method were 22.05 and 8 kHz and 22.05 and 32 kHz for the reverse-polarity stereo echo method, the *dss* method, and the *echo* method. The sample rate of 22.05 kHz is one-half of the original sample rate, and the effective bandwidth is halved. However, this is a simple 2-to-1 decimation. On the other hand, 32 and 8 kHz is not an integer fraction of the original rate, and thus is first up-sampled and then down-sampled, which potentially adds significant degradation into the process. Up-sampling to 48 kHz is also not an integer multiple, and so the same multistage up-sampling and down-sampling is necessary. We used the built-in sample rate conversion in CoolEdit 2000 lite (after being acquired by Adobe, this software was renamed Soundbooth, and is now called Audition). All filters, including the anti-alias filters, were applied within this tool. Tables 5 and 6 show the BERs when random bits were embedded. As shown in this table, the sample rate conversion has no significant effect on the embedded bits for the interchannel delay stereo method and the reverse-polarity stereo echo method. Surprisingly, down-sampling (even to 8 kHz, which is less than one-fifth of the original rate) has no significant

Table 3. BER (%) for additive noise with bit pattern (interchannel delay stereo method)

a. Interchannel Delay Stereo Method				
Source	***Bit pattern***	**SNR [dB]**		
		10	**20**	**30**
trumpet	**Random (p1)**	37.3	0.0	0.0
	Alternating (p2)	36.0	1.6	0.0
b. Reverse-Polarity Stereo Echo Method				
Source	***Bit pattern***	**SNR [dB]**		
		10	**20**	**30**
ABBA	**Random (p1)**	8.9	1.6	0.0
	Alternating (p2)	8.9	1.6	0.0
Beethoven	**Random (p1)**	3.4	0.6	0.0
	Alternating (p2)	4.0	0.6	0.0

Table 4. BER (%) of stereo encoded audio

Source	Interchannel Delay Stereo				Reverse-Polarity Stereo Echo			
	MP3		AAC		MP3		AAC	
	96 kbps	128 kbps	96 kbps	128 kbps	96 kbps	128 kbps	96 kbps	128 kbps
ABBA	1.5	0.4	0.4	0.0	0.3	0.3	0.3	0.3
Beethoven	0.6	0.0	0.0	0.0	0.0	0.0	0.0	0.0
Mozart	0.0	1.0	0.0	0.0	4.5	5.1	5.1	4.5
piano	0.0	1.1	1.1	0.0	1.6	1.6	1.6	1.1
trumpet	0.8	0.0	0.8	0.0	2.2	1.1	1.8	1.4

effect on the BER and shows the significant robustness of both of the proposed algorithms to sample rate conversion. The *dss* method shows large BERs by down-sampling, especially at 22 kHz. The echo method shows modest BERs, but this is source dependent, showing no errors with some sources and numerous errors with others.

EMBEDDED AUDIO QUALITY EVALUATION

The embedding process introduces a small, noticeable alteration in quality for some of the sources, while for others, no degradation was perceived. We conducted the multiple stimulus tests with hidden reference and anchors (MUSHRA) subjective listening tests (ITU BS.1534-1, 2003) to quantify these degradations. We tested the audio clips described above with the proposed data embedding method using the random bit pattern 1 (**p1**) and the "0" and "1" alternating bit pattern 2 (**p2**). Because bit pattern 2 forces polarity inversions in every frame, the impact on the quality is expected to be larger. The delays for the decorrelator used in the reverse-polarity stereo echo method were set to 20% of the frame length.

For comparison, embedded audio with the *dss* method and the echo method were included in the test set. Separate bit sequences were embedded in each channel, and the total bit rate was adjusted to match the bit rates of the proposed methods for *dss*. The bit rate was halved for the echo method.

For reference, we included the original audio clip (**ref**), a 3.5 kHz low-pass-filtered audio clip, as an anchor (**lp35**). We also included the MP3 transcoded audio clips at 128 kbps (**m128**), 96 kbps (**m96**), 64 kbps (**m64**), and 48 kbps (**m48**).

Table 5. BER (%) of sample rate converted audio (proposed methods)

Source	Interchannel Delay			Reverse-Polarity Stereo Echo		
	8 kHz	22 kHz	48 kHz	22 kHz	32 kHz	48 kHz
ABBA	3.1	0.0	0.0	0.0	0.0	0.0
Beethoven	0.0	0.0	0.0	0.0	0.0	0.0
Mozart	1.0	0.0	0.0	5.1	4.5	0.0
piano	1.1	0.0	0.0	1.6	1.6	0.0
trumpet	0.0	0.0	0.0	1.4	1.4	0.4

Table 6. BER (%) of sample rate converted audio (dss and echo)

Source	Direct Spread Spectrum (dss)			Echo Hiding Method (echo)		
	22 kHz	32 kHz	48 kHz	22 kHz	32 kHz	48 kHz
ABBA	33.3	0.0	0.0	0.0	0.0	0.0
Beethoven	29.9	0.0	0.0	0.0	0.0	0.0
Mozart	24.8	1.3	2.0	7.9	6.6	3.9
piano	26.5	0.8	0.0	10.6	10.6	7.6
trumpet	34.2	0.0	12.8	5.4	1.4	5.4

For the interchannel delay stereo samples, twelve subjects, all in their twenties with normal hearing (confirmed with annual audiogram checks), participated in the tests. For the reverse-polarity stereo echo samples, the *dss* samples, and the echo samples, ten subjects were employed. All subjects were requested to rate each processed audio, including the hidden reference on a 100-point scale. 100 to 80 points on this scale was categorized as "excellent," 80 to 60 as "good," 60 to 40 as "fair," 40 to 20 as "bad," and 20 to 0 as "very bad." The subjects rated the processed audio for only one source in a single session. Thus, each subject conducted five sessions, one session per source. The rated scores were averaged for all subjects (ITU, 2003).

As shown in Table 7, the subjective quality of the embedded audio is quite source-dependent. Generally, the embedded quality for the interchannel delay stereo method showed significantly lower quality compared to the reverse-polarity stereo echo method, from 12 to 20 points.

For the interchannel delay stereo method, the embedded audio showed approximately the same quality as the MP3 encoded audio at 64 kbps for **ABBA**. For **piano**, however, the embedded audio showed significantly lower quality than the MP3 encoded audio at any rate. The quality of the other sources falls between these two sources. On average, the embedded quality is equivalent to slightly lower than MP3 coding at 48 kbps. The quality rating for this range of MUSHRA scores (40 to 60) is equivalent to a "fair" rating. Thus, the embedded audio quality is apparently not transparent, but not objectionable either. The audio quality still does need significant improvement for wide application. The embedded quality does not seem to depend on the embedded bit patterns (pattern 1 and pattern 2). This suggests that altering the echo delay does not affect audio quality.

For the reverse-polarity-echo method, in some of the sources the quality of the embedded audio is close to the reference and was graded as "excellent" (**ABBA**, **Beethoven**). With other sources, the embedded quality is approximately equivalent to MP3 encoded audio at 48 kbps (m48) and was graded as "good" (**Mozart**, **trumpet**). In the extreme case (**piano**), the embedded quality was significantly worse and was scored lower than any of the MP3 encoded audio samples. The quality grading for this audio sample was rated as "fair." The overall quality of the embedded audio over all of the sources can be rated as "good," and its quality is between MP3 coding at 48 and 64 kbps.

The embedded bit pattern seems to affect the embedded audio quality for the reverse-polarity stereo echo method. The quality for the random bit pattern (**p1**) was better than the "0" "1" alternating pattern (**p2**) for all sources except **ABBA**, which showed equivalent quality. This was expected because the alternating pattern forces polarity re-

Table 7. Subjective quality of embedded audio samples

Source	Reference (no data embedded)						Interchannel Delay Stereo		Reverse-Polarity Stereo Echo		*dss*	*echo*
	ref	lp35	m48	m64	m96	m128	p1	p2	p1	p2	p1	p1
ABBA	90.08	18.75	38.17	69.58	90.92	70.83	69.42	67.25	81.30	84.60	13.20	84.30
Beethoven	89.92	17.17	43.25	80.58	86.00	94.67	49.58	50.67	87.00	85.10	11.80	92.50
Mozart	78.75	12.25	49.42	77.67	77.67	72.08	42.33	56.08	66.00	52.70	11.00	59.60
piano	79.83	12.92	89.92	75.92	77.83	73.25	41.08	40.08	56.70	45.80	9.60	48.10
trumpet	85.58	27.17	64.50	82.17	86.50	82.50	47.75	52.58	69.80	58.40	12.70	66.90
average	84.83	17.65	57.05	77.18	83.78	78.67	50.03	53.33	72.16	65.32	11.60	70.28

versal of the added echo at every frame boundary. However, this difference is small when averaged over all sources.

Interestingly, the echo method shows relatively high quality, almost equal to the reverse-polarity-echo method. On the other hand, large quality degradation is observed for *dss*. This degradation is due to the additive white noise quality that is inherent with this method.

DISCUSSION

Two similar data-hiding algorithms that embed data by altering the high frequency regions of the host audio signal were proposed in this chapter. The first algorithm, the interchannel stereo method, embeds data by introducing a data-dependent interchannel delay to the high frequency mid-channel signal. The motivation for this algorithm was that if the delay alteration was small, and if the alteration was smoothed out, these alterations should be unperceivable because the HAS is relatively insensitive to phase.

The second algorithm, the reverse-polarity stereo echo method, adds reversed polarity echo to the host signal. The motivation for this algorithm was that if the delay of the echo is small, the echoes are unperceivable. Moreover, by adjusting the level of the echoes, the interchannel correlation can be adjusted to match the original signal and preserve the stereo image size. Parametric stereo coding, which has recently been introduced to the Highly Efficient Advanced AUDIO coding (HE-AAC) standard (Meltzer & Moser, 2006), inspired us in the proposal of this algorithm. The parametric stereo coding assumes that stereo signals can be compressed into a single mid-channel, the Interchannel Level Difference (ILD), the Interchannel Phase Difference (IPD), and the Interchannel Coherence (IC). In the proposed algorithm, because we are embedding in the high-frequency region, IPD does not significantly affect the quality and thus was ignored. It was also found that ILD can be ignored to some extent, and only the IC needs to be preserved to retain the stereo image of the host signal.

The large difference in the embedded audio quality is most likely due to the accuracy of the different methods in preserving the original stereo image. The first method significantly alters the stereo image and thus was rated low for some of the sources. The change in the frame-by-frame delay also appears to degrade overall quality. Note that in the second algorithm, the delay itself is fixed for all frames. Only the polarity is reversed.

Additionally, the embedded data bit rate was found to be higher by approximately 30% on average compared to the second algorithm. This bit rate difference exists because the signal level needs to be significantly high to detect the interchannel delay using correlation with the first algorithm. If the signal level is small, the correlation peak showing the interchannel delay becomes difficult to distinguish from the correlation of the host signal itself, and so we were forced not to embed data in these frames. With the second algorithm, the data are detected by differentiating the stereo channels, which proved to be much more stable than interchannel correlation, enabling us to employ lower threshold levels for detection. These lower thresholds resulted in more frames being available for embedding data.

The robustness, as well as the embedded audio quality, was also compared to two conventional methods. The direct spread spectrum (*dss)* was extremely robust to additive noise but showed a large number of errors with down-sampling. The embedded audio quality was also extremely poor due to the noise-like characteristics of the embedded data. The other tested method, the echo-hiding method (*echo)*, was rated to be "good" in terms of quality but proved to be fragile to all forms of degradations tested in this chapter.

FUTURE RESEARCH DIRECTIONS

As described in this chapter, we have shown that it is possible to transparently embed data by exploiting the interchannel redundancy in stereo audio signals. Both of the proposed algorithms use blind detection. However, if the reference host signal is available, direct correlation can be used with the reference high frequency signals to improve detection robustness. There is no need to change the embedding process. Moreover, we may be able to increase the embedded data bit rate if we employ informed detection by changing the embedding process, perhaps by increasing the frame rate, or by using multiple delay values in the decorrelator. Both of the proposed algorithms also do not have an easy method to distinguish an audio clip with and without embedded data. The algorithms do include a mechanism to detect frames without embedded data for which the energy is relatively small, but this mechanism assumes that all frames with substantial energy have embedded data. Thus, a separate mechanism is needed to determine frames with and without data. Perhaps a preamble with embedded data (a predetermined pattern) that shows which subsequent frames contain embedded data may suffice for some applications.

CONCLUSION

This chapter proposed two algorithms to hide data into stereo audio signals transparently. Both of the proposed audio watermarking algorithms exploit the fact that the auditory system's perception of stereo audio images is not affected by phase in high-frequency regions.

In the first proposed method, the interchannel delay stereo method, the high-frequency stereo signals were replaced with a single average middle channel. Data are encoded into the delays between the channels. The detection of embedded data can be achieved without the original signal, i.e., blind detection. Correlations between the right- and left-channel high-frequency signals, both with and without delay, are compared to detect the signals.

In the second proposed method, the reverse-polarity stereo echo method, the data are embedded using the polarity of the echoes added to the high-frequency channel signals. Because the stereo image perception of the human auditory system is known to be relatively insensitive to phase in high-frequency regions, we used one middle channel for the high frequency band and embedded data as the polarity of reverberations added to each channel. The detection of the embedded data was achieved without the original signal, i.e., blind detection. The correlation between the sum and the difference of the high-frequency channels at the detector was used for detection.

The proposed algorithm showed embedded data bit rates between 7 and 30 bps depending on the host audio signal. The reverse-polarity stereo echo method showed approximately 30% higher data rates overall compared to the interchannel delay echo method. The algorithm was also tested for robustness to additive Gaussian noise, MPEG coding (MPEG 1 Layer 3 and Advanced Audio Coding), and sample rate conversion. Few to no errors were observed for additive noise with SNRs above 20 dB for both algorithms. MPEG 1 layer 3 and MPEG AAC coding also do not seem to cause many errors. The proposed watermarks were also surprisingly robust against sample rate conversion. Overall, the robustness of the two proposed algorithms was comparable.

The subjective quality of the data-embedded audio was shown to be source dependent, with some sources showing equivalent quality with MP3-coded audio, while for others the quality was significantly lower. The subjective audio quality for the interchannel delay stereo method was rated as "fair" or "good" depending on the source, while the quality for the reverse-polarity stereo method was rated as "good" to "excellent." Thus, the overall quality of the embedded audio with the reverse-polarity stereo echo method was higher than the interchannel delay stereo method, although the difference was highly source dependent.

Because many of the digital audio samples distributed on a network will be high quality and multi-channel (perhaps stereo for still some time), algorithms that use multiple-channel redundancy to hide information without degrading quality should gain popularity. It is our hope that our algorithm will become a starting point for future proposals of data-hiding algorithms for high-quality multiple-channel audio.

REFERENCES

Apple Inc. (2008). *iTunes*. Retrieved from http://www.apple.com/itunes/download

Bender, W., Gruhl, D., Morimoto, N., & Lu, A. (1996). Techniques for data hiding. *IBM Systems Journal*, *35*(3-4), 313–336. doi:10.1147/sj.353.0313

Blauert, J. (1997). *Spatial hearing*. Cambridge, MA: The MIT Press.

Breebaart, J., & Faller, C. (2007). *Spatial audio processing*. West Sussex, UK: John Wiley & Sons. doi:10.1002/9780470723494

Cvejic, N., & Seppänen, T. (2008). Introduction to digital audio watermarking. In Cvejic, N., & Seppänen, T. (Eds.), *Digital Audio Watermarking Techniques and Technologies* (pp. 1–10). Hershey, PA: IGI Global.

Digital Signal Processing Committee. (1979). *Programs for digital signal processing*. Piscataway, NJ: IEEE Press.

Dittmann, J., Megias, D., Lang, A., & Herrera-Joancomarti, J. (2006). Theoretical framework for a practical evaluation and comparison of audio watermarking schemes in the triangle of robustness, transparency and capacity. *Lecture Notes in Computer Science*, *4300*, 1–40. doi:10.1007/11926214_1

Elliot, L. L. (1969). Masking of tones before, during, and after brief silent periods in noise. *The Journal of the Acoustical Society of America*, *45*, 1277–1279. doi:10.1121/1.1911600

Gibson, J. D., Berger, T., Lookabaugh, T., Lindberg, D., & Baker, R. L. (1998). *Digital compression for multimedia*. San Francisco, CA: Morgan-Kaufmann.

Gruhl, D. D., Lu, A., & Bender, W. (1996). *Echo hiding*. Paper presented at the 1st International Workshop on Information Hiding. Cambridge, UK.

He, X., Iliev, A. I., & Scordilis, M. S. (2004). *A High capacity watermarking technique for stereo audio*. Paper presented at the IEEE International Conference on Acoustics, Speech & Signal Processing. Montreal, Canada.

He, X., & Scordilis, M. (2007). Spread spectrum for digital audio watermarking. In Cvejic, N., & Seppänen, T. (Eds.), *Digital Audio Watermarking Techniques and Technologies* (pp. 11–49). Hershey, PA: IGI Global. doi:10.4018/978-1-59904-513-9.ch002

Herre, J., Brandenburg, K., & Lederer, D. (1994). *Intensity stereo coding*. Paper presented at the 96th AES Convention. Amsterdam, The Netherlands.

ISO/IEC JTC1/SC29 13818-7. (2006). *Generic coding of moving pictures and associated audio information – Part 7: Advanced audio coding (AAC)*. Retrieved from http://www.mp3-tech.org

ISO/IEC JTC1/SC29/WG11 11172-3. (1999). *Coding of moving pictures and associated audio for digital storage media up to about 1.5 Mbit/s – Part 3: Audio*. Retrieved from http://www.mp3-tech.org

ITU BS. 1534-1. (2003). *Method for the subjective assessment of intermediate quality level of coding systems*. Retrieved from http://www.itu.int

Kondo, K. (2011). A data hiding method for stereo audio signals using interchannel decorrelator polarity inversion. *Journal of the Audio Engineering Society. Audio Engineering Society, 59*(6), 379–395.

Kondo, K., & Nakagawa, K. (2010). A digital watermark for stereo audio signals using variable inter-channel delay in high-frequency bands and its evaluation. *International Journal of Innovative Computing, Information, & Control, 6*(3B), 1209–1220.

Kuo, S. S., Johnston, J. D., Turin, W., & Quackenbush, S. R. (2002). *Covert audio watermarking using perceptually tuned signal independent multiband phase modulation*. Paper presented at the IEEE International Conference on Acoustics, Speech, and Signal Processing. Orlando, FL.

LAME Project. (2008). *LAME aint't an MP3 encoder*. Retrieved from http://lame.sourcforge.net

Lipshitz, S. P., Pocock, M., & Vanderkooy, J. (1982). On the audibility of midrange phase-distortion in audio systems. *Journal of the Audio Engineering Society. Audio Engineering Society, 30*(9), 580–595.

Malik, H. M., Ansari, R., & Khokhar, A. A. (2007). Robust data hiding in audio using allpass filters. *IEEE Transactions on Audio, Speech, and Language Processing, 15*(4), 1296–1304. doi:10.1109/TASL.2007.894509

Megias, D., Herrera-Joancomarti, J., & Minguillon, J. (2004). *An audio watermarking scheme robust against stereo attacks*. Paper presented at the ASM Multimedia and Security Workshop. Magdeburg, Germany.

Meltzer, S., & Moser, G. (2006). MPEG-4 HE-AAC v2 – Audio coding for today's digital media world. *EBU Technical Review*. Retrieved Sept. 2011 from http://tech.ebu.ch/docs/techreview/trev_305-moser.pdf

Modegi, T. (2006). *Nearly lossless audio watermark embedding techniques to be extracted contactlessly by cell phone*. Paper presented at the IEEE International Conference on Mobile Data Management. Nara, Japan.

Nishimura, R., Suzuki, M., & Suzuki, Y. (2001). *Detection threshold of a periodic phase shift in music sound*. Paper presented at the International Congress on Acoustics. Rome, Italy.

Nishimura, R., & Suzuki, Y. (2004). Audio watermark based on periodical phase shift. *Journal of the Acoustical Society of Japan, 60*(5), 268–272.

Nishimura, R., Suzuki, Y., & Ko, B. S. (2008). Advanced audio watermarking based on echo hiding: Time-spread echo hiding. In Cvejic, N., & Seppänen, T. (Eds.), *Digital Audio Watermarking Techniques and Technologies* (pp. 123–151). Hershey, PA: IGI Global.

Takahashi, A., Nishimura, R., & Suzuki, Y. (2005). Multiple watermarks for stereo audio signals using phase-modulation techniques. *IEEE Transactions on Signal Processing, 53*(2), 806–815. doi:10.1109/TSP.2004.839901

Wu, W. C., & Chen, O. (2008). Analysis-by-synthesis echo watermarking. In Cvejic, N., & Seppänen, T. (Eds.), *Digital Audio Watermarking Techniques and Technologies* (pp. 152–171). Hershey, PA: IGI Global.

Zurek, P. M. (1987). The precedence effect. In Yost, W. A., & Gourevitch, G. (Eds.), *Directional Hearing* (pp. 85–105). New York, NY: Springer-Verlag. doi:10.1007/978-1-4612-4738-8_4

Zwicker, E. (1982). *Psychoakustik*. Heidelberg, Germany: Springer-Verlag. doi:10.1007/978-3-642-68510-1

ADDITIONAL READING

Baras, C., & Moreau, N. (2006). Controlling the inaudibility and maximizing the robustness in an audio annotation watermarking system. *IEEE Transactions on Audio, Speech, and Signal Processing*, *14*(5), 1772–1782. doi:10.1109/TASL.2006.879808

Boney, L., Tewfik, A. H., & Hamdy, K. N. (1996). *Digital watermarks for audio signals.* Paper presented at the IEEE International Conference on Multimedia Computing and Systems. Hiroshima, Japan.

Bosi, M., & Goldberg, R. E. (2003). *Introduction to digital audio coding and standards*. Boston, MA: Kluwer Academic Publishers. doi:10.1007/978-1-4615-0327-9

Breebaart, J., van de Par, S., Kohlrausch, A., & Schuijers, E. (2005). Parametric coding of stereo audio. *EURASIP Journal on Applied Signal Processing*, *9*, 1305–1322. doi:10.1155/ASP.2005.1305

Chen, B., & Wornell, G. W. (2000). *Quantization index modulation: A class of provably good methods for digital watermarking and information embedding*. Paper presented at the IEEE International Symposium on Information Theory. Sorrento, Italy.

Craver, S. A., Wu, M., Liu, B., Stubblefield, A., Swartzlander, B., & Wallach, D. S. … Felten, E. W. (2001). *Reading between the lines: Lessons from the SDMI challenge*. Paper presented at the 10th USENIX Security Symposium. Washington, DC.

Cvejic, N., & Seppänen, T. (Eds.). (2008). *Digital audio watermarking techniques and technologies*. Hershey, PA: IGI Global.

Cvejic, N., & Tujkovic, I. (2004). *Increasing robustness of patchwork audio watermarking algorithm using attack characterization.* Paper presented at the IEEE International Symposium on Consumer Electronics. Reading, UK.

Deller, J. R. Jr, Proakis, J. G., & Hansen, J. H. (1993). *Discrete-time processing of speech signals*. New York, NY: Macmillan Publishing Company.

Faller, C., & Baumgarte, F. (2002). *Binaural cue coding: A novel and efficient representation of spatial audio.* Paper presented at the International Conference on Acoustics, Speech, and Signal Processing. Orlando, FL.

Fujimoto, R., Iwaki, M., & Kiryu, T. (2006). *A method of high bit-rate data hiding in music using spline interpolation*. Paper presented at the International Conference on Intelligent Information Hiding and Multimedia Signal Processing. Pasadena, CA.

Gruhl, D., Lu, A., & Bender, W. (1996). Echo hiding. *Lecture Notes in Computer Science*, *1174*, 295–315. doi:10.1007/3-540-61996-8_48

He, X., & Scordilis, M. (2008). Spread spectrum for digital audio watermarking. In Cvejic, N., & Seppänen, T. (Eds.), *Digital Audio Watermarking Techniques and Technologies* (pp. 11–49). Hershey, PA: IGI Global.

Hiratsuka, K., Kondo, K., & Nakagawa, K. (2008). *On the accuracy of estimated synchronization positions for audio digital watermarks using the modified patchwork algorithm on analog channels*. Paper presented at the International Conference on Intelligent Information Hiding and Multimedia Signal Processing. Harbin, China.

Huang, J.-W., Gu, L.-M., & Shi, Y.-Q. (2005). Robustness of watermarking: Is error correcting coding effective? *Acta Automatica Sinica, 31*(5), 683–692.

Kirovski, D., & Malvar, H. S. (2003). Spread-spectrum watermarking of audio signals. *IEEE Transactions on Signal Processing, 51*(4), 1020–1033. doi:10.1109/TSP.2003.809384

Kondo, K. (2009). *A data hiding method for stereo audio signals using the polarity of the inter-channel decorrelator*. Paper presented at the International Conference on Intelligent Information Hiding and Multimedia Signal Processing. Kyoto, Japan.

Kondo, K. (2010). *Evaluation of a stereo audio data hiding method using inter-channel decorrelator polarity*. Paper presented at the IEEE International Conference on Acoustics, Speech and Signal Processing. Dallas, TX.

Kondo, K., & Nakagawa, K. (2008a). Simple watermark for stereo audio signals with modulated high-frequency band delay. *Acoustical Science and Technology, 29*(6), 384–387. doi:10.1250/ast.29.384

Kondo, K., & Nakagawa, K. (2008b). *A digital watermark for stereo audio signals using variable interchannel delay in high frequency bands*. Paper presented at the International Conference on Intelligent Information Hiding and Multimedia Signal Processing. Harbin, China.

Lang, A., & Dittmann, J. (2006). *Profiles for evaluation – The usage of audio wet*. Paper presented at the SPIE Security, Steganography and Watermarking of Multimedia Contents VIII. San Jose, CA.

Lubacz, J., Mazurczk, W., & Szczypiorski, K. (2010). Voice over IP. *IEEE Spectrum, 47*(2), 42–47. doi:10.1109/MSPEC.2010.5397787

Marrakchi-Mezghani, I., Alouane, M. T.-H., Djaziri-Larbi, S., Jaidane-Saidane, M., & Mahe, G. (2006). *Speech processing in the watermarked domain: Application in adaptive acoustic echo cancellation*. Paper presented at the 14th European Signal Processing Conference. Florence, Italy.

Mintzer, F., & Braudaway, G. W. (1999). *If one watermark is good, are more better?* Paper presented at the IEEE International Conference on Acoustics, Speech, and Signal Processing. Phoenix, AZ.

Nishimura, A. (2006). *Audio watermarking based on sinusoidal amplitude modulation*. Paper presented at the IEEE International Conference on Acoustics, Speech, and Signal Processing. Toulouse, France.

Nishimura, A. (2010a). Audio data hiding that is robust with respect to aerial transmission and speech codecs. *International Journal of Innovative Computing, Information, & Control, 6*(3B), 1389–1400.

Nishimura, A. (2010b). *Aerial acoustic modem with decoding capabilities using a CELP-based speech encoder*. Paper presented at the International Conference on Intelligent Information Hiding and Multimedia Signal Processing. Darmstadt, Germany.

Nishimura, A. (2011). *Reversible audio data hiding using linear prediction and error expansion.* Paper presented at the International Conference on Intelligent Information Hiding and Multimedia Signal Processing. Dalian, China.

Nishimura, R. (2009). *Information hiding into interaural phase difference for stereo audio signals.* Paper presented at the International Conference on Intelligent Information Hiding and Multimedia Signal Processing. Kyoto, Japan.

Nishimura, R. (2010). *Audio information hiding based on spatial masking.* Paper presented at the International Conference on Intelligent Information Hiding and Multimedia Signal Processing. Darmstadt, Germany.

Steinbach, M., Petitcolas, F. A. P., Dittmann, J., Fates, N., Fontaine, C., Raynal, F., & Seibel, C. (2001). *Stirmark benchmark: Audio watermarking attacks.* Paper presented at the International Symposium on Information Technology. Las Vegas, NV.

Suzuki, Y., Nishimura, R., & Tao, H. (2006). *Audio watermark enhanced by LDPC coding for air transmission.* Paper presented at the International Conference on Intelligent Information Hiding and Multimedia Signal Processing. Pasadena, CA.

Swanson, M. D., Zhu, B., Tewfik, A. H., & Boney, L. (1998). Robust audio watermarking using perceptual masking. *Signal Processing, 66*(3), 337–355. doi:10.1016/S0165-1684(98)00014-0

Tachibana, R. (2004). Sonic watermarking. *EURASIP Journal on Applied Signal Processing, 13*, 1955–1964. doi:10.1155/S1110865704403138

Unoki, M., & Hamada, D. (2010). Method of digital.-audio watermarking based on cochlear delay characteristics. *International Journal of Innovative Computing, Information, & Control, 6*(3B), 1349–1346.

Unoki, M., & Miyauchi, R. (2011). *Reversible watermarking for digital-audio based on cochlear delay characteristics.* Paper presented at the International Conference on Intelligent Information Hiding and Multimedia Signal Processing. Dalian, China.

van der Waal, R. G., & Veldhuis, R. N. J. (1991). *Subband coding of stereophonic digital audio signals.* Paper presented at the IEEE International Conference on Acoustics, Speech, and Signal Processing. Toronto, Canada.

Wong, W. C., Steele, R., & Xydeas, C. S. (1982). Transmitting data on the phase of speech signals. *The Bell System Technical Journal, 61*(19), 2970–2987.

Yeo, I.-K., & Kim, H. J. (2001). *Modified patchwork algorithm: A novel audio watermarking scheme.* Paper presented at the International Symposium on Information Technology. Las Vegas, NV.

KEY TERMS AND DEFINITIONS

Advanced Audio Coding (AAC): Lossy compression standard for MPEG 2 and 4 which is generally considered to be much more efficient compared to the MP3 standard. Default coder used for Apple Computer's iPods and iPhones.

Decorrelation: A process to alter the cross-correlation between sets of signals, for example between left and right channels of a stereo signal.

Interarual Coherence (IC): The degree of similarity (normalized interaural cross-correlation) between left and right ear entrance.

Interaural Level Difference (ILD): The level difference between left and right ear signal.

Interaural Time Difference (ITD): The time difference between left and right ear signal.

MPEG 1 Audio Coding Layer 3 (MP3): A lossy audio compression that adaptively assigns adaptive number of bits to each frequency band according to the estimated masking threshold.

Parametric Stereo: An efficient stereo coding method for the Advanced Audio Coding (AAC) standard. Parametric stereo coding attempts to code stereo signals using a mixed-down mono signal and an inter-channel coherence term as side information. Part of the MPEG 4 Audio standard.

Stereo Signals: Also called stereophonic sound or signals. Refers to any method of sound reproduction to create an illusion of directionality and perspective. Usually two or more independent audio channels are used to create this illusion.

Chapter 7
Advanced Information Hiding for G.711 Telephone Speech

Akinori Ito
Tohoku University, Japan

Yôiti Suzuki
Tohoku University, Japan

ABSTRACT

G.711 is the most popular speech codec for Voice over IP (VoIP). This chapter proposes a method for embedding data into G.711-coded speech for conveying side information for enhancing speech quality such as bandwidth extension or packet loss concealment. The proposed method refers to a low-bit rate encoder to determine how many bits are embedded into each sample. First, a variable-bit rate data hiding method is proposed as a basic framework of the proposed method. Then, the proposed method is extended to achieve fixed bit rate data hiding. According to comparison experiments, the proposed method is proved to achieve higher speech quality compared with the conventional method. Moreover, the authors developed a low-complexity speech bandwidth extension method that uses the proposed data hiding method.

INTRODUCTION

Voice over Internet Protocol (VoIP) technology has been extensively used as a new infrastructure of the public phone network (Varshney, et al., 2002). Although several codecs are available for VoIP, G.711 (ITU, 1988), the simplest codec, is the most common one at present and is expected to remain so for the immediate future.

G.711 uses 64 kbit/s for conveying telephone-quality speech. Although its quality is enough to convey linguistic information, its quality is much lower than so-called wideband speech. Besides, as VoIP uses a connectionless communication channel such as Real-time Transport Protocol (RTP) (Schulzrinne, et al., 2003), the packet losses are not recovered by the transport protocol, therefore further degradation of speech is inevitable.

There have been several attempts to enhance G.711-coded speech, for both packet loss concealment (Komaki, et al., 2003) and bandwidth expansion (Aoki, 2006; Larsen & Aarts, 2004;

DOI: 10.4018/978-1-4666-2217-3.ch007

Vary & Geiser, 2007; Kataoka, et al., 2008). Packet loss concealment reduces the degradation of speech that is specific to IP-based communication (Perkins, et al., 1998), whereas bandwidth expansion provides users with a value-added speech communication experience. These enhancement methods require side information to the speech data coded by the G.711 codec. As the bit rate of the additional data is not very high, adding more side information to the original speech data is not a major problem in terms of bit rate. The problem with the additional side information is how to convey the side information with the speech itself. If we simply add the side information to the original speech data, we have to remodel the existing data format or communication protocol, but using one's own data format or protocol prevents communication with most terminals that can handle only the standard protocols. Therefore, it is desirable that the speech data containing the additional data for enhancement is downward compatible with ordinary speech data coded by G.711.

An approach based on data hiding solves this problem. Data hiding is a technique to embed certain data into the original media data (or host signal) such as image, video, and speech, without significantly degrading the quality of the original media data (Petitcolas, et al., 1999).

Data hiding has been usually used for steganography and watermarking. Steganography is a method of secret communication, where the existence of a communication channel is kept secret. If data hiding is applied to steganography, the embedded information is regarded as more important than the host signal and so must be kept secret. Watermarking is a method to embed secret information into media data to keep track of the distribution of that data, and its most common purpose is copyright protection. If data hiding is applied to watermarking, the embedded information must be kept secret and degradation of the host signal should be imperceptible. Moreover, in these applications, the embedding methods must be robust against attacks.

Conversely, in the present study, data hiding is used to embed side information for enhancing the host signal and is hidden for the sake of compatibility. Thus, the embedded information need not be kept secret. In addition, we do not need to consider any attack on the hidden data in this case because the VoIP data are transmitted digitally. On the other hand, a data hiding method for compatibility should embed much data compared with a data hiding for steganography or watermarking, while keeping the quality of the host signal high.

Several data hiding methods have been developed with the aim of enhancing of multimedia data with backward compatibility. Marvel et al. (1999) proposed a spread spectrum image steganography, which is the very first work for using spread spectrum technique for data hiding. They pointed out that the steganography technique can be used to convey additional information such as in-band captioning. Yilmaz and Alatan (2003) proposed a method for using data hiding to carry side information for error concealment of video stream. Moreover, Smith et al. (2005) proposed a method to embed sensor data to RFID time series, which enables to create a new communication channel without changing a protocol. As our target is an audio signal, especially speech signal for VoIP, we are now studying other data hiding methods for VoIP. Several methods for hiding data in VoIP based on G.711 have been developed. For example, Aoki proposed a data-hiding-based speech enhancement approach for the G.711 codec (Aoki, 2007), based on LSB substitution for packet loss concealment and bandwidth expansion. Although this approach degrades the speech quality, it can be used for any protocol. Similar approach was also proposed by Vary and Geiser (2007), Tian et al. (2009), and Mazurczyk and Lubacz (2010).

In this chapter, we propose a novel data hiding method for G.711-coded speech. Our approach is similar to Aoki's method but with superior performance; our method can embed more data into the speech with less degradation. In addition, we propose a new frequency band extension method that can be used with the proposed data hiding method.

LSB SUBSTITUTION FOR G.711-CODED SPEECH

Basics of G.711 Codec

G.711 (ITU, 1988) is a kind of nonlinear Pulse Code Modulation (PCM) codec, where a speech signal up to 3.4 kHz wide is coded at 64 kbit/s. The input speech is sampled at the rate of 8 kHz, and each sample is quantized into usually eight bits (sometimes seven bits) using nonlinear quantization. Since G.711 coding is also used in the existing digital phone network, it is easy to communicate between the existing (non-IP) phone network and a G.711-based VoIP network without any transcoding.

Let us briefly explain how G.711 encodes and decodes the input speech. Let o_i be the i-th sample of the input speech, linearly quantized into 14 bits. Let $f(o)$ and $g(x)$ be nonlinear functions for encoding and decoding a speech sample, respectively. Then, encoding and decoding of speech is like this:

$$x_i = f(o_i) \tag{1}$$

$$\hat{o}_i = g(x_i) \tag{2}$$

In G.711, two kinds of nonlinear functions are applied: the μ-law and the A-law. Although we apply the μ-law in this chapter, the proposed framework can also be applied to the A-law. The nonlinear functions of the μ-law are as follows.

$$f(o) = \mathrm{sgn}(o)\left\lfloor x_{\max}\frac{\ln\left(1+\mu\frac{|o|}{o_{\max}}\right)}{\ln(1+\mu)}\right\rfloor \tag{3}$$

$$g(x) = \mathrm{sgn}(x)\left\lfloor o_{\max}\frac{(1+\mu)^{\frac{|x|}{x_{\max}}}-1}{\mu}\right\rfloor \tag{4}$$

where

$\mu = 255,\ x_{\max} = 2^7,\ o_{\max} = 2^{13},$

$-o_{\max} \le o < o_{\max}$

and

$-x_{\max} \le x < x_{\max}.$

Note that $g(x)$ is a monotonically increasing function, i.e. $g(a) \le g(b)$ whenever $a \le b$.

Information Hiding Based on LSB Substitution

In this section, we briefly explain the conventional data hiding method based on LSB substitution. LSB substitution (Latzenbeisser, 2000) is the simplest method for embedding information into speech data.

Let $x_1,\ldots,x_n$ be a sequence of scalar values, where x_i is encoded into M bits. Let $b_1,\ldots,b_n$ be the data we want to embed, where $b_i \in \{0,1\}$. Let $m(x)$ be a bitmask function, which clears the least significant bit (LSB) of x, defined as follows.

$$m(x) = x - (x \bmod 2) \tag{5}$$

Here, mod is a modulo operator defined as

$$a \bmod b = a - \left\lfloor \frac{a}{b} \right\rfloor b \quad (6)$$

where a is an integer and b is a natural number.

If M is sufficiently large, we can expect that there is no big difference between x and $m(x)$. Therefore, we can use the LSB of x_i as the payload for embedding information. Now let y_i be

$$y_i = m(x_i) + b_i . \quad (7)$$

Then we can use the data $y_1, \ldots, y_n$ as new data where the information $b_1, \ldots, b_n$ is embedded. The embedded information b_i can be recovered by

$$b_i = y_i - m(y_i) . \quad (8)$$

One problem of applying the simple LSB substitution method to G.711-coded speech is that distortion of the decoded speech depends on the magnitude of the input speech. When linear quantization is applied, it is ensured that $0 \le (x_i - y_i)^2 \le 1$ for any x_i. On the other hand, when a nonlinear quantization method such as G.711 is applied, the distortion of a decoded sample is calculated as

$$\varepsilon_i^2 = (g(x_i) - g(y_i))^2 . \quad (9)$$

which depends on the magnitude of x_i. When x_i is large, we obtain larger ε_i^2. Figure 1 shows the relationship between $|x_i|$ and the upper bound of ε_i. Therefore, when the magnitude of the signal is large, the distortion audibly degrades the sound quality of the embedded speech signal.

Conventional Data Hiding Methods for G.711

To improve the quality of embedded speech, Aoki (2007) invented a selective embedding method, which embeds a fixed number of information for samples that have small magnitudes. In this chapter, we shall refer to this method as the "selective LSB substitution method."

Figure 1. Absolute value of G.711 codeword (μ-law) and the upper bound of absolute error

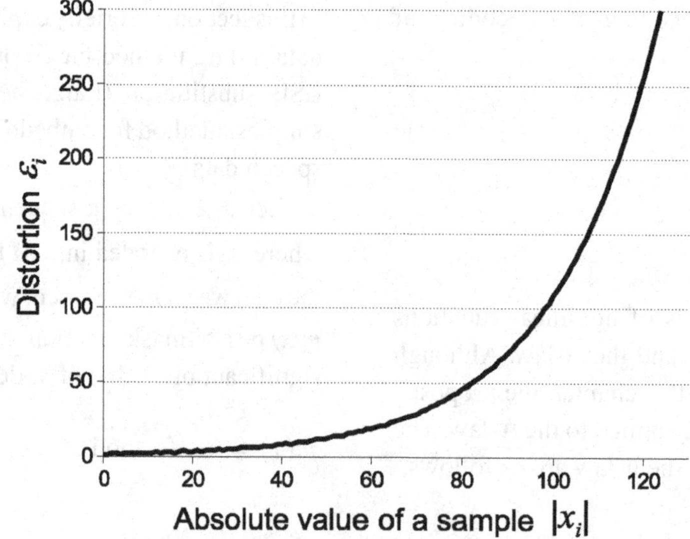

Consider embedding K bits of information into a packet with N samples $(K \leq N)$. The basic idea is to embed only K bits of information into samples that have small magnitude.

Let $i_1, i_2, \ldots, i_N$ be a permutation of 1, 2,..., N such that

$$| m(x_{i_1}) | \leq | m(x_{i_2}) | \leq \cdots \leq | m(x_{i_N}) |. \quad (10)$$

Here, $i_j < i_{j+1}$ when $m(x_{i_j}) = m(x_{i_{j+1}})$. We can determine i_j the following procedure.

1. Clear all LSBs of $x_1, \ldots, x_N$.
2. Sort them in ascending order of their absolute values. Let them be $x'_1, \ldots, x'_N$.
3. For $j = 1, \ldots, N$ perform 4. and 5.
4. Set i_j to the value i so that i be the smallest number such that $x_i = x'_j$ and x_i is not marked.
5. Set mark to x_i.

Then we calculate the embedded signal y_i such that

$$y_{i_j} = \begin{cases} m(x_{i_j}) + b_j & \text{if } j \leq k \\ x_{i_j} & \text{otherwise} \end{cases} \quad (11)$$

By using samples with smaller magnitude for embedding, this method minimizes the total distortion of the embedded signal. Moreover, the bit rates of the embedded data can be controlled up to 8 kbit/s (i.e. the bit rate of LSB) by changing K in balance with the speech quality.

Although the selective LSB substitution method can reduce total distortion of the embedded signal when $K<N$, it has a problem; the selective LSB substitution method (and the original LSB substitution) only uses the least significant one bit for embedding. We could use more than one bit, i.e. multiple lower significant bits including LSB, if subjective degradation is small.

Wu and Yang (2006) proposed a method for embedding multiple bits into G.711-coded speech. The basic idea of their method is similar to the selective LSB substitution method, where the data should be embedded into those samples that have small absolute values. In addition, their method takes total power of a frame into account, where they embed less information when a frame has large power. Although they proposed a formula for determining the number of bits for embedding, the method is ad hoc and they gave no explanation why they employed that formula. We believe that an embedding method has to be optimum in some sense to guarantee the processed signal has the maximum quality.

ENHANCEMENT OF LSB SUBSTITUTION BASED ON ESTIMATION OF TOLERABLE DISTORTION

Scheme for Embedding

We propose a novel data-hiding algorithm that is based on estimation of tolerable distortion. Here, "tolerable" means that the degradation of the signal is assured to be better than some limit of subjective quality. Figure 2 shows a general schematic diagram of the proposed method.

To judge the limit of subjective quality, we propose employing another encoder as a reference, which encodes the input speech at less than 64 kbit/s by taking human hearing characteristics into account.

Let $m_j^-(x)$ and $m_j^+(x)$ be bitmask functions defined as follows:

$$m_j^-(x) = x - (x \bmod 2^j) \quad (12)$$

Figure 2. Overview of embedding part of the proposed method

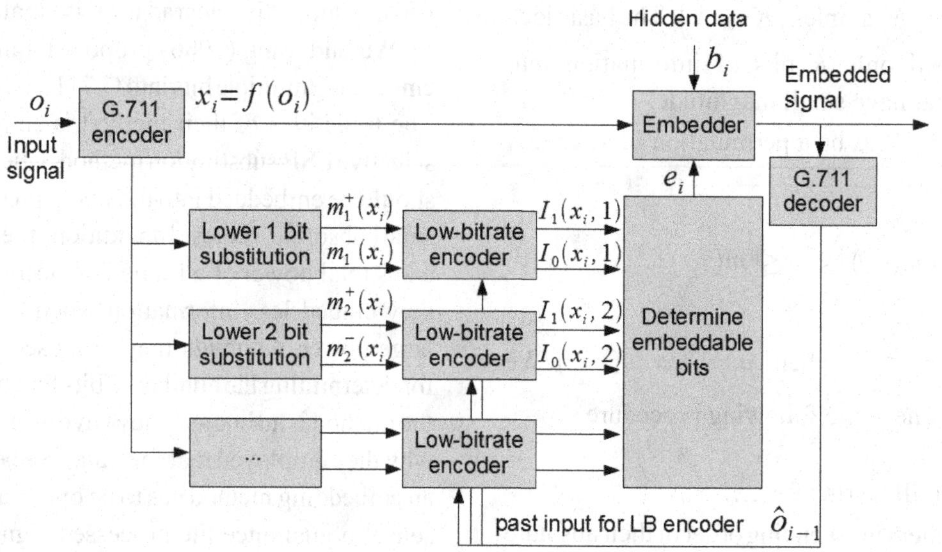

$$m_j^+(x) = m_j^-(x) + 2^j - 1 \tag{13}$$

Here, $m_j^-(x)$ is a function that clears the lowest *j* bits of *x*, and $m_j^+(x)$ is a function that sets the lowest *j* bits of *x*. Here are the basic properties of these functions:

$$m_0^-(x) = m_0^+(x) \tag{14}$$

$$m_j^-(x) < m_j^+(x) \text{ when } j > 0 \tag{15}$$

$$m_j^-(x) \geq m_k^-(x) \text{ when } j \leq k \tag{16}$$

$$m_j^+(x) \leq m_k^+(x) \text{ when } j \leq k \tag{17}$$

$$m_j^-(x) = m_j^-(x+a) \text{ and } m_j^+(x) = m_j^+(x+a) \text{ when } 0 \leq a < 2^j \tag{18}$$

$$m_j^-(m_j^-(x)) = m_j^-(x) \text{ and } m_j^-(m_j^+(x)) = m_j^-(x) \tag{19}$$

$$m_j^+(m_j^-(x)) = m_j^+(x) \text{ and } m_j^+(m_j^+(x)) = m_j^+(x) \tag{20}$$

Next, let $I(o_i \mid o_1, \ldots, o_{i-1})$ be an output of the *i*-th sample using a low-bit rate encoder, given the past input $o_1, \ldots, o_{i-1}$. Here, we make the following assumptions on the low-bit rate encoder:

1. The encoder encodes the input speech sample-by-sample, not considering the past input. Therefore, a frame-based encoder like CELP cannot be applied in our framework.
2. The value of a codeword by the encoder monotonically increases with respect to the original sample value, i.e.:

$$I(a \mid \ldots, o_{i-1}) \leq I(b \mid \ldots, o_{i-1}) \text{ when } a < b \tag{21}$$

Generally speaking, an existing low-bit rate encoder is designed to maximize subjective quality. Therefore, if we determine the number of bits for embedding considering the output of a low-bit rate encoder, we can ensure that the quality of the embedded speech is better than or equals to that by the low-bit rate encoder.

According to this idea, we determine the number of embeddable bits e_i as follows. First, let $\hat{o}_k$ be the k-th speech sample decoded from the data-embedded speech sample, i.e.:

$$\hat{o}_k = g(y_k) \tag{22}$$

Here, y_k is the G.711-coded signal where e_k bits of hidden data are embedded into its LSBs. Next, we define $I_0(i, j)$ and $I_1(i, j)$ as follows:

$$I_0(i, j) = I(g(m_j^-(x_i)) \mid \hat{o}_1, \ldots, \hat{o}_{i-1}) \tag{23}$$

$$I_1(i, j) = I(g(m_j^+(x_i)) \mid \hat{o}_1, \ldots, \hat{o}_{i-1}) \tag{24}$$

Here, $I_0(i, j)$ is the i-th output of the low-bit rate encoder when the least j bits of x_i are cleared, and $I_1(i, j)$ is that when the least j bits are set. Then we define e_i as

$$e_i = \max\{j \mid I_0(i, j) = I_1(i, j)\} \tag{25}$$

Here, e_i is the maximum number of bits where $I_0(i, e_i)$ and $I_1(i, e_i)$ become identical. Now we embed the hidden information b_i $(0 \le b_i < 2^{e_i})$ as follows:

$$y_i = m_{e_i}^-(x_i) + b_i \tag{26}$$

As $m_{e_i}^-(x_i) \le y_i \le m_{e_i}^+(x_i)$, it is guaranteed that

$$I_0(i, e_i) = I_1(i, e_i) = I(g(y_i) \mid \hat{o}_1, \ldots, \hat{o}_{i-1}) \tag{27}$$

and therefore the embedded information b_i does not affect the output of the low-bit rate encoder, which means that the quality of the decoded signal from y_i is better than or, at least, equals to that using the low-bit rate encoder. The overall procedure of embedding is shown in Figure 3. Note that Equations 23 and 24 depend on $e_1, \ldots, e_{i-1}$ because they affects the value of $y_1, \ldots, y_{i-1}$, and thus $\hat{o}_1, \ldots, \hat{o}_{i-1}$. This means that we have to determine $e_1, \ldots, e_{i-1}$ and e_i in order.

Figure 3. Procedure for embedding

```
for i ← 1 to n
  j ← 0
  do
    j ← j + 1
    I0(i, j) ← I(g(m_j^-(x_i))|ô1, ..., ô_{i-1})
    I1(i, j) ← I(g(m_j^+(x_i))|ô1, ..., ô_{i-1})
  while I0(i, j) = I1(i, j) and j < 8
  e_i ← j − 1
  y_i ← x_i with embedded data into the least e_i bits
  ô_i ← g(y_i)
end for
```

Scheme for Extraction

On extracting the embedded information from the signal, we only have $y_1, \ldots, y_i$ for determining e_i. Figure 4 shows the block diagram of the extractor. Let us define

$$I_0'(i,j) = I(g(m_j^-(y_i)) \mid \hat{o}_1, \ldots \hat{o}_{i-1}) \tag{28}$$

and

$$I_1'(i,j) = I(g(m_j^+(y_i)) \mid \hat{o}_1, \ldots \hat{o}_{i-1}) \tag{29}$$

When $j \le e_i$, it is guaranteed that

$$I_0'(i,j) = I_1'(i,j) \tag{30}$$

because, $I_0(i,e_i) = I_1(i,e_i)$ and

$$m_{e_i}^-(y_i) \le m_j^-(y_i) \le m_j^+(y_i) \le m_{e_i}^+(y_i) \tag{31}$$

$$\begin{aligned} m_{e_i}^-(y_i) &= m_{e_i}^-(m_{e_i}^-(x_i) + b_i) \\ &= m_{e_i}^-(m_{e_i}^-(x_i)) = m_{e_i}^-(x_i) \end{aligned} \tag{32}$$

$$\begin{aligned} m_{e_i}^+(y_i) &= m_{e_i}^+(m_{e_i}^-(x_i) + b_i) \\ &= m_{e_i}^+(m_{e_i}^-(x_i)) = m_{e_i}^+(x_i) \end{aligned} \tag{33}$$

and thus

$$I_0(i,e_i) \le I_0'(i,j) \le I_1'(i,j) \le I_1(i,e_i) \tag{34}$$

When $j > e_i$ it is obvious that $m_j^-(x_i) = m_j^-(y_i)$ and $m_j^+(x_i) = m_j^+(y_i)$ because other than the least e_j bits of x_i and y_i are identical. Therefore,

$$I_0'(i,j) = I_0(i,j) \ne I_1(i,j) = I_1'(i,j)\,. \tag{35}$$

From these facts, we can say that

$$\begin{aligned} &j = e_i \text{ if } I_0'(i,j) = I_1'(i,j) \text{ and} \\ &I_0'(i,j+1) \ne I_1'(i,j+1) \end{aligned}\,. \tag{36}$$

Figure 4. Overview of extraction part of the proposed method

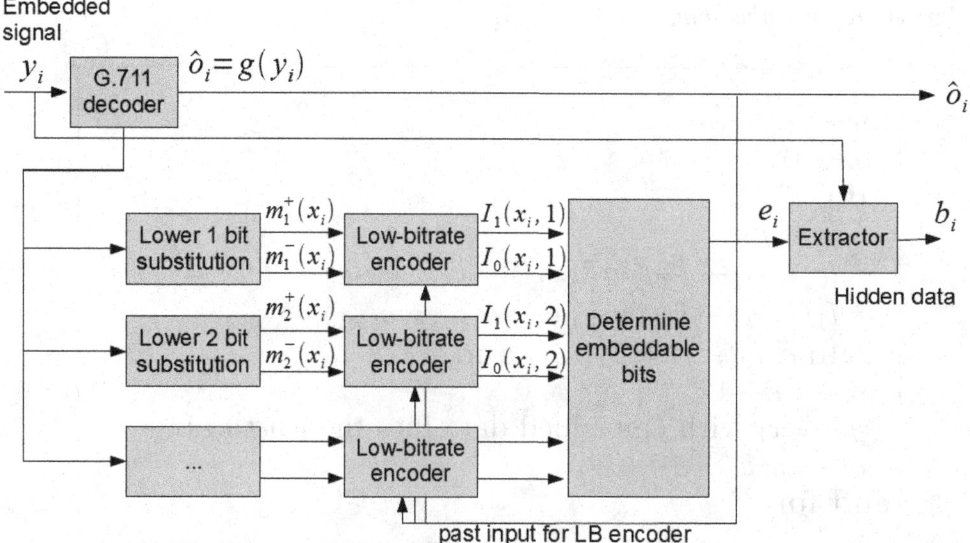

According to the above discussion, it is clear that we can determine the number of embedded bits in a sample exactly same manner as the embedding process.

Selection of a Low Bit Rate Encoder

In the present proposal, we chose G.726 ADPCM (ITU, 1990) as a low-bit rate encoder on implementing this algorithm, since G.726 has several features that meets the requirements for the low-bit rate encoder in our framework. First, it determines the code sample-by-sample. Next, G.726 has several bit rate configurations, which allow us to control the amount of embedded information.

G.726 ADPCM is a codec that encodes telephone speech into from 16 kbit/s up to 40 kbit/s. Basically, an ADPCM encoder encodes speech samples adaptively using variable quantization steps. Figure 5 shows an overview of G.726 encoder and decoder. In the encoding process (Figure 5a), difference between the input signal *x(k)* and the predicted signal $x_e(k)$ is calculated, and the difference *d(k)* is quantized into the ADPCM output *I(k)* using an adaptive quantizer, which determines the quantization step according to the previous difference signal $d(1),\ldots,d(k-1)$. The encoded signal $I(k)$ is decoded again, and sent to a signal predictor to predict the next signal. In the decoding process (Figure 5b), an ADPCM-coded sample is decoded using the adaptive de-quantizer, which is the exactly same one that is used in the encoding process. The decoded difference signal is added to the predicted signal to generate the decoded signal.

On using G.726 encoder, we make an exceptional rule for determining the number of embeddable bits. Let *N* be the bit length of a sample coded by ADPCM. The number depends on the bit rate of ADPCM; *N* = 5 for the 40 kbit/s configuration, *N* = 4 for 32 kbit/s and *N* = 3 for 24 kbit/s. When $I_0(i,0) = 2^{N-1} - 1$ it means that the distortion between the true sample and the predicted value is maximum. In this case, $I_0(i,j)$ and $I_1(i,j)$ coincide with high probability. This happens because the absolute value of the code

Figure 5. Block diagrams of G.726 encoder and decoder

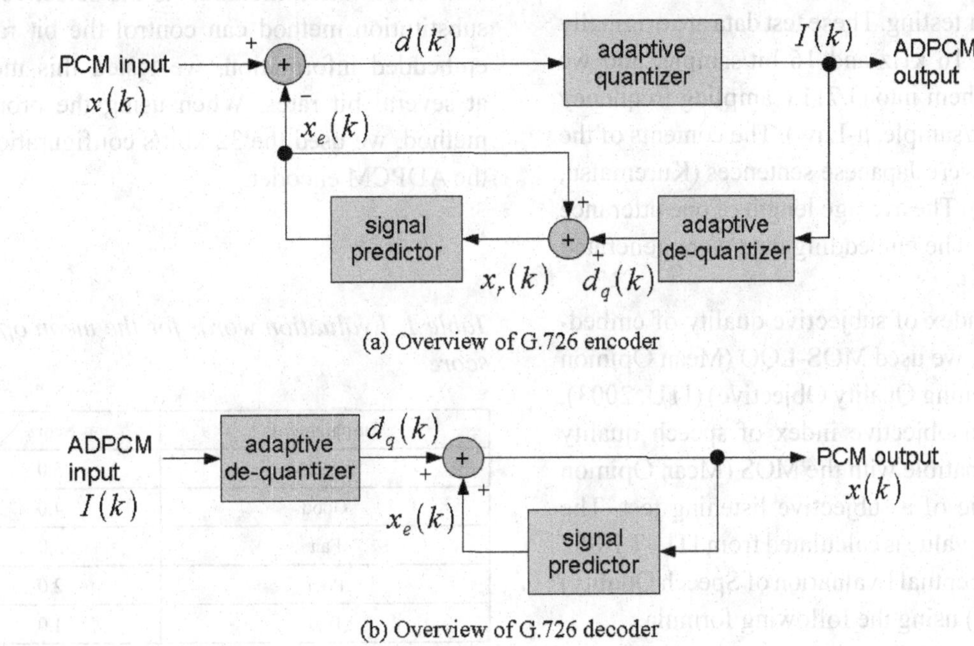

cannot become any larger, and we cannot trust the fact that $I_0(i,j) = I_1(i,j)$ as an index of subjective quality, so we use the following e_i' instead of e_i, which is defined as follows:

$$e_i' = \begin{cases} 0 & if \mid I_0(i,0) \mid = 2^{N-1} - 1 \\ e_i & \text{otherwise} \end{cases}. \quad (37)$$

This equation means that we do not embed any data to the sample where the ADPCM-coded value of the sample has the maximum absolute value $\left(2^{N-1} - 1\right)$.

EVALUATION OF THE PROPOSED METHOD

Experimental Conditions of Experiment 1

We conducted experiments to investigate the bit rate of embedded information and the degradation of the original signal by the proposed and the conventional methods. We used 10 utterances extracted from the NTT-AT phone-balanced speech database for testing. These test data are originally sampled at 16 kHz and 16 bit/sample, and we converted them into G.711 (sampling frequency 8 kHz, 8 bit/sample, μ-Law). The contents of the utterances were Japanese sentences (Kurematsu, et al., 1990). The average length of one utterance was 4.01 s. The embedding data were generated randomly.

As an index of subjective quality of embedded speech, we used MOS-LQO (Mean Opinion Score-Listening Quality Objective) (ITU, 2003), which is an objective index of speech quality that is compatible with the MOS (Mean Opinion Score) value of a subjective listening test. The MOS-LQO value is calculated from ITU-T P.862 PESQ (Perceptual Evaluation of Speech Quality) (ITU, 2001) using the following formula.

$$x_{LQO} = 0.999 + \frac{4.999 - 0.999}{1 + e^{-1.4945 x_{PESQ} + 4.6607}}. \quad (38)$$

Here, x_{LQO} is a MOS-LQO value and x_{PESQ} is a score calculated by PESQ. Table 1 shows the levels of MOS ratings. We used Opticom OPERA for calculating PESQ. PESQ was designed to have high correlation to the human-evaluated score (more than 0.9 for evaluation of codec), and MOS-LQO improves correlation further compared to raw PESQ score (ITU, 2003), and thus these were adopted as the recommendations of ITU-T as P.862 and P.862.1, respectively. With such a background, MOS-LQO is widely accepted as a quality measure of telephone-quality speech (Lundberg, et al., 2005; Broom, 2006; Valin & Montgomery, 2006). Therefore, we used MOS-LQO to measure the quality of speech instead of subjective evaluations.

Experimental Results for 32 kbit/s ADPCM Setting (Experiment 1a)

First, we compared the proposed method with the simple LSB substitution and the selective LSB substitution method. As the selective LSB substitution method can control the bit rate of embedded information, we tested this method at several bit rates. When using the proposed method, we used the 32 kbit/s configuration for the ADPCM encoder.

Table 1. Evaluation words for the mean opinion score

Impairment	Score
Excellent	5.0
Good	4.0
Fair	3.0
Poor	2.0
Bad	1.0

Figure 6 shows the result. The error bars in the figure shows the standard deviations. Compared with the selective LSB substitution method, our method achieved higher MOS-LQO, proving its effectiveness. Table 2 shows the ratio of embeddable bits for a sample. From this result, no information is embedded in more than half of the sample. Our method, nevertheless, can embed more than two bits of information into almost 20% of the samples.

Figure 7 shows frame-by-frame PESQ intermediate values for the proposed method and the selective LSB substitution method. Although the final PESQ value is not a simple average of these intermediate values, we can investigate partial degradation of speech quality by observing these intermediate values. The bit rate settings of the payload are set to be equal for both methods. From this result, we can confirm that frames with low PESQ values are observed in the result of the selective LSB substitution method, while such frames are hardly observed in the result of the proposed method.

Effect of ADPCM Bit Rate Settings on the Payload Bit Rate and Speech Quality (Experiment 1b)

In the previous experiment, we used the ADPCM encoder at 32 kbit/s bit rate. We can change the bit rate of payload by changing the bit rate of the ADPCM encoder. If we use high bit rate ADPCM encoder, the speech quality increases while the bit rate of payload decreases, and vice versa.

Thus, we investigated the trade-off between the speech quality and the bit rate of payload. We examined the speech quality and bit rate of the payload for four ADPCM settings, 16 kbit/s, 24 kbit/s, 32 kbit/s, and 40 kbit/s. Figure 8 shows the experimental result. This result shows that we can control the bit rate of the payload by changing the setting of ADPCM encoder. However, the

Figure 6. Experimental results using 32 kbit/s ADPCM

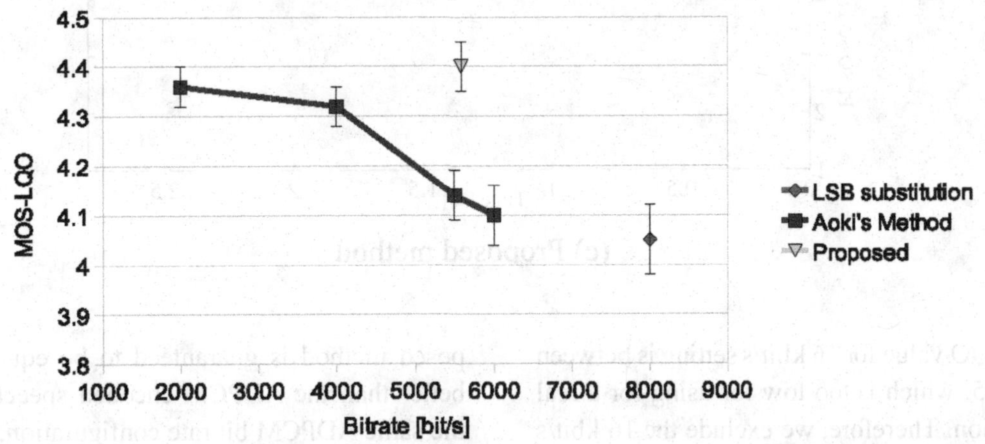

Table 2. Ratio of embeddable bits

e_i'	0	1	2	3	≥ 4
Ratio [%]	51.6	30.0	13.1	4.1	1.3

Figure 7. Temporal change of PESQ intermediate values

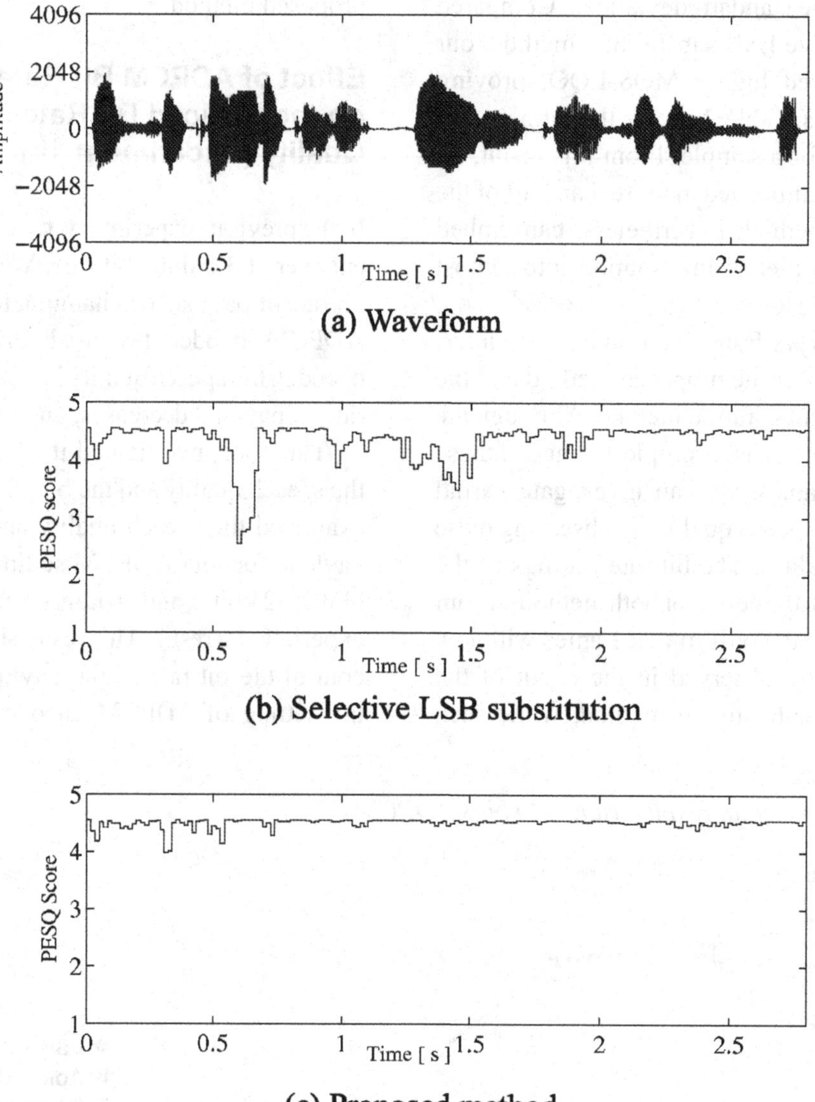

MOS-LQO value for 16 kbit/s setting is between 2 and 2.5, which is too low for using for a real application. Therefore, we exclude the 16 kbit/s condition thereafter.

In addition, we compared the speech quality of the data-embedded speech and the speech encoded by the ADPCM encoder. As explained above, one advantage of our method is that quality of the data-embedded speech using the proposed method is guaranteed to be equal to or better than the ADPCM-encoded speech using the same ADPCM bit rate configuration. Figure 9 shows the comparison results between the data-embedded speech by the proposed method using various ADPCM settings and the speech simply encoded by the G.726 ADPCM encoder. This result clearly proves the above-mentioned advantage.

Figure 8. Bit rate vs. MOS for various configurations

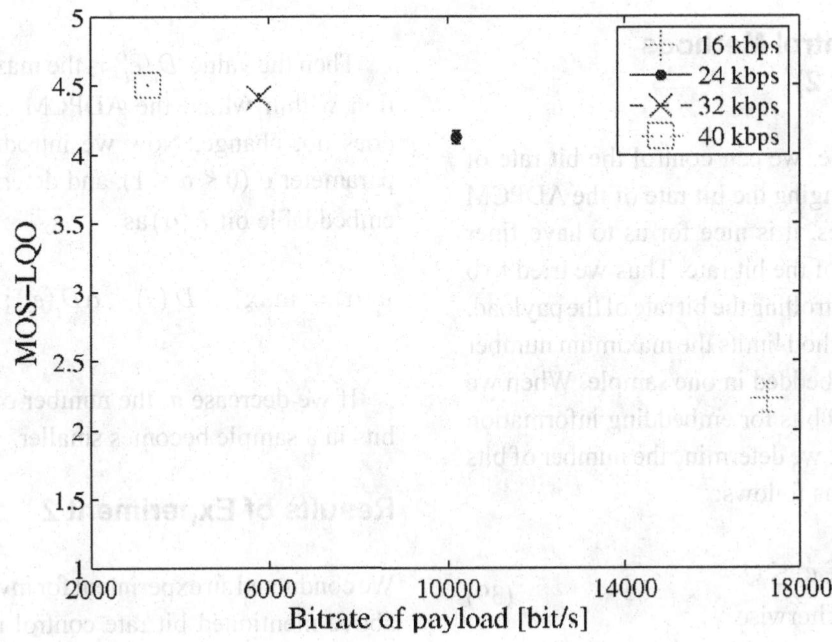

Figure 9. Comparison of speech quality of ADPCM-encoded speech and the embedded speech by the proposed method

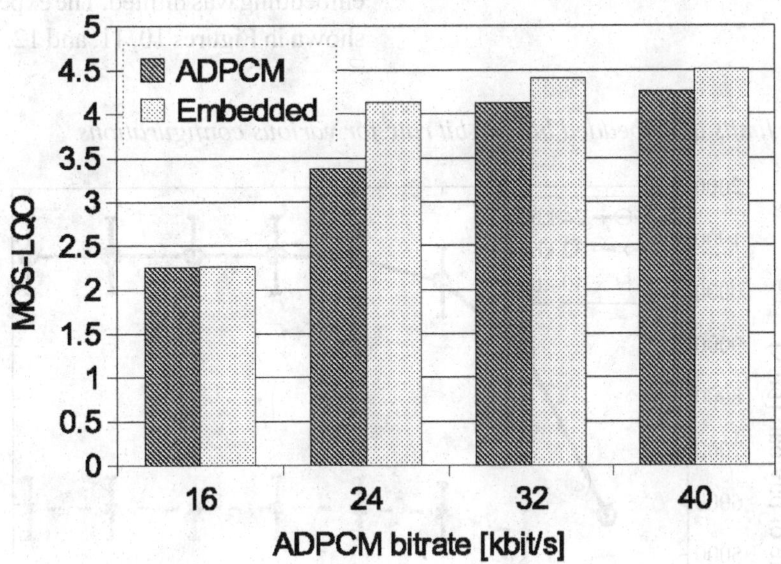

BIT RATE CONTROL OF PAYLOAD

Bit Rate Control Methods (Experiment 2)

As shown above, we can control the bit rate of payload by changing the bit rate of the ADPCM encoder. Besides, it is nice for us to have finer tuning method of the bit rate. Thus we tried two methods for controlling the bit rate of the payload.

The first method limits the maximum number of bits to be embedded in one sample. When we allow at most Q bits for embedding information into one sample, we determine the number of bits for embedding as follows:

$$\tilde{e}_i(Q) = \begin{cases} e_i' & \text{if } e_i' \le Q \\ Q & \text{otherwise} \end{cases} \tag{39}$$

The second method is based on distortion of samples. Let $D_i(k)$ be the absolute distortion of the i-th sample when k bits are substituted.

$$D_i(k) = \mid g(m_k^+(x_i)) - g(m_k^-(x_i)) \mid \tag{40}$$

Then the value $D_i(e_i')$ is the maximum distortion within which the ADPCM-encoded value does not change. Now we introduce a control parameter α ($0 < \alpha \le 1$), and determine the new embeddable bit $\tilde{e}_i(\alpha)$ as

$$\tilde{e}_i(\alpha) = \max_j \{ j \mid D_i(j) < \alpha D_i(e_i') \} \tag{41}$$

If we decrease α, the number of embeddable bits in a sample becomes smaller.

Results of Experiment 2

We conducted an experiment for investigating the above-mentioned bit rate control methods. The experimental conditions were same as that in the previous section.

We examined the first bit rate control method, where the maximum number bits per sample for embedding was limited. The experimental result is shown in Figures 10, 11, and 12. Figure 10 shows

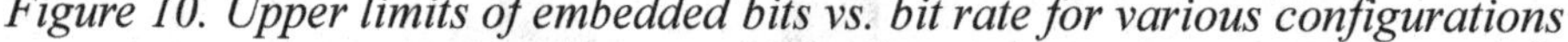

Figure 10. Upper limits of embedded bits vs. bit rate for various configurations

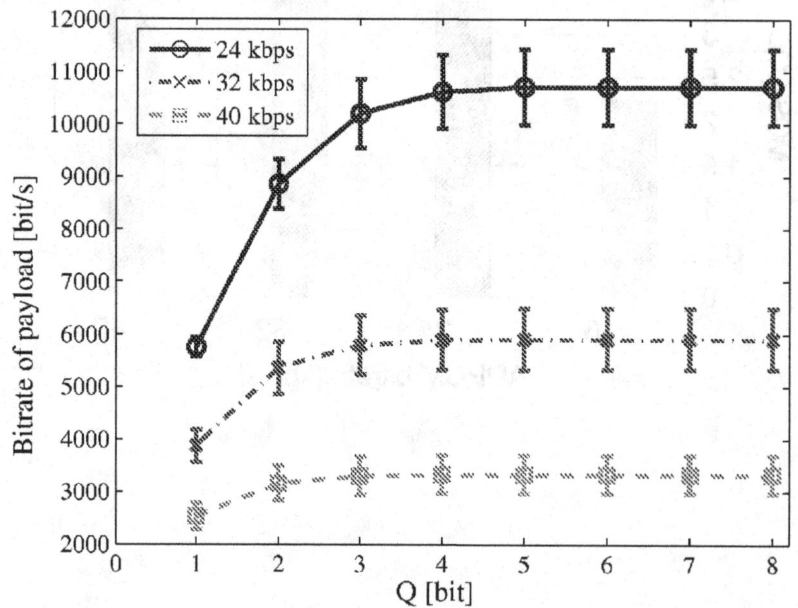

Figure 11. Upper limits of embedded bits vs. MOS for various configurations

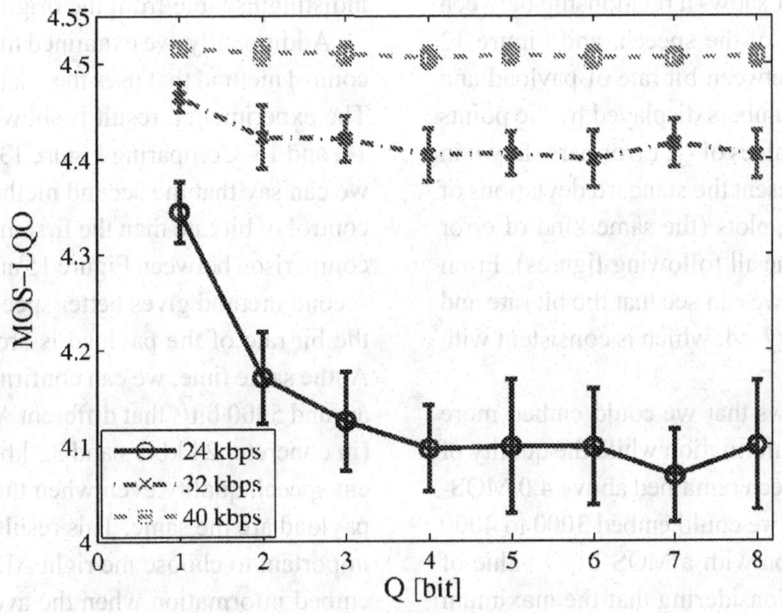

Figure 12. Bit rate vs. MOS for various configurations

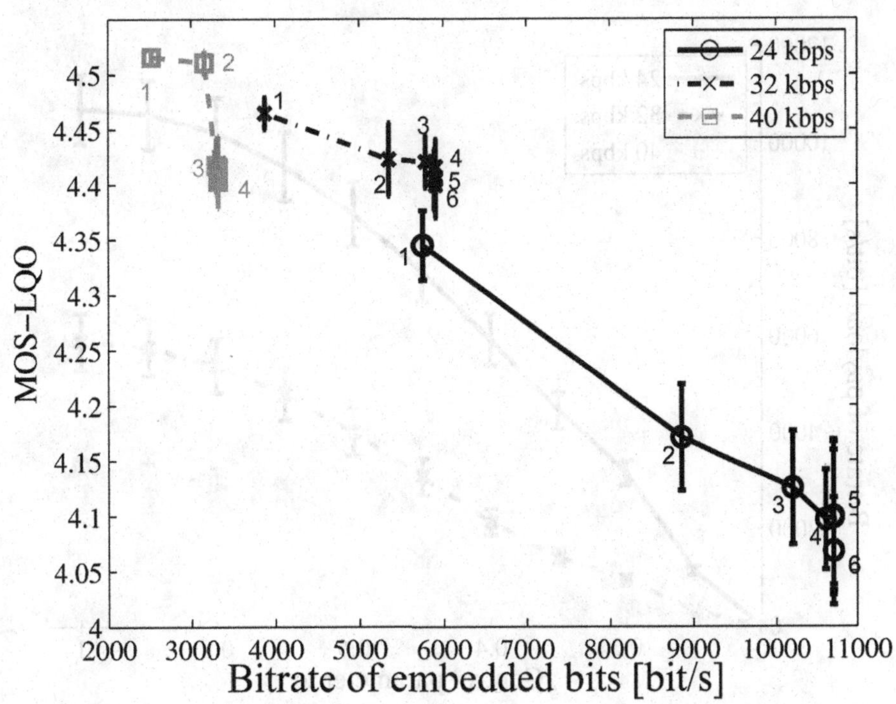

a relationship between Q and the bit rate of the payload, Figure 11 shows a relationship between Q and the quality of the speech, and Figure 12 shows trade-off between bit rate of payload and speech quality. Numbers displayed by the points in Figure 12 are values of Q. Error bars shown in these figures represent the standard deviations of the corresponding plots (the same kind of error bars are used in the all following figures). From Figures 9 and 10, we can see that the bit rate and MOS saturates at $Q = 4$, which is consistent with Table 2.

Figure 12 shows that we could embed more than 10 kbit/s of information while the quality of the embedded speech remained above 4.0 MOS-LQO. In contrast, we could embed 3000 to 4000 bit/s of information with a MOS-LQO value of more than 4.45. Considering that the maximum value of MOS-LQO is 4.5, the speech with 4000 bit/s of hidden data is considered to be almost indistinguishable from the original speech.

Additionally, we examined the second bit rate control method that uses the control parameter α. The experimental result is shown in Figures 13, 14, and 15. Comparing Figure 13 with Figure 10, we can say that the second method enables finer control of bit rate than the first method. From the comparison between Figure 15 and Figure 12, the second method gives better speech quality when the bit rate of the payload is around 5000 bit/s. At the same time, we can confirm from the result around 5000 bit/s that different ADPCM settings (in concrete, 24 kbit/s and 32 kbit/s) give different speech quality even when the bit rates of the payload are the same. This result shows that it is important to choose the right ADPCM setting to embed information when the average bit rate of payload is determined.

Figure 13. α vs. bit rate

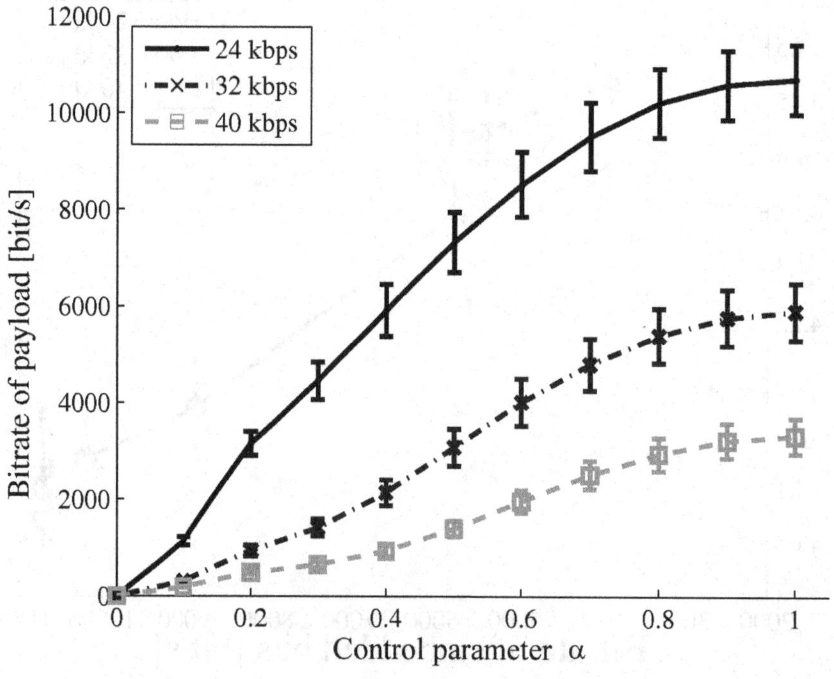

Figure 14. α vs. MOS

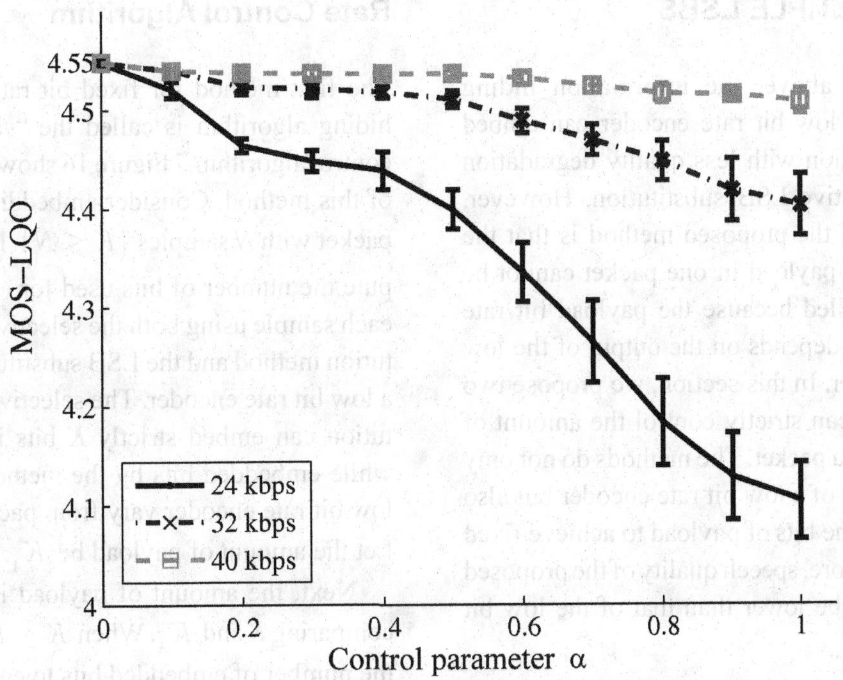

Figure 15. Bit rate vs. MOS when using α

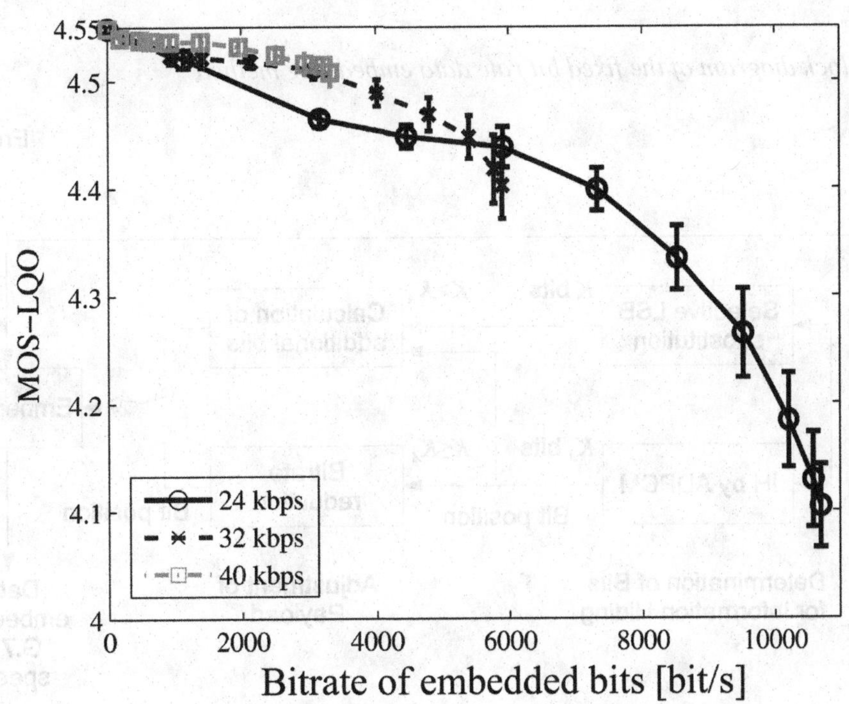

FIXED BIT RATE DATA HIDING USING MULTIPLE LSBS

As described above, the information hiding method using low bit rate encoder can embed more information with less quality degradation than the selective LSB substitution. However, a drawback of the proposed method is that the amount of the payload in one packet cannot be strictly controlled because the payload bit rate of the method depends on the output of the low bit rate encoder. In this section, we propose two methods that can strictly control the amount of the payload in a packet. The methods do not only refer the result of a low bit rate encoder but also add or delete the bits of payload to achieve fixed bit rate. Therefore, speech quality of the proposed method could be lower than that of the low bit rate encoder.

Overview of the Simple Bit Rate Control Algorithm

The first method for fixed bit rate information hiding algorithm is called the "simple bit rate control algorithm." Figure 16 shows an overview of this method. Consider embedding K bits in a packet with N samples $\left(K \leq N\right)$. First, we compute the number of bits used for embedding for each sample using both the selective LSB substitution method and the LSB substitution based on a low bit rate encoder. The selective LSB substitution can embed strictly K bits in the packet, while embedded bits by the method based on a low bit rate encoder vary from packet to packet. Let the amount of payload be K_A.

Next, the amount of payload is adjusted by comparing K and K_A. When $K \leq K_A$, we reduce the number of embedded bits to embed K bits in a packet. Otherwise, we add the embedding samples determined by the selective LSB substitution method to that determined by the low-bit rate-encoder-based method to increase the amount of payload.

Figure 16. A block diagram of the fixed bit rate data embedding method

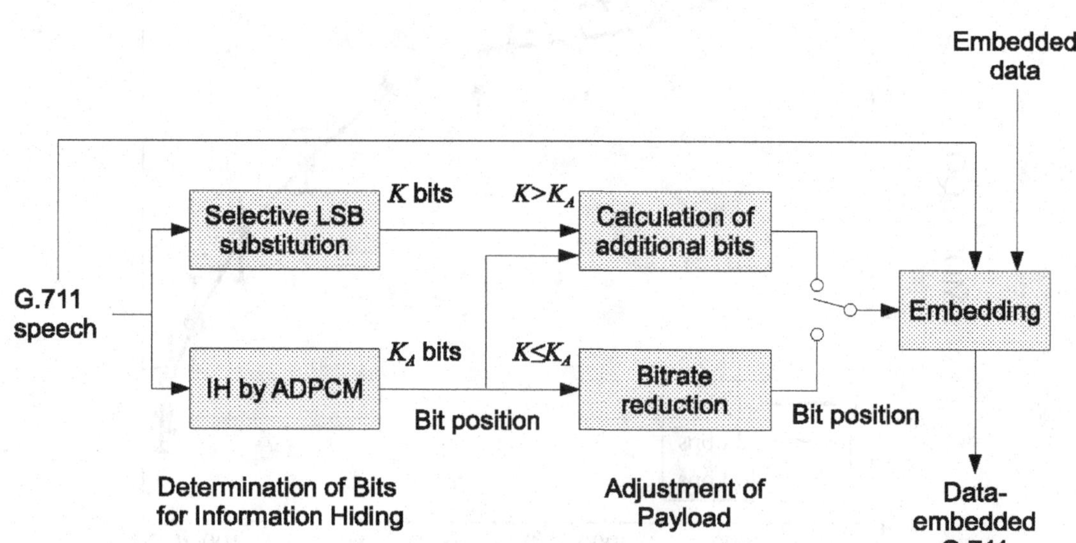

After determining number of embedding bits for each sample in a packet, we actually embed the data in the samples to generate the embedded speech.

An Algorithm for Payload Bit Rate Adjustment

Let $x_1,\ldots,x_N$ be samples in a packet encoded in G.711. We first determine the number of bits used for the payload, denoted as $e_1,\ldots,e_N$, using the LSB substitution method based on a low-bit rate encoder (in this case, G.726 ADPCM). Note that e_i here can be e_i', $e_i'(Q)$ or $e_i'(\alpha)$ described in the previous sections. Then the number of bits for payload in the packet can be written as

$$K_A = \sum_{i=1}^{N} e_i \,. \tag{42}$$

Now, we switch the procedure according to the relationship between K and K_A.

When $K \le K_A$, we can embed sufficient amount of bits into the packet. Then we reduce the payload by reducing the embedding bits from samples with the largest number of embedding bits.

When $K > K_A$, we need to add payload. Here, we employ the selective LSB substitution for determining extra bits into the samples. Let r_i be the rank of $|m(x_i)|$ in the samples of the packet. Then we determine h_i as follows:

$$h_i = \begin{cases} 1 & r_i < K \\ 0 & \text{otherwise} \end{cases} \tag{43}$$

Next, we choose candidate samples to embed extra bits using the selective LSB substitution. Then we embed the extra bits into those samples, which have smaller absolute values. Figure 17 shows the procedure for determining e_i. We first determine $e_1,\ldots,e_N$ using this procedure, and then we actually embed the data according to $e_1,\ldots,e_N$.

Figure 17. Algorithm for embeddable bit adjustment

```
if K_A > K then
    while K_A > K do
        E ← max_{1≤j≤N} e_j
        k ← min_{e_i=E} i
        e_k ← e_k − 1,   K_A ← K_A − 1
    end while
else if K_A < K then
    while K_A < K do
        k ← argmin_{i:h_i=1,e_i=0} r_i
        e_k ← e_k + 1, K_A ← K_A + 1
    end while
end if
```

Evaluation of the Proposed Method (Experiment 3)

We conducted an evaluation experiment for the proposed fixed-bit rate data embedding method. We compared the proposed method with the selective LSB substitution method. We did not compare the proposed method with the previously proposed method based on a low-bit rate encoder, because it cannot achieve fixed-bit rate data embedding. The experimental conditions are identical to those in the previous experiments.

Figure 18 shows a comparison result (the label "conventional" show the result by the selective LSB substitution). This result suggests the following two observations: quality of the speech signal degrades when the bit rate of the embedded data is high, and the proposed method gives better speech quality under several conditions. Then we checked the conditions where the proposed method gives statistically significant improvement. To this end, we conducted a one-way ANOVA with embedding method ("conventional" and "proposed" with different ADPCM bit rate) as a factor. As a result, we obtained significant difference among the embedding methods ($p < 0.01$). Then we conducted multiple comparison test (one-sided t-test) for all of results with different embedding bit rate and different embedding methods to check if the proposed method gave better result over the conventional one. Table 3 shows the comparison result; in this table, "n.s" and "**" denote "not significant" and "significant at 1% level," respectively. This result shows that the proposed method shows significant improvements when the embedding bit rate is 4 kbit/s or more, and larger improvements are observed when the embedding bit rate is 8 kbit/s. This result suggests that the proposed method is advantageous under a condition when embedding bit rate is high. Especially, when the embedding bit rate is 8 kbit/s, the conventional method is a simple LSB substitution. The proposed method, on the other hand, can improve the speech quality even under 8 kbit/s embedding bit rate because it embeds more than one bit into samples with less degradation while avoiding embedding data into the samples that causes severe degradation.

Figure 18. Speech quality of the proposed method with respect to the bit rate of payload

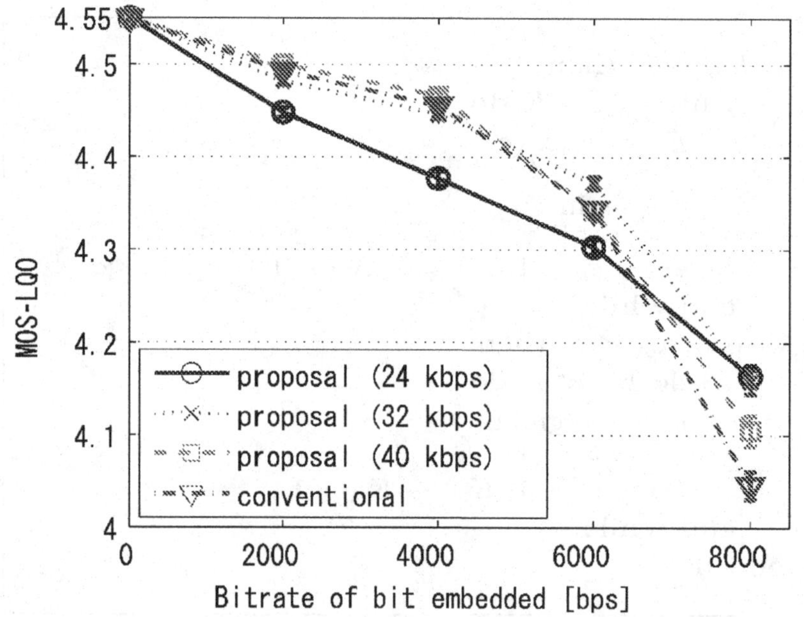

*Table 3. Result of statistical tests between the conventional method [10] and the proposed method (n.s.: not significant, **: $p < 0.01$)*

Embedding Bit rate (bit/s)	ADPCM Bit rate (kbit/s)		
	24	32	40
2000	n.s.	n.s.	n.s.
4000	n.s.	n.s.	**
6000	n.s.	**	n.s.
8000	**	**	**

Figure 19 shows an example of host signal along with temporal PESQ values using the LSB substitution and the proposed method under 8 kbit/s embedding bit rate condition. The uppermost figure shows the waveform of the host signal, the middle figure is the temporal PESQ values of the LSB substitution, and the lowermost figure is a result of the proposed method when the 24 kbit/s ADPCM encoder is employed as a low-bit rate encoder. This figure clearly depicts that the proposed method improves PESQ values of the low quality samples. For example, in the region marked as A in the figure, we can observe that the number of frames with low PESQ values is reduced. In the region B, the proposed method improves the minimum PESQ values.

Improvement of the Proposed Method by Bit rate Reduction based on Tolerable Quantization Step

The algorithm explained above reduces bit rate when $K < K_A$ by reducing the number of embedding bits from the samples with the largest number of embedding bits, the earliest samples first. However, even when reducing the number of embedding bits, it is desirable to reduce them so that the maximum quality of speech signal is obtained. Therefore, besides the simple method,

Figure 19. Waveform of the speech and temporal change of PESQ value (embedding bit rate 8 kbit/s)

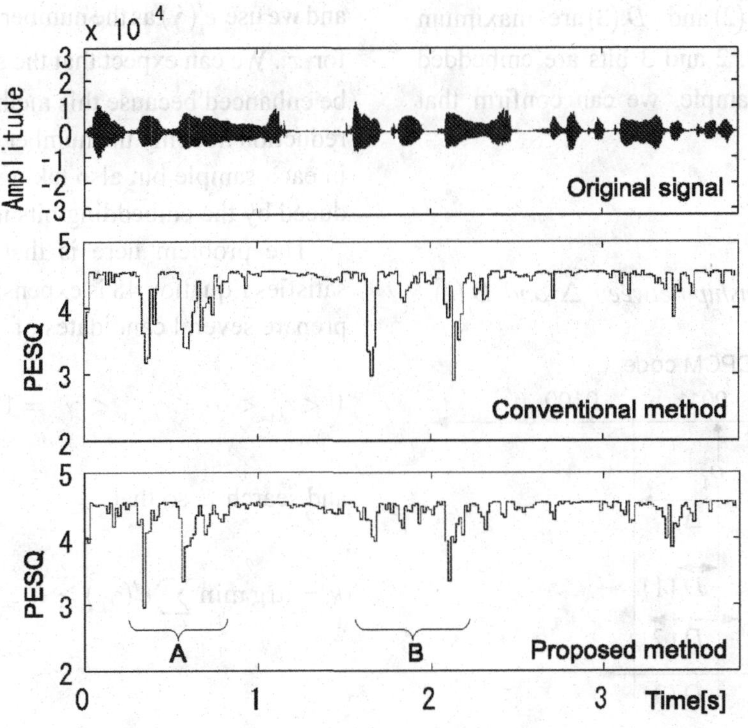

we propose another method based on control of tolerable distortion.

Let $o_i = g(x_i)$. Let o_i^+ and o_i^- be

$$o_i^+ = \max_o\{o \mid I(g(x_i) \mid \ldots, \hat{o}_{i-1}) = I(g(x_i) \mid \ldots, \hat{o}_{i-1})\} \quad (44)$$

$$o_i^- = \min_o\{o \mid I(g(x_i) \mid \ldots, \hat{o}_{i-1}) = I(g(x_i) \mid \ldots, \hat{o}_{i-1})\} \quad (45)$$

and let us define

$$\Delta_i = o_i^+ - o_i^- \quad (46)$$

Here, Δ_i is a range where the low-bit rate encoder gives the same code as the output code for $g(x_i)$. Then we compare this Δ_i and $D_i(e)$ defined by Equation 40. Note that, if $e \leq e_i$ then $D_i(e) \leq \Delta_i$, but not vice versa.

Figure 20 shows the relationship between Δ_i and $D_i(e)$. In this example, the input sample o_i is encoded into the code 0011 using an ADPCM encoder. $D_i(1), D_i(2)$ and $D_i(3)$ are maximum distortions when 1, 2 and 3 bits are embedded into x_i. In this example, we can confirm that $e_i = 2$

Figure 20. Relationship between Δ_i and $D_i(e)$

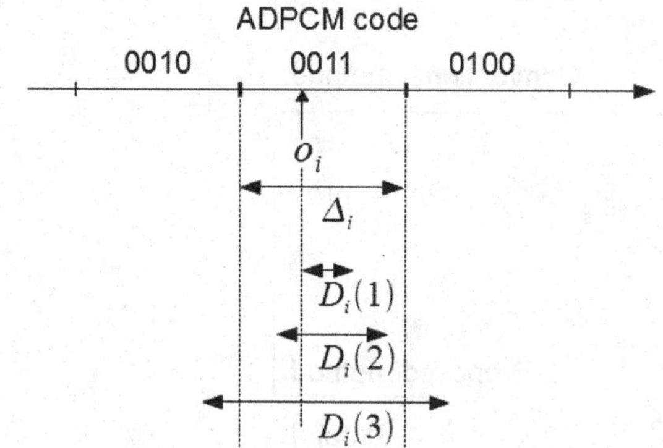

The point of the proposed method is to consider the relationship between $D_i(e_i)$ and Δ_i when deciding if we reduce the embedding bits of x_i. If $D_i(e_i)$ is sufficiently smaller than Δ_i it means that embedding e_i bits into x_i does not cause much distortion. Conversely, if $D_i(e_i) \approx \Delta_i$, it means that the distortion caused by embedding e_i bits into x_i is almost as large as the tolerable limit. Therefore, we reduce the embedding bits from the samples that have small values of $\Delta_i - D_i(e_i)$. To achieve this, we use a coefficient $0 < \gamma \leq 1$ and determine $e_i'(\gamma)$ as follows.

$$e_i'(\gamma) = \arg\max_{j \leq e_i}\{j \mid d_i(j) \leq \gamma\Delta_i\}. \quad (47)$$

By changing γ we can control the number of embedding bits. Then we search $\hat{\gamma}$ such that

$$\sum_{i=1}^{N} e_i'(\hat{\gamma}) = K. \quad (48)$$

and we use $e_i'(\hat{\gamma})$ as the number of embedding bits for x_i. We can expect that the speech quality can be enhanced because this method determines bit reduction not only the number of embedding bits in each sample but also taking the distortion induced by the embedding bits into account.

The problem here is that searching $\hat{\gamma}$ that satisfies Equation 48 is expensive. Therefore, we prepare several candidates of $\hat{\gamma}$,

$$0 < \gamma_1 < \cdots < \gamma_{n-1} < \gamma_n = 1, \quad (49)$$

and search $\hat{k}$ so that

$$\hat{k} = \arg\min_k \sum_{i=1}^{N} e_i'(\gamma_k) \geq K. \quad (50)$$

Next, we use $e_i'(\gamma_{\hat{k}})$ for $i = 1, \ldots, N$ as initial values of embedding bits, and apply the embedding bit adjustment shown in Figure 17.

Result of the Proposed Method (Experiment 4)

We conducted an evaluation experiment of the proposed method. In this section, we call the previous bit reduction method as "simple bit rate reduction method" and that in this section as "tolerable quantization step method." The experimental conditions are same as those in the previous sections. We prepared 10 candidates for γ such as 0.1, 0.2, ..., 1.0.

Figure 21 shows the relationship between embedding bit rate and speech quality using the tolerable quantization step method. Comparing this result with Figure 17, we could obtain larger improvement when using the 24 kbit/s ADPCM encoder.

Next, we conducted the one-sided t-test to check if the tolerable quantization step method is better than the simple bit rate reduction method, as shown in Table 4. This result suggests that the proposed method improves the speech quality when using the 24 kbit/s ADPCM encoder regardless of the embedding bit rate, and when using the 32 kbit/s ADPCM encoder and lower embedding bit rate.

Next, we conducted a statistical comparison between the selective LSB method and the tolerable quantization step method. We carried out a one-way ANOVA with embedding method as a factor. As a result, we obtained significant difference among the embedding methods ($p < 0.01$). Then we conducted multiple comparison tests (one-sided t-test) for all of results with different embedding bit rate and different embedding methods to check if the proposed method is better than the conventional method. Table 5 shows the comparison result; in this table, "n.s," "*," and "**" denote "not significant," "significant at 5%

Figure 21. Speech quality of the tolerable quantization step based bit rate reduction method with respect to the bit rate of payload

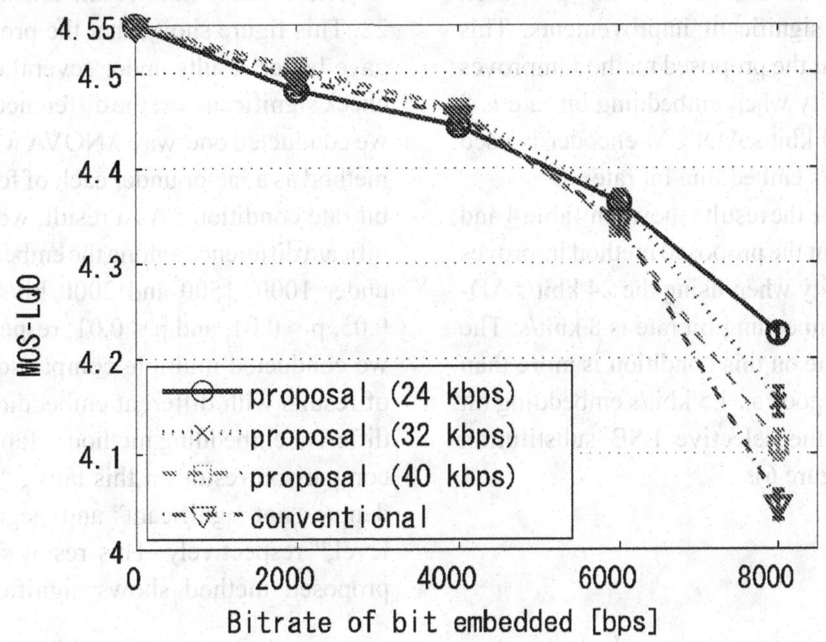

*Table 4. Result of statistical tests between the simple bit rate reduction method and the tolerable quantization step based bit rate reduction method (n.s.: not significant, **:p < 0.01)*

Embedding Bit Rate (kbit/s)	ADPCM Bit rate (kbit/s)		
	24	32	40
2	**	**	n.s.
4	**	**	n.s.
6	**	n.s.	n.s.
8	**	n.s.	n.s.

*Table 5. Result of statistical tests between the selective LSB substitution method and the tolerable quantization step based bit rate reduction method (n.s.: not significant, *: p < 0.05, **: p < 0.01)*

Embedding Bit Rate (kbit/s)	ADPCM Bit rate (kbit/s)		
	24	32	40
2	n.s.	n.s.	**
4	n.s.	n.s.	n.s.
6	n.s.	n.s.	*
8	**	**	**

level," and "significant at 1% level," respectively. This result shows that the proposed method shows significant improvements. This result shows that the proposed method improves the speech quality when embedding bit rate is 8 kbit/s, or the 40 kbit/s ADPCM encoder is used except at 4 kbit/s embedding bit rate.

To summarize the results shown in Table 4 and 5, we can say that the proposed method improves the speech quality when using the 24 kbit/s ADPCM and the embedding bit rate is 8 kbit/s. The MOS-LQO value on this condition is more than 4.2, which is as good as 4.5 kbit/s embedding bit rate given by the selective LSB substitution method (see Figure 6).

Application to 56 kbit/s G.711 Speech (Experiment 5)

The ordinary G.711 codec encodes a speech signal sampled at 8 kHz into 8 bits, and then the bit rate becomes 64 kbit/s. Here, there are several options for bit length of a sample, When a sample is quantized in 6 or 7 bits, the bit rate becomes 48 or 56 kbit/s, respectively. Especially, 56 kbit/s G.711 is frequently used because it is compatible with PSTN used in North America. Therefore, we examined the quality of data-embedded speech when applied to 56 kbit/s G.711. As speech signal encoded by 56 kbit/s G.711 has only 7 bit/sample, the LSB substitution can cause severe degradation because of the limited dynamic range.

We conducted an experiment to embed data in 56 kbit/s G.711 speech. The bit rate of the embedded data was changed from 500 to 2000 bit/s. In this experiment, we used 56 kbit/s G.711 speech without embedding as a reference for MOS-LQO evaluation to observe the difference of speech quality between the "normally encoded" signal and the embedded signals. The other experimental conditions were identical to those in the previous section.

The experimental result is shown in Figure 22. This figure shows that the proposed method gave better results under several conditions. To check significance of the difference of the results, we conducted one-way ANOVA with embedding method as a factor under each of four embedding bit rate conditions. As a result, we obtained significant difference among the embedding methods under 1000, 1500 and 2000 bit/s bit rate ($p < 0.05$, $p < 0.01$, and $p < 0.01$, respectively). Then we conducted multiple comparison tests for all of results with different embedding bit rate and different embedding methods. Table 6 shows the comparison result; in this table, "n.s" and "**" denote "not significant" and "significant at 1% level," respectively. This result shows that the proposed method shows significant improve-

Figure 22. Quality of data-embedded speech for 56 kbit/s G.711 codec

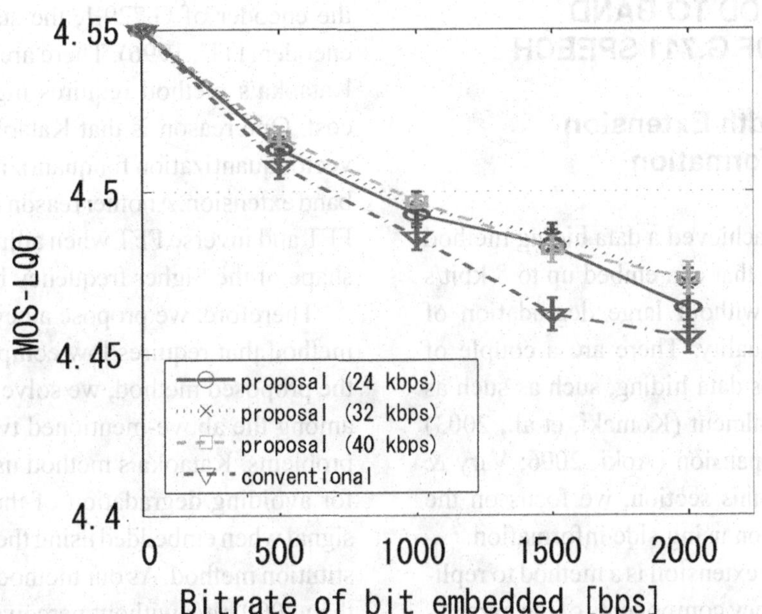

ments. This result shows that the proposed method improves the speech quality when embedding bit rate is 1000 bit/s or more.

On the Computational Cost of the Proposed Methods

As explained, the proposed methods can embed more information bits than the conventional selective LSB substitution method with less degradation of cover speech. In this section, we consider the computational cost of the proposed method. According to Yang (2004), G.711 encoder requires 0.01 MIPS, while G.726 ADPCM requires 5 MIPS. As our method need to calculate ADPCM-encoded values as many as the maximum number of embedding bits in one sample. For example, when using the lowest 3 bits for embedding, we need 15 MIPS for calculation of e_i. This computational cost is much higher than G.711 itself and several times higher than that of G.726, it is comparable with other CELP-based codec. For example, G.728 LD-CELP requires 30 MIPS, which is twice as heavy as the proposed method. Therefore, computational cost of the proposed method is sufficiently small considering current technologies for real-time data embedding.

*Table 6. Result of statistical tests between the selective LSB substitution method and the proposed method under 56 kbit/s G.711 codec (n.s.: not significant, **: $p < 0.01$)*

Embedding Bit rate (bit/s)	ADPCM Bit rate (kbit/s)		
	24	32	40
500	n.s.	n.s.	n.s.
1000	n.s.	n.s.	**
1500	**	**	**
2000	**	**	**

APPLICATION OF THE DATA HIDING METHOD TO BAND EXTENSION OF G.711 SPEECH

G.711 Bandwidth Extension Using Side Information

As explained, we achieved a data hiding method into G.711 speech that can embed up to 8 kbit/s side information without large degradation of the host speech quality. There are a couple of applications of this data hiding, such as such as packet loss concealment (Komaki, et al., 2003) and bandwidth expansion (Aoki, 2006; Vary & Gaiser, 2007). In this section, we focus on the bandwidth extension using side information.

The bandwidth extension is a method to replicate higher frequency components of the narrowband speech to obtain pseudo-wideband speech, first proposed by Makhoul and Berouti (1979). There have been many methods that generate high frequency bands from only the narrowband speech (Epps & Holmes, 1999; Larsen & Aarts, 2004). The other approach uses side information that is used to adjust the spectral shape of the higher frequency band. Using small amount of side information, we can improve the quality of the bandwidth-extended speech.

There are several works that use side information for bandwidth extension. Aoki (2006) proposed a framework for extending frequency band using data hiding for G.711. Vary and Geiser (2007) also proposed similar approach. This approach is promising, but there is room for enhancement for extending the frequency band. Several methods with similar idea have also been proposed. Kataoka et al. (2008) proposed a band extension method using 600 bit/s side information. Kataoka's method utilizes LPC analysis, and it encodes the LSP parameters and spectral shape using vector quantization. Although Kataoka's method gives high-quality wideband speech, it has a drawback that it requires high computational cost. The encoder for Kataoka's method requires 3.2 times high computational cost than the encoder of G.729.1, the standard wideband encoder (ITU, 1996). There are two reasons why Kataoka's method requires high computational cost. One reason is that Kataoka's method uses vector quantization for quantizing parameters for band extension. Another reason is that it calculates FFT and inverse FFT when adjusting the spectral shape of the higher frequency band.

Therefore, we propose a new band extension method that requires low computational cost. In the proposed method, we solve the first problem among the above-mentioned two computational problems. Kataoka's method uses only 600 bit/s for avoiding degradation of the original speech signal when embedded using the simple LSB substitution method. As our method can embed more than 2000 bit/s without perceivable degradation, we can use more bits for the side information. Therefore, we used scalar quantizer instead of vector quantizer for coding the LSP parameters and the spectral gain vector.

Band Extension using LPC and Spectral Shape

As our method is based on the method by Kataoka et al. (2008), we first describe their method. Figure 23 and 24 show the encoder and decoder of Kataoka's method. Their method encodes wideband speech that is sampled at 16 kHz. The wideband speech is down-sampled into 8 kHz sampling rate, and then quantized by G.711 encoder. At the same time, the wideband speech and the narrowband speech are analyzed by the linear prediction analysis, and LSP parameters for wideband and narrowband speech, respectively, are also calculated. The LSP parameters are quantized using vector quantizer in two steps; first, we select M code vectors among N codebooks ($M < N$) so that the selected code vectors are nearest to the LSP parameters calculated from the narrowband speech. Then the nearest code vector to the LSP parameters of the wideband speech is

Figure 23. A block diagram of encoder of Kataoka's method

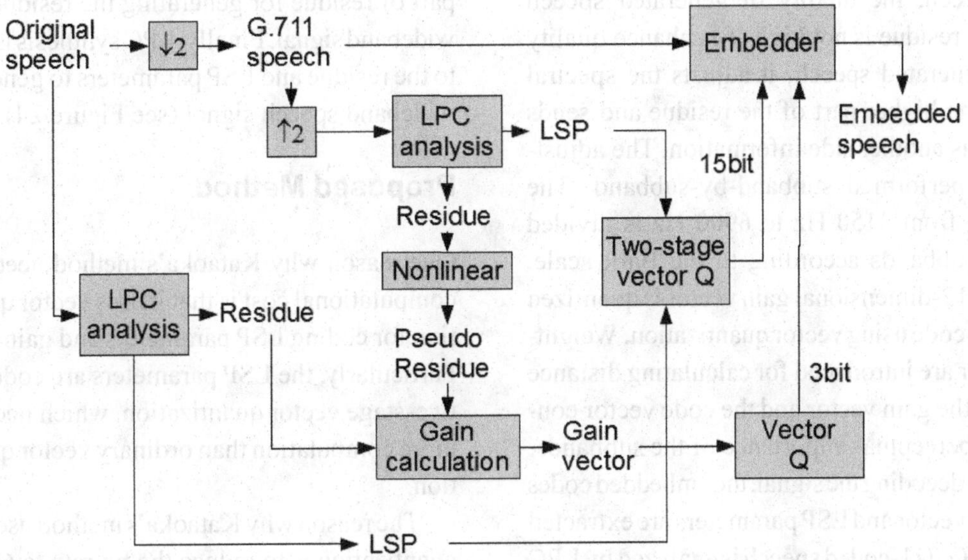

Figure 24. A block diagram of decoder of Kataoka's method

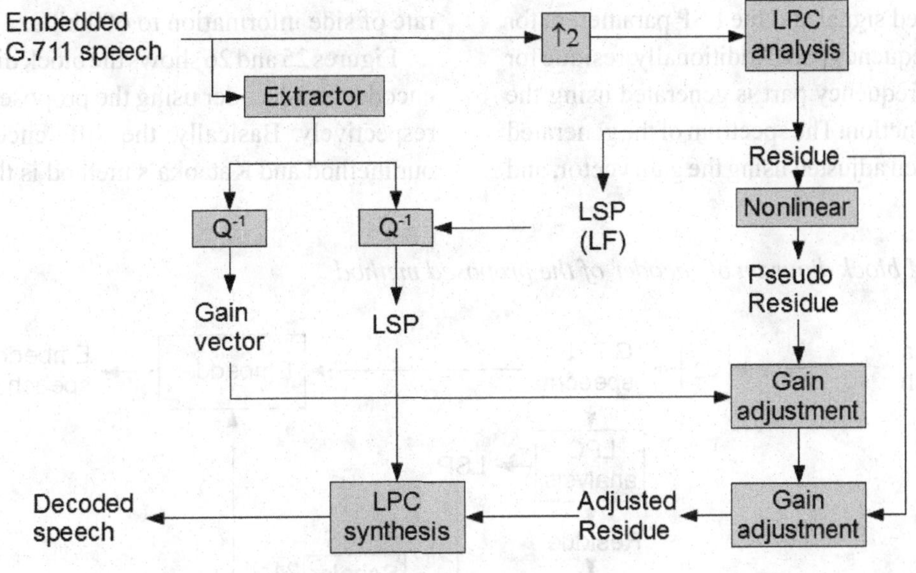

chosen among the pre-selected M code vectors. Next, residue for generating wideband speech is calculated. The residue is basically calculated from only the narrowband speech. A nonlinear function is applied for generating higher frequency part of the residue, as follows.

$$v(n) = \frac{3 \mid u(n) \mid + u(n)}{4} \tag{51}$$

where $u(n)$ is the residue calculated from the narrowband speech encoded by G.711 encoder. However, as the generated residue has different spectral shape from the real residue for the wideband speech, the quality of generated speech using the residue is not high. To enhance quality of the generated speech, it adjusts the spectral gain of the higher part of the residue and sends the gain as another side information. The adjustment is performed subband-by-subband. The spectrum from 3150 Hz to 6900 Hz is divided into 12 subbands according to the Bark scale. Then the 12-dimensional gain vector is quantized into 3-bit code using vector quantization. Weighting vector are introduced for calculating distance between the gain vector and the code vector considering perceptual importance of the subbands.

When decoding the signal, the embedded codes for a gain vector and LSP parameters are extracted first. The G.711-coded speech is analyzed by LPC analysis, and the LSP parameters and residue are generated. Then the LSP parameters for higher frequency part are obtained using the code from the embedded signal and the LSP parameters for the lower frequency part. Additionally, residue for the higher frequency part is generated using the nonlinear function. The spectrum of the generated residue is then adjusted using the gain vector, and the higher part of the residue is added to the lower part of residue for generating the residue for the wideband signal. Finally, LPC synthesis is applied to the residue and LSP parameters to generate the wideband speech signal (see Figure 24).

Proposed Method

One reason why Kataoka's method needs much computational cost is that it uses vector quantization for coding LSP parameters and gain vectors. Particularly, the LSP parameters are coded using two-stage vector quantization, which needs even more computation than ordinary vector quantization.

The reason why Kataoka's method uses vector quantization is to reduce the bit rate to 600 bit/s. However, as our method enables more than 2000 bit/s payload without degrading the quality of the original speech, we do not need to limit the bit rate of side information to 600 bit/s.

Figures 25 and 26 shows the block diagrams of encoder and decoder using the proposed method, respectively. Basically, the difference between our method and Kataoka's method is the method

Figure 25. A block diagram of encoder of the proposed method

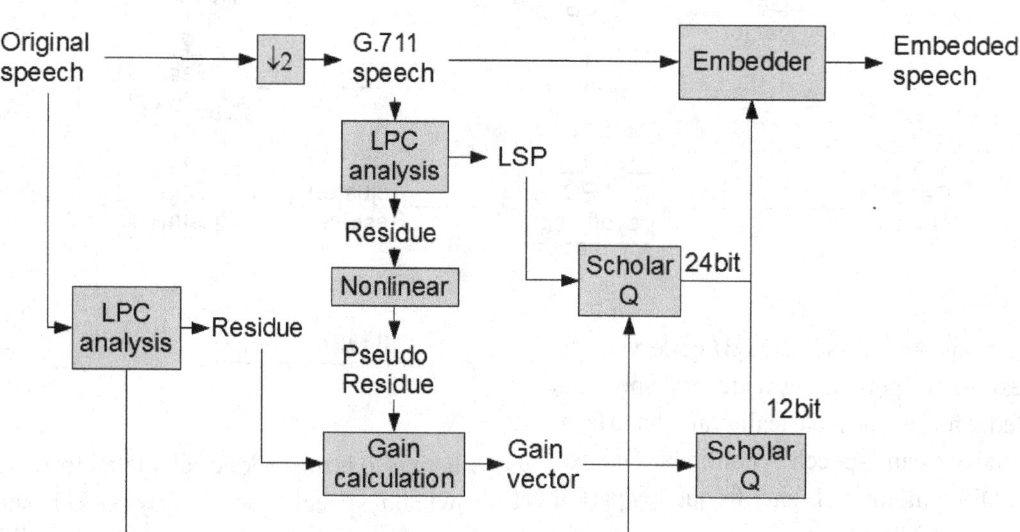

Figure 26. A block diagram of decoder of the proposed method

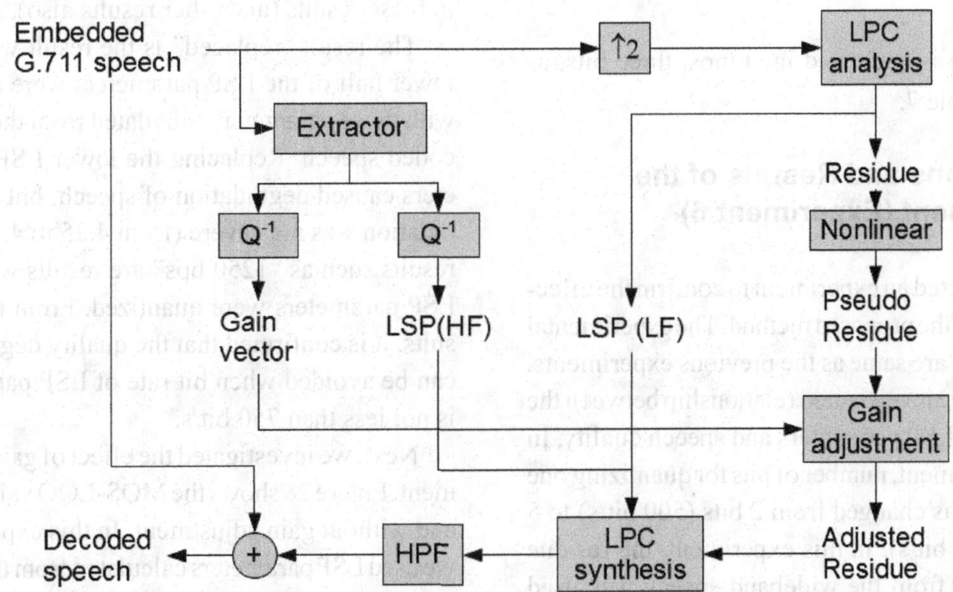

of quantization; Kataoka's method uses vector quantizers, while our method uses scalar quantizers for quantizing LSP parameters and a gain vector. Scalar quantization requires higher bit rate but the computation cost can be significantly lower than that of vector quantization.

There is another difference. In Kataoka's decoder, all the frequency components of the decoded signal are synthesized using the LPC synthesis, including lower frequency part. Conversely, our method only generates the higher frequency part of the decoded signal using the LPC synthesis, and the lower part is substituted by the signal decoded from the G.711-coded speech. We could expect better speech quality by this modification.

We analyze one frame (64 ms) of the wideband speech using the LPC analysis by 50% overlapping window, and 16 LSP parameters are calculated. Then we quantize the intervals of LSP parameters (Soong & Juang, 1984) of the higher 8 LSP parameters. In the decoding process, the lower LSP parameters are estimated from the G.711-coded speech. The limit of quantization was set to 1200 Hz, where 99.5% of intervals of the test set are included. After generating higher part of residue using the nonlinear function, the higher part of the residue spectrum is divided into five subbands. The division is based on the Bark scale.

Table 7 shows the frequency range of each sub-band. After dividing the residue spectrum into subbands, the gain vector is calculated as follows. Let X_i be average of the power spectrum of i-th subband of residue calculated from the wideband speech, and Y_i be that calculated from the G.711-coded speech using the nonlinear function. Now let the i-th gain be

Table 7. Subbands and gain values

Freq. Range [Hz]	# of bits	Gain values
3150-3700	3	0.5,1.0,1.5,2.0,2.5,3.0,4.0,6.0
3700-4400	3	0.5,1.0,1.5,2.0,2.5,3.0,4.0,5.0
4400-5300	3	0.5,1.0,1.5,2.0,2.5,3.0,3.5,4.0
5300-6300	2	0.5,1.0,1.5,2.0
6300-6900	1	0.5,1.0

$$g_i = X_i / Y_i \quad (52)$$

Each g_i is quantized in at most three bits, as shown Table 7.

Conditions and Results of the Experiment (Experiment 6)

We conducted an experiment to confirm the effectiveness of the proposed method. The experimental conditions are same as the previous experiments.

First, we investigated relationship between the bit rate of LSP parameters and speech quality. In this experiment, number of bits for quantizing one interval was changed from 2 bits (500 bit/s) to 5 bits (1250 bit/s). In this experiment, the residue calculated from the wideband speech was used so that only the impact of LSP quantization was measured. On evaluating MOS-LQO, the wideband speech was used as a reference (ITU, 2005). Figure 27 shows the experimental result. The result "original" is the result when using the LSP parameters calculated from the wideband speech directly. Note that the lower frequency part of the speech was replaced with the G.711-coded speech in these results (and other results also).

The result "replaced" is the result where the lower half of the LSP parameters were replaced with those parameters calculated from the G.711-coded speech. Replacing the lower LSP parameters caused degradation of speech, but the degradation was not severe (from 4.25 to 4.16). The results such as "1250 bps" are results where the LSP parameters were quantized. From these results, it is confirmed that the quality degradation can be avoided when bit rate of LSP parameters is not less than 750 bit/s.

Next, we investigated the effect of gain adjustment. Figure 28 shows the MOS-LQO values with and without gain adjustment. In this experiment, we used LSP parameters calculated from the wideband speech without quantization. Quantization of gain vector was not conducted. This result shows that we could improve the quality of speech by adjusting the gain of higher frequency.

Finally, we combined LSP quantization and gain vector quantization. Figure 29 shows the result. From this result, it is clear that the way of

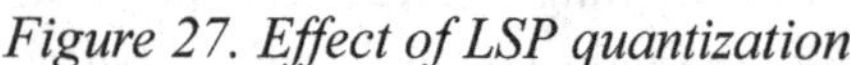

Figure 27. Effect of LSP quantization

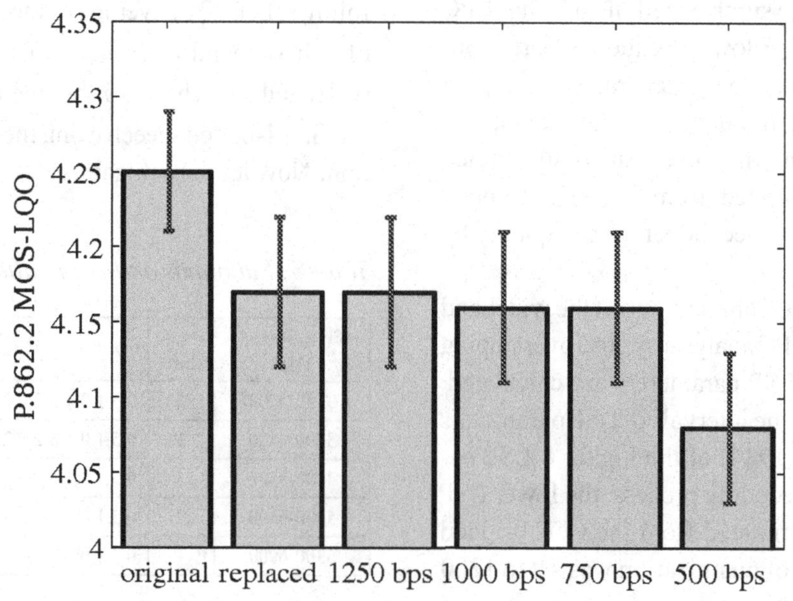

Figure 28. Effect of gain adjustment

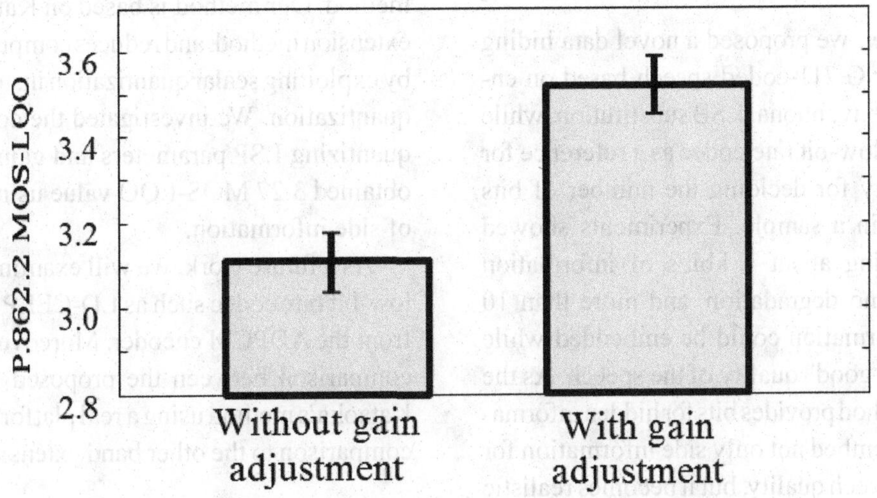

Figure 29. Results of the proposed method

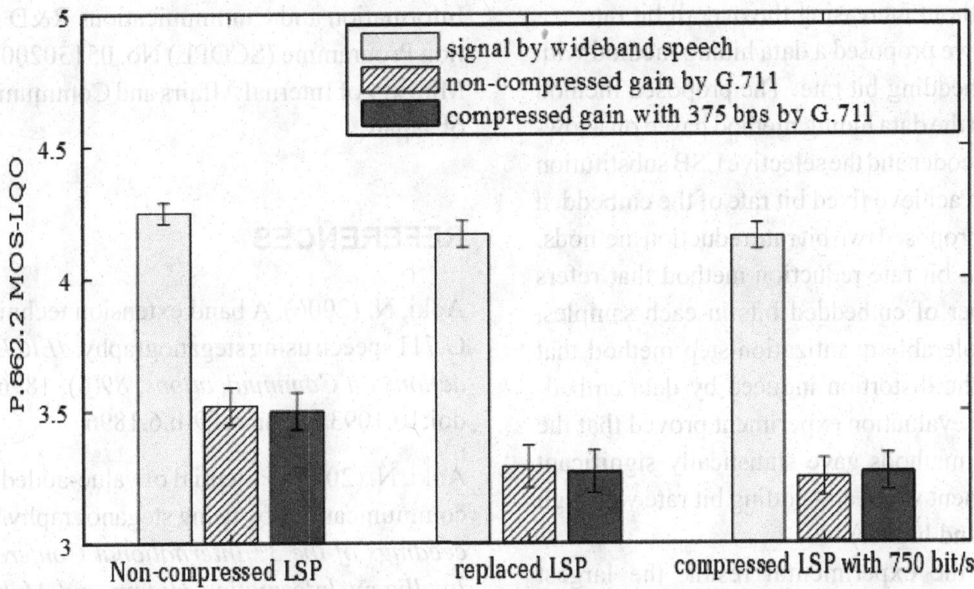

transmitting the LSP parameters, "replaced LSP" and "compressed LSP," and that of transmitting the gains, "non-compressed gain" and "compressed gain," have little influence on the speech quality. Most of degradation was caused by using replicated higher frequency part of the residue.

By quantizing both the LSP parameters and the gain vector, we can send the side information at 1125 bit/s, which is sufficiently small for transmitting by our proposed data hiding method.

CONCLUSION

In this chapter, we proposed a novel data hiding technique for G.711-coded speech based on enhancing the conventional LSB substitution, while employing a low-bit rate codec as a reference for speech quality for deciding the number of bits embeddable in a sample. Experiments showed that embedding about 4 kbit/s of information gave almost no degradation, and more than 10 kbit/s of information could be embedded while maintaining "good" quality of the speech. As the proposed method provides bits for hidden information, we can embed not only side information for enhancing speech quality, but it becomes realistic to embed information for making the speech signal into wide-band stereo (Hiwasaki, et al., 2008), or to embed another low-quality speech into G.711 speech for steganographic purposes (Wu & Yang, 2006) without increasing the overall bit rate.

Next, we proposed a data hiding method with fixed embedding bit rate. The proposed method combines the data hiding method based on a low-bit rate encoder and the selective LSB substitution method to achieve fixed bit rate of the embedded data. We proposed two bit rate reduction methods: the simple bit rate reduction method that refers the number of embedded bits in each samples, and the tolerable quantization step method that controls the distortion induced by data embedding. The evaluation experiment proved that the proposed methods gave statistically significant improvement when embedding bit rate was high (4 kbit/s and higher).

From the experimental result, the largest advantage of the proposed method is obtained when the embedding bit rate is 8 kbit/s. Under this condition, the selective LSB substitution method cannot achieve any improvement over the simple LSB substitution, while the proposed method could improve the quality while the embedding bit rate was exactly 8 kbit/s.

Finally, we proposed a band extension method for G.711-coded speech with low computational cost as an application of the proposed data hiding method. Our method is based on Kataoka's band extension method, and reduces computational cost by exploiting scalar quantization instead of vector quantization. We investigated the conditions for quantizing LSP parameters and gain vector, and obtained 3.27 MOS-LQO value using 1125 bit/s of side information.

As a future work, we will examine a different low-bit rate codec such as LD-CELP (ITU, 1992) from the ADPCM encoder. Moreover, we need a comparison between the proposed method and Kataoka's method using a real platform, as well as comparison to the other band extension methods.

ACKNOWLEDGMENT

This study was partly supported by the Strategic Information and Communications R&D Promotion Programme (SCOPE) No. 051302004 of the Ministry of Internal Affairs and Communications of Japan.

REFERENCES

Aoki, N. (2006). A band extension technique for G.711 speech using steganography. *IEICE Transactions on Communications*, *89*(6), 1896–1898. doi:10.1093/ietcom/e89-b.6.1896

Aoki, N. (2007). Potential of value-added speech communications by using steganography. In *Proceedings of the 3rd International Conference on Intelligent Information Hiding and Multimedia Signal Processing,* (pp. 251-254). IEEE.

Beerends, J. G., Hekstra, A. P., Rix, A. W., & Hollier, M. P. (2002). Perceptual Evaluation of speech quality (PESQ): The new ITU standard for end-to-end speech quality assessment, part 2 – Psychoacoustic model. *Journal of the Audio Engineering Society. Audio Engineering Society*, *50*(10), 765–778.

Broom, S. R. (2006). VoIP quality assessment: Taking account of the edge-device. *IEEE Transactions on Audio. Speech & Language Processing*, *14*(6), 1977–1983. doi:10.1109/TASL.2006.883233

Epps, J., & Holmes, W. H. (1999). A new technique for wideband enhancement of coded narrowband speech. In *Proceedings of the IEEE Workshop on Speech Coding*, (pp. 174-176). IEEE Press.

Hiwasaki, Y., Mori, T., Sasaki, S., Ohmuro, H., & Kataoka, A. (2008). A wideband speech and audio coding candidate for ITU-T G.711 WBE standardization. In *Proceedings of the IEEE International Conference on Acoustics, Speech and Signal Processing*, (pp. 4017–4020). IEEE Press.

ITU. (1988). *G.711: Pulse code modulation (PCM) of voice frequencies*. Retrieved from http://www.itu.int

ITU. (1990). *G.726: 40, 32, 24, 16 kbit/s adaptive differential pulse code modulation (ADPCM)*. Retrieved from http://www.itu.int

ITU. (1992). *G.728: Coding of speech at 16 kbit/s using low-delay code excited linear prediction*. Retrieved from http://www.itu.int

ITU. (2001). *Perceptual evaluation of speech quality (PESQ): An objective method for end-to-end speech quality assessment of narrow-band telephone networks and speech codecs*. Retrieved from http://www.itu.int

ITU. (2003). *Mapping function for transforming of P.862 to MOS-LQO*. Retrieved from http://www.itu.int

ITU. (2005). *P.862.2 wideband extension to recommendation P.862 for the assessment of wideband telephone networks and speech codecs*. Retrieved from http://www.itu.int

ITU. (2006). *G.729.1: G.729 based embedded variable bit-rate coder: An 8-32 kbit/s scalable wideband coder bitstream interoperable with G.729*. Retrieved from http://www.itu.int

Kataoka, A., Mori, T., & Hayashi, S. (2008). Bandwidth extension of G.711 using side information. *IEICE Transactions on Information and Systems*, *91*(4), 1069–1081.

Komaki, N., Aoki, N., & Yamamoto, T. (2003). A packet loss concealment technique for VoIP using steganography. *IEICE Transactions on Fundamentals of Electronics, Communications and Computer Science*, *86*(8), 2069–2072.

Kurematsu, A., Takeda, K., Sagisaka, Y., Katagiri, S., Kuwabara, H., & Shikano, K. (1990). ATR Japanese speech database as a tool of speech recognition and synthesis. *Speech Communication*, *19*(4), 357–363. doi:10.1016/0167-6393(90)90011-W

Larsen, E., & Aarts, R. M. (2004). *Audio bandwidth extension: Application of psychoacoustics, signal processing and loudspeaker design*. Hoboken, NJ: John Wiley & Sons, Inc. doi:10.1002/0470858710

Latzenbeisser, S. (2000). *Information hiding techniques for steganography and digital watermarking*. New York, NY: Artech House.

Lundberg, T., de Bruin, P., Bruhn, S., Hakansson, S., & Craig, S. (2005). Adaptive thresholds for AMR codec mode selection. In *Proceedings of the IEEE Vehicular Technology Conference*, (pp. 2325–2329). IEEE Press.

Makhoul, J., & Berouti, M. (1979). High frequency regeneration in speech coding systems. In *Proceedings of the International Conference on Acoustics, Speech, Signal Processing*, (pp. 428-431). IEEE.

Marvel, L. M., Boncelet, C. G., & Retter, C. T. (1999). Spread spectrum image steganography. *IEEE Transactions on Image Processing*, *8*(8), 1075–1083. doi:10.1109/83.777088

Mazurczyk, W., & Lubacz, J. (2010). LACK—A VoIP steganographic method. *Telecommunication Systems*, *45*(2-3), 153–163. doi:10.1007/s11235-009-9245-y

Perkins, C., Hodson, O., & Hardman, V. (1998). A survey of packet loss recovery techniques for streaming audio. *IEEE Network*, *12*(5), 40–48. doi:10.1109/65.730750

Petitcolas, F. A. P., Anderson, R. J., & Kuhn, M. G. (1999). Information hiding—A survey. *Proceedings of the IEEE*, *87*(7), 1062–1078. doi:10.1109/5.771065

Schulzrinne, H., Casner, S., Frederick, R., & Jacobson, V. (2003). *RTP: A transport protocol for real-time applications, RFC 3550*. Retrieved from http://www.ietf.org

Smith, J. R., Jiang, B., Roy, S., Philipose, M., Sundara-Rajan, K., & Mamishev, A. (2005). ID modulation: Embedding sensor data in an RFID time series. *Lecture Notes in Computer Science*, *3727*, 234–246. doi:10.1007/11558859_18

Soong, F., & Juang, B. (1984). Line spectrum pair (LSP) and speech data compression. In *Proceedings of the IEEE International Conference on Acoustics, Speech and Signal Processing,* (pp. 37–40). IEEE Press.

Tian, H., Zhou, K., Jiang, H., Liu, J., Huang, Y., & Feng, D. (2009). An m-sequence based steganography model for voice over IP. In *Proceedings of the International Conference on Communications,* (pp. 1-5). IEEE.

Valin, J.-M., & Montgomery, C. (2006). Improved noise weighting in CELP coding of speech - Applying the vorbis psychoacoustic model to speex. In *Proceedings of the 120th AES Convention*. AES.

Varshney, U., Snow, A., McGivern, M., & Howard, C. (2002). Voice over IP. *Communications of the ACM*, *45*(1), 89–96. doi:10.1145/502269.502271

Vary, P., & Geiser, B. (2007). Steganographic wideband telephony using narrowband speech codecs. In *Proceedings of the 41st Asilomer Conference on Signals, Systems and Computers,* (pp. 1475-1479). Asilomer.

Wu, Z., & Yang, W. (2006). G.711-based adaptive speech information hiding approach. In *Proceedings of the International Conference of Intelligent Computing,* (pp. 1139-1144). IEEE.

Yang, M. (2004). Low bit rate speech coding. *IEEE Potentials*, *23*(4), 32–36. doi:10.1109/MP.2004.1343228

Yilmaz, A., & Alatan, A. A. (2003). Error concealment of video sequences by data hiding. In *Proceedings of the International Conference on Image Processing,* (pp. 679–682). IEEE.

ADDITIONAL READING

Bender, W., Gruhl, D., Morimoto, N., & Liu, A. (1996). Techniques for data hiding. *IBM Systems Journal*, *35*(3/4), 313–336. doi:10.1147/sj.353.0313

Goode, B. (2002). Voice over Internet protocol (VoIP). *Proceedings of the IEEE*, *90*(9), 1495–1517. doi:10.1109/JPROC.2002.802005

Heute, U. (2008). Telephone-speech quality. In Hänsler, E., & Schmidt, G. (Eds.), *Speech and Audio Processing in Adverse Environments* (pp. 287–337). Berlin, Germany: Springer-Verlag. doi:10.1007/978-3-540-70602-1_9

Janssen, J., De Vleeschauwer, D., Buchli, M., & Petit, G. H. (2002). Assessing voice quality in packet-based telephony. *IEEE Internet Computing*, *6*(3), 48–56. doi:10.1109/MIC.2002.1003131

Petitcolas, F. A. P., Anderson, R. J., & Kuhn, M. G. (1999). Information hiding—A survey. *Proceedings of the IEEE*, *87*(7), 1062–1078. doi:10.1109/5.771065

Petrovic, R., Winograd, J. M., Jemili, K., & Metois, E. (1999). Data hiding within audio signals. In *Proceedings of the International Conference on Telecommunications in Modern Satellite, Cable and Broadcasting,* (pp. 88-95). IEEE.

Rix, A. W., Beerends, J. G., Hollier, M. P., & Hekstra, A. P. (2001). Perceptual evaluation of speech quality (PESQ)-A new method for speech quality assessment of telephone networks and codecs. In *Proceedings of the IEEE International Conference on Acoustics, Speech, and Signal Processing,* (pp. 749-752). IEEE Press.

Spanias, A. S. (1994). Speech coding: A tutorial review. *Proceedings of the IEEE, 82*(10), 1541–1582. doi:10.1109/5.326413

Yang, M. (2004). Low bit rate speech coding. *IEEE Potentials, 23*(4), 32–36. doi:10.1109/MP.2004.1343228

Chapter 8
Enhancement of Speech Quality in Telephony Communications by Steganography

Naofumi Aoki
Hokkaido University, Japan

ABSTRACT

Steganography can transmit supplementary data without changing conventional data formats. The concept of high value-added communications is drawn from this advantage of steganography. As a specific application of the concept, this chapter describes two topics about the enhancement of the speech quality in telephony communications by steganography. A packet loss concealment technique and a band extension technique are explained. These techniques employ steganography for transmitting side information for improving the performance of signal processing. In addition, this chapter describes an efficient steganography technique devised for G.711, the most common codec for telephony speech standardized by ITU-T. The proposed technique, named selective LSB replacement technique, outperforms the conventional one in order to decrease the degradation caused by embedding side information into speech data by steganography.

INTRODUCTION

There is a somewhat negative image of steganography since it may be employed for illegal secret communications (Singh, 2000). However, any technology can be a poison or a medicine depending on its usage. The concept of high value-added communications potentially indicates a positive usage of steganography. Transmitting supplementary data by steganography, new functions may be realized without changing conventional data formats.

Of course, it might be easier to design completely new systems for such new functions. However, it costs enormously to replace conventional standards that are used widespread. The concept of high value-added communications based on steganography can be a solution for adding new functions to the conventional standards without losing their compatibility (Aoki, 2007b).

DOI: 10.4018/978-1-4666-2217-3.ch008

This concept gives a research framework of steganography that employs supplementary data as side information for improving the performance of signal processing. One of the practical targets is controlling the quality of multimedia information without increasing its apparent data size. It mainly focuses on the enhancement of communications quality at the receiver by using secret side information embedded at the sender. It has been indicated that the concept may potentially be applicable to some practical applications such as packet loss concealment for reliable speech communications (Aoki, 2007b; Ito, Konno, Ito, & Makino, 2010), band extension for high-fidelity speech communications (Aoki, 2007b; Ito, Handa, & Suzuki, 2009), and the improvement of a speech codec (Ito & Makino, 2009), and so on. Other recent trends are controlling the quality of entertainment applications such as manipulating vocal signal in music data at the receiver by using secret side information embedded at the sender (Sasaki, Hahm, & Ito, 2011).

In order to appeal the effectiveness of the concept, this article describes two topics about the enhancement of the speech quality in telephony communications by steganography. A packet loss concealment technique and a band extension technique are explained (Aoki, 2007b).

A packet loss concealment technique is employed for reliable telephony communications. Packet loss causes silent gaps that degrade the speech quality in telephony communications. It inevitably occurs in recent telephony communications systems based on VoIP (Voice over IP) that transmits speech data in best-effort networks such as the Internet. In order to enhance the speech quality, this article proposes a technique in which side information is embedded into speech data by steganography, and employed for restoring the gap frames caused by packet loss (Aoki, 2003a, 2003b). This article describes how the proposed technique outperforms the conventional one.

A band extension technique is employed for high-fidelity telephony communications. It enhances the clarity of the telephony speech. Since the sampling rate of the conventional telephony speech is 8 kHz, the frequency components higher than 4 kHz are not transmitted. Due to this limitation, the speech quality is somewhat muffled. In order to enhance the speech quality, this article proposes a technique in which side information is embedded into speech data by steganography, and employed for restoring the frequency components higher than 4 kHz (Aoki, 2006b, 2006c, 2007a). This article describes how the proposed technique outperforms the conventional one.

STEGANOGRAPHY FOR TELEPHONY SPEECH

As shown in Figure 1, steganography embeds secret message into the redundancy of cover data. Such redundancy may be a container for transmitting the secret message. The capacity for the secret message depends on the size of the redundancy.

In this article, speech data encoded with G.711 is chosen to be the cover data. G.711 is the most common codec for telephony speech standardized by ITU-T (International Telecommunication Union Telecommunication Standardization Sector) (ITU-T, 1988). It consists of μ-law and A-law schemes designated PCMU and PCMA, respectively. PCMU is mainly employed in North America and Japan. It encodes 14 bit speech data into 8 bit compression data at an 8 kHz sampling rate. PCMA is mainly employed in Europe. It encodes 13 bit speech data into 8 bit compression data at an 8 kHz sampling rate. Due to the simple logarithmic quantization algorithms, there remains a plenty of redundancy in the speech data encoded with G.711.

The LSB (Least Significant Bit) replacement technique is known as one of the simplest steganography technique (Cox, 2008). It just embeds the secret message into the LSB of the cover data. It is based on the fact that the LSB of the cover data obtained from multimedia information such

Figure 1. Embedding procedure of steganography

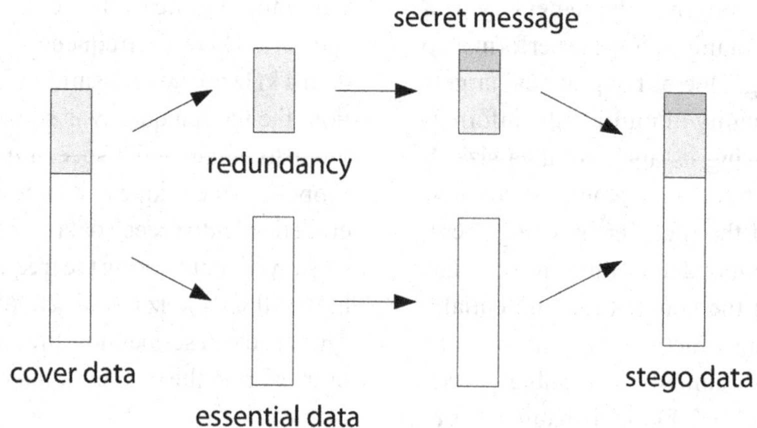

as audio and visual data is not very important in perception. The embedding procedure of the LSB replacement technique for 8 bit speech data encoded with G.711 is shown in Figure 2 in which b represents a 1 bit secret message and c represents a sample of 8 bit speech data.

SELECTIVE LSB REPLACEMENT TECHNIQUE

Although the LSB replacement technique is sufficient enough in many practical cases, some degradation in the cover data by embedding the secret message is inevitable. In order to decrease the degradation as much as possible, this article proposes a technique named selective LSB replacement technique. It embeds the secret message by taking account of the characteristic of G.711.

The magnitude of the LSB of speech data encoded with G.711 depends on the magnitude of speech data itself due to its logarithmic quantization algorithm (ITU-T, 1988). Exploiting this characteristic of G.711, the selective LSB replacement technique embeds the secret message into the speech data of small magnitude.

Figure 3 shows the schematic procedure of embedding 4 bit secret message with the selective LSB replacement technique. In order to detect correctly the speech data in which the secret message is embedded, the magnitude of speech data is defined as follows for the sorting procedure. This ignores the LSB of the speech data that may be replaced with the secret message.

$$| s(n) |= \begin{cases} 2\lfloor s(n) / 2 \rfloor + 1 & s(n) \geq +0 \\ 2\lfloor -s(n) / 2 \rfloor & s(n) \leq -0 \end{cases} \quad (1)$$

where $s(n)$ represents a sample of 8 bit speech data, $\lfloor x \rfloor$ represents the integer that does not exceed x. After the sorting procedure, the secret message is embedded into the LSB of the speech data. Then, the stego speech data is sorted back into its original order.

Figure 4 shows the SNR (Signal-to-Noise Ratio) of stego speech data processed by the selective LSB replacement technique as well as the conventional one. In this comparison, two pieces of speech data phonated by a male and a female speaker are employed as the cover data. The length of each speech data is 5 s. A binary sequence is embedded as the secret message in the every frame of the speech data. The frame length is 20 ms. It is equivalent to 160 samples at an 8 kHz sampling rate, so that 160 bits are the maximum capacity of the secret message in each

Figure 2. Embedding procedure of the LSB replacement technique programmed in C language

```
if (b == 0) c &= 0xFE;
if (b == 1) c |= 0x01;
```

frame. Figure 4 shows the average SNR calculated from all the frames of the speech data.

This comparison indicates that the speech quality is less degraded by the selective LSB replacement technique especially when the size of the secret message is small enough. Consequently, it is indicated that the selective LSB replacement technique outperforms the conventional one in order to decrease the degradation caused by embedding the secret message into speech data by steganography.

A PACKET LOSS CONCEALMENT TECHNIQUE BY USING STEGANOGRAPHY

The end-to-end speech quality in best-effort telephony communications systems is not necessarily guaranteed. Packet loss causes silent gaps that degrade the speech quality in telephony communications. In order to reduce the degradation, a number of packet loss concealment techniques have been studied (Perkins, 1998).

One of the practical techniques for restoring the silent gaps is standardized by ITU-T as G.711 Appendix 1 (ITU-T, 1999). This technique restores the silent gap by copying repeatedly the pitch waveform extracted from the backward frame of the gap frame. This technique just extends the waveform of the backward frame, so that it is designated as one-side PWR (Pitch Waveform Replication) in this article.

Figure 3. Schematic procedure of embedding 4 bit secret message into speech data encoded with G.711 by means of the selective LSB replacement technique: (a) original speech data, (b) sorting procedure, (c) embedding procedure, and (d) stego speech data

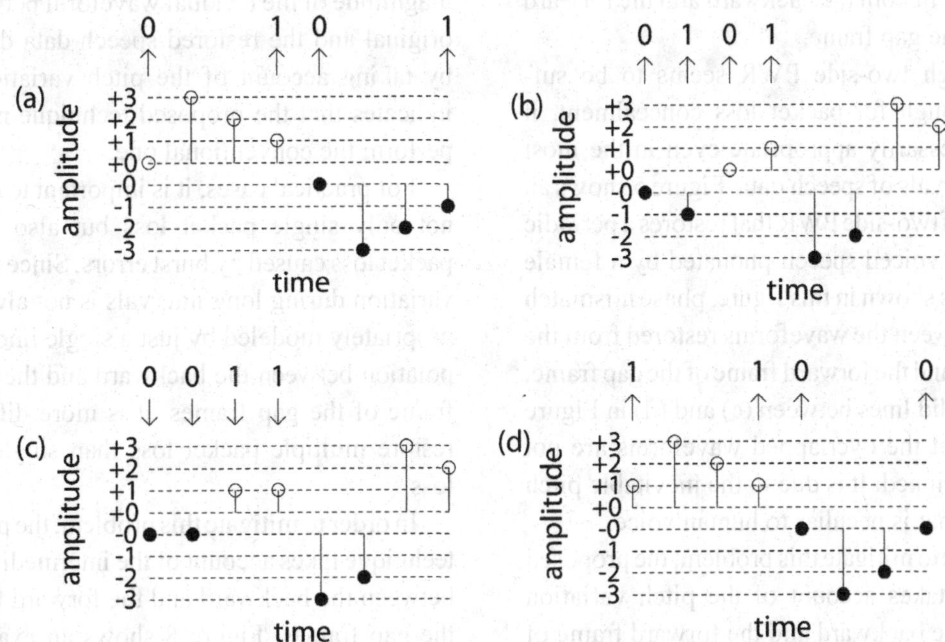

Figure 4. SNR of stego speech data: (a) selective LSB replacement technique and (b) conventional LSB replacement technique

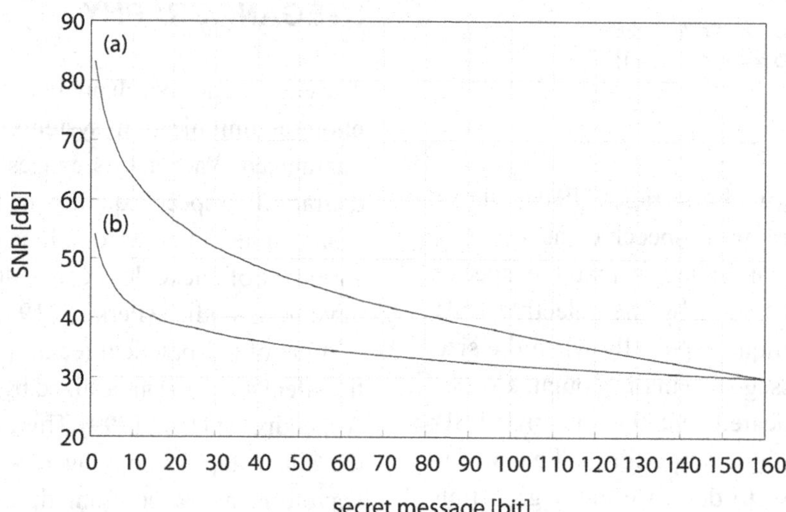

Since one-side PWR does not consider the pitch variation in the gap frame, the restored speech data may have some discrepancy at the boundary between the gap frame and the forward frame. In order to reduce such discrepancy, two-side PWR is proposed instead of one-side PWR (Aoki, 2004a, 2004b, 2004c, 2006a). It crossfades the waveform restored from both the backward and the forward frame of the gap frame.

Although two-side PWR seems to be sufficient enough for packet loss concealment, it is not necessarily appropriate even in the most stable intervals of speech data. Figure 5 shows an example of two-side PWR that restores a periodic interval of voiced speech phonated by a female speaker. As shown in this figure, phase mismatch occurs between the waveforms restored from the backward and the forward frame of the gap frame. Vertical solid lines between (c) and (d) in Figure 5 show that the overlapped waveforms are not properly aligned. It is due to the inevitable pitch variation that is peculiar to human voice.

In order to mitigate this problem, the proposed technique takes account of the pitch variation between the backward and the forward frame of the gap frame. As shown in Figure 6, the proposed technique models the pitch variation by linear interpolation. Figure 7 shows an example of packet loss concealment with the proposed technique. Vertical solid lines between (c) and (d) in Figure 7 show that the overlapped waveforms are properly aligned. Compared with Figure 5, the magnitude of the residual waveform between the original and the restored speech data decreases by taking account of the pitch variation. This indicates that the proposed technique may outperform the conventional one.

For practical cases, it is important to consider not only single packet loss but also multiple packet loss caused by burst errors. Since the pitch variation during long intervals is not always appropriately modeled by just a single linear interpolation between the backward and the forward frame of the gap frames, it is more difficult to restore multiple packet loss than single packet loss.

In order to mitigate this problem, the proposed technique takes account of the intermediate pitch between the backward and the forward frame of the gap frames. Figure 8 shows an example of

Figure 5. Procedure of two-side PWR technique: (a) original speech data, (b) degraded speech data, (c) extrapolation from the backward frame, (d) extrapolation from the forward frame, (e) restored speech data, and (f) residual between the original and the restored speech data

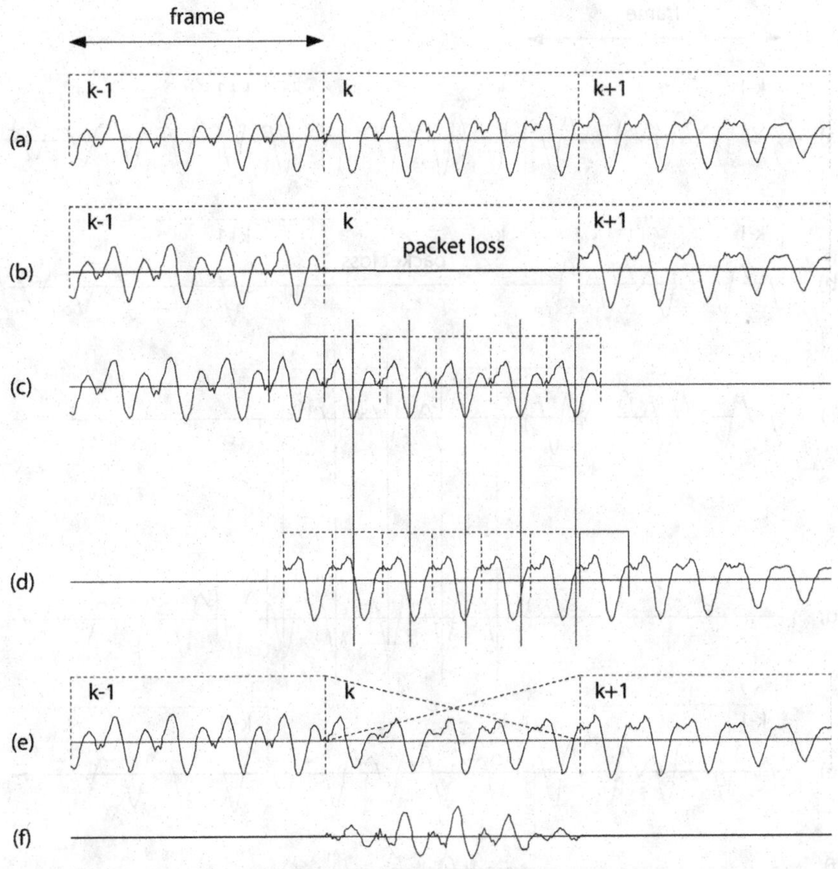

Figure 6. Linear interpolation of pitch variation in a gap frame

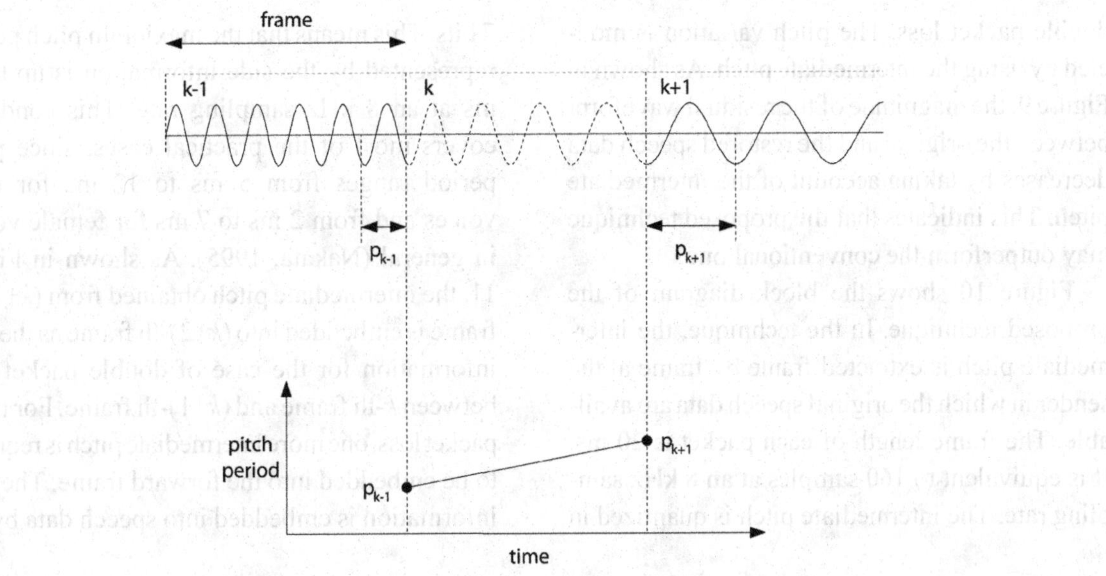

Figure 7. Procedure of the proposed technique: (a) original speech data, (b) degraded speech data, (c) extrapolation from the backward frame, (d) extrapolation from the forward frame, (e) restored speech data, and (f) residual between the original and the restored speech data

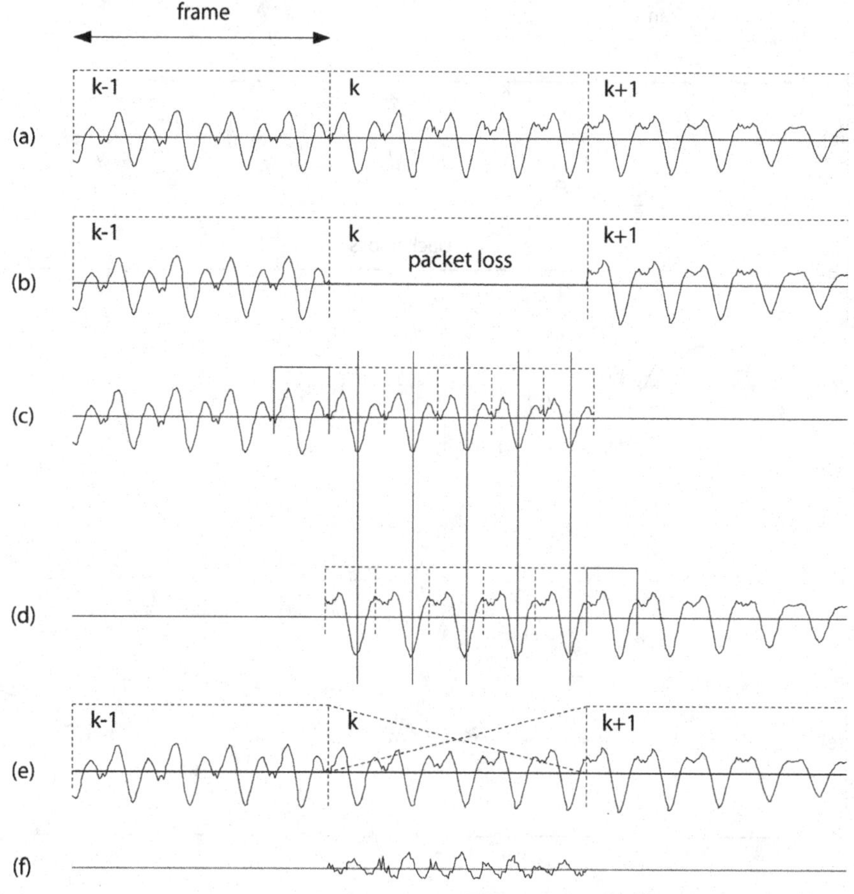

double packet loss. The pitch variation is modeled by using the intermediate pitch. As shown in Figure 9, the magnitude of the residual waveform between the original and the restored speech data decreases by taking account of the intermediate pitch. This indicates that the proposed technique may outperform the conventional one.

Figure 10 shows the block diagram of the proposed technique. In the technique, the intermediate pitch is extracted frame by frame at the sender in which the original speech data are available. The frame length of each packet is 20 ms. It is equivalent to 160 samples at an 8 kHz sampling rate. The intermediate pitch is quantized in 7 bits. This means that the maximum pitch period represented by the side information is up to 16 ms at an 8 kHz sampling rate. This condition covers most of the practical cases, since pitch period ranges from 5 ms to 12 ms for male voices and from 2 ms to 7 ms for female voices in general (Nakata, 1995). As shown in Figure 11, the intermediate pitch obtained from (k+1)-th frame is embedded into (k+2)-th frame as the side information for the case of double packet loss between k-th frame and (k+1)-th frame. For triple packet loss, one more intermediate pitch is required to be embedded into the forward frame. The side information is embedded into speech data by us-

Figure 8. Linear interpolation of pitch variation in gap frames for double packet loss by taking account of the intermediate pitch

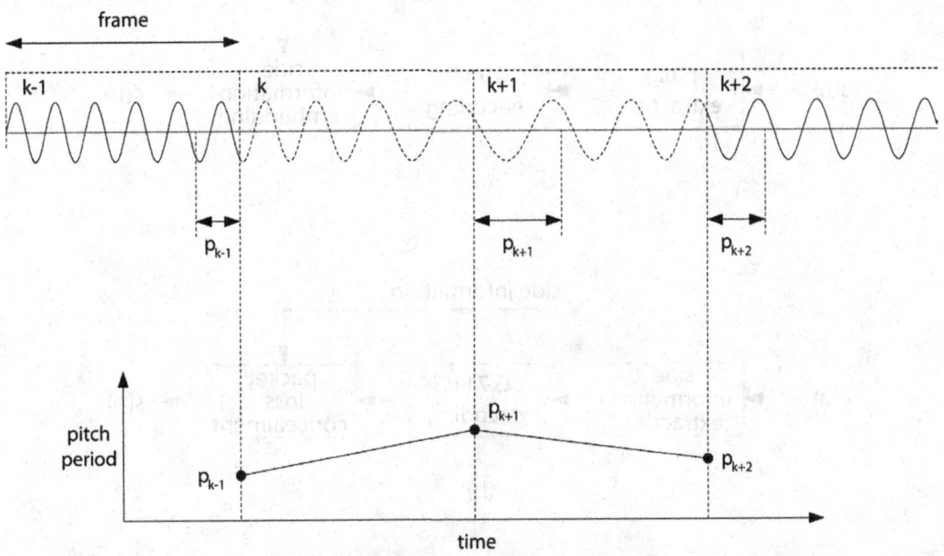

Figure 9. Packet loss concealment for double packet loss: (a) original speech data, (b) degraded speech data, (c) restored speech data without taking account of the intermediate pitch, (d) its residual from the original speech data, (e) restored speech data with taking account of the intermediate pitch, and (f) its residual from the original speech data

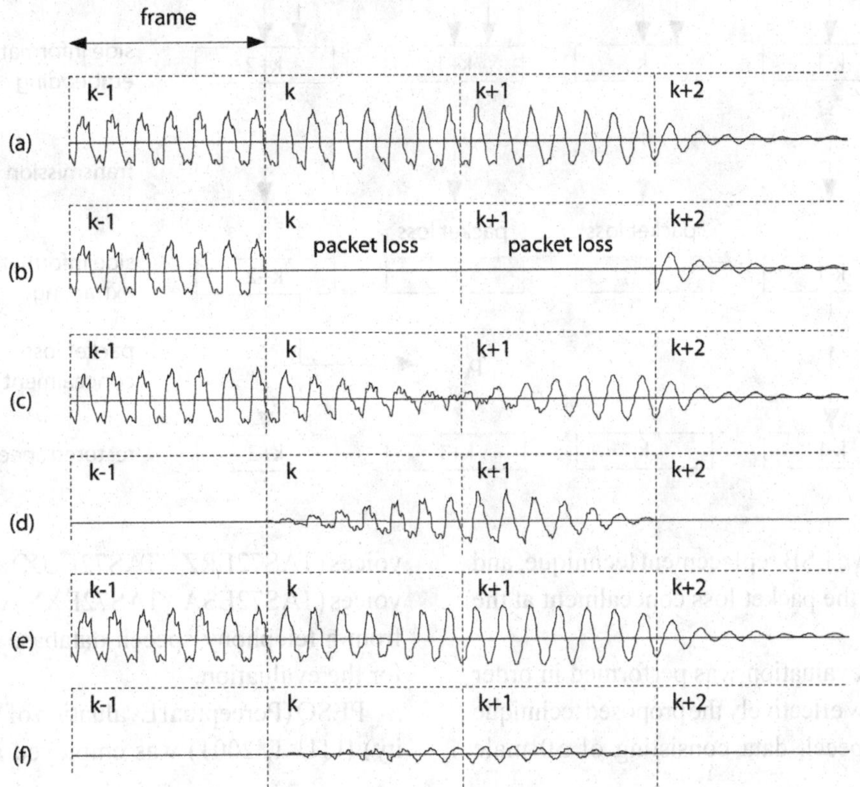

Figure 10. Procedure of the proposed technique at (a) sender and (b) receiver

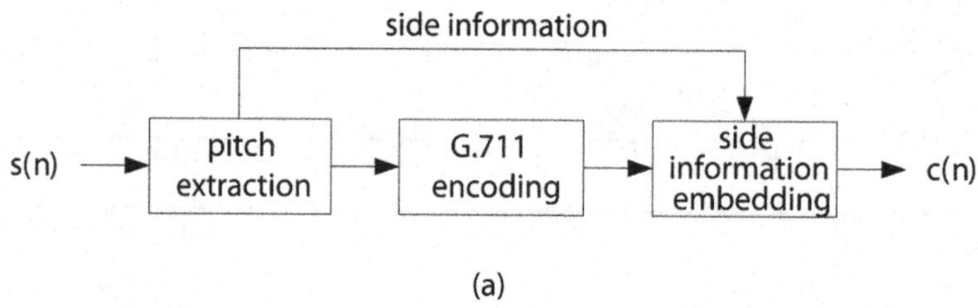

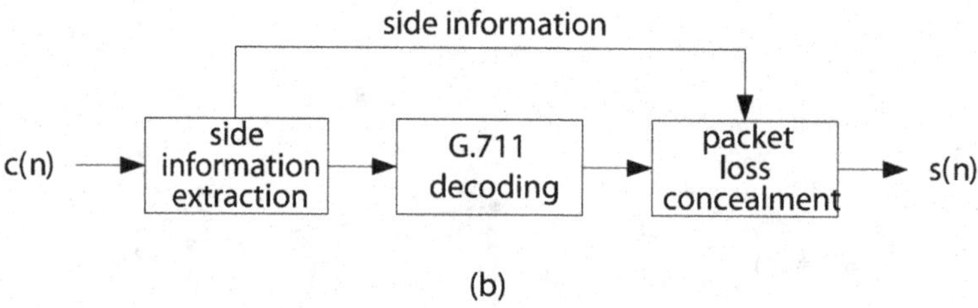

Figure 11. Procedure of the proposed technique for double packet loss

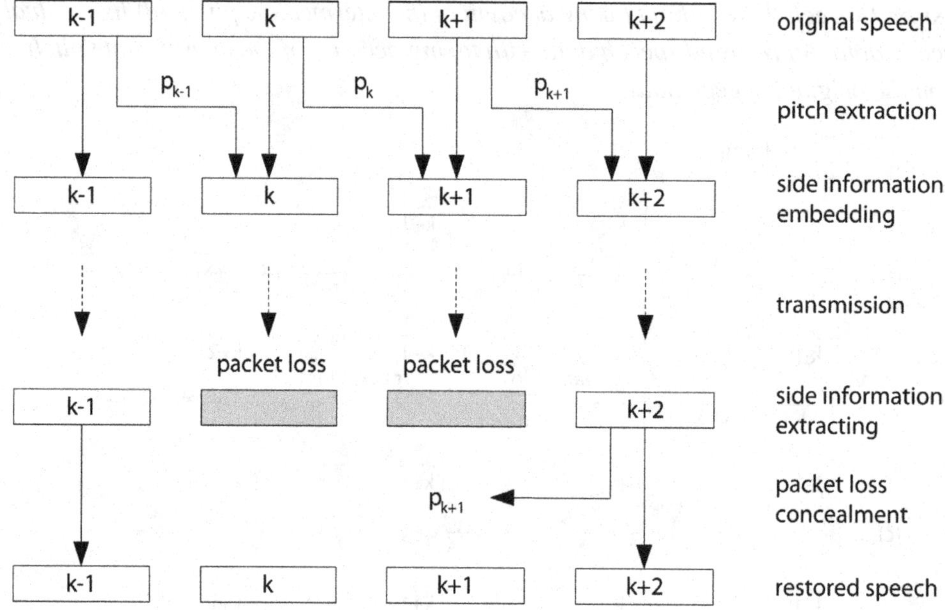

ing the selective LSB replacement technique, and employed for the packet loss concealment at the receiver.

Objective evaluation was performed in order to examine how effectively the proposed technique works. 100 speech data consisting of 50 male voices (TAS72ERZ–TAS72EUX) and 50 female voices (TAS72ESA–TAS72EXN) were obtained from a telephony speech database (ATR, 1997) for the evaluation.

PESQ (Perceptual Evaluation of Speech Quality) (ITU-T, 2001) was employed as a measure of the speech quality as well as SNR. It is widely employed as an objective measure evaluating the speech quality in telephony communications. Taking account of the characteristics of human auditory perception, PESQ positively correlates with a subjective measure employed for evaluating MOS (Mean Opinion Score). PESQ score ranges from 4.5 to -0.5. The higher the PESQ score, the better the speech quality.

In the evaluation, each speech data was artificially degraded by packet loss at the rate between 0.5% and 10%. The conditions of single, double, and triple packet loss were evaluated. The degraded speech data were restored with one-side PWR and two-side PWR as well as the proposed technique.

The experimental results are shown in Figures 12, 13, 14, 15, 16, and 17. These figures also show the 95% confidence intervals of the averages. Although the degradation increases according to the packet loss rate as well as the duration of burst errors, the results show that both the SNR and the PESQ of the proposed technique are larger than those of the other conventional techniques at the same packet loss rate. This means that the speech quality of the proposed technique exceeds those of the other conventional techniques in the same conditions. It is indicated that the speech quality may be enhanced by restoring appropriately the gap frames by taking account of the pitch variation.

A BAND EXTENSION TECHNIQUE BY USING STEGANOGRAPHY

A band extension technique is employed for high-fidelity telephony communications. It enhances the clarity of the telephony speech. Figure 18 compares the frequency characteristics between the narrow-band telephony speech in the conventional systems and the wide-band telephony speech in the high-fidelity systems. This is an example obtained from a periodic interval of voiced speech phonated by a female speaker. As shown in this figure, harmonic tones of voiced speech are still found over 4 kHz. However, the frequency components higher than 4 kHz are not transmitted in the conventional systems, since the sampling rate is set to be 8 kHz for the narrow-band telephony speech. This limitation makes the speech quality somewhat muffled.

In order to enhance the speech quality, non-linear signal processing such as full wave rectification is often employed for generating harmonic tones higher than 4 kHz. Figure 19 shows the procedure of the band extension technique for the narrow-band telephony speech that models a periodic interval of voiced speech. As shown in this figure, full wave rectification can artificially restore the frequency components higher than 4 kHz by referring the harmonic structure of the frequency components lower than 4 kHz (Aarts, Larsen, & Schobben, 2002).

In order to simplify the explanation of the method, the conventional technique does not consider the gain variation of the high band (Aarts, Larsen, & Schobben, 2002). The gain parameter for the high band is time-invariant in the conventional technique. However, this is not always reasonable for the band extension of unvoiced speech. In general, the magnitude of the high band is large for unvoiced speech compared with voiced speech. In order to improve the conventional technique, the proposed technique takes account of gain variation according to the characteristics of speech data (Aoki, 2008, 2009, 2010).

Figure 20 shows the spectrogram obtained from a Japanese speech data "shiro" phonated by a female speaker. The high band is restored from the low band with the conventional and the proposed technique as shown in Figure 21 and Figure 22. Compared with the conventional technique, the proposed technique can restore the high band more appropriately especially in the part of unvoiced speech. It is due to the gain control of the high band in the proposed technique.

Figure 23 shows the block diagram of the proposed technique. In the proposed technique, the magnitude of the high band is estimated frame

Figure 12. SNR of single packet loss: (a) proposed technique, (b) two-side PWR, and (c) one-side PWR

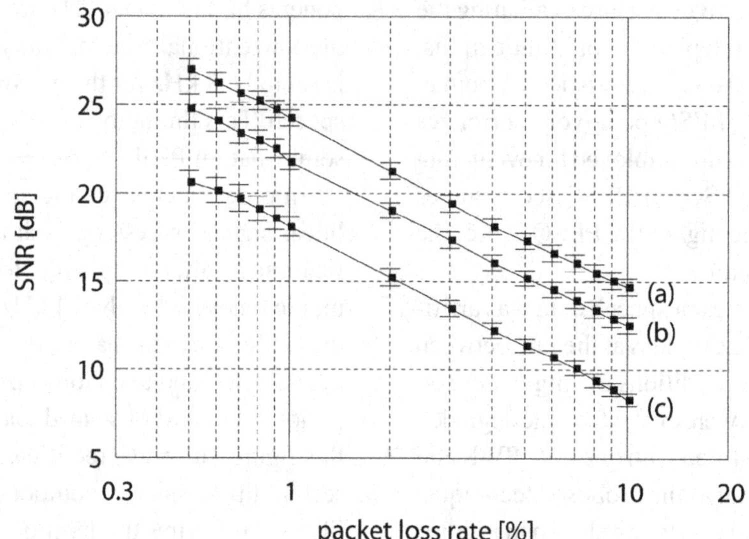

by frame at the sender in which the original speech data are available. The frame length of each packet is 20 ms. It is equivalent to 160 samples at an 8 kHz sampling rate. The magnitude of the high band is quantized in 15 bits. This means that the maximum magnitude represented by the side information is up to 32767. The side information is embedded into speech data by using the selective LSB replacement technique, and employed for the band extension at the receiver.

Subjective evaluation was performed in order to examine how effectively the proposed technique works. 10 speech data consisting of 5 male voices (TAS72ESB, TAS72ETR, TAS72ETX, TAS72EXM, TAS72EYG) and 5 female voices (TAS72ESG, TAS72ETM, TAS72ETU,

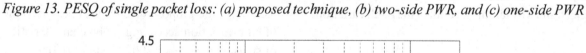

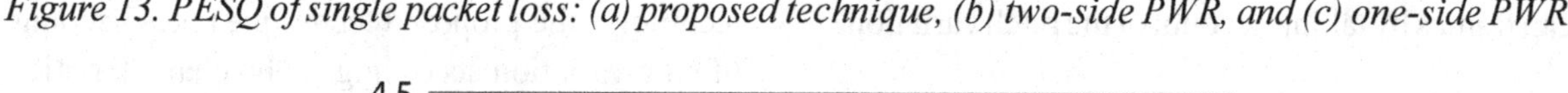
Figure 13. PESQ of single packet loss: (a) proposed technique, (b) two-side PWR, and (c) one-side PWR

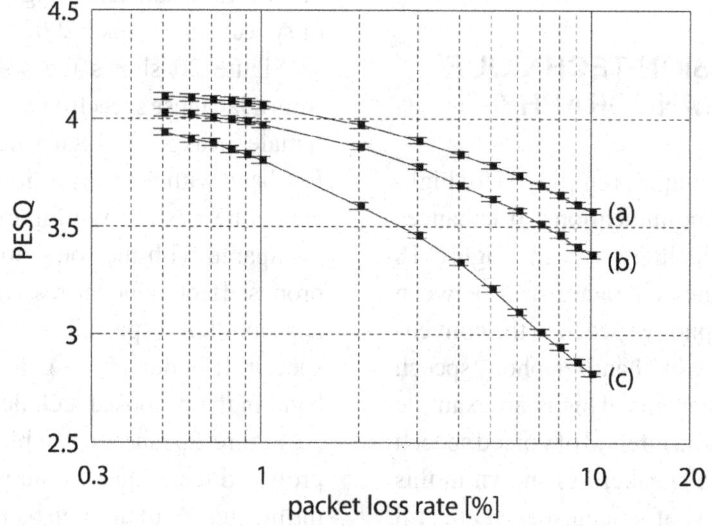

Figure 14. SNR of double packet loss: (a) proposed technique, (b) two-side PWR, and (c) one-side PWR

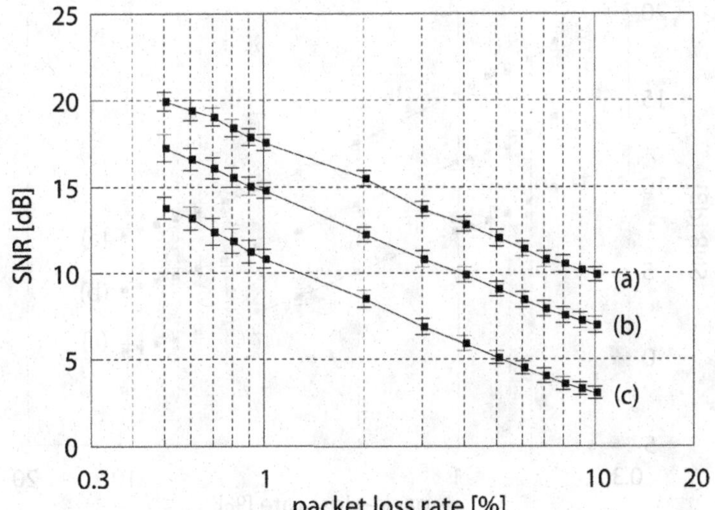

TAS72EYF, TAS72EYJ) were obtained from a telephony speech database (ATR, 1997) for the evaluation. The male voices were labeled (m1 – m5) and the female voices were labeled (f1 – f5) in the evaluation.

CMOS (Comparison Mean Opinion Score) (ITU-T, 1996) was employed as a measure of the speech quality. In each trial of comparison test, a reference stimulus, stimulus A, and stimulus B were presented to the listeners in this order. The reference stimulus was the unprocessed original speech data, while stimulus A and B were the band-extended speech data processed by means of either the proposed or the conventional technique. 10 listeners rated the speech quality of stimulus B compared with stimulus A according to Table 1. Each combination of stimulus A and B was presented twice by reversing the order, so

Figure 15. PESQ of double packet loss: (a) proposed technique, (b) two-side PWR, and (c) one-side PWR

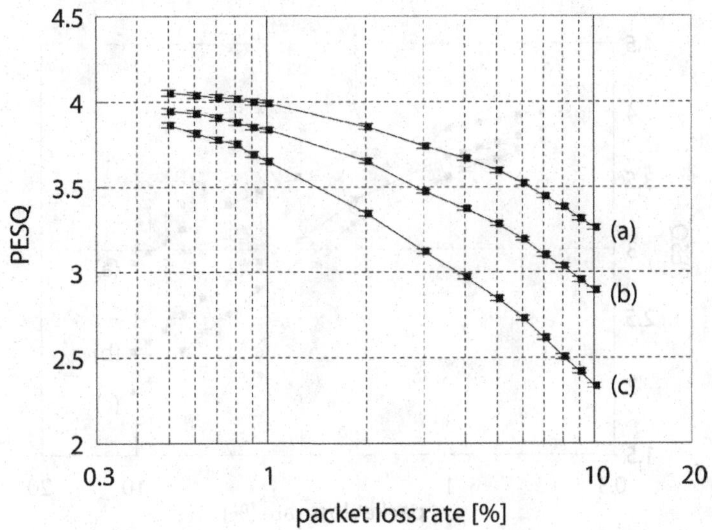

Figure 16. SNR of triple packet loss: (a) proposed technique, (b) two-side PWR, and (c) one-side PWR

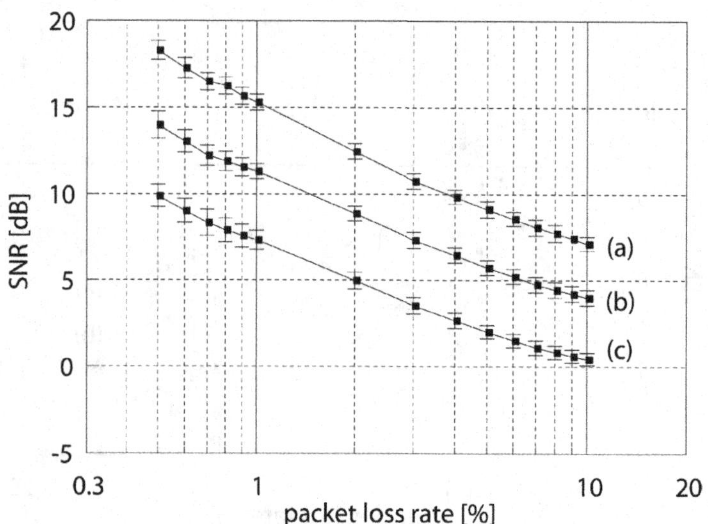

that each condition was evaluated 20 times by the 10 listeners.

Figure 24 shows the experimental result. This figure also shows the 95% confidence intervals of the averages. The results show that the proposed technique outperforms the conventional technique. It is indicated that the speech quality may be enhanced by restoring appropriately the high band by taking account of the gain variation.

DISCUSSION

Both of the proposed techniques intend to preserve the information that is lost in the transmission. Such information is difficult to estimate at the receiver, although it is easy at the sender, where the original information is available. The proposed techniques perform the signal processing more efficiently than the conventional ones due to the availability of the side information.

Figure 17. PESQ of triple packet loss: (a) proposed technique, (b) two-side PWR, and (c) one-side PWR

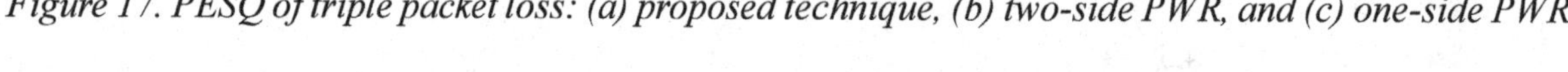

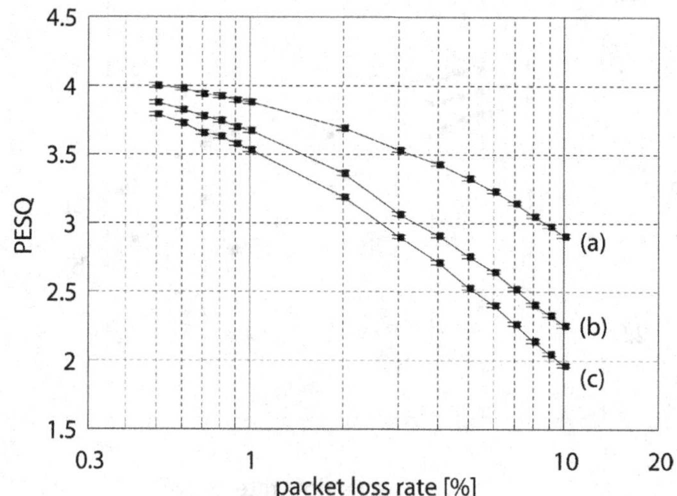

Figure 18. Frequency characteristics of the narrow-band and the wide-band telephony speech

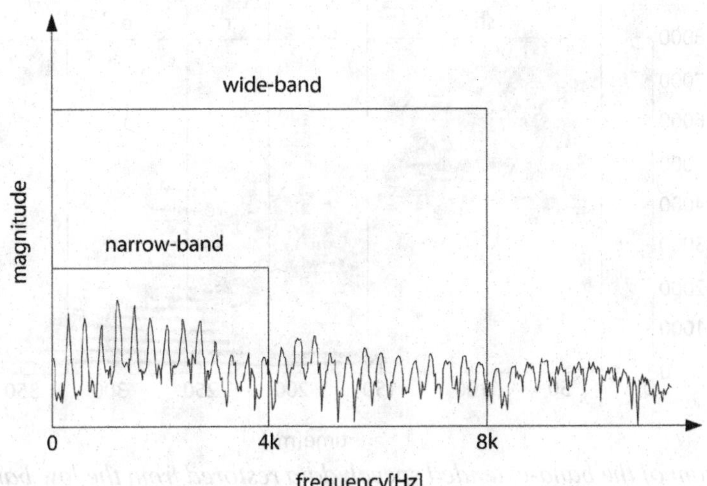

Figure 19. Procedure of the band extension technique: (a) narrow-band speech data, (b) band-pass filtering, (c) full wave rectification, (d) high-pass filtering, and (e) mixing the high and the low bands

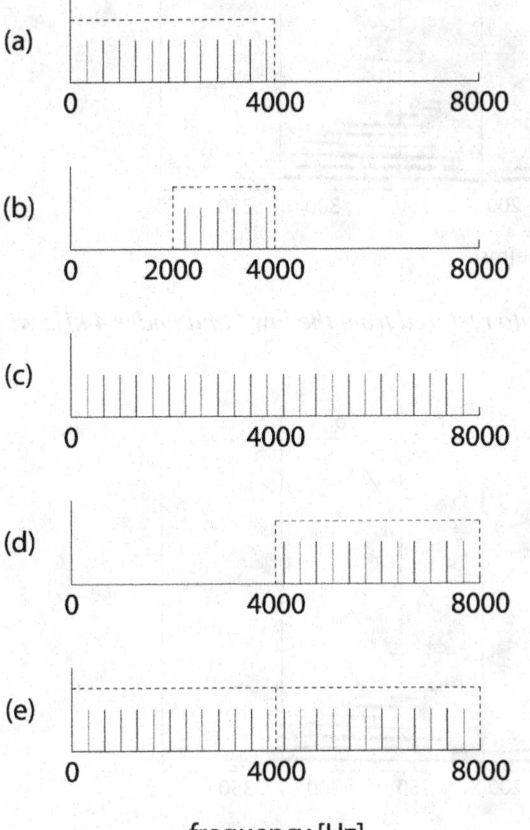

Table 1. Seven-point scale in CMOS

Point	Quality
+3	much better
+2	better
+1	slightly better
0	about the same
-1	slightly worse
-2	worse
-3	much worse

The proposed techniques do not require new data formats for transmitting the side information, since steganography can secretly transmit the side information along with the speech data itself without increasing its apparent data size. Stego speech data processed by the proposed techniques do not lose the compatibility with the conventional standards, so that it is still available in the conventional telephony communications systems.

Although embedding the side information causes some degradation, it is negligible when the size of the side information is small enough. On the contrary, the speech quality is much enhanced by embedding the side information. It should be

Figure 20. Spectrogram obtained from a Japanese speech data "shiro" phonated by a female speaker

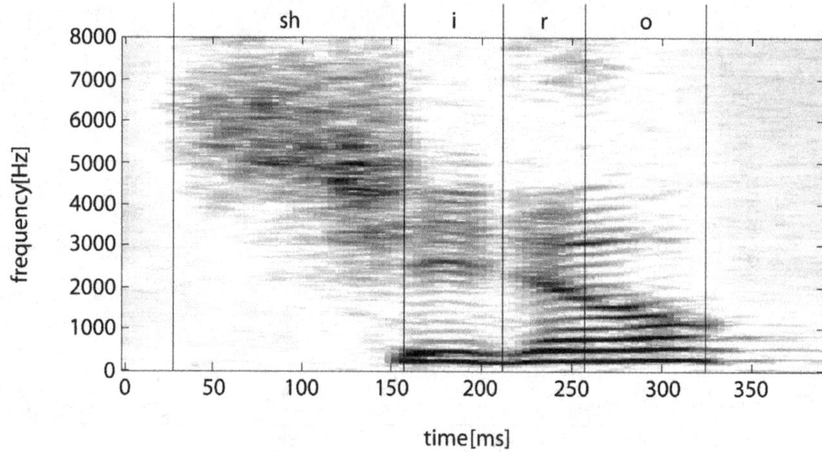

Figure 21. Spectrogram of the band-extended speech data restored from the low band under 4 kHz with the conventional technique

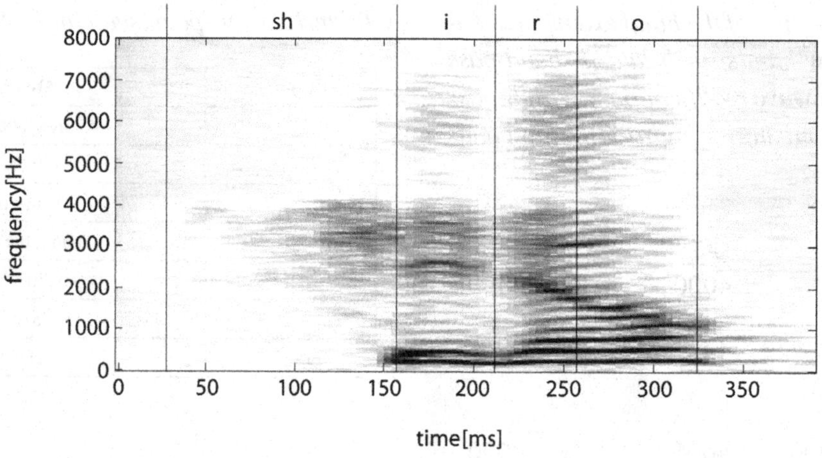

Figure 22. Spectrogram of the band-extended speech data restored from the low band under 4 kHz with the proposed technique

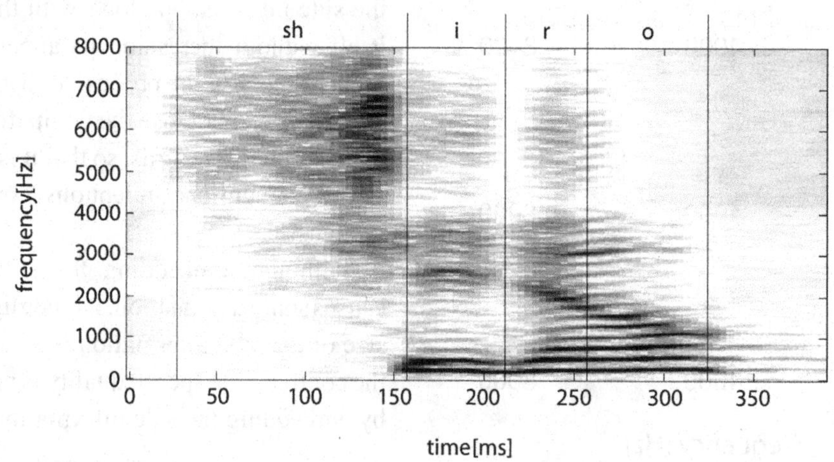

Figure 23. Procedure of the proposed technique at (a) sender and (b) receiver

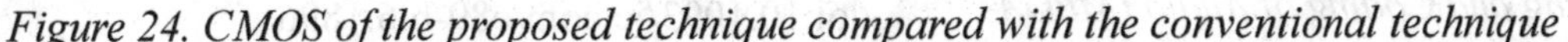

Figure 24. CMOS of the proposed technique compared with the conventional technique

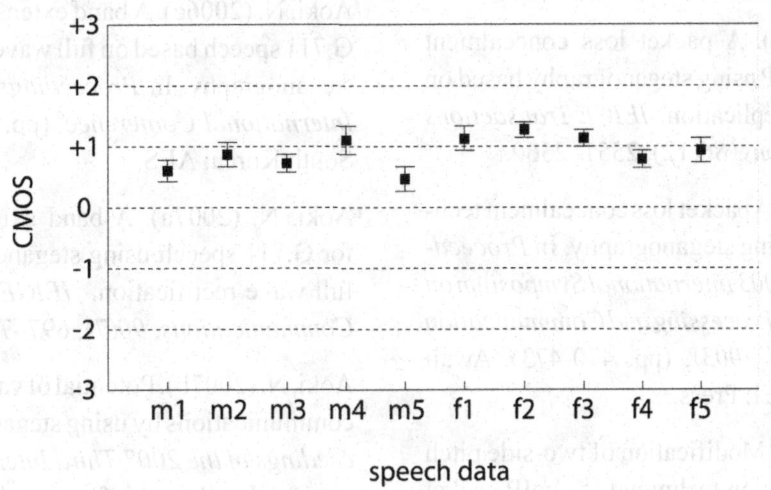

remarked that the proposed techniques indicate an attractive paradox that the speech quality can be enhanced by degrading the speech quality.

CONCLUSION

This article described two topics about the enhancement of the speech quality in telephony communications by steganography. A packet loss concealment technique and a band extension technique were explained. These applications appeal the effectiveness of the concept of high value-added communications based on steganography. The experimental results indicate that the speech quality may be enhanced by taking account of the appropriate side information. Steganography can be a solution for transmitting such side information without losing the compatibility with the conventional telephony communications systems.

The main focus of the research activities on steganography is to discover efficient embedding techniques that allow more capacity for transmitting the secret message with less degradation of the cover data. In order to promote furthermore the research activities, it is also important to propose some practical applications of steganography. The topics described in this article can be pilot cases for such applications. These examples indicate that steganography can be a promising methodology for realizing the concept of high value-added communications.

REFERENCES

Aarts, R. M., Larsen, E., & Schobben, D. (2002). Improving perceived bass and reconstruction of high frequencies for band limited signals. In *Proceedings of IEEE Benelux Workshop on Model based Processing and Coding of Audio (MPCA-2002)*, (pp. 59-71). IEEE Press.

Aoki, N. (2003a). A packet loss concealment technique for VoIP using steganography based on pitch waveform replication. *IEICE Transactions on Communications*, *86*(12), 2551–2560.

Aoki, N. (2003b). A packet loss concealment technique for VoIP using steganography. In *Proceedings of the IEEE 2003 International Symposium on Intelligent Signal Processing and Communication Systems (ISPACS 2003)*, (pp. 470-473). Awaji Island, Japan: IEEE Press.

Aoki, N. (2004a). Modification of two-side pitch waveform replication technique for VoIP packet loss concealment. *IEICE Transactions on Communications*, *87*(4), 1041–1044.

Aoki, N. (2004b). Modification of two-side pitch waveform replication technique for VoIP packet loss concealment using steganography. In *Proceedings of the IEICE and IEEK 2004 International Technical Conference on Circuits/Systems, Computers and Communications (ITC-CSCC 2004)*. Matsushima, Japan: IEICE/IEEK.

Aoki, N. (2004c). VoIP packet loss concealment based on two-side pitch waveform replication technique using steganography. In *Proceedings of the IEEE Region 10 Conference TENCON*, (pp. 52-55). Chiang Mai, Thailand: IEEE Press.

Aoki, N. (2006a). A VoIP packet loss concealment technique taking account of pitch variation in pitch waveform replication. *Electronics and Communications in Japan (Part I Communications)*, *89*(3), 1–9. doi:10.1002/ecja.20268

Aoki, N. (2006b). A band extension technique for G.711 speech using steganography. *IEICE Transactions on Communications*, *89*(6), 1896–1898. doi:10.1093/ietcom/e89-b.6.1896

Aoki, N. (2006c). A band extension technique for G.711 speech based on full wave rectification and steganography. In *Proceedings of the AES 29th International Conference*, (pp. 124-127). Seoul, South Korea: AES.

Aoki, N. (2007a). A band extension technique for G.711 speech using steganography based on full wave rectification. *IEICE Transactions on Communications*, *90*(7), 697–704.

Aoki, N. (2007b). Potential of value-added speech communications by using steganography. In *Proceedings of the 2007 Third International Conference on Intelligent Information Hiding and Multimedia Signal Processing (IIHMSP2007)*, (vol 2), (pp. 251-254). Kaohsiung, Taiwan: IIHMSP.

Aoki, N. (2008). Improvement of band extension technique for G.711 telephony speech based on full wave rectification. In *Proceedings of the 11th International Conference on Digital Audio Effects (DAFx-08)*, (pp. 161-164). Espoo, Finland: DAFx.

Aoki, N. (2009). Improvement of a band extension technique for G.711 telephony speech by using steganography. In *Proceedings of the 2009 Fifth International Conference on Intelligent Information Hiding and Multimedia Signal Processing (IIHMSP2009)*, (pp. 487-490). Kyoto, Japan: IIHMSP.

Aoki, N. (2010). A band extension technique for narrow-band telephony speech based on full wave rectification. *IEICE Transactions on Communications*, *93*(3), 729–731. doi:10.1587/transcom.E93.B.729

ATR. (1997). *Speech dialogue database for spontaneous speech recognition*. ATR.

Cox, I., Miller, M., Bloom, J., Fridrich, J., & Kalker, T. (2008). *Digital watermarking and steganography* (2nd ed.). San Francisco, CA: Morgan Kaufmann Publishers.

Ito, A., Handa, H., & Suzuki, Y. (2009). A band extension of G.711 speech with low computational cost for data hiding application. In *Proceedings of the 2009 Fifth International Conference on Intelligent Information Hiding and Multimedia Signal Processing (IIHMSP2009)*, (pp. 491-494). Kyoto, Japan: IIHMSP.

Ito, A., Konno, K., Ito, M., & Makino, S. (2010). Improvement of packet loss concealment for MP3 audio based on switching of concealment method and estimation of MDCT signs. In *Proceedings of the 2010 Sixth International Conference on Intelligent Information Hiding and Multimedia Signal Processing (IIHMSP2010)*, (pp. 518-521). Darmstadt, Germany: IIHMSP.

Ito, A., & Makino, S. (2009). Data hiding is a better way for transmitting side information for MP3 bitstream. In *Proceedings of the 2009 Fifth International Conference on Intelligent Information Hiding and Multimedia Signal Processing (IIHMSP2009)*, (pp. 495-498). Kyoto, Japan: IIHMSP.

ITU-T. (1988). *G.711: Pulse code modulation (PCM) of voice frequencies*. Retrieved from http://www.itu.int

ITU-T. (1996). *P.800: Methods for subjective determination of transmission quality*. Retrieved from http://www.itu.int

ITU-T. (1999). *G.711: Appendix 1: A high quality low-complexity algorithm for packet loss concealment with G.711*. Retrieved from http://www.itu.int

ITU-T. (2001). *P.862: Perceptual evaluation of speech quality (PESQ), an objective method for end-to-end speech quality assessment of narrow-band telephone networks and speech codecs.* Retrieved from http://www.itu.int

Nakata, K. (1995). *Speech.* Tokoyo: Corona Publishing.

Perkins, C., Hodson, O., & Hardman, V. (1998, September/October). A survey of packet loss recovery techniques for streaming audio. *IEEE Network Magazine*, 40-48.

Sasaki, Y., Hahm, S. J., & Ito, A. (2011). Manipulating vocal signal in mixed music sounds using small amount of side information. In *Proceedings of the 2011 Seventh International Conference on Intelligent Information Hiding and Multimedia Signal Processing (IIHMSP2011)*, (pp. 298-301). Dalian, China: IIHMSP.

Singh, S. (2000). *The code book: The science of secrecy from ancient Egypt to quantum cryptography*. New York, NY: Anchor Books.

Chapter 9
Spatial and Temporal Position Information Delivery to Mobile Terminals Using Audio Watermarking Techniques

Toshio Modegi
Dai Nippon Printing Co., Ltd., Japan

ABSTRACT

These authors are developing audio watermarking techniques that enable the extraction of embedded data by mobile phones. They applied acoustic interpolation of human auditory organs to embed data in full phone-line frequency ranges, where human auditory response is important for facilitating data extraction, using 3G mobile phones. They are interested in applying this technique to a mobile guide system for use in museums. In particular, they are considering applying audio watermarking techniques for synchronizing the stored contents of mobile terminals based on the spatial positions of the terminal and the temporal positions of playback contents in surrounding media. For this purpose, they are developing five linear spatial location identification codes that transfer to mobile terminals via two-channel stereo audio media that have embedded watermarks. They are also developing time codes that continuously transfer to mobile terminals via audio media. In this chapter, the authors initially describe their proposed audio watermarking algorithm and then present the main topic of novel audio watermarking applications for position information delivery to mobile terminals.

DOI: 10.4018/978-1-4666-2217-3.ch009

INTRODUCTION

In these days, "Ubiquitous Acoustic Spaces," a term that has been defined by the author (Modegi, 2007), are growing to be popular. In these spaces, each sound source can emit certain link address information using audio signals, thereby allowing automatic access to related cyberspace using mobile terminals, such as mobile phones. For example, QR codes (quick response bar codes) shown during TV commercials can be used to indicate related shopping site URLs and these can be transmitted visually to allow site access by capturing with a mobile phone camera. However, it is not so simple to implement such site linking services in radio commercials.

A further example is a museum guide system, which the authors focus on in this chapter, where real object exhibits can be linked to their respective virtual museum sites via mobile terminals. This application requires that exhibit showcases send spatial position information to visitors via their mobile terminals. In museum video presentation areas, video equipment must send temporal position information to mobile terminals before the video contents are played back on the terminals. In order to implement these applications, the requisite technical topics are described in this chapter.

Proposed Basic Watermark Technology: Development of an Analogue-Robust Audio Watermark Embedding Technique, "G-Encoder Mark," Enabling the Extraction of Embedded Data Using a 3G Mobile Phone

To implement this application, the authors aimed to develop a novel audio watermark technique to extract embedded data simply by directing a mobile phone at a loudspeaker that emits watermark embedded audio signals. They addressed the following problems.

Current 3G mobile phones and public phone networks cannot capture audio frequency components higher than 4 kHz. Recorded sound data are automatically compressed by the 3GPP specification format, so the sound quality can be highly degraded. Stego audio signals can also be distributed via analogue broadcasting, digital broadcasting, or IP network streaming, but frequency components higher than 4 kHz may be degraded by signal modulation or compression operations. Thus, data needs to be embedded in frequency components lower than 4 kHz when we implement audio watermark extraction functions for mobile phones. These frequency components are within the most sensitive auditory ranges, so we had to make extensive modifications to allow them to be detected by mobile phones. We also had to reduce additional auditory noises caused by these modifications during the playback of embedded signals.

The application of acoustic interpolation of human auditory organs (interpolation of missing signal components by the auditory stream segregation phenomenon) allowed us to embed data in full phone-line frequency ranges without adding any audible noises. Thus, the data signals were embedded in major auditory response ranges to facilitate data extraction using commonly available 3G mobile phones.

Proposed Main Functions: Provision for Extended Functions that Facilitate Spatial and Temporal Position Information Delivery of Embedded Audio Watermarks

The authors proposed an extended audio watermark method to extract new codes at the center of a stereo audio playback environment. Specifically, they developed five linear spatial location identification codes with embedded watermarks that can be transferred to mobile terminals via two-channel stereo audio media.

A major feature of audio watermark technology that cannot be implemented in image watermarks is the embedding of variable temporal codes into audio signals. The authors developed time codes that continuously transfer to mobile terminals via audio media, which allows a mobile terminal to play back its stored content synchronously with external audio media. Using this technology, we can listen to translated Japanese audio content via mobile terminals while native foreign language audio content is played back in a theater.

BACKGROUND

Museum guide systems are used as a substitute for curator communication with museum visitors. This is the very important for museum businesses because it maintains a steady flow of museum visitors. Several highly advanced multimedia guide systems have been proposed, but methods other than mobile audio guide devices have never been successfully implemented.

A team at the National Museum of Ethnology built digital archives that initially contained all the Japan treasures in their possession, where visitors' access is facilitated by video consoles (Hong, et al., 1995). Subsequently, this group proposed a laptop-based mobile guide terminal (Kurita, 2003) that could recognize displayed objects using an infrared light technology before receiving video content via PHS wireless communications. Another group at the University of Tokyo constructed a real experimental digital museum where many exhibition trails can be followed physically and virtually, and they also introduced a multimedia guidance terminal model (Yura, et al., 1998). This project later integrated advanced infrared ID or RFID-based object or location detection technologies and the group proposed a "Ubiquitous Communicator" (UC; Personal Media Corp, 2009) device, which has undergone several field tests in museums.

In contrast to these custom-made electronic consoles, Chou et al. (2004) proposed the use of general-purpose PDA (Personal Digital Assistant) devices as museum guide handy terminals. Brans (2007) proposed using the camera-equipped mobile phones of visitors as handy museum guide terminals, and a QR code-based object detection method was introduced. Kusunoki (2008) proposed using RFIDs to determine visitor locations and the use of a loudspeaker array system to present audio guidance in limited areas. Visible light communications technology (VLCC, 2007) has also been applied, where full audio or visual content is transmitted to mobile terminals via visible light waveforms. However, in such systems, a receiver hardware module needs to be installed in mobile terminals with additional costs. Furthermore, an AR (augmented reality) technique was introduced into the Louvre museum (Louvre-DNP, 2009) to display virtual digital contents in front of real display objects. However, this technique had the disadvantage of involving the labeling of real objects with relatively large unattractive ID marks to allow machine recognition, and the content production cost was high.

These highly advanced methods highlight several problems faced during facility installation such as the utility costs and the restrictions of radio wave regulations. Thus, it is not easy to introduce these technologies into public museums, compared with traditional audio guide systems.

Proposed Basic Watermark Technology

The authors propose "Ubiquitous Acoustic Spaces" (Modegi, 2007) where sound sources can emit audio signals containing certain link address information, allowing the automatic access of related cyberspace using mobile devices, such as mobile phones. In order to implement this concept, the authors considered three types of information transmission methods via acoustic signals, namely, acoustic modulation, audio fingerprints, and the audio watermark technique. They selected the audio watermark technique because it offered the most technological potential. Therefore, they began developing a novel audio watermark technique that enables the extraction of embedded data simply by directing a mobile phone at a loudspeaker that emits watermark-embedded audio signals. Previous watermark techniques are mainly applied for copyright protection (Ono, 2001). These techniques embedded data by modifying the less sensitive auditory frequency ranges of host audio signals, thereby avoiding additional sound production during playback. These methods demanded relatively low robustness against any compression or modulatory processing of embedded audio signals to prevent these modifications from damaging the content quality. In contrast, we required high robustness against analogue audio signal conversion and audio signal processing for capturing by the mobile phone when implementing contactless watermark extraction using a mobile phone to capture watermark-embedded sound signals.

Several studies (Ko, 2005; Matsuoka, 2006; Nishimura, 2006; Munekata, 2009) have analyzed the provision of analogue robustness to audio watermarks, and this has facilitated contactless extraction functions for audio watermarks using microphones directed at sound sources. Ko (2005) addressed this issue by proposing a spread echo method with an embedded data rate of 4 bps, and Munekata (2009) applied this technique to a handy caption display terminal for assisting deaf or hard-of-hearing people. Matsuoka (2006) proposed acoustic OFDM modulation with an embedded data rate of 1 kbps, while Nishimura (2006) proposed an amplitude modulation method with an embedded data rate of 40 bps. However, no previous trials have been conducted for contactless audio watermark extraction using commercially available 3G-standard mobile phone device with extraction function implemented. It was difficult to implement this using the proposed methods because all these methods embedded data in higher or broader frequency ranges than the voice communication ranges used by mobile phones.

As we described before, current 3G mobile phones and public phone networks cannot capture audio frequency components higher than 4 kHz. We need to embed data in frequency components lower than 4 kHz to provide mobile phones with audio watermark extraction functions. However, as these frequency components are in the most sensitive auditory ranges, we have to reduce additional auditory noises caused by these modifications during the playback of embedded signals.

The authors proposed the application of a noise canceling method to these embedded noises via two-channel stereo playback, where noises generated by the embedded L-channel signal are cancelled by the R-channel signal (Modegi, 2006). They proposed three different embedding methods, namely, a spatial division method, frequency division method, and temporal division method. The temporal division method best facilitated contactless watermark extraction using mobile phones (Modegi, 2006). The embedding rate of our proposed method was 10 bps, which was much higher than that of previously proposed audio watermark embedding methods. As an alternative to mobile phones, the use of mobile terminals with high sampling-rate audio recording functions would have allowed embedding at a maximum data rate of 61.5 bps at frequency ranges of less than 400 Hz (Modegi, 2007). Moreover, they allowed more flexible extraction operations by capturing from both stereo channel loudspeakers. When data was embedded at frequency ranges between 1.7 kHz and 3.4 kHz, we could embed at a maximum data rate of 80 bps (Modegi, 2007).

However, their previous method was difficult to use in monaural playback situations or headphone playback auditory environments because of the occurrence of annoying embedded noises. There was also a problem in stereo playback environments, where the receiver terminal location imposed certain restrictions. The authors could not extract data properly at locations distant from the sound source because of disturbances in the R-channel noise canceling signal and room reverberation.

The authors proposed an improved method that synthesized the R-channel canceling signal with the single L-channel signal to allow extraction operations in a monaural playback environment (Modegi, 2009). In this method, the synthesized monaural signal patterns use the segregation phenomenon to allow listeners to hear an auditory stream (Nakajima, 2009) without sensing the watermarks as audible noises while microphones faithfully capture the data embedded signal patterns. They also proposed a wide-band embedding method to produce a dual auditory stream segregation phenomenon, which allowed data embedding over all public phone frequency ranges while reducing a wide range of audible noises. This method increased the extraction sensitivity with 3G mobile phones when compared with previous methods, while also reducing the content quality degradation.

Proposed Main Functions of Position Information Delivery

The authors implemented the audio watermark extraction algorithm in Windows Mobile-based PDA devices, and they used them to identify the locations of museum visitor via BGM audio media (Modegi, 2008). Their method had the advantages of lower installation costs, lower usage of regulated radio waves, and a lower electric power requirement compare with the UC device (UC; Personal Media Corp, 2009). They had to install multiple spatial sound sources that transmitted different codes to implement an application such as a museum guide system (Modegi, 2008) in which each mobile terminal can present different content appropriate to its spatial location. However, it was difficult to install too many different sound sources in a limited space because of acoustic interference problems. Therefore, they had to consider extending their proposed audio watermarking technique such that it enabled the extraction of different codes depending on the spatial location of a watermark-extracting mobile terminal by applying stereo audio playback characteristics. There have been other proposals of applying audio watermarking technologies for measuring the spatial positions of a receiver terminal (Nakashima, 2007; Kanetou, 2009; Nakashima, 2009). However, these previous studies found it difficult to identify stable position owing to the instability of the watermark extraction precision, which made this method unsuitable for applications such as museums (Modegi, 2008).

In their previously proposed audio watermarking method, they applied auditory stream segregation (Nakajima, 2009) to freely modify the watermark embedding level. The watermark embedding level could be modulated for each bit-embedding frame to generate new codes in the mixed acoustic signals between the left and right loudspeaker. They then proposed a single-dimensional location detection method, which enabled the extraction of five different codes by moving the extracting microphone between the left and right loudspeakers, each of which emitted different code embedded signals (Modegi, 2009).

PROPOSED BASIC WATERMARK TECHNOLOGY

Conceptual Basis of the Proposed Audio Watermark Embedding Method

Figure 1 shows three frames containing the typical signal components found in the embedding frequency ranges (1.7–3.4 kHz, the divided center frequency: 2.55 kHz), where each frame is divided into two sections in both the horizontal/ temporal and vertical/ frequency directions. If we embed a bit 0, we decrease the level of U1 and D2 to 30%, whereas if we embed a bit 1, we decrease the level of D1 and U2 to 30%. These checkered patterns will allow listeners to experience an auditory stream segregation phenomenon, and the decreased components will be compensated for psychologically to almost their original level, thereby preventing the recognition of any noises. In contrast, a microphone can physically recognize these checkered patterns and extract the embedded data patterns.

We also propose the production of dual auditory stream segregation patterns to extend the embedding frequency ranges to the entire public phone network frequency range between 340 Hz–3.4 kHz without any distinct audible noises. We can produce similar patterns to those shown Figure 1 between 340 Hz and 1.7 kHz (the divided middle frequency: 1.02 kHz) and add these two-band patterns below the two-band patterns shown in Figure 1. Using these four-band patterns, we can increase extraction sensitivity to allow the extraction of a 40 bps data with mobile phones.

Watermark Embedding Algorithm

1. Converting the Source Acoustic Signal to Frequency Dimension

In the following sections, we describe a monaural source acoustic signal, but this method can be used with any type of stereo signals by applying the same algorithm to each channel. We initially extract the number of N-sample length frames $x(i)$ (i=0,…,N−1) for N/2 intervals from the source acoustic signal, sampled with a frequency f_s. We embed 1-bit data in a set of consecutive odd and even frames. The value of N is selected from 4096 (10 bps), 2048 (20 bps), 1024 (40 bps), and 512 (80 bps), where f_s=44.1[kHz]. The two types of window functions $W_k(i)$ (k=1,2) are defined in Equation 2. We multiply the first function $W_1(i)$ with odd frames and the second function $W_2(i)$ with even frames, and we then calculate the discrete

Figure 1. Conceptual basis of an audio watermark embedding method applying auditory stream segregation. Single auditory stream segregation patterns are found in the embedding frequency ranges (1.7–3.4 kHz, the divided center frequency: 2.55 kHz)

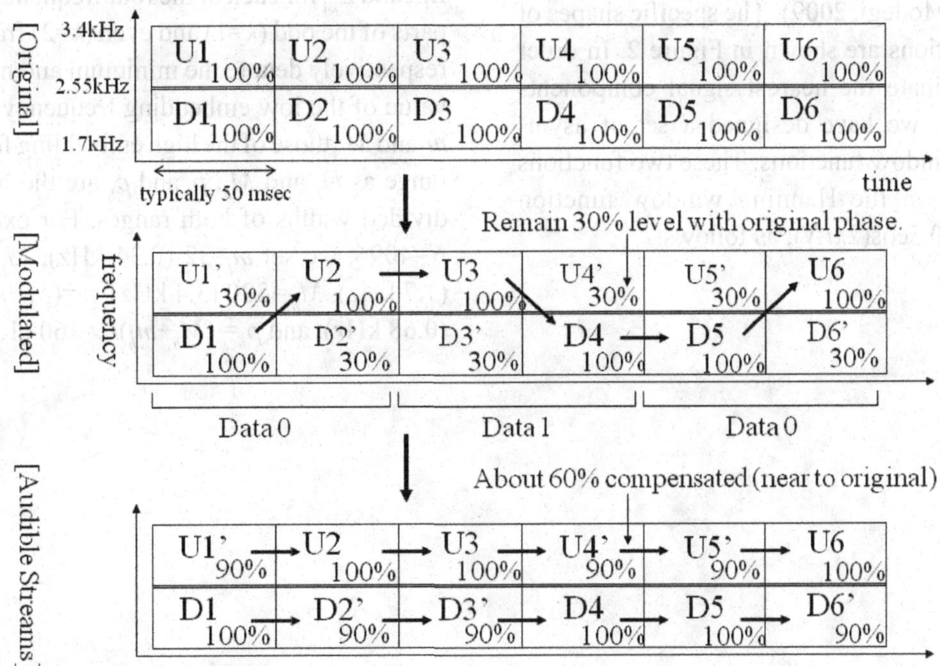

Fourier transform of these multiplied frames. The real parts $A_k(j)$ (j=0,…,N−1, k=1,2) and imaginary parts $B_k(j)$ (j=0,…,N−1, k=1,2) of the transformed values are given as follows:

$$Ak(j) = \sum_{i=0}^{N-1} W_k(i)\{x(i) + R(i)\}\cos(2\pi ij / N)$$
$$Bk(j) = \sum_{i=0}^{N-1} W_k(i)\{x(i) + R(i)\}\sin(2\pi ij / N)$$
$$(j = 0, \ldots, N-1,\ \text{k=1,2}) \qquad (1)$$

R(*i*) are white noise signals that can be added optionally to the source acoustic signals. Data embedding cannot proceed correctly if there are many silent sections, as found in voice signals, so white noise signals are required in that case. When the bit-depth of the source acoustic signal is 16-bit, we provide uniform random noise as *R*(*i*) within ±32 (the maximum value is 32768), which allows us to correctly embed data in the silent sections without degrading the source signal quality.

The two window functions $W_k(i)$ (k=1,2) are designed such that they can completely compensate for each other with a half-length pitch N/2 shift (Modegi, 2009). The specific shapes of these functions are shown in Figure 2. In order to discriminate the nearest signal components temporally, we have designed a set of asymmetrical window functions. These two functions are based on the Hanning window function $W(i)$=0.5−0.5cos(2πi/N), as follows:

$$W_1(i) = 0.0\ (i \le N/8)$$
$$W_1(i) = 0.5 - 0.5\cos(4\pi(i - N/8)/N)$$
$$(\text{N/8} < i \le 3N/8)$$
$$W_1(i) = 1.0\ (3N/8 < i \le 11N/16)$$
$$(11N/16 < i \le 13N/16)$$
$$W_1(i) = 0.5 + 0.5\cos(8\pi(i - 11N/16)/N)$$
$$(11N/16 < i \le 13N/16)$$
$$W_1(i) = 0.0\ (13N/15 < i)$$
$$W_2(i) = 0.0\ (i \le 3N/16)$$
$$W_2(i) = 0.5 - 0.5\cos(8\pi(i - 3N/16)/N)$$
$$(3N/16 < i \le 5N/16)$$
$$W_2(i) = 1.0\ (5N/16 < i \le 5N/8)$$
$$W_2(i) = 0.5 + 0.5\cos(4\pi(i - 5N/8)/N)$$
$$(5N/8 < i \le 7N/8)$$
$$W_2(i) = 0.0\ (7N/8 < i) \qquad (2)$$

2. Determination of Optimal Embedding Scaling Ratio

We calculate the energy summation values E_{k1}, E_{k2}, E_{k3}, and E_{k4} for each of the four frequency divided parts of the odd (k=1) and even (k=2) frames. We respectively denote the minimum and maximum value of the low embedding frequency range as m_l and M_l; those of the high embedding frequency range as m_h and M_h; p_l and p_h are the frequency divided widths of both ranges. For example, if N=4096, we set m_l=32 (0.34 kHz), M_l=m_h=160 (1.7 kHz), M_h= 320 (3.4 kHz), p_l=(M_l−m_l)/2= 64 (0.68 kHz), and p_h= (M_h−m_h)/2=160 (1.7 kHz).

Figure 2. A set of proposed asymmetrical window functions based on the Hanning window function

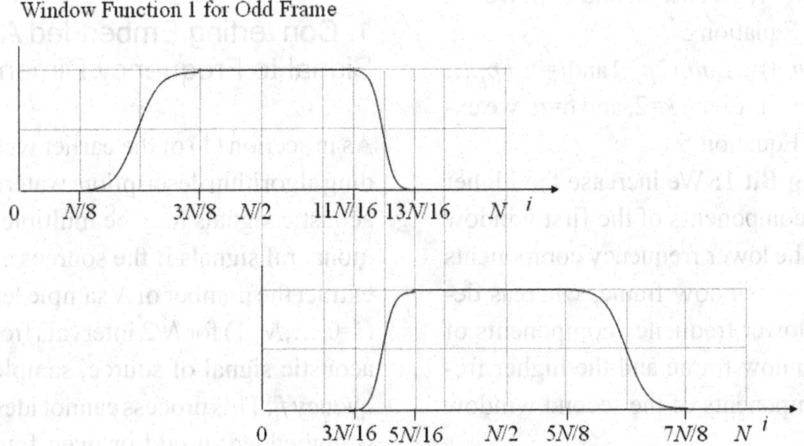

$$E_{kl} = \sum_{j=ml}^{ml+pl-1} \left\{ Ak(j)^2 + Bk(j)^2 \right\}$$
$$E_{k2} = \sum_{j=ml+pl}^{ml+2pl-1} \left\{ Ak(j)^2 + Bk(j)^2 \right\}$$
$$E_{k3} = \sum_{j=mh}^{mh+ph-1} \left\{ Ak(j)^2 + Bk(j)^2 \right\}$$
$$E_{k4} = \sum_{j=mh+ph}^{mh+2ph-1} \left\{ Ak(j)^2 + Bk(j)^2 \right\} \quad (k=1,2) \tag{3}$$

Then, we calculate $\gamma = (E_{11} \cdot E_{21} \cdot E_{13} \cdot E_{24}) / (E_{12} \cdot E_{21} \cdot E_{14} \cdot E_{23})$. If an embedding bit is 1, we transform γ as $\gamma = 1/\gamma$. We define the embedding scaling ratios, which determine watermark robustness and quality damage level, α and β with initial values of 0.7 and 0.3, respectively. If $\gamma < 1.0$, we correct the α and β values as follows.

$$\alpha = 0.7 \cdot \gamma^{-1/4}, \ \beta = 0.3 \cdot \gamma^{1/4} \tag{4}$$

However, we set a limit within $\alpha \leq 7.0$ and $\beta \geq 0.03$ to suppress pulse-like noise production with large scaling.

3. Converting the Frequency Components

Using our determined embedding scaling ratios α and β, we modify the frequency components $A_k(j)$ and $B_k(j)$ (k=1,2) within the specified ranges based on the following equation, where δ is an embedding scaling ratio, either α or β.

$$A_k{}'(j) = A_k(j)\delta$$
$$B_k{}'(j) = B_k(j)\delta \tag{5}$$

1. **Embedding Bit 0:** We increase the lower frequency components of the first window frame and the higher frequency components of the second window frame, whereas decrease the higher frequency components of the first window frame and the lower frequency components of the second window frame.
   a. For $j=m_l,\ldots,m_l+p_l-1$ and $j=m_h,\ldots m_h+p_h-1$, given k=1, and $\delta=\alpha$, we execute Equation 5.
   b. For $j=m_l,\ldots,m_l+p_l-1$ and $j=m_h,\ldots m_h+p_h-1$, given k=2, and $\delta=\beta$, we execute Equation 5.

c. For $j=m_l+p_l,\ldots,m_l+2p_l-1$ and $j=m_h+p_h,\ldots m_h+2p_h-1$, given $k=1$, and $\delta=\beta$, we execute Equation 5.

d. For $j=m_l+p_l,\ldots,m_l+2p_l-1$ and $j=m_h+p_h,\ldots m_h+2p_h-1$, given $k=2$, and $\delta=\alpha$, we execute Equation 5.

2. **Embedding Bit 1:** We increase the higher frequency components of the first window frame and the lower frequency components of the second window frame, whereas decrease the lower frequency components of the first window frame and the higher frequency components of the second window frame.
   a. For $j=m_l,\ldots,m_l+p_l-1$ and $j=m_h,\ldots,m_h+p_h-1$, given $k=1$ and $\delta=\beta$, we execute Equation 5.
   b. For $j=m_l,\ldots,m_l+p_l-1$ and $j=m_h,\ldots,m_h+p_h-1$, given $k=2$ and $\delta=\alpha$, we execute Equation 5.
   c. For $j=m_l+p_l,\ldots,m_l+2p_l-1$ and $j=m_h+p_h,\ldots,m_h+2p_h-1$, given $k=1$ and $\delta=\alpha$, we execute Equation 5.
   d. For $j=m_l+p_l,\ldots,m_l+2p_l-1$ and $j=m_h+p_h,\ldots,m_h+2p_h-1$, given $k=2$ and $\delta=\beta$, we execute Equation 5.

4. Reconverting the Modified Frequency Components to Temporal Dimension

The updated time-scale frame data $x'(i)$ is defined as the addition of time-scale reconverted data from the current frequency-scale frame components and the previously reconverted frame data $x'(i-N/2)$ with an $N/2$ offset. We execute the following equation based on the inverse discrete Fourier transform, given $k=1$ for odd frames and $k=2$ for even frames.

$$X'(i)=\\1/N\left\{\sum_{j=0}^{N-1}A_k'(j)\cos(2\pi ij/N)-\sum_{j=0}^{N-1}B_k'(j)\sin(2\pi ij/N)\right\}\\+\{1-W_k(i)\}X'(i-N/2) \quad (6)$$

Watermark Extraction Algorithm

1. Converting Embedded Acoustic Signal to Frequency Dimension

As in section (1) of the earlier watermark embedding algorithm description, watermark embedded acoustic signals may be multiple-channel mixed monaural signals if the sources are stereo, so we extract the number of N sample length frames $x(i)$ ($i=0,\ldots,N-1$) for $N/2$ intervals from the monaural acoustic signal of source, sampled with the frequency f_s. This process cannot identify where data is embedded in odd or even frames. Therefore, we define H (e.g., $H=6$) types of analyzed frame sets by shifting the phase h ($h=0,..,H-1$) of the given signals. Using the same window functions $W_k(i)$ ($k=1,2$) found in Equation 1, we calculate the discrete Fourier transform for each phase h shifted set of analyzed frames. The transformed values, the real parts $A_k(j,h)$ ($j=0,\ldots,N'-1, k=1,2, h=0,..,H-1$) and imaginary parts $B_k(j,h)$ ($j=0,\ldots, N'-1, k=1,2, h=0,..,H-1$), are given as follows:

$$A_k(j,h)=\sum_{i=0}^{N'-1}W_k(i)x(i+hN/H)\cos(2\pi ij/N)\\B_k(j,h)=\sum_{i=0}^{N'-1}W_k(i)x(i+hN/H)\sin(2\pi ij/N)\\(j=0,\ldots,N'-1;\ k=1,2;\ h=0,\ldots,H-1) \quad (7)$$

2. Scaling Amplitude of the Virtual Dimension

Before determining the bit patterns by comparing the amplitude levels between consecutive frames, we remove the level fluctuation components included in the original audio signals by flattening the amplitude of the temporal distribution. We calculate the summation of energy levels for H types of odd and even frames, and define the scaling conversion parameters, $S_1(h)$ and $S_2(h)$, to convert these energy summation values to a fixed value S_o.

$$S_k\left(h\right) = S_0 / \left[\sum_{j=ml}^{Mh-1}\left\{A_k\left(j,h\right)^2 + B_k\left(j,h\right)^2\right\}\right]^{1/2}$$
$$(k = 1,2;\ h = 0,\ldots,H-1)$$

(8)

We perform a scaling conversion of each $A_k(j,h)$ and $B_k(j,h)$ component for $j=ml,\ldots,Mh$ and $k=1,2$. We then calculate the energy summation values of the four divided bands in both the odd and even frames, $E_{k1}(h)$, $E_{k2}(h)$, $E_{k3}(h)$, and $E_{k4}(h)$, based on Equation 9.

$$E_{kl}\left(h\right) = \sum_{j=ml}^{ml+pl-1}\left\{A_k\left(j,h\right)^2 + B_k\left(j,h\right)^2\right\}$$
$$E_{k2}\left(h\right) = \sum_{j=ml+pl}^{ml+2pl-1}\left\{A_k\left(j,h\right)^2 + B_k\left(j,h\right)^2\right\}$$
$$E_{k3}\left(h\right) = \sum_{j=mh}^{mh+ph-1}\left\{A_k\left(j,h\right)^2 + B_k\left(j,h\right)^2\right\}$$
$$E_{k4}\left(h\right) = \sum_{j=mh+ph}^{mh+2ph-1}\left\{A_k\left(j,h\right)^2 + B_k\left(j,h\right)^2\right\}$$
$$(k = 1,2)$$

(9)

3. Reverb Correction and Determination of Extracted Bit Data

We assume that the calculated energy summation values described in the previous section include some level q ($0\leq q\leq 1$) of the previous frame energy values $E_{k1}{}^{P}(h)$, $E_{k2}{}^{P}(h)$, $E_{k3}{}^{P}(h)$, and $E_{k4}{}^{P}(h)$. Considering this, we correct these energy summation values as shown in equation 10, where $E_{k1}'(h)\geq 0$, $E_{k2}'(h)\geq 0$, $E_{k3}'(h)\geq 0$, and $E_{k4}'(h)\geq 0$. The specific value of the reverb parameter q under typical room conditions is given as $q=0.06\bullet 4096/N$, which is inversely proportional to the analyzed frame length N. The typical room is an office conference room, whose size are about W: 3×D:5×H:3 [m].

$$\begin{aligned}
E_{11}'\left(h\right) &= E_{11}\left(h\right) - qE_{21^P}\left(h\right)\\
E_{12}'\left(h\right) &= E_{12}\left(h\right) - qE_{22^P}\left(h\right)\\
E_{13}'\left(h\right) &= E_{13}\left(h\right) - qE_{23^P}\left(h\right)\\
E_{14}'\left(h\right) &= E_{14}\left(h\right) - qE_{24^P}\left(h\right)\\
E_{21}'\left(h\right) &= E_{21}\left(h\right) - qE_{11}\left(h\right)\\
E_{22}'\left(h\right) &= E_{22}\left(h\right) - qE_{12}\left(h\right)\\
E_{23}'\left(h\right) &= E_{23}\left(h\right) - qE_{13}\left(h\right)\\
E_{24}'\left(h\right) &= E_{24}\left(h\right) - qE_{14}\left(h\right)
\end{aligned} \qquad (10)$$

We determine whether these corrected values or the original uncorrected values are to be used for estimating bit patterns by calculating the phase-fitted evaluation parameters, $D(h)$ and $D'(h)$, which indicate signal contrast between increased four sets of components and decreased four sets of components by embedding, as follows:

$$D\left(h\right) = \frac{\left\{E_{11}\left(h\right)E_{22}\left(h\right)E_{13}\left(h\right)E_{24}\left(h\right)\right\}^{1/4} - \left\{E_{12}\left(h\right)E_{21}\left(h\right)E_{14}\left(h\right)E_{23}\left(h\right)\right\}^{1/4}}{\left\{E_{11}\left(h\right)E_{22}\left(h\right)E_{13}\left(h\right)E_{24}\left(h\right)\right\}^{1/4} + \left\{E_{12}\left(h\right)E_{21}\left(h\right)E_{14}\left(h\right)E_{23}\left(h\right)\right\}^{1/4}}$$

$$D'\left(h\right) = \frac{\left\{E_{11}'\left(h\right)E_{22}'\left(h\right)E_{13}'\left(h\right)E_{24}'\left(h\right)\right\}^{1/4} - \left\{E_{12}'\left(h\right)E_{21}'\left(h\right)E_{14}'\left(h\right)E_{23}'\left(h\right)\right\}^{1/4}}{\left\{E_{11}'\left(h\right)E_{22}'\left(h\right)E_{13}'\left(h\right)E_{24}'\left(h\right)\right\}^{1/4} + \left\{E_{12}'\left(h\right)E_{21}'\left(h\right)E_{14}'\left(h\right)E_{23}'\left(h\right)\right\}^{1/4}}$$

(11)

If $|D'(h)|>|D(h)|$, the correction described in the Equation 10 is assumed to be effective, otherwise it is assumed to be not effective. We define a candidate code table $B(h)$ and a phase determination $T(h)$ (all initial values are 0) corresponding to phase h, and we estimate the candidate codes using the following number-ordered rules.

1. If $|D(h)|>|D'(h)|$, $E_{11}(h)E_{13}(h)>E_{21}(h)E_{23}(h)$, $E_{22}(h)E_{24}(h)>E_{12}(h)E_{14}(h)$: $B(h)=0$, $T(h)\leftarrow T(h)+D(h)$.
2. If $|D(h)|>|D'(h)|$, $E_{11}(h)E_{13}(h)<E_{21}(h)E_{23}(h)$, $E_{22}(h)E_{24}(h)<E_{12}(h)E_{14}(h)$: $B(h)=1$, $T(h)\leftarrow T(h)-D(h)$.
3. If $|D'(h)|>|D(h)|$, $E_{11}'(h)E_{13}'(h)>E_{21}'(h)E_{23}'(h)$, $E_{22}'(h)E_{24}'(h)>E_{12}'(h)E_{14}'(h)$: $B(h)=0$, $T(h)\leftarrow T(h)+D'(h)$.
4. If $|D'(h)|>|D(h)|$, $E_{11}'(h)E_{13}'(h)<E_{21}'(h)E_{23}'(h)$, $E_{22}'(h)E_{24}'(h)<E_{12}'(h)E_{14}'(h)$: $B(h)=1$, $T(h)\leftarrow T(h)-D'(h)$.
5. If $|D(h)|>|D'(h)|$, $E_{11}(h)E_{13}(h)E_{22}(h)E_{24}(h) > E_{21}(h)E_{23}(h)E_{12}(h)E_{14}(h)$: $B(h)=0$, $T(h)\leftarrow T(h)+D(h)$.
6. If $|D(h)|>|D'(h)|$, $E_{11}(h)E_{13}(h)E_{22}(h)E_{24}(h) \leq E_{21}(h)E_{23}(h)E_{12}(h)E_{14}(h)$: $B(h)=1$, $T(h)\leftarrow T(h)-D(h)$.
7. If $|D'(h)|>|D(h)|$, $E_{11}'(h)E_{13}'(h)E_{22}'(h)E_{24}'(h) > E_{21}'(h)E_{23}'(h)E_{12}'(h)E_{14}'(h)$: $B(h)=0$, $T(h)\leftarrow T(h)+D'(h)$.
8. If $|D'(h)|>|D(h)|$, $E_{11}'(h)E_{13}'(h)E_{22}'(h)E_{24}'(h) \leq E_{21}'(h)E_{23}'(h)E_{12}'(h)E_{14}'(h)$: $B(h)=1$, $T(h)\leftarrow T(h)-D'(h)$.

We then estimate H types of candidate codes for all h phases and determine the extracted bit data from an analyzed frame as $B(h_{max})$ from the candidate codes, where h_{max} is $T(h_{max})$ for the maximum of H types of $T(h)$, which were summed from the initial frame analyzed.

Extraction Process Acceleration Techniques for Mobile Terminals

Compared with personal computers, mobile terminals such as mobile phones have a lower CPU performance (especially floating point calculation performance), a smaller memory capacity, and a lower sound recording specification (in terms of sampling frequency and quantized bit-length). Therefore, we have to modify the algorithm, as described in the previous sections. In this section, we describe improvements in the watermark extraction algorithm to be implemented on 3G mobile phones.

In the previous sections, we proposed H-times repeated calculation methods based on Equation 7 and subsequent equations because we could not identify where the data was embedded in odd or even frames. The length of a recorded voice file on a mobile phone is practically 1 to 3 seconds. Thus, if the optimum phase h_{max} is determined as the beginning position of the file (e.g., the estimated optimum phase values h_{max} are the same in three consecutive frames), we can consider that the optimum phase value will remain unchanged until the end of the file. Thus, if the optimum phase h_{max} is determined, we only have to make a single calculation as $h=h_{max}$, and the calculation load will be decreased to $1/H$. We conducted experiments and found that when the length of a voice file was less than 10 seconds, the extraction results were no different with or without abbreviated calculations.

As described in section (1), the sampling frequency f_s during extraction processes should be the same (for example, f_s=44.1 kHz) as that of the source acoustic signals used in the embedding processes described in section (1) of the watermark embedding algorithm description. However, the voice sampling frequency in 3G mobile phones is typically limited to 8 kHz. Therefore, we need to up-convert the recorded signals to the same sampling frequency format (for example, 44.1 kHz) as that of the source acoustic signals. We propose to up-convert the recorded signals to the same $f_s/4$ reduced sampling frequency format (for example, 11.025 kHz) as that of the source acoustic signals. In this case, no modifications are required for the described extraction algorithm other than replacing the frame length N with $N/4$. The extraction load will also be lowered by reducing the frame length to 1/4. There was a highly significant decrease in the calculation load of the discrete Fourier transform based on Equation 7, which had the highest calculation load in the entire extraction processes. Moreover, the phase information of the analyzed frequency components is not required by the extraction process, so we can use a real-value specific simplified FFT algorithm, which can reduce the number of FFT points to 1/2 of the frame length, *N*/8. Our experiments showed that the extraction results were almost the same regardless of which of these reduced FFT calculations were used.

We aimed to construct a watermark extraction system for mobile phones, as shown in Figure 3. To test this system, we initially used a mobile phone with a preinstalled voice recorder or video camera to record short lengths (around 3 seconds) of an audio clip from a loudspeaker playing watermark embedded audio signals. We then sent an e-mail with a recording of the 3GPP encoded video or sound file as an attachment to the specific server using a preinstalled mobile phone e-mail function. The server then decoded the audio track and extracted the watermark text before returning the text. If the text was interpreted as the URL string of a specific website, we could access it directly. In this case, the text may include ID codes for identifying specified URLs, but need not include full URL strings. The server has a URL conversion table and can link the client terminal to the converted URL site directly.

The proposed system did not require the installation of any specific software, such as a Java application (*i-appli* in NTT-docomo), on our mobile phone devices and it was not dependent on the device specification. However, smart phones, such as the Apple iPhone and Android terminals, are now becoming increasingly popular, so we will also consider implementing our watermark extraction software for several smart phone devices.

Byte Data Embedding Sequence

In the previous sections, we described algorithms for embedding 1-bit data into or extracting 1-bit data from each frame. In this section, we describe the embedding of a sequence of frequently used 7-bit ASCII data, including error detection bits.

Various types of error detection or correction codes have been developed for data communi-

Figure 3. Watermark extraction system for 3G mobile phones (e.g., NTT-docomo FOMA) cooperating with signal processing PC servers

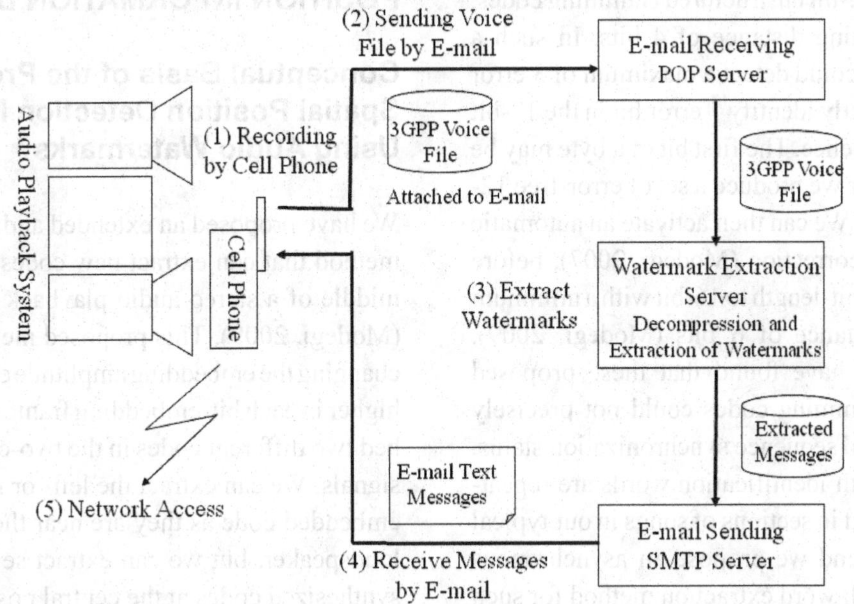

cation applications, and these are effective for dealing with bit errors caused by unpredictable disturbances. However, other types of bit errors occurred in our proposed watermark embedding methods. For example, we could not embed data properly if the level of the original signal in the embedding frame was low or close to zero, and this frame would cause a bit error for extraction. This problem can be solved by intentionally adding white noise signals, but this method is not always applicable due to the degradation of playback quality (Modegi, 2006).

In serial data communication, we generally need to insert a synchronous bit code indicating the first bit of a byte, and we tested several types of byte data embedding sequences discussed by Modegi (2007). Our experiments showed that the best method was not the insertion of additional synchronous bit data, but instead, it was the use of error detection bits (Modegi, 2006).

We considered giving multiple inspection functions to error detection codes. These allow the detection of bit errors based on a low signal level in the original frames used for embedding, identification errors in the first bit of each embedded byte, and bit errors due to environmental noise disturbances. We previously proposed (Modegi, 2007) using 12-bit unstructured Hamming codes, with a Hamming distance of 4 bits. In such a sequence, we could detect a maximum of 3 error bits and correctly identify 1 error bit in the 12-bit extracted sequence. The first bit of a byte may be identified after we produce a set of error-free 12-bit sequences. We can then activate an automatic one bit error correction (Modegi, 2007), before extending the bit-length to 16-bit with a minimum Hamming distance of 6 bits (Modegi, 2009). However, we have found that these proposed structured Hamming codes could not precisely detect the word sequence synchronization status.

Short-length identification words are repeatedly embedded in sections of songs in our typical applications, and we propose an asynchronous fixed bit length word extraction method for such an application. We define a set of bit-shifting unique 16-bit cyclic unstructured Hamming codes, as shown in Figure 4, with a minimum Hamming distance of 3 that can express 124 variations. If we embed a code selected from Figure 4, we can identify the embedded code simply by extracting one of the cyclic patterns in the embedded codes, without synchronizing the embedded sequence of a word. For example, if we embed a 16-bit code '28655 (0110 1111 1110 1111, 6FEFh)' for a 7-bit code '130 (82h),' 15 types of 16-bit extracted cyclic code patterns are produced, '57310 (1101 1111 1101 1110),' '49085 (1011 1111 1011 1101),' '32635 (0111 1111 0111 1011),' ' 65270 (1111 1110 1111 0110),' '65005 (1111 1101 1110 1101),' ' 64475 (1111 1011 1101 1011),' '63415 (1111 0111 1011 0111),' '61295 (1110 1111 0110 1111),' '57055 (1101 1110 1101 1111),' '48575 (1011 1101 1011 1111),' '31615 (0111 1011 0111 1111),' '63230 (1111 0110 1111 1110),' '60925 (1110 1101 1111 1101),' '56315 (1101 1011 1111 1011),' and '47095 (1011 0111 1111 0111),' that can be identified as corresponding to the 7-bit code '130 (82h)' (Modegi, 2009).

PROPOSED MAIN FUNCTIONS OF POSITION INFORMATION DELIVERY

Conceptual Basis of the Proposed Spatial Position Detection Method Using Audio Watermarks

We have proposed an extended audio watermark method that can extract new codes found in the middle of a stereo audio playback environment (Modegi, 2009). This proposed method features changing the embedding amplitude either lower or higher in each bit-embedding frame when we embed two different codes in the two-channel audio signals. We can extract the left- or right-channel embedded code as they are near the left or right loudspeaker, but we can extract several hybrid-synthesized codes at the central position that are

Figure 4. Code book of [16,7] bit cyclic unstructured Hamming codes for encoding 7-bit ASCII codes

Code	16-bit Cyclic Codes (Minimum Hamming Distance: 3)							
00-07	1	F	33	55	5B	9D	A5	C3
08-0F	EF	117	163	17F	1A9	1C5	239	249
10-17	293	303	325	34F	39F	3E7	3F1	42B
18-1F	465	4B9	4D1	4DF	505	51B	5A3	5BF
20-27	5CB	62D	637	653	6CD	6EB	6F5	75D
28-2F	787	799	869	887	889	8F7	91D	92B
30-37	975	9B1	9DB	9ED	A5F	A63	AAB	AB5
38-3F	B8D	C3F	CAD	CB3	D47	D79	D8F	DDD
40-47	E7B	E97	EE7	F27	F6D	FA9	FFF	1147
48-4F	1159	11F7	1227	1273	**12BD**	12CF	**12D5**	131D
50-57	1369	13AF	14FB	1537	1539	15AD	165F	16D9
58-5F	172B	1765	17B3	17D7	18EB	1997	19A5	19F9
60-67	1A6F	1A75	1B33	1B4B	1BDF	1D7F	1DAB	1E49
68-6F	1EAF	1EB9	1FB5	1FCD	256F	**26BD**	2777	**27BB**
70-77	295F	29EB	2BB3	**2D3B**	2DBD	2DE7	2EDF	334D
78-7F	33FD	36EF	3AB7	3CFD	3EFB	3F3F	5555	55DF
80-83	575B	5AFF	**6FEF**	FFFF				

composed of selected higher-level embedded bits from either the left or right embedded signals.

Figure 5 shows an example of changing the embedding amplitude in two steps of our previously proposed audio watermarking method, based on Figure 1 (Modegi, 2009). As before, we embed data by changing the amplitude proportions between diagonal paired signal components created by dividing an embedding frame (temporal width of 50 ms and frequency range of 0.34–3.4 kHz) into four sections in the horizontal/temporal dimension and the vertical/frequency dimension. We use psychological acoustic interpolation, and expect the decreased component pairs be compensated for by the sections with the original amplitude (Nakajima, 2009), but observe that a microphone can physically detect the decreased components. We define the two types of embedding modes shown in the upper and lower parts of Figure 4 and select either mode frame-by-frame, based on the code extracted at the middle.

The model described in Figure 6 extends the embedding amplitudes to three steps (decrease/increase amplitude ratios designated as weak: 34%/166%; middle: 28% /172%; and strong: 22%/178%) based on the Figure 5 description, which allows the extraction of the five different codes in a single dimension of the stereo audio environment. Extending the 8-bit codes described in Figure 6, we define 5 position codes as 'L (12D5h),' 'LC (12BDh),' 'C (26BDh),' 'RC (27BBh),' and 'R (2D3Bh)' within a 16-bit cyclic unstructured Hamming code, which is conditioned with a minimum Hamming distance of 3 based on the error detection codes described in Figure 4. By embedding the 'L' code to the left-channel signal and the 'R' code to the right-channel signal with 3-step embedding level changes, we can extract the other three code 'LC,' 'C,' and 'RC' at the position located in the middle of the left and right loudspeakers.

Conceptual Basis of a Two-Dimensional Extended Spatial Position Detection Method Using Audio Watermarks

We can extend the proposed method described in the previous section to two-dimensional location detection applied to surround sound audio features. For example, Figure 7 shows that using a 5.1 channel surround audio system allows us to construct a 3 × 3 two-dimensional location detection model. By dividing the 8-bit code embedding into two parts, we can embed the first 4-bit code and use it for detecting the vertical direction of the front-to-back linear spatial locations, while we can embed the second 4-bit code and use it for detecting the horizontal direction of the left to right linear spatial locations.

Using the three-step amplitude embedding model described in Figure 6, we can extract nine different codes in two dimensions of 4-channel surround sound audio environment. Extending the 8-bit codes described in Figure 7, we define 9 position codes as 'FL (0001h),' 'FC (00C3h),' 'FR (00EFh),' 'ML (0505h),' 'MC (05CBh),' 'MR (0FFFh),' 'BL (5555h),' 'BC (55DFh),' and 'BR (FFFFh)' within the 16-bit cyclic unstructured Hamming code, which is conditioned with a minimum Hamming distance of 3 based on the error detection codes described in Figure 4. By embedding the 'FL' code to the front-left-channel signal, the 'FR' code to the front-right-channel signal, the 'BL' code to the back-left-channel signal, and the 'BR' code to the back-right-channel signal using 3-step embedding level changes, we can extract the other five codes 'FC,' 'ML,' 'MC,' 'MR,' and 'BC' at the middle posi-

Figure 5. Example showing the definition of two-step embedding amplitudes, based on the previously proposed watermark method (Modegi, 2009)

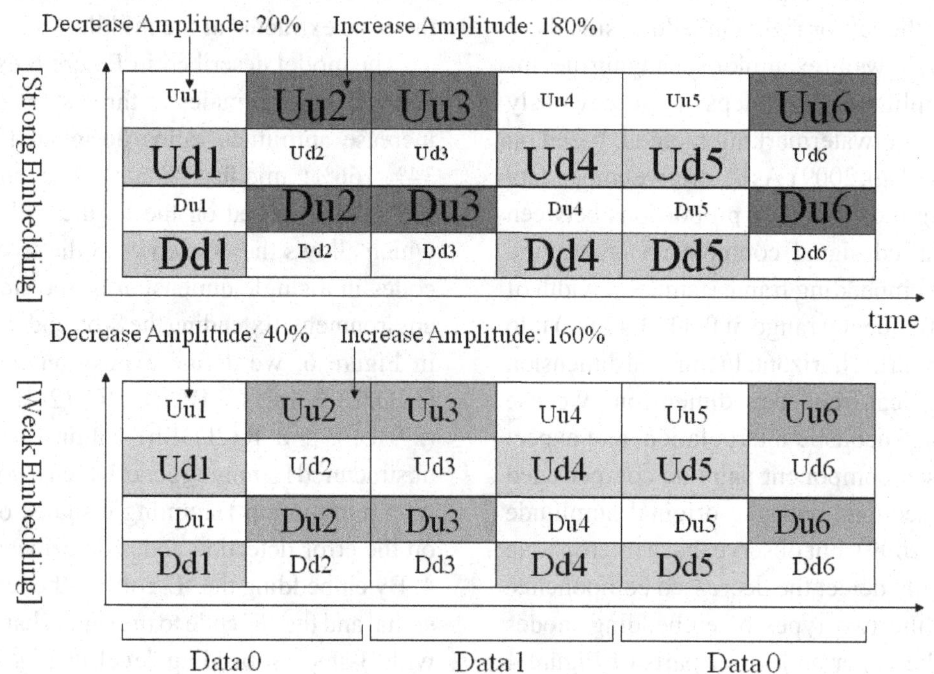

Figure 6. Extended watermark method for providing 5-step mobile terminal position detection functions in a stereo audio environment

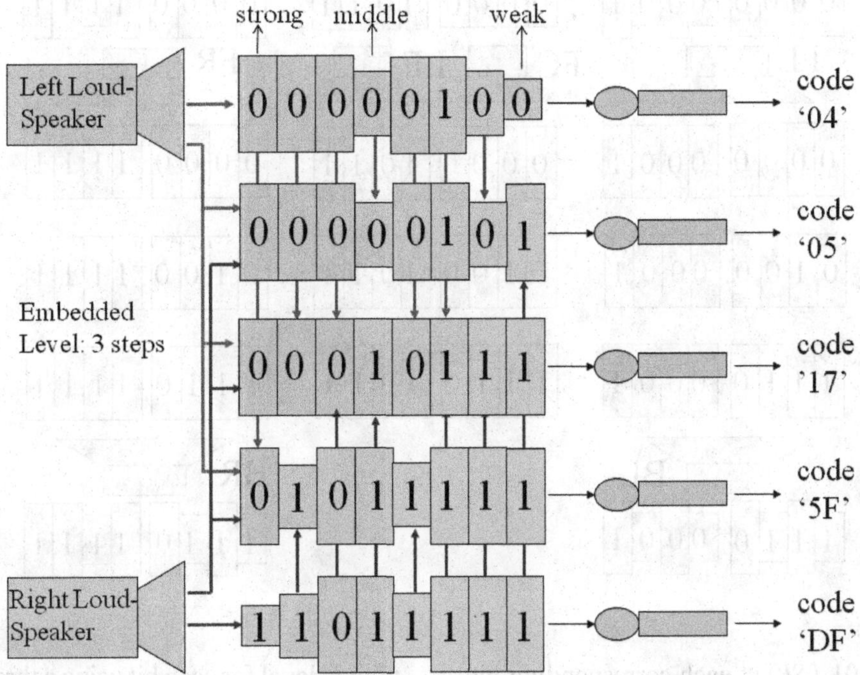

tions of the front-left, front-right, back-left, and back-right loudspeakers.

Modification of the Proposed Watermark Embedding Algorithm for Spatial Position Detection

The specific watermark for spatial position detection embedding algorithm proposed in this section can be easily implemented using the algorithm described in the previous section, simply by adding a modulation process in the embedding level for each bit embedding frame. Moreover, the previously proposed algorithm can be used for extraction without any modifications.

Thus, in section (2) of the previous watermark embedding algorithm description, we calculate a γ value and define the embedding scaling ratios α and β using Equation 4. We modify Equation 4 for the following three types of equations corresponding with the three types of embedding level shown in Figure 3.

As described in the previous section, we change these values for each bit-embedding frame. In the case of the middle embedding level, we define the embedding scaling ratios α and β with initial values of α_o=0.72 and β_o=0.28, respectively. If γ<1.0, we correct the α and β values as shown in Equation 12. However, we limit $\alpha \leq 72.0$ and $\beta \geq 0.028$.

$$\alpha = \alpha_o \cdot \gamma^{-1/4}, \ \beta = \beta_o \cdot \gamma^{1/4} \tag{12}$$

Similarly, in the case of strong embedding, we define the initial values of α_o and β_o as 0.78 and 0.22, whereas in the case of weak embedding, we define the initial values of α_o and β_o as 0.66 and 0.34, respectively.

In the case of the 5-step spatial location detection application described in Figure 5, we can select 5 position codes from Figure 4 as 'L(12D5h),' 'LC (12BDh),' 'C (26BDh),' 'RC (27BBh),' and 'R (2D3Bh),' rather than the 8-bit codes '04h,' '05h,' '17h,' '5fh,' and 'dfh.' In the left channel signal, we embed the 16-bit code '12D5h' (*MSB* 0001

Figure 7. Two-dimensional extended location detection method in a 5.1 channel surround sound system

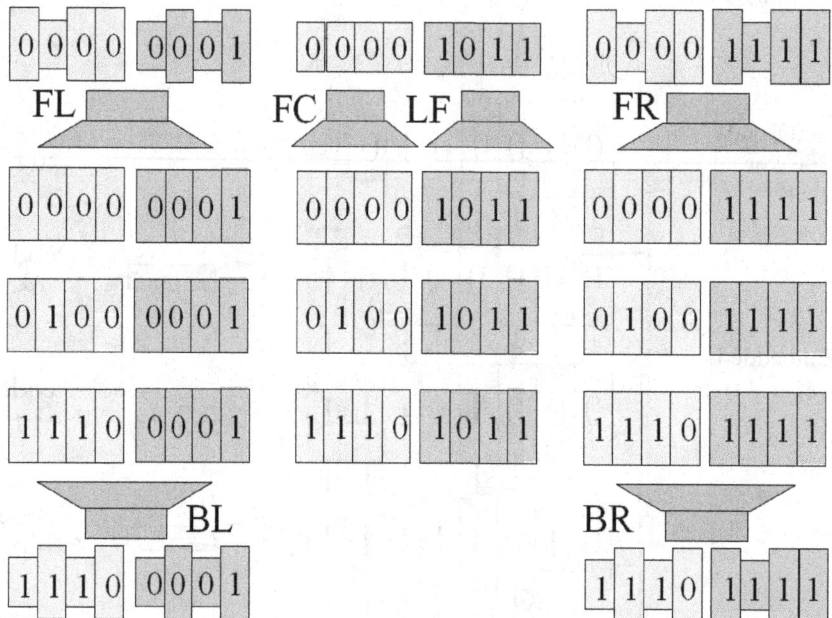

0010 1101 0101 *LSB*) at each corresponding bit embedding level as '*MSB* SSMM SMSS SWWS WSSS *LSB* (S: strong, M: middle, W: weak),' while in the right channel signal, we embed the other 16-bit code '2D3Bh' (0010 1101 0011 1011) at each corresponding bit embedding level as 'SSSS WSWM WSSS SMMS.' We can then extract three more types of 16-bit code—'12BDh' (0001 0010 1011 1101) at the near-left center position, the 16-bit code '26BDh' (0010 0110 1011 1101) at the center position, and the 16-bit code '27BBh' (0010 0111 1011 1011) at the near-right center position—as well as the 16-bit code '12D5h' at the left position and the 16-bit code '2D3Bh' at the right position.

In the case of the 3 × 3 two-dimensional spatial location detection application described in Figure 7, we can select 9 position codes from Table 1—'FL (0001h),' 'FC (00C3h),' 'FR (00EFh),' 'ML (0505h),' 'MC (05CBh),' 'MR (0FFFh),' 'BL(5555h),' 'BC (55DFh),' and 'BR (FFFFh)'—rather than the 8-bit codes '01h,' '0Bh,' '0Fh,' '41h,' '4Bh,' '4Fh,' 'E1h,' 'EBh,' and 'EFh.' We initially determine the two-step embedding amplitude level for each bit using a three-step single dimensional spatial location model. In order to extract the 16-bit code '00C3h' (0000 0000 1100 0011) at the front-center position between the FL and FR locations in the front-left channel signal, we embed the 16-bit code '0001h' (*MSB* 0000 0000 0000 0001 *LSB*) in each corresponding bit embedding level as '*MSB* SSSS SSSS WWSS SSWS *LSB* (S: strong, W: weak),' while in the other front-right channel signal, we embed the other 16-bit code '00EFh' (0000 0000 1110 1111) in each corresponding bit embedding level as 'SSSS SSSS SSWS WWSS.' Similarly, to extract the 16-bit code '55DFh' (0101 0101 1101 1111) at the back-center position between the BL and BR locations in the back-left channel signal, we embed the 16-bit code '5555h' (*MSB* 0101 0101 0101 0101 *LSB*) in each corresponding bit embedding level as '*MSB* SSSS SSSS WSSS WSWS *LSB*,' while in the other back-right channel signal we embed the other 16-bit code 'FFFFh' (1111 1111 1111 1111) in each corresponding bit embedding level as 'WSWS WSWS SSWS SSSS.'

In the vertical direction, we embed the 16-bit code '0001h' in each corresponding bit embedding level as '*MSB* SSSS SWSW SSSS SWSS *LSB* (S: strong, W: weak)' in order to extract the 16-bit code '0505' (0000 0101 0000 0101) at the middle-left position between the FL and BL locations, in the front-left channel signal, while we embed the other 16-bit code 5555h' at each corresponding bit embedding level as 'SWSW SSSS SWSW SSSS' in the other back-left channel signal. Similarly, we embed the 16-bit code '00EFh' in each corresponding bit embedding level as '*MSB* SSSS WWWW SSSW SSSS *LSB*' in order to extract the 16-bit code '0FFFh' (0000 1111 1111 1111) at the middle-right position between the FR and BR locations in the front-right channel signal, while we embed the other 16-bit code 'FFFFh' in each corresponding bit embedding level as 'WWWW SSSS SSSS SSSS' in the other back-right channel signal.

Therefore, we determine three-step embedding level patterns by multiplying the previously determined horizontal and vertical two-step embedding patterns in the single three-step spatial model with each other in the two-dimensional spatial mode. We embed the following: the16-bit code '0001h' (*MSB* 0000 0000 0000 0001 *LSB*) in each corresponding bit embedding level as '*MSB* SSSS SMSM MMSS SMMS *LSB* (S: strong, M: middle, W: weak)' in the front-left channel signal; the 16-bit code '00EFh' (0000 0000 1110 1111) in each corresponding bit embedding level as 'SSSS MMMM SSMM MMSS' in the front-right channel signal; the 16-bit code '5555h' (0101 0101 0101 0101) in each corresponding bit embedding level as 'SMSM SSSS MMSM MSMS' in the back-left channel signal; and the 16-bit code 'FFFFh' (1111 1111 1111 1111) in each corresponding bit embedding level as 'WMWM MSMS SSMS SSSS' in the back-right channel signal. We can then extract five more types of 16-bit code—'00C3h' (0000 0000 1100 0011) at the front center position; '0505h' (0000 0101 0000 0101) at the middle-left position; '05CBh' (0000 0101 1100 1011) at the middle-center position; '0FFFh' (0000 1111 1111 1111) at the middle-right position; '55DFh' (0101 0101 1101 1111) at the back-center position—as well as the 16-bit code '0001h' at the front-left position, '00EFh' at the front-right position, '5555h' at the back-left position, and 'FFFFh' at the back-right position.

Conceptual Basis of the Proposed Temporal Position Detection Method Using Audio Watermarks

Our proposed audio watermarking method can also be used for transmitting the temporal position information of sound sources. Figure 8 shows the synchronization of audio contents (foreign language translated version) to be played back via a PDA device along with the surrounding PA (Public Address) audio content (Japanese language version) by transmitting the time codes of the currently played PA audio content. In this example, the serial number codes or time codes are continuously embedded temporally into all of the PA audio channels at 3-second intervals, (four 18-bit word number codes repeated at a 20 bps embedding rate for 48 kHz sampled audio signals). These 18-bit codes are also cyclic unstructured Hamming codes similar to those shown in Table 1, with a minimum Hamming distance of 3 bits, allowing the expression of 212 variations. If one of the time codes is extracted successfully by a PDA device, it can be used to forward the playback start position of the PDA internal content. Therefore, even if several embedded time codes cannot be extracted properly, the synchronization process can be successfully achieved using a single properly extracted time code. This is a highly suitable application for audio watermarks even if its extraction reliability is relatively low compared with that of the acoustic modulation method. A maximum time delay of 3 seconds may occur between the PDA and the PA playback position, which does not present a problem in language translation applications.

Other watermark extraction processes using a microphone device cannot be executed when using off-the-shelf PDA devices for the playback of audio contents. The specification of our used PDA device is the iPAQ rx5965 Travel Companion (CPU: Samsung SC32442 400MHz, Memory: 64Mbytes, OS: Japanese Windows Mobile 5.0). This is because the sound device driver does not support simultaneous recording and playback due to the lack of PDA I/O processing performance. Therefore, we need to allow for several idling periods during audio playback to receive a further synchronization time code or alternative types of control codes, such as stopping audio playback.

Design of a Museum Guide System by Integrating the Proposed Spatial and Temporal Position Detection Methods

Our proposed museum guide system consists of multiple audio player systems installed at each exhibition spot and Microsoft Windows Mobile-based PDA devices that are rented to museum visitors. Each PDA device contains multimedia guide contents including stored photos, videos, and audio media that are presented to the user after receiving codes from the nearest sound sources. When implementing the proposed methods described in the previous sections, we can use two types of codes for indicating the spatial positions of the user and the temporal positions of the playback content in the nearest media player. The spatial position code is used for selecting an appropriate multimedia file, whereas the temporal position code is used for positioning start playback point of the time-based media content, such as audio or video files.

Figure 9 shows our proposed museum guide system using the audio watermarking technology. Each of the 3 exhibition spots on the left has a set of stereo audio players that can transmit spot identification codes, and they can also transmit 2 to 5 different codes depending on the linear

Figure 8. Method for synchronizing time-based PDA contents with PA contents by transmitting the temporal playing position codes of the PA contents

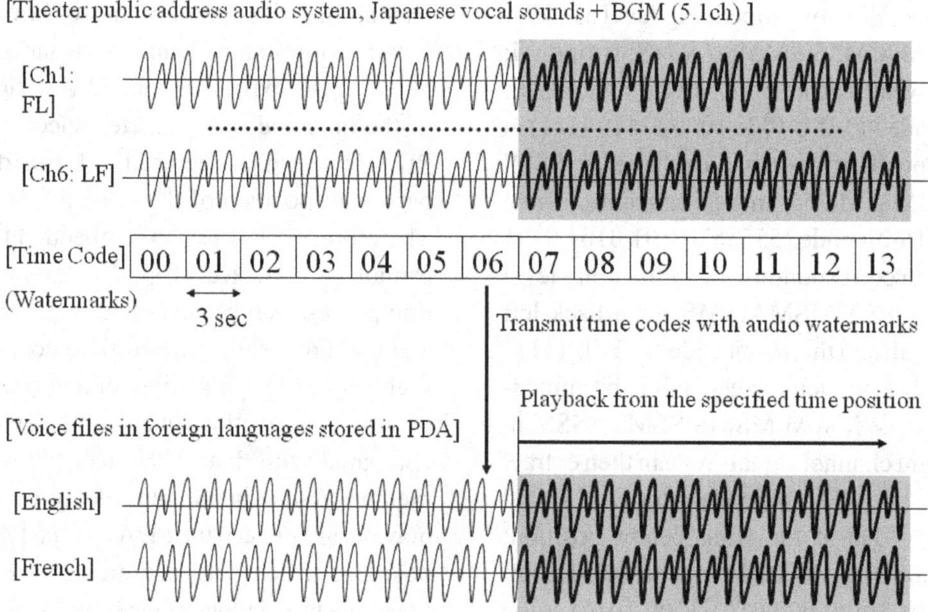

spatial location. Figure 6 showed that 2 to 5 sets of art works can be displayed horizontally in these spots and their respective guide content can be automatically selected by a visitor's PDA, based on its spatial location. In our implemented prototype system, the greatest distance between the PDA and the nearest loudspeaker was less than 50 cm, the response time was 2 to 10 seconds, and the correctly extracted 16-bit code rate was 0.4 to 2.0 words/second.

Figure 9 shows a typical auditorium on the right, where movie content related to exhibition topics can be viewed. Figure 7 showed that this room can have 3 × 3 two-dimensional seat zone codes that can be sent to a visitor's PDA and supplemental information will be presented depending on visitor's seat position, such as translated texts for foreign visitors or detailed internal data for curators. Multiple foreign language translations that narrate audio content can also be stored in the PDA. This supplementary audio content can be played back synchronously at any time along with the theater public address audio content in the domestic language edition by receiving temporal position codes from the nearest PA loudspeaker. In our implemented prototype system, the distance between the four loudspeakers (FL, FR, BL, BR) was around 6 m, the response time was 6 to 22 seconds, and the correctly extracted 16-bit code rate was 0.18 to 0.6 words/second.

FUTURE RESEARCH DIRECTIONS

During the trial in our laboratory museum, LDML (Louvre-DNP, 2009), we experienced difficulties in determining appropriate watermark embedding parameters, which led to several response failure problems on site. In order to overcome these problems, we are considering the following topics as important future research areas.

Figure 9. Proposed museum guide system using audio watermarking technology

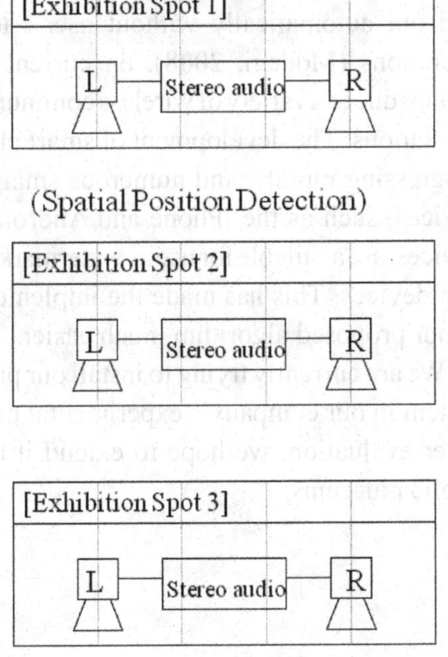

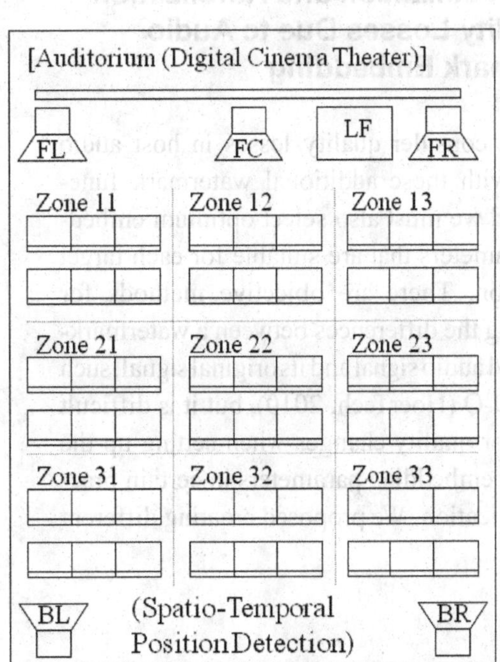

Proposed Additional Functions: Providing Extended Functions to Ensure the Room Reverberation Robustness of Embedded Audio Watermarks

The development of a robust audio watermarking technique against room reverberation was also important when implementing the application described because there is often some distance between the mobile terminals and the watermark embedded sound sources. The influence of room reverberation was especially apparent in our proposed spatial position information delivery application. We have proposed adding room reverberation robustness to our proposed audio watermark method without degrading host content quality by rotating the phases of the decreased signal components using information embedded to decrease the influence of temporally emitted signal components (Modegi, 2010b). However, this cannot satisfy all types of room acoustics specifications.

An Evaluation Tool for Practical Use: Visualization and Auralization of Quality Losses Due to Audio Watermark Embedding

We must consider quality losses in host audio signals with these additional watermark functions, and we must also select optimum embedding parameters that are suitable for each target application. There are objective methods for evaluating the differences between a watermark-embedded audio signal and its original signal, such as PEMO-Q (HoerTech, 2010), but it is difficult to monitor quality changes when setting up the optimum embedding parameters in certain practical application. We proposed creating different MIDI data to allow the evaluation of a watermark-embedded audio signal and its original signal along with visualized and auralized sound quality losses due to our watermark embedding processes. This could be achieved by applying our proposed MIDI encoding technique known as "Auto-F®" (Modegi, 2010a). In future work, we also intend to propose quantitative evaluation methods that consider human auditory response characteristics and several subjective evaluation databases for watermark-embedded acoustic signals.

CONCLUSION

In this chapter, we described our proposed audio watermark embedding method and its application to mobile museum guide systems. In particular, we focused on transmitting spatial or temporal position information to mobile terminals using our proposed audio watermarking methods. Our proposed audio watermark method supports 3G mobile feature phones for watermark extraction. However, we had to use a Windows Mobile-based PDA or a smart phone device as a mobile terminal because it was difficult to implement push-type information delivery, where delivery will be carried out automatically without user's terminal operations (Modegi, 2008), on current mobile phones due to a variety of wireless communication regulations. The development of smart phones is progressing rapidly, and numerous smart phone devices, such as the iPhone and Android-based devices, are available for use as watermark extraction devices. This has made the implementation of our proposed algorithm much easier.

We are currently trying to install our proposed system in our company's experimental museum. After evaluation, we hope to extend it to other public museums.

REFERENCES

Brans, E., Brombach, B., Zeidler, T., & Bimber, O. (2007). Enabling mobile phones to support large-scale museum guidance. *Journal of IEEE Multimedia, 14*(2), 16–25. doi:10.1109/MMUL.2007.33

Chou, L. D., Wu, C. H., Ho, S. P., Lee, C. C., & Chen, J. M. (2004). Requirement analysis and implementation of palm-based multimedia museum guide systems. In *Proceedings of IEEE 18th International Conference on Advanced Information Networking and Applications,* (Vol. 1), (pp. 352-357). IEEE Press.

HoerTech. (2010). *Home page of PEMO-Q by HoerTech.* Retrieved from http://www.hoertech.de/web_en/produkte/pemo-q.shtml

Hong, J. K., Takahashi, J., Kusaba, M., Yamada, S., & Sugita, S. (1995). *Multimedia applications in the national museum of ethnology.* IPSJ SIG Technical Report, 1995-CH-026, 31-35. IPSJ.

Kanetou, R., Nakashima, Y., & Babaguchi, N. (2009). Position estimation using detect strength of digital watermarking for audio signals. In *Proceedings of IEICE General Conference: DS-3-10,* (pp. S37-38). IEICE.

Ko, B. S., Nishimura, R., & Suzuki, Y. (2005). Time-spread echo method for digital audio watermarking. *IEEE Transactions on Multimedia,* 7(2), 212–221. doi:10.1109/TMM.2005.843366

Kurita, Y. (2000). *Minpaku denshi guide (electronic guide of the national museum of ethnology).* Osaka, Japan: The Senri Foundation.

Kusunoki, F., Satoh, I., Mizoguchi, H., & Inagaki, S. (2008). SoundSpot: Location-bound audio guide system for exhibition supports in museums. *IEICE Transactions on Information and Systems, 91*(2), 229–237.

Louvre-DNP. (2009). *Augmented reality museum – YouTube, Metaio's cooperation with Japanese company DNP within the Louvre - DNP museum lab in Tokyo.* Retrieved August 22, 2011, from http://www.youtube.com/watch?v=lQfCndsnXUc

Matsuoka, H., Nakashima, Y., & Yoshimura, T. (2006). *Aerial acoustic communications in audible band-acoustic OFDM.* Technical Report of IEICE, EA2006-24, 106(125), 25-29. IEICE.

Modegi, T. (2006). Development of audio watermark technology to be extracted contactlessly by cell phone. *IEEJ Transactions on Electronics. Information Systems, 126*(7), 825–831.

Modegi, T. (2007). Construction of ubiquitous acoustic spaces using audio watermark technology and mobile terminals. *IEEJ Transactions on Electrical and Electronic Engineering, 2*(6), 608–619. doi:10.1002/tee.20216

Modegi, T. (2008). Prototyping of push-type information delivery system using audio watermark technology. In *Proceedings of IEICE General Conference,* (Vol. DS-4-5), (pp. S27-28). IEICE.

Modegi, T. (2009). Detection method of mobile terminal spatial location using audio watermark technique. In *Proceedings of ICROSS-SICE International Joint Conference,* (pp. 5479-5484). ICROSS-SICE.

Modegi, T. (2010a). Evaluation method for quality losses generated by miscellaneous audio signal processing using MIDI encode tool auto-F. In *Proceedings of IEEE Region10 TENCON,* (pp. 2066-2071). IEEE Press.

Modegi, T. (2010b). Robust audio watermark method resistant to room reverberation for realizing ubiquitous acoustic spaces. In *Proceedings of IEICE General Conference: DS-3-3,* (pp. S19-20). IEICE.

Munekata, T., Yamaguchi, T., Handa, H., Nishimura, R., & Suzuki, Y. (2009). Portable acoustic caption decoder using IH techniques for enhancing lives of the people who are deaf or hard-of-hearing - System configuration and robustness for airborne sound. *International Journal of Innovative Computing, Information, & Control*, *5*(7), 1829–1836.

Nakajima, Y. (2009). *Home page of Yoshitaka Nakajima Laboratory in Kyushu University*. Retrieved August 22, 2011, from http://www.design.kyushu-u.ac.jp/~ynhome/ENG/index.html

Nakashima, Y., Tachibana, R., Nishimura, M., & Babaguchi, N. (2007). Determining recording location based on synchronization positions of audio watermarking. In *Proceedings of ICASSP2007*, (vol. 2), (pp. 253-256). ICASSP.

Nakashima, Y., Tachibana, R., Nishimura, M., & Babaguchi, N. (2009). Watermarked movie soundtrack finds the position of the camcorder in a theater. *IEEE Transactions on Multimedia*, *11*(3), 443–454. doi:10.1109/TMM.2009.2012938

Nishimura, A. (2006). Audio watermarking based on sinusoidal amplitude modulation. In *Proceedings of IEEE International Conference on Acoustics, Speech and Signal Processing ICASSP2006*, (Vol. 4), (pp. 797-800). IEEE Press.

Ono, T. (2001). Watermark embedded in sound. In *Watermark and Content Protection* (pp. 122–138). Tokyo, Japan: Ohm Publishing.

Personal Media Corp. (2009). *Technical resources of UC (ubiquitous communicator)*. Retrieved August 22, 2011, from http://www.uid4u.com/products/uc.html

VLCC. (2007). *Home page of visible light communications consortium*. Retrieved August 22, 2011, from http://www.vlcc.net/?ml_lang=en

Yura, S., Fujimori, K., Mori, H., & Sakamura, K. (1998). A multimedia MUD (multi-user dungeon) system for the digital museum. In *Proceedings of IEEE 3rd Asia Pacific Computer Human Interaction* (pp. 32–37). IEEE Press.

ADDITIONAL READING

Amold, M. (2004). *Digital audio watermarking*. New York, NY: Logos.

Aoki, N. (2008). *Sound programming in C language–Signal processing of sound effect*. Tokyo, Japan: Ohmsha Publishing.

Arnold, M., Wolthusen, S. D., & Schmucker, M. (2003). *Techniques and applications of digital watermarking and content protection*. New York, NY: Artech House.

Bailey, K. (2005). *Steganography*. New York, NY: BookSurge Publishing.

Barni, M. (Ed.). (2005). Digital watermarking. In *Proceedings of the 4th International Workshop on Digital Watermarking Secure Data Management*. Berlin, Germany: Springer Publishing.

Bassia, P., Pitas, I., & Nikolaidis, N. (2001). Robust audio watermarking in the time domain. *IEEE Transactions on Multimedia*, *3*(2), 232–241. doi:10.1109/6046.923822

Chandramouli, R. (2003). *Digital data-hiding and watermarking with applications*. Boca Raton, FL: CRC Press.

Cox, I. J., Miller, M. L., & Bloom, J. A. (2002). *Digital watermarking*. San Francisco, CA: Morgan Kaufmann Publishers.

Cvejic, N. (2007). *Digital audio watermarking techniques and technologies: Applications and benchmarks*. Hershey, PA: IGI Global. doi:10.4018/978-1-59904-513-9

Dutoit, T., & Marques, F. (2009). *Applied signal processing: A MATLAB(TM)-based proof of concept (signals and communication technology)*. Berlin, Germany: Springer Publishing.

Fridlich, J. (2009). *Steganography in digital media: Principles, algorithms, and applications*. Cambridge, UK: Cambridge University Press.

Furht, B., Muharemagic, E., & Socek, D. (2010). *Multimedia encryption and watermarking (multimedia systems and applications)*. Berlin, Germany: Springer Publishing.

He, X. (2008). *Watermarking in audio: Key techniques and technologies*. New York, NY: Cambria Press.

Hi, S. (2011). *Signal processing, perceptual coding and watermarking of digital audio: Advanced technologies and models*. Hershey, PA: IGI Global.

Icon Group International. (2009). *Watermarking: Webster's timeline history, 1972–2007*. New York, NY: Icon Group International.

Inoue, A. (1997). *Digital watermark – Encryption system in multimedia era*. Tokyo, Japan: Maruyama Gakugei Publishing.

Johnson, N. F., Duric, Z., & Jajodia, S. (2000). *Information hiding: Steganography and watermarking - Attacks and countermeasures*. Berlin, Germany: Springer Publishing. doi:10.1007/978-1-4615-4375-6

Katzenbeisser, S. (Ed.). (1999). *Information hiding techniques for steganography and digital watermarking*. New York, NY: Artech House. do i:10.1201/1079/43263.28.6.20001201/30373.5

Katzenbeisser, S., & Petitcolas, F. (2002). *Information hiding techniques for steganography and digital watermarking*. New York, NY: Artech House Publishers. doi:10.1201/1079/43263.28.6.20001201/30373.5

Kientzle, T. (1998). *A programmer's guide to sound*. Reading, MA: Addison-Wesley.

Kim, H. J., Shi, Y. O., & Barni, M. (Eds.). (2010). *Digital watermarking: 9th international workshop, IWDW 2010*. Berlin, Germany: Springer Publishing.

Kirovski, D. (2006). *Multimedia watermarking techniques and applications (internet and communications)*. New York, NY: Auerbach Publications.

Kitayama, H. (2008). *WAV programming–Acoustic processing by C language*. Tokyo, Japan: CUTT System Publishing.

Komatsu, N., & Tanaka, K. (Eds.). (2004). *Digital watermark technology – Digital content security*. Tokyo, Japan: The Institute of Image Electronic Engineers of Japan.

Lee, M.-J., Kim, K.-S., & Lee, H.-K. (2010). Digital cinema watermarking for estimating the position of the pirate. *IEEE Transactions on Multimedia*, *12*(7), 605–621. doi:10.1109/TMM.2010.2061221

Lie, W.-N., & Chang, L.-C. (2006). Robust and high-quality time-domain audio watermarking based on low-frequency amplitude modification. *IEEE Transactions on Multimedia*, *8*(1), 46–59. doi:10.1109/TMM.2005.861292

Matsui, K. (1993). *Image concealment method*. Tokyo, Japan: Morikita Publishing.

Matsui, K. (1998). *Fundamentals of digital watermark – New protect technology for multimedia*. Tokyo, Japan: Morikita Publishing.

Matsuoka, H., Nakashima, Y., & Yoshimura, T. (2008). Acoustic OFDM system and performance analysis. *IEICE Transactions on Fundamentals of Electronics, Communications and Computer Science, 91*(7), 1652–1658. doi:10.1093/ietfec/e91-a.7.1652

Meana, H. P. (2007). *Advances in audio and speech signal processing: Technologies and applications*. Hershey, PA: IGI Global. doi:10.4018/978-1-59904-132-2

Miller, I. J., Bloom, M. L., Fridrich, J. A., Kalker, J., & Cox, T. (2007). *Digital watermarking and steganography*. London, UK: Elsevier Science Ltd.

Modegi, T. (2007). Expansion techniques of embedding audio watermark data rate for constructing ubiquitous acoustic spaces. *IEEJ Transactions on Electronics. Information Systems, 127*(7), 1013–1021.

Modegi, T. (2007). Technical review and future scope of digital watermark technologies – The third wave on the mobile phone network infrastructure. *Material Stage, Technical Information Institute Co. Ltd., 7*(2), 70–76.

Modegi, T. (2008). Audio watermark embedding technique applying auditory stream segregation: 'G-encoder mark,' extractable by mobile phone. *IEEJ Transactions on Electronics. Information Systems, 128*(7), 1087–1095.

Modegi, T. (2008). Increasing the audio watermark data rate in the construction of ubiquitous acoustic spaces. *Electrical Engineering in Japan, 165*(1), 42–51. doi:10.1002/eej.20758

Modegi, T. (2009). Audio watermark embedding technique applying auditory stream segregation: 'G-encoder *mark*,' extractable by mobile phone. *Electronics and Communications in Japan, 92*(12), 1–12. doi:10.1002/ecj.10245

Mohammad, A. (2010). *Advanced techniques in multimedia watermarking: Image, video and audio applications*. Hershey, PA: IGI Global.

Munekata, T., Yamaguchi, T., Handa, H., Nishimura, R., & Suzuki, Y. (2007). A portable acoustic caption decoder using IH techniques for enhancing lives of the people who are deaf or hard-of-hearing: System configuration and robustness for airborne sound. *Proceedings of IIH-MS, P2007*, 271–274.

Murata, H., Ogihara, A., Iwata, M., & Shiozaki, A. (2008). A method of capacity increase for time-domain audio watermarking based on low-frequency amplitude modification. In *Proceedings of 125th AES Convention*. AES.

Nakashima, Y. N., Tachibana, R., & Babaguchi, N. (2009). Watermarked movie soundtrack finds the position of the camcorder in a theater. *IEEE Transactions on Multimedia, 11*(3), 443–454. doi:10.1109/TMM.2009.2012938

Nishimura, A. (2008). Data hiding for audio signals that are robust with respect to air transmission and a speech codec. In *Proceedings of the 4th International Conference on Intelligent Information Hiding and Multimedia Signal Processing*, (pp. 601-604). IEEE.

Nishimura, A. (2010). Audio data hiding that is robust with respect to aerial transmission and speech codecs. *International Journal of Innovative Computing, Information, & Control, 6*(3), 1389–1400.

Ono, T. (2001). *Digital watermark and content protection*. Tokyo, Japan: Ohmsha Publishing.

Petitcolas, F., & Kim, H. J. (Eds.). (2002). *Digital watermarking: First international workshop, IWDW 2002*. London, UK: Springer Publishing.

Sasaki, H. (Ed.). (2007). *Intellectual property protection for multimedia information technology (premier reference source)*. Hershey, PA: IGI Global. doi:10.4018/978-1-59904-762-1

Sencar, H. T., Ramkumar, M., & Akansu, A. N. (2004). *Data hiding fundamentals and applications: Content security in digital multimedia*. San Francisco, CA: Academic Press.

Shih, F. I. (2011). *Digital watermarking and steganography: Fundamentals and techniques*. Boca Raton, FL: CRC Press.

Spanias, A., Painter, T., & Atti, V. (2007). *Audio signal processing and coding*. New York, NY: Wiley-Interscience. doi:10.1002/0470041978

Visvanathan, A. (2011). *Application of binary image in digital audio watermarking, lap lambert*. San Francisco, CA: Academic Publishing.

Wayner, P. (2008). *Disappearing cryptography: Information hiding: Steganography & watermarking* (3rd ed.). San Francisco, CA: Morgan Kaufmann.

Wu, M., & Liu, B. (2003). *Multimedia data hiding*. Berlin, Germany: Springer Publishing.

Xian, Y. Y., Xin, N., & Zhu, X. B. (1991). *Digital watermarking theory and technology*. New York, NY: Higher Education.

KEY TERMS AND DEFINITIONS

Acoustic Interpolation: Interpolation of missing signal components by the auditory stream segregation phenomenon.

Analogue Robustness: Watermarks having robustness against D/A (loudspeaker), A/D (microphone) conversion, and aerial transmission.

Audio Watermark: Embedded or hided data in audio signals without audible sounds.

Cyclic Unstructured Hamming Codes: Error detection codes that are robust against bit shifting.

Museum Guide System: Explanations of exhibited objects via audio, image, and video.

Mobile Terminal: Mobile feature phone, smart phone, and PDA (Personal Digital Assistant) that can capture sound signals, execute user applications, and play multimedia contents.

Position Information: Spatial location of users or temporal position of audio or movie contents.

Push-Type Information Delivery: Information will be delivered automatically without user's terminal operations like traditional radio or TV broadcasting.

Ubiquitous Acoustic Space: Information transmitting sound sources distributed in 3 dimensional spaces.

Section 2
Information Hiding for Images and Video

Chapter 10
Introduction to Image Steganography and Steganalysis

Michiharu Niimi
Kyushu Institute of Technology, Japan

Hideki Noda
Kyushu Institute of Technology, Japan

ABSTRACT

This chapter reviews information hiding methods, with a focus on steganography and steganalysis. First, the authors summarize image data structures and image formats required by computers and the Internet. They then introduce several information hiding methods based on image formats including lossless (non-compression based), limited color-based image data, JPEG, and JPEG2000. The authors describe a steganographic method in detail, which is based on image segmentation using a complexity measure. They also introduce a method for applying this to palette-based image formats, reversible information hiding for grayscale images, and JPEG2000 steganography. The steganographic methods for JPEG and JPEG2000 described in this chapter give particular consideration to the naturalness of cover data. In the steganalysis section, the authors introduce two methods, i.e., a specific steganalysis method for LSB steganography and Bit-Plane Complexity Segmentation (BPCS) stegnography.

QUICK SUMMARY OF IMAGE DATA AND FORMAT

Before describing detailed methods for the embedding and extraction of information in image data, we provide a summary of image data storage on computers and transmission over the Internet.

Digital Images

Digital images can be represented as a 2-dimensional discrete signal $f(x,y)$ where x and y represent a sampled point in the image, ranging from $0 \leq x \leq S_x - 1$ and $0 \leq y \leq S_y - 1$, if the image size is S_x and S_y respectively. The value of $f(x,y)$

DOI: 10.4018/978-1-4666-2217-3.ch010

is quantized using *N* bits, i.e., $0 \leq f(x, y) \leq 2^N - 1$. If *f*(x,y) is a scalar, the image is a grayscale image. The black-and-white color corresponds to 0 and 255, if *N* = 8. When dealing with a color image, *f*(*x,y*) can be regarded as a vector with three components: R, G, and B. In general, a full color image is represented as *f*(*x,y*) with 8 bits quantized for each component, i.e., 24 bits are quantized in total.

Palette-Based Images

The intensity of the three colors, i.e., red, green, and blue (denoted as R, G, and B), must be provided to display a color on a screen via a computer's frame buffer. This information is provided from the image data. We designate three images, the R image, G image, and B image, which correspond to the intensities of the R, G, and B color components for the color image, respectively. We refer to these R, G, and B images as the color component images.

A pixel is regarded as a triplet vector (R, G, B), known as a color vector. We assume that the values of R, G, and B are less than 256, which means that each can be represented using 8 bits. A palette contains a set of color vectors with a unique index assigned to each vector. If the palette contains less than 256 color vectors, the index can itself be represented using 8 bits. In a palette-based image, a pixel value does not directly contain color information, but instead it contains an index for the palette. We refer to such an image as an index image.

Lossless, Lossy, and Non-Compression Image Formats

Digital images are stored in computers, USB drives, DVDs, and other media, and they can be transmitted via the Internet. We need different formats to achieve this. Compression-based image formats consist of two types, i.e., lossless compression-based formats and lossy compression-based formats. With the compression-based image format, a bit sequence of compressed data is stored on a computer, whereas the pixel values are stored directly. The original pixel value is reconstructed from the compressed bit sequence. Lossless compression-based image formats can completely recover the original pixel value, e.g., PNG, whereas the lossy compression-based image format can make errors when recovering the original pixel value from the recovered pixel value, e.g., JPEG and JPEG2000. Non-compression based image formats store pixel values on computers without any compression.

INFORMATION HIDING IN IMAGE DATA

In this section, we introduce several information hiding methods for image data. The hiding methods are categorized as lossless compression (non-compression-based) methods, limited color-based methods, JPEG-based methods, and JPEG2000-based methods. A reversible information hiding method for lossless and JPEG2000 formats is also introduced.

Information Hiding for Lossless Compression/Non-Compression Base Image Format

It is simple and easy to implement an algorithm for information hiding with lossless compression and such methods are also applicable to non-compression-based image formats. This subsection introduces LSB-based steganography and Bit-Plane Complexity Segmentation (BPCS) steganography (Niimi, et al., 1999). A method for applying a complexity measure to reversible information hiding (Niimi, et al., 2006) is also introduced.

LSB Steganography and LSB Matching

Let $f_{ORG}(x,y)$ and $f_{EMB}(x,y)$ be a cover image and a stego-image where the cover image is a natural image in which we want to hide secret data, whereas the stego-image is the cover image with information embedded. Let $B=(b_1,b_2,\ldots)$, $b_i \in \{0,1\}$ be the secret data we want to hide.

LSB steganography is a method for replacing the LSB bits of pixels with the information we want to embed. Thus,

$$f_{EMB}(x,y)=((f_{ORG}(x,y)>>1)<<1)\mid b_i \tag{1}$$

where $>>$ and $<<$ represent a right shift and a left shift operator, respectively, and | represents an OR operation between the LSB bit of a pixel and b_i. LSB matching is an improved version of LSB steganography and it is formalized as follows:

$$f_{EMB}(x,y)=\begin{cases} f_{ORG}(x,y)+1 & \text{if } (f_{ORG}(x,y)\,\&\,0x01 \neq b_i) \text{ and } (r>0 \text{ or } f_{ORG}(x,y)=255) \\ f_{ORG}(x,y)-1 & \text{if } (f_{ORG}(x,y)\,\&\,0x01 \neq b_i) \text{ and } (r<0 \text{ or } f_{ORG}(x,y)=0) \\ f_{ORG}(x,y) & \text{if } (f_{ORG}(x,y) \text{ and } 0x01=b_i) \end{cases} \tag{2}$$

where *r* represents an iid random variable with a uniform distribution on $\{-1,+1\}$

BPCS Steganography

This method is based on image segmentation using complexity measures for binary images. To understand this method we first explain the complexity measures, before describing how to embed using image segmentation.

Complexity Measures and Conjugation

We use the four-connectivity neighborhood method in the following discussion. The total length of the black-and-white border equals the sum of the number of color changes among the rows and columns of an image. For example, a single black pixel surrounded by white background pixels has a border length of 4. We assume that the image frame is always a square measuring $m \times m$ pixels in size. We count the number of color changes in the interior parts of the image. Thus, the minimum border length is 0 (in either black or white pattern), whereas the maximum is $2 \times m \times (m-1)$ (in checkerboard patterns). Thus, the image complexity measure is defined as follows:

$$\alpha=\frac{k}{2m(m-1)} \tag{3}$$

where *k* is the total length of the black-and-white border of the image. Thus, the value range is as follows:

$$0 \le \alpha \le 1 \tag{4}$$

In the following discussion, we assume that a value of 0 indicates a black pixel and a value of 1 indicates a white pixel. Let *P* be a binary image. The background of *P* is assumed to be white. *W* and *B* are defined as all white pixels and all black pixels, respectively. In addition, the two checkerboard patterns are assumed to be *Wc* and *Bc*. Here, the leftmost pixel is white in *Wc* whereas *Bc* is black (Figure 1) in the opposite case.

The foreground is considered as *B* and the image background is *W* in *P*. Based on the above definition, the "conjugate image" P^* of *P* is defined as follows:

$$P^* = P \oplus Wc$$

Figure 1. Example of conjugate operation using simple binary pattern (m = 16)

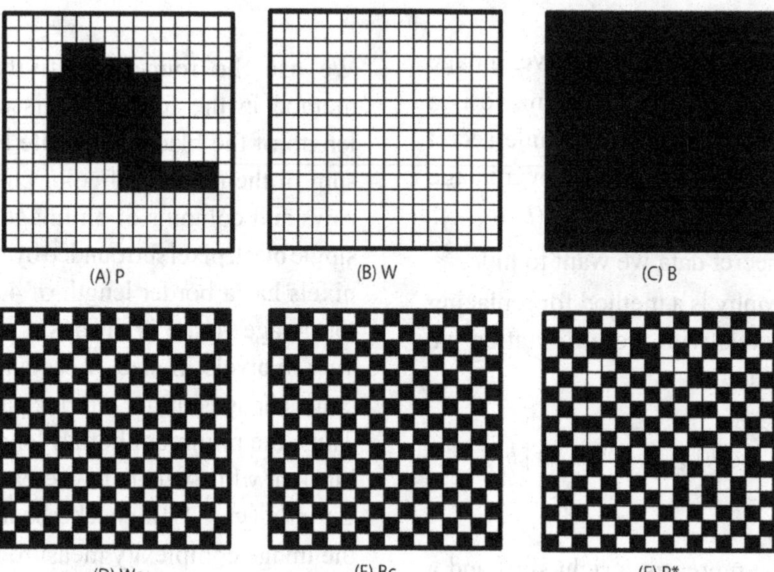

where $\oplus$ represents the exclusive-OR operation for each pixel. We call the operation to obtain the conjugate image. P^* is regarded as an image that satisfies the following conditions.

1. The foreground area shape is the same as P
2. The foreground area has the Bc pattern
3. The background area has the Wc pattern

Thus, P and P^* correspond one-to-one. The following properties apply to P and P^*. $\alpha(P)$ represents the complexity of P.

A. $(P^*)^* = P$
B. $P^* \neq P$
C. $\alpha(P^*) = 1 - \alpha(P)$

Here, the most important property of the conjugation is (c). This property indicates that the conjugation provides a technique for transforming a simple image to a complex image, or vice versa, without losing any shape information.

Embedding Method Using Complexity

It would not be noticeable if we replaced noise-like regions in a binary image generated from a natural image with random patterns. This means that it is possible to replace noise-like regions with secret data. The criterion of a noise-like region is different depending on the dummy image, so it is necessary to obtain a suitable threshold for each.

In the binary image, the complexity of a local region $(m \times m)$ to be replaced with secret data satisfies the following condition.

$$\alpha_{TH} \geq \alpha \quad (5)$$

To embed the secret data file into the dummy image, we divide the file into subfiles (m x m bits) and replace the noise-like region with the binary pattern mapped from the subfile. However, not all of the replaced patterns have a complexity greater than α_0. Thus, the binary pattern is complicated by the conjugate operation. Using this operation, we can embed any secret file within the cover image. However, we need information about the location of the simple pattern that has had a conjugate operation applied when extracting the secret information completely. We call this information the conjugation map.

The steganography proposed in this chapter consists of the following five steps:

1. An $M \times M$, N-bits/pixel dummy image in natural binary form is transformed to N-bits gray-code form.
2. The image is decomposed into N bit-planes using a bit-slicing operation. Each bit-plane image is a binary image.
3. Each plane is divided into $m \times m$ small blocks. Let us denote those blocks as $P_i; i = 1,2,...,\lfloor M/m \rfloor^2$. Thus, the n-th bit-plane image can be expressed as follows:

$$I_n = \{P_1^n, P_2^n, ..., P_{\lfloor M/m \rfloor^2}^n\}$$

In the same manner, the n-th conjugation map can be expressed as

$$C_n = \{Q_1^n, Q_2^n, ..., Q_{\lfloor M/m \rfloor^2}^n\}$$

where each Q is 0 or 1. A value of 1 indicates that a conjugate operation is applied.

The embedded data is denoted by E and it contains three sections, i.e., the header, body, and pad. The header shows the size of the embedded data, the body is the secret data (such as a cover image), and the pad is data that is only used to adjust the total length of E such that the size of E is exactly equal to a multiple of $m \times m$. E_j, $(j = 1,2,..,J)$ is a segmented block of E with a size of $m \times m$ bits. The binary pattern of E_j mapped on the $m \times m$ region in the cover data is designated by makes (E_j).

The threshold value is denoted α_{TH} and the embedding algorithm is described as follows, where each Q in C_n is initialized at 0.

The embedding procedure in Box 1 is executed on the lowest bit plane first, before proceeding to higher planes, because the lower bit-planes are less significant. If the complexity of makeS(E_j) is smaller than the threshold, makeS(E_j) has the conjugate operation applied. Thus, a mark 1 is placed at the location of E_j in the conjugation map.

4. **Bit-planes embedded with secret data using (3) are composed into an N bit image. Pixel values in the N bit image are in gray code.**
5. **The N bit image is transformed into a natural binary image.**

The embedded information, i.e., the secret data, within the dummy image is extracted by executing the steps of the embedding method in reverse. It is impossible to extract the embedded information without knowing α_{TH} and the conjugation map.

Box 1. Embedding procedure

```
for (n=N, j=1; n >= 1 && j < J ; n--) {
    for (i=1; i <= ⌊M / m⌋² && j < J; i++) {
        if (α (P_i^n) >= α_TH ) {
            if (α (makeS(E_j)) >= α_TH )
                P_i^n = makeS(E_j)
            else {
                P_i^n = makeS(E_j)*
                Q_i^n = 1
            }
            j++;
        }
    }
}
```

Reversible Information Hiding for Image Data

Most data embedding techniques modify pixel value directly or indirectly to embed information within it, hence, distort the pixel value. Usually the distortion is very small so that the human visual system cannot detect unnaturalness. However, it cannot be removed to recover the original image by usual information hiding. The reversible information hiding, which is also referred as lossless, invertible, or distortion free information hiding, as we call it, is a technique to embed information within image data and extract embedded information; then the original cover image can be recovered from the stego image. The easiest way to realize this can be referred as Fridrich et al. (2001a) and Fridrich et al. (2002). A plane of gray scale image can be regarded as a binary image. We can compress it, then, make space for information for embedding. This is the simplest way to realize the reversible information hiding in which the compressed binary image and the information are embedded in the gray scale image.

We introduce two of reversible information hiding: Tians's method and Niimi's method which is an application of the complexity measure for reversible information hiding in gray scale images.

Tian's Method

We assume here a cover image can be given as a gray scale image, and two adjacent pixel values are denoted by *x* and *y*. An average value (*l*) and the difference (*h*) of the two values are defined by

$$l := \left\lfloor \frac{x+y}{2} \right\rfloor, \quad h := x - y$$

where $\lfloor a \rfloor$ means the largest integer not greater than *a*. From *l* and *h*, *x* and *y* are calculated by

$$x = l + \left\lfloor \frac{h+1}{2} \right\rfloor \text{ and } y = l - \left\lfloor \frac{h+1}{2} \right\rfloor$$

Base on this reversible transformation, Tian (2003) proposed the reversible information hiding called Deference Expansion (DE) method. The difference between two pixels carries information. To realize this, *h* is modified by

$$h' = 2 \times h + b$$

where *h'* is the deference with the information embedded and *b* is a message bit. From *h'*, the modified pixel values for two pixels are calculated by the following:

$$x' = l + \left\lfloor \frac{h'+1}{2} \right\rfloor, \quad y' = l - \left\lfloor \frac{h'+1}{2} \right\rfloor$$

We will give an example of the embedding and extraction of DE. Let $x = 206$, $y = 201$. *l* and *h* are calculated by

$$l = \left\lfloor \frac{206+201}{2} \right\rfloor = \left\lfloor \frac{407}{2} \right\rfloor = 203,$$

$$h = 206 - 201 = 5$$

When we embed "1" into the difference *h*, where *h'* is given by

$$h' = 2 \times h + b = 2 \times 5 + 1 = 11$$

From this, the value of two pixel with information embedded is given by

$$x' = 203 + \left\lfloor \frac{11+1}{2} \right\rfloor = 209 \text{ and}$$

$$y' = 203 - \left\lfloor \frac{11}{2} \right\rfloor = 198$$

From the pair of pixel value (x', y') we can recover the original value as the following.

First, we calculate the average and the difference of (x', y'), that is:

$$l' = \left\lfloor \frac{209 + 198}{2} \right\rfloor = 203,\ h' = 209 - 198 = 11$$

The embedded information is located in the LSB position of the difference h', that is:

$$b = \mathrm{LSB}(h') = \mathrm{LSB}(11) = 1$$

and the original difference of h' can be recovered by dividing it by 2, that is:

$$h = \left\lfloor \frac{h'}{2} \right\rfloor = \left\lfloor \frac{11}{2} \right\rfloor = 5$$

From the these values, we can recover the original pixel value of (x, y) by

$$x = l' + \left\lfloor \frac{h+1}{2} \right\rfloor = 203 + \left\lfloor \frac{5+1}{2} \right\rfloor = 206 \text{ and}$$
$$y = l' - \left\lfloor \frac{h}{2} \right\rfloor = 203 + \left\lfloor \frac{5}{2} \right\rfloor = 201$$

In order to apply DE to image data, we need to define two categories for the difference between two pixel values: expandable if the difference satisfies

$$\left|2 \times h + b\right| \leq \min(2(255 - l), 2l + 1)$$

for both $b = 0$ and 1, and changeable if the difference satisfies

$$\left|\left\lfloor \frac{h}{2} \right\rfloor \times 2 + b\right| \leq \min(2(255 - l), 2l + 1)$$

for both $b = 0$ and 1. We can directly apply DE to expandable difference. However, for changeable difference, we need to store the location of changeable difference because we replace the LSB of the difference with a message bit to be hidden.

Application of Complexity Measure for Reversible Information Hiding in Grayscale Images

This subsection introduces a technique for reversible information hiding using binary image processing based on the complexity measure. Using the complexity measure, we can classify blocks on bit-planes of cover images into three groups, i.e., L (left), R (right), and M (middle) groups. By assigning a 0 to L and a 1 to R, we can then scan all blocks of an image and the status of the image is obtained as a bit sequence. The additional information and the compressed bit sequence are embedded to recover the original sequence. We can embed one message bit in each L and R group. To obtain a match for a bit in a message and the group type of the blocks, we apply a logical operation known as the conjugate operation that can flip each group and completely recover the original sequence. The embedded information is easily extracted by scanning the L and R blocks during the extraction procedure. We can recover the status of the original image from the bit-stream. Therefore, we can obtain the original image by applying the conjugate operation to match the group types and the status of the original image.

The complexity measure is used to define three types of block groups: *L*, *R*, and *M*:

$$\begin{aligned} &\mathit{Left\ Group} : P \in L \Leftrightarrow 0 \leq \alpha(P) < 0.5 \\ &\mathit{Right\ Group} : P \in R \Leftrightarrow 0.5 < \alpha(P) \leq 1 \\ &\mathit{Middle\ Group} : P \in M \Leftrightarrow \alpha(P) - 0.5 \end{aligned} \tag{6}$$

From the definition of conjugate operation, the following conditions are always satisfied.

$$P \in L \quad \Leftrightarrow \quad P^* \in R$$
$$P \in R \quad \Leftrightarrow \quad P^* \in L$$
$$P \in M \quad \Leftrightarrow \quad P^* \in M$$

where P^* represents the binary image where the conjugate operation is applied to P. In other words, the L and R groups are flipped into each other due to the conjugate operation, whereas the middle groups M remain unchanged. We further note that application of the conjugate operation to any group twice restores it to its original binary pattern.

We can embed one message bit in each L and R group by assigning a 0 to L and 1 to R (or 1 to R and 0 to L). If the message bit and the group type do not match, we apply the conjugate operation to the group to match their bit correspondence. Before the embedding begins, we scan the image by groups and compress the status of the image in a lossless manner. The bit-stream of the L and R groups is denoted by the LR-vector C.

We take the compressed LR-vector C and append it with the message bits, before embedding the resulting bit-stream in the image using the procedures described above.

The capacity of the message bits for embedding using the proposed method is

$$\text{Capacity[bits]} = N_L + N_R - |C| \tag{7}$$

where N_L and N_R is the number of left and right groups in the image, and $|C|$ is the length of the bit-stream C. If we are to embed the message bits, C must be less than $N_L + N_R$.

We now formulate the data embedding method as follows:

1. The cover image in the natural binary code is transformed to N-bit gray code (the binary-reflected gray-code). The gray-code image is decomposed into N bit-planes.
2. Each bit-plane is divided into small block squares of size $m \times m$. The blocks are categorized into three groups using the group definitions described above.
3. By assigning a 0 to L and a 1 to R group, and scanning the R blocks on all the bit-planes we obtain the status of the image as the LR-vector C.
4. The LR vector C is compressed in a lossless fashion and the message bits are appended, i.e., the information to be embedded is a bit-stream consisting of the compressed LR-vector and the message bits.
5. We embed the bit-stream such that there is match between the bit extracted from the bit-stream and group type of the block.
6. The N-bit gray-code image is recovered from the N binary image and is transformed to natural binary code.

The receiver can extract the bit-stream from all the L and R groups (L=1, R=0) by scanning the image in the same order as the embedding. The extracted bit-stream is separated into the compressed LR-vector C and the message bits. The bit-stream C is decompressed to reveal the original status of all L and R groups. The image is then processed and the status of all groups is adjusted if necessary by applying the conjugate operation. Thus, the original image can be completely restored.

Limited Color Image-Based Data Hiding

A number of steganographic techniques for palette-based images have been proposed and developed. We can place these methods into two categories, i.e., methods that embed information by manipulation of the palette and methods that change the pixel value of the index image.

A variation of the first method embeds a small amount of information in the palette by controlling color rearrangement in the palette. This technique does not affect image quality at all. However, there is no guarantee that the order of the color vectors in the palette does not change with many image manipulation tools or during lossless compression. A second variation of the first method was proposed by Fridrich (1999), which embeds information by controlling the parity of the color components in each vector. The data hiding capacity is insignificant with both of these palette-based methods.

The second method embeds information in the index image rather than in the palette, thereby providing the potential for a larger embedding capacity. Such methods typically rely on maintaining a fixed order of color vectors in the palette; therefore, they are also not robust to changes in the palette that can occur with many image manipulation tools or during lossless compression. Furthermore, such methods slightly reduce image quality.

Another method (Niimi, et al., 2002) is independent of the order of color vectors in the palette, and is therefore more robust. Furthermore, it provides high embedding capacity with limited color images. This method operates on an image that is decomposed into its R, G, and B component images. Color space transformations are not used and the embedding and color reductions described below only occur in the RGB color space.

Three Typical Methods for Palette-Based Images

We deal with here three methods for palette-based image: LSB steganography of index image, LSB steganography of index image ordered by the luminance value and Fridrich's (1999) method.

LSB steganography of index image embeds data by replacing the least significant bit of index image with a bit sequence of data. In LSB steganography of index image ordered by the luminance value, we firstly reorder the color vector on the palette by the luminance value and then we reassign the pixel value of index image so that the color value of pixels is the same as the original one. Then, we apply LSB steganography to the index image whose pixel value is reassigned. Fridrich's method embeds data into the parity of color vector. If the parity is not equal to a bit of data to be embedded, we find a color vector on the color table which parity is the same as a bit so that the difference between color vectors is smaller in the color space. For a 880x660 palette-based image (Figure 2a), we embedded a random bit sequence whose size is the limit for the image, that is, 880x660 bit. As we can see from Figure 2b, the distortion by the data embedding is easily detectable. This is because two adjacent color vectors in the color map is not similar color. In Figure 2c, we reorder the color vectors in the color map by the luminance value, and then we apply LSB steganography with the index color image. The distortion of this is smaller than the color vectors are not ordered. Figure 2d is the result of Fridrich's method. It is difficult to see the distortion by the embedding from the stego image.

Method for Applying BPCS Steganography to Palette-Based Images by Luminance Quasi-Preserving Color Quantization

Approach to Using BPCS for Embedding in Palette-Based Images

With this approach, one problem is selecting the number and type of color component images that we should embed secret information within. The human visual system is most sensitive to changes in the luminance of a color. The luminance component of a color corresponds to its *Y* component in the *YIQ* color space. A transformation from *RGB* to *YIQ* is achieved as follows:

Figure 2. Demonstration of typical information hiding for palette-based images: (a) original palette-based image, (b) LSB steganography for index image, (c) LSB steganography for index image whose color palette is ordered by luminance value, (d) Fridrich's method

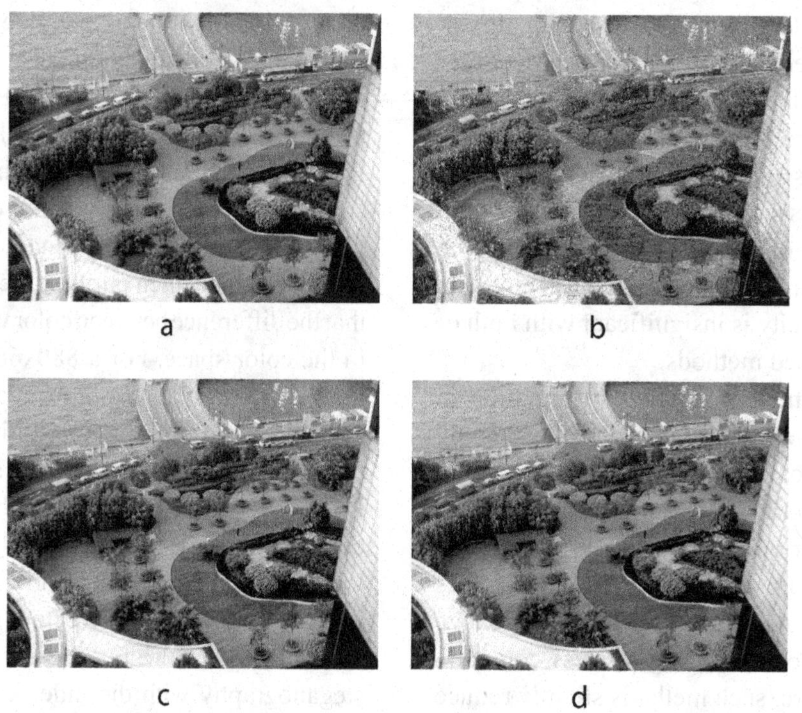

$$
\begin{aligned}
Y &= 0.299R + 0.587G + 0.114B \\
I &= 0.596R - 0.275G + 0.321B \\
Q &= 0.207R - 0.497G - 0.290B
\end{aligned}
\tag{8}
$$

This color space transformation is difficult to use in a steganographic system using Bit-Plane Complexity Segmentation (BPCS). As mentioned above, BPCS is restricted to lossless compression schemes, because lossy schemes do not allow embedded information to be extracted correctly. To investigate this, we assume that BPCS is applied to one of the *YIQ* components and we ignore the number of color vectors in a palette after embedding. Each element of the color vectors in a palette-based image must be represented as an *RGB* value, so we must transform from *YIQ* to *RGB* space. When extracting the embedded information, we need to transform from *RGB* to *YIQ*. During the above data process, floating point numerical processing will typically produce truncation errors and the *YIQ* value of color vectors before embedding may not be equal to the value after embedding. For this reason, it is simpler to directly embed in *RGB* color space.

When computing the Y value, the *G* value has the largest gain of the three color components. Thus, if we store the *G* value as accurately as possible, we can maximize the preservation of luminance information. One consideration is that even if we embed secret information within only one color component of an *R*, *G*, and *B* image using BPCS, the number of color vectors in a palette after embedding would not be less than 256. Therefore, we need a color quantization scheme. The color component image that contains the secret information must be stored without any information loss. Thus, we must reduce the colors only by changing the values of the color component images that do not contain secret information.

The degradation of images after manipulation to reduce color is worse than the degradation that occurs during the embedding of information. Based on the above discussions, we can hide secret information in palette-based images by embedding secret information into the G component image and then reducing the number of colors by changing the pixel values of the R and B component images. An outline of these steps is as follows:

1. Produce R, G, and B color component images from the original palette-based image.
2. Apply BPCS steganography to the G image. We denote a G image with information embedded as a G' image.
3. Produce a palette from the G', R, and B images.

If the number of color vectors in the palette is more than 256, we need to reduce the number of colors in the palette using a quantization method.

Color Quantization Algorithm

The number of colors in a palette after embedding may exceed 256; thus, we require a color quantization scheme. Color quantization can only change the R and B values and it must not change the G values, because this is where the information is embedded. One method for color quantization is to make a new color vector from color vectors that share the same G value. This method guarantees that the number of color vectors in the palette after color reduction need not exceed 256, because the G value is represented using 8 bits.

We classify the color vectors in the palette according to their G value. Let A_i, $i = 0, 1, \ldots, m$ be sets of color vectors. The total number of elements in all the color vector sets is equal to the number of color vectors in the palette. It is possible to reduce the colors to one color in sets that have two or more elements.

Color reduction is based on preparing a new color vector from two color vectors. The new color vector is prepared to minimize the square error. Let R_k and R_l be the red component of the k-th and l-th color vectors in the palette, whereas R_{kl} is the red component of the new color vector that will be prepared by combining the two color vectors.

Let m_k and m_l be the number of pixels with the k-th and l-th color vectors, respectively. Therefore, the number of pixels that have the new color is m_k and m_l. We can calculate the error, denoted as Total Error (TER), which is caused by substituting the two color vectors with one color vector according to the following equation:

$$\mathrm{TER}(R_{(kl)}) = (R_k - R_{(kl)})^2 m_k + (R_l - R_{(kl)})^2 m_l \tag{9}$$

The derivative of TER is

$$(m_k + m_l) R_{(kl)} - (R_k m_k + R_l m_l) \tag{10}$$

The global minimum can be derived as

$$R_{(kl)} = \frac{R_k m_k + R_l m_l}{m_k + m_l} \tag{11}$$

In the same manner, we can find the new B value that minimizes the error using the following formula.

$$B_{(kl)} = \frac{B_k m_k + B_l m_l}{m_k + m_l} \tag{12}$$

When we use this method repeatedly, the number of elements in the color set can be reduced to $n-1$, $n-2$, $n-3$, etc.

We now consider a set of color vectors with the same G value and we assume that the number of elements in the set is n. We propose a color-reduction measure (CRM) that determines the order of combining the color vectors. CRM is based on the total square error when reducing colors, and it therefore can be regarded as the similarity between two colors. We calculate CRM using the square errors of red color (SER), and blue color (SEB), which are defined using the following equations.

$$\mathrm{SER}_{kl} = (R_k - R_{(kl)})^2 m_k + (R_l - R_{(kl)})^2 m_l \tag{13}$$

$$\mathrm{SEB}_{kl} = (B_k - B_{(kl)})^2 m_k + (B_l - B_{(kl)})^2 m_l \tag{14}$$

Using SER and SEB, CRM is defined as follows:

$$\mathrm{CRM}_{ij} = \sqrt{\mathrm{SER}_{\mathrm{ij}}^2 + \mathrm{SEB}_{\mathrm{ij}}^2} \tag{15}$$

Smaller CRM values will not have a serious influence on the image quality; therefore, we combine the color vectors starting with those that have the smallest CRM and continue until the number of colors is reduced by the desired amount. For the color vectors in a set (each with the same G value) the process is as follows:

1. Calculate the CRM between all color vectors.
2. Pick the minimum value of CRM. The color vectors that yield the minimum value are denoted as U and V respectively.
3. Make a new color vector from U and V. The $_{R \text{ and } B}$ values of the new color vector are calculated using Equations 11 and 12, respectively. Color vectors corresponding to U and V are deleted from the palette and the new color vector is added to the palette.
4. n is changed to $n-1$ and the above steps are repeated until n is reduced by the desired amount.

From the above steps, we can calculate the final color of A_i using the following equation.

$$R_{(A_i)} = \frac{\sum_{j \in A_i} R_j m_j}{\sum_{j \in A_i} m_j} \qquad B_{(A_i)} = \frac{\sum_{j \in A_i} B_j m_j}{\sum_{j \in A_i} m_j} \tag{16}$$

We have assumed that the reduction algorithm is operating on a set of color vectors with same G value. We can extend this idea to the whole set of color vectors that contains many G values. The problem is now how to best decide the order for combining pairs of color vectors. We can use CRM to achieve this in a way that minimizes image degradation. The following algorithm illustrates this approach.

1. Make a palette from the G', R, B image. Produce color sets from the palette, where each set has a single G value.
2. Calculate all the CRM values between all color vectors in each set with more than two elements and sort them from lowest to highest, to create a single table as shown in Table 1.

Table1. CRM table

CRM	Index of the color vectors combined with one
80.89	444,445
91.00	468,469
96.00	896,898
97.13	121,130

3. Combine the two colors from the entry at the top of table (the pair with the lowest CRM).
4. Remove all CRM values involving either of the combined color components. Generate new CRM values between the newly generated color vector and the remaining color vectors in its set. Put the new CRM values in the table in the appropriate positions.
5. Repeat the combination process until the number of color vectors is less than 256.

In order to embed data into G image, we apply BPCS-steganography, which is described in the section: Information hiding for lossless compression/non-compression base image format (level 2), to the G image directly.

JPEG Format-Based Data Hiding

Several steganographic techniques for JPEG images have already been proposed such as J-Steg (Upham, 1997), F5 (Westfeld, 2001), and OutGuess (Provos, 2001). It is well known that embedding using J-Steg is detectable with a chi-square attack (Westfeld, 2001), because it is based on flipping the Least Significant Bits (LSBs). F5 cannot be detected using the chi-square attack method. However, it can be detected with a specific technique (Fridrich, et al., 2003) that exploits a significant change in the histogram of quantized DCT coefficients that is caused by embedding. J-Steg and F5 are known as high-capacity steganographic methods. OutGuess was developed to counter chi-square attacks. OutGuess embeds data in a similar way to J-Steg, but LSB flipping is applied to part of the usable coefficients. The remaining part is used to make the post-embedding histogram of the quantized DCT coefficients match the histogram of the cover image. Therefore, the embedding capacity of OutGuess is much lower than that of J-Steg. Note that OutGuess can preserve only the global histogram for all frequencies and it cannot preserve histograms for individual frequencies.

Another high-capacity JPEG steganographic method has been developed (Eggers, et al., 2002) using Quantization Index Modulation (QIM) (Chen & Wornell, 2001). In reality, only the spirit of QIM is utilized to embed data into quantized DCT coefficients. Its main feature is that histograms of DCT coefficients for individual frequencies after embedding are kept same as those before embedding, which makes it robust against histogram-based attacks. Data embedding using QIM with two different quantizers is generally conducted in such a way that one of two quantizers is used during the DCT coefficient quantization step in order to embed zero, while the other quantizer is used to embed one. The Histogram-Preserving Data Mappings (HPDM) of Eggers et al. (2002) apply a data mapping technique to quantized DCT coefficients. Given two different mappings that map DCT coefficients onto different sets of representatives of two quantizers, one mapping is used to embed zero and the other mapping is used to embed one. Histogram-preserving embedding is achieved given the condition that the probability of zero in the binary data to be embedded is equal to the probability of the quantized DCT coefficients of the cover image belonging to representatives of one of two quantizers. Note that this condition also means that the probability of one in binary embedding data is equal to the probability of quantized coefficients belonging to representatives of the other quantizer. However, this condition cannot generally be met. Secret data are processed by two steps to meet the condition and overcome this problem. First, binary encryption is applied to the secret data to make the probability of zero equal to that of one, i.e., both probabilities are 0.5. Entropy decoding is then applied to the encrypted data to set both probabilities of zero and one to those of the DCT coefficients. Note that different entropy decoders should be used for each frequency component, because the two DCT coefficient probabilities differ significantly among frequency components.

This subsection introduces two steganographic methods using QIM in the DCT domain (Noda, et al., 2006). In these two methods, embedding is conducted only during quantization of the DCT coefficients (not after the quantization step) and this is different from previously proposed methods, including Histogram-Preserving Data Mapping (HPDM). The first is a histogram-preserving method using two quantizers, where the representatives of each quantizer are provided in advance and the intervals for each representative are set so as to preserve the histogram of cover image. This method can meet this condition in a different manner to that proposed by Eggers et al. (2002) and it does not need an entropy decoder to meet the condition. The second is a histogram quasi-preserving method that uses QIM in a straightforward way with a device, which does not change the post-embedding histogram excessively.

QIM in the DCT Domain

QIM (Chen & Wornell, 2001) can be applied using two different quantizers to embed binary data during the quantization step of DCT coefficients in JPEG compression. Each bit (zero or one) of binary data is embedded in such a way that one of the two quantizers is used for quantization of a DCT coefficient, which corresponds to embedding zero whereas the other quantizer is used to embed one. Given a quantization table and a quality factor for JPEG compression, the quantization step size Δ_k, $1 \le k \le 64$ for each frequency component can be set. Then, two codebooks C^0 and C^1 for two quantizers are chosen as

$$C^0 = \{2j\Delta_k; j \in Z\}$$

and

$$C^1 = \{(2j+1)\Delta_k; j \in Z\}$$

for k-th frequency. For example, given a k-th frequency DCT coefficient x, $2q$ with $q = \arg\min_j \|x - 2j\Delta_k\|$ becomes the quantized coefficient when embedding zero and $2q+1$ with $q = \arg\min_j \|x - (2j+1)\Delta_k\|$ when embedding one.

Assuming that the probabilities of zero and one are the same in the binary data to be embedded, we consider how the histograms of the quantized DCT coefficients will change after embedding. We assume that the DCT coefficients belonging to k-th frequency are divided by its quantization step size Δ_k in advance and then two codebooks, C^0 and C^1 are defined as $C^0 = \{2j; j \in Z\}$ and $C^1 = \{2j+1; j \in Z\}$ for all frequency components. Let h_i, $i \in Z$ denote the number of DCT coefficients where the values x are in the interval $i - 0.5 < x < i + 0.5$. Let h_i^- and h_i^+ denote the number of DCT coefficients in the interval $i - 0.5 < x < i$ and $i < x < i + 0.5$ respectively, so $h_i^- + h_i^+ = h_i$. After embedding using QIM, the histogram h_i is changed to $h_i^{'}$ as follows:

$$h_i^{'} = \frac{1}{2}h_i + \frac{1}{2}(h_{i-1}^+ + h_{i+1}^-) \tag{17}$$

The change in (17) can be understood as follows. If i is an even number, $i \in C^0$ and C^0 are used for embedding zero, while half of the DCT coefficients in the interval $i - 0.5 < x < i + 0.5$ are used for embedding zero and their quantized coefficients remain unchanged after embedding. However, the other half $(h_i^- + h_i^+)/2$ of the coefficients is used for embedding one, with the result that $h_i^{'}/2$ coefficients are quantized to $i-1$ and $h_i^+/2$ coefficients to $i+1$. Alternatively, $h_{i-1}^+/2$ coefficients from the bin $i-1$ and $h_{i+1}^-/2$ coefficients from the bin $i+1$ are quantized to i for embedding zero. Thus, it is easily understood that the change shown in (17) also holds true for odd numbers, i.

A typical example of pre- and post-embedding histograms is shown in Figure 3. These histograms are for a (2,2) frequency component among 64 components (k,l), $1 \leq k,l \leq 8$ for the Lena image (512 x 512 pixels in size; 8 bits per pixel, i.e., bpp) that has been compressed with quality factor 80. It can be seen that the number of quantized coefficients for low absolute values around zero changes significantly after embedding. Equation 17 shows that if $h_i = h^+_{i-1} + h^-_{i+1}$, then the number in the bin i does not change. However, for $i = 0, \pm 1$ a large difference between h_i and $h^-_i + h^+_i$ causes a significant change in h_i after embedding. Therefore a straightforward application of QIM in the DCT domain cannot be possible in secure steganography against histogram-based attacks.

Histogram-Preserving and Quasi-Preserving JPEG Steganography

This section described two JPEG steganographic methods that use QIM (or its spirit) in the DCT domain. The first is a histogram-preserving method based on histogram-matching that is similar in its nature to HPDM (Eggers, et al., 2002). The histogram-matching scheme may not be directly related to QIM in the sense that the closest representative of a relevant quantizer to a given DCT coefficient is not necessarily chosen as a quantized coefficient. Our method differs from HPDM in that embedding is conducted during DCT coefficient quantization and the condition of matching the post-embedding histogram with the pre-embedding is met in a different way. This means that we do not have to use the entropy decoder to meet the condition and we can send the receiver information on the probabilities of zero (or one) with each frequency component. The second is a histogram quasi-preserving method that uses QIM in a straightforward manner with a device and it does not change the post-embed-

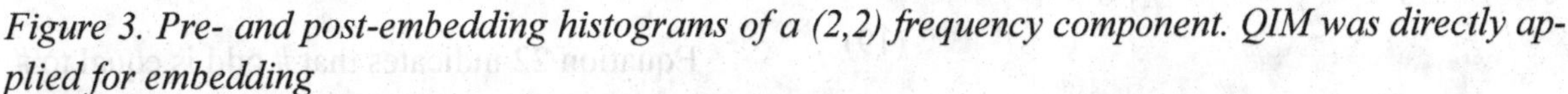

Figure 3. Pre- and post-embedding histograms of a (2,2) frequency component. QIM was directly applied for embedding

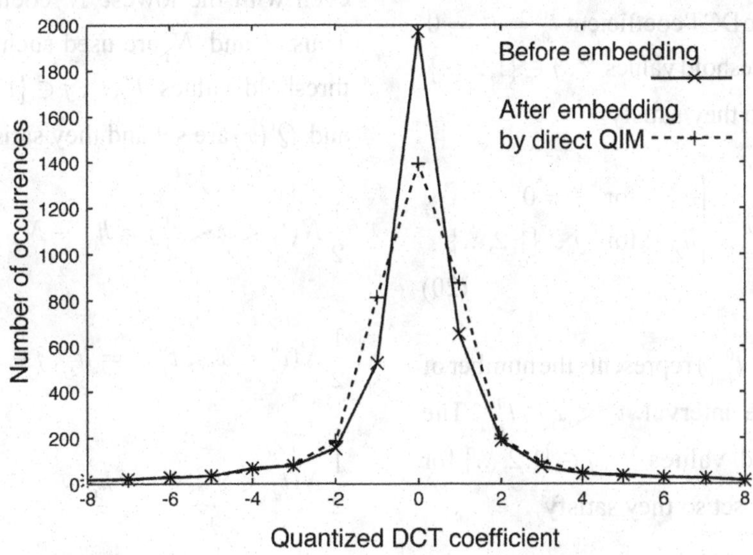

ding histogram excessively. We refer to the first method as histogram-matching JPEG (HM-JPEG) steganography and the second as QIM-JPEG steganography.

HM-JPEG Steganography

During the histogram matching in the DCT coefficient quantization step, we assume that the probabilities of zero and one are the same in the binary data to be embedded. This assumption is quite natural because any compressed data has such a property. Histogram-matching is considered separately for the positive and negative coefficient parts, because there is sometimes an asymmetry between both parts. Matching for the positive part is only described here (the negative part can be treated in the same way).

Two quantizers $Q^0(x)$ and $Q^1(x)$ are prepared where the first is used to embed zero and the second is used to embed one, as follows:

$$Q^0(x) = 2j, t_j^0 < x < t_{j+1}^0, j \in \{0,1,2,...\} \tag{18}$$

$$Q^1(x) = 2j+1, t_j^1 < x < t_{j+1}^1, j \in \{0,1,2,...\} \tag{19}$$

where x is a positive DCT coefficient $t_0^0 = t_0^1 = 0$

The decision threshold values $t_j^0, j \in \{1,2,...\}$ for $Q^0(x)$ are set so they satisfy

$$\frac{1}{2}N(t_j^0 < x < t_{j+1}^0) = \begin{cases} h_0^+ & \text{for } j=0 \\ h_{2j} & \text{for } j \in \{1,2,...\} \end{cases} \tag{20}$$

where $N(t_j^0 < x < t_{j+1}^0)$ represents the number of coefficients in the interval $t_j^0 < x < t_{j+1}^0$. The decision threshold values $t_j^1, j \in \{1,2,...\}$ for $Q^1(x)$ are similarly set so they satisfy

$$\frac{1}{2}N(t_j^0 < x < t_{j+1}^0) = h_{2j+1}, j \in \{0,1,2,...\} \tag{21}$$

From Equations 20 and 21, it is found that histogram preservation can be achieved if

$$h_0^+ + \sum_{j=1}^{\infty} h_{2j} = \sum_{j=0}^{\infty} h_{2j+1} = N(0 < x < \infty)/2$$

The number of coefficients with even values (# even) = the number of coefficients with odd values (# odd) is rarely satisfied approximately in histograms with very low frequency components, but it does not hold true in general.

We next consider how to match the post-embedding histogram with the pre-embedding one, given the relationship # even > # odd. We introduce a dead zone, $0 < x < t_d (t_d < 0.5)$, where DCT coefficients are not used for embedding, t_d is determined such that it satisfies

$$N_d = N(0 < x < t_d) = \#\text{even-}\#\text{odd} \tag{22}$$

Equation 22 indicates that # odd is equal to # even with the lowest N_d coefficients removed. Thus, t_d and N_d are used such that the decision threshold values $t_j^0, t_j^1, j \in \{1,2,...\}$ for $Q^0(x)$ and $Q^1(x)$ are set and they satisfy

$$\frac{1}{2}N(t_d < x < t_1^0) = h_0^+ - N_d \tag{23}$$

$$\frac{1}{2}N(t_j^0 < x < t_{j+1}^0) = h_{2j}, j \in \{1,2,...\} \tag{24}$$

$$\frac{1}{2}N(t_d < x < t_1^1) = h_1 \tag{25}$$

$$\frac{1}{2}N(t_j^1 < x < t_{j+1}^1) = h_{2j+1}, j \in \{1,2,...\} \quad (26)$$

respectively. Equations 23, 24, 25, and 26 indicate that # odd and # even - N_d are equal to $N(t_d < x < \infty)/2$, which makes histogram matching possible. Figure 4 shows histogram-matching using two quantizers with a dead zone.

QIM-JPEG Steganography

HM-JPEG steganography is a histogram-matching method that uses two quantizers, where the representatives of each quantizer are provided in advance and the intervals for each representative are set to preserve the histogram of the cover image. HM-JPEG is in the spirit of QIM because it uses two quantizers, but it differs from QIM in that the chosen representative of a relevant quantizer is not necessarily the closest to a given input. We now consider the application of QIM in a straightforward manner, where the closest representative to a given DCT coefficient is chosen as the quantized coefficient. We can expect to obtain less distorted stego-images using QIM-JPEG when compared with HM-JPEG.

The most significant changes caused by the direct application of QIM are a decrease in h_0 and an increase in h_1 and h_{-1}. Let us consider preserving h_0 after embedding. Here, we consider only the positive coefficient part for preserving h_0^+. The negative part can be treated in the same manner for preserving h_0^-

With the direct application of QIM, h_0^+ is changed as follows:

$$h_0^{+'} = \frac{1}{2}h_0^+ + \frac{1}{2}h_1^- \quad (27)$$

The relation $h_0^+ > h_1^-$ generally holds true, and in high frequency components, $h_0^+ >> h_1^-$. Therefore $h_0^{+'}$ becomes smaller than h_0^+ and much smaller in the high frequency components. We can generally preserve h_0^+ by introducing a dead zone, $0 < x < t_d (t_d < 0.5)$, where DCT coefficients are not used for embedding. t_d is determined such that is satisfies the following:

$$N_d = N(0 < x < t_d) = h_0^+ - h_1^- \quad (28)$$

Figure 4. Histogram-matching using two quantizers with a dead zone. The black area corresponds to the dead zone

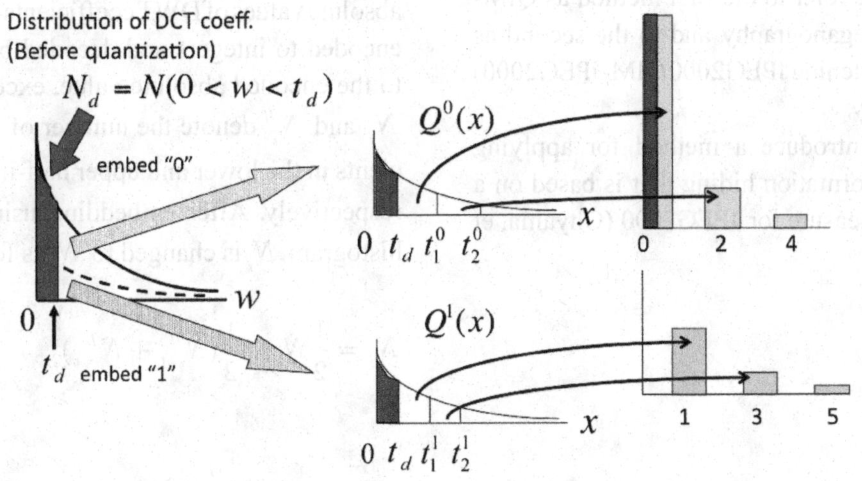

Thus, it is easy to achieve the preservation of h_0^+, as follows:

$$h_0^{+'} = N_d + \frac{1}{2}(h_0^+ - N_d) + \frac{1}{2}h_1^- \quad (29)$$

JPEG2000 Format-Based Data Hiding

JPEG2000 using the Discrete Wavelet Transform (DWT) is an incoming image coding standard that has improved features compared with JPEG and it is widely used. Therefore, steganographic methods for JPEG2000 images may be commonly used in the near future, but only a few methods have been proposed to date (Ando, et al., 2002; Noda, et al., 2002; Su & Kuo, 2003).

This subsection introduces two steganographic methods (Noda, et al., 2007) for securing JPEG2000 still images that can preserve the histograms of quantized DWT coefficients. Histogram preservation should be a necessary requirement for secure JPEG2000 steganography, because future steganalysis for JPEG2000 steganography will probably exploit histogram changes that occur after embedding. Both methods use two quantizers. The first method is a histogram quasi-preserving method that uses Quantization Index Modulation (QIM) (Chen & Wornell, 2001) in the DWT domain. The second is a histogram preserving method that uses a histogram-matching technique. We refer to the first method as QIM-JPEG2000 steganography and to the second as histogram-matching JPEG2000 (HM-JPEG2000) steganography.

We also introduce a method for applying reversible information hiding that is based on a complexity measure for JPEG2000 (Ohyama, et al., 2007).

Secure Steganography for JPEG2000

Histogram Quasi-Preserving JPEG2000 Steganography

We apply QIM (Chen & Wornell, 2001) using two different quantizers to embed the binary data at the DWT coefficient quantization step. Each bit (zero or one) of the binary data is embedded such that one of the two quantizers is used for DWT coefficient quantization, corresponding to embedding zero, whereas the other quantizer is used to embed one.

We assume that DWT coefficients belong to a codeblock that is divided by its quantization step size in advance and the two codebooks, C^0 and C^1, for the two quantizers can be defined as

$$C^0 = \{0, \pm(2j + 0.5); j \in \{1, 2, ...\}$$

and

$$C^1 = \{\pm(2j + 1.5); j \in \{0, 1, 2, ...\}$$

for all frequency sub-bands. Let N_i and N_{-i}, $i \in \{1, 2, ...\}$ denote the number of DWT coefficients where the value w is in the interval $i \leq w < i + 1$ and $-i - 1 < w \leq -i$, respectively, and N_0 in the interval $-1 < w < 1$. These settings reflect the feature of JPEG2000 that the absolute values of DWT coefficients are bit-plane-encoded to integers and decoded by adding 0.5 to the encoded absolute value, except for 0. Let N_i^L and N_i^H denote the number of DWT coefficients in the lower and upper half-interval of N_i respectively. After embedding using QIM, the histogram N_i is changed to N_i' as follows:

$$N_i' = \frac{1}{2}N_i + \frac{1}{2}(N_{i-1}^H + N_{i+1}^L) \quad (30)$$

Equation 30 indicates that if $N_i = N^H_{i-1} +^L_{i+1}$, then the number in the bin i does not change. However, for $i = 0, \pm 1$ a large difference between N_i and $N^H_{i-1} +^L_{i+1}$ causes a significant change in N'_i after embedding. N_0 is usually larger than N_1 and N_{-1} so the most significant changes are decreases in N_0 and increases in N_1 and N_{-1}. Therefore, a straightforward application of QIM in the DWT domain cannot be possible with secure steganography against histogram-based attacks.

We now try to preserve N_0, N_1, and N_{-1} after embedding. We introduce a dead zone for DWT coefficients w:

$$t_d^- < w < t_d^+ (-1 < t_d^- < 0 < t_d^+ < 1)$$

where DWT coefficients are not used for embedding. Let N_d^+ and N_d^- denote the number of positive DWT coefficients and negative coefficients in the dead zone, i.e., the number of coefficients in the interval $0 < w < t_d^+$ and $t_d^- < w < 0$ respectively. t_d^+ and t_d^- are determined using the optimum N_d^+ and N_d^- values that minimize the histogram changes for the bins 0 and ± 1

Introducing dead zone means that parts of N_0^H and N_o^L are used for embedding, so N'_0, N'_1, and N'_{-1} become as follows:

$$N'_0 = N_d^+ + N_d^- + \frac{1}{2}\{(N_0^H - N_d^+) + (N_0^L - N_d^-)\} + \frac{1}{2}(N_{-1}^H + N_1^L) \tag{31}$$

$$N'_1 = \frac{1}{2}(N_1^L + N_1^H) + \frac{1}{2}\{(N_0^H - N_d^+) + N_2^L\} \tag{32}$$

$$N'_{-1} = \frac{1}{2}(N_{-1}^L + N_{-1}^H) + \frac{1}{2}\{N_{-2}^H + (N_0^L - N_d^-)\} \tag{33}$$

The optimum values for N_d^+ and N_d^- can be derived by minimizing the sum of squared histogram changes over the bin indices 0 and ± 1:

$$\sum_{i=-1}^{1} (N_i - N'_i)^2$$

Histogram Preserving HM-JPEG2000 Steganography

Histogram matching is here considered separately for positive and negative coefficient parts, because there is sometimes an asymmetry between both parts. Thus, matching only for the positive part is only described (the negative part can be treated in the same way).

Two quantizers, $Q^0(w)$ and $Q^1(w)$ are produced and the first is used for embedding zero, whereas the second is used to embed one.

$$Q^0(w) = \begin{cases} 0, & t_0^0 < w < t_1^0, \\ 2j + 0.5 & t_j^0 < w < t_{j+1}^0, \quad j \in \{1, 2, ...\} \end{cases} \tag{34}$$

$$Q^1(w) = 2j + 1.5, t_j^1 < w < t_{j+1}^1, j \in \{0, 1, 2, ...\} \tag{35}$$

where w is a positive DWT coefficient and $t_0^0 = t_0^1 = 0$. The decision threshold values t_j^0, $j \in \{1, 2, ...\}$ for $Q^0(w)$ are set so they satisfy

$$\frac{1}{2} N_{t_j^0 < w < t_{j+1}^0} = \begin{cases} N_0^H & \text{for } j = 0 \\ N_{2j} & \text{for } j \in \{1, 2, ...\} \end{cases} \tag{36}$$

where $N_{t_j^0 < w < t_{j+1}^0}$ represents the number of coefficients in the interval $t_j^0 < w < t_{j+1}^0$. The decision threshold values t_j^1, $j \in \{1, 2, ...\}$ for $Q^1(w)$ are similarly set so they satisfy

$$\frac{1}{2}N_{t_j^1<w<t_{j+1}^1} = N_{2j+1}, j \in \{0,1,2,...\} \quad (37)$$

From Equations 36 and 37, histogram preservation can be achieved if

$$N_0^H + \sum_{j=1}^{\infty} N_{2j} = \sum_{j=0}^{\infty} N_{2j+1} = N_{0<w<\infty} / 2$$

The condition

$$N_0^H + \sum_{j=1}^{\infty} N_{2j} = \sum_{j=0}^{\infty} N_{2j+1}$$

does not hold true in general. The relation $N_{even} > N_{odd}$ usually holds true and in high frequency (low level) sub-bands, $N_{even} >> N_{odd}$ because N_0^H is much larger.

We now consider how to match the post-embedding histogram with the pre-embedding given the relation $N_{even} > N_{odd}$. We introduce a dead zone $0 < w < t_d (t_d < 1)$ where DWT coefficients are not used for embedding. t_d is determined such that is satisfies the following:

$$N_d = N_{0<w<t_d} = N_{even} - N_{odd} \quad (38)$$

Equation 38 means that N_{odd} is equal to N_{even} with the lowest N_d coefficients removed. Using t_d and N_d the decision threshold values t_j^0, t_j^1, $j \in \{1,2,...\}$ for $Q^0(w)$ and $Q^1(w)$ are set so they satisfy

$$\frac{1}{2}N_{t_d<w<t_1^0} = N_0^H - N_d \quad (39)$$

$$\frac{1}{2}N_{t_j^0<w<t_{j+1}^0} = N_{2j}, j \in \{1,2,...\} \quad (40)$$

$$\frac{1}{2}N_{t_d<w<t_1^1} = N_1 \quad (41)$$

$$\frac{1}{2}N_{t_j^1<w<t_{j+1}^1} = N_{2j+1}, j \in \{1,2,...\} \quad (42)$$

respectively. Equations 39, 40, 41, and 42 indicate that N_{odd} and $N_{even} - N_d$ are equal to $N_{t_d<w<\infty} / 2$, so histogram-matching is possible.

Implementation of the Proposed JPEG2000 Steganography

The JPEG2000 encoder contains several fundamental components, i.e., pre-processing, DWT, quantization, arithmetic coding (tier-1 coding), and bit-stream organization (tier-2 coding) (Rabbani, 2002) (see the left part of Figure 4). Pre-processing includes intercomponent transformation for multi-component images that are typically color images. After the DWT is applied to each component, wavelet coefficients are quantized uniformly in the dead zone. The quantized wavelet coefficients are then bit-plane encoded by arithmetic coding. In JPEG2000, each sub-band of the wavelet-transformed image is encoded independently of the other sub-bands. Furthermore, each sub-band is partitioned into small blocks called code-blocks, where each code-block is independently encoded. The compressed data from the code-blocks is organized into units known as packets and layers in the tier-2 coding, where the bit-stream of each code-block is truncated in an optimal manner to minimize distortion, subject to a constraint on the bit rate. This rate-distortion optimization determines the optimal number of bit-planes for each code-block with the given bit rate. Thus, the true quantization step sizes for DWT coefficients are determined during the final stage of compression.

Given the aforementioned feature of JPEG2000, data embedding using the proposed JPEG2000 steganography must be performed after the arithmetic decoding in decoding process, where the optimal bit-plane structure and the true quantization step sizes for a given bit rate are available. The procedure for data embedding and extraction using the proposed JPEG2000 steganography is shown in Figure 5.

The entire process of embedding data follows the solid line arrows shown in Figure 5. An image is encoded into a JPEG2000 bit-stream, the size of which can be matched almost exactly to a target bit rate. The JPEG2000 bit-stream is then decoded, but decoding is halted after the arithmetic decoding. At this point, data embedding can be performed using the two quantizers given the raw DWT coefficients and the true quantization step sizes. The quantized DWT coefficients modified by embedding are then subjected to JPEG2000 encoding once more, which produces a secret data-embedded JPEG2000 bit-stream.

The data extraction procedure follows the dashed arrows in the middle section of Figure 5. JPEG2000 decoding of the secret data-embedded bit-stream begins with bit-stream disorganization and it is halted after the arithmetic decoding. At this point, the extraction of the secret data is conducted using the quantized DWT coefficients.

Reversible Information Hiding for JPEG2000 Using a Complexity Measure for Binary Images

We assume that the data for the cover image is given as a JPEG2000 compressed bit-stream with three color components YC_rC_b and perform the embedding procedures with the Y color component in the bit-stream. As a consequence, stego-images are produced as a JPEG2000 compressed bit-stream. The quantized wavelet coefficients in cover images are completely recovered from the stego-image.

A block diagram for encoding using the proposed method is shown in Figure 6. The embedding procedure proceeds as follows. In JPEG2000, the bit-depth that represents quantized wavelet coefficients for code-blocks is allowed to vary

Figure 5. Flowchart of data embedding and extraction for the proposed JPEG2000 steganography. The solid line arrows and dashed arrows show the embedding flow and extraction flow, respectively.

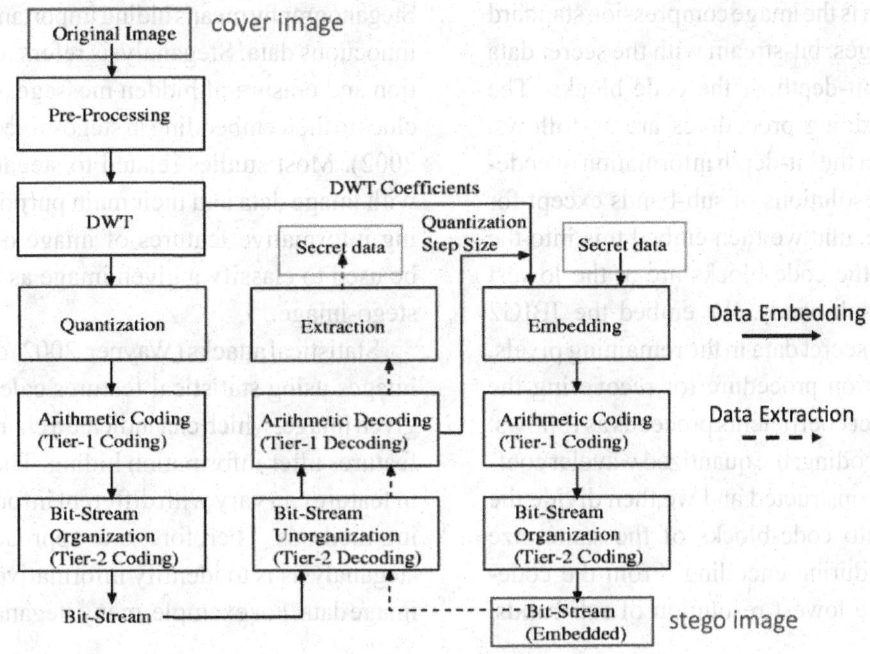

Figure 6. Block diagram of embedding using this method

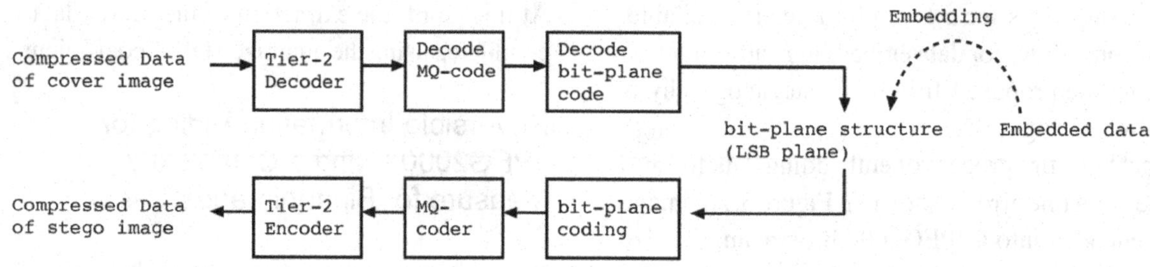

within ±32 bits and this depth is determined after the tier-2 encoding. Therefore, we can extract the least significant bit from each wavelet coefficient encoded in the JPEG2000 bit-stream using the bit-depth information.

Basically, we apply our reversible information hiding method for binary images (Tanaka, et al., 2007) to the LSB plane that has been extracted from quantized wavelet coefficients, which is regarded as a binary image.

However, we found a problem where the bit-depth of code-blocks containing wavelet coefficients values of 0, 1, or -1 were increased by the embedding in several experiments. This led to the incorrect extracting of embedded information.

In order to solve this problem, we need to embed a JBIG2, which is the image compression standard for binary images, bit-stream with the secret data and also the bit-depth of the code-blocks. The detailed embedding procedures are as follows. First, we collect the bit-depth information of code-blocks at all resolutions of sub-bands except for the lowest one, and we then embed this into the region where the code-blocks are at the lowest resolution of sub-bands. We embed the JBIG2 bit-stream and secret data in the remaining pixels.

The extraction procedure for recovering the original wavelet coefficients proceeds as follows. After tier-1 decoding, the quantized wavelet coefficients are reconstructed and we then divide the coefficients into code-blocks of the same size as those used during encoding. From the code-blocks with the lowest resolution of sub-bands, we extract the original bit-depth information for the rest of code-blocks and we then use the bit-depth information for extracting the embedded bit-stream containing the secret data and the JBIG2 bit-stream.

The recovery of the original wavelet coefficients proceeds as follows. The extracted JBIG2 bit-stream is initially decoded and the pixel value located on changeable pixels of the decoded image is then replaced. After this replacement, we completely reconstruct the original quantized wavelet coefficients.

STEGANALYSIS OF IMAGE DATA

Steganography means hiding important message in innocuous data. Steganalysis refers to the extraction and erasure of hidden message, or detecting clues to their embedding in stego-objects (Wayner, 2002). Most studies related to steganalysis deal with image data and their main purpose is detecting informative features of image data that can be used to classify a given image as a cover or a stego-image.

Statistical attacks (Wayner, 2002) detect stego-images using statistical features calculated for a given image, which can indicate a change in image features after information hiding. These changes in feature can vary with different information hiding methods. Therefore, one approach to image steganalysis is to identify informative features in image data. For example, many steganalyzers have been proposed for LSB steganography that embed message data into the least significant planes of digital images (Dumitrescu, 2003). Fridrich et al.'s method can estimate the amount of embedded data with particularly high accuracy (Fridrich, et al., 2001). However, these methods are specifically for LSB steganography.

Universal steganalysis means a type of steganalysis that is not particular to an embedding technique. Farid proposed the first method for universal steganalysis (Farid, 2002). The outline of this method is as follows. First, we need to collect natural images that are used for cover data. Stego-images are then produced from the cover images. The cover images and stego-images are then used training a two-class classifier with a supervised learning algorithm. Finally, given images are inputted into the classifier to determine whether they are stego-images.

The types of image features and the supervised learning algorithms used are very important in universal steganalysis. The main concern of steganalysis research is to select image features that can be effectively used for stego-image detection, rather than the supervised learning algorithms used. The informative features of image data used by Farid's method were the higher statistics of wavelet coefficients and the linear predictive error of wavelet coefficients. Goljan et al.'s method uses the central moment of the estimated noise of wavelet coefficients with a Wiener filter (Goljan, et al., 2006). Wang and Moulin's method uses the higher moments of wavelet coefficients and linear predictive errors (Wang & Moulin, 2007).

We introduce two steganalysis methods in this section: a high performance LSB steganalysis and an example of steganalysis for BPCS steganography (Niimi, et al., 2001).

Steganalysis for LSB Steganography Based on RS-Diagram

We assume here that an $M \times N$ gray scale image whose pixel value $P = \{0, 1, ..., 255\}$ is given to a steganalyzer for LSB steganography. From the image, we make pixel groups of *n*, and we define this as

$$G = (x_1, x_2, ..., x_n)$$

$\lfloor MN / n \rfloor$ is the maximum size of the group.

For a group, we define the discrimination function as

$$f(G) = \sum_{i=1}^{n-1} | x_{i+1} - x_i |$$

In addition, we introduce an operation for pixel value called flipping as following:

$$\begin{array}{llllll} F_1 : & 0 \leftrightarrow 1, & 2 \leftrightarrow 3, & ..., & 254 \leftrightarrow 255 \\ F_{-1} : & -1 \leftrightarrow 0, & 1 \leftrightarrow 2, & ..., & 255 \leftrightarrow 256 \\ F_0 : & 0 \leftrightarrow 0, & 1 \leftrightarrow 1, & ..., & 255 \leftrightarrow 255 \end{array}$$

F_1 and F_{-1} are the reversible operation, that is:

$$F(F(x)) = x, \quad \text{all } x \in P$$

Using the discrimination function and the flipping operation, we can classify the pixel groups into three groups, regular (R), singular (S), and unusable (U), as follows:

$$\begin{array}{ll} \text{Regular} & : G \in R \Leftrightarrow f(F(G)) > f(G) \\ \text{Singular} & : G \in S \Leftrightarrow f(F(G)) < f(G) \\ \text{Unusable} & : G \in U \Leftrightarrow f(F(G)) = f(G) \end{array}$$

Figure 7. RS-diagram for natural images $\left(M = [0\ 1\ 1\ 0]\right)$

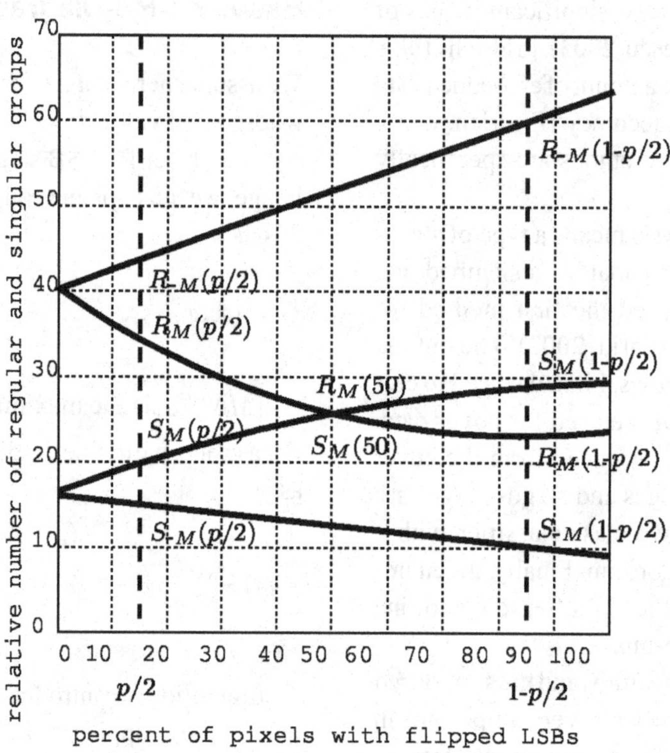

$F(G)$ in the group classification stands for to apply the flipping operation to each pixel in the group G. We define mask M which is the n-tuples

$$\left(M(1), M(2), \ldots, M(n) \in \{1, -1, 0\}\right)$$

so that we can apply other flipping operations by each pixel. Using this mask, we can apply different flipping operation by each pixel, that is, $F_{M(1)}(x_1),\ F_{M(2)}(x_2), \ldots,\ F_{M(n)}(x_n)$

We denote the ratio of regular group and singular group which is calculated using mask M as R_M and S_M. Here, $R_M + S_M \leq 1$ and $R_{-M} + S_{-M} \leq 1$. In RS-steganalysis, natural images are assumed that

$$R_M \cong R_{-M} \text{ and } S_M \cong S_{-M}$$

Figure 7 shows the typical graph of R_M, S_M, R_{-M}, and S_{-M} $\left(M = [0\ 1\ 1\ 0]\right)$ for natural images whose horizontal axis stands for the ratio of flipped pixels to whole image, which is called RS-diagram. In RS-steganalysis, four curves are estimated and the cross points are evaluated. Here R_{-M} and S_{-M} can be modeled as straight line and R_M and S_M can be modeled as quadratic curve.

We assume here a stego image that p percent to whole image size is replaced with a random bit sequence by LSB steganography. We can evaluate R_M and S_M from the stego image. This means that $R_M(p/2)$, $R_{-M}(p/2)$, $S_M(p/2)$, and $S_{-M}(p/2)$ are calculated. The reason why p is divided by 2 is the half of p is still original value because a random bit sequence is embedded.

When we flip all pixels, we can evaluate $R_M(1-p/2)$, $R_{-M}(1-p/2)$, $S_M(1-p/2)$, and $S_{-M}(1-p/2)$. $R_M(1/2)$ and $S_M(1/2)$ are calculated by embedding the maximum capacity with randomly selected bits.

We can evaluate a straight line from $R_{-M}(p/2)$ and $R_{-M}(1-p/2)$ and a straight line from $S_{-M}(p/2)$ and $S_{-M}(1-p/2)$. In addition, we can estimate two quadratic curves: one is from $R_M(p/2)$, $R_M(1/2)$, and $R_M(1-p/2)$, and another is from $S_M(p/2)$, $S_M(1/2)$ and $S_M(1-p/2)$. The straight line intersects the quadratic curve at the left end in RS-diagram.

By rescaling $p/2$ to 0 and $100-p/2$ to 1, the intersection point at the left end is given as the solution of the following quadratic equation:

$$2(d_1+d_0)x^2+(d_{-0}-d_{-1}-d_1-3d_0)x+d_0-d_{-0}=0$$

$$d_0=R_M(p/2)-S_M(p/2)$$

$$d_1=R_M(1-p/2)-S_M(1-p/2)$$

$$d_{-0}=R_{-M}(p/2)-S_{-M}(p/2)$$

$$d_{-1}=R_{-M}(1-p/2)-S_{-M}(1-p/2)$$

We can get the message to be hidden ratio p to the image using the solution of the quadratic equation and the p is given by

$$p=\frac{x}{x-1/2}$$

Steganalysis for BPCS Steganography: An Example

We consider changes in the statistical features of cover images embedded with data using Bit-Plane Complexity Segmentation (BPCS). We begin with a brief experiment of the connection with complexity histograms.

We then consider the influence of the substitution of image data with random patterns in the color component images. We then extend this by considering luminance histograms.

Let P_{ORG} be a block that is replaced with secret data, while P_{EMB} is a squared binary pattern mapped from the secret data. Based on the principle of embedding using BPCS, the complexity of P_{ORG} and P_{EMB} satisfies

$$\alpha_{TH}\le\alpha(P_{ORG})\text{ and }\alpha_{TH}\le\alpha(P_{EMB})\qquad(43)$$

where α is the complexity of a sub-image and α_{TH} represents the threshold used to determine whether the sub-image is noise-like. However, the following equation is not always satisfied.

$$\alpha(P_{ORG})=\alpha(P_{EMB})\qquad(44)$$

This causes a change in the shape of the complexity histogram. To understand this, we will look at the complexity histogram in greater detail. The complexity histogram used in this study represents the relative frequency of occurrence of the various complexities in a binary pattern. The complexity of an original binary pattern is not always equal to that of a binary pattern mapped from secret data, so a change in the shape of the complexity histogram will generally occur. Binary patterns with a complexity value larger than the threshold are substituted with noise-like binary patterns with the complexity distribution described below.

One might assume that the complexities of random binary patterns of size $n\times n$ would follow a normal distribution and we have confirmed this assumption through several practical experiments (Niimi, et al., 1999). Patterns in bit-plane images that are substituted with secret information generally distribute as a normal distribution, because the secret information is noise-like.

We embedded pseudo-random data into the full color image referred to as GIRL (256 x 256) using BPCS with $\alpha_{TH} = 0.36$. Local regions on all bit-planes > 0.36 in complexity were substituted with pseudo random data. In the original data, 62.2% corresponded to such regions. Image degradation due to the embedding was not noticeable. Figure 8 shows the complexity histograms of the 3rd, 4th, and 5th bit-planes, while Figure 9 shows complexity histograms of the 6th, 7th, and 8th bit-planes. The complexity histograms of the 5th and 6th bit-planes have an unusual shape in the form of a valley around the threshold, whereas the substituted pattern (complexities greater than the threshold) is a normal distribution. In the lowest bit-planes, the complexity histogram hardly changes after embedding, because most patterns on these bit-planes were already noise-like. However, noise-like patterns and non-noise-like patterns are mixed in the middle bit-planes. When embedding in these planes, patterns that are above the threshold change to the normal distribution and a discontinuity around the threshold becomes noticeable.

Figure 8. Changes in the complexity histograms (lower 3rd, 4th, and 5th bit-planes)

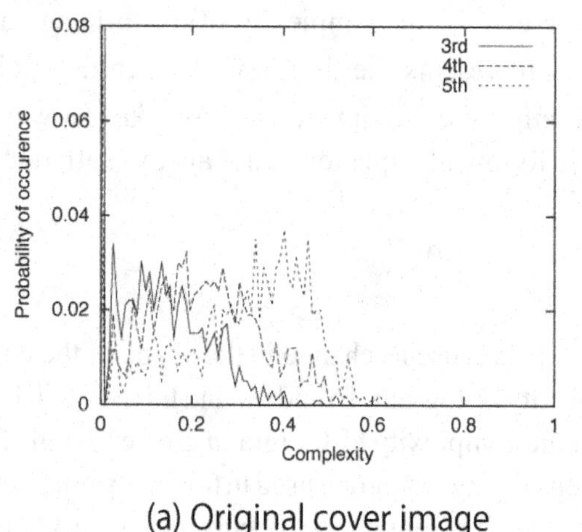

(a) Original cover image

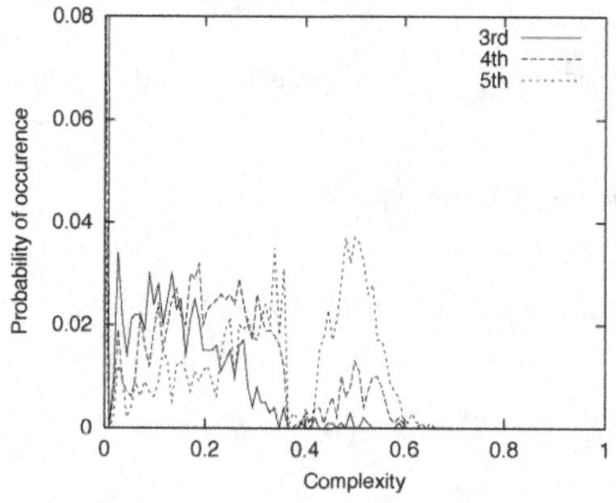

(b) Cover image with data embedded

Figure 9. Changes in the complexity histogram (lower 6th, 7th, and 8th bit-planes)

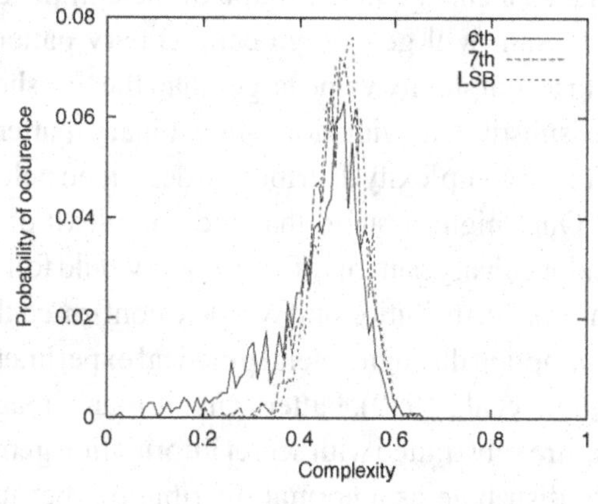

(a) Original cover image

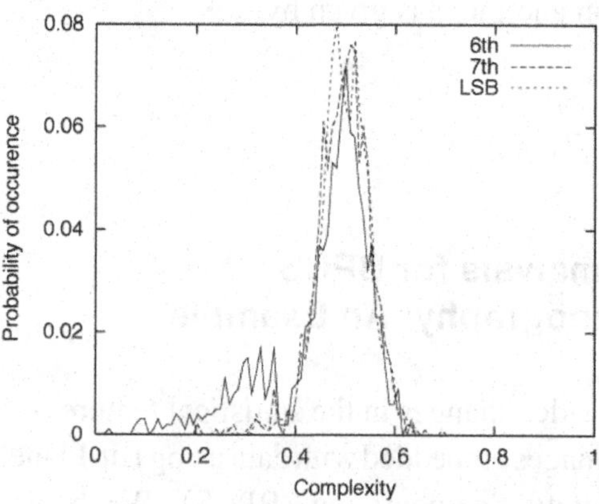

(b) Cover image with data embedded

FUTURE RESEARCH DIRECTIONS

Information hiding is not a final goal to do something but a way to realize a purpose. So far, two purposes have been known well. One is watermarking that embeds information which may be used to verify the authenticity or the identity of the original signal, and another is steganography that embeds important information for someone into digital media without drawing any suspicious from a third party person. In other words, information hiding is regarded as a technique to protect information security. Fundamental techniques to realize these purposes have been proposed and developed well.

From now on, we expect to increase papers and researches that not only tackle how to embed messages into cover media but also propose what its purpose is. This means that we should pay attention to practical applications more. From the definition of steganography, it is for very limited field. Indeed, fundamental techniques for information hiding are being researched. However, to be noted from people more, we need practical applications of information hiding in the real world, which are able to give many people the benefit of information hiding.

For steganalysis, we may make a model of natural images using the knowledge of steganalysis methods that have been proposed before, because the purpose of steganalysis is to find out what information is better to distinguish between original one and stego data, and to find out which quality is usually distorted by information hiding. The model is applicable to many practical fields, such as tamper detection for digital media.

CONCLUSION

In this chapter, we reviewed several steganographic methods and two steganalysis methods for a specific steganography. First, we summarized image data structures and image formats required by computers and the Internet. We then introduced several information hiding methods based on image formats including lossless (non-compression based), limited color-based image data, JPEG, and JPEG2000. For limited color-based images, we showed experimental results using three typical methods: LSB steganography of index image, LSB steganography of index image ordered by the luminance value and Fridrich's parity-based method. For lossless image format, we introduced reversible information hiding that is able to completely recover the original cover media. Then, we described steganographic methods for JPEG and JPEG2000, which make a particular consideration to the naturalness of cover data. In the steganalysis section, we introduced RS-Steganalysis and a detection method for BPCS-Steganography. Last, we showed future research direction for information hiding and steganalysis.

REFERENCES

Ando, K., Kobayashi, H., & Kiya, H. (2002). A method for embedding binary data into JPEG2000 bit streams based on the layer structure. In *Proceedings of 2002 EURASIP EUSIPCO*, (vol 3), (pp. 89–92). EURASIP.

Chen, B., & Wornell, G. W. (2001). Quantization index modulation: A class of provably good methods for digital watermarking and information embedding. *IEEE Transactions on Information Theory*, *47*, 1423–1443. doi:10.1109/18.923725

Dumitrescu, S., Wu, X., & Wang, Z. (2003). Detection of LSB steganography via sample pair analysis. *IEEE Transactions on Signal Processing*, *51*(7), 1995–2007. doi:10.1109/TSP.2003.812753

Eggers, J. J., Bauml, R., & Girod, B. (2002). A communications approach to image steganography. *Proceedings of the Society for Photo-Instrumentation Engineers*, *4675*, 26–37. doi:10.1117/12.465284

Farid, H. (2002). Detecting hidden messages using higher-order statistical models. In *Proceedings of the International Conference on Image Processing 2002*, (vol 2), (pp. 905-908). IEEE.

Fridrich, J., & Du, R. (1999). Steganographic methods for palette images. In *Proceedings of the Third International Workshop on Information Hiding*, (pp. 47–60). IEEE.

Fridrich, J., Goljan, M., & Du, R. (2001a). Invertible authentication. *Proceedings of the Society for Photo-Instrumentation Engineers*, *4314*, 197–208. doi:10.1117/12.435400

Fridrich, J., Goljan, M., & Du, R. (2001b). Reliable detection of LSB steganography in color and grayscale images. *IEEE MultiMedia*, *8*, 22–28. doi:10.1109/93.959097

Fridrich, J., Goljan, M., & Du, R. (2002). Lossless data embedding: New paradigm in digital watermarking. *EURASIP Journal on Applied Signal Processing*, *1*, 185–196. doi:10.1155/S1110865702000537

Fridrich, J., Goljan, M., & Hogea, D. (2003). New methodology for breaking steganographic techniques for JPEGs. *Proceedings of the Society for Photo-Instrumentation Engineers*, *5020*, 143–155. doi:10.1117/12.473142

Goljan, M., Fridrich, J., & Holotyak, T. (2006). New blind steganalysis and its implications. In *Proceedings of the SPIE, Electronic Imaging, Security, Steganography, and Watermarking of Multimedia Contents VIII*, (vol 6072), (pp. 1–13). SPIE.

Niimi, M., Eason, R., Noda, H., & Kawaguchi, E. (2001). Intensity histogram steganalysis in BPCS-steganography. *Proceedings of the Society for Photo-Instrumentation Engineers*, *4314*, 555. doi:10.1117/12.435440

Niimi, M., Eason, R., Noda, H., & Kawaguchi, E. (2002). A method to apply BPCS-steganography to palette-based images using luminance quasi-preserving color quantization. *IEICE Transactions on Fundamentals of Electronics, Communications and Computer Science*, *85*(9), 2141–2148.

Niimi, M., Nakamura, T., & Noda, H. (2006). Application of complexity measure to reversible information hiding. In *Proceedings of the International Conference on Image Processing 2006*, (pp. 113–116). IEEE.

Niimi, M., Noda, H., & Kawaguchi, E. (1999). Steganography based on region segmentation with a complexity measure. *Systems and Computers in Japan*, *30*(3), 1–9. doi:10.1002/(SICI)1520-684X(199903)30:3<1::AID-SCJ1>3.0.CO;2-M

Noda, H., Niimi, M., & Kawaguchi, E. (2006). High-performance JPEG steganography using quantization index modulation. *Pattern Recognition Letters*, *27*(5), 455–461. doi:10.1016/j.patrec.2005.09.008

Noda, H., Spaulding, J., Shirazi, M. N., & Kawaguchi, E. (2002). Application of bit-plane decomposition steganography to JPEG2000 encoded images. *IEEE Signal Processing Letters*, *9*(12), 410–413. doi:10.1109/LSP.2002.806056

Noda, H., Tsukamizu, Y., & Niimi, M. (2007). JPEG2000 steganography which preserves histograms of DWT coefficients. *IEICE Transactions on Information and Systems*, *90*(4), 783–786. doi:10.1093/ietisy/e90-d.4.783

Ohyama, S., Nimi, M., & Noda, H. (2009). Lossless data hiding using bit-depth embedding for JPEG2000 compressed bit-stream. *Journal of Communication and Computer*, *6*(2), 35–39.

Provos, N. (2001). Defending against statistical steganalysis. In *Proceedings of the 10th USENIX Security Symposium*, (vol 10), (pp. 323–336). USENIX.

Rabbani, M., & Joshi, R. (2002). An overview of JPEG 2000 still image compression standard. *Signal Processing Image Communication, 17*, 3–48. doi:10.1016/S0923-5965(01)00024-8

Su, P. C., & Kuo, C. C. (2003). Steganography in JPEG2000 compressed images. *IEEE Transactions on Consumer Electronics, 49*(4), 824–832. doi:10.1109/TCE.2003.1261161

Tanaka, S., Niimi, M., & Noda, H. (2007). A study on reversible information hiding using complexity measure for binary images. *IEEE Proceedings of the Intelligent Information Hiding and Multimedia Signal Processing, 2007*, 29–32.

Tian, J. (2003). Reversible data embedding using a difference expansion. *IEEE Transactions on Circuits and Systems for Video Technology, 13*(8), 890–896. doi:10.1109/TCSVT.2003.815962

Upham, D. (1997). *Website.* Retrieved from http://ftp.funet.fi/pub/crypt/cypherpunks/steganography/jsteg/

Wayner, P. (2002). *Disappearing cryptography.* San Francisco, CA: Morgan Kaufmann Publishers.

Westfeld, A. (2001). F5 - A steganographic algorithm: High capacity despite better steganalysis. *Lecture Notes in Computer Science, 2137*, 289–302. doi:10.1007/3-540-45496-9_21

KEY TERMS AND DEFINITIONS

Complexity Measure for Binary Image: Complexity measure is a measure for binary images. The value is calculated using border length of binary images. The border length is counted by the number of color changes in the interior parts of the image.

Information Hiding: To hide message into digital media, such as digital image, digital audio, digital text, and so on.

Joint Photographic Experts Group (JPEG): A commonly used method of lossy compression for digital image, and is based on a Discrete Cosine Transform (DCT) and a quantization to reduce redundant part of image data.

JPEG2000: JPEG2000 uses wavelet transformation instead of DCT in JPEG, and adds several features such as scalability.

Quantization Index Modulation (QIM): Embedding information by first modulating an index or sequence of indices with the embedded information and then quantizing the host signal with the associated quantizer or sequence of quantizers.

Steganalysis: To detect the clue of information hiding from digital media.

Steganography: To hide important message into digital media without drawing any suspicious from third party people.

Watermarking: To hide message into digital media to protect the owner ship of the original media.

Chapter 11
Reversible Information Hiding and Its Application to Image Authentication

Masaaki Fujiyoshi
Tokyo Metropolitan University, Japan

Hitoshi Kiya
Tokyo Metropolitan University, Japan

ABSTRACT

This chapter addresses a new class of Reversible Information Hiding (RIH) and its application to verifying the integrity of images. The method of RIH distorts an image once to hide information in the image itself, and it not only extracts embedded information but also recovers the original image from the distorted image. The well-known class of RIH is based on the expansion of prediction error in which a location map, which indicates the pixel block positions of a certain block category, is required to recover the original image. In contrast, the method described in this chapter is free from having to memorize any parameters including location maps. This feature suits the applications of image authentication in which the integrity of extracted information guarantees that of a suspected image. If image-dependent parameters such as location maps are required, the suspected image should first be identified from all possible images. The method described in this chapter reduces such costly processes.

INTRODUCTION

Information Hiding (IH) technology has been diligently studied to not only solve security-related problems, particularly to protect the intellectual property rights of digital content and covert communication, but also non security-oriented issues, such as the monitoring of broadcasts and multiplexing of captions (Cox, Miller, Bloom, Fridrich, & Kalker, 2008; Wu & Liu, 2003). IH techniques are used to embed information referred to as a payload into a target signal that is called the original or host signal. They then generate a slightly distorted signal carrying the payload by exploiting the redundancy of the original signal in the human perceptual system, and this distorted signal is referred to as a stego signal. Many IH techniques extract hidden information from a stego signal, but the stego signal is left as it is.

DOI: 10.4018/978-1-4666-2217-3.ch011

As the original image needs to be accurately restored in military, medical, and heritage imagery applications as well as the hidden payload to be extracted, Reversible IH (RIH) methods that restore the original image from a stego image have been proposed. Of several RIH implementations (Caldelli, Filippini, & Becarelli, 2010), this chapter focuses on prediction error expansion-based RIH (PEE-RIH) (Conotter, Boato, Carli, & Egiazarian, 2010; Thodi & Rodríguez, 2007; Yang, Chung, Yu, & Liao, 2010), which is one major class in RIH because of its capabilities of accepting large payloads or serving large capacities. The method of PEE-RIH hides a portion of the payload into a pixel block of the original image by expanding or rounding prediction error, which is the difference between the target pixel value and its corresponding prediction in the block.

The choice between expansion and rounding for a pixel block is based on its corresponding prediction error; expansion is for expandable blocks and rounding is for changeable blocks. Consequently, the recovery of the original image with PEE-RIH should distinguish between the two types of blocks, but expandable blocks become changeable through the IH process. To overcome this problem, a location map, which indicates the block positions for a certain block group, is used in PEE-RIH (Kamstra & Heijmans, 2005; Thodi & Rodríguez, 2007). This location map is image-dependent, and should be memorized in a database or transmitted along with a stego image. This fact narrows its applications and decreases its practicality.

This chapter describes a new method of PEE-RIH that does not require parameters to be memorized including location maps. It can classify pixel blocks as expandable and unexpandable, even in stego images, by utilizing a threshold parameter that is introduced based on block statistics. Part of the information is hidden in each expandable block in an error expansion-based manner. These strategies free the method from location maps. In addition, the method described in this chapter is completely free from having to memorize parameters by adapting the capacity to the payload size. This feature of the method suits image authentication applications (Mahdian & Saic, 2010; Rey & Dugelay, 2002) in which the integrity of extracted information guarantees the integrity of the suspected stego image.

Digital signature technology is applied to images by considering them to be media-unaware data (Schneier, 1994) in basic image authentication. This approach should be used to transmit or store the signature along with the image itself. IH-based image authentication hides a predefined pattern in the image with a fragile IH technique in which image editing of the stego image corrupts the hidden payload (Rey & Dugelay, 2002). Image tampering is exposed by comparing the pattern and the payload extracted from the suspected image. This framework results in distorted images even if the images are genuine when an irreversible IH technique is used. Consequently, RIH-based image authentication is needed, which is free from having to transmit or store signatures, and can deliver undistorted images when the images are genuine.

BACKGROUND

This section briefly presents some implementations of RIH (Caldelli, Filippini, & Becarelli, 2010), and it then describes the most fundamental method of PEE-RIH (Thodi & Rodríguez, 2007) to clarify the problem on which this chapter is focused. The fundamental frameworks for image authentication (Mahdian & Saic, 2010) including those that are RIH-based are also mentioned to emphasize the advantages of the new method in its application to image authentication.

First, four major classes of RIH are presented here, viz., compression-based, histogram modification-based, difference expansion-based, and PEE-based. Compression-based RIH losslessly compresses a portion of the original image to prepare room for a payload. For example, the least significant bit plane of the image is compressed by the Joint Bi-Level Image Experts Group (JBIG) standard. This class, however, requires a costly compression technique to provide enough capacity.

A method of histogram modification-based RIH changes pixel values by one in a portion of the original image to make room for the payload, based on its tonal distribution or the image histogram. Pixel values between the zero frequency pixel value (i.e., there are no pixels with this value in the image), and the highest frequency pixel value (the number of pixels with the pixel value is the largest in the image) are shifted by one. A pixel with the highest frequency pixel value is left as is, or shifted by one based on a payload bit, so the capacity is limited up to the highest frequency in its image histogram.

Difference expansion-based RIH and PEE-RIH are closely related. To secure room for a payload bit(s), the difference between a pixel pair, which consists of a target pixel and its corresponding pixel, is expanded or rounded in the former, whereas the latter expands or rounds prediction error, which is the difference between the target pixel value and its corresponding prediction value. The prediction error instead of the pixel difference is used to increase capacity. As will be explained next, these two classes have to memorize an image-dependent location map to restore the original image.

The most fundamental PEE-RIH is described here that has been generalized for hiding a portion of information of D-bits in a block. It is assumed that a payload consisting of L information portions of D-bits is hidden in an $X \times Y$-sized quantized image of Q-bits where a pixel is in $[0, 2^Q - 1]$ and $D < Q$. A block diagram for the IH of this method is shown in Figure 1.

The method first segments the image into B blocks in which the b-th block is expected to convey information portion $\mathbf{w}_l \in [0, 2^D - 1]$ of l-th D-bits, where $b = 0, 1, \ldots, B - 1$, $l = 0, 1, \ldots, L - 1$, and $L \leq B$. Note that blocks of any size or shape can be employed (Fujiyoshi, Sato, Jin, & Kiya, 2007). One target pixel t_b and the J of other pixels, $s_{b,j}$'s, exist in the b-th block where $j = 0, 1, \ldots, J-1$, and prediction value p_b is obtained from the $s_{b,j}$'s by using a predictor. Prediction error e_b is derived as

$$e_b = t_b - p_b \tag{1}$$

The method then classifies the block as expandable, if the block satisfies

$$2^D e_b + \mathrm{w}_l \in [-p_b, 2^Q - 1 - p_b], \forall \mathrm{w}_l \tag{2}$$

Even if the block is not expandable, it can be changeable, as long as the block satisfies

Figure 1. Information hiding process in most fundamental method of prediction error expansion-based reversible information hiding

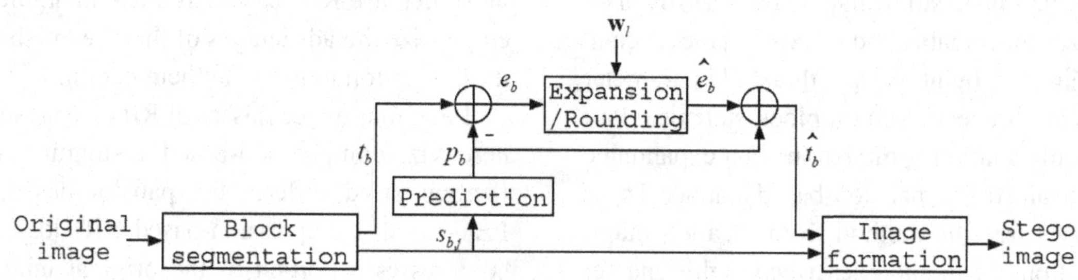

$$2^D\left\lfloor\frac{e_b}{2^D}\right\rfloor+\mathbf{w}_l\in\left[-p_b,2^Q-1-p_b\right],\forall\mathbf{w}_l \quad (3)$$

where $\lfloor\cdot\rfloor$ rounds its input toward negative infinity. A block that is neither expandable nor changeable is unchangeable, and the method does not use the unchangeable blocks for IH, i.e., unchangeable blocks are not modified by this IH process.

Finally, the method hides $\mathbf{w}_l$ in the block by

$$\hat{e}_b=2^De_b+\mathbf{w}_l \quad (4)$$

if the block is expandable, and by

$$\hat{e}_b=2^D\left\lfloor\frac{e_b}{2^D}\right\rfloor+\mathbf{w}_l \quad (5)$$

as long as the block is changeable, where $\hat{e}_b$ is the modified prediction error. In blocks that convey $\mathbf{w}_l$, t_b is replaced by $\hat{t}_b$ to form the stego pixel, where

$$\hat{t}_b=p_b+\hat{e}_b \quad (6)$$

Let the number of expandable blocks and changeable blocks be represented by N_{EX} and N_{CH}. The capacity, which is the conveyable payload size, is defined as $N=N_{\mathrm{EX}}+N_{\mathrm{CH}}$ in this method, where N is the capacity and $L\leq N\leq B$.

As long as prediction value p_b is derived from the b-th block in a stego image, the method can obtain modified prediction error $\hat{e}_b$ by

$$\hat{e}_b=\hat{t}_b-p_b \quad (7)$$

and it can then extract l-th information portion $\mathbf{w}_l$ from the block, unless the block is unchangeable, by

$$\mathbf{w}_l=\hat{e}_b-2^D\left\lfloor\frac{\hat{e}_b}{2^D}\right\rfloor \quad (8)$$

Once $\mathbf{w}_l$ is extracted, original prediction error e_b is obtained by

$$e_b=\frac{\hat{e}_b-\mathbf{w}_l}{2^D} \quad (9)$$

if the block is expandable. As Equation 5 shows, note that the original status of e_b in each changeable block has to be memorized to recover the original image, because Equation 5 substitutes the least D-bits of e_b with the information portion $\mathbf{w}_l$ of D-bits. After original prediction error e_b is recovered, original target pixel t_b is simply recovered by

$$t_b=p_b+e_b \quad (10)$$

Even though the method has to distinguish expandable from changeable blocks to recover the original image as previously mentioned, all expandable blocks become changeable in a stego image through the IH process mentioned above and as shown in Figure 2. A location map that memorizes the positions of blocks in a certain group is introduced to overcome this problem, i.e., either expandable or originally changeable blocks. This location map is image-dependent and should be stored in an extra database or transmitted along with the stego image, and the original status of prediction error in originally changeable blocks should be memorized. Even though hiding a (compressed) location map in an image as well as a payload has been studied (Kamstra & Heijmans, 2005; Kim, Sachnev, Shi, Nam, & Choo, 2008; Thodi & Rodríguez, 2007), treating a location map still causes trouble.

Now, image authentication that verifies the integrity of suspected images is focused on. The

Figure 2. Block classification in original and stego images in ordinary methods of prediction error expansion-based reversible information hiding

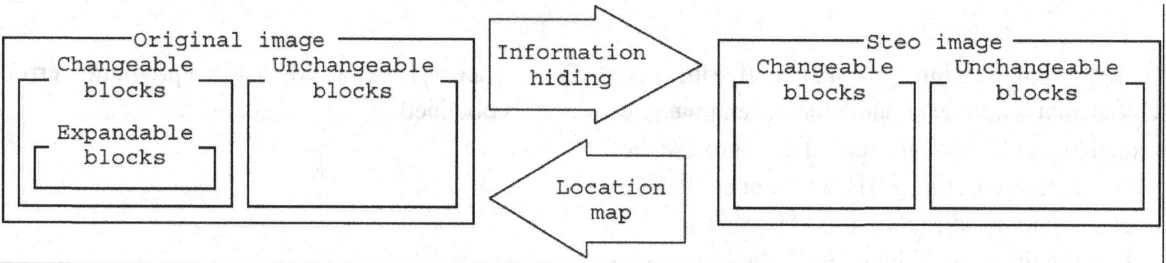

most basic image authentication framework uses a feature descriptor, in particular, a digital signature. The feature description or signature of an original image is generated before the image is transmitted or distributed. When the signature of a suspected image is identical to the previously generated signature, the suspected image is determined to be genuine. A signature in this framework should be memorized in a database or transmitted along with the image itself. In addition, the image that corresponds to the suspected image should first be identified to derive the corresponding signature from the database.

IH-based image authentication embeds a predefined pattern as a payload into the original image with a fragile IH method in which the hidden payload is damaged by applying image processing to the stego image, whereas ordinary robust IH methods are required to make the hidden payload capable of surviving image processing. If the pattern extracted from a suspected image is the same as the predefined pattern, the suspected image is determined to be genuine. Since this framework is based on ordinary irreversible IH methods, the verified image is distorted even it is genuine.

Finally, the fundamental framework for RIH-based image authentication is described (Celik, Sharma, Saber, & Tekalp, 2006). Note that this chapter focuses on the block-based authentication in Figure 3. An original image in this framework is first segmented into non-overlapping blocks where a block feature is obtained by using a feature descriptor in each block. A cryptographic one-way hash function is often used as the descriptor because its description has fixed length and the ability to avoid collisions. The acquired description is encrypted by an encryption algorithm and is hidden in the block from which the description was obtained with a method of RIH, i.e., the encrypted description is the payload and the non-overlapping block is the original image for the RIH method. The stego image is distributed or transmitted.

The embedded description is first extracted in each non-overlapping block of a suspected stego image to verify the integrity of the image as shown

Figure 3. Sign process in reversible information hiding-based image authentication

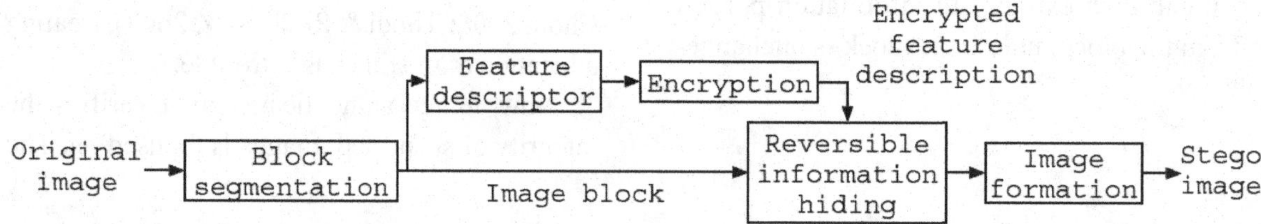

Figure 4. Process of verifying integrity in reversible information hiding-based image authentication

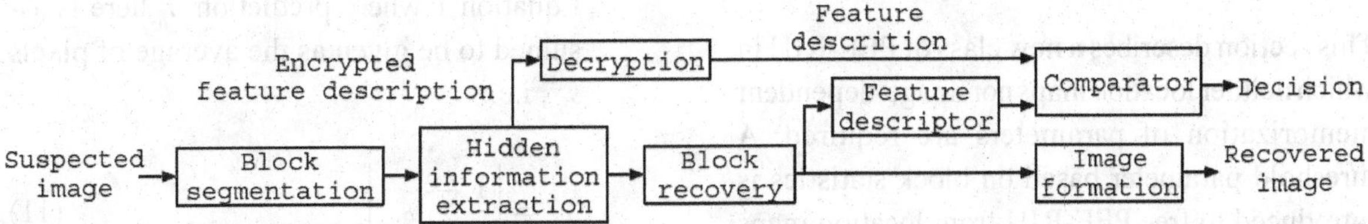

in Figure 4. Then, an image, which is identical to the original image unless the stego image has been tampered with, is recovered from the stego image. The descriptor is now reapplied to non-overlapping blocks of the recovered image to obtain a description, and this regenerated description is compared with the extracted description block-by-block. If the descriptors differ in any block, the suspected image is determined to be a tampered image. The recovered image is considered genuine when no differences are found in any block. Consequently, RIH-based image authentication does not need the description to be either memorized or transmitted and it serves as the genuine image without any distortion.

However, if the method of RIH that is used requires an image-dependent parameter such as a location map, the method first has to identify the suspected image from all possible images that the authentication system has treated. After the image is identified, the required parameter is obtained from the parameter database to extract the hidden descriptor and to recover the original image. The costs of identifying and acquiring parameters are high for authentication systems that treat huge numbers of images or numerous numbers of frames in large numbers of videos (Han, Fujiyoshi, & Kiya, 2009).

THE LOCATION MAP-FREE PEE-RIH

Issues, Controversies, and Problems

An image-dependent location map is required by most PEE-RIH methods including the most fundamental method that was described in the previous section. Even though the map is sometimes hidden in an image as well as the original payload, treating the map still causes trouble. The next section describes the new class of PEE-RIH to remove the map from it in which no location map is required. The approach employed in the next section is an introduction to the threshold parameter that is based on block statistics. The parameter distinguishes expandable from unexpandable blocks not only in the original image but also in a stego image; thus, a location map is projected onto the parameter.

Furthermore, an image-dependent parameter in RIH methods applied in image authentication increases the cost of authentication as mentioned in the previous section. No image-dependent parameters should be memorized in applications to image authentication. The new class of PEE-RIH described in the next section is further freed from having to memorize parameters. In addition to the above mentioned approach that frees PEE-RIH from location maps, the next section further employs a strategy in which the parameter value is decreased unless the capacity controlled by the parameter is smaller than the size of the payload so that the parameter can be estimated in a process of extracting hidden information and recovering the original image.

Solutions and Recommendations

This section describes a new class of PEE-RIH in which neither location maps nor image-dependent memorization of parameters are required. A threshold parameter based on block statistics is introduced to free PEE-RIH from location maps as mentioned in the previous section. Furthermore, the parameter value is controlled to free PEE-RIH from having to memorize the parameter. The five definite algorithms in this PEE-RIH class are described as examples of implementation in the subsequent sections, viz., deriving parameters, hiding information, estimating parameters, extracting information, and recovering the original image. It has again been assumed here that a payload consisting of L information portions of D-bits is hidden in an $X \times Y$-sized and Q-bits quantized image that has been segmented into B blocks. Figure 5 shows the IH process in the PEE-RIH class here described.

Derivation of Parameters

The introduced parameter is derived with this algorithm based on block statistics.

1. $b = 0$.
2. Prediction error e_b is obtained by using Equation 1 where prediction p_b here is assumed to be given as the average of pixels $s_{b,j}$, i.e.:

$$p_b = \left\lfloor \frac{1}{J} \sum_{j=0}^{J-1} s_{b,j} \right\rfloor \tag{11}$$

3. Check whether the b-th block is expandable by using Equation 2 and set parameter candidate τ_b as

$$\tau_b = \begin{cases} 2^Q, & \text{expandable} \\ a_b, & \text{others} \end{cases} \tag{12}$$

where a_b is a block statistic given by

$$a_b = \max(|s_{b,\max} - p_b|, |s_{b,\min} - p_b|) \tag{13}$$

$$s_{b,\max} = \max_j s_{b,j} \tag{14}$$

$$s_{b,\min} = \min_j s_{b,j} \tag{15}$$

Figure 5. Information hiding process for described prediction error expansion-based reversible information hiding

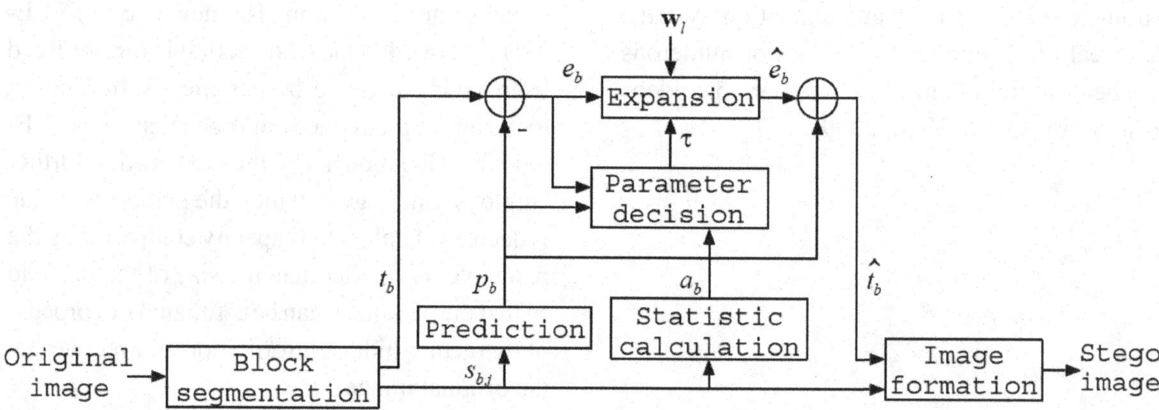

and a_b describes the smoothness of the block.

4. $b = b + 1$. Continue to Step 2 unless $b = B$.

5. Tentative parameter $\tilde{\tau}$ is determined from candidates τ_b's as

$$\tilde{\tau} = \min_b \tau_b \tag{16}$$

to guarantee that blocks satisfying $a_b < \tilde{\tau}$ are expandable (c.f., Figure 6).

6. Find threshold parameter τ as

$$\tau = \arg\min_{\tau} N_{\tau}, \text{ subject to: } \tau \in \left[1, \tilde{\tau}\right] \text{ and } N_{\tau} \geq L \tag{17}$$

where N_τ is the number of blocks where a block satisfies

$$a_b < \tau \tag{18}$$

as seen in Figure 6.

This algorithm derives image-dependent positive integer parameter τ, where the number of blocks satisfying Equation 18 is equal to or greater than payload size L, i.e., the capacity is sufficient for the payload. The blocks satisfying $a_b < \tau \leq \tilde{\tau}$ are guaranteed to be expandable, i.e., neither changeable nor unchangeable, because a_b's in expandable blocks tend to be smaller than those in unexpandable blocks and $\tilde{\tau}$ is the smallest a_b of all unexpandable blocks. Therefore, a location map in the algorithm is considered to be projected onto a single Q-bit parameter by using Steps 3 and 5 to free PEE-RIH from location maps. In addition, the parameter value is decreased to its smallest possible value by using Step 0 to free PEE-RIH from having to memorize the parameter.

Note that block statistic a_b describing the smoothness of the block has been selected here to adapt it to natural images having smooth blocks, based on the definition of prediction p_b. Other predictors and statistics may be appropriate for images having other characteristics.

Figure 6. Derivation and estimation of threshold parameter

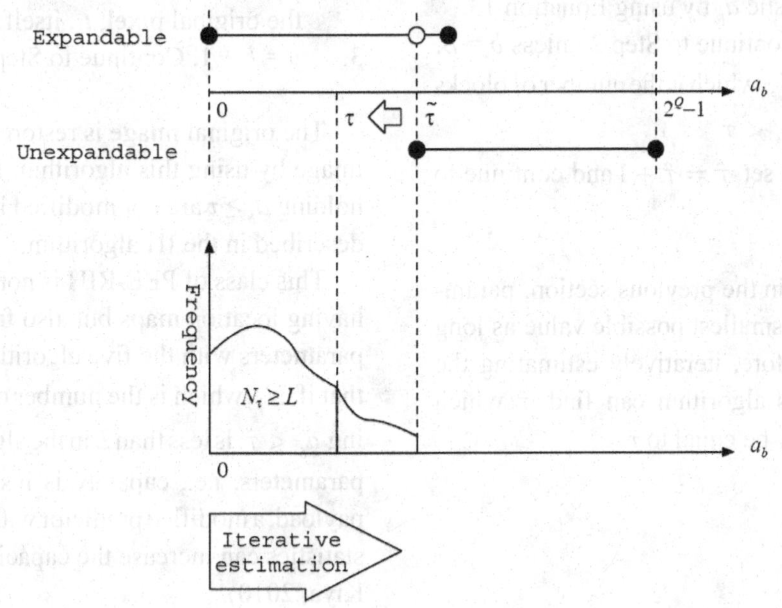

Information Hiding

By using parameter τ derived in the previous section, the l-th information portion $\mathbf{w}_l$ of D-bits is hidden in a block satisfying Equation 18 with the following algorithm.

1. $b = 0$ and $l = 0$.
2. If $a_b < \tau$, $\mathbf{w}_l$ is hidden in the b-th block by using Equations 4 and 6, and $l = l + 1$ is set.
3. $b = b + 1$. Continue to Step 2 unless $b = B$.

The payload with information of $L \times D$-bits is hidden in the image with this algorithm. Note that blocks with $a_b \geq \tau$ are not modified in this algorithm. Stego pixel $\hat{t}_b$ in such blocks is exactly the same as its original state t_b, i.e., $\hat{t}_b = t_b$

Estimation of Parameter τ

Before the hidden payload is extracted and the original image is recovered, parameter τ is estimated from a stego image with this algorithm. Note that the other pixels in a block, $s_{b,j}$'s, are not modified through an IH process.

1. $b = 0$ and $\hat{\tau} = 1$
2. Obtain statistic a_b by using Equation 13.
3. $b = b + 1$. Continue to Step 2 unless $b = B$.
4. Calculate $N_{\hat{\tau}}$, which is the number of blocks satisfying $a_b < \hat{\tau}$
5. If $N_{\hat{\tau}} < L$, set $\hat{\tau} = \hat{\tau} + 1$ and continue to Step 4.

As described in the previous section, parameter τ is set to its smallest possible value as long as $N_\tau \geq L$. Therefore, iteratively estimating the parameter in this algorithm can find $\hat{\tau}$, which should essentially be equal to τ.

Extraction of Hidden Information

With estimated parameter $\hat{\tau}$, which should be equal to the parameter used for the IH process, τ, the hidden payload is extracted from the stego image with the following algorithm.

1. $b = 0$ and $l = 0$.
2. If $l < L$ and $a_b < \hat{\tau}$, hidden information portion $\mathbf{w}_l$ is extracted by using Equation 8 and $l = l + 1$ is set.
3. $b = b + 1$. Continue to Step 2 unless $b = B$.

This algorithm extracts the hidden payload consisting of L information portions of D-bits from a stego image.

Recovery of Original Image

After the hidden payload is extracted, the following algorithm is used to recover the original image from the stego image.

1. $b = 0$ and $l = 0$.
2. If $l < L$ and $a_b < \hat{\tau}$, original target pixel t_b is restored by using Equations 9 and 10, and $l = l + 1$ is set. Otherwise, stego pixel $\hat{t}_b$ is the original pixel, t_b, itself.
3. $b = b + 1$. Continue to Step 2 unless $b = B$.

The original image is restored from the stego image by using this algorithm. Note that blocks holding $a_b \geq \tau$ are not modified in the IH process described in the IH algorithm.

This class of PEE-RIH is not only freed from having location maps but also from memorizing parameters with the five algorithms above. Note that if $N_{\tilde{\tau}}$, which is the number of blocks satisfying $a_b < \tilde{\tau}$, is less than L in the algorithm to derive parameters, i.e., capacity is insufficient for the payload, a modified predictor with modified block statistics can increase the capacity (Jin, Choe, & Kiya, 2010).

A method of PEE-RIH consisting of the five algorithms is applied to image authentication in which an $X \times Y$-sized image with Q-bits representation is segmented to the R of $U \times V$-sized non-overlapping blocks for authentication, i.e., block-based authentication, where $XY = RUV$. Note that the r-th authentication block is considered to be the input image for IH in this application, where $r = 0, 1, \ldots, R - 1$. The five algorithms are described in the subsequent sections, viz., those for generating the block descriptions, hiding the descriptions, extracting the hidden descriptions, recovering blocks and regenerating the descriptions, and comparing the descriptions. The content of an image in this scenario is assumed to be modified and the size of a suspected image is also is assumed to be identical to that of the original image.

Generation of Block Descriptions

It is assumed that a cryptographic one-way hash function is used as a feature descriptor and that the generated description is encrypted with an encryption algorithm to be resistant to replacement attacks or collage attacks. The following algorithm is applied to the image to be protected.

1. $r = 0$.
2. The cryptographic one-way hash function is applied to the r-th authentication block to generate hash string $\mathbf{h}_r$.
3. The encryption algorithm is applied to $\mathbf{h}_r$ to generate encrypted hash string $\mathbf{c}_r$.
4. $r = r + 1$. Continue to Step 2 unless $r = R$.

This algorithm generates R encrypted hash strings, $\mathbf{c}_r$'s, that will be hidden in the image itself. It is assumed that $\mathbf{c}_r$ is an LD-bit string to simplify explanation and that all $\mathbf{c}_r$'s are the same size.

Hiding of Descriptions

The above generated $\mathbf{c}_r$'s are hidden in their corresponding r-th authentication blocks with the following algorithm.

1. $r = 0$.
2. Encrypted hash string $\mathbf{c}_r$ is hidden in the r-th authentication block with the IH algorithm described in the section entitled "Hiding of Information," while considering the r-th authentication block to be an image and $\mathbf{c}_r$ to be a payload.
3. $r = r + 1$. Continue to Step 2 unless $r = R$.

This algorithm outputs a stego image that will be distributed to the public or transmitted through an unreliable channel.

Extraction of Hidden Descriptions

The following algorithm is applied to a suspected stego image to extract a hidden description from the image.

1. $r = 0$.
2. Hidden encrypted description $\hat{\mathbf{c}}_r$ is extracted from the r-th block of the suspected image by using the algorithm described in the section entitled "Extraction of Hidden Information," while considering the r-th authentication block in the suspected stego image to be a stego image.
3. $r = r + 1$. Continue to Step 2 unless $r = R$.

Extracted description $\hat{\mathbf{c}}_r$ may differ from its original state $\mathbf{c}_r$ due to modifications to the stego image, and it will be compared with a hash string regenerated from an image that has been recovered from the stego image.

Recovery of Blocks and Regeneration of Descriptions

After hidden description $\hat{\mathbf{c}}_r$ is extracted from the suspected stego image, an image is recovered from the suspected stego image by using the following algorithm.

1. $r = 0$.
2. The r-th authentication block is recovered from the suspected stego image with the algorithm described in the section entitled "Recovery of Original Image," while considering the r-th authentication block in the suspected stego image to be a stego image and $\hat{\mathbf{c}}_r$ to be the extracted payload.
3. The cryptographic one-way hash function used in the algorithm for generating block descriptions is applied to the recovered r-th authentication block to regenerate hash string $\breve{\mathbf{h}}_r$.
4. $r = r + 1$. Continue to Step 2 unless $r = R$.

Hash string $\breve{\mathbf{h}}_r$ is generated from the recovered r-th authentication block to be compared with extracted hidden string $\hat{\mathbf{c}}_r$.

Comparison of Descriptions

Extracted hash string $\hat{\mathbf{c}}_r$ is compared to regenerated hash string $\breve{\mathbf{h}}_r$ block-by-block to verify the integrity of the suspected stego image.

1. $r = 0$.
2. Extracted encrypted hash string $\hat{\mathbf{c}}_r$ is decrypted with the decryption algorithm that corresponds to the encryption algorithm used in the algorithm for generating block descriptions to obtain hash string $\hat{\mathbf{h}}_r$.
3. If $\hat{\mathbf{h}}_r$ and $\breve{\mathbf{h}}_r$ are the same, the r-th authentication block is determined to be genuine, i.e., no modifications are applied to the block in the stego image. Otherwise, the block is determined to have been modified.
4. $r = r + 1$. Continue to Step 2 unless $r = R$.

The integrity of the suspected stego image is verified block-by-block using this algorithm. If no differences between $\hat{\mathbf{h}}_r$ and $\breve{\mathbf{h}}_r$ are found in any authentication block, the recovered image is exactly the same as the original image.

Note that the process of estimating parameters has been omitted from the above description to focus on the process of image authentication. Forged blocks are occasionally detected before descriptions are actually compared, i.e., no parameters serving the appropriate capacity can be found in the algorithm for estimating parameters, no encrypted hash string with an appropriate length can be extracted in the algorithm for extracting hidden descriptions, or the extracted hash string fails to be decrypted in the algorithm to compare descriptions.

Some experimental results are given here. Table 1 summarizes the maximum capacity for seven natural images obtained by using the PEE-RIH algorithms that have been described above. The seven images for evaluation are shown in Figure 7 where each image consists of 512×512 pixels with 8-bit representation, i.e., $X = Y = 512$ and $Q = 8$. Here, an image is segmented into 3×3-sized overlapping blocks as an example implementation, and the central pixel of a block is the target pixel, t_b, i.e., $B = 65025$ and $J = 8$ (c.f. Figure 8). For simplicity, one bit information has been hidden in an expandable block here, i.e., $D = 1$.

The number of expandable blocks, N_{EX}, is almost the same as the number of blocks, B, in all images except for "Barbara" and "Baboon."

Table 1. Maximum capacity of described method of prediction error expansion-based reversible information hiding

Image	Number of Blocks, B	Number of Expandable Blocks, N_{EX}	Number of Blocks with $a_b < \tilde{\tau}$, $N_{\tilde{\tau}}$	Averaged Stego Image Quality (PSNR [dB])
Airplane	65025	65021	63847	39.82
Baboon	65025	64953	41050	36.60
Barbara	65025	64221	36486	45.34
Lena	65025	65016	61686	40.66
Peppers	65025	64996	61565	41.81
Sailboat	65025	65019	64921	36.06
Tiffany	65025	64955	61454	42.13

As mentioned in the section entitled "Derivation of Parameters," averaging the other pixels, $s_{b,j}$'s, yields a prediction and statistic a_b represents the smoothness of the b-th block. This thus results in "Barbara" and "Baboon," which have complex textures or a high frequency component, to decrease N_{EX}, and the number of blocks satisfying $a_b < \tilde{\tau}$, $N_{\tilde{\tau}}$, and the peak signal-to-noise ratio between a stego and an original image averaged over 50 different payloads to also decrease. Other predictors and other statistics provide different results.

Figure 9 indicates that capacity N_τ can be controlled by decreasing threshold parameter τ. The quality of the stego image varies according to N_τ or τ. Capacity N_τ may not be linearly decreased whereas τ is decreased one-by-one. The most important point here, however, is that the described method can control N_τ by controlling τ. Due to this feature, the method is free from having to memorize parameters, which makes it practical, i.e., no identification is required before hidden data are extracted and the original image is recovered. In addition, no database for the parameters is needed.

An example of the application of the method for authenticating images is given in Figure 10, where the stego image conveys encrypted hash string(s), and the three circles are on the stego image to form a tampered image. Tampered areas are detected and localized as shown in Figure 11 in this application. Due to the number of authentication blocks, R, or the size of authentication blocks, $U \times V$, the accuracy with which tampered areas are localized fluctuates; the greater the number of authentication blocks there are, the more accurately the tampered regions are localized.

If an image-dependent parameter is required in such situations, the cost of treating parameters is quite high even if the parameter is Q-bits represented by τ. Table 2 lists the required storage size for an image or a video. Even though τ is represented by $Q = 8$ [bits] for an authentication block, the total parameter size for an image or a video becomes huge because each authentication block may have different τ. In contrast, the described class of PEE-RIH estimates τ rather than memorizing it, and the image authentication system based on the described PEE-RIH requires no storage for memorizing parameters. Since an image authentication system manages many images, this difference in the required storage for memorizing parameters is increased. Moreover,

Figure 7. Seven natural images used in evaluation. Each image consists of 512 × 512 pixels where each pixel has representation of 8 bits, i.e., X = Y = 512 and Q = 8: (a) Airplane, (b) Baboon, (c) Barbara, (d) Lena, (e) Peppers, (f) Sailboat, (g) Tiffany

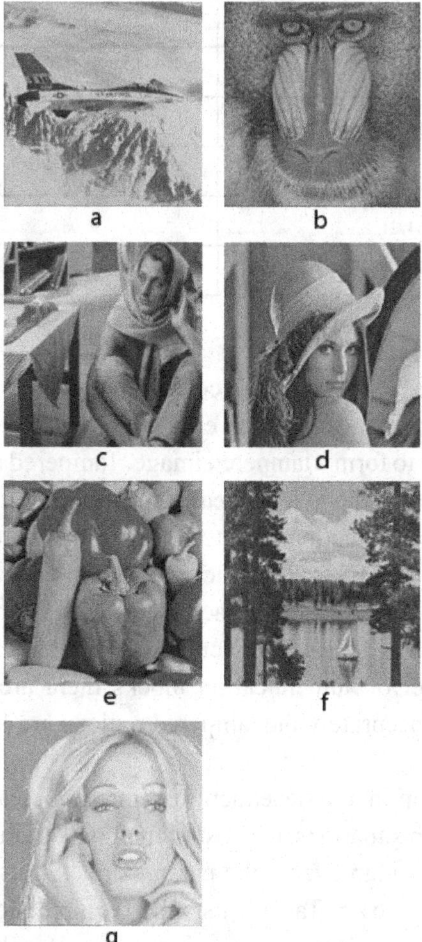

Figure 8. Example block segmentation used for evaluation: (a) block segmentation, (b) pixel block

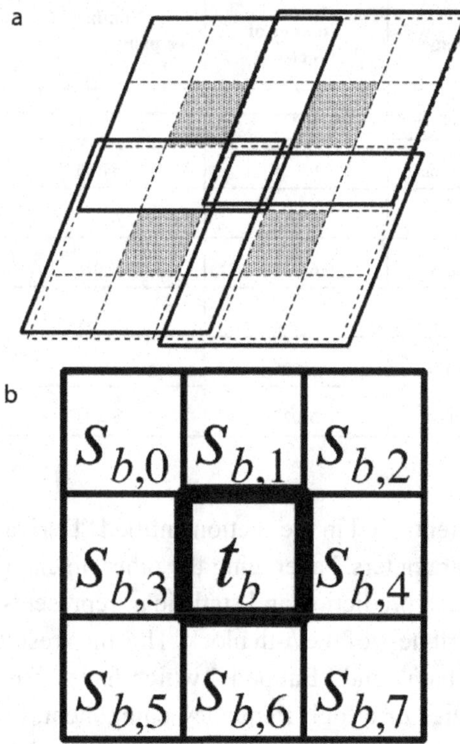

this feature of the described PEE-RIH class, which frees a system of managing videos with many frames from having to memorize parameters, helps the system by purging the parameter database.

In addition, a system memorizing parameter(s) has to identify a suspected image from many possible images in the system to acquire parameter(s) corresponding to the suspected image before hidden information is extracted. The described class of PEE-RIH frees the system from such costly processes. Consequently, the class of PEE-RIH described in this chapter is practical and also makes image authentication based on RIH practical.

FUTURE RESEARCH DIRECTIONS

As mentioned in the section entitled "Derivation of Parameters," other predictor and block parameters can be employed according to the characteristics of images to be watermarked. In addition, an appropriate block parameter and rule can be used for selecting blocks so that those having other characteristics convey information, e.g., blocks on image edges convey information (Ono, Han, Fujiyoshi, & Kiya, 2009). Various modified meth-

Figure 9. Control of capacity by decreasing value of threshold parameter: (a) capacity N_τ versus threshold parameter τ, (b) averaged PSNR versus threshold parameter τ, (c) averaged PSNR versus capacity N_τ

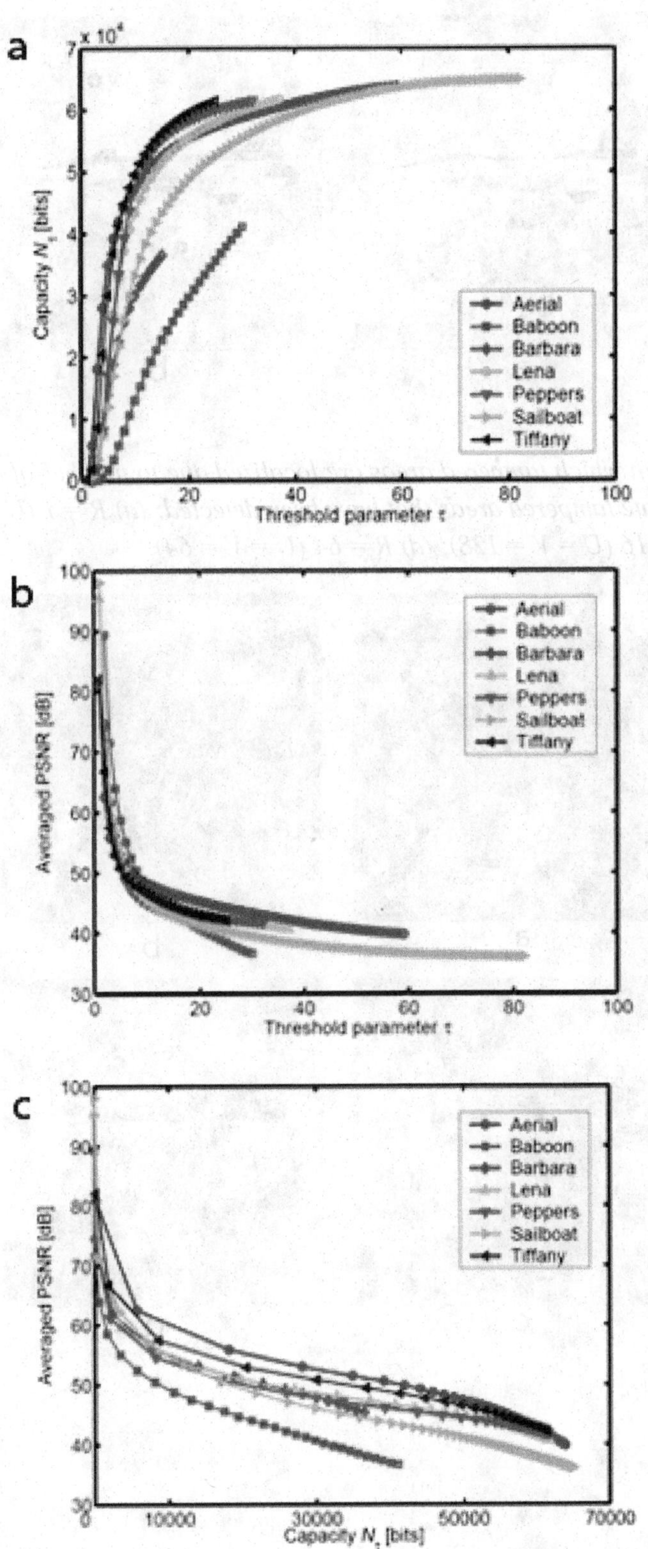

Figure 10. Example of image authentication: (a) stego image (64 authentication blocks in which each block conveys encrypted hash string of 256 bits, PSNR: 52.2 dB), (b) tampered image

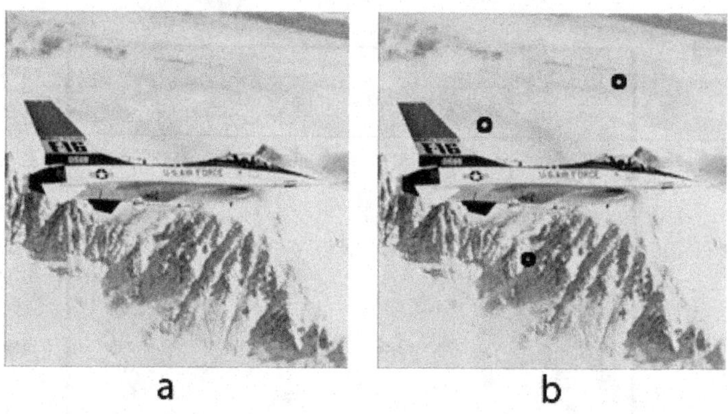

Figure 11. Accuracy with which tampered areas are localized due to number of authentication blocks. R shaded squares indicate tampered areas that have been detected: (a) R = 1 (U = V = 512), (b) R = 4 (U = V = 256), (c) R = 16 (U = V = 128), (d) R = 64 (U = V = 64).

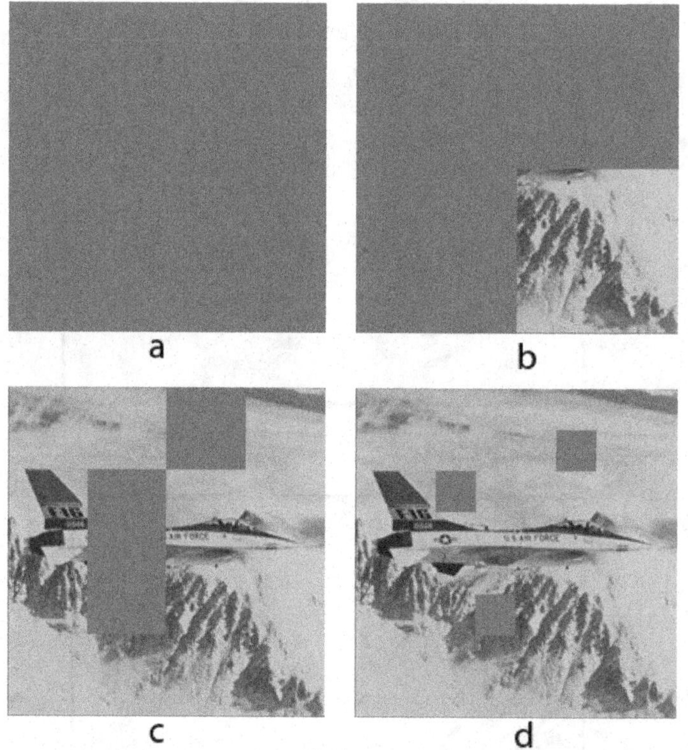

Table 2. Storage consumption to memorize parameter τ, which is represented by Q = 8 [bits]

Medium	Parameter Unit	Storage Size [bits]	
		τ is memorized	Memorization-free
Image ($X = Y = 512$)	Image ($U = V = 512$, $R = 1$)	8	0
	Block ($U = V = 64$, $R = 64$)	512	
Video ($X = 640$, $Y = 480$, 1 minute, and 30 frames/sec)	Frame ($U = 640$, $V = 480$, $R = 1$, and 1,800 frames)	14,400	
	Block in frame ($U = 64$, $V = 60$, $R = 80$, and 1,800 frames)	1,152,000	
Video ($X = 4096$, $Y = 2160$, 2 hours, 24 and frames/sec)	Frame ($U = 4096$, $V = 2160$, $R = 1$, and 172,800 frames)	1,382,400	
	Block in frame (U = 64, V = 80, R = 1728, and 172,800 frames)	2,388,787,200	

ods of PEE-RIH can be developed conforming to these perspectives based on the class of PEE-RIH described in this chapter.

All payloads were assumed to have fixed size L in the previous section. Although the memorization of parameters can be removed from this class of PEE-RIH under this assumption, the fixed payload size does not suit some applications. Other variations need to be determined from this point of view so that the method can accept any arbitrarily sized payloads. Instead of a location map, the size of a payload, which is represented by several bits of information, is hidden in the image prior to the payload itself (Fujiyoshi, Tsuneyoshi, & Kiya, 2010).

As seen in Equation 18, a payload is hidden over blocks with small a_b's. By utilizing this fact, the algorithm described in the previous sections can be made to be more sophisticated. Blocks are sorted in ascending order of a_b before the IH process so that successive expandable blocks from the first block convey the payload. Even parameter τ can be removed from algorithms (Fujiyoshi, Tsuneyoshi, & Kiya, 2010) through this sophistication, and a ploy to indicate the payload size is required. More sophistications and improvements based on additional knowledge and facts can be introduced.

Moreover, the costs of treating parameters including memorization and transmission should be focused on much more in further developments of IH methods, just as this chapter has focused on. Using image-dependent parameters requires the stego image to be identified to obtain parameters from a parameter database in some applications including image authentication. Practical IH methods should be designed while taking into account such costs, particularly in target applications.

CONCLUSION

This chapter described a new class of PEE-RIH in which neither location maps nor image-dependent memorization of parameters is required. The method described in this chapter not only frees PEE-RIH from location maps but also from memorizing parameters by introducing a threshold parameter and setting it to its smallest possible value as long as the capacity is equal to or greater than the payload size. These features suit applications in image authentication in which the integrity of feature descriptions guarantees the integrity of suspected images. The method described in this chapter does not have to identify a suspected image from all possible images that the authentication system treats, whereas a method using image-dependent parameters requires such costly processes. The method described in this chapter broadens the fields in which RIH can be applied and increases its practicality.

REFERENCES

Caldelli, R., Filippini, F., & Becarelli, R. (2010). Reversible watermarking techniques: An overview and a classification. *European Association for Signal Processing Journal on Information Security, 2*.

Celik, M. U., Sharma, G., Saber, E., & Tekalp, A. M. (2006). Lossless watermarking for image authentication: A new framework and an implementation. *Institute of Electrical and Electronics Engineers Transactions on Image Processing, 15*(4), 1042–1049.

Conotter, V., Boato, G., Carli, M., & Egiazarian, K. (2010). Near lossless reversible data hiding based on adaptive prediction. In *Proceedings of the International Conference on Image Processing of Institute of Electrical and Electronics Engineers*, (pp. 2585-2588). Hong Kong, China: IEEE.

Cox, I. J., Miller, M. L., Bloom, J. A., Fridrich, J., & Kalker, T. (2008). *Digital watermarking and steganography* (2nd ed.). Burlington, MA: Morgan Kaufmann.

Fujiyoshi, M., Sato, S., Jin, H., & Kiya, H. (2007). A location-map free reversible data hiding method using block-based single parameter. In *Proceedings of the International Conference on Image Processing of Institute of Electrical and Electronics Engineers*, (pp. 257-260). San Antonio, TX: IEEE.

Fujiyoshi, M., Tsuneyoshi, T., & Kiya, H. (2010). A parameter memorization-free lossless data hiding method with flexible payload size. *Institute of Electronics. Information and Communication Engineers Electronics Express, 7*(23), 1702–1708.

Han, S., Fujiyoshi, M., & Kiya, H. (2009). A reversible image authentication method without memorization of hiding parameters. *Institute of Electronics, Information and Communication Engineers Transactions on Fundamentals of Electronics. Communications and Computer Sciences, 92*(10), 2572–2579.

Jin, H., Choe, Y., & Kiya, H. (2010). Reversible data hiding based on adaptive modulation of statistics invertibility. *Institute of Electronics, Information and Communication Engineers Transactions on Fundamentals of Electronics. Communications and Computer Sciences, 93*(2), 565–569.

Kamstra, L., & Heijmans, H. J. (2005). Reversible data embedding into images using wavelet techniques and sorting. *Institute of Electrical and Electronics Engineers Transactions on Image Processing, 14*(12), 2082–2090.

Kim, H., Sachnev, V., Shi, Y., Nam, J., & Choo, H.-G. (2008). A novel difference expansion transform for reversible data embedding. *Institute of Electrical and Electronics Engineers Transactions on Information Forensics and Security, 3*(3), 456–465.

Mahdian, B., & Saic, S. (2010). A bibliography on blind methods for identifying image forgery. *Signal Processing Image Communication, 25*(6), 389–399. doi:10.1016/j.image.2010.05.003

Ono, M., Han, S., Fujiyoshi, M., & Kiya, H. (2009). A location map-free reversible data hiding method for specific area embedding. *Institute of Electronics. Information and Communication Engineers Electronics Express, 6*(8), 483–489.

Rey, C., & Dugelay, J.-L. (2002). A survey of watermarking algorithms for image authentication. *European Association for Signal Processing Journal on Applied Signal Processing, 1*, 613–621. doi:10.1155/S1110865702204047

Schneier, B. (1994). *Applied cryptography: Protocols, algorithms, and source code in C* (2nd ed.). New York, NY: John Wiley & Sons.

Thodi, D. M., & Rodríguez, J. J. (2007). Expansion embedding techniques for reversible watermarking. *Institute of Electrical and Electronics Engineers Transactions on Image Processing, 16*(3), 721–730.

Wu, M., & Liu, B. (2003). *Multimedia data hiding*. New York, NY: Springer-Verlag.

Yang, W.-J., Chung, K.-L., Yu, W.-K., & Liao, H.-Y. M. (2010). Edge-sensing prediction-based reversible data hiding. In *Proceedings of the Annual Summit and Conference of Asia-Pacific Signal and Information Processing Association*, (pp. 919-922). Biopolis, Singapore: IEEE.

ADDITIONAL READING

Alattar, A. M. (2004). Reversible watermark using the difference expansion of a generalized integer transform. *Institute of Electrical and Electronics Engineers Transactions on Image Processing, 13*(8), 1147–1156.

Celik, M. U., Sharma, G., Tekalp, A. M., & Saber, E. (2005). Lossless generalized-LSB data embedding. *Institute of Electrical and Electronics Engineers Transactions on Image Processing, 14*(2), 253–266.

Coltuc, D. (2011). Improved embedding for prediction-based reversible watermarking. *Institute of Electrical and Electronics Engineers Transactions on Information Forensics and Security, 6*(3), 873–882. doi:10.1109/TIFS.2011.2145372

De Vleeschouwer, C., Delaigle, J.-F., & Macq, B. (2003). Circular interpretation of bijective transformations in lossless watermarking for media asset management. *Institute of Electrical and Electronics Engineers Transaction on Multimedia, 5*(1), 97–105.

Fridrich, J. (1998). Image watermarking for tamper detection. In *Proceedings of the International Conference on Image Processing of Institute of Electrical and Electronics Engineers*, (pp. 404-408). Chicago, IL: IEEE.

Fridrich, J., Goljan, M., & Du, R. (2001). Invertible authentication. In P. W. Wong & E. J. Delp III (Eds.), *Proceedings of SPIE: Security and Watermarking of Multimedia Contents III*, (pp. 197-208). SPIE.

Fridrich, J., Goljan, M., & Du, R. (2002). Lossless data embedding — New paradigm in digital watermarking. *European Association for Signal Processing Journal on Applied Signal Processing, 2*, 185–196. doi:10.1155/S1110865702000537

Fridrich, J., Goljan, M., & Du, R. (2002). Lossless data embedding for all image formats. In E. J. Delp III & P. W. Wong (Eds.), *Proceedings of SPIE: Security and Watermarking of Multimedia Contents IV*, (pp. 572-583). SPIE.

Fujiyoshi, M., & Kiya, H. (2011b). PE expansion-based reversible data hiding without location maps. In *Proceedings of the Annual Summit and Conference of Asia-Pacific Signal and Information Processing Association*. Xi'an, China: APSIPA.

Fujiyosih, M., & Kiya, H. (2011a). Reversible data hiding for sparse histogram images. In *Proceedings of the International Technical Conference on Circuits/Systems, Computers and Communications*, (pp. 510-513). Gyeongju, Korea: IEEE.

Hongmei, L., Zhefeng, Z., Huang, J., Huang, X., & Shi, Y.-Q. (2003). A high capacity distortion-free data hiding algorithm for palette image. In *Proceedings of the International Symposium on Circuits and Systems of Institute of Electrical and Electronics Engineers*, (pp. 916-919). Bangkok, Thailand: IEEE.

Jin, H. L., Fujiyoshi, M., & Kiya, H. (2007). Lossless data hiding in the spatial domain for high quality images. *Institute of Electronics, Information and Communication Engineers Transactions on Fundamentals of Electronics. Communications and Computer Sciences*, *90*(4), 771–777.

Kihara, M., Fujiyoshi, M., & Kiya, H. (2008). Morphological image tamper detecting method considering robustness against compression. In *Proceedings of the International Workshop on Advanced Image Technology*. Taiwan, China: IEEE.

Kihara, M., Fujiyoshi, M., Wan, Q. T., & Kiya, H. (2007). Image tamper detection using mathematical morphology. In *Proceedings of the International Conference on Image Processing of Institute of Electrical and Electronics Engineers*, (pp. 101-104). San Antonio, TX: IEEE.

Lin, C.-C., Tai, W.-L., & Chang, C.-C. (2008). Multilevel reversible data hiding based on histogram modification of difference images. *Pattern Recognition*, *41*(12), 3582–3591. doi:10.1016/j.patcog.2008.05.015

Ni, Z., Shi, Y.-Q., Ansari, N., & Su, W. (2006). Reversible data hiding. *Institute of Electrical and Electronics Engineers Transactions on Circuits and Systems for Video Technology*, *16*(3), 354–362.

Saleha, N. A., Boghdadya, H. N., Shaheenb, S. I., & Darwish, A. M. (2010). High capacity lossless data embedding technique for palette images based on histogram analysis. *Digital Signal Processing*, *20*(6), 1629–1636. doi:10.1016/j.dsp.2010.02.004

Simmons, G. J. (Ed.). (1992). *Contemporary cryptology: The science of information integrity*. New York, NY: Institute of Electrical and Electronics Engineers.

Stamm, M. C., & Liu, K. J. R. (2009). Forensic detection of image tampering using intrinsic statistical fingerprints in histograms. In *Proceedings of the Annual Summit and Conference of Asia-Pacific Signal and Information Processing Association*, (pp. 563-527). Sapporo, Japan: APSIPA.

Swaminathan, A., Wu, M., & Liu, K. J. R. (2006). Image tampering identification using blind deconvolution. In *Proceedings of the International Conference on Image Processing of Institute of Electrical and Electronics Engineers*, (pp. 2309-2312). Atlanta, GA: IEEE.

Tian, J. (2003). Reversible data embedding using a difference expansion. *Institute of Electrical and Electronics Engineers Transactions on Circuits and Systems for Video Technology*, *13*(8), 890–896.

Tsai, P., Hu, Y.-C., & Yeh, H.-L. (2009). Reversible image hiding scheme using predictive coding and histogram shifting. *Signal Processing*, *89*(6), 1129–1143. doi:10.1016/j.sigpro.2008.12.017

Wang, X., Li, X., Yang, B., & Guo, Z. (2010). Efficient generalized integer transform for reversible watermarking. *Institute of Electrical and Electronics Engineers Signal Processing Letters*, *17*(6), 567–570.

Watanabe, K., Fujiyoshi, M., & Kiya, H. (2010). Multi-keyed hierarchical image authentication. In *Proceedings of the Annual Summit and Conference of Asia-Pacific Signal and Information Processing Association*. Biopolis, Singapore: APSIPA.

KEY TERMS AND DEFINITIONS

Capacity: The conveyable payload size for an original signal. The capacity depends on both the information hiding method and original signal.

Image Authentication: An application in which the integrity of images is verified. Tamper detection.

Information Hiding: A technology multiplexing a signal and its related/unrelated information in which the information is directly hidden into the signal in an imperceptible manner.

Location Map: A map memorizing the position of signal segments that belong to a certain segment group.

Original Signal: The signal into which information is hidden. Another input to an information hiding process.

Payload: The information to be hidden into a signal. An input to an information hiding process.

Prediction Error Expansion: A way of accomplishing reversible information hiding in which a prediction error in a signal segment is expanded to convey a portion of information.

Reversible Information Hiding: A category of information hiding in which the original signal is recovered from a stego signal as well as in which the hidden information is extracted.

Stego Signal: The signal that is slightly distorted from the original signal to convey hidden information. The output of an information hiding process.

Chapter 12
New Proposals for Data Hiding in Paper Media

Kitahiro Kaneda
Tokyo University of Science, Japan

Keiichi Iwamura
Tokyo University of Science, Japan

ABSTRACT

Digital watermarks provide the capability to insert additional information onto various media such as still images, movies, and audios, by utilizing features of the media content. Several techniques that use content features such as text or images have already been proposed for printed documents. The authors propose two new techniques using a single dot pattern and an Artificial Fiber (AF) pattern in order to address the disadvantages of conventional information hiding technologies for paper media. In this chapter, the authors describe each scheme's characteristics, and how to improve its robustness. As a result, they have attained greater than 80% extraction rate with an information hiding capacity of 91 Kbits in the case of the single dot pattern, and a 100% extraction rate with color characters as the foreground in the case of using artificial fiber patterns.

INTRODUCTION

In 2010, 69% of the incidents in which information was leaked in Japan, involved paper media, and the percentage has been increasing each year (NPO Japan Network Security Association, 2010). In addition, paper media are the major source of information that is leaked over the Internet because these are more accessible than electronic data. For this reason, information hiding technologies for paper media have become increasingly important.

There are two general techniques for hiding information in paper media:

1. Embedding digital watermarks as characters or pictures in the content.
2. Embedding bar codes or other special patterns in the background of the paper.

Both techniques have its advantages and disadvantages, and there is currently no technique that meets all of the requirements of robustness,

DOI: 10.4018/978-1-4666-2217-3.ch012

adequate information hiding capacity, fast processing speed, accuracy, and low cost.

We propose two new techniques, one using a single dot pattern (Kaneda, Nagai, Iwamura, & Hangai, 2008) and the other using an artificial fiber pattern (Kaneda, Hirano, Iwamura, & Hangai, 2008), to address the disadvantages of conventional information-hiding technologies for paper media. The single dot pattern information-hiding scheme for paper media provides both good visual quality and good information hiding capacity, which is commonly problematic with conventional techniques. The artificial fiber pattern is a texture pattern for embedding information, and owing to the random nature of the paper fiber, it is expected that there will not be visually discernible incongruities. Figure 1 illustrates the position of our proposed techniques with respect to visual quality and information hiding capacity. In this figure, (1) and (2) correspond to techniques (1) and (2) mentioned above. In this chapter, we introduce the characteristics of our schemes and explain how to improve their robustness.

Figure 1. Position of our proposed techniques with respect to visual quality and information hiding capacity

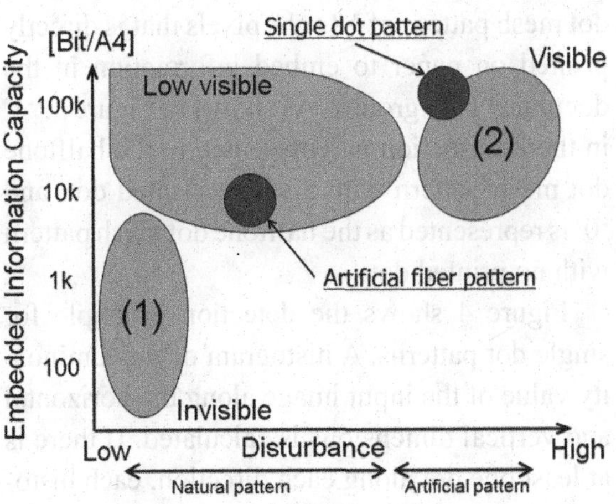

BACKGROUND

As mentioned in the introduction, information-hiding technologies for paper media can be divided roughly into techniques that embed digital watermarks directly into the foreground and techniques that embed information in the background using dot or line patterns.

Bender et al. proposed a technique for embedding information into a text image by shifting a word interval (Bender, Gruhl, Morimoto, & Lu, 1996). Fujii et al. proposed changing character forms to embed information (Fujii, Nakano, Echizen, & Yoshino, 2005). These have the drawback of degrading the document's visual quality, and the information hiding capacity is influenced by the number of characters that are available.

On the other hand, techniques for embedding information in the background are not directly influenced by the foreground. Tow proposed embedding information as a difference in the printing direction of a predetermined pattern (Figure 2a) (Palo Alto Research Center Incorporated, 2012; Tow, 1994). Ito et al. proposed hiding information using a combination of two different types of line screen on a halftone dot background, which produces a predetermined gradation for a binary image (Ito, Soda, Ihara, Kimura, & Fuse, 2005).

Suzaki et al. proposed a technique that embeds information in a document that has an 18 halftone dot mesh pattern of 18 × 18 pixels arranged in the background (Suzaki & Sudo, 2005). This pattern, which includes dots arranged at equal intervals, is called a "basic" halftone dot mesh pattern and is used when there is no embedded information. To embed binary information, dot-mesh patterns representing '0' and '1' are obtained by shifting some of the dots in the basic halftone dot-mesh pattern, and these are used to embed the information. The halftone dot-mesh patterns representing '0' and '1' are shown in Figure 2b. When extracting information from a document using this technique, the dot pattern may degrade during the printing and scanning processes. Therefore, to

Figure 2. Existing information-hiding patterns

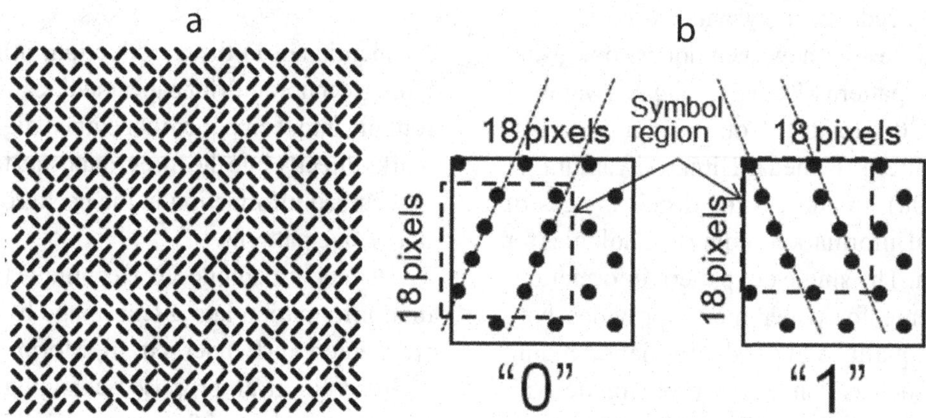

discriminate between the '0' and '1' patterns, wave features generated from the two dot patterns of slanted lines (see Figure 2) are utilized. The wave features are detected by a 2-D Gabor filter. The Gabor filter uses a Gauss function as its windowing function and can reliably detect the direction of the wave, even in a noisy image.

Because this technique uses a small pattern of 18 dots with size 18 × 18 pixels, or 0.75 mm^2, the background density is high; thus, degrading the visual quality of the document. Furthermore, although the Gabor filter is successfully used for extraction, it is believed to have a negative influence on processing speed because of its computational complexity.

Because the pattern and the dots are relatively large and artificial, these techniques have weaknesses with respect to:

- The document's visual quality.
- Computational complexity.
- Robustness against geometric modifications and physical attacks.

SINGLE DOT PATTERN

The Basic Technique

We first set the following as basic requirements that must be met when addressing the problems associated with conventional techniques for information hiding in paper media:

- Improvement of the document's visual quality.
- Increase in information hiding capacity.
- Simple calculation.

Our single dot pattern technique uses a halftone dot mesh pattern of 18 × 18 pixels that is directly printed on paper to embed information in the document background. As shown in Figure 3, '1' in the information is represented in the halftone dot mesh pattern with a single printed dot, and '0' is represented as the halftone dot mesh pattern with no printed dot.

Figure 4 shows the detection principle for single dot patterns. A histogram of the luminosity value of the input image along the horizontal and vertical dimensions is calculated. If there is at least one dot along each direction, each histogram has a peak. We define the ith vertical peak position and the jth horizontal peak position of the

Figure 3. Halftone dot-mesh patterns for '1' and '0' using a single dot pattern

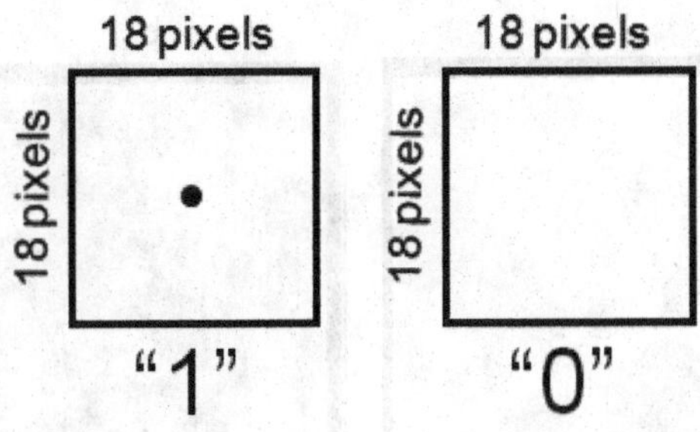

histogram as the tile coordinates_ij (pcxi,pcyj), and we define the corresponding area to be tile area_ij. When at least one pixel above a predetermined value exists in tile area_ij, it is interpreted as '1,' and when none exists, it is interpreted as '0.'

The resolutions of the printer and scanner are set at 600 dpi because we experimentally confirmed that a dot diameter of 0.042 mm and an interval of 0.75 mm are difficult to differentiate at 600 dpi. We assume that there are no skewed or bent areas when the document is scanned.

Because a single dot pattern uses only one dot in 0.75 mm², the single dot technique is superior to the existing halftone dot-mesh technique in terms of the document's visual quality. Moreover, because this technique expresses information through the existence of a '1' dot, it can be used in fundamental addition and comparison operations. In addition, extraction is computationally less complex than the existing technique using the Gabor filter. Furthermore, the single dot technique can be used to further reduce the pattern size to 9 × 9 or 7 × 7 pixels.

We prove these advantages and our technique's robustness against the foreground through two experiments presented in the following sections.

Experiment for Verifying the Technique's Basic Advantages

In this experiment, we compare our proposed technique with the conventional technique proposed by Suzaki et al. (2005) with respect to the document's visual quality and information hiding capacity under conditions in which there are no foreground objects, dirt, bending, or skew.

We used the following experiment conditions:

- Printing is 600 dpi with normal document print mode (black and white).
- Scanning is 600 dpi with 8-bit gray, default setting.
- The scanning area is limited to business card size (2016 × 1296 pixels @ 600 dpi), to save memory resources.

Moreover, the extraction rate for the embedded data is thoroughly verified through different combinations of input/output devices.

Figure 4. Detection principle for a single dot pattern

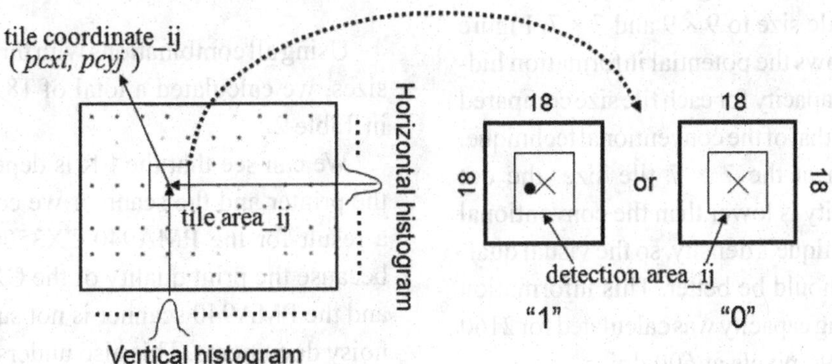

1. Equipment
    a. Standard Equipment (Printer/ Scanner): MP960, Canon
    b. Printers for checking device combinations
        i. Satera LBP5000, Canon
        ii. IPSiO CX3500, RICOH
    c. Scanners for checking device combinations
        i. MP960, Canon
        ii. PM-A940, Epson
    d. Printing Specifications: 600 dpi, monochrome, A4
    e. Scanning Specifications: 600 dpi, 8-bit gray, default configuration
    f. Paper Media: Business-cut paper
    g. Computer and Software
        i. PC: Hewlett-Packard dx5150 with AMD Sempron™ processor 3000+@1.79 GHz, 448 MB RAM
        ii. Software: Microsoft Visual C++ 6.0
2. Result
    a. *Improvement of the document's visual quality*. The actual printing result for each technique using the standard equipment is shown in Figure 5. It is clear that the visual quality of the background produced by our proposed technique is better than that produced by the conventional technique.
    b. *Improvement of information hiding capacity.* In order to increase the information hiding capacity, we reduced the tile size to 9 × 9 and 7 × 7. Figure 6 shows the potential information hiding capacity for each tile size compared with that of the conventional technique. Even at the 7 × 7 tile size, the dot density is lower than the conventional technique's density, so the visual quality should be better. This information hiding capacity was calculated for 2160 × 1296 pixels at 600 dpi.

Figure 5. Printing results based on 600 dpi: (a) proposed technique, (b) conventional technique

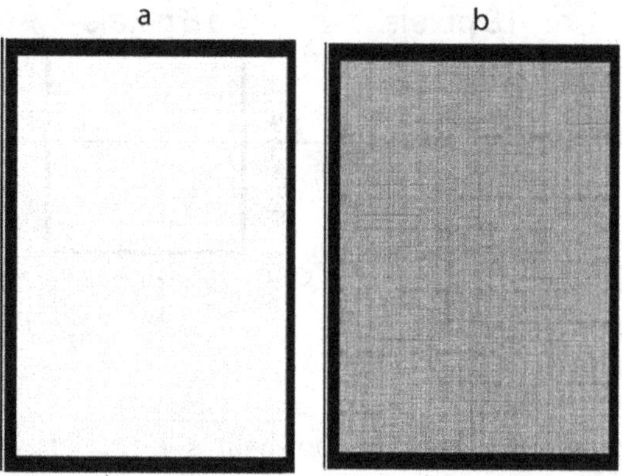

Next, we verified the extraction rate for the hidden information. The Extraction Rate (ER) is defined as follows:

ER = Number of bits correctly detected/ potential information hiding capacity (in bits)

We show the extraction rate ER for different tile sizes using the standard equipment in Table 1. The embedded data "11001100" and "00110011" are repeated on each line. We can see that the ER is greater than 90% for all three tile sizes.

c. *Printer and scanner dependency.* We also examined the ER with all combinations of the following devices:
    i. Printer: MP960, LBP5000, and CX3500
    ii. Scanner: MP960, PMA940

Using all combinations with three different tile sizes, we calculated a total of 18 ERs as shown in Table 2.

We can see that the ER is dependent on both the printer and the scanner. We could not obtain a result for the PMA940/CX3500 combination because the print quality of the CX3500 is noisy and the PMA940 scanner is not suitable for such noisy documents. This also underscores the ER's device dependency.

Figure 6. Tile size and potential information hiding capacity in a business card size document

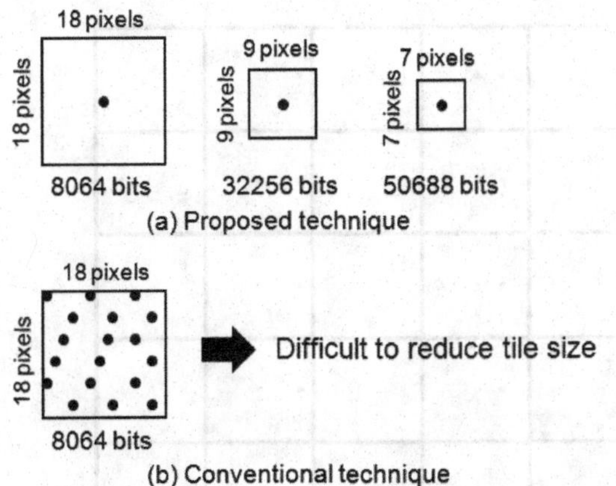

Table 1. ER for different tile sizes

	Tile Size (pixel)		
	18 × 18	9 × 9	7 × 7
Possible Information Capacity	8064	32256	50688
Error bit	189	682	3828
ER (%)	97.68	97.89	92.45

Table 2. ER for different equipment combinations (%)

	Tile Size (pixel)		
Scanner/Printer	18 × 18	9 × 9	7 × 7
MP960/MP960	97.68	97.89	92.45
MP960/CX3500	81.04	89.80	82.26
MP960/LBP5000	91.75	95.56	94.83
PMA940/MP960	89.62	88.48	86.00
PMA940/CX3500	error	error	error
PMA940/LBP5000	68.54	74.17	79.94

Experiment for Verifying Robustness

In this section, we expanded the target size of the embedded document from business card size to A4 size, and we experimented both with and without a foreground object. We also verified the extraction accuracy when information was embedded between characters, making it difficult to remove only a dot (Kaneda, Tachibana, & Iwamura, 2011).

1. Equipment
   a. Standard Equipment (Printer/ Scanner): MP970, Canon
   b. Printing Specifications: 600 dpi, monochrome, A4
   c. Scanning Specifications: 600 dpi, 8-bit gray, default configuration
   d. Paper Media: Business-cut paper
   e. Computer and Software
      i. PC: Hewlett-Packard xw4550 Workstation with Dual Core AMD Opteron™ processor model 1212@2.00 GHz, 896 MB RAM
      ii. OCR: Yomitori Kakumei, Version 12 (Japanese OCR)
      iii. Development environment: Microsoft Visual C++ 6.0
2. *Experiment method.* First, we examined the difficulty of extraction caused by distortion of a document in the A4 size range. We found that when we expanded the extraction range from name-card size to A4 size, the printed dots were slightly shifted horizontally and vertically, based on the printers' individual mechanical characteristics. The gradual shifting of the printed dots is shown in Figure 7.

Figure 7 clearly indicates that is the dots are not printed correctly within each 18 × 18 pixel tile. We attempted to isolate the reason for the dot shift as follows. We considered that the shift could either be the result of a bug in the program that controls the print position of the dots or the result of shifting that occurred during the printing and scanning processes. To determine whether the program contained a bug, we altered the program to directly output the dot image to a BMP file rather than print the dot image on the document.

Figure 7. Printed dot shift

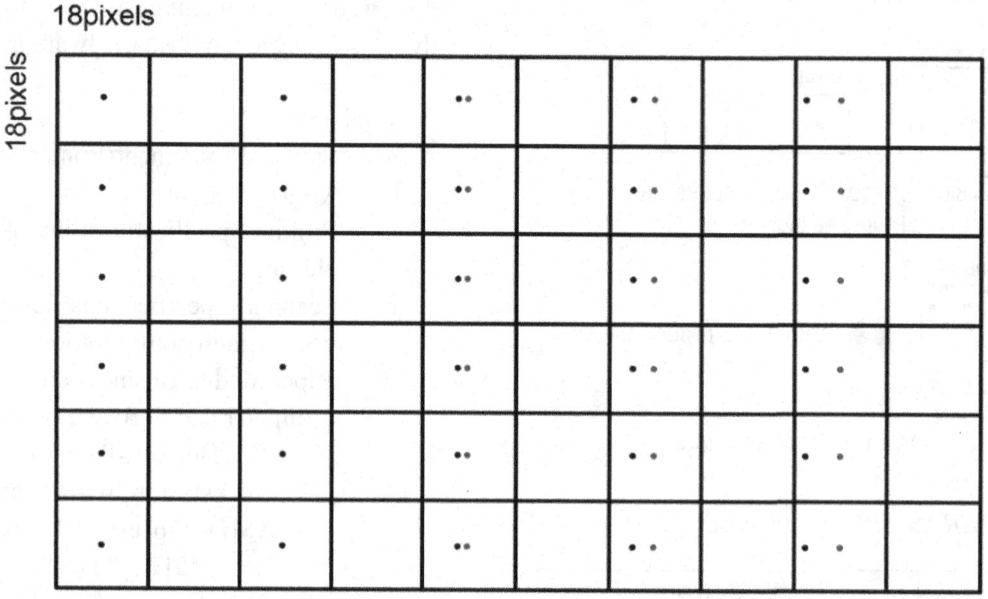

As a result, we did not observe any dot shift in the BMP file. To examine the second possibility, we replaced the printer and checked the output dot image on the document. We found that other printers had the same problem, resulting in a similar printed dot shift.

Thus, we confirmed that the reason for the printed dot shift is not a bug in the program, but rather lies in the printing and scanning processes used for information hiding. Figure 8 shows the printed dot shift on an A4 page.

Embedding information at equal intervals on A4 size paper with a program produced a result that was similar to the red rectangle in Figure 8. However, when we used a printer and scanner to embed and extract the information in a document, the result was a dot image area similar to the black skewed rectangle in Figure 8. Because we have to assume that common printers and scanners will be used for the single dot pattern technique, extraction of information from a shifted dot pattern with reasonable accuracy is required.

We devised a new technique for solving this problem as follows. Figure 9 is an enlargement of the skewed region in Figure 8. Based on experimental observation, we assume that the dot shift direction is linear and horizontal. Using the location of the leftmost side and of the rightmost side in Figure 9, we can obtain a gradient between "a" and "b." Then, the next printed dot at a certain point along that line can be predicted.

Therefore, to investigate the horizontal range of the printed dots, we constructed a vertical histogram of the pixel density. The calculated histogram shows a relatively high value at the no dot position and a relatively low value at the printed dot position. As a result, the left and right extremes of the printed dot range can be predicted by observing the vertical histogram distribution. Similarly, the positions of the upper right end ("b" in Figure 9) and lower left end can be predicted. However, the vertical positions of the upper left end ("a" in Figure 9) and lower right end cannot be obtained because, as shown in Figure 9, "a" is not an upper edge. To obtain the vertical position of "a," we add the number of vertical tiles, which is a multiple of 18 pixels, to the vertical position of the lower left end. As a

Figure 8. Overall printed dot shift (the skewed black rectangle represents the actual printing area; the red rectangle indicates the target printing area)

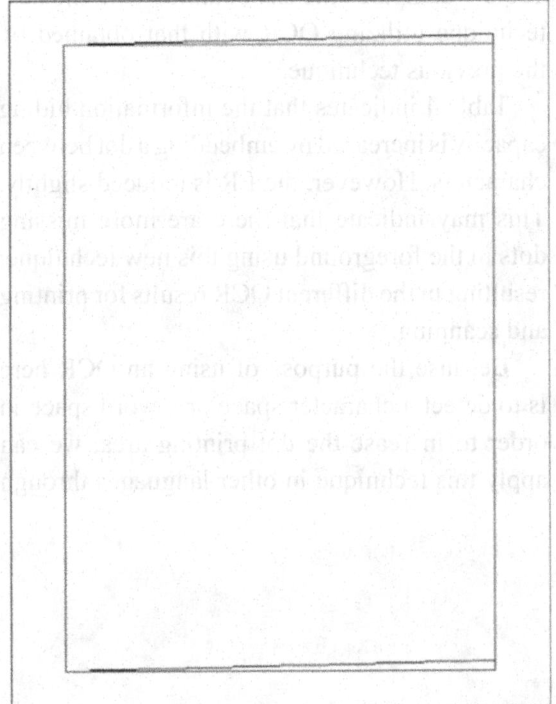

result, the correct position of a shifted dot can be detected by changing the extraction point and the gradient of positions "a" and "b." Because the second line and the subsequent ones have shifted in the same direction, we only investigated the gradient.

Next, to verify robust extraction from the dot area, we updated the program to enable printing and extracting a dot between characters. Earlier, the character component was treated as a block of text or a paragraph unit by using XML data outputted from an OCR application, and a dot was printed by bypassing this unit. Now we utilized each character's position and the recognition result obtained from an OCR application to enable precise printing and extraction of a dot between characters. This was not possible before, and it improves this technique with respect to both robustness and information hiding capacity. Figure 10 shows an abstract flowchart for embedding a dot between characters.

For extracting a dot, the "PRINT DOT" blocks in Figure 10 are replaced with "EXTRACT DOT" blocks whereas the other blocks remain the same.

3. *Result.* Figure 11 shows the A4 size document sample used in the experiment. The extraction accuracy obtained using the improved single dot pattern technique, but without the new technique utilizing OCR, is shown in Table 3.

Table 3 shows that the ER for an A4 size document is lower than the ER for a name card size document, both with and without a foreground object. Furthermore, in the case of an A4 size document with a foreground object, the ER fell to 80%. Based on the difference in the OCR results for printing and scanning the sample document, we believe that this is caused by missing dots in the foreground.

Figure 9. Enlargement of Figure 8 (the skewed black line represents the actual printed dot line; the red line indicates the target printed dot line)

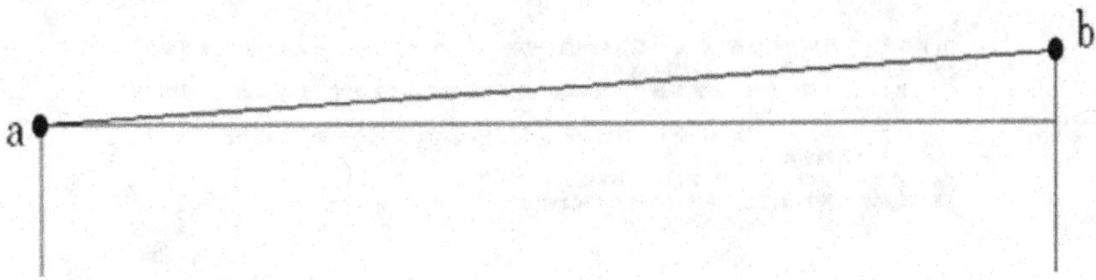

Figure 10. Flowchart for embedding a dot between characters

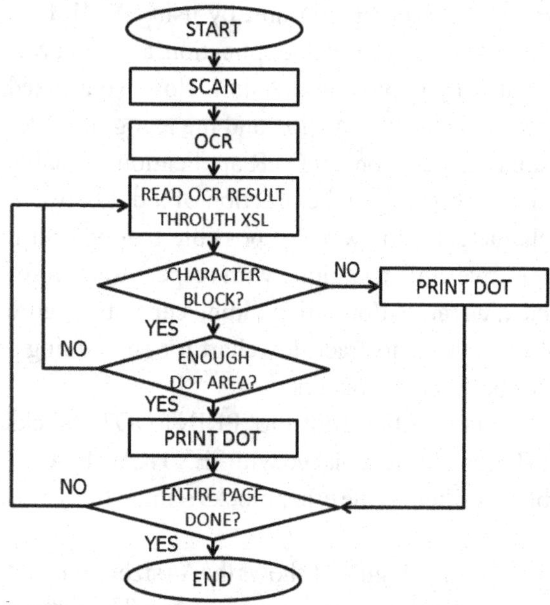

Figure 11. Experimental sample document

(電子協標準パターンＪ１／Ｖｅｒ．１）
社員各位殿

１９９△年１０月１日
総務課

＊社員旅行のお知らせ＊

温泉が楽しい季節になってきました。そこで今期は温泉旅行を企画しました。山間の渓流を眺めながら、露天風呂でチョット一杯、なんていうのもトレンディではないでしょうか？もちろん露天風呂は混浴だけではなく女性専用もあります。女性の方も安心して露天風呂が楽しめます。
また、パソコン、ＣＤプレーヤー、テレビなどの豪華賞品が当たる抽選会もありますので楽しみにしてください。
尚、翌日は下記の３コースに分かれます。希望するコースを１０月７日までに幹事へご連絡ください。コース毎の詳しい内容は追って連絡します。

記

☆日　時　　１９９△年１１月１６日～１１月１７日
☆場　所　　栃木県鬼怒川温泉
☆宿泊先　　ホテル◎◎◎
☆集合場所　本社ビル前　ＡＭ８：２０
☆スケジュール
　１１月１６日　８：３０出発
　　１２：００日光到着
　　　昼食（湯葉懐石）
　　１３：３０東照宮など寺社観光
　　１６：３０鬼怒川温泉ホテル◎◎◎到着
　　　露天風呂、大浴場、遊戯施設などご自由に
　　１８：００宴会
　　　ショー、演芸大会、抽選会（二次会もお楽しみに！）
　１１月１７日　第１コース　鬼怒川周辺観光
　　９：３０ホテル出発
　　１４：００ホテル着
　　第２コース　テニス
　　９：３０ホテル出発
　　１４：３０ホテル着
　　第３コース　ゴルフ
　　７：００ホテル出発
　　１４：３０ホテル着

全コース（バス）
１４：４５ホテル出発
１８：３０本社ビル到着・解散

メモ
（１）日光・鬼怒川方面は都心に比べて気温が低いので、カーディガンかジャンパーなど寒さを防ぐものを用意したほうが良いでしょう。
（２）第１コース選択の方は天候が良ければ鬼怒川渓谷を散策する予定です。散策に適した履物を用意ください。
（３）第２コースの方はテニスに適した服装を用意ください。テニス用具を借りたい方はコース申し込み時に幹事に申し出ください。
（４）第３コースの方はプレー費は各自払いとなります。
（５）道路の混雑具合により帰着時間は若干変わります。

以　上
（担当：山中）

Next, we show the result for our new technique utilizing OCR, which enables embedding and extracting a dot between characters. Figure 12 enlarges the dots embedded between characters. Table 4 compares the ER obtained with the new technique utilizing OCR with that obtained by the previous technique.

Table 4 indicates that the information hiding capacity is increased by embedding a dot between characters. However, the ER is reduced slightly. This may indicate that there are more missing dots in the foreground using this new technique, resulting in the different OCR results for printing and scanning.

Because the purpose of using an OCR here is to detect a character space or a word space in order to increase the dot printing area, we can apply this technique in other languages through

Table 3. Comparison of the ER of the business card size and A4 size documents

	Business Card Size Document		A4 Size Document	
Foreground	No	Yes	No	Yes
Ideal Information Capacity [bit]	8064	7450	101572	88963
Extraction Failures [bit]	189	108	3827	17296
ER[%]	97.68	98.55	96.23	80.56

Table 4. ER when embedding a dot between characters

	Embedding a Dot between Text Blocks	Embedding a Dot between Characters
Ideal Information Capacity [bit]	88963	91615
Extraction Failures [bit]	17296	18110
ER [%]	80.56	80.23

use of suitable independent OCRs. Therefore, this technique is not specific to the Japanese language.

ARTIFICIAL FIBER PATTERN

The Basic Technique

In order to address the problems associated with conventional information hiding techniques as described in the Background section, we propose an "artificial fiber pattern" (abbreviated as "AF pattern") technique that aims at satisfying the following requirements:

- Combined low visibility and robustness for printing.
- Robustness against various geometric conversions, physical attacks, and foreground objects.First, we analyzed blank paper on microscale to observe the concavo–convex pattern formed by the fiber in the paper and its frequency distribution. The fiber pattern was scanned with a professional-use high-resolution 2400 dpi scanner, and its spatial frequency components were calculated with a 2-D Fourier transform (MATLAB FFT2 function). These are shown in Figures 13a and b. The paper is a normal business-cut paper, and its scanned image was automatically adjusted by Photoshop. From these observations, we found that the spatial frequency components of the paper

Figure 12. Enlargement of dots embedded between characters

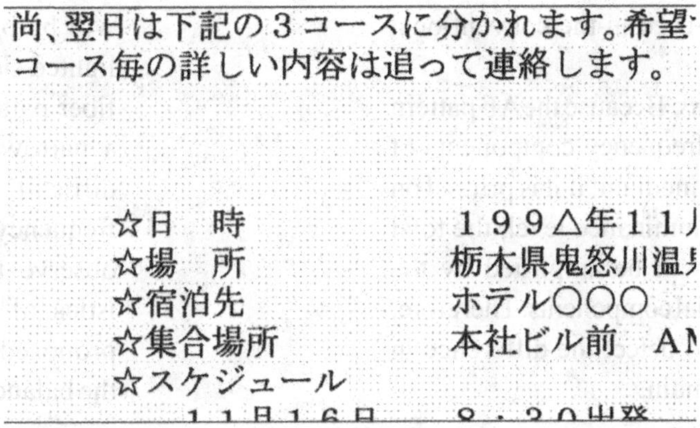

尚、翌日は下記の３コースに分かれます。希望
コース毎の詳しい内容は追って連絡します。

☆日　時　　１９９△年１１
☆場　所　　栃木県鬼怒川温
☆宿泊先　　ホテル○○○
☆集合場所　本社ビル前　A
☆スケジュール

Figure 13. Fiber pattern and its Fourier spectrum

a

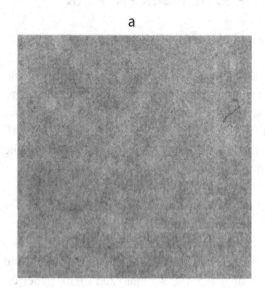

b

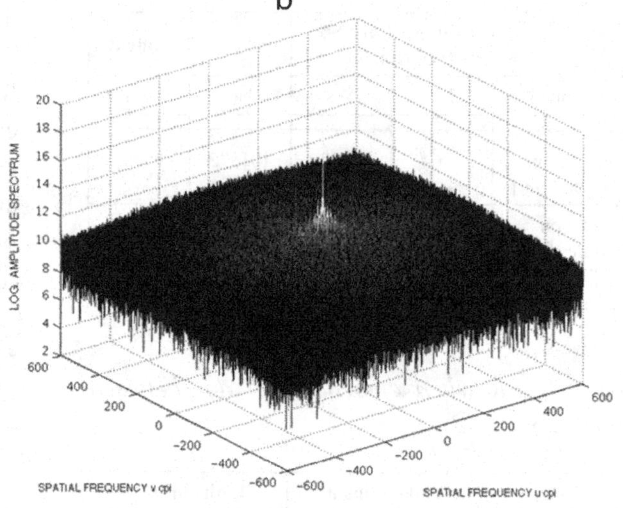

medium concentrate up to a maximum of 100 cpi.

The original AF pattern is defined on basis of the concave-convex pattern formed by the paper fiber, and it is generated from the 2-D Fourier inverse transform of the high frequency components of the detailed power spectrum obtained from the high-resolution scan.

The following advantages of employing this AF pattern were anticipated:

1. *Improvement of the visual quality of the document.* Since an AF pattern is based on the natural fiber pattern of the paper itself, the pattern should be less visible than the artificial patterns used in the conventional technique.
2. *Printing robustness.* Because the AF pattern utilizes the high frequency components of the original paper medium, if it is printed on paper with a low luminance level, the total luminance level will be amplified by the pattern's own spatial components. Therefore, it becomes easy to detect the difference in the frequency domain.
3. *Rotation robustness.* Because the frequency distribution of a fiber pattern has no directivity, an AF pattern is not sensitive to the skewing of paper media in the spatial domain or to rotation.
   a. *Embedding procedure using the AF pattern.* The procedure for generating the AF pattern, shown in Figure 14, is as follows:
      i. Scan the target blank paper to produce the blank paper image and cut a 0.5 square inch pattern for subsequent processing.
      ii. The reflection rate of normal paper is nearly 100%, so the density histogram after scanning will be biased toward the highlighted side, causing the original fiber pattern to be distributed in a narrow range. This makes it difficult to correctly perform a frequency analysis. To accurately observe the original characteristics of the fiber pattern, our proposed technique optimizes the balance of highlight, shadow,

Figure 14. AF pattern generation procedure

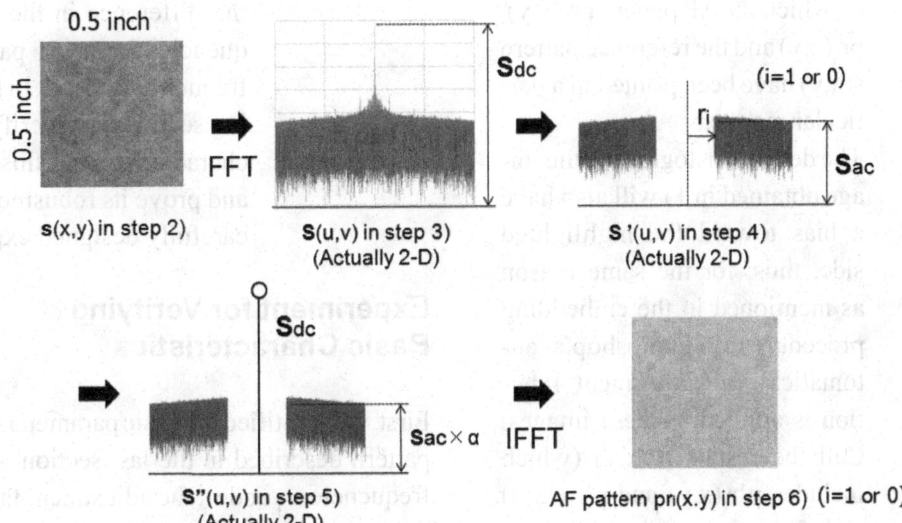

and gamma using Photoshop's automatic level adjustment function to equalize the gray density level prior to performing the 2-D Fourier transform. Thus, all of the density information included in the original shadowed and highlighted areas can be utilized. Let s(x,y) be the resulting 0.5 square inch reference pattern.

iii. The 2-D Fourier transform of the reference pattern s(x,y) is carried out using MATLAB software, with the result S(u,v) distributed as concentric circles.

iv. The low-frequency component of S(u,v) is cut off two-dimensionally with a radius r to produce S'(u,v). Here r is assumed to take values r_1 and r_0 corresponding to the data bits 1and 0, respectively. Let Sac(u,v) be the remaining AC component of S(u,v).

v. Because the DC component is missing, Sac(u,v) cannot be used to form a luminosity signal, even if it is converted back to the spatial domain. Therefore, the DC component Sdc of S(u,v) is added. In addition, Sac(u,v) is multiplied by a visibility adjustment factor α ($0 < \alpha < 1$) that adjusts the visibility (gray density level) and changes the DC component in the spatial domain by utilizing the linearity of the Fourier transform. Let this processing result be S"(u,v).

vi. Performing a 2-D inverse Fourier transform on S"(u,v) results in the AF patterns pr_1(x,y) and pr_0(x,y) corresponding to r_1 and r_0.

vii. Print the AF patterns pr_1(x,y) and pr_0(x,y) corresponding to the data bits 1 and 0 and the reference pattern s(x,y) on one page for extraction. We explain the reason for this in the next section.

b. *Extraction procedure for the AF pattern.* The extraction procedure for the information embedded in the AF pattern is as follows:

i. Scan and digitize the paper image on which the AF pattern $pr_1(x,y)$, $pr_0(x,y)$ and the reference pattern **s**(x,y) have been printed in a particular manner.
ii. The density histogram of the image obtained in 1) will also have a bias toward the highlighted side; thus, for the same reason as mentioned in the embedding procedure a), Photoshop's automatic level adjustment function is applied to these images. Call the results **p'**(x,y) (which includes $p'r_1(x,y)$ and $p'r_0(x,y)$) and **s'**(x,y), respectively.
iii. The 2-D Fourier transform is performed on **p'**(x,y) to produce the amplitude spectrum **P'**(u,v).
iv. The 2-D Fourier transform is performed on **s'**(x,y) to produce the amplitude spectrum **S'**(u,v).
v. To evaluate the reduction rate of the low-frequency components of **P'**(u,v) against **S'**(u,v), we define the intensity ratio *d*(R) as follows:

$$d(\mathrm{R}) = \frac{\iint_{0}^{\mathrm{R}} \left|\mathrm{P}'(\mathrm{u},\mathrm{v})\right| \mathrm{dudv}}{\iint_{0}^{\mathrm{R}} \left|\mathrm{S}'(\mathrm{u},\mathrm{v})\right| \mathrm{dudv}} \quad (1)$$

The double integral expresses the integration value of the amplitude spectrum in a circle of radius R in the 2-D spatial frequency domain (u, v).

vi. The bit information that was previously related to the intensity ratio is extracted as embedded information. The intensity ratio *d*(R), which normalizes the amplitude spectrum of the scanned AF pattern using the reference pattern, is employed to identify the difference in the cutoff frequencies for the AF pattern in the frequency domain. In the following sections, we verify the basic characteristics of this technique and prove its robustness through carefully designed experiments.

Experiment for Verifying Basic Characteristics

First, we identified the basic parameters for the AF pattern described in the last section—the cutoff frequencies r_1 and r_0, the adjustment factor α, and the integration radius R identified through the intensity ratio *d*(R)—by using a high-resolution Kodak scanner and a Canon MP970 IJ printer as the reference equipment with two types of paper (business-cut paper and high-quality paper). Then we evaluated the technique's robustness against several physical attacks. Finally, we performed information embedding and extraction tests with three types of printer and two types of paper to verify paper/printer independence(Kaneda, Fujii, Iwamura, & Hangai, 2010).

1. Equipment
   a. Printer
      i. MP970 (print resolution 2400 dpi), Canon
      ii. PM-A940 (print resolution 5760 × 1440 dpi), Epson
      iii. Photosmart C8180 (print resolution 4800 × 1200 dpi), Hewlett-Packard
   b. Scanner: IQSmart2 (maximum optical resolution 4300 dpi), Kodak
   c. Printing Specifications: Color/high definition
   d. Scanning Specifications: 8-bit gray, default configuration, pattern size 1200 × 1200 pixels (0.5 square inches)

e. Paper Media: Business-cut paper and high-quality paper
f. Computer and Software
   i. PC: Epson Endeavor Pro4300 with Intel Core2 Duo CPU, E6850@3.00GHz, 2.50GB RAM
   ii. Software: MATLAB, Version 7.5.0(R2007b); Adobe Photoshop CS2, Version 9.0

2. *Basic parameter identification.* We identified a stable condition to maximize the difference between the two intensity ratios *d*(R). We needed to carefully choose the cutoff frequency *r* and integration radius R by observing the intensity ratio *d*(R) for different values of R and *r*.

   Figure 15 shows the relationship between the cutoff frequency *r* and the intensity ratio *d*(R) as we varied the integration radius R with normal business-cut paper, using the fixed value $\alpha = 1/2$. Table 5 displays the differences in the intensity ratio *d*(R) for different values of α with the fixed value R = 10. It is observed that the intensity ratio *d*(R) is proportional to the cutoff frequency *r*, so that the integration radius R should be large. Moreover, the integration radius R is not necessarily proportional to the cutoff frequency *r* under the influence of power spectrum noise, when *r* is small. In most case, the maximum difference between different *r* is observed when it is 2 and 20. Also, in the case of the fixed value $\alpha = 1/2$, we can observe the largest differences for *d*(R) in Table 5.

   Based on these observations, we defined the basic parameters for the AF pattern on business-cut paper as follows:

   $R = 10, \alpha = 1/2, r_1 = 2$, and $r_0 = 20$.

   In addition, we did not find a parameter dependency based on business-cut vs. high-quality paper.

   Figure 16 shows the AF patterns created with the parameters defined as above.

Table 5. Intensity ratio d for different values of α and fixed values r

	α		
	1/2	**1/4**	**1/8**
$r_1 = 2$	0.9760	0.9631	0.9647
$r_0 = 20$	0.8676	0.8879	0.9570

Figure 15. Intensity ratio d for different values of R and r, with α= 1/2

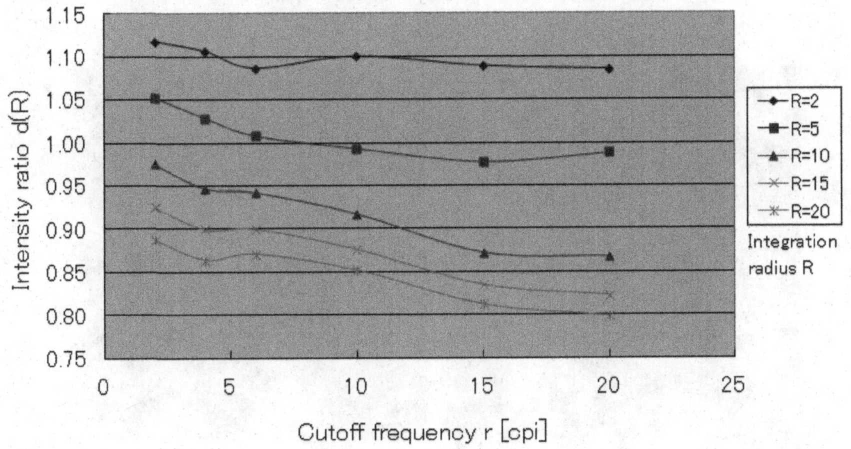

By scanning these patterns and calculating the threshold of the intensity ratio d(R) for discriminating between r_1 and r_0, we were able to extract the embedded information from each AF pattern. For example, in the case where a pattern was recognized as r_1, the embedded information was identified as 1.

3. *Robustness against several physical attacks.* Using the basic parameters identified in (2), we verified the robustness of our proposed technique against the following physical attacks:
   a. **Distortion:** Place the paper on a window facing the sun for one week.
   b. **Eraser:** Scratch the pattern with an eraser.
   c. **Tape:** Mask half of the pattern with transparent adhesive tape.
   d. **Add-On:** Draw pencil lines on the pattern by hand.

Figure 17 shows the actual samples that we used for the add-on attacks.

Table 6 compares the resulting intensity ratio d and the threshold after these physical attacks, using business-cut paper. From these results, we can see that satisfactory information extraction is possible with the same threshold as the original technique (0.9122)

Figure 16. AF pattern: (a) $pr_1(x,y)$, (b) $pr_0(x,y)$

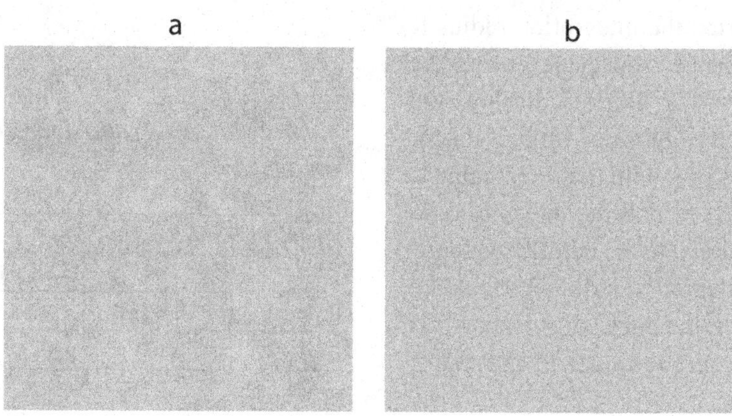

Figure 17. Add-on attacks on the AF pattern: (a) $pr_1(x,y)$, (b) $pr_0(x,y)$

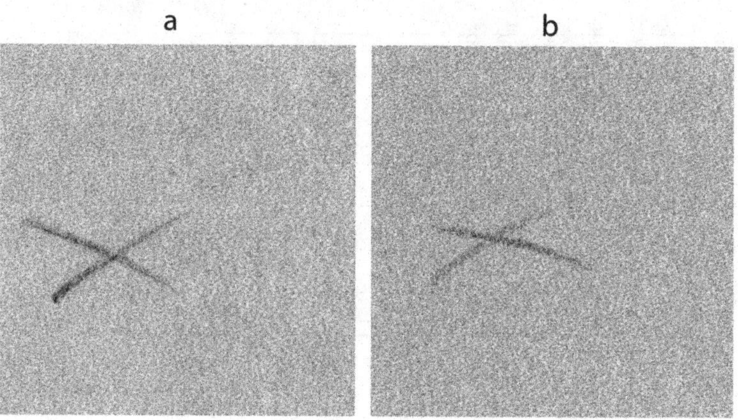

Table 6. Intensity ratio d and threshold under several physical attacks and cutoff frequencies r_1 and r_0 (using business-cut paper)

	Original	Distortion	Eraser	Tape	Add-On
$r_1 = 2$	0.9604	0.9648	0.9609	0.9905	1.013
$r_0 = 20$	0.8639	0.8488	0.8654	0.8994	0.8761
Threshold	0.9122	<- OK	<- OK	<- OK	<- OK

in all physical attacks. We obtained the same results with the high-quality paper.

4. *Printing robustness and equipment dependency.* Using the basic parameters for information hiding with the AF pattern—R = 10, $\alpha = 1/2$, $r_1 = 2$, and $r_0 = 20$—we evaluated the accuracy of our technique's information extraction with the three types of printer and the two types of paper described in a). The evaluation procedure is as follows.
   a. Print the AF and the reference patterns on business-cut and high-quality paper with the Canon, HP, and Epson printers, using the above parameters. Ten printings at a time were performed for each combination of the three printers and the two types of paper, for a total of 60 samples.
   b. Scan each sample created by (a) with the high-resolution scanner, and find the 2-D Fourier transforms of these scans.
   c. Calculate the intensity ratio *d* using the above parameters and the threshold for extracting information.
   d. Perform round-robin extraction evaluation by the intensity ratio *d* of the 10 samples, to which we shall refer by number, for each combination of printer and type of paper type.

The round-robin extraction evaluation is as follows. Using the threshold of sample 1, identify the first difference in the cutoff frequency for the AF pattern in samples 2–10. Next use the threshold of sample 2 to identify the first cutoff frequency difference in samples 1 and 3–10, and so on. As a result, 9 judgments are performed 10 times with each threshold; i.e., 90 evaluations are performed for each printer/paper combination. Overall, we evaluated 540 information extractions in this way.

Figure 18 shows the intensity ratio *d* with $r_1 = 2$ and $r_0 = 20$ for every sample in the three combinations of printer with the high-quality paper.

We can see that every AF pattern could be discriminated in terms of its cutoff frequencies by using common criteria, for example, the dotted line in the graph. We observed the same results for the business-cut paper.

Experiment for Verifying Robustness with Foreground Characters

In this section, we present our experimental verification of the robustness of the technique when a character foreground is present by using color AF patterns that contain different gray density levels of the AF pattern that is attached to an actual character pattern.

1. Equipment
   a. Printer: MP970 (print resolution 2400 dpi), Canon
   b. Scanner: IQSmart2 (maximum optical resolution 4300 dpi), Kodak
   c. Pattern Size
      i. Reference pattern: 0.5 square inches, 1200 × 1200 pixels
      ii. AF pattern: 1 square inch, 2400 × 2400 pixels

Figure 18. Intensity ratio d under cutoff frequencies r_1 and r_0 for every sample using high-quality paper

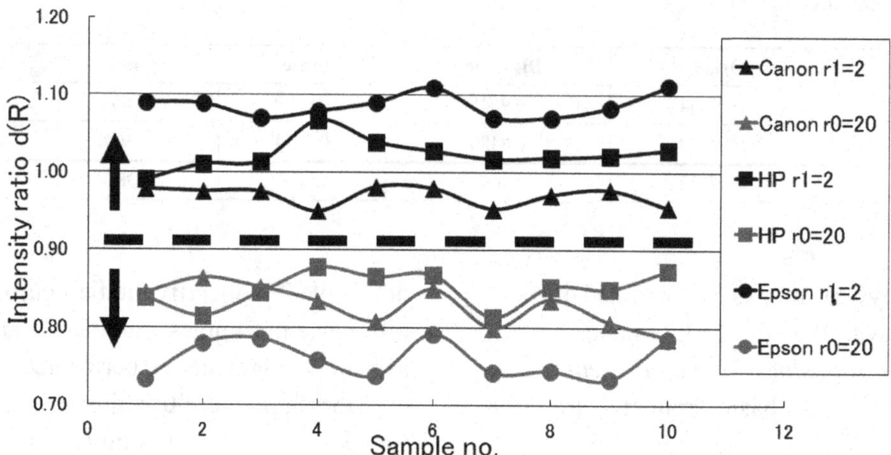

d. Print Specifications: Color/high definition/2400 dpi
e. Scanning Specifications: 8-bit gray, default configuration, 2400 dpi
f. Paper Media: Business-cut paper
g. Computer and Software
   i. PC: Epson Endeavor Pro4300 with Intel Core2 Duo CPU@3.00 GHz, 2.50 GB RAM
   ii. Software: MATLAB Version 7.5.0 (R2007b); Adobe Photoshop CS2 Version 9.0

2. *Basic parameters*. The cut-off frequency r_1 and r_0, the visibility adjustment factor α, and the integral radius R are set as

   $r_1 = 2$, $r_0 = 20$, $\alpha = 1/2$, and $R = 10$.

3. *Experiment method.* We overlaid the color AF character patterns for the characters '0'–'9' on the normal AF pattern that is generated using the basic parameters. The character size is 400 pt, with a 2400 dpi conversion. We chose this value so that all of the numbers can fit within an area of 0.5 square inches. The colors are Magenta 80% (gray level 16%, henceforth M80%), Magenta 100% (gray level 20%, henceforth M100%), Cyan 100% (gray level 22%, henceforth C100%). Magenta and cyan are used instead of different gray-level signals because it is easy to see colored characters on a gray background, it is easy to control the gray density level, since the inkjet printer contains pure color ink, and because we intended to perform this verification for a small difference in gray level. The experimental procedure is as follows:
   a. Using the IQSmart2, and A4 business-cut sheets, create the reference pattern s(x,y) and the AF patterns $pr_1(x,y)$ and $pr_0(x,y)$ as described in the embedding procedure. These are created using the basic parameters and are shown in Figures 19 and 20.
   b. Using Photoshop, overlay the color AF patterns using M80%, M100%, and C100% on the AF patterns $pr_1(x, y)$ and $pr_0(x, y)$. These are shown in Figures 21, 22, and 23.
   c. Arrange the color AF patterns as shown in Figure 24. We used 11 pieces of $pr_1(x,y)$ and 10 pieces of $pr_0(x,y)$, and these were printed on a business-cut sheet.

Figure 19. Reference pattern **s***(x,y)*

d. Using the IQSmart2, scan an 8-bit gray-scale square inch at the positions where the AF patterns are embedded. Then calculate 21 intensity ratios as described in the extraction procedure, using the reference pattern **s**(x,y) that was generated in (a).

4. *Results.* The intensity ratio distribution results for M80%, M100%, and C100% with no foreground are shown in Figures 25, 26, and 27. The horizontal axis in each figure corresponds to the data number in Figure 24.

In the case of M80%, there was a sufficient difference between the intensity ratios for pr_1(x,y) and pr_0(x,y), making it possible to extract information from the color AF pattern using the present technique. Moreover, it was possible to discriminate using the same threshold as used for the AF pattern without a foreground.

In the case of M100%, although the intensity ratio distribution was generally higher than in the case with no foreground, it was possible to identify the difference in the intensity ratios for discrimination, but it was not easily identified using a common threshold.

In the case of C100%, there was neither a difference nor a similarity to the intensity ratios in the case with no foreground, and it was not possible to distinguish between pr_1(x,y) and pr_0(x,y).

A New Approach for Suppressing the Effect of the Foreground

In the case of M80% with a gray density level of 16%, the robustness of the foreground characters that used the color AF pattern was verified. However, in the cases of M100% and C100%, both of which have a higher gray density level than M80%, our previous experiments showed that the current technique for extracting information is inadequate. Therefore, we propose a new

Figure 20. AF pattern: (a) $pr_1(x,y)$, (b) $pr_0(x,y)$

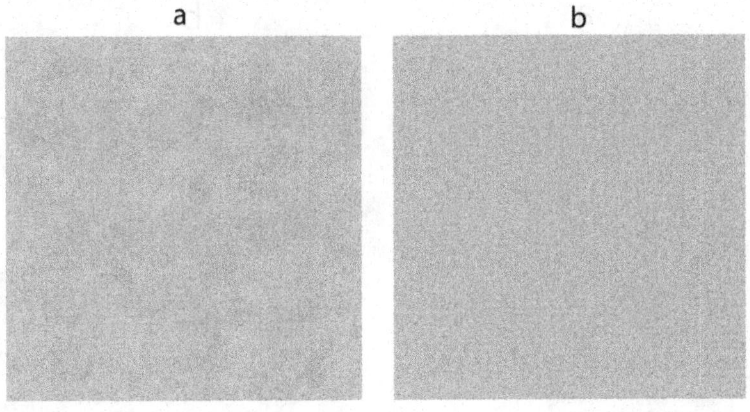

Figure 21. AF pattern (M80%): (a) $pr_1(x,y)$, (b) $pr_0(x,y)$

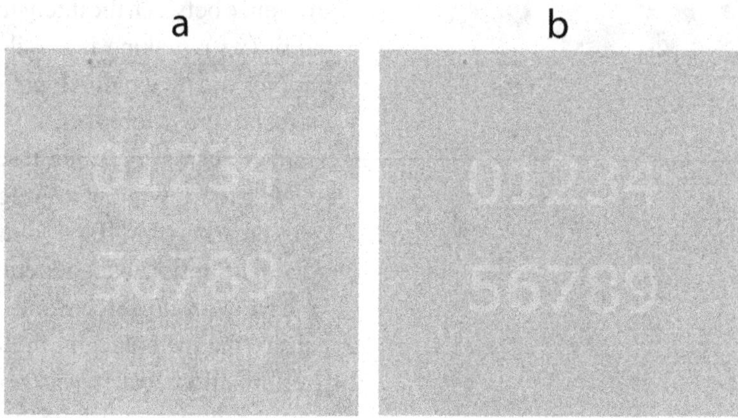

Figure 22. AF pattern (M100%): (a) $pr_1(x,y)$, (b) $pr_0(x,y)$

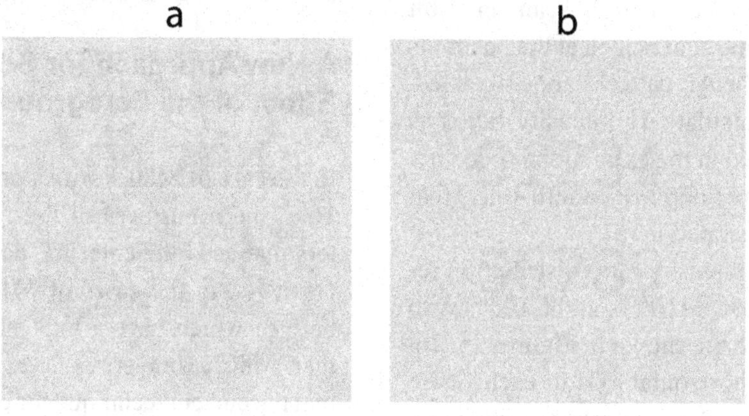

Figure 23. AF pattern (C100% color): (a) $pr_1(x,y)$, (b) $pr_0(x,y)$

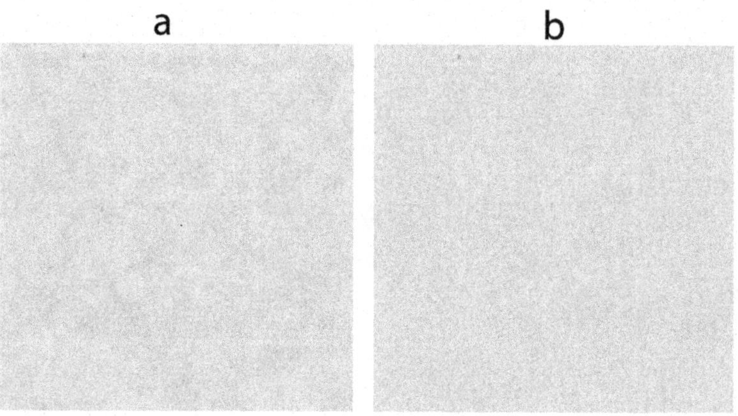

Figure 24. AF pattern-checking sheet

pr1(x,y) Data No.1	pr0(x,y) Data No.1	pr1(x,y) Data No.2
pr0(x,y) Data No.2	pr1(x,y) Data No.3	pr0(x,y) Data No.3
pr1(x,y) Data No.4	pr0(x,y) Data No.4	pr1(x,y) Data No.5
pr0(x,y) Data No.5	pr1(x,y) Data No.6	pr0(x,y) Data No.6
pr1(x,y) Data No.7	pr0(x,y) Data No.7	pr1(x,y) Data No.8
pr0(x,y) Data No.8	pr1(x,y) Data No.9	pr0(x,y) Data No.9
pr1(x,y) Data No.10	pr0(x,y) Data No.10	pr1(x,y) Data No.11

technique that removes the change in gray density level by separating the foreground components from the scanned color AF pattern used to be gray scanned (Kaneda, Kito, & Iwamura, 2011). The generation procedure for AF patterns does not need to be changed. The updated extraction procedure is as follows.

Extraction Procedure Using Our New Approach

In this section, we describe the extraction procedure for our proposed technique for color AF patterns. The reference pattern s(x,y) created during the generation procedure is used as originally generated.

1. Scan and perform the imaging of the paper, on which the color AF pattern p(x, y) (for information embedding, $pr_1(x,y)$ and $pr_0(x,y)$) will be printed in RGB, and divide the image into 0.5-square-inch areas.
2. Convert the color AF pattern image into CMYK and extract the cyan, magenta, and yellow components.
3. Define gray density level thresholds c, m, and y with values in the range 0–1, and create new image components by setting the pixel gray density levels to zero to be greater than c, m, and y for the cyan, magenta, and yellow components, respectively. Below, we will explain in detail the reason for setting up the thresholds c, m, and y.
4. Convert the images to gray scale and perform an automatic level adjustment for the converted images, storing the result in the form p'(x,y).
5. Perform steps (c)–(f) of the extraction procedure, calculating an intensity ratio and extracting information.

The following experiment verifies the validity of this proposed technique.

1. *Equipment and basic parameters.* The equipment is the same as that used in the last section, except for the addition of RGB (24 bits, 3 × 8 bits) to the scanning specifications. The basic specifications are also the same.
2. *Experiment method.* We used steps (1)–(3) from the previous section to generate the color AF pattern. We also created a new

Figure 25. Intensity ratio (M80%)

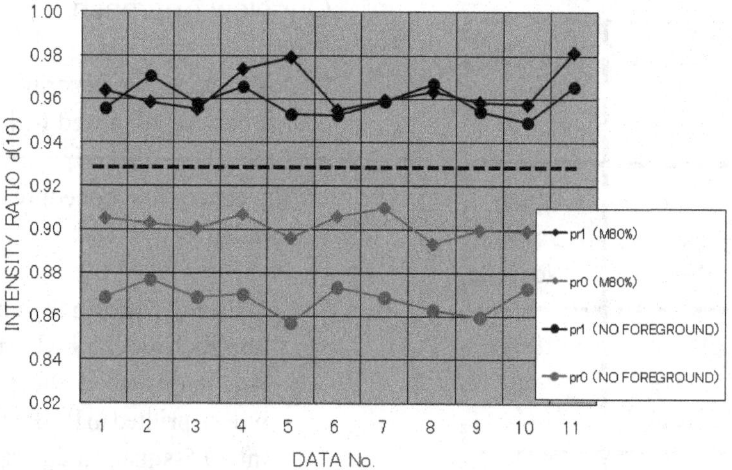

Figure 26. Intensity ratio (M100%)

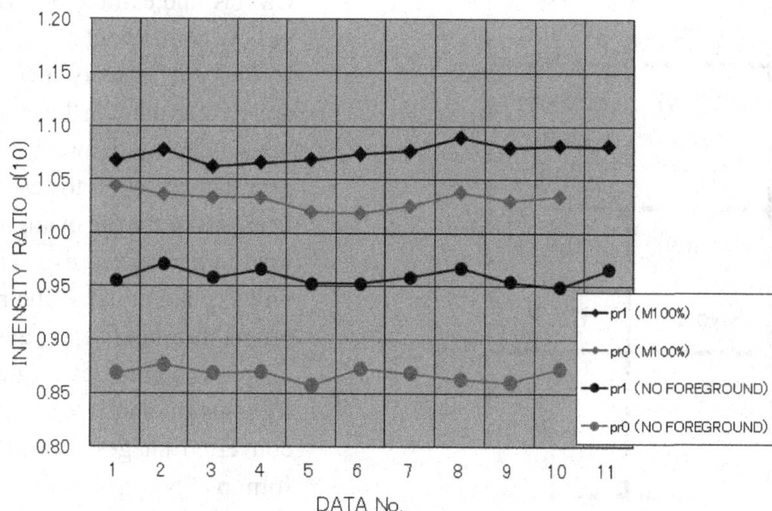

Figure 27. Intensity ratio (C100%)

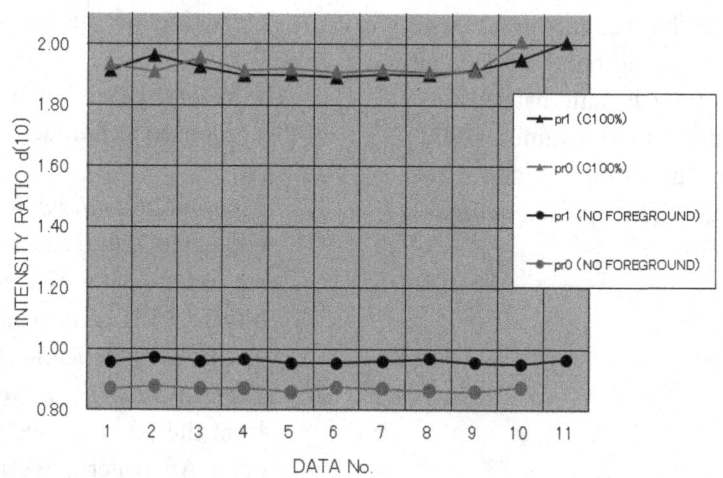

color AF pattern by adding C100%+M100% to M100% and C100%. The new color AF patterns are shown in Figure 28.

In the extraction procedure, we used the IQSmart2 to scan the square inch position, at which each color AF pattern is embedded. Then, 21 intensity ratios were calculated using the reference pattern s(x, y) from the last section.

3. Result

a. The thresholds for the C100% foreground used for extraction were

c = 0.1 (10%), m = 1, and y = 1

with the results shown in Figure 29. The horizontal axis corresponds to the data numbers in Figure 24. Because the difference in the intensity ratio between $pr_1(x, y)$ and $pr_0(x, y)$ is sufficiently large, it is clear that information can be extracted from the C100% color AF pattern.

b. The thresholds for the M100% foreground used for extraction were

c = 1, m = 0.1 (10%), and y = 1

with the results shown in Figure 30. It is clear that we can extract information from the M100% color AF pattern.

c. The thresholds for the C100% + M100% foreground used for extraction were

c = 0.1 (10%). m = 0.1 (10%), and y = 1

with the results shown in Figure 31. It is clear that we can extract information from the C100% + M100% color AF pattern.

d. We also performed an experiment to determine whether our proposed technique can be applied without a foreground. Using a gray-scale image converted from the scanned RGB color AF patterns $pr_1(x,y)$ and $pr_0(x,y)$ shown in Figure 20, we calculated the intensity ratios. The result in Figure 32 shows that it is possible to discern the AF patterns $pr_1(x,y)$ and $pr_0(x,y)$ without a foreground.

Figure 28. New color AF patterns (after adding C100% + M100%): (a) $pr_1(x,y)$, (b) $pr_0(x,y)$

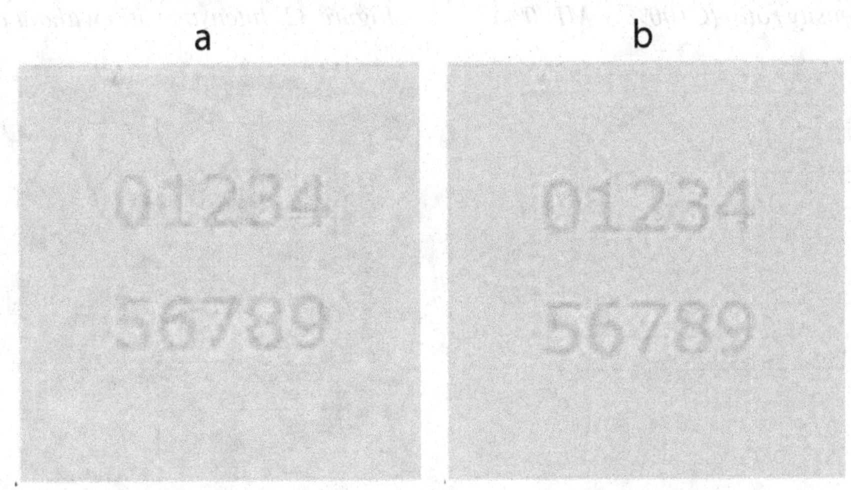

Figure 29. Intensity ratio (C100%)

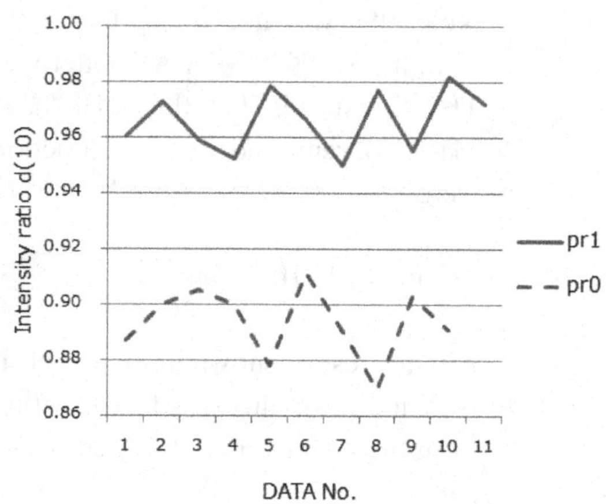

Figure 30. Intensity ratio (M100%)

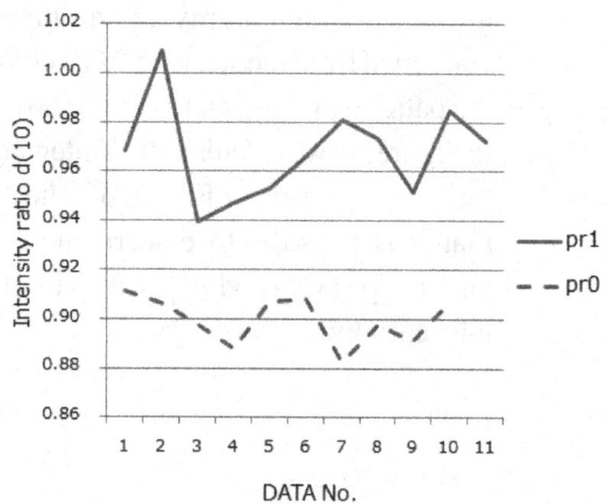

Discussion

The aim of our proposed technique is to scan with color and delete the foreground. Figures 33 and 34, which we will use to explain the process, reproduce the histograms of the cyan component of the C100% color AF pattern $pr_1(x,y)$ from Figure 28a and the no foreground AF pattern $pr_1(x,y)$ from Figure 20a. The horizontal axis shows the gray density level for 8 bits that has been normalized from 0 to 1, and the vertical axis shows the number of accumulated pixels. Comparing the normalized gray density levels in these histograms, we see that more cyan components are above 0.1 in the color AF pattern than in the no foreground AF pattern. Therefore, since it can be assumed that 0.1 or more portions were influenced by the cyan foreground, a stable extraction from the intensity ratio can be achieved by eliminating the portion of the normalized density that is greater than or equal to 0.1. Figure 35 shows the color-scanned C100% color AF pattern for $pr_1(x,y)$ in 0.5 square inch areas, the reconstructed image based on normalized density values of 0.1 or greater for the deleted cyan component, and the image that has been converted into gray scale. It is clear that the visual effect of the foreground has been removed

Figure 31. Intensity ratio (C100% + M100%)

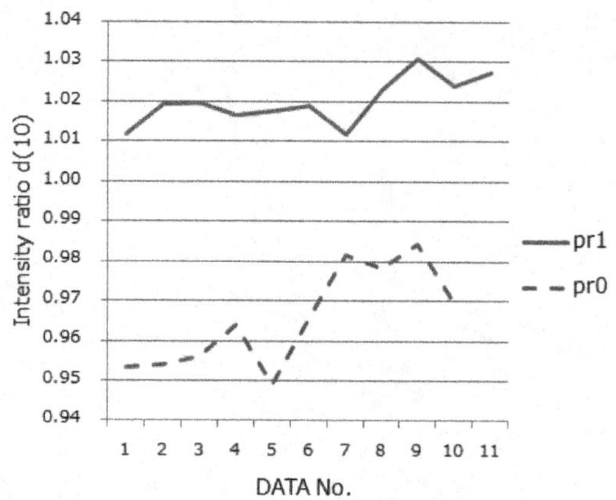

Figure 32. Intensity ratio without a foreground

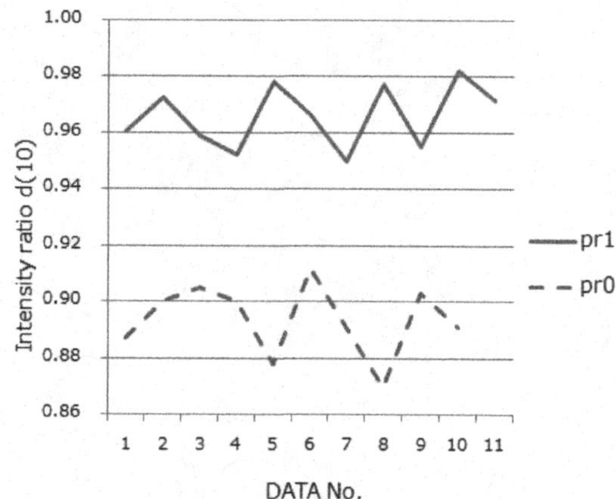

Figure 33. Histogram of the cyan component for $pr_1(x,y)$ with no foreground

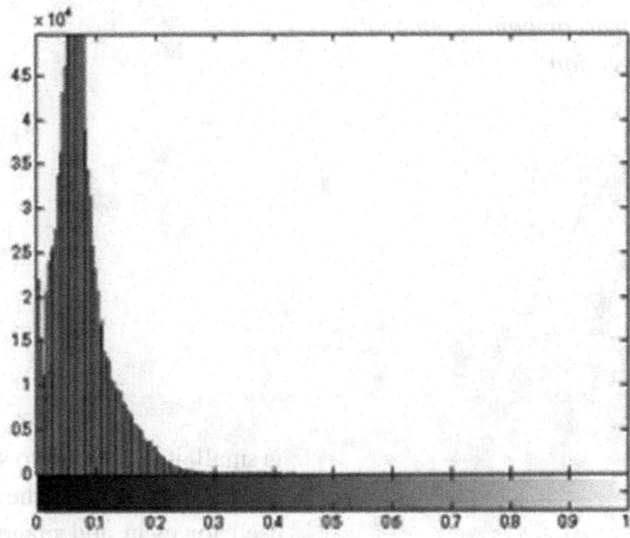

Figure 34. Histogram of the cyan component for $pr_1(x,y)$ with C100%

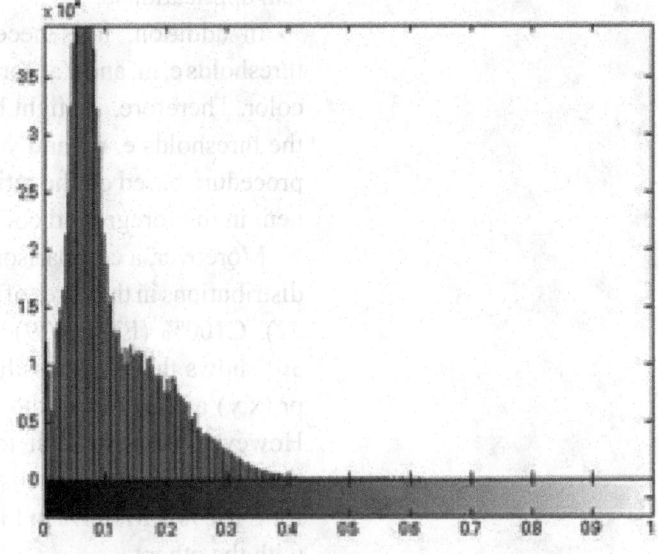

and results in the difference between the intensity ratio distributions shown in Figures 27 and 29. The same results hold for the magenta foreground.

However, the reflection factor for the yellow foreground is close to the original reflection factor of the paper, and as a consequence, the differences between the relevant density distributions are small. Therefore, it is difficult to detect yellow components when scanning. Figures 36 and 37 show the actual result. Figure 36 shows the image with Y100%-colored characters as the foreground of the AF pattern $pr_1(x,y)$, and Figure 37 shows

Figure 35. Process of removing the foreground C100% image for $pr_1(x,y)$: (a) before cyan component removal, (b) after cyan component removal, (c) after gray-scale conversion

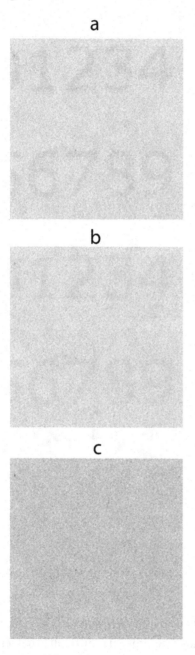

the histogram of the yellow component of the image in the 0.5-square-inch area. Because the histogram for the yellow component in Figure 37 is small, it is difficult to separate the background and foreground using the same technique that was used for cyan and magenta. However, because the color mixture CMY (C100% + M100% + Y100%) is frequently used for black in actual print documents, this problem must be solved for real applications.

Figure 36. Y100% color AF pattern for $pr_1(x\ y)$

In addition, it is necessary to change the thresholds c, m, and y according to the foreground color. Therefore, it might be necessary to adjust the thresholds c, m, and y in the new extraction procedure based on the ratio of the color component in the foreground color.

Moreover, a comparison of the intensity ratio distributions in the cases of no foreground (Figure 32), C100% (Figure 29), and M100% (Figure 30) shows that it is possible to discern between $pr_1(x,y)$ and $pr_0(x,y)$ with a common threshold. However, it is difficult to identify a common threshold when the intensity ratio distributions for C100% + M100% in Figure 31 are compared with the others.

Based on these observations, even if the thresholds c, m, and y are increased (in the case of a mixed color) and an applicable component can be eliminated using these thresholds, the difference between the densities of the foreground and background patterns is not sufficient to break down the distribution of the intensity ratio, but it may slightly affect on the intensity ratio.

Figure 37. Histogram of the yellow component

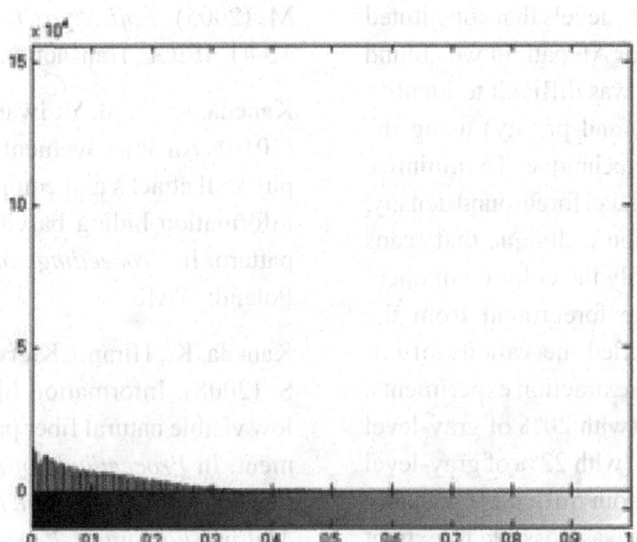

CONCLUSION AND FUTURE RESEARCH

In this chapter, we introduced two novel information hiding techniques for paper media that have several advantages over previous conventional techniques.

First, we described a single dot pattern scheme. Then, through several experiments, we established its superiority with respect to the visual quality of the document, information hiding capacity, and foreground robustness with a reasonable embedding area. In particular, an intensive experiment to verify robustness achieved an ER of 80.56% with an 88963 bit information hiding capacity for an A4 size document. Moreover, it was possible to embed a dot between characters to increase the robustness cutoff for the foreground portion of a document. In addition, we were able to create embedded printed documents with minimal incongruity. The ER was maintained at 80.23% with 3% more information hiding capacity than the case in which no dots were embedded between characters.

The ER for an A4 size document with a foreground object was 18% lower than the rate for a name card size document. We believe this was caused by missing dots in the foreground, resulting in different OCR results for printing and scanning. Moreover, because the foreground part cannot be accurately examined with graphs and figures, there are character recognition errors and information cannot be extracted correctly.

Next, we described an artificial fiber pattern scheme and proved its robustness through carefully designed experiments. We explained the information embedding and extraction procedures using the AF pattern. Then we identified the basic parameters: the cutoff frequencies $r_1 = 2$ (cpi) and $r_0 = 20$ (cpi), the adjustment factor $\alpha = 1/2$, and the integration radius R = 10 (cpi). We verified the equipment dependence and robustness against several physical attacks: distortion, eraser, tape-banding, and add-on.

In order to verify the robustness of the characters in the AF pattern, we defined characters with AF patterns using different (colored) gray density levels from that of the background AF pattern, calling these character patterns "color AF patterns." The robustness of the technique for foreground characters was verified using a color AF pattern, in which the foreground contains 16%

gray level in the character. However, the foreground robustness for gray levels that constituted 20% and 22% of the color AF pattern was found to be insufficient, and it was difficult to identify the AF patterns $pr_1(x,y)$ and $pr_0(x,y)$ using the conventional extraction technique. To minimize the influence of the high-level foreground density, we proposed an extraction technique that scans by color and removes only the color component that is applicable to the foreground from the histogram. We then verified the validity of our proposed technique with extraction experiments. In the cases of M100% (with 20% of gray-level conversion) and C100% (with 22% of gray-level conversion), which are both difficult to visually discern, we found that it was possible to extract the information from the color AF pattern using our proposed technique.

We plan to improve our single dot pattern technique so that it is applicable to foreground objects such as graphs and figures, in addition to characters. It is also necessary to devise an error-correcting code to improve the overall accuracy. For the AF pattern technique, we plan improvements to make the scanning of both the yellow components and the color AF pattern for the color mixture possible without extraction problems.

Finally, we would like to continue to make our proposed techniques available for practical purposes.

REFERENCES

Bender, W., Gruhl, D., Morimoto, N., & Lu, A. (1996). Techniques for data hiding. *IBM Systems Journal*, *35*(3-4), 313–336. doi:10.1147/sj.353.0313

Fujii, Y., Nakano, K., Echizen, I., & Yoshiura, H. (2005). *Method of watermarking for binary images*. US Patent 2005 0 025 333. Washington, DC: US Patent Office.

Ito, K., Soda, H., Ihara, F., Kimura, T., & Fuse, M. (2005). *Fuji Xerox technical report, No.15*, 32-41. IEICE Transactions.

Kaneda, K., Fujii, Y., Iwamura, K., & Hangai, S. (2010). An improvement of robustness against physical attacks and equipment independence in information hiding based on the artificial fiber pattern. In *Proceedings of WAIS-2010*. Krakow, Poland: WAIS.

Kaneda, K., Hirano, K., Iwamura, K., & Hangai, S. (2008). Information hiding method utilizing low visible natural fiber pattern for printed document. In *Proceedings of the 2008 International Conference on Intelligent Information Hiding and Multimedia Signal Processing, IIHMSP-2008-IS05-007*. IIHMSP.

Kaneda, K., Kito, Y., & Iwamura, K. (2011). Information hiding based on the artificial fiber pattern with improved robustness against foreground objects. In *Proceedings of the 2011 International Conference on Intelligent Information Hiding and Multimedia Signal Processing, IIH-MSP-2011-233*. IIHMSP.

Kaneda, K., Nagai, F., Iwamura, K., & Hangai, S. (2008). A study of information hiding performance using simple dot pattern with different tile sizes. In *Proceedings of the 2008 International Conference on Intelligent Information Hiding and Multimedia Signal Processing, IIHMSP-2008-IS05-008*. IIHMSP.

Kaneda, K., Tachibana, Y., & Iwamura, K. (2011). Information hiding based on a single dot pattern method with improved extraction and robustness against foreground objects. In *Proceedings of the 2011 International Conference on Intelligent Information Hiding and Multimedia Signal Processing, IIH-MSP-2011-238*. IIHMSP.

NPO Japan Network Security Association. (2010). *2009 investigation report about a year information security incident*. Tokyo, Japan: NPO.

Palo Alto Research Center Incorporated. (2012). *Website.* Retrieved from http://www.microglyphs.com/english/html/dgtech.shtml

Suzaki, M., & Sudo, M. (2005). A watermark embedding and extracting method for printed documents. *ECJC*, *88*(7), 43–51.

Tow, R. F. (1994). *Methods and means for embedding machine readable digital data in halftone images*. US Patent 5 315 098. Washington, DC: US Patent Office.

Chapter 13
Watermarking for Still Images Using a Computation of the Watermark Weighting Factor and the Human Visual System in the DCT Domain

O-Hyung Kwon
Sogang University, Korea & ETRI, Korea

Rae-Hong Park
Sogang University, Korea

ABSTRACT

In this chapter, the authors propose a Discrete Cosine Transform (DCT)-based watermarking method using the calculation of the watermark weighting factor and the Human Visual System (HVS) for the given peak signal to noise ratio of still image as well as the specified length of watermarks to be inserted. Using the energy relationship of the DCT, they derive the equation that directly computes the watermark weighting factor in the DCT domain. In addition, the authors propose a digital watermarking method for still images, in which the HVS is used in the DCT domain. The modulation transfer function of the HVS model is employed to increase the invisibility of the inserted watermark in images. Experimental results show that the proposed watermarking method is an effective objective evaluation method to compare the performances of watermarking algorithms.

DOI: 10.4018/978-1-4666-2217-3.ch013

INTRODUCTION

Recently, a huge usage of video on demand services and social network services has increased the commercial potential of providing multimedia resources through various digital networks such as the Internet. However, it is possible to illegally copy and transfer the digital multimedia to others through the Internet. To prevent this, the digital watermark methods were suggested (Vahedi, et al., 2012; Jayanthi, et al., 2011; Patra, et al., 2010; Cox, et al., 1996; Craver, et al., 1998; Barni, et al., 1997; Pitas, 1998; Motwani, et al., 2010). The owner of the digital image or video can insert his/her own particular signal (watermark) into digital image or video to insist ownership, where the watermark can be a random number with a specific seed number and size or a specific code identifying the owner. If a malicious user gets and transfers this image or video to others, the owner can extract the watermark, which has been inserted into the image or video using a specific watermark method and can insist the ownership who is the real owner of that image or video. The encryption techniques have been used to protect illegal reproduction of the digital multimedia. However, the piracy problem could not be solved perfectly by this method because nobody can insist copyrights or ownership of the decrypted digital multimedia contents. To solve this problem, many digital watermarking techniques have been studied to protect the ownership of the digital contents (Cox, et al., 1996, 1997; Cox & Miller, 1997; Craver, et al., 1996, 1998; Barni, et al., 1997; Pitas, 1998; Piva, et al., 1997; Kwon, et al., 1999, 2006). The digital watermarking is an information hiding technique to insert secret data into the original contents. The secret data that is information including an ownership can be easily extracted from the watermarked digital multimedia contents and it can be decided who the right owner of the watermarked digital contents is. The main requirements of digital watermarking method to protect the copyright of a digital image or video are:

- Watermarks cannot be distinguished visibly after inserting it into original image or video
- It is impossible to statistically detect the watermark information
- Watermarks can be detected after general signal processing
- Watermarks can be extracted even under malicious attacks (Cox, et al., 1997)

The digital watermarking methods can be categorized into text watermarking, still image watermarking, video watermarking, and audio watermarking according to where watermarks will be inserted. The digital watermarking method can satisfy the requirements mentioned above and there are two kinds of watermarking methods for still image watermarking to satisfy those requirements: one is to insert watermark in the spatial domain and the other in the frequency domain. Watermarking methods in the spatial domain have a merit that the watermark can be inserted and detected easily. Frequency domain watermarking methods have been studied because they are more robust than the spatial domain watermarking against several malicious attacks and noise.

A method was proposed, in which the identification string was inserted in digital audio signals by substituting Least Significant Bit (LSB) of audio samples with identification bit strings (Schyndel, et al., 1994). The LSB of insignificant bit means the smallest audio signal level that human can hardly distinguish. This method was applied to two-dimensional (2-D) still image, however it turns out that this method has a drawback of easy forgery.

Caronni proposed a method by inserting the geometrical patterns into the quantized luminance level that can be hardly distinguished visibly (Caronni, 1995). However, the method of inserting watermark in the spatial domain can be easily attacked by filtering and re-digitization and thus has weakness against geometrical transformation and cropping especially.

Recently, Shrivastava et al. proposed a general method to improve the robustness of watermark by exploiting the masking effect of surface roughness on watermark in three-dimensional (3-D) image (Shrivastava & Choubey, 2011). Motwani et al. proposed a digital right management system for 3-D graphics that makes use of biometric watermarking technology (Motwani, et al., 2010).

Agarwal et al. and Kwon et al. proposed methods to improve the invisibility of the inserted watermark using the HVS (Agarwal, et al., 2011; Kwon & Park, 1999) and Vahedi et al. proposed a method for color image in the wavelet domain (Vahedi, et al., 2012).

In this chapter, a watermarking algorithm (Kwon, et al., 1999) for still image is reviewed and a computation of the watermark weighting factor in the Discrete Cosine Transform (DCT) domain (Kwon & Park, 2006) is described. The contribution of this chapter is to propose an objective evaluation method to compare watermarking methods by maintaining the same Peak Signal to Noise Ratio (PSNR) value after inserting watermark. In addition, the watermarking process can be automated using the computation of the watermark weighting factor in the DCT domain.

This chapter is organized as follows: in the second section, 2-D DCT and energy relationship, Modulation Transfer Function (MTF), and watermarking method in the frequency domain used in the proposed algorithm are reviewed. We use MTF using the HVS in the watermark inserting process in order to increase the invisibility of the inserted watermark. In the next section, a computation of the watermark weighting factor for the specified PSNR of still image and still image watermarking in the DCT domain using the HVS are described. In the fourth section, performance comparisons of the proposed algorithm with Cox et al.'s algorithm (Cox, et al., 1997) are given. The chapter is concluded in the final section.

BACKGROUND

The watermarking method can be applied in the spatial domain and the transformed domain (Mario, et al., 2006). Most of the watermarking methods are studied in the transformed domain because the spatial domain methods are not robust against various attacks. The DCT is more frequently used to compress images and videos rather than the Fourier transform, or the wavelet transform in many applications and the DCT is used as a basic technique to compress images or videos in moving picture experts group standard. So, we propose the watermarking method in DCT domain. In addition, our methods can be easily extended to the Fourier transform based method and the wavelet transform based method. For this reason, we review the 2-D DCT and energy relationship between the watermark weighting factor and the PSNR, and describe the MTF to increase the invisibility of the inserted watermark. Next, we review Cox et al.'s algorithm (Cox, et al., 1997) proposed in the DCT domain.

2-D DCT and Energy Relationship

The 2-D DCT is defined in Box 1, where $f(i, j)$ and $F(u, v)$ denote pixel values in the spatial domain and DCT coefficients, respectively, and N is the size of original image. In addition, the Inverse DCT (IDCT) is defined in Box 2.

The energy relationship between the spatial and DCT domains can be expressed as in Box 3, where E represents the energy of the original image.

Box 1. 2-D DCT

$$F(u,v) = \begin{cases} \sum_{i=0}^{N-1}\sum_{j=0}^{N-1} f(i,j)\ \cos\frac{\pi}{2N}u(2i+1)\ \cos\frac{\pi}{2N}v(2j+1), & \text{for } 0 \le u,v \le N-1 \\ 0, & \text{otherwise} \end{cases} \quad (1)$$

Box 2. Inverse DCT

$$f(i,j) = \begin{cases} \sum_{u=0}^{N-1}\sum_{v=0}^{N-1} p(u)p(v)F(u,v)\ \cos\frac{\pi}{2N}u(2i+1)\ \cos\frac{\pi}{2N}v(2j+1), & \text{for } 0 \le i,j \le N-1 \\ 0, & \text{otherwise} \end{cases} \quad (2)$$

$$p(u) = \begin{cases} \frac{1}{2}, & u = 0 \\ 1, & \text{otherwise.} \end{cases} \quad (3)$$

Box 3. Energy between spatial and DCT domains

$$E = \sum_{i=0}^{N-1}\sum_{j=0}^{N-1} f^2(i,j) = \frac{1}{4N^2}\sum_{u=0}^{N-1}\sum_{v=0}^{N-1} p(u)\ p(v)\ F^2(u,v) \quad (4)$$

MTF

Using the assumption that the HVS is isotropic, the HVS was modeled as a nonlinear point transformation followed by the MTF of the form (Chitprasert & Rao, 1990):

$$H(f) = a(b + cf)\exp(-cf)^d \quad (5)$$

where *a*, *b*, *c*, and *d* are constants. The frequency variable *f* in cycles/degree of the MTF needs to be changed to the normalized spatial frequency f_n in cycles/sample or cycles/pixel, which requires a conversion factor f_s :

$$f(\text{cycles/degree}) = f_n(\text{cycles/pel})\ f_s(\text{pels/degree}) \quad (6)$$

where f_n (the corresponding frequency in polar form) is given by:

$$f_n = \frac{\sqrt{u^2+v^2}}{2N}, \quad 0 \le \quad u,v \le N-1 \quad (7)$$

Thus, Equation 5 can be converted into 2-D form:

$$H(u,v) = a\left(b + c\,\frac{\sqrt{u^2+v^2}}{2N}f_s\right)\exp\left(-c\,\frac{\sqrt{u^2+v^2}}{2N}f_s\right)^d \quad (8)$$

Watermarking Methods in the Frequency Domain

Cox et al. (1997) proposed an algorithm that inserts watermarks on visibly important DCT coefficients. In this algorithm, the random vector x, $x = x_1, \cdots\cdots, x_n$, which has normal distribution with zero mean and unit variance is used. Also, Cox et al. (1997) proposed three equations to produce the watermarking image I' based on the original image I. Those equations are expressed as:

$$i_j' = i_j + \alpha x_j \quad (9)$$

$$i_j' = i_j(1 + \alpha x_j) \quad (10)$$

$$i_j' = i_j e^{\alpha x_j} \quad (11)$$

where α represents watermark weighting factor, i_j and i_j' are j-th visually important frequency component and watermarked frequency component, respectively. Equation 9 is used in case where the difference between the smallest DCT coefficient and the largest DCT coefficient of the selected DCT coefficients is small. Equations 10 and 11 have the similar characteristic when αx_j is small, and in most cases, these two equations are used to insert the watermark into images.

To decide whether or not any watermark is inserted into a given image, the similarity function using the normalized correlation coefficient can be expressed as:

$$sim(x, x^*) = \frac{x \otimes x^*}{\sqrt{x^* \otimes x^*}} \quad (12)$$

where x and x^* are the original watermark and a possibly corrupted extracted watermark, respectively, and $\otimes$ is the inner product operator between x and x^*

PREVIOUS WORKS

Overview

The previous watermarking algorithms for still image are described. Kwon et al.'s approaches (Kwon, et al., 1999, 2006) are based on an existing MTF (Chitprasert & Rao, 1990) and DCT domain algorithm (Cox, et al., 1997). They applied the existing DCT domain algorithm to the MTF and directly calculated the watermark weighting factor in the DCT domain.

Their algorithm consists of three steps: watermark insertion with the MTF, calculation of the watermark weighting factor, and watermark detection. First, the original image is transformed to the DCT domain and watermark is inserted using the MTF function. In the step of calculation of the watermark weighting factor, they used the equation to calculate the watermark weighting factor in the DCT domain with a given PSNR and watermark length. Finally, both the contaminated image and the original image are transformed to the DCT domain, and the watermarks are extracted from both sets of DCT coefficients. So, they can decide the owner of the contaminated image by comparing the inserted watermark with the extracted watermark. Figure 1 shows the overall block diagram of the watermark insertion and detection process.

Cox et al.'s method (Cox, et al., 1997) has a problem to decide the watermark weighting factor heuristically to insert watermarks into the

Figure 1. Overall block diagram of watermarking process in the DCT domain: (a) insertion process, (b) detection process

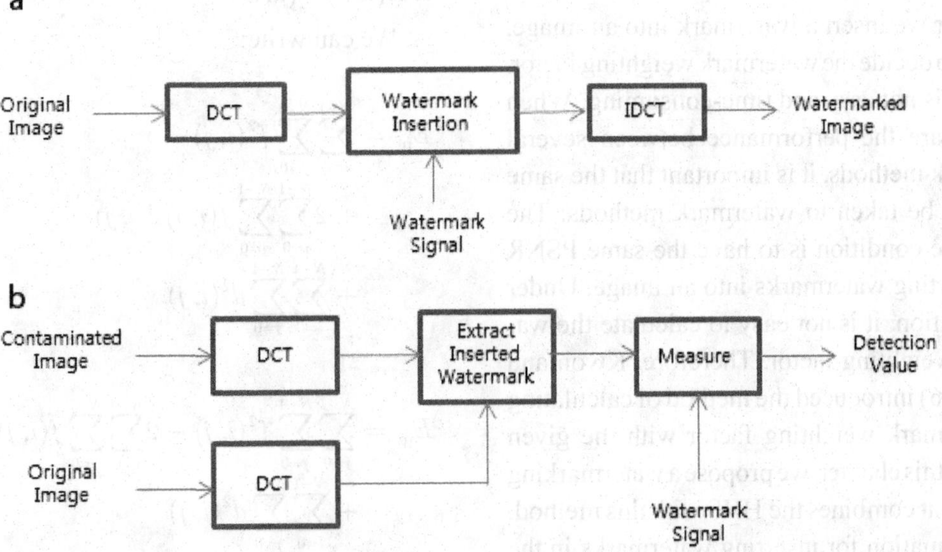

images. To solve this problem, we derived the equation to calculate watermark weighting factor with the given PSNR and apply this equation to Cox et al.'s method (Cox, et al., 1997). Moreover, to increase the invisibility of watermark inserted, we modified the Equation 10 by Cox et al.'s method (Cox, et al., 1997) with Equations 13 and 14 using HVS.

Watermark Insertion

In this process as shown in Figure 1a, the main concept of the encoding process is to insert the watermark into the DCT coefficients. As in Cox et al.'s method (Cox, et al., 1997), their watermark $W = [w_1, w_2, \ldots w_M]$ consists of a pseudo-random sequence of length M, where each value w_k is a random number having a normal distribution with zero mean and unit variance for any k satisfying $1 \leq k \leq M$.

The procedure of the DCT based watermarking insertion algorithm using the HVS is described as follows (Kwon, et al., 1999). In the first step, the original image $I(x, y)$ is transformed to the DCT domain. In the second step, they choose the set of the transformed 2-D DCT coefficients, where the size of the set is M, and each coefficient has the largest absolute value except for the DC component. In the third step, the watermark is inserted to the M DCT coefficients using

$$I'_{wk}(u, v) = I'_k(u, v)\ (1 + \beta_k(u, v)\ w_k) \tag{13}$$

$$\beta_k(u, v) = \frac{\alpha}{H(u, v)} \tag{14}$$

and the watermarked image I'_{wk} is obtained from the original image I'_k, where $I'_k(u, v)$ and $I'_{wk}(u, v)$ denote k-th non-watermarked and watermarked DCT coefficient selected in the second step, respectively, and $\beta_k(u, v)$ is a modified watermark weighting factor using the HVS.

Calculation of the Watermark Weighting Factor

Whenever we insert a watermark into an image, we have to decide the watermark weighting factor. This step is not easy and time-consuming. When we compare the performance between several watermark methods, it is important that the same condition be taken to watermark methods. The reasonable condition is to have the same PSNR after inserting watermarks into an image. Under this condition, it is not easy to calculate the watermark weighting factor. Therefore, Kwon and Park (2006) introduced the method of calculating the watermark weighting factor with the given PSNR. In this chapter, we propose a watermarking method that combines the HVS with this method.

The equation for inserting watermarks in the DCT-based watermarking methods is expressed in the 2-D space as:

$$F_W(u,v) = F(u,v) \ + \alpha \ w(u,v) \ F(u,v) \tag{15}$$

where α and $w(u,v)$ represent the watermark weighting factor and the watermark to be inserted at (u,v)-th component in the DCT domain, respectively. Then, we can write an auxiliary equation:

$$F'_W(u,v) = F(u,v) \ - \alpha \ w(u,v) \ F(u,v) \tag{16}$$

by replacing $w(u,v)$ with $-w(u,v)$ in Equation 15. By inverse transformation of Equations 15 and 16, we obtain:

$$f_W(i,j) = f(i,j) \ + d(i,j) \tag{17}$$

$$f'_W(i,j) = f(i,j) \ - d(i,j) \tag{18}$$

where $d(i,j)$ represents the difference image in the spatial domain, or equivalently the IDCT of $\alpha \ w(u,v) \ F(u,v)$.

We can write:

$$\begin{aligned} E_W = & \sum_{i=0}^{N-1}\sum_{j=0}^{N-1} f^2(i,j) \\ & + 2\sum_{i=0}^{N-1}\sum_{j=0}^{N-1} f(i,j)\, d(i,j) \\ & + \sum_{i=0}^{N-1}\sum_{j=0}^{N-1} d^2(i,j) \end{aligned} \tag{19}$$

$$\begin{aligned} E'_W = & \sum_{i=0}^{N-1}\sum_{j=0}^{N-1} f^2(i,j) - 2\sum_{i=0}^{N-1}\sum_{j=0}^{N-1} f(i,j)\, d(i,j) \\ & + \sum_{i=0}^{N-1}\sum_{j=0}^{N-1} d^2(i,j) \end{aligned} \tag{20}$$

where E_W and E'_W denote the energies of the $N \times N$ images $f_W(i,j)$ and $f'_W(i,j)$ respectively, computed in the spatial domain, when watermarks of $w(u,v)$ and $-w(u,v)$ are inserted in the DCT domain. Also, using Equations 19 and 20, we have:

$$\sum_{i=0}^{N-1}\sum_{j=0}^{N-1} d^2(i,j) = \frac{1}{2}(E_W \ + E'_W) - E \tag{21}$$

where E signifies the energy of the original image $f(i,j)$

Moreover, we can derive the energy E_W of $f_W(i,j)$ in the DCT domain as in Box 4.

In the same way, E'_W of $f'_W(i,j)$ can be expressed as in Box 5.

If S and E_W are defined as:

$$S = \frac{3}{4}F_W^2(0,0) + \frac{1}{2}\sum_{v=1}^{N-1} F_W^2(0,v) + \frac{1}{2}\sum_{u=1}^{N-1} F_W^2(u,0) \tag{24}$$

Box 4. Derivation of energy in the DCT domain

$$E_W = \frac{1}{4N^2}\left\{\sum_{u=0}^{N-1}\sum_{v=0}^{N-1} F_W(u,v)^2 - \left[\frac{3}{4}F_W^2(0,0) + \frac{1}{2}\sum_{v=1}^{N-1} F_W^2(0,v) + \frac{1}{2}\sum_{u=1}^{N-1} F_W^2(u,0)\right]\right\} \quad (22)$$

Box 5.

$$E'_W = \frac{1}{4N^2}\left\{\sum_{u=0}^{N-1}\sum_{v=0}^{N-1} F'_W(u,v)^2 - \left[\frac{3}{4}F'^{\,2}_W(0,0) + \frac{1}{2}\sum_{v=1}^{N-1} F'^{\,2}_W(0,v) + \frac{1}{2}\sum_{u=1}^{N-1} F'^{\,2}_W(u,0)\right]\right\} \quad (23)$$

$$E_W = \frac{1}{4N^2}\left\{\hat{E}_W - S\right\} \quad (25)$$

The above energy relationship equation is expressed as:

$$E'_W = \frac{1}{4N^2}\left\{\hat{E}'_W - S'\right\} \quad (26)$$

$$E = \frac{1}{4N^2}\left[\hat{E} - S_0\right] \quad (27)$$

where S' and S_0 are computed as:

$$S' = \frac{3}{4}F'^{\,2}_W(0,0) + \frac{1}{2}\sum_{v=1}^{N-1} F'^{\,2}_W(0,v) + \frac{1}{2}\sum_{u=1}^{N-1} F'^{\,2}_W(u,0) \quad (28)$$

$$S_0 = \frac{3}{4}F^2(0,0) + \frac{1}{2}\sum_{v=1}^{N-1} F^2(0,v) + \frac{1}{2}\sum_{u=1}^{N-1} F^2(u,0) \quad (29)$$

Equation 21 can be written as:

$$\sum_{i=0}^{N-1}\sum_{j=0}^{N-1} d^2(i,j) = \frac{1}{4N^2}\left[\frac{1}{2}\left(\hat{E}_W + \hat{E}'_W - S - S'\right) - \left(\hat{E} - S_0\right)\right] \quad (30)$$

and the PSNR in the spatial domain can be expressed as:

$$PSNR = 10\,\log\left(\frac{255^2\,N^2}{\sum_{i=0}^{N-1}\sum_{j=0}^{N-1}\left(f_w(i,j) - f(i,j)\right)^2}\right) = 10\,\log\left[\frac{255^2\,N^2}{\sum_{i=0}^{N-1}\sum_{j=0}^{N-1} d^2(i,j)}\right] \quad (31)$$

Finally, the PSNR of the $N \times N$ watermarked image $f_W(i,j)$ quantized to 8 bits in the spatial domain can be written as:

$$PSNR = 10 \times \log \left[\frac{255^2 N^2}{\frac{1}{4N^2}\left\{\frac{1}{2}\left(\hat{E}_W + \hat{E}_W' - S - S'\right) - \left(\hat{E} - S_0\right)\right\}} \right] \quad (32)$$

Using the energy relationship of the DCT, Kwon et al. derived the equation that directly computes the watermark weighting factor in the DCT domain, without calculating the IDCT when both the desired PSNR in the spatial domain and the length of watermarks to be inserted in the DCT domain are given (Kwon, et al., 2006). In this chapter, Kwon et al.'s method (Kwon, et al., 2006) is used to calculate the weighting factor in the DCT domain using the given PSNR without processing the IDCT. To insert watermark into images or videos, the watermark weighting factor have to be calculated from Equations 13, 14, and 31. Thus, the watermark insertion processing time can be decreased and the watermark insertion process can be automatized by Equation 31. Without using this method, it is required that the watermark weighting factor should be heuristically decided in the initial state of the watermark insertion step, which is time-consuming and bothersome. If we choose a high value of the watermark weighting factor by manually, we have a detection value close to 1 even though there are various attacks against the watermarked images or videos. If we choose a small value of the watermark weighting factor, we cannot extract the inserted watermark from the watermarked and attacked images or videos.

Watermark Detection

The watermark detection process is very similar to the insertion process, as shown in Figure 1b. In the first step of watermarking detection process, the possibly contaminated image or watermarked image is transformed into the DCT domain. In the second step to extract the possibly contaminated watermark, M large coefficients are selected, except for the DC component, from DCT coefficients of an original image. From that information, the watermarks inserted in the insertion process are extracted by comparing DCT coefficients of the original image and the watermarked image. Then, the contaminated watermark is extracted. In the final step, we calculate the similarity between the original watermark W and a possibly corrupted extracted watermark W'_{cw} using Equation 15 (Cox, et al., 1997).

The final step of detection process is to measure the similarity between the original watermark W and a possibly corrupted extracted watermark W'_{cw} (Kwon, et al., 1999). This similarity function is used (Cox, et al., 1997):

$$D = \frac{W'_{cw} \otimes W}{\sqrt{W'_{cw} \otimes W'_{cw}}\ \sqrt{W \otimes W}} \quad (33)$$

If there no attack on the watermarked images, the value of the similarity function by Equation 33 is close to 1. If some malicious attacks such as smoothing and cropping happen to the watermarked image, the value of the similarity function tend to be far from 1. When we compare the performance of watermark methods, it can be concluded that the watermark method having the higher detection value against various attacks is superior to the other methods.

PROPOSED METHOD

Issues and Problems

It is needed to decide the watermark weighting factor or the length of watermarks to be inserted when a watermarking method is employed to protect digital contents (Cox, et al., 1997). However, in DCT-based methods it is difficult to select the optimal weighting factor for the given PSNR of the still image as well as the specified length of watermarks to be inserted. Kwon et al.'s method (Kwon, et al., 2006) is used to calculate the weighting factor in the DCT domain using the given PSNR without processing the IDCT. This method can be applied to other transform methods such as the Discrete Wavelet Transform (DWT). In addition, we use Kwon et al.'s method (Kwon, et al., 1999) in the DCT domain using the HVS in order to increase the invisibility of the inserted watermark. We adopt MTF using the HVS in the watermark inserting process in order to increase the invisibility of the inserted watermark (Agarwa, et al., 2011; Chitprasert, et al., 1990). Before we insert a watermark into an image or video, we modify the watermark weighting factor α with β_k using Equations 8 and 14. In Equation 8, $H(u, v)$ has a relatively high value at the visually sensitive frequencies. Equation 14 means that the MTF is used to adjust the relatively small watermark weighting factor at the visually sensitive DCT coefficients.

Figure 2 shows the proposed watermarking process. In the first step, the desired PSNR after

Figure 2. Proposed watermarking method in the DCT domain: (a) insertion process, (b) detection process

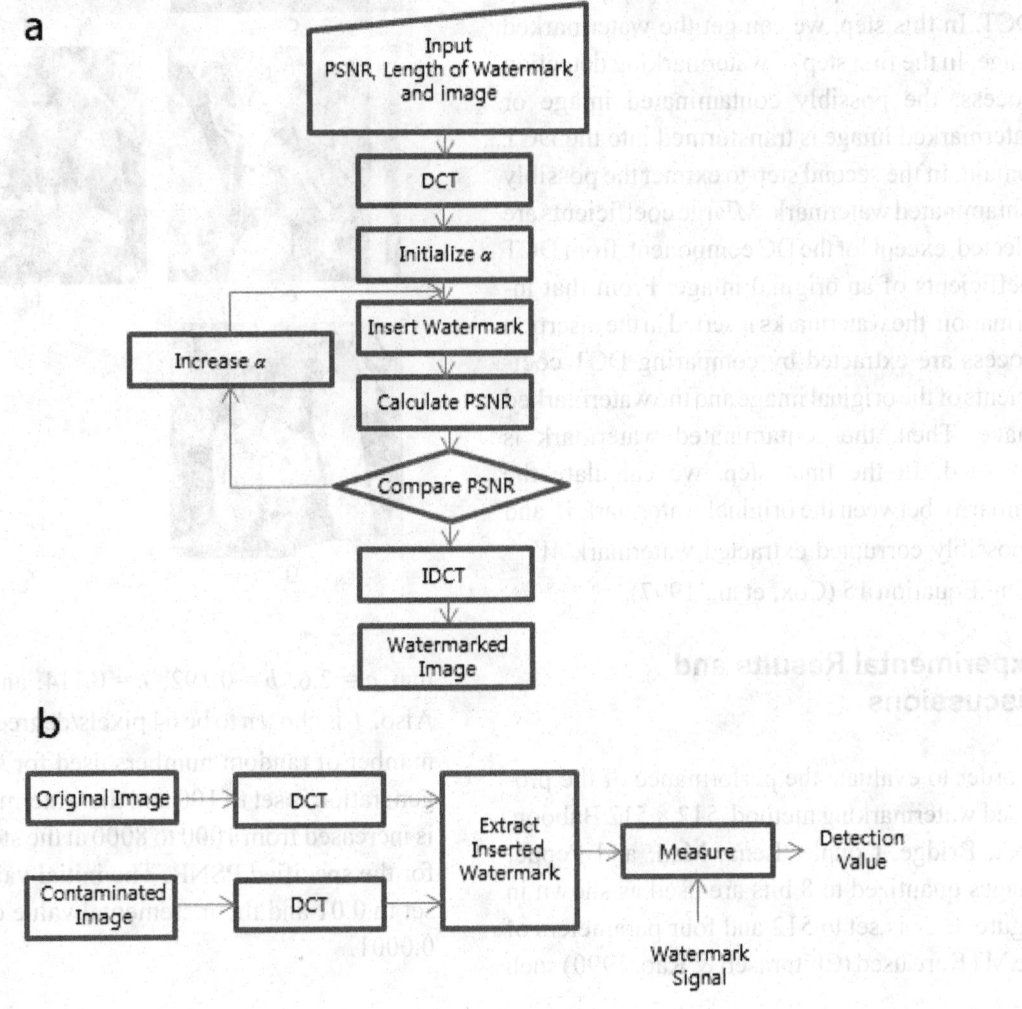

inserting watermark in the original image, the watermark length, and source images are input. In the second step, the original image is transformed into the DCT domain and watermark is inserted into the DCT coefficients using Equations 13 and 14. In this step, we choose the significant DCT coefficients except for the DC coefficient to insert watermarks. In the third step, the PSNR in the DCT domain is calculated by Equation 32 and compared with the desired PSNR in the spatial domain. In this step, if the desired PSNR value is larger than the PSNR value in the DCT domain, α is increased by 0.001 and the second step is repeated again, otherwise, α is stored and the watermark insertion process is terminated. In the final step, the watermarked image is transformed into the spatial domain by performing IDCT. In this step, we can get the watermarked image. In the first step of watermarking detection process, the possibly contaminated image or watermarked image is transformed into the DCT domain. In the second step to extract the possibly contaminated watermark, M large coefficients are selected, except for the DC component, from DCT coefficients of an original image. From that information, the watermarks inserted in the insertion process are extracted by comparing DCT coefficients of the original image and the watermarked image. Then, the contaminated watermark is extracted. In the final step, we calculate the similarity between the original watermark W and a possibly corrupted extracted watermark W'_{cw} using Equation 15 (Cox, et al., 1997).

Figure 3. Original images: (a) Baboon, (b) Boat, (c) Bridge, (d) Couple, (e) Lena, (f) Man, (g) Pepper

Experimental Results and Discussions

In order to evaluate the performance of the proposed watermarking method, 512 × 512 Baboon, Boat, Bridge, Couple, Lena, Man, and Pepper images quantized to 8 bits are used as shown in Figure 3. N is set to 512 and four parameters of the MTF are used (Chitprasert & Rao, 1990) such that $a = 2.6$, $b = 0.192$, $c = 0.114$, and $d = 1.1$. Also, f_s is chosen to be 64 pixels/degree. The seed number of random numbers used for watermark generation is set to 100 and the watermark length is increased from 1000 to 8000 at the step of 1000 for the specified PSNR. The initial value of α is set to 0.01 and the incremental value of is set to 0.0001.

Figure 4 shows the calculated watermark weighting factor after inserting watermark on the Baboon image, where the desired PSNR varies from 30 dB to 50 dB, incremented at the step of 4 dB. In this case, the watermark weighting factor was precisely calculated and the difference of the desired PSNR and the PSNR directly calculated in the DCT domain is very small. In addition, we can get similar results on the other test images and it is observed that the proposed method has merits to increase the invisibility by the HVS and to minimize to calculate the watermark weighting factor. In Figure 5, the length of watermarks are in the first column, the calculated watermark weighting factors are in the second column, and the PSNRs in the DCT domain and in the spatial

Figure 4. Calculated watermark weighting factor (Baboon): (a) as a function of the length of watermarks, (b) as a function of the desired PSNR

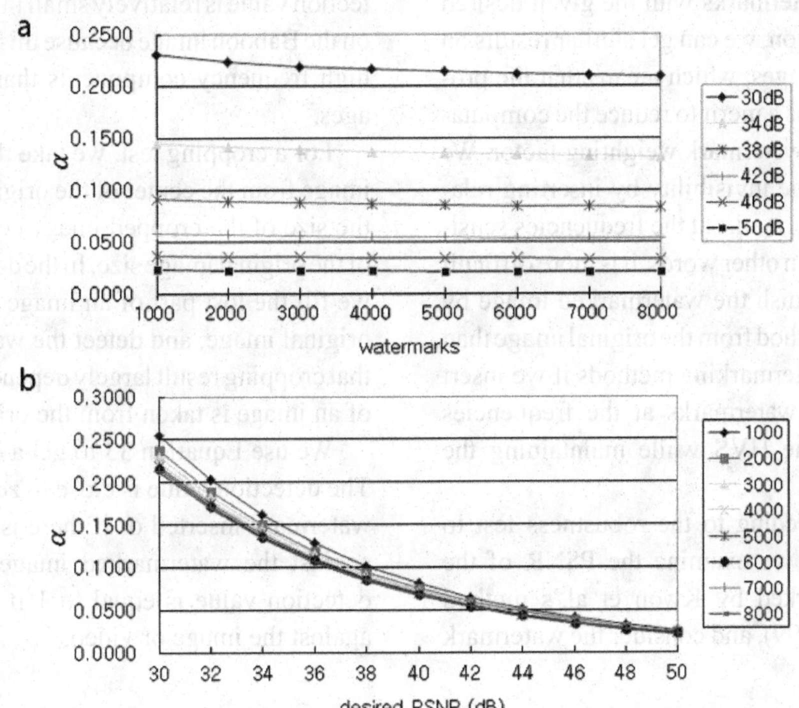

Figure 5. Calculated watermark weighting factor (Pepper, PSNR=40 dB)

Length of watermark	α	PSNR (dB,DCT Domain)	PSNR (dB,Spatial Domain)
1000	0.0478	39.991175	39.938974
2000	0.0470	39.987750	39.934088
3000	0.0466	39.996379	39.943488
4000	0.0464	39.993480	39.937143
5000	0.0463	39.983539	39.928764
6000	0.0462	39.983302	39.933548
7000	0.0461	39.987267	39.935230
8000	0.0460	39.995391	39.942030

domain are in the third and fourth columns, respectively. Figure 5 shows that the watermark weighting factor can be calculated to minimize the difference of the desired PSNR and the PSNR computed in the DCT domain, If we set the incremental value of the watermark weighting factor to value smaller than 0.0001 in this experiment, we can get the watermark weighting factor so that the PSNR after watermarking is very close to the given PSNR. From this experiment, it is shown that the watermark weighting factor does not vary as much as the increment of the length of watermarks with the given desired PSNRs. In addition, we can get similar results on the other test images, which means that the proposed method has a merit to reduce the computation time of the watermark weighting factor. We try to increase the invisibility by inserting relatively small watermarks at the frequencies sensitive to the HVS. In other words, it is more difficult for us to distinguish the watermarked image by the proposed method from the original image than that by other watermarking methods if we insert relatively large watermarks at the frequencies insensitive to the HVS while maintaining the desired PSNR.

Before proceeding to the robustness test to various attacks, we examine the PSNR of the image watermarked by Kwon et al.'s method (Kwon, et al., 1999), and consider the watermark detection value as a function of the PSNR for the cases without any attacks. Figure 6 shows the watermark detection result for seven test images without any attack, where the length of watermarks is 1000. The similarities are very close to 1 and the inserted watermarks are very well detected.

The watermarked image is filtered with a 3 × 3 lowpass filter and we obtain fairly good results with lowpass filtered images, which are shown in Figure 7 and Figure 8, even though the watermarked images appear a little bit degraded. In addition, Figure 7 shows that the watermark detection value is relatively small in both algorithms on the Baboon image because this image has more high frequency components than other test images.

For a cropping test, we take the watermarked image from the center of the original image, with the size of the cropped image equal to a quarter of the original image size. In the detection process, we fill the lost part of an image with that of the original image, and detect the watermarks. Note that cropping result largely depends on which part of an image is taken from the original image.

We use Equation 33 to get a detection value. The detection value is close to zero if there is no watermark inserted or if there is a severe attack against the watermarked image or video. The detection value is equal to 1 if there no attack against the image or video.

Figure 6. Watermark detection result (no attack, length of watermarks = 1000)

PSNR	Baboon	Boat	Bridge	Couple	Lena	Man	Pepper
30	0.999643	0.999956	0.999880	0.998340	0.999957	0.999961	0.999903
32	0.999667	0.999930	0.999882	0.998714	0.999919	0.999932	0.999920
34	0.999635	0.999859	0.999848	0.998993	0.999841	0.999830	0.999898
36	0.999585	0.999667	0.999760	0.999139	0.999614	0.999671	0.999792
38	0.999373	0.999296	0.999455	0.998869	0.999033	0.999130	0.999589
40	0.998920	0.998207	0.998778	0.998257	0.997937	0.998029	0.999284
42	0.997126	0.995885	0.997543	0.996441	0.994823	0.995146	0.998139
44	0.994376	0.989692	0.993836	0.991490	0.987429	0.988717	0.994494
46	0.984230	0.978916	0.985623	0.980508	0.972497	0.974899	0.984995
48	0.964964	0.954546	0.968662	0.958235	0.946442	0.944577	0.961780
50	0.924940	0.918845	0.932701	0.912914	0.892681	0.895413	0.935207

Figure 7. Watermark detection result as a function of the PSNR (no attack, smoothing, and cropping): (a) Baboon, (b) Boat, (c) Bridge, (d) Couple

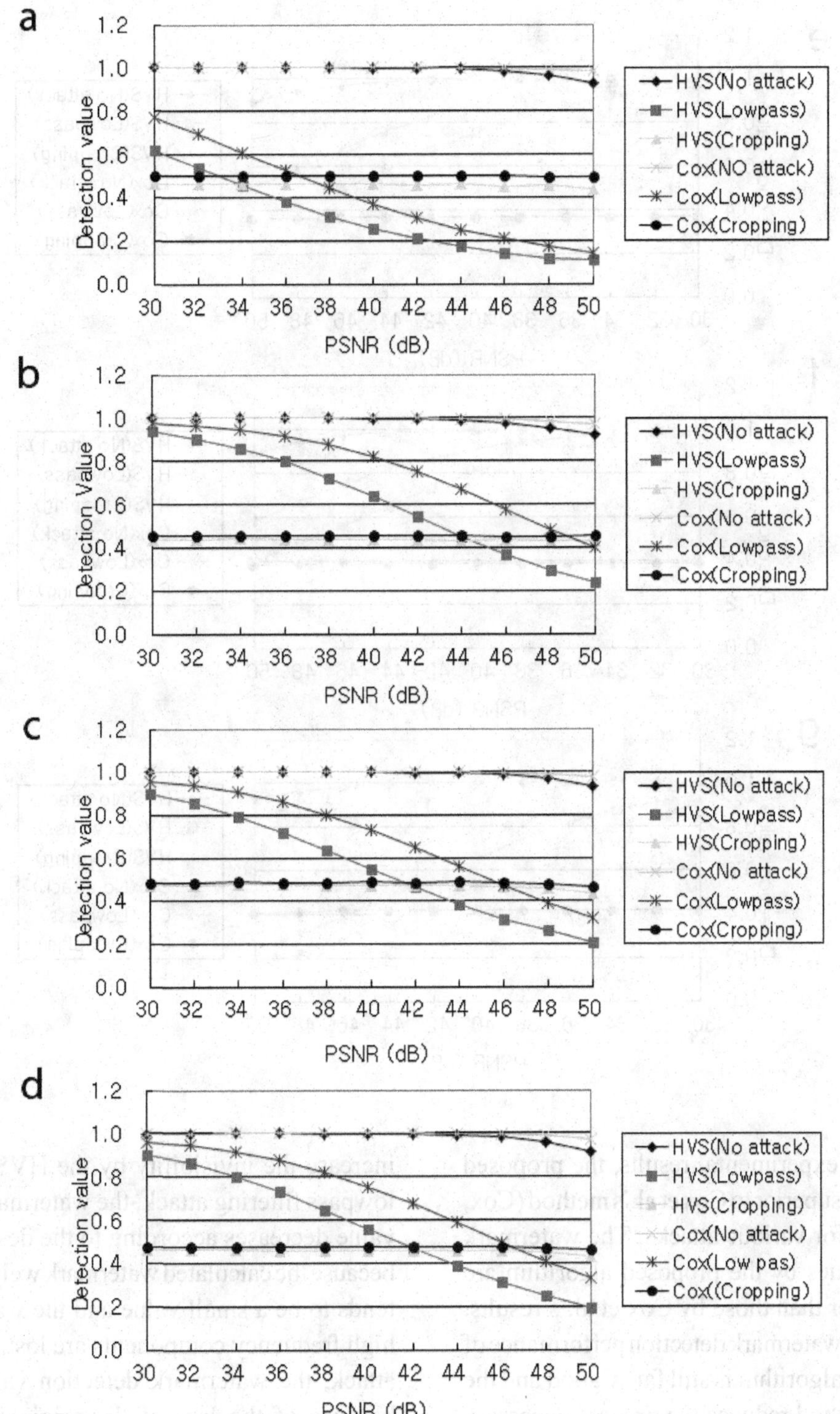

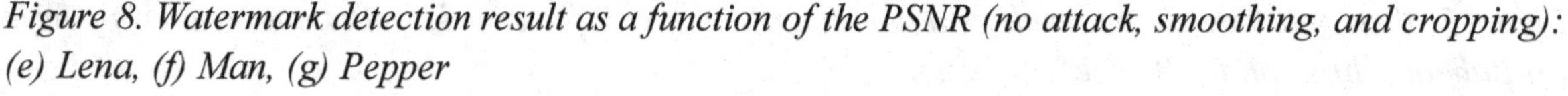

Figure 8. Watermark detection result as a function of the PSNR (no attack, smoothing, and cropping): (e) Lena, (f) Man, (g) Pepper

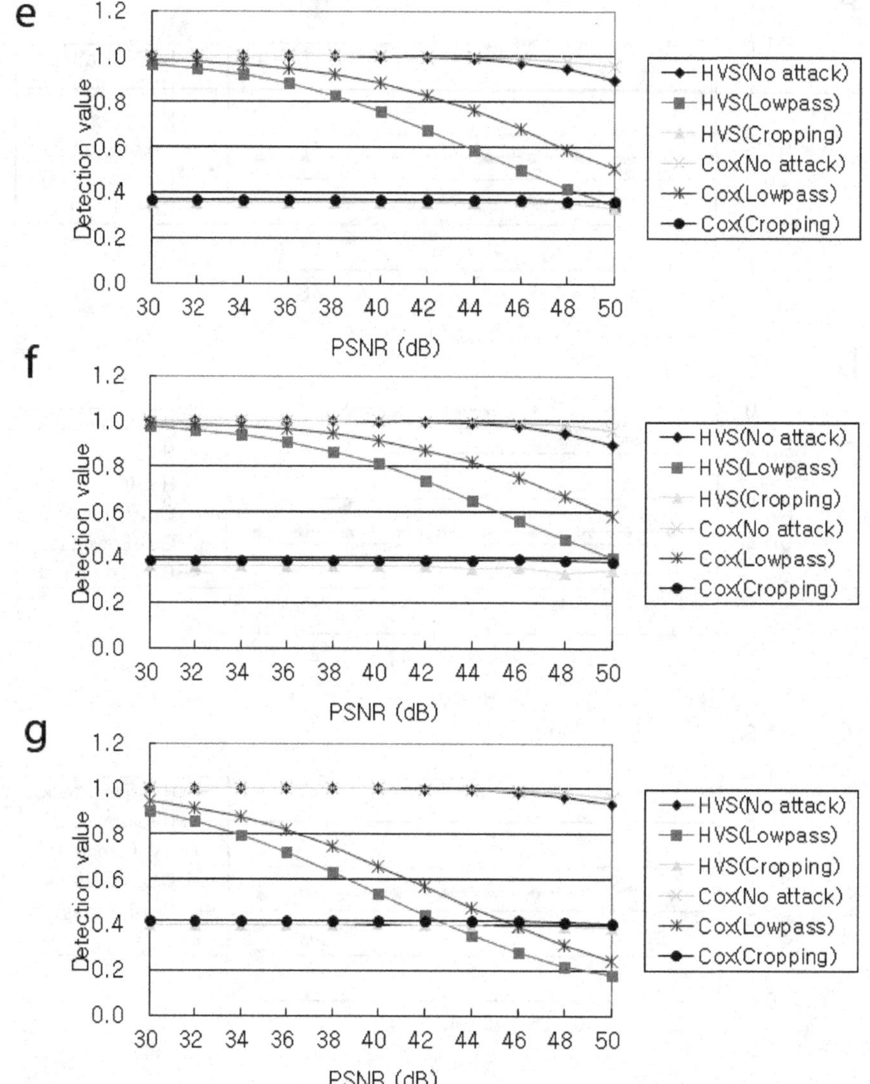

From our experimental results, the proposed method is not superior to Cox et al.'s method (Cox, et al., 1997) for various attacks. The watermark detection values by the proposed algorithm are a little smaller than those by Cox et al.'s results. However, the watermark detection performance of the proposed algorithm is still fairly good and the proposed method reduces the process necessary to insert the watermark in a certain image and increase the invisibility by the HVS. In case of lowpass filtering attack, the watermark detection value decreases according to the desired PSNRs because the calculated watermark weighting factor tends to be a small value and the watermarks in high frequency components are lost. In cropping attack, the watermark detection value is small because of the loss of the original image and watermark information.

CONCLUSION

This chapter proposes a watermarking method, where computation of the watermark weighting factor for the specified PSNR of still image (Kwon, et al., 2006) and still image watermarking in the DCT domain using the HVS (Kwon, et al., 1999) are combined. The formula for calculating the weighting factor in the DCT-based watermarking methods has been used in the DCT domain when both the desired PSNR and the length of watermarks are given. Experimental results show that the formula derived in the DCT domain works very well and it can be applied to automating the watermark insertion process in practice.

Note that the proposed method simplifies the process necessary to insert the watermarks in an image. To prove that our proposed method increases the invisibility, the subjective image quality evaluation can be performed. However, we can infer that the proposed method increases the invisibility of the watermark by using the HVS.

When we compare the performance of watermark methods, it can be concluded that the watermark method having the higher detection value against various attacks is superior to the other methods. If there are no attacks on the watermarked image, the value of the similarity function for most watermark methods is very close to 1. Therefore, it is definitely concluded who the right owner is on a certain image. However, if there are attacks on the watermarked image, the value of the similarity function tends to decrease to a small value and sometimes we cannot decide who the right owner is on that image. The concrete and objective decision criteria are difficult to define and should be further studied. Further research will focus on the extension of the proposed method to other transform-based watermarking methods such as the DWT-based watermarking methods. Also the proposed algorithm using the HVS will be extended to watermarking of 2-D video and 3-D still image/video.

REFERENCES

Agarwal, C., Mishra, A., & Sharma, A. (2011). Genetic algorithm-backpropagation network hybrid architecture for grayscale image watermarking in DCT domain. In *Proceedings of the 7th International Conference on Intelligent Information Hiding and Multimedia Signal Processing*, (pp. 177-180). Dalian, China: IEEE.

Barni, M., Bartolini, F., Cappellini, V., & Piva, A. (1997). *A DCT-domain system for robust image watermarking*. London, UK: Elsevier. doi:10.1016/S0165-1684(98)00015-2

Caronni, G. (1995). *Reliable IT systems*. Wiesbaden, Germany: Vieweg Publishing Company.

Chitprasert, B., & Rao, K. R. (1990). Human visual weighted progressive image transmission. *IEEE Transactions on Communications*, *38*, 1040–1044. doi:10.1109/26.57501

Cox, I. J., Kilian, J., Leighton, F. T., & Shamoon, T. (1997). Secure spread spectrum watermarking for multimedia. *IEEE Transactions on Image Processing*, *6*, 1673–1687. doi:10.1109/83.650120

Cox, I. J., Kilian, J., Leighton, T., & Shamoon, T. (1996). Secure spread spectrum watermarking for images, audio and video. *IEEE Transactions on Image Processing*, *3*, 243–246.

Cox, I. J., & Miller, M. L. (1997). A review of watermarking and the importance of perceptual modeling. In *Proceedings of SPIE Conference of Human Vision and Electronic Imaging II*, (vol 3016), (pp. 92-99). San Jose, CA: SPIE.

Craver, S., Memon, N., Yeo, B. L., & Yeung, M. (1996). *Can invisible watermarking resolve rightful ownership? IBM Research Report*. Armonk, NY: IBM.

Craver, S., Memon, N., Yeo, B. L., & Yeung, M. (1998). Resolving rightful ownerships with invisible watermarking technique: Limitations, attacks, and implications. *IEEE Journal on Selected Areas in Communications*, *16*, 573–586. doi:10.1109/49.668979

Jayanthi, V. E., Rajamani, V., & Karthikayen, P. (2011). Performance analysis for geometrical attack on digital image watermarking. *International Journal of Electronics*, *98*, 1565–1580. doi:10.1080/00207217.2011.601444

Kwon, O. H., Kim, Y. S., & Park, R.-H. (1999). Watermarking for still images using the human visual system. In *Proceedings of IEEE International Symposium on Circuits and Systems,* (vol 4), (pp. 76-79). Orlando, FL: IEEE Press.

Kwon, O. H., & Park, R.-H. (2006). Computation of the watermark weighting factor in the DCT-based watermarking methods for the specified PSNR of the still image. In *Proceedings of 7th International Workshop Image Analysis for Multimedia Interactive Services*, (pp. 41-43). Incheon, Korea: IEEE.

Mario, G. L., Mariko, N. M., & Meana, H. M. P. (2006). Optimal detection system of digital watermarks in spatial domain. *Telecommunications and Radio Engineering*, *65*, 739–751. doi:10.1615/TelecomRadEng.v65.i8.60

Motwani, R., Harris, F. C., & Bekris, K. (2010). A proposed digital rights management system for 3D graphics using biometric watermarks. In *Proceedings of International Conference on Signal Acquisition and Processing*, (pp. 125-129). Bangalore, India: IEEE.

Patra, J. C., Phua, J. E., & Bornand, C. (2010). A novel DCT domain CRT-based watermarking scheme for image authentication surviving JPEG compression. *Digital Signal Processing*, *20*, 1597–1611. doi:10.1016/j.dsp.2010.03.010

Pitas, I. (1998). A method for watermark casting on digital images. *IEEE Transactions on Circuits and Systems for Video Technology*, *8*, 775–780. doi:10.1109/76.728421

Piva, A., Barni, M., Bartolini, F., & Cappellini, V. (1997). DCT-based watermark recovering without resorting to the uncorrupted original images. In *Proceedings of IEEE International Conference on Image Processing*, (vol 1), (pp. 520-523). Santa Barbara, CA: IEEE Press.

Schyndel, R. G., Tirkel, A. Z., & Osborne, C. F. (1994). A digital watermark. In *Proceedings of International Conference on Image Processing*, (vol 2), (pp. 86-90). Austin, TX: IEEE.

Shrivastava, S., & Choubey, S. (2011). A secure image based watermark for 3D images. In *Proceedings of the 2011 International Conference on Communication Systems and Network Technologies*, (pp. 559-562). Katra, India: IEEE.

Vahedi, E., Zoroofi, R. A., & Shiva, M. (2012). Toward a new wavelet-based watermarking approach for color images using bio-inspired optimization principles. *Digital Signal Processing*, *22*, 153–162. doi:10.1016/j.dsp.2011.08.006

ADDITIONAL READING

Barni, M. (2002). Color image watermarking in the Karhunen-Loeve transform domain. *Journal of Electronic Imaging*, *11*, 87–95. doi:10.1117/1.1426383

Brassil, J., Low, S., & O'Gorman, L. (1994). Electronic marking and identification techniques to discourage document copying. *Proceedings of Infocom*, *94*, 1278–1287. Toronto, Canada: Infocom.

Delaigle, J. F., Vleeschouwer, C. D., & Macq, B. (1998). Watermarking algorithm based on a human visual model. *Signal Processing*, *66*, 319–335. doi:10.1016/S0165-1684(98)00013-9

Fei, C., Kundur, D., & Kwong, R. H. (2004). Analysis and design of watermarking algorithms for improved resistance to compression. *IEEE Transactions on Image Processing*, *13*, 126–144. doi:10.1109/TIP.2004.823830

Feng, C., & Liu, Q. (2011). A study of digital watermark algorithm based on HVS for half-tone images. *Advanced Materials Research*, *174*, 127–131. doi:10.4028/www.scientific.net/AMR.174.127

Griswold, N. C. (1980). Perceptual coding in the cosine transform domain. *Optical Engineering (Redondo Beach, Calif.)*, *19*, 306–311.

Hernadez, J. R., Gonzalez, F. P., Rodriguez, J. M., & Nieto, G. (1998). Performance analysis of a 2-D-multipulse amplitude modulation scheme for data hiding and watermarking of still images. *IEEE Journal on Selected Areas in Communications*, *16*, 510–524. doi:10.1109/49.668974

Hernandez, J. R., Amado, M., & Perez-Gonzalez, F. (2000). DCT-domain watermarking techniques for still images: Detector performance analysis and a new structure. *IEEE Transactions on Image Processing*, *9*, 55–68. doi:10.1109/83.817598

Hsu, C. T., & Wu, J. L. (1998). DCT-based watermarking for video. *IEEE Transactions on Consumer Electronics*, *44*, 206–216. doi:10.1109/30.663749

Jin, X., & Feng, Z. (2011). A digital watermarking algorithm based on wavelet transform and singular value segmentation of the watermark image. In *Proceedings of the 30th Chinese Control Conference*, (pp. 2327-2330). Yantai, China: CCC.

Kang, H. S., Choi, J. G., Lee, S. W., & Cho, S. J. (2000). Reliable watermark detection method based on analysis of correlation. *Optical Engineering (Redondo Beach, Calif.)*, *39*, 3308–3316. doi:10.1117/1.1327900

Karakos, D., & Papamarcou, A. (2003). A relationship between quantization and watermarking rates in the presence of additive Gaussian attacks. *IEEE Transactions on Information Theory*, *49*, 1970–1982. doi:10.1109/TIT.2003.814474

Kim, Y. S., Kwon, O. H., & Park, R.-H. (1999). Wavelet based watermarking method for digital images using the human visual system. *Electronics Letters*, *35*, 466–468. doi:10.1049/el:19990327

Kutter, M., & Petitcolas, F. A. P. (2000). Fair evaluation methods for image watermarking systems. *Journal of Electronic Imaging*, *9*, 445–455. doi:10.1117/1.1287594

Kwon, O. H., Kim, Y. S., & Park, R.-H. (1998). A DCT-domain watermarking method using human visual system. In *Proceedings of International Workshop on HDTV 1998*, (pp. 252-260). Seoul, Korea: HDTV.

Lin, S. D., & Chen, C. F. (2000). A robust DCT-based watermarking for copyright protection. *IEEE Transactions on Consumer Electronics*, *46*, 415–421. doi:10.1109/30.883387

Ma, B. (2011). Experimental research of image digital watermark based on DWT technology. In *Proceedings of the International Conference on Uncertainty Reasoning and Knowledge Engineering*, (pp. 9-12). Bali, Indonesia: IEEE.

Mannos, J. L., & Sakrison, D. (1974). The effects of a visual fidelity criterion on the encoding of images. *IEEE Transactions on Information Theory*, *20*, 525–536. doi:10.1109/TIT.1974.1055250

Marc, B. M., & Quisquater, J. J. (1995). Crytology for digital TV broadcasting. *Proceedings of the IEEE*, *83*(6), 944–957. doi:10.1109/5.387094

Moulin, P., & O'Sullivan, J. A. (2003). Information-theoretic analysis of information hiding. *IEEE Transactions on Information Theory*, *49*, 563–593. doi:10.1109/TIT.2002.808134

Podilchuk, C. I., & Zeng, W. (1998). Image-adaptive watermarking using visual models. *IEEE Journal on Selected Areas in Communications*, *16*, 525–539. doi:10.1109/49.668975

Qiao, L., & Nahrstedt, K. (1998). Watermarking schemes and protocols for protecting rightful ownership and customer's right. *Journal of Visual Communication and Image Representation*, *9*, 194–210. doi:10.1006/jvci.1998.0391

Stone, H. S. (1996). *Analysis of attacks on image watermarks with randomized coefficients*. Tokyo, Japan: NEC Research Institute.

Swanson, M. D., Zhu, B., & Tewfik, A. H. (1998). Multiresolution scene-based video watermarking using perceptual models. *IEEE Journal on Selected Areas in Communications*, *16*, 540–550. doi:10.1109/49.668976

Tanaka, K., Nakamura, Y., & Matsui, K. (1990). Embedding secret information into a dithered multilevel image. In *Proceedings of 1990 IEEE Military Communication Conference*, (pp. 216-220). Monterey, CA: IEEE Press.

Van Schyndel, R. G., Tirkel, A. Z., & Osborne, C. F. (1994). A digital watermark. In *Proceedings of International Conference on Image Processing*, (vol 2), (pp. 86-90). Austin, TX: IEEE.

Vleeschouwer, C. D., Delaigle, J., & Macq, B. (2002). Invisibility and application functionalities in perceptual watermarking – An overview. *Proceedings of the IEEE*, *90*, 64–77. doi:10.1109/5.982406

Wong, K. K., Tse, C. H., Ng, K. S., Lee, T. H., & Cheng, L. M. (1997). Adaptive watermarking. *IEEE Transactions on Consumer Electronics*, *43*, 1003–1009. doi:10.1109/30.642365

Ye, T. (2011). A robust zero-watermark algorithm based on singular value decomposition and discrete cosine transform. *Communications in Computer and Information Science*, *137*, 1–8. doi:10.1007/978-3-642-22706-6_1

Yeung, M. M., & Mintzer, F. C. (1998). Invisible watermarking for image verification. *Journal of Electronic Imaging*, *7*(3), 578–591. doi:10.1117/1.482612

Zeng, W., & Liu, B. (1999). A statistical watermark detection technique without using original images for resolving rightful ownerships of digital images. *IEEE Transactions on Image Processing*, *8*, 1534–1548. doi:10.1109/83.799882

KEY TERMS AND DEFINITIONS

Discrete Cosine Transform: A sequence of finitely many data points in terms of a sum of cosine functions oscillating at different frequencies.

Human Visual System: A system that human observer perceives the visual information in an image.

JPEG Compression: A standard method to compress a still image.

Lowpass Filtering: A method for filtering the low frequency components.

Peak Signal to Noise Ratio: A power ratio of the peak value of an image to a noise to be inserted or to the difference between the two images.

Watermark: A signal that is inserted into an image or a video to guarantee the ownership.

Watermark Weighting Factor: A parameter to control the amount of the watermark to be inserted into image or video.

Chapter 14
Self-Embedding Watermarking with Content Restoration Capabilities

Rong Huang
Kyushu University, Japan

Kyung-Hyne Rhee
Kyushu University, Japan & Pukyong National University, Korea

ABSTRACT

In this chapter, the authors give a survey about self-embedding watermarking, which enables not only detection of tampered regions but also recovering the damaged information. They introduce the pioneering method as well as the representative schemes, including adjacent-block detection, hierarchical detection and self-recovery, dual watermarks, reference sharing, and flexible self-recovery. The authors analyze the distinguishing features and loopholes by considering four key techniques, namely the secure block-mapping function, the unambiguous authentication, the reference information extraction, and the watermark embedding approaches. They make comparative studies on the above works and then outline further research directions and a conclusion.

1. BACKGROUND

With the proliferation of the sophisticated and powerful digital image processing software, such as PhotoShop, PaintShop, and FreeHand, tampering images becomes easier even for an amateur. As a result, those tools threaten to diminish the credibility of digital images. Professor Hany Farid warns that we are living in a world where seeing (or hearing) is no longer believing. The severe situation has spurred a great deal of intensive research activities in the study of multimedia security. Several concepts such as image encryption, steganography, watermarking, signature, and blind/passive, forensic and corresponding methods have been proposed as a protection against illegal access to private information or as means for authentication and tampering detection. For

DOI: 10.4018/978-1-4666-2217-3.ch014

ease of exposition, in this chapter, we assume that the target being protected is a still image, although there exist a great many multimedia security techniques designed for audio (Kirovski & Malvar, 2003; Wang & Zhao, 2006; Wu, et al., 2005) and video data (Bloom, et al., 1999; Doerr & Dugelay, 2003).

Generally speaking, encryption techniques (Chen, Mao, & Chui, 2004; Cheng & Li, 2000; Wu & Kuo, 2005) transform the original image to a non-recognizable form under the control of key while steganography techniques (Chang, Chen, & Lin, 2004; Lee, et al., 2008; Marvel, Boncelet, & Retter, 1999; Petitcolas, Anderson, & Kuhn, 1999; Tsai, Hu, & Yeh, 2009) hide the existence of one target image through embedding itself to the cover/host image. Of course, the above two types of techniques are not independent. Obviously, a designer can combine them by implementing encryption prior to embedding for enhancing the security. The common objective of encryption and steganopraphy is to protect the target image's information from being stolen by the eavesdropper. On the other hand, watermarking, signature and blind/passive forensic focus on authentication and tampering detection. Watermarking (Celik, et al., 2002; Cox, et al., 1997; Hartung & Kutter, 1999; Thodi & Rodriguez, 2007) can be considered as an active and invasive technique. Here, we use term "active" to indicate that the watermark should be embedded by the sender and must be present in the host image before the tampering occurs, while invasiveness specifies that the insertion manipulation alters the pixel values of the host image inevitably. The signature (Cano, et al., 2002; Wu, 2002) can be a hash value of image contents or extracted characteristics. Although it is one type of non-invasive technique, the attached signature requires an additional storage in Certification Authority (CA). Besides, the signature techniques only can judge whether an image has been changed or not but cannot locate the tampered regions. Blind/passive forensic techniques (Farid, 2009; Fridrich, 2009; Lukas, Fridrich, & Goljan, 2006; Popescu & Farid, 2005; Wang, Dong, & Tan, 2009) enable detecting traces of digital forgeries in the complete absence of any form of pre-embedding or pre-registered information. Although the inactive and non-invasive image forensic methods appear in bursts and attract more attention, digital watermarking is still an immediate and mature authentication approach.

In this chapter, we attempt to survey and summarize the self-embedding watermarking which is first proposed in Fridrich and Goljan (1999). For completeness, we quote the definition of watermarking from Cox et al. (2008). Watermarking is defined as the practice of imperceptibly altering an image to embed a message about that image. Hereinafter, we give the generic classification of watermarking for drawing forth the concept of self-embedding watermarking.

According to different missions and considerations, various watermarking schemes have been proposed. Conventional invisible watermark techniques can be classified into robust watermarking, fragile watermarking and semi-fragile watermarking on the basis of the functionality. Robust watermarking (Barni, et al., 1998; Nikolaidis & Pitas, 1998; Tang & Hang, 2003), as the name suggests, possesses the ability to resist against malicious attacks and is used to declare the ownership of the image. Fragile watermarking (Barreto, et al., 2002; Li, 2004), on the other hand, is destroyed by any manipulations of pixels thus being able to locate the altered areas. However, due to the extreme sensibility, it cannot distinguish between malicious attacks and innocent manipulations such as compression, sharpening, or contrast adjustment. To address this problem, semi-fragile watermarking (Lin & Chang, 2000; Maeno, et al., 2006) is designed. It is capable of authenticating an image even after undergoing some legitimate manipulations mentioned above. In general, hash value, owner's logo or serial number etc. serves as digital watermark for multifarious intentions. Although watermarks may survive some malicious attacks, alterations introduced in the host image is perceptually visible and may lead to the disparate semantics. This problem becomes acute especially when retransmission mechanism or original host image is not available.

As a remedy, the self-embedding watermarking (Fridrich & Goljan, 1999) preserves the structure of the host image, and enables not only detection of areas that have been tampered, but also recovering the missing information. It should be noted that the dominating objectives of self-embedding watermarking and so-called reversible watermarking (Alattar, 2004; Tian, 2003) are quite different, although they do share similarity. The former is contrived for maintaining the same semantics even if the watermarked image has undergone malicious attacks or unintentional disturbance. The latter focuses on recovering fidelity after removing watermark. In this chapter, we restrict our attention to the self-embedding watermarking.

The rest of this chapter is organized as follows. Section 2 is devoted to the description of preliminaries. Section 3 elaborates the state of the art in self-embedding watermarking. We summarize of current works and give conclusions in section 4. We expect the readers can grasp the basic concept, classical methods and research directions of self-embedding watermarking after reading.

2. PRELIMINARIES

To facilitate understanding, the essential knowledge is sorted out and introduced in this section. Experienced reader can directly skip this section and immediately proceed to the next part.

2.1. Watermarking

Suppose that a watermark is defined as $\mathbf{W}$, $\mathbf{X}$ is the host image, and K is denoted as the key. The watermark embedding procedure can be depicted as follows:

$$\mathbf{X}' = e_K\left(\mathbf{X}, \mathbf{W}\right) \quad (1)$$

where $e\left(\bullet\right)$ is the embedding function which takes the host image $\mathbf{X}$ and watermark $\mathbf{W}$ as input parameters. The watermarked image is represented as $\mathbf{X}'$. Here, K is the user's insertion key.

The watermark extraction works as follow:

$$\mathbf{W}' = d_{K'}\left(\hat{\mathbf{X}}'\right) \quad (2)$$

During the above watermark extraction stage, the original host image is not required. This type of technique is called oblivious watermarking. In the equation 2, the extraction function is denoted as $d\left(\bullet\right)$ which is governed by the extraction key K'. The symbol $\hat{\mathbf{X}}'$ stands for the possibly corrupted watermarked image.

Several general requirements of typical watermarking system should be satisfied:

1. The watermarked image $\mathbf{X}'$ should be as close to the host image $\mathbf{X}$ as possible.
2. If the watermarked image does not undergo any changes, which means $\mathbf{X}' = \hat{\mathbf{X}}'$, the extracted watermark $\mathbf{W}'$ should be identical to the original one $\mathbf{W}$.
3. Using different extraction key $K_1' \neq K_2'$, the outputted watermarks should be different.
4. The watermark extraction process is nonreversible. It means that relying on the extraction function $d\left(\bullet\right)$ or the watermark $\mathbf{W}'$, the extraction key K' can hardly be deductive.

2.2. Introduction of MSB and LSB

The letters MSB stand for Most Significant Bit. Likewise, the letters LSB are short for Least Significant Bit. As their names imply, LSB and MSB refer to those bits that have the least weight and most weight in a digital word. The Figure 1 shows

Figure 1. Bit position and the corresponding relative bit weight

	MSB							LSB
Bit Position	Bit 7	Bit 6	Bit 5	Bit 4	Bit 3	Bit 2	Bit 1	Bit 0
Power of two	128	64	32	16	8	4	2	1

the bit position and the corresponding relative bit weight of an eight-bit word.

We display eight-bit planes of the gray "Lena" image in Figure 2. The contributions of planes to the original gray image are different. Apparently, the LSB plane contains much less information and be commonly regarded as the embedding space. The MSB plane preserves the outline and should remain unchanged.

2.3. Introduction of JPEG

JPEG stands for the Joint Photographic Experts Group that formulated and finalized the standard in 1992. Here, we just review the essential parts, which are relevant to subsequent statement. A completed description of the standard can be found in Pennebaker and Mitchell (1993).

JPEG compression constitutes the following five steps:

1. **Color Model Transformation:** The RGB model is transformed to the YC_rC_b model. The first component Y represents for luminance. Both C_r and C_b are chrominance components.
2. **Division and Subsampling:** The luminance signal Y is divided into 8×8 blocks while chrominance signals should be subsampled before implementing division operation.
3. **Discrete Cosine Transform (DCT):** Each block is transformed from the spatial domain to the frequency domain using the DCT.
4. **Quantization:** The resulting transform coefficients are quantized by dividing them by quantization steps and rounded to the nearest integers

Figure 2. Eight-bit planes of the gray Lena image

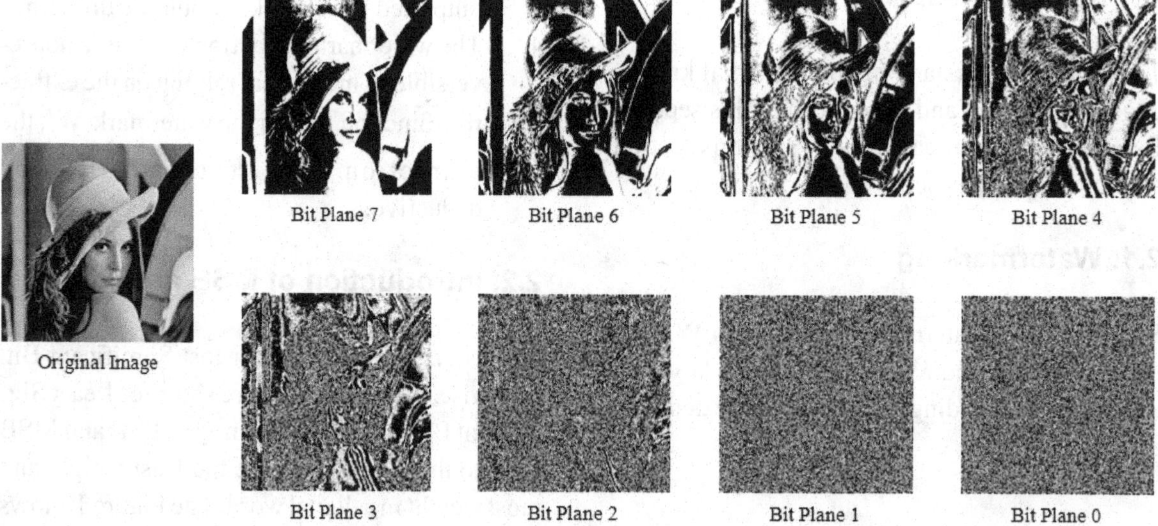

$$\tilde{\mathbf{c}}(i,j) = \left[\frac{\mathbf{c}(i,j)}{\mathbf{Q}(i,j)}\right], \quad i,j \in \{0,\cdots,7\} \tag{3}$$

In Equation 3, the function $[\bullet]$ is round operation. It should be noted that because of the difference in visual sensitivity between luminance and chrominance, different quantization matrix may be used. The JPEG standard recommends a set of quantization matrices indexed by a quality factor $q_f \in \{1,2,\cdots,100\}$. Any quantization matrix can be obtained using the following formula:

$$\mathbf{Q}_{q_f} = \begin{cases} \max\left\{1, \left[2\mathbf{Q}_{50}\left(1 - q_f/100\right)\right]\right\}, & q_f > 50 \\ \min\left\{255 \cdot \mathbf{1}, \left[\mathbf{Q}_{50}\ 50/q_f\right]\right\}, & q_f \leq 50 \end{cases} \tag{4}$$

The boldface **1** in Equation 4 is a 8 x 8 matrix of ones. Quantization matrix $\mathbf{Q}_{50}$ with $q_f = 50$ is a fixed reference as shown in Figure 3. Larger values of the quantization steps (or smaller quality factor) generate a higher compression ratio but introduce more perceptual distortion.

5. **Encoding:** The quantized DCT coefficients are scanned according to a zig-zag pattern as shown in Figure 4. Each integer value is encoded using bits and further compressed using Huffman or arithmetic coding.

2.4. Counterfeiting Attack

Holliman and Memon (2000) propose the vector quantization counterfeiting attack which is effective on the block-wise independent watermarking technique. Given one or more watermarked images containing an owner's watermark, it is possible for an attacker to forge this authenticated

Figure 3. JPEG quantization table with q_f=50: (a) quantization table for luminance, (b) quantization table for chrominance

16	11	10	16	24	40	51	61
12	12	14	19	26	58	60	55
14	13	16	24	40	57	69	56
14	17	22	29	51	87	80	62
18	22	37	56	68	109	103	77
24	35	55	64	81	104	113	92
49	64	78	87	103	121	120	101
72	92	95	98	112	100	103	99

(a)

17	18	24	47	99	99	99	99
18	21	26	66	99	99	99	99
24	26	56	99	99	99	99	99
47	66	99	99	99	99	99	99
99	99	99	99	99	99	99	99
99	99	99	99	99	99	99	99
99	99	99	99	99	99	99	99
99	99	99	99	99	99	99	99

(b)

Figure 4. Scanning path of zig-zag pattern

watermark and embed it into the target image **Y** without the consent of the original watermark owner.

The block-wise watermarking technique partitions a host image **X** into non-overlapping blocks $X_1, X_2, \cdots X_n$. One watermarked block X_i' is only dependent on block X_i, watermark W_i and sub-key K_i. Each sub-key is scheduled by the user's insertion key K.

Then, the embedding and extraction function can be rewritten as follows:

$$\mathbf{X}' = e_{K_1}\left(X_1, W_1\right)\left\|e_{K_2}\left(X_2, W_2\right)\right\|\cdots\left\|e_{K_n}\left(X_n, W_n\right) \quad (5)$$

$$\mathbf{W}' = d_{K_1'}\left(\hat{X}_1'\right)\left\|d_{K_2'}\left(\hat{X}_2'\right)\right\|\cdots\left\|d_{K_n'}\left(\hat{X}_n'\right) \quad (6)$$

where the symbol Π denotes the concatenation operation.

For giving a detailed description of the counterfeiting attack, K-equivalent is defined in advance here. Given a key K, blocks $X_i, X_{i+1}, \cdots, X_j$ are K-equivalent if

$$d_K\left(X_i\right) = d_K\left(X_{i+1}\right) = \cdots = d_K\left(X_j\right) = W \quad (7)$$

This equation means that blocks $X_i, X_{i+1}, \cdots, X_j$ are K-equivalent if the same watermark W is extracted from all of them using the key K. All image blocks are classified into equivalence classes $\left\{C_1, C_2, \cdots, C_m\right\}$ according to the K-equivalent property. After doing so, any block belonging to an equivalence class C_i is K-equivalent and results in the same watermark being extracted with key K. The above property forms a significant consequence. For making the target image **Y** pass the authentication process, an attacker can replace each block of **Y** with an approximated one by searching within the corresponding equivalence class. The counterfeit process can be loosely represented by the following procedure: The block Y_i is replaced by Y_i' as long as $Y_i \approx Y_i'$ and $Y_i' \in C_K$. The attacker is successful in generating a counterfeit watermarked image such that $\mathbf{Y}' \approx \mathbf{Y}$. Intuitively, the more watermarked images containing same watermark one has, the higher quality counterfeit can be constructed.

An immediate resistance means is to diminish the degree of freedom by increasing dependence of a watermark signal on surrounding image contents. In literature (Holliman & Memon, 2000), authors give a modified insertion process:

$$\mathbf{X}' = e_{K_1}\left(\chi_1, W_1\right)\left\|e_{K_2}\left(\chi_2, W_2\right)\right\|\cdots\left\|e_{K_n}\left(\chi_n, W_n\right) \quad (8)$$

where the block set χ_i but not a single block X_i is used to construct the watermarked block X_i'. The composition of one block set χ_i satisfies $X_i \in \chi_i$ and $\chi_i \cap \left\{X_j \middle| j \neq i\right\} \neq \varnothing$. In the block-wise independent watermarking scheme, we have $\chi_i = X_i$. We end this subsection by giving a straightforward example of introducing dependence between blocks. The literature (Coppersmith, et al., 1999) suggests using a large surrounding neighborhood to be hashed and inserted in each block.

2.5. Compressive Sensing

Compressive Sensing (CS) (Baraniuk, 2007; Candès, Romberg, & Tao, 2006; Donoho, 2006) can sample a sparse or compressible signal at a rate below the Nyquist theorem required. Intuitively, most digital images are not simple in the spatial domain. Fortunately, the sparse representation of one original signal can be derived from decomposition algorithms such as Discrete Cosine Transform (DCT), Discrete Wavelet Transform (DWT) and overcomplete basis transform. Suppose x is a signal with length N. We deal with image data by first vectorizing it into one-dimension vector. For simplicity, assume that $\{\Psi_i\}(i=1,\cdots,N)$ is a normal orthonormal basis in $\mathbb{R}^N$. Basis matrix with the Ψ_i as columns is denoted by $\mathbf{\Psi}$. The decomposition coefficient s is the equivalent representation of x in $\mathbf{\Psi}$ domain. If only K entries of s are non-zero, where $K \ll N$, x is termed as K-sparse signal. The linear measurement process is expressed as:

$$y = \mathbf{\Phi}x = \mathbf{\Phi\Psi}s = \mathbf{\Theta}s \tag{9}$$

This formula describes $M \times N$ inner products between x and M rows of measurement matrix $\mathbf{\Phi}$. The array $\mathbf{\Theta} = \mathbf{\Phi\Psi}$ can be called sensor matrix. The asymmetric size of measurement matrix results in an ill-posed problem with respect to reconstruction, which means Equation 9 has infinitely many solutions. To simplify this problem, a necessary and sufficient condition has been proposed in Candès, Romberg, and Tao (2006), namely Restricted Isometry Property (RIP), which can be cast as following:

$$\left(1-\varepsilon_K\right)\|s\|_2 \le \|\mathbf{\Theta}s\|_2 \le \left(1+\varepsilon_K\right)\|s\|_2 \tag{10}$$

If the above condition is satisfied, a steady solution can be obtained from this underdetermined system. An alternative prerequisite is that the measurement matrix $\mathbf{\Phi}$ must be incoherent with basis matrix $\mathbf{\Psi}$. This related condition requires that the rows $\{\Phi_i\}$ of $\mathbf{\Phi}$ cannot sparsely represent the columns $\{\Psi_i\}$ of $\mathbf{\Psi}$. (and vice versa). In general, this requirement can be satisfied with overwhelming probability, when elements of measurement matrix $\mathbf{\Phi}$ are independent and identically distributed (i.i.d) random variables taking on their values from a Gaussian probability density function with mean zero and variance $1/N$. Meanwhile, the measurement data length M is restricted by the inequality below:

$$M \ge cK\log\left(N/K\right) \tag{11}$$

where c is a small constant. The parameter M in Equation 11 is one crucial factor of compression rate. Another one is quantization level.

These projections y obtained from Equation 9 retain structure of the original signal. The recovery boils down to a convex optimization process:

$$\hat{s} = \arg\min \|s'\|_1 \text{ subject to } s' = \mathbf{\Theta}y \tag{12}$$

There exist too many reconstruction techniques to enumerate here. Typical representatives include orthogonal matching pursuit (Tropp & Gilbert, 2007), gradient pursuit (Blumensath & Davies, 2008), iterative shrinkage thresholding algorithms (Bioucas & Figueiredo, 2007), FOCUSS (Gorodnitsky & Rao, 1997), and SPARLS (Babadi, et al., 2010).

3. STATE OF THE ART

In this section, five existing works are introduced including the pioneering method, the adjacent-block detection, the hierarchical detection and self-recovery, the dual watermarks, the reference sharing and flexible self-recovery. We analyze each method and give summaries.

3.1. Pioneering Work

At the International Conference on Image Processing 1999 (ICIP-99), Fridrich et al. put forward the idea, namely self-embedding watermarking (Fridrich & Goljan, 1999), in which the compressed host image is treated as watermark and embedded into the host image itself for the purpose of not only detection of tampered areas but also recovering the missing information. This proposal is generally looked upon as the pioneering work. We give the description of their proposed methods in the following.

The method starts with partitioning image into non-overlapping blocks and transforming each block using a DCT. A specified numbers of low-frequency DCT coefficients are quantized using the quantization matrix **Q** that is directly taken from luminance quantization table of JPEG standard. The quantized values are encoded using an assigned number of bits. Information about one block is embedded into the LSB of another block. We call the extracted information reference data.

In order to be compatible with JPEG standard, the block size 8×8 is recommended. A recessive prerequisite should be satisfied prior to executing the algorithm. That is, both height and width of the host image are multiple of 8. The reference information extraction and embedding processes are represented by the following procedure:

[Step 1] Initialization: Gray levels of a $M \times N$ host image are transformed into the interval [-127,128]. The LSB of all pixels are initialized to zero.

[Step 2] Partitioning: The host image is divided into 8×8 blocks. Use the denotation $\mathbf{B}_{(m,n)}$ to represent the block at position (m, n), where $m = 1, \cdots, \frac{M}{8}$ and $n = 1, \cdots, \frac{N}{8}$

[Step 3] DCT and Selecting Coefficient: Each 8×8 block is transformed into the frequency domain using DCT. The coefficients are sorted in a zig-zag pattern. For obtaining a compact representation, the first *K* coefficients are selected by simply truncating the ordered sequence. In this way, the *K* selected coefficients lie in low-frequency domain and contain information important for recognition. In this original proposal, *K* = 11. Let **K** denote the set composed of coordinates (i, j) of *K* selected coefficients, where $i, j \in \{1, 2, \cdots, 8\}$

[Step 4] Quantization and Encoding: The quantization processing is expressed in Equation 3 and the quality factor is fixed to be 50. The bit lengths for encoding are sophisticatedly designed so that the resulting bit-string for each block is exactly 64 bits long. Here, we directly reproduce a same matrix **L** as that in the original paper. The matrix L consists of the bit lengths in different position as shown in Figure 5. The positions of selected coefficients are painted by the gray background (in the case that *K*= 11). We will discuss later that in fact, one can redesign this matrix and also reset the value of *K* by oneself as long as an equation is satisfied.

[Step 5] Encrypting and Embedding: Although the encryption processing is not emphasized, actually it is indispensable for enhancing the security. The raw reference information without encrypting lacks resistivity to dictionary attack. In the embedding stage, the 64 bits information of block $\mathbf{B}_{(m,n)}$ is first encrypted and then embedded into the LSB

Figure 5. Matrix **L**. *The components of this matrix are bit lengths for encoding quantized values*

7	7	7	5	4	3	2	1
7	6	5	5	4	2	1	0
6	5	5	4	3	1	0	0
5	5	4	3	1	0	0	0
4	4	3	1	0	0	0	0
3	2	1	0	0	0	0	0
2	1	0	0	0	0	0	0
1	0	0	0	0	0	0	0

of another block $\mathbf{B}_{(m',n')}$. The position of block $\mathbf{B}_{(m',n')}$ is indexed using a shift vector $\mathbf{p} = (x, y)$.

$$m' = (m + x) \bmod M \text{ and } n' = (n + y) \bmod N \quad (13)$$

The shift vector $\mathbf{p} = (x, y)$ is set below:

$$x = \left\lceil \frac{M}{3} \right\rceil \text{ and } y = \left\lceil \frac{N}{3} \right\rceil \quad (14)$$

The direction of shift vector is chosen randomly.

There is a conspicuous tradeoff between the quality of reconstruction and the extent of distortion caused by embedding manipulation. To improve the quality of reconstruction, an immediate approach is to use two least significa-tion bit planes for embedding 128 bits reference information extracted from a certain block. The encoding procedure is redesigned as shown in Figure 6. The matrix **L** is fixed without changing and also plays the same role.

The bit length allocation is explained in the following:

- The first three quantized coefficients are encoded using seven bits as listed in matrix **L**.
- Check the following eighteen quantized coefficients and return the binary results. A binary one indicates that the corresponding quantized coefficient is not equal to zero. Analogically, a zero quantized coefficient outputs a binary zero.
- Pick out the non-zero quantized coefficients and encoding them according to the matrix **L**.

Figure 6. Bit length allocation when two least significant bit planes are used

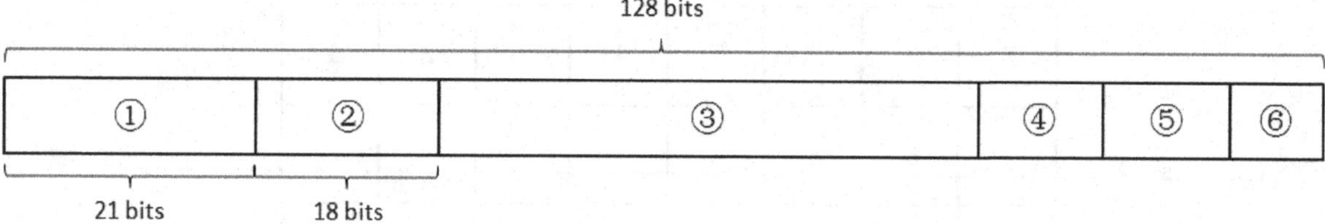

- If the total number of bits ①+②+③ is less than 128, the quantized coefficients between the 22nd and 36th position are further checked one by one until two consecutive binary zeros are outputted.
- Pick out the non-zero quantized coefficients and encoding them. As listed in matrix **L**, the higher-frequency quantized coefficients are encoded with fewer bits.
- If the total number of bits ①+②+③+④+⑤ is still less than 128, zero padding is applied.

The absolute value of the quantized coefficient locating at (i, j) may rarely be greater than $2^{\mathbf{L}(i,j)-1}$, in this case, only this upper limit will be encoded.

The verification and information recovery processes are described below.

[Step 1] Partitioning and Decryption: The watermarked image is first divided into 8×8 blocks. The block at position (m, n) which may have been subjected to disturbance and tampering is denoted by $\hat{\mathbf{B}}_{(m,n)}$ where $m = 1, \cdots, \frac{M}{8}$ and $n = 1, \cdots, \frac{N}{8}$. Decrypt the LSBs of all pixels block by block, then copy the decrypted results and store them in a newly created table **T**. Gray levels of the watermarked image are transformed into the interval [-127,128]. Then initialize the used LSB planes to zeros.

[Step 2] Initialization: Be same as the **[Step 1]** of reference information extraction process.

[Step 3]: DCT and Selecting Coefficient: Be same as the **[Step 3]** of reference information extraction process.

[Step 4] Quantization and Encoding: Be same as the **[Step 4]** of reference information extraction process.

[Step 5] Verification and Recovery: In order to facilitate the elaboration of verification mechanism, we suppose a block-mapping sequence:

$$(m_0, n_0) \rightarrow (m_1, n_1) \rightarrow (m_2, n_2) \rightarrow (m_3, n_3) \rightarrow (m_4, n_4) \rightarrow \cdots \rightarrow (m_0, n_0) \tag{15}$$

The above path indicates that the reference information of $\mathbf{B}_{(m_0,n_0)}$ is embedded into the LSBs of $\mathbf{B}_{(m_1,n_1)}$. In the detection and recovery stage, the back-up of $\mathbf{B}_{(m_0,n_0)}$ is copied and stored in $\mathbf{T}_{(m_1,n_1)}$. The rest of the mapping relationship may be deduced by analogy. We take the block $\hat{\mathbf{B}}_{(m_2,n_2)}$ as an example. This block will be verified as valid if the following two requirements are satisfied:

1. The information extracted from $\hat{\mathbf{B}}_{(m_2,n_2)}$ is consistent with the content stored in $\mathbf{T}_{(m_3,n_3)}$
2. The content stored in $\mathbf{T}_{(m_2,n_2)}$ matches the information extracted from $\hat{\mathbf{B}}_{(m_1,n_1)}$

When the mismatching occurs, the additional predecessor and successor blocks are taken into account. The block $\hat{\mathbf{B}}_{(m_2,n_2)}$ will be judged as invalid if the following four items are achieved simultaneously:

1. The information extracted from $\hat{\mathbf{B}}_{(m_2,n_2)}$ is not consistent with the content stored in $\mathbf{T}_{(m_3,n_3)}$
2. The content stored in $\mathbf{T}_{(m_2,n_2)}$ is not consistent with the information extracted from $\hat{\mathbf{B}}_{(m_1,n_1)}$
3. The content stored in $\mathbf{T}_{(m_1,n_1)}$ is consistent with the information extracted from $\hat{\mathbf{B}}_{(m_0,n_0)}$
4. The information extracted from $\hat{\mathbf{B}}_{(m_3,n_3)}$ is consistent with the content stored in $\mathbf{T}_{(m_4,n_4)}$

If the block $\hat{\mathbf{B}}_{(m_2,n_2)}$ is declared to be valid, the inspection proceeds to the next block. Otherwise, the damaged block $\hat{\mathbf{B}}_{(m_2,n_2)}$ is reconstructed using its corresponding back-up $\mathbf{T}_{(m_3,n_3)}$

Here, to more vividly demonstrate the effectiveness of self-embedding watermarking technique, we directly display the original paper's experimental result. In the experiment, two least significant bit planes are used as the embedding space, thus providing 128 bits of embedding capacity for each block. One utilizes the crop-and-replacement attack to tamper with the license plate. As a result, the alteration to the semantics may cause dispute and then lead to miscarriage of justice. As shown in Figure 7, the license plate in each image is scaled up for comparison. The experimental result indicates that the self-embedding watermarking is successful in recovering the damaged information with the approximate but degraded version.

We analyze this method and draw some conclusions:

1. In the case that using one LSB plane, the recovered region is perceptually indistinguishable from a 50% quality JPEG compressed original.
2. The approximate PSNR of watermarked image can be estimated. Let v_o and v_n denote the original and modified pixel value, respectively. Suppose that v_o and v_n belong to the interval $\left[0, 2^{num} - 1\right]$, where '*num*' is the number of used LSB plane. Due to the embedding manipulation, the average energy of distortion per pixel is

$$E_D = \sum_{v_o=0}^{2^{num}-1} \sum_{v_n=0}^{2^{num}-1} \left(v_o - v_n\right)^2 \cdot P\left(v_o\right) \cdot P\left(v_n\right) \tag{16}$$

A reasonable assumption is that the distribution of v_o and v_n is approximately uniform. The probability distribution function is

$$P\left(v_o\right) = P\left(v_n\right) = \frac{1}{2^{num}}$$

In the case that only one least significant bit plane is used, $P\left(v_o\right) = P\left(v_n\right) = \frac{1}{2}$, thus $E_D = 0.5$. Analogously, when two planes are used, the corresponding results are $P\left(v_o\right) = P\left(v_n\right) = \frac{1}{4}$ and $E_D = 2.5$

So, the approximate PSNR is calculated by

$$\text{PSNR} = 10 \cdot \log_{10}\left(255^2 / E_D\right) \tag{17}$$

We have PSNR=51.1dB (one plane) and PSNR=44.1dB (two planes).

3. As mentioned above, one can adjust the quality of reconstruction by redesigning the matrix **L** or resetting the value *K*. The adjustment should be restricted by the following equation.

Figure 7. The experimental result: (a) the original image, (b) the watermarked image, (c) the tampered image (the license plate is cropped and replaced by a forged one), and (d) the reconstructed image

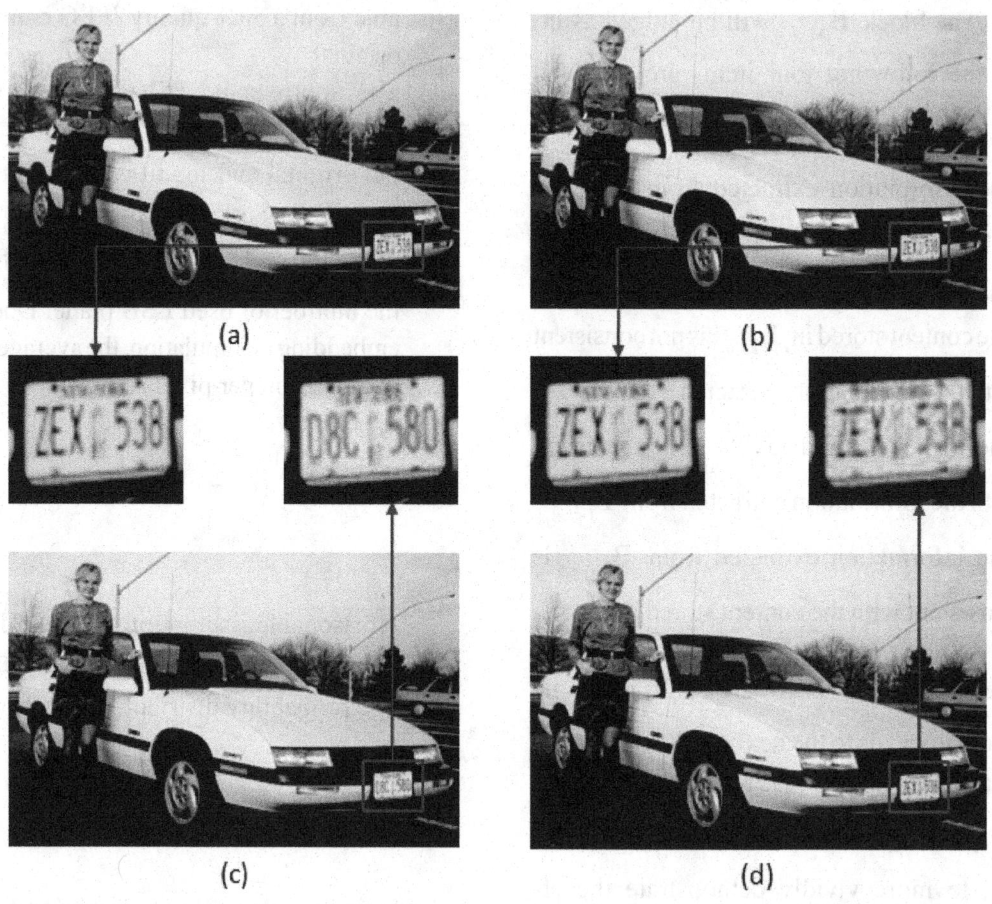

$$\sum_{(i,j)\in \mathbf{K}} \mathbf{L}(i,j) = 64, \quad |\mathbf{K}| = K \tag{18}$$

In the case that two LSB planes are used, the quality can also be adjusted. However, due to its sophisticated encoding approach, the adjustment is hard to boil down to a formula. Certainly, using two LSB planes will improve the quality of reconstruction dramatically.

4. It is a block-wise watermarking method, in which the reference data are forbidden from embedding the block itself, namely $m \neq m'$ and $n \neq n'$. The watermark consists of the compact representation of host image, which means that the watermark is particularly dependent on the content of host image. Moreover, since the insertion function takes both $\mathbf{B}_{(m,n)}$ and $\mathbf{B}_{(m',n')}$ as parameters, one watermarked block is obtained from

$$\mathbf{B}'_{(m',n')} = e_K\left(\mathbf{B}_{(m,n)}, \mathbf{B}_{(m',n')}\right)$$

The self-embedding watermarking naturally introduces the dependence between blocks thus resisting against the vector quantization counterfeiting attack.

5. There exist loopholes in the authentication system. The so-called tampering coincidence

problem (also can be called double loss problem) results in a confusing situation. Along the block-mapping path, if two connected blocks are both damaged, the tampering coincidence problem occurs. Let us recall the verification and recovery step, we suppose that $\hat{\mathbf{B}}_{(m_2,n_2)}$ and $\hat{\mathbf{B}}_{(m_3,n_3)}$ are both damaged. In this case, the fourth item: "The information extracted from $\hat{\mathbf{B}}_{(m_3,n_3)}$ is consistent with the content stored in $\mathbf{T}_{(m_4,n_4)}$." cannot be satisfied. Therefore, the block $\hat{\mathbf{B}}_{(m_2,n_2)}$ is declared neither valid nor invalid. One may attempt to relax the authentication requirements by directly abrogating the third and the fourth item. If in doing so, although this confusing situation will be shielded, false alarm appears. For example, assume that only two blocks, $\hat{\mathbf{B}}_{(m_1,n_1)}$ and $\hat{\mathbf{B}}_{(m_3,n_3)}$ are damaged. Unluckily, the innocent block $\hat{\mathbf{B}}_{(m_2,n_2)}$ will also be judge as invalid. This becomes a dilemma.

6. If the tampering coincidence problem occurs, the back-up of $\hat{\mathbf{B}}_{(m_2,n_2)}$, namely $\mathbf{T}_{(m_3,n_3)}$ is also damaged. As a result, information restoration fails.
7. In order to obtain the convincing tampering results, the altered region denoted as Λ generally covers several adjacent blocks. It means that if one block is tampered, its neighboring blocks may be tampered as well with high probability. Under this assumption, the immediate way to avoid the tampering coincidence problem is that the reference data of one block should be embedded far from the block itself. In doing so, the probability of double loss is reduced to some extent. So, in this proposal, the shift vector is assigned a value approximately 1/3 of the image size. This way is only an expedient to reduce the probability of double loss.
8. The block-mapping path is almost public because the shift vector is assigned a fixed value with a random direction. This will lead to insecurity. He et al. (2006) propose the synchronous counterfeiting attack which exploits the vulnerability of shift vector.

Assume that $(m,n) \rightarrow (m',n')$ is a short-chain of block-mapping sequence and has been exposed to attackers. The synchronous counterfeiting attack is carried out according to the following procedure: Block $\mathbf{B}_{(m,n)}$ is replaced by an artificial block $\mathbf{B}$. The reference data extracted from the block $\mathbf{B}$ is embedded into the LSB of $\mathbf{B}_{(m',n')}$ synchronously. Tampering both the content and the corresponding back-up forms the medley consistency, and slips the forged image through the authentication without alerting.

We suggest that the confidential block-mapping path and the encrypted watermark are the first step to ensure security. As the above analysis, the former is an obvious requirement. The latter is equally important. If the encryption system is not applied, the artificial block $\mathbf{B}$ can be designed or selected arbitrarily as long as the size of block is compatible. In contrast, the availability of encryption process greatly reduces the freedom of tampering. In addition, it is an effective means of resisting against the dictionary attack.

In response to these existing problems, lots of meaningful efforts are put into this research topic for improving performance. Unfortunately, it is difficult to enumerate all related research works due to the limited space. Instead, we only survey five representative works and attempt to cover a variety of different technologies. In addition, it should be noted that we consider the security issues in self-embedding watermarking but not from the purely cryptographic perspective.

3.2. Adjacent-Block Detection

In the above work, the design of the shift vector is almost public even if the directions are chosen randomly. He et al. (2009) adopt the random sequence to generate the block-mapping sequence. Each block is assigned a unique and consecutive integer from left to right and top to bottom. Let N denote the total number of blocks. The generation algorithm is governed by a key K_m and described in the following:

[Step 1]: A pseudo-random sequence $b_1, b_2, \cdots, b_N$ is generated using a key K_m

[Step 2]: The pseudo-random sequence is sorted in ascending order $b_{a_1}, b_{a_2}, \cdots, b_{a_N}$. We obtain an index sequence $a_1, a_2, \cdots, a_N$ which is a scrambled version of sequence $1, 2, \cdots, N$

[Step 3]: The one-to-one block-mapping: $a_i = i$ where $1 \leq i \leq N$

Through implementing the above steps, we obtain a one-to-one block-mapping sequence. The information extracted from block $\mathbf{B}_i$ is embedded into block $\mathbf{B}_{a_i}$. Compared with the fixed shift vector, the key-based mapping sequence indeed improves the security. However, it is difficult to guarantee that there is a sufficient distance between block $\mathbf{B}_i$ and $\mathbf{B}_{a_i}$. In other words, the probability of double loss is dependent on not only the altered region Λ but also the used key K_m. In our opinion, this key-based block-mapping sequence generation is far from practical.

The reference data extraction and embedding are almost same with the proposal (Fridrich & Goljan, 1999) except the block-mapping sequence. We do not repeat the description of these processes and switch over to the authentication and recovery stage directly.

[Step 1] Block-Mapping Sequence Generation: Reproduce the block-mapping sequence using the key K_m.

[Step 2] Computation and Extraction: Compute the reference data $\hat{\mathbf{R}}_i$ from block $\hat{\mathbf{B}}_i$. The back-up $\mathbf{T}_{a_i}$ is obtained from the LSB of block $\hat{\mathbf{B}}_{a_i}$

[Step 3] Marking Dubious Blocks: If $D_i = \left|\hat{\mathbf{R}}_i - \mathbf{T}_{a_i}\right| \neq 0$, mark the block $\hat{\mathbf{B}}_i$ dubious, otherwise, mark it valid.

[Step 4] Judgment: For each dubious block $\hat{\mathbf{B}}_i$ judge this block $\hat{\mathbf{B}}_i$ valid if $\eta_i < \eta_{a_i}$; otherwise, it is judged as invalid. The measure η_i counts the number of dubious blocks around the block $\hat{\mathbf{B}}_i$

[Step 5] Post-Processing: For each valid block $\hat{\mathbf{B}}_i$ re-judge this block invalid if there are five or more invalid blocks around it. Similarly, an invalid block $\hat{\mathbf{B}}_i$ is re-judged as valid as long as there are no invalid blocks around it.

All invalid blocks are recovered by accessing the corresponding back-ups.

This adjacent-based detection method provides an approach to overcoming the authentication dilemma. We clarify the improved point hereinafter. Let us come back to the block-mapping sequence given in Equation 15.

Assuming that the reference information extracted from $\hat{\mathbf{B}}_{(m_1,n_1)}$ is not consistent with the content stored in $\mathbf{T}_{(m_2,n_2)}$, the block $\hat{\mathbf{B}}_{(m_1,n_1)}$ is marked as dubious instead of checking the information consistency with its forward block $\hat{\mathbf{B}}_{(m_0,n_0)}$. The final judgment is made on each dubious block by taking the status of all its adjacent blocks into account. In a nutshell, a dubious block tends to be judged as invalid if it is immersed in the dubious blocks. On the contrary, a dubious block can be cleared of suspicion as long as the valid blocks are majority in its adjacent blocks. This mechanism is similar with the slang "One takes the attributes of one's associates." We remark that adoption of the mechanism is reasonable. The reason is that in order to obtain a forged image without leaving visual traces, the altered region generally covers several adjacent blocks. However, it is predictable that the above mechanism is extremely fragile to some global operations, such as compression, filter, or noise contamination.

We conclude that this method develops a judgment mechanism which distinguishes tampered blocks from dubious blocks based on the status of adjacent blocks.

3.3. Hierarchical Detection and Self-Recovery

Lin et al. (2005) propose an efficient and effective digital watermarking method for detection and self-recovery. Authors explain that their method is efficient because only simple operations such as parity check and comparison between average intensities are used. The effectiveness refers to the hierarchical structure, which ensures the accuracy of tamper localization. The so-called hierarchical structure consists of four inspections from fine to coarse scope. If a tampered block is not detected in level-1 inspection, it can be detected in level-2 or level-3 inspection with a probability of nearly 1. Level-4 inspection is designed for resisting against vector quantization counterfeiting attack.

The proposed method starts with the preparation stage, namely block-mapping sequence generation. A 1-D transformation derived from the Arnold scrambling is utilized to produce the one-to-one block-mapping sequence. The transformation rule is formulated by the following equation.

$$a = \left(k \times b\right) \bmod N + 1 \qquad (18)$$

where a and b belonging to the interval $\left[0, N-1\right]$ are the block numbers. A prime number $k \in \left[0, N-1\right]$ can be regarded as a secret key K_m. Total number of blocks is denoted as N.

Different from the pseudo-random sequence sorting, this 1-D transformation provides another way to generate the one-to-one block-mapping sequence. However, it shares the same disadvantage. That is, this transformation is unable to ensure a sufficient distance between block $\mathbf{B}_a$ and $\mathbf{B}_b$. What is worse is that the small key space (only a prime number between 0 and $N-1$ can be used as key) makes this transformation difficult to resist against brute-force attack. How to design a reliable and secure block-mapping transformation is one of the main issues in the self-embedding watermarking techniques.

In this method, since the average intensity is extracted as reference data instead of using JPEG compression, the watermark generation and embedding algorithm become different with the method (Fridrich & Goljan, 1999). We give a completed description in the following.

[Step 1]: Set the two LSBs of each pixel to zero. The two LSBs are used as the reserved space for embedding watermark.

[Step 2]: Divide the image into non-overlapping blocks of size 4x4. This partitioning way implies that both height and width should be a multiple of 4.

[Step 3]: Randomly pick a prime number between 0 and $N-1$ as a secret key K_m. For each block, apply the Equation 18 to get the corresponding mapping block.

[Step 4]: Divide each block $\mathbf{B}_a$ into four sub-blocks sub$\mathbf{B}_a$ with size 2x2. Compute the average intensity of the block and each sub-block, denoted by $\mathrm{avg}\left(\mathbf{B}_a\right)$ and $\mathrm{avg}\left(\mathrm{sub}\mathbf{B}_a\right)$, respectively.

[Step 5]: For each sub-block, the authentication bit v and parity-check bit p are generated as two formulas below:

$$v = \begin{cases} 1 & \text{if } \operatorname{avg}\left(\text{sub}\mathbf{B}_a\right) \geq \operatorname{avg}\left(\mathbf{B}_a\right) \\ 0 & \text{otherwise} \end{cases} \tag{19}$$

$$p = \begin{cases} 1 & \text{if } sum \text{ is odd} \\ 0 & \text{otherwise} \end{cases} \tag{20}$$

where the variable *sum* counts the total number of bit 1 in the six MSBs of $\operatorname{avg}\left(\text{sub}\mathbf{B}_a\right)$

The 2x2 sub-block is the smallest unit and its six MSBs average intensity is regarded as the reference data. We have $\mathbf{R}_b = \operatorname{avg}\left(\text{sub}\mathbf{B}_b\right)$. According to Equation 18, the reference data $\mathbf{R}_b$ is embedded into the two LSBs of the sub-block sub$\mathbf{B}_a$

[Step 6]: The 3-tuple-watermark $\{v, p, \mathbf{R}\}$ containing eight bits is embedded into the two LSBs of sub-block sub$\mathbf{B}_a$. Figure 8 illustrates the detailed embedding position within one sub-block.

We draw a diagram shown in Figure 9 for well exhibiting the watermark generation and embedding processes.

The proposed tampering detection algorithm has a hierarchical structure. In the level-1 inspection, the checking target is the smallest unit, namely the sub-block of size 2x2. In the level-2 inspection, the checking view is adjusted to the block level. In the level-3 inspection, the checking view is further extended to the block-group which consists of the 3x3 adjacent blocks. Level-4 inspection is specially designed to frustrate the vector quantization certification attack. The details of hierarchical tampering detection scheme are described as follows.

[Step 1]: Level-1 inspection. For each sub-block sub$\hat{\mathbf{B}}_a$, extract authentication bit v and parity-check bit p from corresponding position as shown in Figure 9.

[Step 2]: Compute the average intensity $\operatorname{avg}\left(\text{sub}\hat{\mathbf{B}}_a\right)$ from the 6 MSBs of sub-block sub$\hat{\mathbf{B}}_a$. The computed parity-check bit p' is obtained according to the Equation 20.

[Step 3]: Compare p' with p. If they are not equal, mark the sub$\hat{\mathbf{B}}_a$ invalid and end the judgment for sub$\hat{\mathbf{B}}_a$. Otherwise, continue to the next step.

[Step 4]: Compute the average intensity $\operatorname{avg}\left(\hat{\mathbf{B}}_a\right)$ from the 6 MSBs of block $\hat{\mathbf{B}}_a$. The authentication bit v' can be determined according to the Equation 19.

[Step 5]: Compare v' with v. If they are not equal, mark the sub$\hat{\mathbf{B}}_a$ invalid and end the judgment for sub$\hat{\mathbf{B}}_a$. Otherwise, mark it valid.

[Step 6]: Level-2 inspection. The block $\hat{\mathbf{B}}_a$ is marked as invalid if any of its sub-block sub$\hat{\mathbf{B}}_a$ has been marked as invalid. Otherwise, mark the block $\hat{\mathbf{B}}_a$ valid.

[Step 7]: Level-3 inspection. For each valid block, re-mark the block invalid if there are five or more invalid blocks in its 3x3 adjacent blocks.

[Step 8]: Level-4 inspection. For resisting against vector quantization attack, the following sub-steps are performed on each valid block. Assume that the reference data of block $\hat{\mathbf{B}}_a$ is embedded into the LSBs of block $\hat{\mathbf{B}}_z$. This mapping block is accessible by using secret key K_m and 1-D transformation (18).

a. If block $\hat{\mathbf{B}}_z$ is marked as invalid, then directly re-mark block $\hat{\mathbf{B}}_a$ invalid.

b. If block $\hat{\mathbf{B}}_z$ is valid, compare four pairs of average intensities, namely

Figure 8. The eight-bit watermark embedded in pixel-1,2,3,4

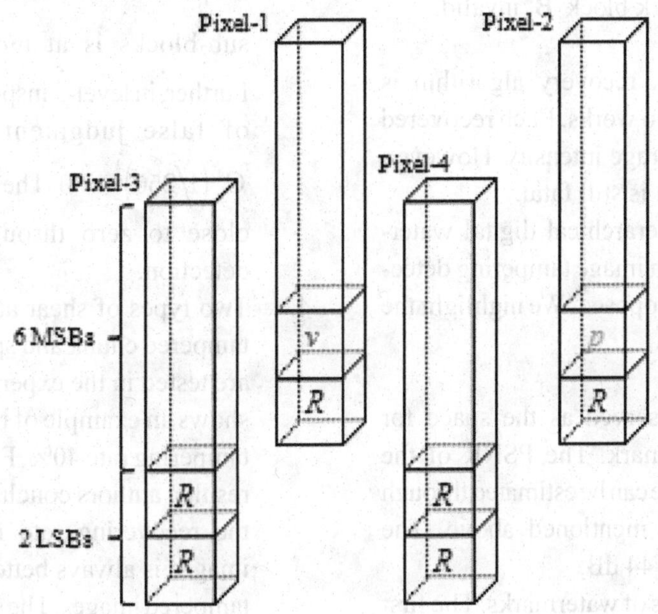

Figure 9. The diagram of the watermark generation and embedding procedure

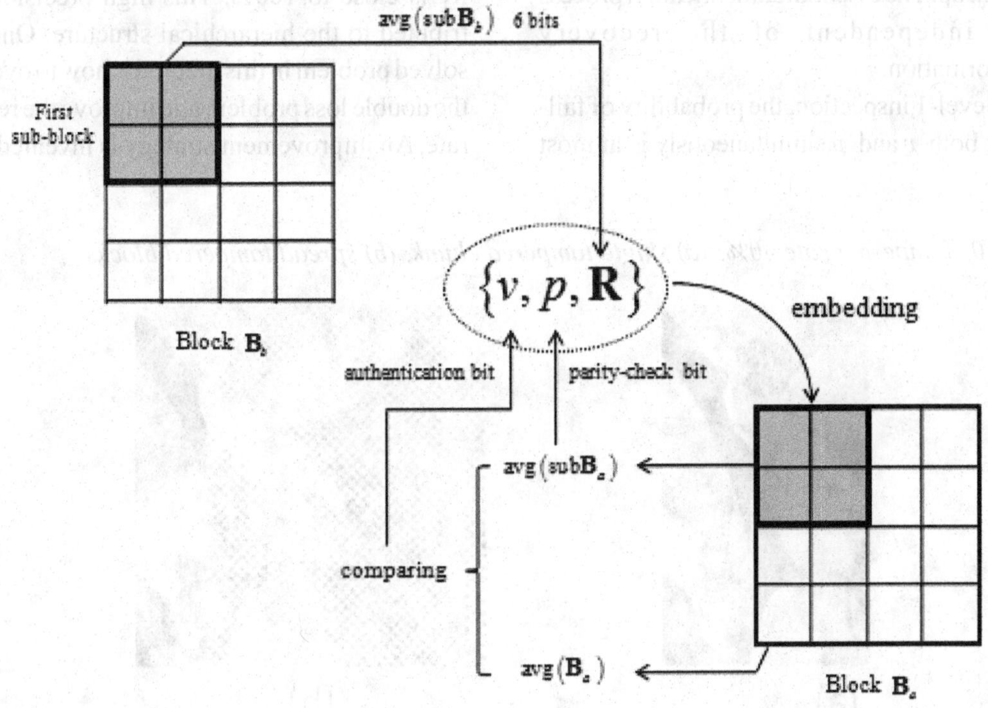

avg$\left(\text{sub}\hat{\mathbf{B}}_a\right)$ with sub$\mathbf{T}_z$. If they are different, mark block $\hat{\mathbf{B}}_a$ invalid.

The tampered block recovery algorithm is similar with previous two works. Each recovered pixel shares a same average intensity. However, the double loss problem is still fatal.

In this method, a hierarchical digital watermarking scheme for both image tampering detection and restoration is proposed. We highlight the important points:

1. Two LSBs are reserved as the space for embedding watermark. The PSNR of the watermarked image can be estimated through the same way as mentioned above. The estimated result is 44 dB.
2. There are two types of watermarks. The first type is designed for authentication. As an essential verification, the extracted bit v and p are embedded back to the sub-block itself. The second type is used for restoration. The average intensity of a sub-block acts as its back up. The essential authentication process is independent of the recovery information.
3. In level-1 inspection, the probability of failing both v and p simultaneously is at most (1/2 x (1/2) = 1/4. So in level-2 inspection, the probability of false judgment for all four sub-blocks is at most $\left(1/4\right)^4 \approx 0.39\%$. Further, in level-3 inspection, the probability of false judgment can be deduced: $C_9^4\left(1/256\right)^4 \approx 0$. The miss rate is almost close to zero through the hierarchical detection.
4. Two types of shear attacks, namely single tampered chunk and spread tampered block are tested in the experiment. The Figure 10 shows an example of two types of attacks at tampering rate 40%. From the experimental results, authors conclude in their paper that the recovering rate for spread tampered images is always better than that for single tampered images. The single tampered block is made up of a continuous shear zone, which gets trapped in double loss problem with higher probability.

The error detection and localization capability is close to 100%. This high precision is attributed to the hierarchical structure. One unresolved problem in this method is how to overcome the double loss problem and improve the recovery rate. An improvement strategy is invented in Lee

Figure 10. Tampering rate 40%: (a) single tampered chunk, (b) spread tampered blocks

(a)

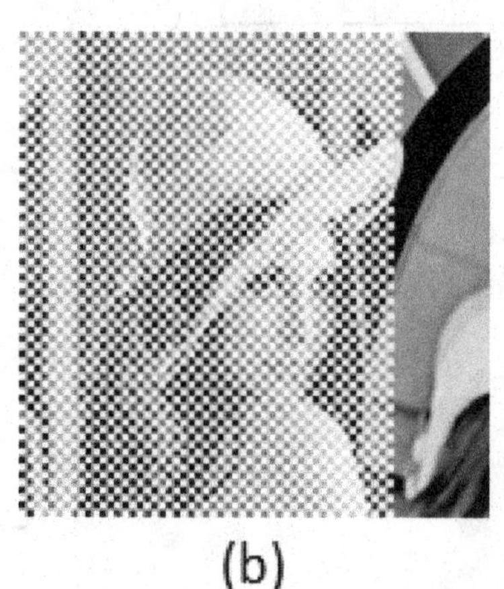

(b)

and Lin (2008). We now move to introduce this method.

3.4. Dual Watermark

As the title suggests, for each block, two copies are extracted. This mechanism provides second chance for block restoration in case one back-up is destroyed (Lee & Lin, 2008).

The authors first simplify the 1-D transformation in equation (18) to a look-up table, and then sum up two inherent properties.

The first one is so-called partner-block property. Two blocks **P** and **Q** are defined as partner-block pair if two conditions are always satisfied before and after the transformation.

1. The distance between two blocks equals to $N/2$
2. If either block is located in the upper half part, the other one must be located in the lower half of the image. (The original image is horizontally divided into two equal parts.)

Let $\langle \mathbf{P}, \mathbf{Q} \rangle$ denote a partner-block pair. We directly cite an example from Lee and Lin (2008) as shown in Figure 11. The basic settings are $N = 64$ and $k = 13$. The look-up table is the output transformed from the original table.

For instance, the reference data of block $\mathbf{B}_0$ is embedded into $\mathbf{B}_1$. Likewise, block $\mathbf{B}_{33}$ reserves space for storing the reference data of $\mathbf{B}_{32}$. In addition, we can find that $\mathbf{B}_0$ and $\mathbf{B}_{32}$ satisfy the above two conditions thus composing a partner-block pair. Also, block $\mathbf{B}_1$ and $\mathbf{B}_{33}$ have the same relationship.

In this dual watermarking scheme, two blocks with different position should be available. The following gives a brief description:

1. Extract the joint reference information from a partner-block pair $\langle \mathbf{B}_0, \mathbf{B}_{32} \rangle$
2. Embed the joint reference information into $\mathbf{B}_1$ which is the mapping block of $\mathbf{B}_0$
3. Embed the same joint reference information into $\mathbf{B}_{33}$ which is the mapping block of $\mathbf{B}_{32}$

Even if the upper half or the lower half of the image is totally damaged, the loss information can be entirely recovered by the back-up hidden in the other half of the image.

The second property is whole-column moving phenomenon. The 1-D transformation builds a mapping relationship taking the column as the

Figure 11. Block mapping transformation table: (a) original table, (b) look-up table, (c) modified look-up table after push-aside operation

(a)

0	1	2	3	4	5	6	7
8	9	10	11	12	13	14	15
16	17	18	19	20	21	22	23
24	25	26	27	28	29	30	31
32	33	34	35	36	37	38	39
40	41	42	43	44	45	46	47
48	49	50	51	52	53	54	55
56	57	58	59	60	61	62	63

(b)

1	14	27	40	53	2	15	28
41	54	3	16	29	42	55	4
17	30	43	56	5	18	31	44
57	6	19	32	45	58	7	20
33	46	59	8	21	34	47	60
9	22	35	48	61	10	23	36
49	62	11	24	37	50	63	12
25	38	51	0	13	26	39	52

(c)

14	53	15	28	1	27	40	2
54	29	55	4	41	3	16	42
30	5	31	44	17	43	56	18
6	45	7	20	57	19	32	58
46	21	47	60	33	59	8	34
22	61	23	36	9	35	48	10
62	37	63	12	49	11	24	50
38	13	39	52	25	51	0	26

unit. In other words, the elements in a column are exactly the same before and after transformation only in a different order. For example, all elements of the first column $[0, 8, 16, 24, 32, 40, 48, 56]^T$ are mapped to the second column, and the elements of the second column $[1, 9, 17, 25, 33, 41, 49, 57]^T$ are mapped to the seventh column.

The above two properties are the main causes of double loss problem. Even when using double back-ups, the improvement of recovery rate is limited.

We can observe from Figure 11. Two components of a partner-block pair $\langle \mathbf{P}, \mathbf{Q} \rangle$ come from the same column. The joint reference information of $\langle \mathbf{B}_0, \mathbf{B}_{32} \rangle$ is embedded into the second column. In fact, all partner-block pairs in the first column, namely $\langle \mathbf{B}_8, \mathbf{B}_{40} \rangle$, $\langle \mathbf{B}_{16}, \mathbf{B}_{48} \rangle$, and $\langle \mathbf{B}_{24}, \mathbf{B}_{56} \rangle$ are mapped to the second column. As mentioned above, the contiguous blocks are generally tampered concurrently for obtaining a good visual effect. If the tampered region includes both the first and second column, the double back-ups are both damaged. It means that the restoration for the first column fails.

A push-aside operation is designed to modify the look-up table. The core idea of this operation is to expand the distance between the source block and its mapping block. The operation is simple column moving. Push right the columns, which originally belong to the left half and push left the columns, which originally belong to the right half. The result of a modified look-up table is shown in Figure 11c. Therefore, even if the left half or the right half of the image is totally damaged, the information of the tampered region can be entirely recovered by the back-ups hidden in the other half of the image.

The main procedure is similar with the hierarchical structure watermarking. However, since double back-ups should be stored, naturally, more space is need. In this method, three LSBs are reserved for embedding watermark.

Assume that $\langle \mathbf{B}_a, \mathbf{B}_b \rangle$ is a partner-block pair. The block $\mathbf{B}_c$ and $\mathbf{B}_d$ are corresponding mapping blocks. Note that the size of each block is 2x2. The average intensity $\mathbf{R}$ is computed from the five MSBs of all pixels in the block. The parity-check bits p and v are generated as below:

$$p = R_{a7} \oplus R_{a6} \oplus R_{a5} \oplus R_{a4} \oplus R_{a3} \oplus R_{b7} \oplus R_{b6} \oplus R_{b5} \oplus R_{b4} \oplus R_{b3} \quad (21)$$

$$v = \begin{cases} 1 & \text{if } p = 0 \\ 0 & \text{otherwise} \end{cases} \quad (22)$$

In Equation 21, the subscripts refer to the block position and bit planes. The symbol $\oplus$ stands for the XOR operator.

As shown in Figure 12, the joint 12-bit watermark consists of average intensities $\text{avg}(\mathbf{B}_a)$, $\text{avg}(\mathbf{B}_b)$, as well as parity-check bits p and v.

Figure 12. Configuration of the joint 12-bit watermark

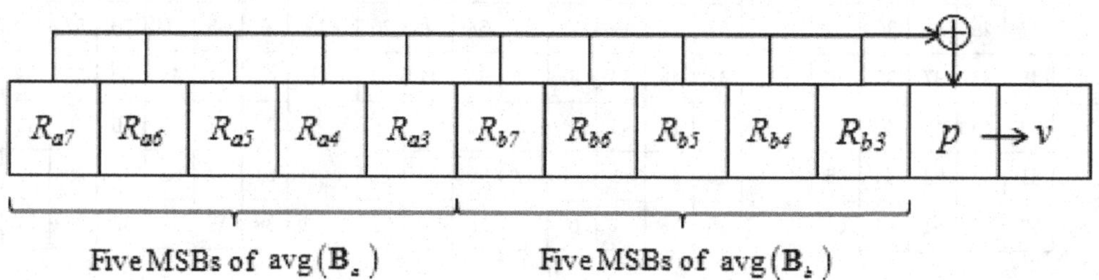

Then, the watermark is embedded into the three LSBs of the mapping blocks $\mathbf{B}_c$ and $\mathbf{B}_d$

A smoothing function is designed to minimize the difference between the original and the watermarked image. The smoothing function is given by

$$\hat{x} = \begin{cases} x+\alpha & \text{if } \left|\alpha\right| < 5 \\ x+\alpha+8 & \text{if } \alpha \leq -5 \\ x+\alpha-8 & \text{if } \alpha \geq 5 \end{cases} \tag{23}$$

For example, the value of pixel x is 232 $\left(11101000\right)_2$, and $\left(111\right)_2$ is the watermark bit which will be embedded into the three LSBs of pixel *x*. After embedding the watermark, the value of pixel becomes $\hat{x} = 239\left(11101111\right)_2$. The difference is 239-232 = 7. We apply the smoothing function to improve the quality of watermarked image. In this example, because $\alpha = 7 > 5$, the modified value is 239-8 = 231. The difference becomes 232-232 = 1. After applying the smoothing function, the difference is controlled within the interval [-4,4].

The detection and recovery procedures are almost similar with Lin et al.'s proposal. We will not repeat it here but highlight important points:

1. In Lin et al.'s proposal, the size of one block is 4x4. If and only if no sub-blocks are marked as invalid, the block is judged as valid. The above process is implemented in the level-2 inspection. Intuitively, at the edge of tampering region, some innocent sub-blocks are judged as invalid. However, in this proposal, much less false alarms are introduced because smaller block size is adopted.
2. The dual watermark technique provides double back-ups. If one back up is damaged, there is second chance to restore the loss information using another back up. Adoption of multiple back-ups is one way to exalt the recovery rate. We conclude two challenging issues for in-depth consideration. The first one is how to balance the trade-off between the number of back up and the quality of watermarked image. The second one is how to optimize the distribution of multiple back-ups so as to keep sufficient distance between any two back-ups. If the optimized distribution is achieved, we can expect that the probability of recovery failure is reduced.

In fact, this method has the same framework with the hierarchical structure watermarking technique. It can be looked upon as an advanced version.

The proposed two hierarchical detection methods fail to withstand the four-scanning attack (Chang, et al., 2008). The objective of this attack is to counterfeit a different image and pass the authentication successfully. A dictionary is generated by collecting the average intensities. For each block, the corresponding mapping block can be located through looking up its average intensity throughout the dictionary. After matching all mapping pairs, the block-mapping sequence is resolved. As explained above, the block-mapping sequence is the protection against synchronous counterfeiting attacks. Once this mapping information is exposed to attackers, the received images are no longer faithful. Although using encryption systems can indeed obstruct the dictionary searching, the real loophole is that the authentication bit v and parity-check bit p are both dependent on the average intensity. We can find that the 3-tuple-watermark $\left(v, p, \mathbf{R}\right)$ is constant as long as the average intensity does not change. In other words, a forged image is successful in passing the authentication when the tampered blocks hold their original average intensity. The four-scanning attack shows that the insecure factors in the hierarchical structure watermarking technique.

Recently, two new self-embedding watermarking techniques (Zhang, Wang, Qian, & Feng, 2011; Zhang, Qian, Ren, & Feng, 2011) based on compressive sensing are designed. We introduce this new structure hereinafter.

3.5. Reference Sharing and Flexible Self-Recovery

Zhang, Wang, Qian, and Feng (2011) propose a self-embedding watermarking with reference sharing mechanism. In its advanced version, the flexible self-recovery ability is endowed under similar sharing mechanism. Therefore, we focus more on the advance version.

Authors sum up two issues: tampering coincidence problem and watermark-data waste problem. The former has been explained in the above. Once again, it means that when double loss occurs, it is impossible to recover the damaged content. The latter means the embedded watermark data are not efficiently exploited. In the case that the tampered area is small, a large number of fresh watermark data do not contribute to improving the recovery quality.

The details of the procedure are as follows.

[Step 1]: Set the three LSBs of each pixel to zero. The three LSBs are used as the reserved space for embedding watermark.

[Step 2]: Segment the image into blocks of size 8x8. This partitioning way implies that both height and width should be a multiple of 8. Let N denote the total number of blocks.

[Step 3]: Perform DCT in each block. By the zigzag scanning, the 64 coefficients of a block are reshaped as a vector $\left[C_n(1), C_n(2), \cdots, C_n(64)\right]$. The subscript n stands for the label of one block.

[Step 4]: Permute and divide the N blocks into $N/16$ block-groups, each of which containing 16 blocks. The block permutation manipulation is governed by a key. The blocks in a same group come from different regions of the image. Collect the DCT coefficients of each block-group and form a longer vector **v**:

$$\begin{aligned}\mathbf{v} = [&C_{n1}(1),\ C_{n1}(2),\ \ldots, C_{n1}(64),\\ &C_{n2}(1),\ C_{n2}(2),\ \ldots, C_{n2}(64),\\ &\ldots \ldots,\\ &C_{n16}(1),\ C_{n16}(2),\ \ldots, C_{n16}(64)]^T\end{aligned}$$

[Step 5] Dimensionality Reduction Measurement: The 1024 DCT coefficients are projected onto a pseudo-random low-dimensional space. This process is similar with the random measurement of compressive sensing. Get the reference data **R** through the following equation.

$$\mathbf{R} = \mathbf{\Phi} \cdot \mathbf{v} \tag{24}$$

where $\mathbf{\Phi}$ is a pseudo-random matrix of size 368×1024. Elements of matrix $\mathbf{\Phi}$ are produced by a pseudo-random number generator and then normalized by column. We call $\mathbf{\Phi}$ the measurement matrix. The total number of reference values is $368 \times \left(N/16\right) = 23N$

[Step 6] Quantization: Each reference value is converted into an integer within the interval [-64,63]. Each quantized reference value is represented by 7 bits. The quantization function is given by

$$\hat{R} = \begin{cases} 63 & \text{if } R \geq f(64) \\ t & \text{if } f(t) \leq R \leq f(t+1) \\ -t-1 & \text{if } -f(t+1) \leq R \leq -f(t) \\ -64 & \text{if } R < -f(64) \end{cases}$$
$$t = 0,1,\cdots,63 \tag{25}$$

where

$$f(t) = \frac{t}{6} + \frac{t^2}{300}$$

So, the reference information in each block has $23 \times 7 = 161$ bits.

[Step 7] Generate Check-Bits: The check-bits are used for authentication and locating the tampered regions. For each block, the check-bits c_n are the output of a XOR operation between the hash-bits h_n and label-bits l. We mention here that each check-bits c_n contains 31 bits.

$$c_n(i) = h_n(i) \oplus l(i)$$
$$n = 1,2,\cdots,N \tag{26}$$
$$i = 1,2,\cdots,31$$

We explain how to obtain the hash-bits h_n and label-bits l in the following.

For each block, the position-bits with length 64 bits are converted from the coordinate of its upper left corner pixel. The 320 original bits in the 5 MSBs, 161 bits quantized reference information as well as 64 position-bits are taken as inputs to a hash function. Therefore, any change in the input leads to a totally different output. The label-bits with length 31 bits are generated randomly.

It should be noted that same label-bits are commonly used for all blocks.

[Step 8] Form Watermark and Embed: The 161 bits quantized reference information and 31 bits check-bits are combined and then permuted governed by a key. This 192 bits block watermark is to replace the 3 LSBs of the block.

In the image authentication and recovery stage, the 31 check-bits are exploited for locating the tampered blocks.

The 31 label-bits are calculated from each block using the corresponding reverse operations.

$$\hat{l}_n(i) = \hat{h}_n(i) \oplus \hat{c}_n(i)$$
$$n = 1,2,\cdots,N \tag{27}$$
$$i = 1,2,\cdots,31$$

If a certain block is not damaged, the extracted label-bits $\hat{l}_n(i)$ must be same as the original label-bits. Relatively, a tampered block results in different label-bits with a probability $(1-2^{-31})$. Although the receiver has no knowledge about the original label-bits $l(i)$, it can pairwise compare the extracted label-bits $\hat{l}_n(i)$. If the extracted label-bits $\hat{l}_n(i)$ is different with most others, the nth block is marked as invalid.

The recovery procedure is described as follows:

[Step 1] Inverse Quantization: Assume that each block-group which contains q tampered blocks. From the unspoiled blocks, we can extract the reference values whose number is $(16-q) \times 64$, less than 1024. Through the inverse quantization given in Equation 28, the range of extractable reference values can be retrieved approximatively.

$$\tilde{R} = \begin{cases} \dfrac{f(\hat{R}) + f(\hat{R}+1)}{2} & \text{if } 0 \le \hat{R} \le 63 \\ \dfrac{-f(-\hat{R}) - f(-\hat{R}-1)}{2} & \text{if } -64 \le \hat{R} \le -1 \end{cases} \tag{28}$$

[Step 2] Content Recovery: In the case that $(16-q) \times 64 = 1024$, namely $q = 0$, there are no damaged blocks in this block-group. Therefore, the content recovery is needless.

If one block-group contains damaged blocks, the following content recovery stage is switched on. Firstly, the Equation 24 can be rewritten as

$$\tilde{\mathbf{R}} = \mathbf{\Phi}^{(E)} \cdot \mathbf{v} \tag{29}$$

where $\tilde{\mathbf{R}}$ is the output of the inverse quantizer and its length is $(16-q) \times 64 < 368$. Matrix $\mathbf{\Phi}^{(E)}$ is made up by taking rows from original measurement matrix $\mathbf{\Phi}$ corresponding to the positions of extractable reference values. One coefficient vector $\mathbf{v}$ is divided into the reserved part $\mathbf{v}_R$ and the tampered part $\mathbf{v}_T$. The Equation 29 implies

$$\tilde{\mathbf{R}} = \mathbf{\Phi}^{(E,R)} \cdot \mathbf{v}_R + \mathbf{\Phi}^{(E,T)} \cdot \mathbf{v}_T \tag{30}$$

Since the reserved part $\mathbf{v}_R$ has not been damaged, only vector $\mathbf{v}_T$ is waiting for reconstruction. Then,

$$\mathbf{s} = \tilde{\mathbf{R}} - \mathbf{\Phi}^{(E,R)} \cdot \mathbf{v}_R = \mathbf{\Phi}^{(E,T)} \cdot \mathbf{v}_T \tag{31}$$

If there are many tampered blocks in the block-group, the length of $\mathbf{v}_T$ is greater than that of $\mathbf{s}$. In this way, the reconstruction becomes an underdetermined problem. Most of compressive sensing reconstruction methods (Babadi, et al., 2010; Bioucas & Figueiredo, 2007; Blumensath & Davies, 2008; Gorodnitsky & Rao, 1997; Tropp & Gilbert, 2007) can be directly applied.

On the contrary, if the length of $\mathbf{v}_T$ is less than that of $\mathbf{s}$, Equation 31 forms an overdetermined problem. An iterative deviation shrink algorithm is designed for getting an approximate solution. The quantization cased error is restricted by the lower bound $\mathbf{b}_l$ and the upper bound $\mathbf{b}_u$. The estimated bound values are listed in Box 1.

Hence, the following inequality should be hold for each data $s(m)$:

$$s(m) + b_l(m) \le \mathbf{\Phi}_m^{(E,T)} \cdot \mathbf{v}_T < s(m) + b_u(m) \tag{33}$$

where $\mathbf{\Phi}_m^{(E,T)}$ is the mth row of matrix $\mathbf{\Phi}^{(E,T)}$, and $m = 1, \cdots, (16-q) \times 64$.

Box 1. Estimated bound values

$$\mathbf{b}_l = \begin{cases} \dfrac{f(63) - f(64)}{2} \\ \dfrac{f(\hat{R}) - f(\hat{R}+1)}{2} \\ \dfrac{f(-\hat{R}-1) - f(-\hat{R})}{2} \\ -\infty \end{cases} \text{ and } \mathbf{b}_u = \begin{cases} +\infty & \text{if } \hat{R} = 63 \\ \dfrac{f(\hat{R}+1) - f(\hat{R})}{2} & \text{if } 0 \le \hat{R} \le 62 \\ \dfrac{f(-\hat{R}) - f(-\hat{R}-1)}{2} & \text{if } -63 \le \hat{R} \le -1 \\ \dfrac{f(64) - f(63)}{2} & \text{if } \hat{R} = -64 \end{cases} \tag{32}$$

The iterative deviation shrink algorithm is performed as follows:

1. **Initialization:** Pseudo-inverse method. We get an initial solution $\mathbf{v}'_{\mathrm{T}}$ from

$$\mathbf{v}'_{\mathrm{T}} = \left[\mathbf{\Phi}^{(\mathrm{E,T})}\right]^{-1} \cdot \mathbf{s} \tag{34}$$

2. Let $\mathbf{v}''_{\mathrm{T}} = \mathbf{v}'_{\mathrm{T}}$, and $m = 1$. Calculate $\overline{s}\left(m\right) = \Phi^{(\mathrm{E,T})}_{m} \cdot \mathbf{v}''_{\mathrm{T}}$.
3. **Update:** This process, shown in Box 2, is to force $\mathbf{v}''_{\mathrm{T}}$ to meet the constraint in Equation 33.
4. **Two Termination Conditions:**

    a. $m > \left(16 - q\right) \times 64$

    b. $D = \dfrac{\left\|\mathbf{v}''_{\mathrm{T}} - \mathbf{v}'_{\mathrm{T}}\right\|}{64 \times q} < T$

Here, the symbol T is a threshold and should be set as a small constant. The second termination condition is prescribed to ensure two last versions of $\mathbf{v}_{\mathrm{T}}$ have been close enough and the update will not reduce the deviation further.

The proposed method provides a way to solve the tampering coincidence problem. The block-wise embedding style is abandoned instead by the one-to-many mapping fashion. A trade-off mechanism is built. It moderates the double loss problem by scattering the whole block loss over multiple blocks. In doing so, the alteration of semantics is avoided at the expense of multiple blocks' degraded recovery.

3.6. Summary

In this section, we introduce five existing works according to a series of questions. We hope that authors can answer these questions when they review this section.

1. What is self-embedding watermarking?
2. Why the one-to-one block mapping function should be kept secret?
3. Why the one-to-one block mapping function should be modified by push-side operation?
4. How to judge one block as valid or invalid?
5. Why the extracted information should be encrypted?
6. How to withstand the four-scanning attack?
7. How to overcome the tampering coincidence problem?

There exist too many meaningful self-embedding watermarking works to include them into this chapter. Zhu et al. (2007) propose a semi-fragile watermarking method for the automatic authentication and restoration of the loss content of digital images. Semi-fragile watermarks are used for locating the malicious tampering on the image. The restoration problem is formulated as

Box 2. Updating

$$\begin{cases} \mathbf{v}''_{\mathrm{T}} = \mathbf{v}''_{\mathrm{T}} - \left[\overline{s}\left(m\right) - s\left(m\right) - b_{\mathrm{l}}\left(m\right)\right] \cdot \dfrac{\Phi^{(\mathrm{E,T})}_{m}}{\left\|\Phi^{(\mathrm{E,T})}_{m}\right\|} & \text{if } \overline{s}\left(m\right) - s\left(m\right) < b_{\mathrm{l}}\left(m\right) \\ \mathbf{v}''_{\mathrm{T}} = \mathbf{v}''_{\mathrm{T}} - \left[\overline{s}\left(m\right) - s\left(m\right) - b_{\mathrm{u}}\left(m\right)\right] \cdot \dfrac{\Phi^{(\mathrm{E,T})}_{m}}{\left\|\Phi^{(\mathrm{E,T})}_{m}\right\|} & \text{if } \overline{s}\left(m\right) - s\left(m\right) > b_{\mathrm{u}}\left(m\right) \end{cases} \tag{35}$$

an irregular sampling problem. Luo et al. (2008) exploit a digital halftoning technique to extract the reference data. Their method combines the pixel-wise and block-wise property. The watermark is pixel-wise permuted and embedded into the host image, while tampering detection and recovery are performed in a block-wise strategy. Yang and Shen (2010) first create an index table of the original image via vector quantization, which is used to recover the tampered regions. They imitate Wong's watermarking scheme (Wong & Memon, 2001) to authenticate image.

Finally, we summarize this chapter and outline the further works in the conclusion section.

4. CONCLUSION

In this chapter, we focus on self-embedding watermarking techniques, which enable not only locating the tampered regions but also recovering the missing information for preserving the semantics of original image. The usual forward routine contains partitioning, extracting authentication bits, extracting recovery information, positioning mapping block, and embedding. The reverse process consists of authentication and reconstruction. Representative methods including hierarchical detection, dual watermarks, reference sharing as well as flexible self-recovery are analyzed and summarized. The key technologies are secure block-mapping function, unambiguous authentication, reference information extraction method and watermark embedding scheme. Table 1 helps readers to clarify the related concepts.

We conclude that although the recent proposals adopt more advanced method, to achieve that is based on the sacrifice of the quality of watermarked image. In addition, since the watermark is embedded into LSB of pixels, the reference data may be destroyed by some legitimate image processing operations, such as compression, filtering and contrast adjustment. What is worse, a naïve attack that erases or cuts the embedding information makes these existing algorithms useless. Moreover, a slight affine transformation destroys the authentication and recovery processes as well. Followings may be suggested for future works: (1) to combine with the content-based authentication method. This research direction requires that the authentication bits have the ability to withstand the various common signal processing as long as the semantics of image is impervious; (2) The reference data should be robustly embedded. Since the reference data is the backup, robustly embedding requires that the damage of reference data should be lowered to the minority if content tampering occurs; (3) To design a more secure embedding algorithm. Intuitively, extracting the reference data should be a hard work without key.

Table 1. Comparison of key technologies

	Block-Mapping Function	Authentication	Extraction	Embedding
Fridrich and Goljan (1999)	Fixed shift vector	Check the consistency between source and mapping block	JPEG	1 LSB
He et al. (2009)	Random sequence	Taking adjacent blocks into account	JPEG	1 LSB
Lin et al. (2005)	1-D transformation	Average intensities comparison and parity check	Average intensities	2 LSB
Lee and Lin (2008)	Improved 1-D transformation	Average intensities comparison and parity check	Average intensities	3 LSB
Zhang et al. (2011)	Permutation algorithm	Hash function	Quantized measurements	3 LSB

REFERENCES

Alattar, A. M. (2004). Reversible watermark using the difference expansion of a generalized integer transform. *IEEE Transactions on Image Processing*, *13*(8), 1147–1156. doi:10.1109/TIP.2004.828418

Babadi, B., Kalouptsidis, N., & Tarokh, V. (2010). SPARLS: The sparse RLS algorithm. *IEEE Transactions on Signal Processing*, *58*(8), 4013–4025. doi:10.1109/TSP.2010.2048103

Baraniuk, R. G. (2007). Compressive sensing. *IEEE Signal Processing Magazine*, *24*(4), 118–121. doi:10.1109/MSP.2007.4286571

Barni, M., Bartolini, F., Cappellini, V., & Piva, A. (1998). A DCT-domain system for robust image watermarking. *Signal Processing*, *66*(3), 357–372. doi:10.1016/S0165-1684(98)00015-2

Barreto, P. S. L. M., Kim, H. Y., & Rijmen, V. (2002). Toward secure public-key blockwise fragile authentication watermarking. *IEEE Proceedings-Vision Image and Signal Processing*, *149*(2), 57-62.

Bioucas, J., & Figueiredo, M. (2007). A new TwIST: Two-step iterative shrinkage/thresholding algorithms for image restoration. *IEEE Transactions on Image Processing*, *16*(12), 2992–3004. doi:10.1109/TIP.2007.909319

Bloom, J. A., Cox, I. J., Kalker, T., Linnartz, J. P. M. G., Miller, M. L., & Traw, C. B. S. (1999). Copy protection for DVD video. *Proceedings of the IEEE*, *87*(7), 1267–1276. doi:10.1109/5.771077

Blumensath, T., & Davies, M. E. (2008). Gradient pursuits. *IEEE Transactions on Signal Processing*, *56*(6), 2370–2382. doi:10.1109/TSP.2007.916124

Candès, E. J., Romberg, J., & Tao, T. (2006). Robust uncertainty principles: exact signal reconstruction from highly incomplete frequency information. *IEEE Transactions on Information Theory*, *52*(2), 489–509. doi:10.1109/TIT.2005.862083

Cano, P., Batlle, E., Kalker, T., & Haitsma, J. (2002). A review of algorithms for audio fingerprinting. In *Proceedings of the 5th IEEE Workshop on Multimedia Signal Processing*. IEEE Press. Retrieved from http://ieeexplore.ieee.org/xpl/freeabs_all.jsp?arnumber=1203274-&abstractAccess=no&userType=

Celik, M. U., Sharma, G., Saber, E., & Tekalp, A. M. (2002). Hierarchical watermarking for secure image authentication with localization. *IEEE Transactions on Image Processing*, *11*(6), 585–595. doi:10.1109/TIP.2002.1014990

Chang, C. C., Chen, G. M., & Lin, M. H. (2004). Information hiding based on search-order coding for VQ indices. *Pattern Recognition Letters*, *25*(11), 1253–1261. doi:10.1016/j.patrec.2004.04.003

Chang, C. C., Fan, Y. H., & Tai, W. L. (2008). Four-scanning attack on hierarchical digital watermarking method for image tamper detection and recovery. *Pattern Recognition*, *41*(2), 654–661. doi:10.1016/j.patcog.2007.06.003

Chen, G. R., Mao, Y. B., & Chui, C. K. (2004). A symmetric image encryption scheme based on 3D chaotic cat maps. *Chaos, Solitons, and Fractals*, *21*(3), 749–761. doi:10.1016/j.chaos.2003.12.022

Cheng, H., & Li, X. B. (2000). Partial encryption of compressed images and videos. *IEEE Transactions on Signal Processing*, *48*(8), 2439–2451. doi:10.1109/78.852023

Coppersmith, D., Mintzer, F. C., Tresser, C. P., Wu, C. W., & Yeung, M. M. (1999). Fragile imperceptible digital watermark with privacy control. In P. M. Wong (Ed.), *Conference on Security and Watermarking of Multimedia Contents,* (pp. 79-84). San Jose, CA: IEEE.

Cox, I. J., Kilian, J., Leighton, F. T., & Shamoon, T. (1997). Secure spread spectrum watermarking for multimedia. *IEEE Transactions on Image Processing*, *6*(12), 1673–1687. doi:10.1109/83.650120

Cox, I. J., Miller, M. L., Bloom, J. A., Fridrich, J., & Kalker, T. (2008). *Digital watermarking and steganography*. Burlington, MA: Morgan Kaufmann Publishers.

Doerr, G., & Dugelay, J. L. (2003). A guide tour of video watermarking. *Signal Processing Image Communication*, *18*(4), 263–282. doi:10.1016/S0923-5965(02)00144-3

Donoho, D. L. (2006). Compressive sensing. *IEEE Transactions on Information Theory*, *52*(4), 1289–1306. doi:10.1109/TIT.2006.871582

Farid, H. (2009). Image forgery dection. *IEEE Signal Processing Magazine*, *26*(2), 16–25. doi:10.1109/MSP.2008.931079

Fridrich, J. (2009). Digital image forensics. *IEEE Signal Processing Magazine*, *26*(2), 26–37. doi:10.1109/MSP.2008.931078

Fridrich, J., & Goljan, M. (1999). Images with self-correcting capabilities. In *Proceedings of the 1999 International Conference on Image Processing*, (pp. 792-796). Kobe, Japan: IEEE Press.

Gorodnitsky, I. F., & Rao, B. D. (1997). Sparse signal reconstruction from limited data using FOCUSS: A re-weighted norm minimization algorithm. *IEEE Transactions on Signal Processing*, *45*(3), 600–616. doi:10.1109/78.558475

Hartung, F., & Kutter, M. (1999). Multimedia watermarking techniques. *Proceedings of the IEEE*, *87*(7), 1079–1107. doi:10.1109/5.771066

He, H. J., Zhang, J. S., & Chen, F. (2009). Adjacent-block based statistical detection method for self-embedding watermarking techniques. *Signal Processing*, *89*(8), 1557–1566. doi:10.1016/j.sigpro.2009.02.009

He, H. J., Zhang, J. S., & Wang, H. X. (2006). Synchronous counterfeiting attacks on self-embedding watermarking schemes. *International Journal of Computer Science and Network Security*, *6*(1).

Holliman, M., & Memon, N. (2000). Counterfeiting attacks on oblivious block-wise independent invisible watermarking schemes. *IEEE Transactions on Image Processing*, *9*(3). doi:10.1109/83.826780

Kirovski, D., & Malvar, H. S. (2003). Spread-spectrum watermarking of audio signals. *IEEE Transactions on Signal Processing*, *51*(4), 1020–1033. doi:10.1109/TSP.2003.809384

Lee, C. C., Wu, H. C., Tsai, C. S., & Chu, Y. P. (2008). Adaptive lossless steganographic scheme with centralized difference expansion. *Pattern Recognition*, *41*(6), 2097–2106. doi:10.1016/j.patcog.2007.11.018

Lee, T. Y., & Lin, S. D. (2008). Dual watermark for image tamper detection and recovery. *Pattern Recognition*, *41*(11), 3497–3506. doi:10.1016/j.patcog.2008.05.003

Li, C. T. (2004). Digital fragile watermarking scheme for authentication of JPEG images. *IEEE Proceedings-Vision Image and Signal Processing*, *151*(6), 460-466.

Lin, C. Y., & Chang, S. F. (2000). Semi-fragile watermarking for authenticating JPEG visual content. *Security and Watermarking of Multimedia Contents II*, *3971*, 140–151.

Lin, P. L., Hsieh, C. K., & Huang, P. W. (2005). A hierarchical digital watermarking method for image tamper detection and recovery. *Pattern Recognition*, *38*(12), 2519–2529. doi:10.1016/j.patcog.2005.02.007

Lukas, J., Fridrich, J., & Goljan, M. (2006). Digital camera identification from sensor pattern noise. *IEEE Transactions on Information Forensics and Security*, *1*(2), 205–214. doi:10.1109/TIFS.2006.873602

Luo, H., Chu, S. C., & Lu, Z. M. (2008). Self embedding watermarking using halftoning technique. *Circuits, Systems, and Signal Processing*, *27*(2), 155–170. doi:10.1007/s00034-008-9024-0

Maeno, K., Sun, Q. B., Chang, S. F., & Suto, M. (2006). New semi-fragile image authentication watermarking techniques using random bias and nonuniform quantization. *IEEE Transactions on Multimedia*, *8*(1), 32–45. doi:10.1109/TMM.2005.861293

Marvel, L. M., Boncelet, C. G., & Retter, C. T. (1999). Spread spectrum image steganography. *IEEE Transactions on Image Processing*, *8*(8), 1075–1083. doi:10.1109/83.777088

Nikolaidis, N., & Pitas, I. (1998). Robust image watermarking in the spatial domain. *Signal Processing*, *66*(3), 385–403. doi:10.1016/S0165-1684(98)00017-6

Pennebaker, W. B., & Mitchell, J. L. (1993). *JPEG: Still image data compression standard*. New York, NY: Springer.

Petitcolas, F. A. P., Anderson, R. J., & Kuhn, M. G. (1999). Information hiding – A survey. *Proceedings of the IEEE*, *87*(7), 1062–1078. doi:10.1109/5.771065

Popescu, A. C., & Farid, H. (2005). Exposing digital forgeries by detecting traces of resampling. *IEEE Transactions on Signal Processing*, *53*(2), 758–767. doi:10.1109/TSP.2004.839932

Tang, C. W., & Hang, H. M. (2003). A feature-based robust digital image watermarking scheme. *IEEE Transactions on Signal Processing*, *51*(4), 950–959. doi:10.1109/TSP.2003.809367

Thodi, D. M., & Rodriguez, J. J. (2007). Expansion embedding techniques for reversible watermarking. *IEEE Transactions on Image Processing*, *16*(3), 721–730. doi:10.1109/TIP.2006.891046

Tian, J. (2003). Reversible data embedding using a difference expansion. *IEEE Transactions on Circuits and Systems for Video Technology*, *13*(8), 890–896. doi:10.1109/TCSVT.2003.815962

Tropp, J. A., & Gilbert, A. C. (2007). Signal recovery from random measurements via orthogonal matching pursuit. *IEEE Transactions on Information Theory*, *53*(12), 4655–4666. doi:10.1109/TIT.2007.909108

Tsai, P., Hu, Y. C., & Yeh, H. L. (2009). Reversible image hiding scheme using predictive coding and histogram shifting. *Signal Processing*, *89*(6), 1129–1143. doi:10.1016/j.sigpro.2008.12.017

Wang, W., Dong, J., & Tan, T. N. (2009). A survey of passive image tampering detection. In A. T. S. Ho (Ed.), *8th International Workshop on Digital Watermarking,* (pp. 308-322). Guildford, UK: University of Surrey.

Wang, X. Y., & Zhao, H. (2006). A novel synchronization invariant audio watermarking scheme based on DWT and DCT. *IEEE Transactions on Signal Processing*, *54*(12), 4835–4840. doi:10.1109/TSP.2006.881258

Wong, P. W., & Memon, N. (2001). Secret an public key image watermarking schemes for image authentication and ownership verification. *IEEE Transactions on Image Processing*, *10*(10), 1593–1601. doi:10.1109/83.951543

Wu, C. P., & Kuo, C. C. J. (2005). Design of integrated multimedia compression and encryption systems. *IEEE Transactions on Multimedia*, *7*(5), 828–839. doi:10.1109/TMM.2005.854469

Wu, C. W. (2002). On the design of content-based multimedia authentication systems. *IEEE Transactions on Multimedia*, *4*(3), 385–393. doi:10.1109/TMM.2002.802018

Wu, S. Q., Huang, J. W., Huang, D. R., & Shi, Y. Q. (2005). Efficiently self-synchronized audio watermarking for assured audio data transmission. *IEEE Transactions on Broadcasting*, *51*(1), 69–76. doi:10.1109/TBC.2004.838265

Yang, C. W., & Shen, J. J. (2010). Recover the tampered image based on VQ indexing. *Signal Processing*, *90*(1), 331–343. doi:10.1016/j.sigpro.2009.07.007

Zhang, X. P., Qian, Z. X., Ren, Y. L., & Feng, G. R. (2011). Watermarking with flexible self-recovery quality based on compressive sensing and compositive reconstruction. *IEEE Transactions on Information Forensics and Security*, *6*(4), 1223–1232. doi:10.1109/TIFS.2011.2159208

Zhang, X. P., Wang, S. Z., Qian, Z. X., & Feng, G. R. (2011). Reference sharing mechanism for watermark self-embedding. *IEEE Transactions on Image Processing*, *20*(2), 485–495. doi:10.1109/TIP.2010.2066981

Zhu, X. Z., Ho, A. T. S., & Marziliano, P. (2007). A new semi-fragile image watermarking with robust tampering restoration using irregular sampling. *Signal Processing Image Communication*, *22*(5), 515–528. doi:10.1016/j.image.2007.03.004

KEY TERMS AND DEFINITIONS

Authentication: The procedure to verify whether a block has been tampered or not.

Compressive Sensing: A new sampling theorem which can sample a sparse or compressible signal at a rate below the Nyquist theorem required.

Counterfeiting Attack: The vector quantization counterfeiting attack which is effective on the block-wise independent watermarking technique.

Mapping Function: A function formulates the location relationship among blocks.

Self-Embedding Watermarking: A type of watermarking which enables not only detection of areas that have been tampered, but also recovering the missing information.

Tampering Coincidence Problem: The original and back-up blocks are both tampered by coincidence.

Watermarking: The practice of imperceptibly altering an image to embed a message about that image.

Chapter 15
A Benchmark Tool for Digital Watermarking

Keiichi Iwamura
Tokyo University of Science, Japan

ABSTRACT

This chapter presents an overview of benchmark tools for digital watermarking and describes a new benchmark tool that supports various attacks and has a graphical user interface. Digital watermarks are used to prevent unauthorized use of digital content such as illegal copying, unauthorized distribution, and falsification. Benchmark tools are required to measure the strength of digital watermarks. Stirmark and JEWELS are well-known benchmark tools. However, the functionality of existing tools is insufficient because they lack evaluation functions for multiple image attacks. In addition, users need to memorize each attack command and check results on another viewer because almost all the existing tools are implemented as command-line-based software without image viewers. Therefore, the authors classify attacks on digital watermarks and develop a new benchmark tool that includes attacking functions using multiple as well as single images. In addition, the tool has a graphical user interface that makes it easy to perform combinations of two or more attacks.

INTRODUCTION

The use of digital media such as pictures, movies, and music has increased in recent years because of advances in computer technology. However, users can easily generate and redistribute illegal copies of this digital content. Digital watermarks are used to protect copyright material from such illegal acts (Bender, 1996). Digital watermarking embeds information such as copyright information or user information in the original content by changing some of its data. When an illegal copy of such content is found, the content owner can extract the embedded watermarks to expose the unauthorized use of that content. Digital watermarks can be embedded in various types of media, including still or moving pictures, animation, and sound. In this chapter, we treat and discuss the digital watermarking of still pictures.

Unauthorized users try to destroy embedded watermarks to prevent discovery of their unauthorized use. Therefore, it is necessary to

DOI: 10.4018/978-1-4666-2217-3.ch015

properly evaluate the robustness of watermarking technologies to prevent the unauthorized use of digital content that uses digital watermarking. Benchmark tools such as Stirmark (1998) and JEWELS (2001) have been developed for this purpose. These tools can determine which attacks have the potential to damage embedded digital watermarks.

However, these conventional tools are difficult to use because they have command line interfaces and do not have image viewers. Therefore, users need to memorize attack commands and use another viewer to check the results. Furthermore, the implemented functions for evaluating robustness are inadequate because they only involve attacks based on a single image. Because of this limitation, most current digital watermarking technologies aim to be robust against single-image attacks. However, attacks that use multiple images are very powerful compared to those that use a single image, and they can be performed quite easily. In addition, these attacks do not degrade images. Therefore, the evaluation of robustness against such attacks is very important and has a practical use in benchmark tools for digital watermarking. We have developed a new benchmark tool that overcomes these limitations. Our tool has attacking functions involving both single and multiple images, and it can easily perform a combination of two or more attacks. In addition, the tool is easy to use because it has a Graphical User Interface (GUI).

In this chapter, we describe attacks on digital watermarking and existing benchmark tools, and we present the features of our new benchmark tool. We discuss its mounting interface and the functions that it implements, and we provide some benchmarking examples.

ATTACKS ON DIGITAL WATERMARKING

Attacks on digital watermarking involve image processing that transforms watermarked information and prevents it from being read. We classify these attacks into two groups.

Single-Image Attacks

A single-image attack is applied to a single image containing a digital watermark. Single-image attacks can employ image-processing operations such as noise addition, JPEG compression, trimming, and scaling. In general, because these operations are frequently performed on images, digital watermarking needs to be robust against these attacks. Some attacks are mounted in many existing image-editing tools, and these are considered to be innocent attacks.

However, malicious attacks intentionally change images to make it impossible to extract the watermark. For example, attacks that create small geometrical distortions in images are well known (Petitcolas, 1998). These attacks warp an image by multiple applications of minute, local rotations, and scaling. In addition, the possibility of Frequency Mode Laplacian Removal (FMLR) attacks has been discovered (Barnett, 1998). These attacks remove watermarks by using Laplacian convolution masks. In general, these single-image attacks degrade image quality.

Multiple-Image Attacks

A multiple-image attack involves two or more images. For example, consider the case where a content owner sends an image to two users. The content owner embeds different watermarks for users to identify. If the users collude and compare their images, the portion where the watermarks differ will be apparent and they can change the watermark of the portion. If many users collude, all portions of watermarks will be apparent and they can freely change the watermarks. This type of attack is known as a collusion attack (Wu, 2006; Feng, 2009).

Another typical multiple-image attack is the averaging attack (Dalkilic, 2010; Braci, 2010). This attack computes an average value of several watermarked images. The greater the number of images that are averaged, the better the image quality will be and the more the average image will approximate the original image. An averaging attack can be described as follows. The original image G is sent to each user i ($i = 1,...,n$) with embedded information A_i. Hence, the watermarked image for i is $W_i = G + A_i$. When an averaging attack is carried out among n users, the average image is

$$\sum_{i=1}^{n} W_i / n = (n \cdot G + \sum_{i=1}^{n} A_i) / n = G + \sum_{i=1}^{n} A_i / n$$

Usually, because it can be assumed that A_i is a different random value for each user, the average value becomes 0. Hence, if n is sufficiently large, colluding users can obtain

$$\sum_{i=1}^{n} W_i / n = G$$

and the watermark information is deleted. Thus, multiple-image attacks constitute the most serious type of threat for digital watermarks.

EXISTING BENCHMARK TOOLS

Benchmark tools attack digital watermarks and then determine whether the digital watermarks were destroyed. We discuss some benchmark tools below.

Stirmark

Stirmark (1998), the most well-known benchmark tool, was developed at Cambridge University (UK) in 1998. The latest edition, the fourth version, was released in October 2007. Stirmark's attack functions use image-processing techniques such as the addition of noise, rotation, JPEG compression, scaling, and cropping. Stirmark's parameters can be fine-tuned. For example, the amount of noise to be added to an image or its degree of rotation can be specified. Stirmark supports some continued attacks such as rotation and cropping as well as rotation and scaling. In addition, Stirmark can introduce geometrical distortions in an image as small random distortion attacks. However, all attacks in Stirmark are single-image attacks, and the combined attacks are limited. Furthermore, Stirmark is command-line-based software and has no image viewer. Therefore, an independent image viewer is necessary for checking the attacked image.

JEWELS

JEWELS (2007) is a software package that was developed in 2000 by the Japan Electronics and Information Technology Industries Association. Like Stirmark, JEWELS has various types of attack functions that use image processing. JEWELS has additional attacks, such as index coloring, gradation processing, and projection transformation, that are not provided in Stirmark. JEWELS uses mainly single-image attacks. Its multiple-image attack function is a single "composite" attack in which two images are compounded (blended) through four parameter-specified steps. Like Stirmark, JEWELS is command-line based.

Checkmark

Checkmark (2001) is a software tool that was developed in 2001 by Shelby Pereira of the University of Geneva. Checkmark also has various types of attack functions including a multiple-image "collage" attack, which pastes an original watermarked image into a larger image (which does not have a digital watermark). However, Checkmark is a MATLAB script rather than an independent software tool. MATLAB is a very useful signal-processing toolkit but a license is required for its use.

Optimark

Optimark (2002) is a software tool developed by the Artificial Intelligence and Information Analysis Laboratory of the Department of Informatics, Aristotle University of Thessaloniki. This tool features a GUI. However, this tool has no multiple-image attack.

FEATURES OF OUR NEWLY DEVELOPED BENCHMARK TOOL

Our newly developed benchmark tool has the following features.

Compatibility with Stirmark and JEWELS in Single-Image Attacks

Our benchmark tool includes the single-image attack functions of Stirmark and JEWELS. Academic use of Stirmark is allowed if written acknowledgement of the copyright is included. JEWELS also allows academic use and any extension with an acknowledgement.

As described above, Stirmark and JEWELS have various single-image attack functions and can also fine-tune their parameters. They have good track records with respect to watermark evaluation. They are efficient, and our tool is compatible with these packages. Our tool was constructed in such a manner that the functions of Stirmark or JEWELS can be called through a menu bar.

Enhancement of Multiple-Image Attacks

In general, multiple-image attacks are stronger than single-image attacks, and they do not degrade images. However, most existing benchmark tools do not have the multiple-image attack functionality. Therefore, we decided to implement multiple-image attacks. Our tool includes an averaging attack and some collusion attacks. In addition, it can easily combine certain attacks. As described below, our tool can easily add other attacks, allowing step-by-step observation of the quality of the attacked image. In addition, it has the potential to launch very large attacks.

Mounting of the GUI

Stirmark and JEWELS both have Command-Line-Based User Interfaces (CUIs). Advantages of CUIs over GUIs include smaller demands on resources (because no resources are assigned to graphics), fast execution speed, ease of program writing, and ease of running a simulation many times. However, GUIs can be easily developed and can process at high speeds because of recent advances in computer capabilities. Images can be intuitively manipulated using GUIs with image viewers. In addition, GUIs allows users to work while observing images, which is very useful in the attacking process, particularly in the case of continuous attacks. The image quality can be observed throughout the continuous addition and repetition of attacks.

FUNCTIONS OF OUR BENCHMARK TOOL

Development Environment

We developed our benchmark tool using Visual Basic v6.0 and Visual C++ v6.0 (Microsoft Corporation, USA). In general, Visual Basic was used for the GUI and file input/output functions because Visual Basic makes it easy to implement GUIs. Visual C++ was used for image processing in the attack functions because programs written in C++ have fast execution times.

Tool Appearance

The appearance of our benchmark tool's display is shown in Figure 1. Two picture boxes are arranged at the center of the display, each displaying an input/output image. File management, watermarking, and attack operations can be chosen from the upper menu bar. Details of the menu items are explained below.

File

The file menu contains submenus for functions such as file open/close/save for each picture box, movement of images between the picture boxes (Picture2→1), and program termination (Exit). Figure 2 shows the submenu. The supported file types for input/output are BMP and JPEG. An input image may be an image with a watermark that has been embedded by other software or an original image into which a watermark will be embedded with our tool (this will be discussed in the subsection "Digital Watermarking"). In general, the picture box on the left is used to input an image

Figure 1. Appearance of our benchmark tool

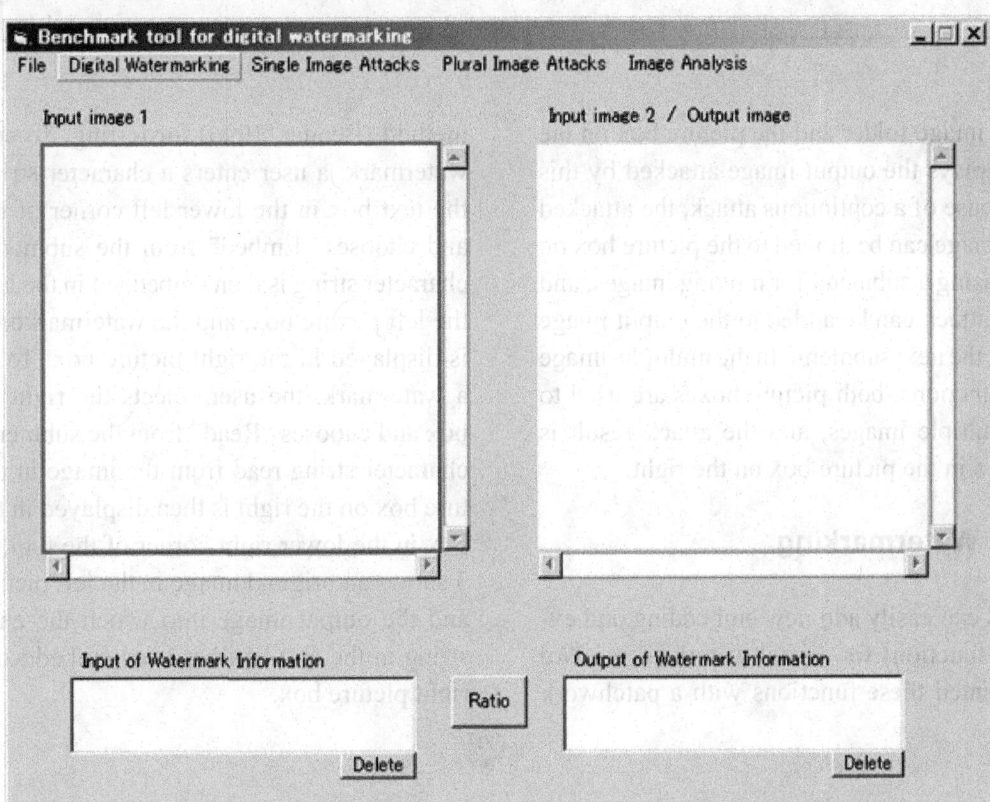

Figure 2. File menu in our benchmark tool

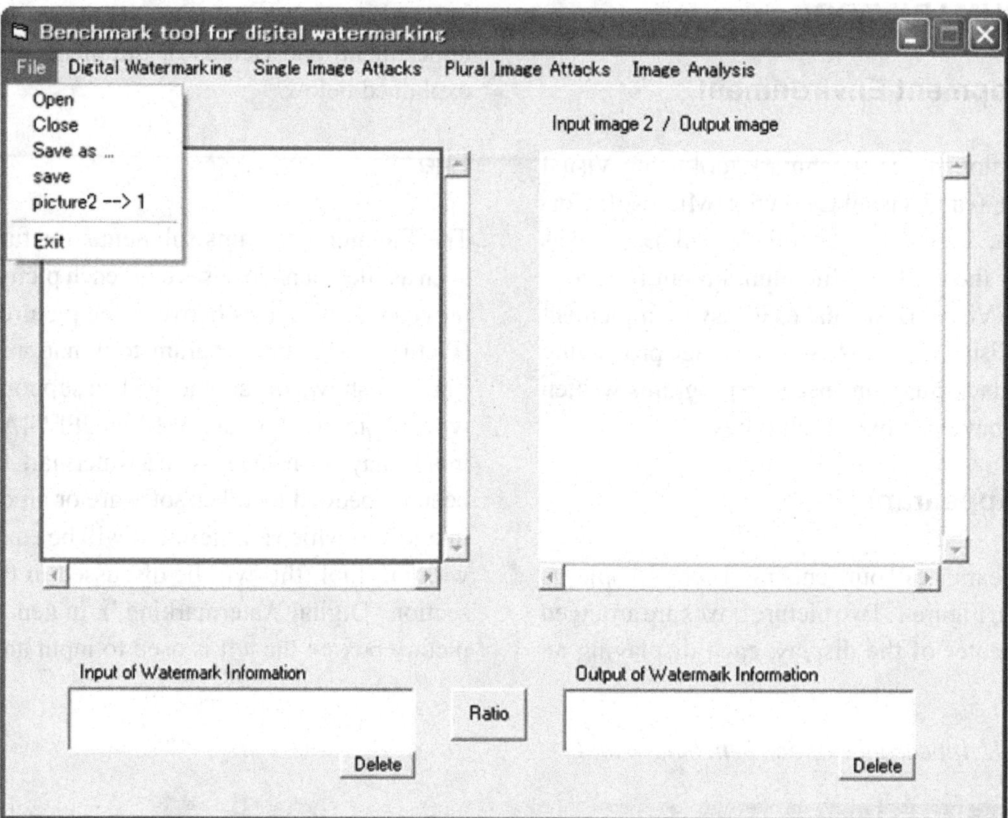

from an image folder and the picture box on the right displays the output image attacked by this tool. In case of a continuous attack, the attacked output image can be moved to the picture box on the left using a submenu for moving images, and another attack can be added to the output image by using the next submenu. In the multiple-image attack functions, both picture boxes are used to input multiple images, and the attack result is displayed in the picture box on the right.

Digital Watermarking

Our tool can easily add new embedding and extracting functions for digital watermarking. We implemented these functions with a patchwork method (Bender, 1996) for testing. To embed a watermark, a user enters a character string into the text box in the lower left corner of the tool and chooses "Embed" from the submenu. The character string is then embedded in the image in the left picture box, and the watermarked image is displayed in the right picture box. To extract a watermark, the user selects the right picture box and chooses "Read" from the submenu. The character string read from the image in the picture box on the right is then displayed in the text box in the lower right corner of the tool. Figure 3 shows an original image in the left picture box and the output image into which the character string in the text box has been embedded in the right picture box.

Figure 3. Digital watermarks in our benchmark tool

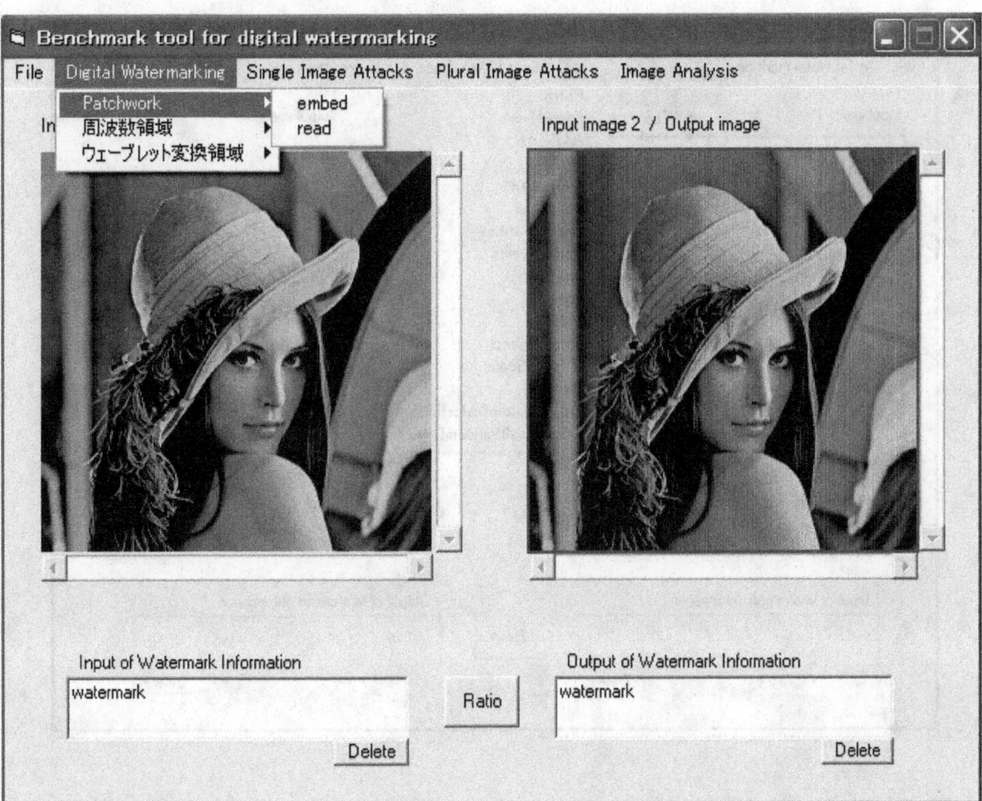

Single-Image Attacks

Single-image attack functions from Stirmark and JEWELS are incorporated in our benchmark tool, as mentioned earlier. Each Stirmark function can be selected from the submenu shown in Figure 4. Because the notation for attack functions in JEWELS is in Japanese, the figure of its menu is omitted. The watermarked image is input into the left picture box and the attacked image is output to the right picture box.

Multiple-Image Attacks

Averaging and collusion attack functions are supported as shown in Plural Image Attacks of Figure 5. For an averaging attack, the user inputs two images to average into the two picture boxes and chooses "Average." The output image is displayed in the right picture box. This operation can be repeated if necessary. We implemented two types of collusion attacks. One compares pixel values at the same position in the two input images, and if the pixels are different, the smaller value becomes the pixel value of the output image. We refer to this as "Collusion-1." The second type of collusion attack computes the average value of pixels in the neighborhood of different pixels and assigns the computed average to the output image. We call this "Collusion-2."

EXAMPLES OF EVALUATION RESULTS

This section shows evaluation results that we obtained using our benchmark tool and discusses how it improves evaluation efficiency.

Figure 4. Single-image attacks in our benchmark tool

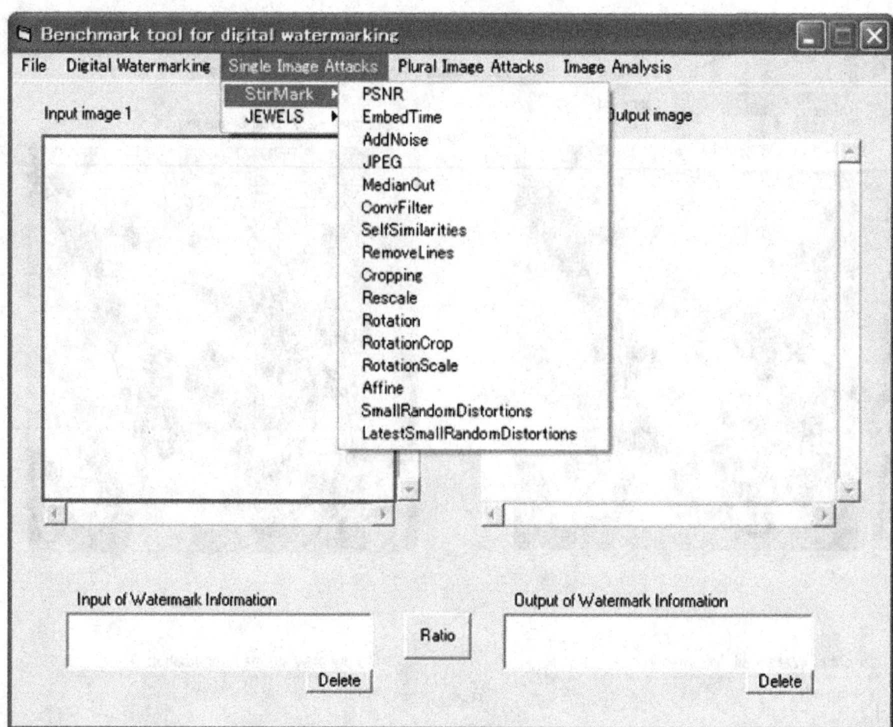

Figure 5. Multiple-image attacks in our benchmark tool

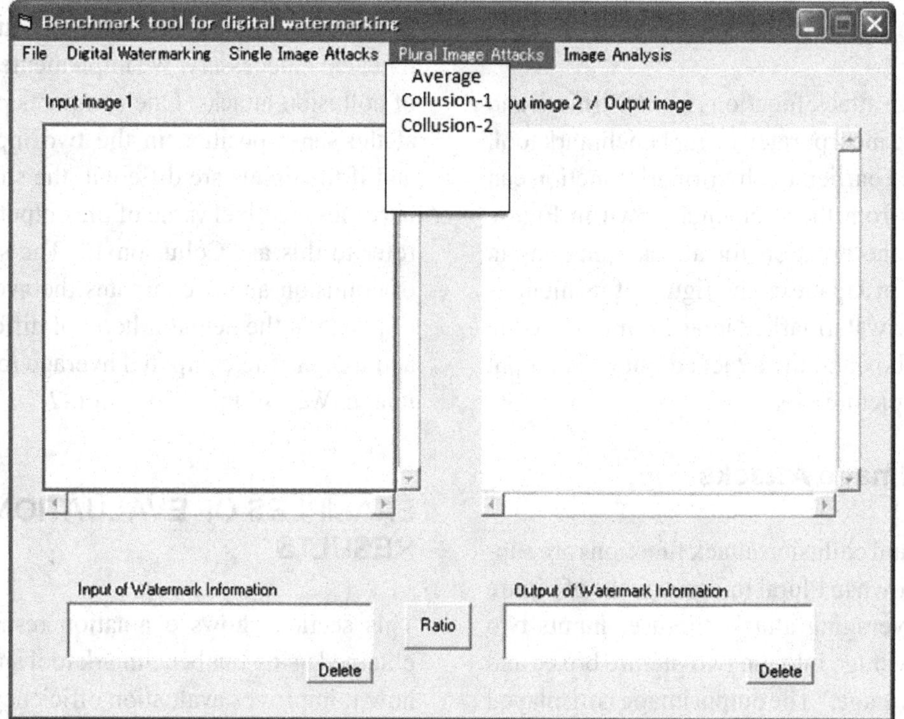

Target Images

Figure 6 shows target images which are 256 × 256 pixel BMP images. We prepared three images—Lena, mandrill, and airplane—and embedded watermarks in these images. The watermarks were developed using the patchwork method and another proprietary commercial method (with a confidential name).

Selected Attacks

As examples of single-image attacks, we selected "rescale," "rotation," "add noise," "JPEG compress," and "index color" functions of Stirmark and JEWELS. In addition, we used a continuous attack that combined the "add noise" and "JPEG compress" functions. As examples of multiple-image attacks, we used the aforementioned collusion attacks and tried to extract the watermark from the attacked images.

Results

The benchmark results for the patchwork method and the other commercial method are shown in Tables 1 and 2, respectively. The parameter set in Table 1 is a parameter set in the Stirmark and JEWELS functions. For the patchwork method, the detection ratio is defined as the ratio of embedded bits to readable bits. For the commercial method, it was not possible to obtain a detection ratio because the algorithm was not disclosed. Hence, we show "readable" or "unreadable" along with the benchmarking result. In Table 2, "weak" and "strong" indicate the strength of embedding. In addition, "O" indicates that the extraction was successful, "X" indicates that the wrong value

Figure 6. Target images: (a) Lena, (b) mandrill, (c) airplane

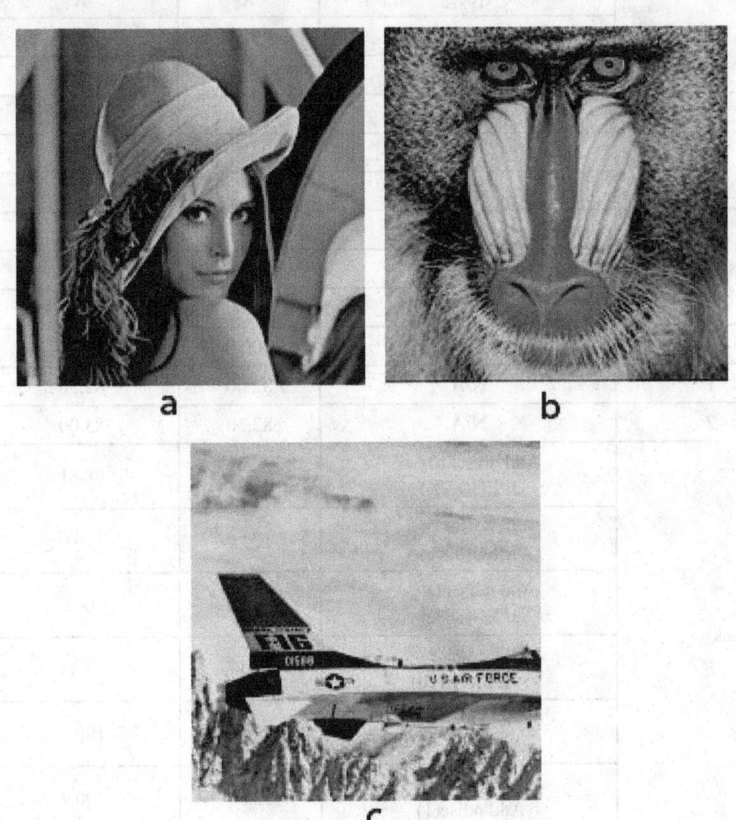

was acquired, and "?" indicates that the extraction was disordered, namely, embedding was not recognized.

Improvement of Evaluation Efficiency

To illustrate the advantages of our tool, we compared user-friendliness and the time required to perform continuous attacks using Stirmark and our tool. We consider the case where a user performs the following attacks as a continuous attack, and each interim result is checked by an image viewer:

Rescale -> Rotation -> JPEG compress

To start evaluation using Stirmark, the user needs to open a command prompt for Stirmark and open the image viewer shown in Figure 7a. The user inputs the first attack command to the command prompt, checks the results using the image viewer by selecting from the output image folder,

Table 1. Result of benchmarking (patchwork method)

Attack Type	Parameter	Detection Ratio[%]		
		Lena	Mandrill	Airplane
Rescale	10[%]	61.50	51.50	46.00
	20[%]	62.25	47.75	55.00
	30[%]	X	49.00	49.17
	40[%]	49.38	45.00	47.50
Rotation	1[deg]	X	X	X
	90[deg]	49.50	X	49.50
	180[deg]	49.50	X	49.50
Add noise	5	100.0	100.0	100.0
	10	96.39	97.22	96.94
	50	52.50	51.04	50.67
JPEG compress	100[%]	100.0	100.0	100.0
	80[%]	82.25	100.0	93.00
	70[%]	65.00	91.00	73.00
Index Color	N/A	100.0	100.0	100.0
Collusion attack - 1	N/A	82.00	82.50	77.50
Collusion attack - 2	N/A	82.50	83.00	80.50
Continuous attack	Add noise(10) -> JPEG(80%)	97.22	98.61	98.61
	Add noise(5) -> JPEG(80%)	100.0	100.0	100.0
	Add noise(1) -> JPEG(80%)	87.50	100.0	98.61
	JPEG(80%) -> Add noise(10)	54.17	93.06	81.94
	JPEG(80%) -> Add noise(5)	55.56	100.0	84.72
	JPEG(80%) -> Add noise(1)	62.50	100.0	88.89

Table 2. Result of benchmarking (watermarking tool on the market)

Attack Type	Parameter	Result (weak/strong)		
		Lena	Mandrill	Airplane
Rescale	80[%]	O / O	O / O	O / O
	110[%]	O / O	X / X	O / O
	150[%]	O / O	X / X	O / O
	200[%]	O / O	O / O	O / O
Rotation	1[deg]	O / O	O / O	O / O
	90[deg]	O / O	O / O	O / O
	180[deg]	O / O	O / O	O / O
Add noise	5	X / O	O / O	X / O
	7	X / O	X / O	X / O
	10	X / X	X / X	X / X
JPEG compress	80[%]	O / O	O / O	O / O
	50[%]	? / O	X / ?	X / O
	20[%]	X / X	X / X	X / X
Index Color	N/A	O / O	O / O	O / O
Collusion attack – 1	N/A	? / ?	? / ?	? / ?
Collusion attack – 2	N/A	? / ?	? / ?	? / ?
Continuous attack	Add noise(10) -> JPEG(80%)	X / X	X / X	X / X
	Add noise(5) -> JPEG(80%)	X / O	X / O	X / O
	Add noise(1) -> JPEG(80%)	O / O	O / O	O / O
	JPEG(80%) -> Add noise(10)	X / X	X / X	X / X
	JPEG(80%) -> Add noise(5)	X / X	X / X	X / X
	JPEG(80%) -> Add noise(1)	X / O	O / O	O / O

returns to the command prompt, and performs the next attack to the stored result images.

To use our tool, the user needs to start the tool as shown in Figure 7b. The user selects the first attack from the menu bar, checks the results on the right picture box, moves the result image to the left picture box, and selects the next attack from the menu bar.

Table 3 shows the time required for the above continuous attacks. From Table 3, we can see that our tool reduces the required time by approximate-

Table 3. Time required for continuous attack

Attempt	Time Required [seconds]	
	Conventional Tool	Our Tool
1st	46	22
2nd	54	30
3rd	47	23
4th	53	26
5th	42	21
Average	48.4	24.4

Figure 7. Conventional Stirmark tool and our benchmark tool: (a) conventional tool, (b) our tool

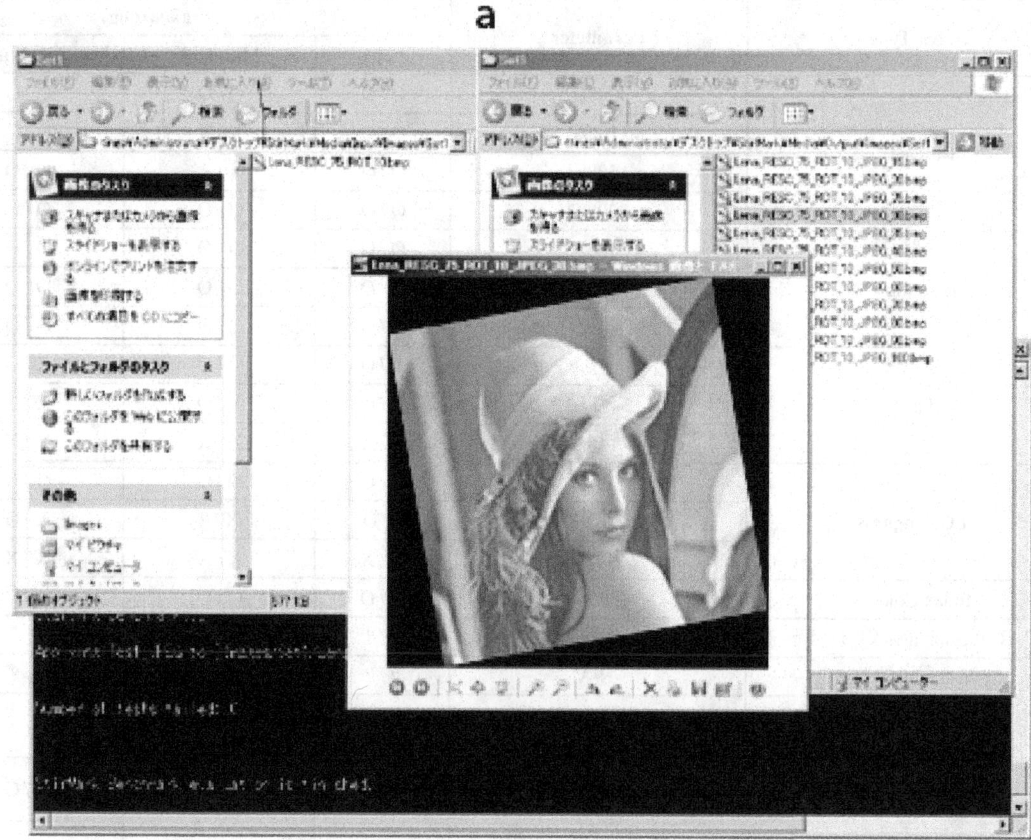

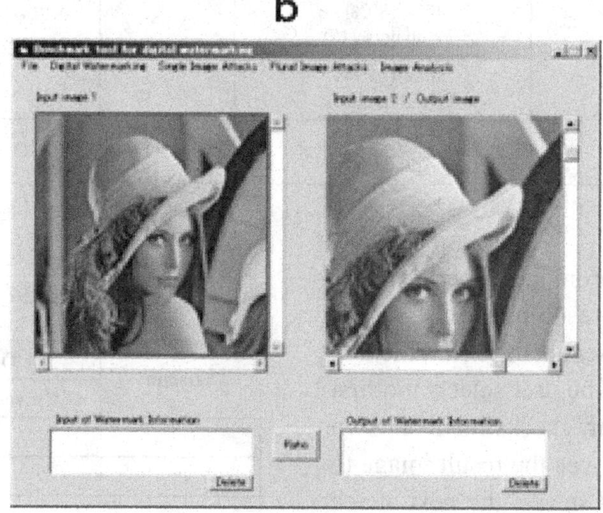

ly half, demonstrating the advantage of using our tool. When more continuous attacks are delivered, the difference in the required time increases. In this evaluation, the Stirmark user was an expert who was aware of all the Stirmark commands. A beginner using this command-line-based conventional tool would require a manual. Hence, more time would be required for the evaluation. In contrast, new users using our tool do not need a manual. Thus, our tool is user-friendly because users can select all the commands from the menu bar and simply click on the target attack. However, it is more convenient and quick to use Stirmark, when checking images in bulk. Therefore, benchmark tools need to be used appropriately according to the users' needs.

CONCLUSION

In this study, we developed a new benchmark tool with a GUI and with single- and multiple-image attack functions.

The GUI was designed for easy image viewing and convenient initiation of attacks (particularly continuous attacks). Using the GUI, command line inputs are not required and it is possible to process an image while observing the image quality.

Some multiple-image attacks are realized in our tool. These are very difficult to implement because there are many methods that realize multiple-image attacks. A significant amount of time was dedicated to their design. We plan to increase the number of multiple-image attack functions in our tool, although it already has more multiple-image functions than any other tools.

This tool has a very high attack capability for watermarking. However, this increases the risk of improper use of our tool. Therefore, we currently have no immediate plans to release it. We hope to make it available publicly for research purposes after we have implemented the necessary restrictions and guidelines for its proper use.

REFERENCES

Barnett, R., & Pearson, D. E. (1998). Frequency mode LR attack operator for digitally watermarked images. *Electronics Letters*, *34*(19), 1837–1838. doi:10.1049/el:19981323

Bender, W., Gruhl, D., Morimoto, N., & Lu, A. (1996). Techniques for data hiding. *IBM Systems Journal*, *35*(3-4), 313–336. doi:10.1147/sj.353.0313

Braci, S., Boyer, R., & Delpha, C. (2010). Analysis of the resistance of the spread transform against temporal frame averaging attack. In *Proceedings of 2010 IEEE 17th International Conference on Image Processing*, (pp. 213-216). IEEE Press.

Checkmark. (2001). *Checkmark*. Retrieved from http://cvml.unige.ch/ResearchProjects/Watermarking/Checkmark/

Dalkilic, O., Ekrem, E., Varlik, S. E., & Mihcak, M. K. (2010). A detection theoretic approach to digital fingerprinting with focused receivers under uniform linear averaging Gaussian attacks. *IEEE Transactions on Information Forensics and Security*, *5*(4), 658–669. doi:10.1109/TIFS.2010.2078505

Feng, H., Ling, H., Zou, F., Lu, Z., & Chen, J. (2009). A performance evaluation of collusion attacks in multimedia fingerprinting. In *Proceedings of the International Conference on Multimedia Information Networking and Security*, (pp. 530-534). IEEE.

JEWELS. (2001). *Research report on watermarking*. Retrieved from http://home.jeita.or.jp/tech/oldfile/report/2001/01-jou-04.pdf

Optimark. (2002). *Optimark*. Retrieved from http://poseidon.csd.auth.gr/optimark/

Petitcolas, F. A. P., Anderson, R. J., & Kuhn, M. G. (1998). Attacks on copyright marking systems. In *Proceedings of the Second Workshop on Information Hiding*, (pp. 218-238). Berlin, Germany: Springer.

Stirmark. (1998). *Stirmark benchmark4.0*. Retrieved from http://www.petitcolas.net/fabien/watermarking/stirmark/

Wu, Y. (2006). Nonlinear collusion attack on a watermarking scheme for buyer authentication. *IEEE Transactions on Multimedia*, *8*(3), 626–629. doi:10.1109/TMM.2006.870720

ADDITIONAL READING

Autrusseau, F., David, S., & Pankajakshan, V. (2010). A subjective study of visibility thresholds for wavelet domain watermarking. In *Proceedings of the IEEE International Conference on Image Processing,* (pp. 201-204). IEEE Press.

Avcba, I., Kharrazi, M., Memon, N., & Sankur, B. (2005). Image steganalysis with binary similarity measures. *EURASIP Journal on Applied Signal Processing*, *17*, 2749–2757.

Boato, G., Conotter, V., De Natale, F. G. B., & Fontanari, C. (2009). Watermarking robustness evaluation based on perceptual quality via genetic algorithms. *IEEE Transaction on Information Forensics and Security*, *4*(2), 207–216. doi:10.1109/TIFS.2009.2020362

Braci, S., Boyer, R., & Delpha, C. (2010). Analysis of the resistance of the spread transform against temporal frame averaging attack. In *Proceedings of the IEEE International Conference on Image Processing,* (pp. 213-216). IEEE Press.

Chandramouli, R., Kharrazi, M., & Memon, N. (2004). Image steganography and steganalysis: Concepts and practice. In *Proceedings of 2nd International Workshop on Digital Watermarking,* (pp. 35–49). IEEE.

Conotter, V., Boato, G., Fontanari, C., & De Natale, F. G. B. (2009). Comparison of watermarking algorithms via a GA-based benchmarking tool. In *Proceedings of the IEEE International Conference on Image Processing,* (pp. 4229-4232). IEEE Press.

Gigaud, G., & Moulin, P. (2010). A geometrically-resilient surf-based image fingerprinting scheme. In *Proceedings of the IEEE International Conference on Image Processing,* (pp. 3669-3672). IEEE Press.

Gokhan, G., & Fatih, K. (2009). A novel universal steganalyser design: LOGSV. In *Proceedings of the IEEE International Conference on Image Processing,* (pp. 4249-4252). IEEE Press.

Guan, Q., Dong, J., & Tan, T. (2011). An effective image steganalysis method based on neighborhood information of pixels. In *Proceedings of the IEEE International Conference on Image Processing,* (pp. 2777-2780). IEEE Press.

Gul, G., Emir Dirik, A., & Avcibas, I. (2007). Steganalytic features for JPEG compression based perturbed quantization. *IEEE Signal Processing Letters*, *14*, 205–208. doi:10.1109/LSP.2006.884010

Leea, M., Kima, K., Suhb, Y., & Leea, H. (2009). Improved watermark detection robust to camcorder capture based on quadrangle estimation. In *Proceedings of the IEEE International Conference on Image Processing,* (pp. 101-104). IEEE Press.

Lyu, S., & Farid, H. (2002). Detecting hidden messages using higher-order statistics and support vector machines. *Lecture Notes in Computer Science*, *2578*, 340–354. doi:10.1007/3-540-36415-3_22

Macq, B., Dittman, J., & Delp, E. J. (2004). Benchmarking of image watermarking algorithms for digital rights management. *Proceedings of the IEEE*, *92*(6), 971–984. doi:10.1109/JPROC.2004.827361

Michiels, B., & Macq, B. (2006). Benchmarking image watermarking algorithms with openwatermark. In *Proceedings of EUSIPCO06*. EUSIPCO.

Mukesh, C. M., Rakhi, C. M., & Frederick, C. H., Jr. (2009). Wavelet based fuzzy perceptual mask for images. In *Proceedings of the IEEE International Conference on Image Processing,* (pp. 4261-4264). IEEE Press.

Nataraj, L., Sarkar, A., & Manjunath, B. S. (2009). Adding Gaussian noise to "DENOISE" JPEG for detecting image resizing. In *Proceedings of the IEEE International Conference on Image Processing,* (pp. 1493-1496). IEEE Press.

Pereira, S., Voloshynovskiy, S., Madueño, M., Marchand-Maillet, S., & Pun, T. (2001). Second generation benchmarking and application oriented evaluation. In *Proceedings of the Information Hiding Workshop,* (pp. 340-353). Pittsburgh, PA: IEEE.

Sadasivam, S., & Moulin, P. (2009). Combating desynchronization attacks on blind watermarking systems: A message passing approach. In *Proceedings of the IEEE International Conference on Image Processing,* (pp. 3641-3644). IEEE Press.

Sato, A., Onishi, J., & Ozawa, S. (1998). Improvement of a digital watermarking method by patchwork. *The Journal of the Institute of Image Information and Television Engineers*, *52*(12), 1852–1855. doi:10.3169/itej.52.1852

Solachidis, V., Tefas, A., Nikolaidis, N., Tsekeridou, S., Nikolaidis, A., & Pitas, I. (2001). A benchmarking protocol for watermarking methods. In *Proceedings of the IEEE International Conference on Image Processing,* (pp. 1023-1026). IEEE Press.

Valizadeh, A., & Wang, Z. J. (2010). Correlation-aware data hiding based on spread spectrum embedding. In *Proceedings of the IEEE International Conference on Image Processing,* (pp. 205-208). IEEE Press.

Voloshynovskiy, S., Herrigel, A., Baumgaertner, N., & Pun, T. (1999). A stochastic approach to content adaptive digital image watermarking. In *Proceeding of the International Workshop on Information Hiding,* (pp. 211-236). IEEE.

Wang, C., Ni, J., Zhuo, H., & Huang, J. (2010). A geometrically resilient robust image watermarking scheme using deformable multi-scale transform. In *Proceedings of the IEEE International Conference on Image Processing,* (pp. 3677-3680). IEEE Press.

Wang, Y., Lei, Y., & Huang, J. (2010). An image copy detection scheme based on radon transform. In *Proceedings of the IEEE International Conference on Image Processing,* (pp. 1009-1012). IEEE Press.

Yamasaki, T., Nakai, Y., & Aizawa, K. (2009). An object-based non-blind watermarking that is robust to non-linear geometrical distortion attacks. In *Proceedings of the IEEE International Conference on Image Processing,* (pp. 3669-3672). IEEE Press.

Section 3
Information Hiding for Text and Binary Data

Chapter 16
Data Hiding for Text and Binary Files

Hirohisa Hioki
Kyoto University, Japan

ABSTRACT

This chapter presents an overview of text-based and binary-based data hiding methods. Text methods, through which secret information is embedded into innocent-looking textual data, are mostly used for steganography. Binary methods are applied to program binary codes: executables and libraries. In binary methods, information is embedded into a binary code so that its functionality is preserved. Data hiding methods for binary codes have been studied intensively to perform watermarking for protecting software from piracy acts. A message can also be embedded into a binary code in a steganographic manner. Another method is also introduced, which is proposed for enhancing the performance of an executable file.

INTRODUCTION

Data hiding methods are mainly applied to multimedia files such as image, video, and audio files to embed information imperceptibly to files. The purpose of data hiding includes discouraging unauthorized copying, concealing the existence of secret messages, and adding extra values to digital files. A data hiding technique for copyright protection is specifically called watermarking. Steganography refers to the technique of concealing secret messages. Multimedia files are indeed suitable for data hiding because they provide a fair amount of exploitable redundancies. For example, slight modification in pixel values of an image will not damage it severely. We can thus embed information into the image while preserving its appearance.

In contrast, text files or binary executable files contain fewer redundancies. Changing a single character in a text file document may be noticeable. Flipping even a single bit of an executable file can make it totally useless. However, it is still possible to use text files or binary executable files for data hiding.

Text data hiding methods date back to the pre-computer era. Secret messages are stealthily embedded into manually composed apparently

DOI: 10.4018/978-1-4666-2217-3.ch016

innocuous texts in order to deceive enemies or even for fun. In our information network era, text steganographic methods are also applied to digital text files. Messages are embedded into texts by modifying their formats or contents on the basis of linguistic knowledge. Texts with hidden data are called "stego" texts and sometimes can be even generated from scratch. Moreover, there are steganographic methods available for non-documental texts such as program sources.

With well-deliberated knowledge, we can transform a binary code to a functionally equivalent code, thereby embedding information. Data hiding methods for binary executable files have been intensively studied to perform watermarking for protecting software from piracy acts. A message can also be embedded into a binary code in a steganographic manner. Another method is also introduced, which is proposed for enhancing the performance of an executable file.

In this chapter, various text data hiding methods including classical ones are presented. Then, binary data hiding methods for watermarking, steganography, and system performance enhancement are described.

TEXT DATA HIDING METHODS

Text data hiding methods are mostly used for steganographic purposes. Text steganographic methods are not limited to digital texts. Steganographic methods have been studied from ancient times.

It has been reported that (Bennett, 2004) digital text steganographic methods include format-based and linguistic methods. In format-based methods, existing text is modified but retains visible characters. Modification is made independent of the textual content. Linguistic methods are those exploiting linguistic knowledge for embedding information. Embedding is done by either modifying the existing text with considering its content or by generating text that looks plausible to the reader.

In this section, before discussing the topics of digital text steganography, several classical steganographic methods are described. Then, the principles of format-based and linguistic methods used in digital steganographic methods are reviewed. Methods for non-documental texts—such as program sources and game logs—are also reviewed.

Classical Methods

Text-based steganographic methods date back to the pre-computer era, because text was the only medium that could be freely edited before computers became widely available. Classical methods include acrostic and null cipher. An acrostic is a text where a message is hidden typically in the initial letters of each line of the text. Null cipher can be regarded as a variant of acrostic. A null cipher hides a message in each word in a text.

An acrostic written by Lewis Carroll appears in his book *Through the Looking-Glass, and What Alice Found There* (Carroll, 1871), as shown in Figure 1. The initial letters of each line spell out "Alice Pleasance Liddell"—the real name of Alice.

The following is a null cipher crafted by a German spy during World War 1 (Kahn, 1996):

PRESIDENT'S EMBARGO RULING SHOULD HAVE IMMEDIATE NOTICE. GRAVE SITUATION AFFECTING INTERNATIONAL LAW. STATEMENT FORESHADOWS RUIN OF MANY NEUTRALS. YELLOW JOURNALS UNIFYING NATIONAL EXCITEMENT IMMENSELY.

Taking the initial letters of each word, the message "Pershing sails from N.Y. June 1" pops up. A check message was returned as another null cipher:

APPARENTLY NEUTRAL'S PROTEST IS THOROUGHLY DISCOUNTED AND IG-

NORED. ISMAN HARD HIT. BLOCKADE ISSUE AFFECTS PRETEXT FOR EMBARGO ON BYPRODUCTS, EJECTING SUETS AND VEGETABLE OILS.

The same message as the first one appears if we pick up the second letters of each word.

Francis Bacon (1561–1626) invented a steganographic method based on the bi-literarie alphabet (Kahn, 1996). In this method, each alphabet is encoded as a five-bit binary code. A message is hidden into an innocuous text. Each character of the text represents a bit. Two different fonts are used to write the text. Characters written in one of the fonts represent bit zero and those written in the other font represent bit one (Bacon used symbols "A" and "B" to represent binary codes). The following example appeared in Bacon's book *Advancement of Learning*:

MANERE TE VOLO DONEC VENERO

This text is written in Latin and means "Stay till I come to you" (The fonts used here are different from the ones that Bacon used). The first 20 characters of this cover text can be interpreted as follows in the binary form:

00101 10011 00110 00100

which represents a hidden message "FUGE" (means Flee) according to Bacon's code.

Figure 1. Lewis Carroll's acrostic

```
A boat beneath a sunny sky,
Lingering onward dreamily
In an evening of July -

Children three that nestle near,
Eager eye and willing ear,
Pleased a simple tale to hear -

Long had paled that sunny sky:
Echoes fade and memories die.
Autumn frosts have slain July.

Still she haunts me, phantomwise,
Alice moving under skies
Never seen by waking eyes.

Children yet, the tale to hear,
Eager eye and willing ear,
Lovingly shall nestle near.

In a Wonderland they lie,
Dreaming as the days go by,
Dreaming as the summers die:

Ever drifting down the stream -
Lingering in the golden gleam -
Life, what is it but a dream?
```

Format-Based Methods

This section introduces digital text steganographic methods based on modification of the format of structured text or plain text. To encode messages secretly in a text file, text data can be modified while keeping textual contents intact. Structured texts, such as HTML files, have components that are not displayed when they are rendered normally, and such components are available for embedding. Plain texts usually include invisible characters that can be added or deleted without significantly affecting the appearance of texts. These types of format-based steganographic methods are explored in this section.

In general, a message embedded in a text file is fragile, in the sense that it is easily corrupted when the text file is edited. Although this lack of robustness in embedded messages is certainly not preferable, but is not fatal as long as messages are not disclosed.

A message can be embedded by manipulating white spaces in plain texts (Bender, Gruhl, Morimoto, & Lu, 1996). The basic idea is to encode a zero bit by a single space character and a one bit by two consecutive space characters. We can adjust the number of spaces at the ends of sentences, ends of lines, or between words for encoding bits. Spaces at the end of lines do not affect text appearance. It is hence possible to encode more than one bit per line by placing more than two spaces at the ends of lines. Figure 2 shows an example of encoding an octet value 65 (=01000001, "A" in ASCII) embedded into the beginning of Lewis Carroll's verse shown in Figure 1. Another example of the use of non-printable characters can be found for structured texts (Khairullah, 2009). Font color data of non-printable characters in a Microsoft Word® document can encode a message without causing visual changes. When K different colors are available, $\log_2 K$ bits can be encoded per non-printable character.

Markup languages are well studied as promising cover objects. Tag descriptions of HTML files are case insensitive. Both upper and lower case letters can appear in a single tag description at the same time. It is hence possible to embed a message into tags by appropriately selecting either upper or lower case for each letter according to the message (Dey, Al-Qaheri, & Sanyal, 2010). Figure 3 depicts an example. A binary message "$01000001 \cdots 10011111$" is encoded using lower case tag letters for '0' and upper case tag letters for '1.'

Cascading Style Sheet (CSS) elements can encode bits (Sun, 2010). A set of CSS classes C is selected and used for embedding. An HTML element with a CSS class $c_i \in C$ encodes a one bit with the element including a nested SPAN element with the same CSS class c_i, whereas an

Figure 2. Encoding an octet by white spaces $(\Box)$ at the ends of lines

```
A boat beneath a sunny sky,□
Lingering onward dreamily□□
In an evening of July -□
□
Children three that nestle near, □
Eager eye and willing ear, □
Pleased a simple tale to hear -□
□□
```

Figure 3. Encoding a message by tag descriptions using upper/lower cases

```
<hTml>
<heaD>
<liNK rEl="stylesheet" hReF="style.css" tyPE="text/css">
<METa htTp-eQUiV="Content-Type" coNtEnt="text/html; charset=UTF-8">
<MetA name="ROBOTS" coNtent="NONE">
<meta name="ROBOTS" cONTenT="NOINDEX,NOFOLLOW">
<TItle>A Web Page</titLe>
</hEad>
<bODy>
</BodY>
</HTML>
```

element that encodes a zero bit does not include a nested SPAN element. Figure 4 depicts an example. This type of nested SPAN elements does not affect the rendering result.

Start-tags and empty-element tags in HTML/XML files can have attributes. The order of attribute specifications is insignificant. We can thus freely arrange attributes without affecting the result of rendering. The names of attributes give a permutation under the lexicographical order. A permutation of n elements can be mapped to a number $x \in \{0,1,\ldots,n!-1\}$ by a bijection. It follows that a message can be represented by attribute lists in an HTML/XML file (Figure 5). A file with M tags including $n_1, n_2, \ldots, n_M$ attributes brings the total to the embedding capacity of $\sum_{i=1}^{M} \log_2(n_i!)$ bits. An embedding method based on this principle is proposed (Huang, Zhong, & Sun, 2008). There is a similar method that uses the order of XML elements (Yang, 2010).

The abovementioned methods are designed for digital files. It is expected that a message is digitally embedded into a certain file and is later extracted from the same file. On the other hand, there is a method by which we can recover the embedded data from printed documents. In this method, lines of a document are shifted upward or downward by a slight amount (e.g., 1/300 in.) to encode data using the varying widths of spacing between lines (Brassil, Low, Maxemchunk, & O'Gorman, 1995).

Figure 6 illustrates the idea of embedding by line-shifting. The beginning of Lewis Carroll's verse (Figure 1) is used here again. A bit is encoded by adjacent three lines. They encode a zero bit when the spacing between the first and second lines is narrower than that between the second and third lines and encode a one bit otherwise. The second line is shifted upward or downward according to the bit to be embedded.

A text consisting of $2k+1$ lines can encode up to k bits by shifting every even line while keeping the position of every odd line.

The data embedded in a printed document are extracted by scanning the document. The spacing

Figure 4. Representation of 0/1 bit using CSS

```
<div class="foo">bar</div>                            →0
<div class="foo"><span class="foo">bar</span></div> →1
```

Figure 5. Encoding a number by an attribute list

```
attributes specification                                permutation           message
<img alt="Foo"  src="foo.jpg"  width="50%"> → (alt,src,width) →    0
<img alt="Foo"  width="50%"  src="foo.jpg"> → (alt,width,src) →    1
<img src="foo.jpg"  alt="Foo"  width="50%"> → (src,alt,width) →    2
<img src="foo.jpg"  width="50%"  alt="Foo"> → (src,width,alt) →    3
<img width="50%"  alt="Foo"  src="foo.jpg"> → (width,alt,src) →    4
<img width="50%"  src="foo.jpg"  alt="Foo"> → (width,src,alt) →    5
```

Figure 6. Embedding by line-shifting

$S_0 < S_1 \rightarrow 0$

A boat beneath a sunny sky,
S_0 Lingering onward dreamily
S_1 In an evening of July –

$S_2 > S_3 \rightarrow 1$

Children three that nestle near,
S_2 Eager eye and willing ear,
S_3 Pleased a simple tale to hear –

between text lines are measured based on their baselines that can be located by the lateral histogram—the histogram counting black pixels along each scanline. Figure 7 shows the lateral histogram for the text in Figure 6. The locations of baselines are marked with the symbol ×.

Linguistic Methods

Natural languages have built-in redundancy, in the sense that the same information can be represented in several ways. Linguistic data hiding methods exploit these redundancies in natural languages using linguistic knowledge in order to embed messages into texts. Secret messages can be embedded into cover texts by modifying them while retaining textual contents. Texts encoding secret messages can even be generated from scratch.

In this section, the principles of methods that are used in digital steganographic methods and based on synonyms, slangs and typographical errors, sentence level features, translations, and auto-summarization are introduced. In addition, methods for generating stego texts from scratch are explained.

Changing words in a text to their synonyms will not affect the textual content. For example, the verb "conceal" is used as an alternative for "hide" in a text. A pair of synonyms provides us with a covert channel for encoding a single bit: one of the synonyms encodes a zero bit and the other encodes a one bit. If a synonym dictionary with bit assignments is prepared, it becomes possible to embed a message in a cover text by selecting words according to the message (Bender, Gruhl, Morimoto, & Lu, 1996; Shirali-Shahreza & Shirali-Shahreza, 2008). The differences in spellings of American and British English can be used in a similar way (Shirali-Shahreza, 2008).

Let us see an example. The following two sentences (a) and (b) are similar to each other:

a. Hide a covert message in a document.
b. Conceal a secret message in a text.

Figure 7. Lateral histogram for the text in Figure 6

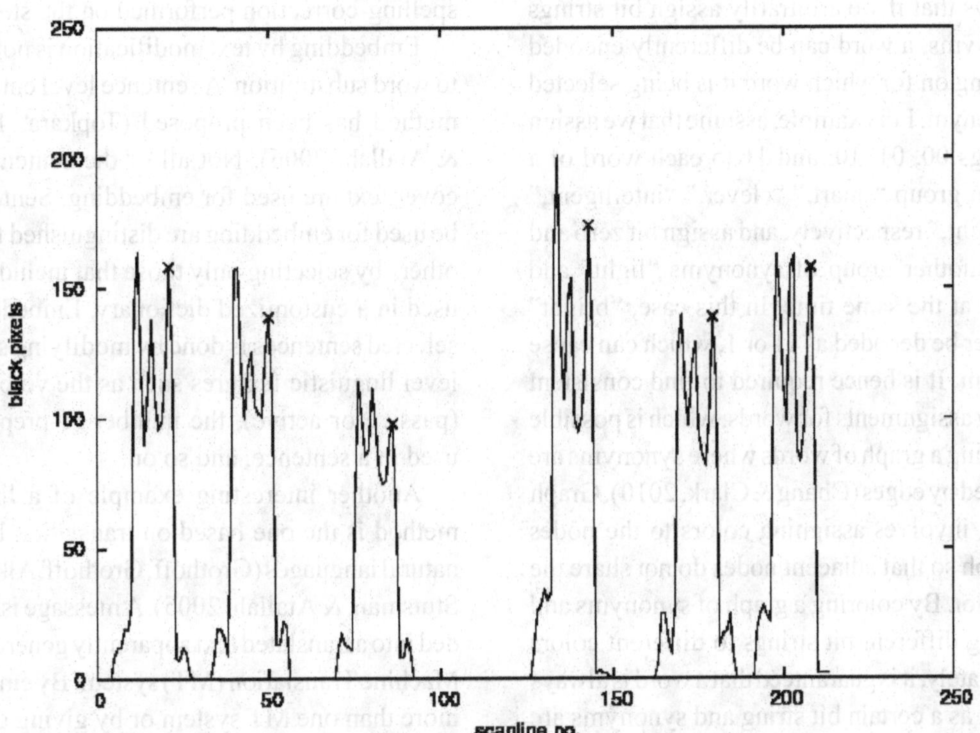

Different bit strings "001" and "110" are encoded by (a) and (b), respectively, under the dictionary shown in Table 1.

One word can encode two or more bits. If there is a set of four synonyms, the set enables us to encode two bits by one word. For example, we may use the adjectives "silent," "soundless," "still," and "quiet" interchangeably.

Unrestricted use of synonyms is however not acceptable for the purpose of data hiding. A stego text might become meaningless if words of the cover text are freely replaced to synonyms without considering the context. For example, the meaning of "bright" depends on the context according to which one of the synonyms can be used—vivid, light, smart, promising, and so on. We can say "a bright color" and this can be rewritten as "a vivid color," but changing it to "a promising color" seldom makes sense. Corpuses can be used to evaluate the appropriateness of a synonym in the context of a cover text to make a stego text more plausible (Chang & Clark, 2010).

Another difficulty in synonym-based steganographic methods arises from the reason that a word often has more than one sense. A word can

Table 1. A synonym dictionary for encoding a 0/1 bit

0	1
autumn	fall
covert	secret
excellent	superior
forest	woods
hide	conceal
movie	film
quick	speedy
state	status
tasty	delicious
text	document

be a synonym of different words at the same time. It follows that if we arbitrarily assign bit strings to synonyms, a word can be differently encoded depending on for which word it is being selected as a synonym. For example, assume that we assign bit strings 00, 01, 10, and 11 to each word of a synonym group "smart," "clever," "intelligent," and "bright," respectively, and assign bit zero and one to another group of synonyms "light" and "bright" at the same time. In this case, "bright" can either be decoded as 11 or 1, which can cause a problem. It is hence required to find consistent bit string assignments for words, which is possible by coloring a graph of words where synonyms are connected by edges (Chang & Clark, 2010). Graph coloring involves assigning colors to the nodes of a graph so that adjacent nodes do not share the same color. By coloring a graph of synonyms and assigning different bit strings to different colors appropriately, it is guaranteed that a word is always encoded as a certain bit string and synonyms are differently encoded at the same time.

Cursory written text is not always syntactically correct and may include chatty expressions. A message can be embedded into a text by injecting unusual expressions such as Internet slang words (e.g., "ne1" for "anyone," "w8," for "wait") (Topkara, Topkara, & Atallah, 2007). Typographical errors are also available for embedding. There are errors that frequently occur, such as the transposition of adjacent letters (e.g., "natoinal" for "national"), duplication/omission of letters (e.g., "neccesary" for "necessary"), and substitution of letters (e.g., "continious" for "continuous"). It sometimes happens that a word is transformed into another word as a result of an error (e.g., "pace" for "peace"). Considering these characteristics of errors along with the corresponding probabilities, a message is embedded into a cover text (Topkara, Topkara, & Atallah, 2007). Groups of similar words (either correct or incorrect ones) are formed and the same bit string is assigned to all the words in one group. This strategy gives a degree of robustness to an embedded message against synonym-substitution and spelling-correction performed on the stego text.

Embedding by text modification is not limited to word substitution. A sentence level embedding method has been proposed (Topkara, Topkara, & Atallah, 2006). Not all of the sentences in a cover text are used for embedding. Sentences to be used for embedding are distinguished from the others by selecting only those that include words used in a customized dictionary. Embedding for selected sentences is done by modifying sentence level linguistic features such as the verb's voice (passive or active), the number of prepositions used in a sentence, and so on.

Another interesting example of a linguistic method is the one based on translation between natural languages (Grothoff, Grothoff, Alkhutova, Stutsman, & Atallah, 2005). A message is embedded into a translated text apparently generated by a Machine Translation (MT) system. By employing more than one MT system or by giving different configurations to a certain MT system, more than one translation is generated for a cover text, and a message is embedded by selecting one translation for each sentence according to the bits to be embedded. At the same time, typical errors found in translations generated by current MT systems have been analyzed, and such errors are exploited for embedding.

There is also an auto-summarization-based method (Desoky, Younis, & El-Sayed, 2008), in which messages are embedded into automatically generated summaries of documents. Different auto-summarization tools are applied to the same document and different summaries are generated. A message is encoded as another summary composed by picking up sentences from the auto-generated summaries. Each sentence of the stego summary is thus one of the sentences in the auto-generated summaries, and bits are encoded according to which of the summaries the sentence is picked up from.

Linguistic data hiding methods do not necessarily require existing cover texts for embedding. A text that secretly encodes a message can be generated from scratch. A customized formal grammar is available for this purpose (Wayner, 2009).

According to grammar, a sentence is derived from a special start symbol by applying production rules specified in the grammar. The start symbol is rewritten to a sequence of symbols by applying a production rule, and derived symbols are rewritten repeatedly by applying production rules until symbols are rewritten as words. A sentence is obtained as a result. In this way, various sentences can be derived if different rules are selected for rewriting a symbol.

The governing principle here, which we will attempt to explore, is that it is possible to embed a message by assigning bits to production rules and by selecting production rules according to the bits to be embedded. If a grammar is designed properly, the derivation process of a sentence can be recovered correctly from the sentence itself. Hence, it is possible to extract the embedded message from sentences that are generated based on such a grammar.

Table 2 shows some examples. Sentences (a)–(c) are generated according to the production rules given below. Each sentence encodes a five-bit message, as shown in the table. These sentences were derived from the same start symbol *S*. According to the production rules, the symbol *S* is rewritten as the sequence of symbols **subj verb obj**, each of which in turn is rewritten as one of the words or phrases specified by the production rules. For example, the production rule

obj → a castle | a museum | a library | a doctor

means that the symbol **obj** can be rewritten as either "a castle," "a museum," "a library," or "a doctor." In this case, we have four alternatives and hence two bits can be embedded by assigning bits to each of them:

obj → a castle(00) | a museum(01) | a library(10) | a doctor(11).

The bit sequence 00 is embedded by selecting "a castle" in this case. The symbols **subj** and **verb** can be similarly rewritten as words or phrases that encode bit-strings. As a result, any five-bit string

Table 2. Messages encoded by sentences

Sentence	Message
(a) A friend of mine visited a doctor	11011
(b) I went to a library	00110
(c) She visited a museum	01001
Production rules (Bit assignments):	
S → **subj verb obj**(ε)	
subj → I(00) | She(01) | He(10) | A friend of mine(11)	
verb → visited(0) | went to(1)	
obj → a castle(00) | a museum(01) | a library(10) | a doctor(11)	
(ε means a null string)	

can be encoded as a sentence by selecting words or phrases appropriately.

There is another grammar-based method (Connell, Tamir, & Guirguis, 2010). In the method, production rules are not directly associated with bit strings, but a prime number or 1 is assigned to each production rule. A message is encoded as the product of all the prime numbers assigned to production rules appeared during the derivation process of the stego text. This scheme enables us to generate various sentences for the same message, which is preferable to make stego texts more plausible. A production rule which is mapped to 1 reduces the amount of embeddable information, but can loosen restriction on the generating process of stego texts, since such a rule can be used repeatedly without affecting the message to be encoded as a number.

In addition to a customized formal grammar, a Markov information source model gives another way to generate a stego text from scratch (Dai, Yu, & Deng, 2009). A text can be approximately modeled as a sequence of symbols obtained from a Markov information source where symbols are generated one by one stochastically depending on a fixed number of preceding symbols. Such a model can be represented by a state diagram with transition probabilities. A state refers to a sequence of previously generated symbols $s_{t-m}s_{t-m+1}\cdots s_{t-1}$ depending on which the next symbol s_t is determined stochastically. After s_t is generated, the state becomes $s_{t-m+1}\cdots s_{t-1}s_t$ and the next symbol s_{t+1} is derived according to this new state. Figure 8 shows a state diagram of a tiny Markov information source. The set of symbols is $\{a, b\}$. A symbol to be generated depends on the state specified by two preceding symbols as indicated in the nodes of the diagram. If the current state is "ab," "a" is generated with the probability 0.4 and the state is changed to "ba," while "b" is generated with the probability 0.6, which brings the transition to the state "bb."

By analyzing a large amount of sample texts of a certain category, we can construct a state diagram of phrases, which provides a way to generate apparently legitimate sentences in a statistical sense. A node of the diagram would normally have more than one state transition edges. We can assign distinct bit strings to each of those edges. Then, a secret message can be hidden as sentences that are generated by selecting phrases at each state according to the message bits.

Figure 8. A state diagram of a Markov information source

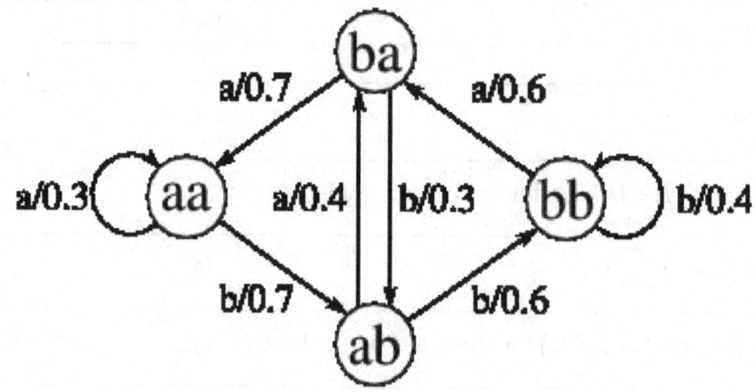

Data Hiding Methods for Non-Documental Texts

Textual data are not necessarily documents. In general, any data described by characters are text. The targets of text data hiding methods extend to non-documental texts.

A commutative operation such as addition in program sources provides space for embedding (Artz, 2001). Because the order of operands is insignificant in a commutative operation, operands can be safely rearranged without affecting a program. The variable names of operands specify a permutation under the lexicographical order. We can thus encode a message as a permutation derived by rearranging operands of a commutative operation.

Secret messages can be shared among a group by playing a game (Hernandez-Castroa, Blasco-Lopezb, Estevez-Tapiadora, & Ribagorda-Garnachoa, 2006). In a game like chess, a player usually has more than one possible move in each turn. Such moves are ordered by some evaluation function, and bits are encoded according to the moves selected by the player. Chess-related materials including game logs can be used for embedding (Desoky & Younis, 2009). A simple poker game has been analyzed for embedding secret information (Diehl, 2008).

Prepending extra zeros to a number does not affect its value. This principle is used to embed a message into the score board of a cricket game (Khairullah, 2011). A bit is encoded based on whether a number is prepended with an extra zero or not.

A steganographic method based on Sudoku—a popular number-placement puzzle—has been proposed previously (Shirali-Shahreza & Shirali-Shahreza, 2008). An 18-bit message can be embedded as a permutation of 1,2, …,9 in a standard 9x9 Sudoku puzzle by shuffling rows and columns according to the message. The receiver of a puzzle with an embedded message first solves it (either by hand or by a solver) and then decodes the message.

Watermarking methods are employed to protect music scores from piracy acts. Since information of a music score can be described by symbols, text-based data hiding methods are applicable. A watermarking method for music scores written in a format called MusicXML has been proposed in a paper (Watanabe, Katoh, Bista, & Takata, 2006). Fingering annotations accompanied with music scores can be used for embedding (Gross-Amblard, Rigaux, Abrouk, & Cullot, 2009). Music scores—as figures composed of black and white regions—can also be watermarked by data hiding methods for binary images (Funk & Schmucker, 2001).

BINARY DATA HIDING METHODS

In this section, we examine cases in which messages are embedded into binary data. Although strictly speaking all of the digital data is intrinsically binary, binary data specifically refers to executable files (including byte codes) and program libraries accompanied with executables in this section. A binary file may become useless by modifying even a single bit. Even so, binary files do have redundancies that can be exploited for data embedding.

The principles of various binary data hiding methods will be reviewed in this section. First, watermarking methods for binary executables, i.e., software watermarking methods, are presented. Then, steganographic methods for binary executables are described. In watermarking methods, identifiers are embedded into software programs for protecting them. In contrast, binary executables are employed just as cover media for hiding secret messages and their values are of no concern in steganographic methods. Apart from these two methods, another binary data hiding method is also introduced, which is used to embed side information for enhancing the performance of an executable file.

Watermarking Methods

Watermarking methods for binary data aim at discouraging software piracy acts. By embedding an identifier into a software program, in the event of piracy, it becomes possible to prove ownership of the software or to find the malicious user who had pirated it. Embedding a watermark should not change the behavior of the program and should not degrade its performance significantly. A more important issue is the robustness of the watermark. A malicious user may transform a piece of watermarked software for removing or invalidating the watermark. Thus, it is imperative that the watermark is robust and will not be damaged by any possible attacks.

Several different types of watermarking methods are introduced in this section. A watermark is embedded either into a dummy method, depths of method calls, statistics values, or graph structures derived from programs.

A watermarking method for a Java class file has previously been proposed (Monden, Iida, Matsumoto, Torii, & Inoue, 2000). The basic idea of this method is to insert a dummy method that encodes watermark information. A watermark is encoded in the opcodes and operands in the method. A complicated, unsatisfiable dummy predicate is inserted along with the method to pretend that the dummy method is called when the predicate becomes true; however, because an unsatisfiable predicate never becomes true, the dummy method will never be executed. Thus, it is possible to insert a watermark without affecting the program through this scheme. At the same time, it becomes difficult to determine that the inserted method is actually a dummy method. In principle, the embedding capacity of this method is unlimited, since the dummy method can be made as large as required. The watermark can be easily removed once the dummy method is identified in the watermarked program. This watermarking method is fragile against code reordering attacks. Decompiling the watermarked method reveals anomalies as shown in Figure 9.

Depths of method calls in a program can be used for watermarking (Curran, Hurley, & Cinnéide, 2003). A redundant recursive call is inserted in a method for encoding a watermark bit. The inserted recursive call is said to be redundant, in the sense that the behavior of the program will not be changed by its insertion. When a watermark is to be extracted from a compiled program, depths of redundant recursive calls are measured by executing the program. To prevent attacks against

Figure 9. A Java method and its corresponding watermarked version

```
private static Timezone[] setup_zone(){
   Timezone tz[] = new Timezone[10];
   tz[0] = new Timezone("Sydney",10);
   tz[1] = new Timezone("Tokyo",9);
   tz[2] = new Timezone("Singapore",8);
   tz[3] = new Timezone("Bangkok",7);
   tz[4] = new Timezone("Moscow",4);
   tz[5] = new Timezone("Paris",2);
   tz[6] = new Timezone("London",1);
   tz[7] = new Timezone("NewYork",-4);
   tz[8] = new Timezone("Galapagos",-6);
   tz[9] = new Timezone("Vancouver",-7);
   return tz;
}
```

(a) Original

```
private static Timezone[] setup_zone(){
   Timezone[] arrayOfTimezone = new Timezone[-121];
   arrayOfTimezone[0] = new Timezone("Sydney", 30);
   arrayOfTimezone[2] = new Timezone("Tokyo", -61);
   arrayOfTimezone[1] = new Timezone("Singapore", -21);
   arrayOfTimezone[3] = new Timezone("Bangkok", -121);
   arrayOfTimezone[3] = new Timezone("Moscow", 4);
   arrayOfTimezone[3] = new Timezone("Paris", 1);
   arrayOfTimezone[-128] = new Timezone("London", 1);
   arrayOfTimezone[29] = new Timezone("NewYork", 30);
   arrayOfTimezone[-16] = new Timezone("Galapagos", -18);
   arrayOfTimezone[-76] = new Timezone("Vancouver", 58);
   return arrayOfTimezone;
}
```

(b) Watermarked(decompiled)

a watermarked program, the watermark is embedded by a spread spectrum approach.

A set of code blocks can be used for watermarking (Stern, Hachez, Koeune, & Quisquater, 2000). Assume that we have n different types of code blocks available for embedding. Let $c_i (0 \leq i < n)$ be the frequency of the i-th code block in a program. Now, $c = (c_0, c_1, \ldots, c_{n-1})$ is formed as its feature vector and is slightly modified according to the watermark $w = (w_0, w_1, \ldots, w_{n-1})$ to be embedded. The vector c is modified by replacing code blocks with functionally equivalent ones. When a program P' is checked to determine whether it is a pirated version of the program P, a similarity measure for the watermark w is computed against the feature vector c' of the program P' using the original feature vector c and the watermark w. The program P' is found to be marked if the degree of similarity is sufficiently high. Because the feature vector is obtained from the frequencies of code blocks, watermarks are rather robust against code reordering attacks.

Graph-based watermarking methods have been extensively studied. Watermark data can be encoded in the structures of various types of graphs (Collberg, Kobourov, Carter, & Thomborson, 2003). A graph representing a watermark data is called a "watermark graph" hereafter.

A graph representation of a program can be derived from its control flow structure consisting of basic blocks (a machine code sequence without jumps or jump targets) and links (jumps and fall-throughs) among them. Watermark information for a program is encoded as a control flow graph in a previous study (Venkatesan, Vazirani, & Sinha, 2001). The watermark graph is then combined into the control flow graph of the program by adding edges so that the watermark graph cannot be separated easily from the combined graph. Figure 10 depicts the idea of this watermarking method. The control flow graph G of a program is combined with a watermark graph W and the graph G' is obtained as a result. The program is not damaged by watermarking if an unsatisfiable predicate is used to add an edge. In order to extract the watermark, it is required to reconstruct the control flow graph of the watermarked program and identify the nodes in the watermark graph. For this purpose, the basic blocks corresponding to the nodes of the watermark graph are marked using unused area of machine codes in the watermarked program. The watermark is corrupted

Figure 10. Watermarking by combining control flow graphs

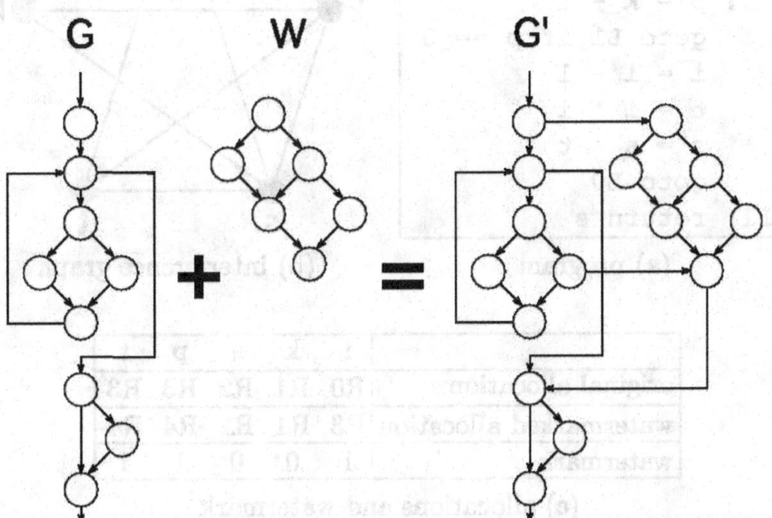

when the watermarked program is transformed by control flow scrambling.

A watermark can be encoded in a graph through graph coloring (Qu & Potkonjak, 1998). As described earlier in this chapter, graph coloring involves assigning colors to the nodes of a graph so that adjacent nodes do not share the same color. Graph coloring can be applied to the task of register allocation. While a program is running, if there are variables used at the same time for a certain duration, they must be allocated to different registers. Such constraints among variables can be represented by a graph called an "interference graph," where a node represents a variable and an edge indicates that the two variables linked by it are used at the same time. Coloring of such a graph gives a solution to allocate registers to variables. An algorithm called QPS (Myles & Collberg, 2004) has been developed for watermarking a method in a program by adding bogus edges to the interference graph of the method and allocating registers according to the watermarked graph. Register allocation is also used in other watermarking methods (Zhu & Thomborson, 2006; Lee & Kaneko, 2008).

In Figure 11, the bit sequence 10011 is embedded into the program shown in Figure 11a by changing register allocation. An algorithm called CC (Lee & Kaneko, 2008) is used in this example. The interference graph for this program is obtained as shown in Figure 11b. Assume that eight registers $R0,\ldots,R7$ are available. By coloring the interference graph, we can find the register allocation in the first row of Figure 11c. This allocation is changed according to the watermark bits under the constraints given by the interference graph. The second row of Figure 11c shows the result. On extracting the watermark from the machine code of the program, variables are numbered in the order as they appear in the code first. The interference graph can be derived from the code and the graph allows us to recover the original allocation through graph coloring. The watermark bits are now identified by comparing

Figure 11. Watermarking by changing register allocation

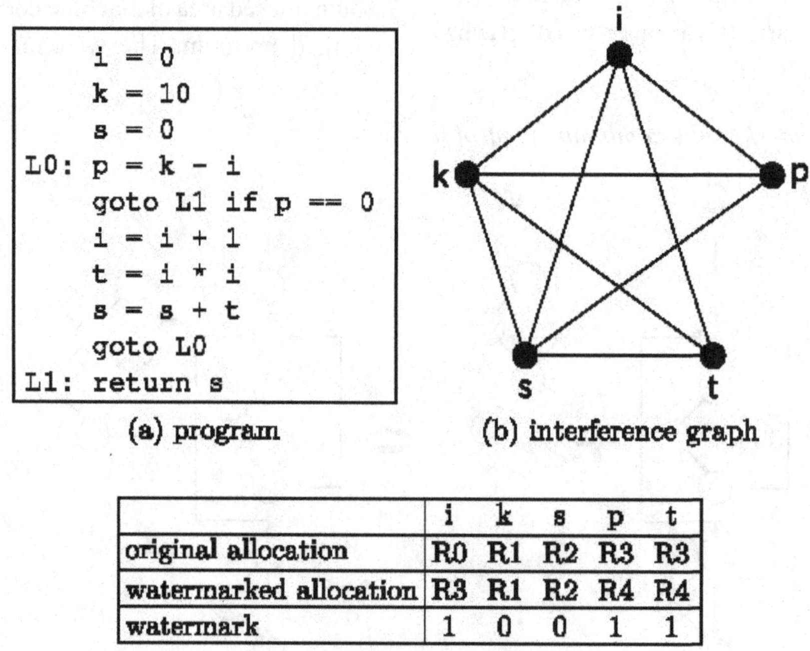

i = 0
k = 10
s = 0
L0: p = k - i
goto L1 if p == 0
i = i + 1
t = i * i
s = s + t
goto L0
L1: return s
(a) program
i
k
p
s
t
(b) interference graph

	i	k	s	p	t
original allocation	R0	R1	R2	R3	R3
watermarked allocation	R3	R1	R2	R4	R4
watermark	1	0	0	1	1

(c) allocations and watermark

the allocation used in the code and the recovered original allocation. A watermark bit is found to be zero or one either the same register is used for the both allocations or not. The size of watermark is limited by the number of variables that appeared in the program. The watermark is easily removed by reallocating the registers.

A dynamic graph watermarking method (Collberg & Thomborson, 1999) does not encode a watermark graph directly into the structure of a program. Instead, a code generating a watermark graph is embedded into the program. When a watermarked program is run with a pre-determined input sequence, the embedded watermark graph is constructed dynamically in memory. The graph generating code is difficult to detect and is robust against watermarking removal attacks such as code optimization. A dynamic graph watermarking method based on a circular linked list (Ping, Xi, & Xu-Guang, 2010) has been proposed to enhance the robustness of a watermark. Another dynamic graph watermarking method based on a variant of a planted plane cubic tree has been developed to improve the watermark encoding rate (Zhu, Liu, & Yin, 2009). A graph can be derived from dependencies among the values of variables during execution of a program. This kind of graph is used in a dynamic graph watermarking method (Feng, Zhang, Xu, Niu, & Hu, 2009). We can obtain a graph for dynamic watermarking from state transitions of the memory stack during program execution (Xu & Zeng, 2010).

An example of a watermark encoded by a circular linked list (Collberg & Thomborson, 1999) is shown in Figure 12. Right pointers of cells are directed to the next cell while left pointers are connected so that they encode watermark digits. A null pointer encodes zero, a self-pointer encodes one, and a pointer to the next cell encodes two and so on. These digits specify the watermark as a number in radix k+1 where k is the number of cells in the list. In Figure 12, the watermark value is 13025 in radix 6 (1961 in decimal). A circular linked list consisting of k-cells can represent one of $(k+1)^k$ different watermarks.

Sandmark (Collberg, Myles, & Huntwork, 2003) is a Java toolkit available for development and analysis of software watermarking techniques. Sandmark includes basic libraries for implementing watermarking algorithms, code analysis tools, performance evaluation, and attack tools for watermarking algorithms.

Besides watermarking, birthmarks provide a way for protecting software. A software birthmark, as its name indicates, is a set of characteristics that a program intrinsically possesses which enables us to identify the program (Myles & Collberg, 2004), i.e., a birthmark method is not based on a technique of data hiding. A software birthmark is obtained either from the static structure (Myles & Collberg, 2005; Choi, Park, Lim, & Han, 2007;

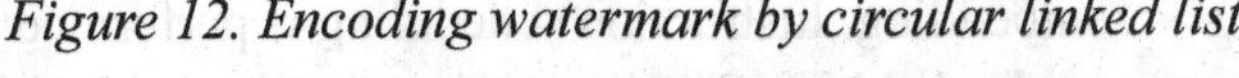
Figure 12. Encoding watermark by circular linked list

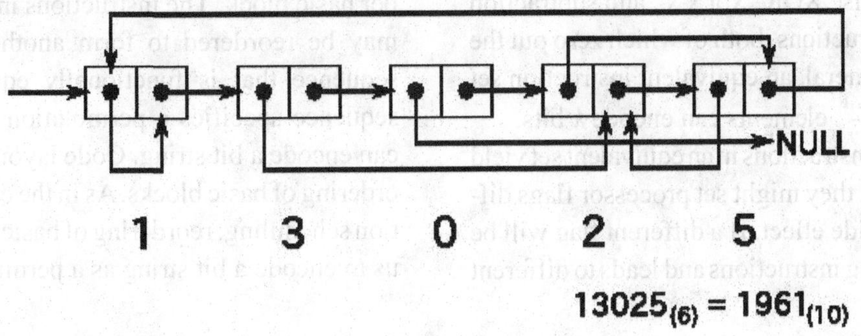

Park, Lim, Choi, & Han, 2011) or dynamic behavior of a program (Lu, Liu, Ge, Liu, & Luo, 2007; Chan, Hui, & Yiu, 2011).

Steganographic Methods

The overview of two representative binary-based steganographic methods called Hydan (El-Khalil & Keromytis, 2004) and Stilo (Anckaert, Sutter, Chanet, & Bosschere, 2005) is described in this section.

Hydan (El-Khalil & Keromytis, 2004) is the pioneering work of this area of steganographic binary data hiding. A message is embedded into a cover executable binary file and a stego binary file is generated as a result. The stego binary file is functionally equivalent to the cover binary file, i.e., the stego binary file remains executable and works identically to the cover binary file.

The basic idea of embedding is to represent bits by equivalent sets of machine instructions. For example, let us see the following pseudo codes (a) and (b):

a. x = x + 2
b. x = x − (−2)

These two codes yield the same result. Hence, it is possible to embed one bit into a machine instruction, such as "add x 2," in a cover binary file by either preserving the instruction as it is or replacing it with its equivalent instruction "sub x −2," depending on the bit we embed. Another example of an equivalent set of machine instructions is a bitwise XOR "xor x x" and subtraction "sub x x" instructions, both of which zero out the entity x. In general, an equivalent instruction set consisting of 2^k elements can encode *k* bits.

Although instructions in an equivalent set yield the same data, they might set processor flags differently as a side effect. If a different flag will be set by replacing instructions and leads to different behaviors of the program, such instructions are not used for embedding.

In Hydan, the x86 architecture is employed. It has been reported that equivalent instruction sets consisting of up to seven elements are found to be available (El-Khalil & Keromytis, 2004). The embedding capacity of Hydan is reported to be approximately 0.91% of the size of a cover executable file.

In addition to equivalents in the instruction set, dead codes and code block ordering are considered as possible sources available for embedding in order to improve the embedding ratio of Hydan. Dead codes are those that are never to be executed regardless of inputs. Such codes can be replaced to any binary string without damaging the program. A message mimicking innocuous machine instructions can be generated, and embedding is done by replacing dead codes with the generated stego instructions. Functionally independent code blocks (e.g., functions), can be reordered without changing the behavior of the program. It is possible to encode a message as a permutation specified by the ordering of code blocks.

Stilo (Anckaert, Sutter, Chanet, & Bosschere, 2005) exploits three different types of redundancies available in program binaries: redundancies in instruction selection, instruction scheduling, and code layout. Instruction selection in Stilo is not just a replacement of a single instruction as in the case of Hydan. Instead, equivalent instruction sequences are exhaustively generated for an operation (under given restrictions) and used for embedding. Instruction scheduling is performed per basic block. The instructions in a basic block may be reordered to form another instruction sequence that is functionally equivalent. The sequence specifies a permutation by which we can encode a bit string. Code layout refers to the ordering of basic blocks. As in the case of instruction scheduling, reordering of basic blocks allows us to encode a bit string as a permutation.

All the three types of abovementioned redundancies are not mutually independent. It is hence assumed that an executable binary is converted into a canonical form before embedding (or extraction), and then embedding (or extraction) is done in a pre-determined way.

Stealthiness of a stego binary program has been analyzed in terms of unusual signatures that may be introduced into codes as a result of embedding (Anckaert, Sutter, Chanet, & Bosschere, 2005). Signatures that possibly reveal the existence of hidden messages include instructions not usually generated by compilers, deviations in relative instruction frequencies, unusual jump behaviors, and basic blocks that have the same logical structure but are scheduled differently. Countermeasures for possible attacks based on these signatures are integrated into Stilo. The embedding ratio of Stilo is about four times as large as that of Hydan when redundancies are fully exploited. Even when stealthiness is considered, Stilo can still achieve an embedding ratio a little higher than that achieved by Hydan.

A Binary Data Hiding Method for Performance Enhancement

Data hiding methods for binary executables are not only used for steganographic purposes or software watermarking but may also be used for enhancing the performance of a program by embedding side information (Swaminathan, Mao, Wu, & Kailas, 2005).

Although system performance can be improved by redesigning the Instruction Set Architecture (ISA) of the CPU, it is impractical to do so, since changing the instruction set requires changing the CPU. Thus, it would be better to improve system performance without modifying the ISA.

A reversible data hiding technique allows us to add side information to each instruction without modifying the ISA, thereby improving system performance. Note that a data hiding method is said to be reversible if it enables us to restore the original cover object from a stego object.

Side information is embedded into operands of instructions. To embed side information in a reversible way, the original operands are losslessly compressed and a lookup table that maps the compressed data to the original operands is stored in the program header. Side information is inserted into the space that is freed up by compression. On executing a program with side information, each operand section is divided into side information and the compressed operands. The original operands are restored from the compressed operands via the lookup table, and side information is fed into the processor pipeline for possible use.

SUMMARY

In the first half of this chapter, text data hiding methods were reviewed. Text data hiding methods have been used since ancient times for steganographic purposes. Classical methods include acrostics and null ciphers. We explored the digital text steganographic methods: format-based and linguistic methods. Format-based methods use text elements such as white space characters, tag descriptions of HTML/XML, and CSS structures to embed information. Embedding for printed documents can be done by slightly shifting the line positions up or down. Linguistic methods that utilize knowledge such as synonyms and sentence features like a verb's voice were introduced. In addition, as we have seen, machine translation, summarization, or even intentional typos can be used for embedding. Stego texts can be generated from scratch according to customized grammars or Markov information source models.

In the second half of this chapter, binary data hiding methods, software watermarking and steganographic methods, and a method for performance enhancement based on embedded side information were described. Watermarks are encoded as dummy methods, depth of method calls, relative frequency of code blocks or graphs derived from structures or dynamic behavior of programs. Steganographic methods use redundancies of programs for embedding: instruction selection, instruction scheduling, and code layout. It may be possible to enhance system performance by embedding side information into executables in a reversible manner.

REFERENCES

Anckaert, B., Sutter, B. D., Chanet, D., & Bosschere, K. D. (2005). Steganography for executables and code transformation signatures. In *Proceedings of the Information Security and Cryptology — ICISC 2004*, (pp. 7-10). ICISC.

Artz, D. (2001). Digital steganography: Hiding data within data. *IEEE Internet Computing*, *5*(3), 75–80. doi:10.1109/4236.935180

Bender, W., Gruhl, D., Morimoto, N., & Lu, A. (1996). Techniques for data hiding. *IBM Systems Journal*, *35*(3-4), 313–336. doi:10.1147/sj.353.0313

Bennett, K. (2004). *Linguistic steganography: Survey, analysis, and robustness concerns for hiding information in text*. Lafayette, IN: Purdue University.

Brassil, J. T., Low, S., Maxemchunk, N. F., & O'Gorman, L. (1995). Electronic marking and identification techniques to discourage document copying. *IEEE Journal on Selected Areas in Communications*, *13*(8), 1495–1504. doi:10.1109/49.464718

Carroll, L. (1871). *Through the looking-glass, and what alice found there*. London, UK: Macmillan.

Chan, P., Hui, L., & Yiu, S.-M. (2011). Dynamic software birthmark for java based on heap memory analysis. In *Proceedings of the Communications and Multimedia Security,* (pp. 94-107). IEEE.

Chang, C.-Y., & Clark, S. (2010). Practical linguistic steganography using contextual synonym substitution and vertex colour coding. In *Proceedings of the 2010 Conference on Empirical Methods in Natural Language Processing,* (pp. 1194-1203). IEEE.

Choi, S., Park, H., Lim, H.-I., & Han, T. (2007). A static birthmark of binary executables based on API call structure. In *Proceedings of the Advances in Computer Science — ASIAN 2007*, (pp. 2-16). ASIAN.

Collberg, C., Kobourov, S., Carter, E., & Thomborson, C. (2003). Error-correcting graphs for software watermarking. In *Proceedings of the Graph-Theoretic Concepts in Computer Science,* (pp. 156-167). IEEE.

Collberg, C., Myles, G., & Huntwork, A. (2003). Sandmark — A tool for software protection research. *IEEE Security and Privacy*, *1*(4), 40–49. doi:10.1109/MSECP.2003.1219058

Collberg, C., & Thomborson, C. (1999). Software watermarking: Models and dynamic embeddings. In *Proceedings of the 26th ACM SIGPLAN-SIGACT Symposium on Principles of Programming Languages*, (pp. 311-324). ACM Press.

Connell, W., Tamir, D., & Guirguis, M. (2010). Prime-based mimic functions for the implementation of covert channels. In *Proceedings of the IEEE International Conference on Wireless Communications, Networking and Information Security 2010,* (pp. 538-543). IEEE Press.

Curran, D., Hurley, N. J., & Cinnéide, M. Ó. (2003). Securing java through software watermarking. In *Proceedings of the 2nd International Conference on Principles and Practice of Programming in Java,* (pp. 145-148). IEEE.

Dai, W., Yu, Y., & Deng, B. (2009). BinText steganography based on Markov state transferring probability. In *Proceedings of the 2nd International Conference on Interaction Sciences: Information Technology, Culture and Human,* (pp. 1306-1311). IEEE.

Desoky, A., & Younis, M. (2009). Chestega: Chess steganography methodology. *Security and Communication Networks*, *2*(6), 555–566.

Desoky, A., Younis, M., & El-Sayed, H. (2008). Auto-summarization-based steganography. In *Proceedings of the International Conference on Innovations in Information Technology 2008,* (pp. 608-612). IEEE.

Dey, S., Al-Qaheri, H., & Sanyal, S. (2010). *Embedding secret data in HTML web page*. Retrieved from http://www.arxiv.org

Diehl, M. (2008). Secure covert channels in multiplayer games. In *Proceedings of the 10th ACM Workshop on Multimedia and Security,* (pp. 117-122). ACM Press.

El-Khalil, R., & Keromytis, A. D. (2004). Hydan: Hiding information in program binaries. In *Proceedings of the International Conference on Information and Communications Security,* (pp. 187-199). IEEE.

Feng, B., Zhang, M., Xu, G., Niu, X., & Hu, Z. (2009). Dynamic data flow graph-based software watermarking. In *Proceedings of the International Conference on Network Infrastructure and Digital Content, 2009,* (pp. 1029-1033). IEEE.

Funk, W., & Schmucker, M. (2001). High capacity information hiding in music scores. In *Proceedings of the First International Conference on Web Delivering of Music,* (pp. 12-19). IEEE.

Gross-Amblard, D., Rigaux, P., Abrouk, L., & Cullot, N. (2009). Fingering watermarking in symbolic digital scores. In *Proceedings of the 10th International Symposium on Music Information Retrieval,* (pp. 141-146). IEEE.

Grothoff, C., Grothoff, K., Alkhutova, L., Stutsman, R., & Atallah, M. (2005). Translation-based steganography. In *Proceedings of Information Hiding* (pp. 219–233). IEEE. doi:10.1007/11558859_17

Hernandez-Castroa, J. C., Blasco-Lopezb, I., Estevez-Tapiadora, J. M., & Ribagorda-Garnachoa, A. (2006). Steganography in games: A general methodology and its application to the game of Go. *Computers & Security, 25*(1), 64–71. doi:10.1016/j.cose.2005.12.001

Huang, H., Zhong, S., & Sun, X. (2008). An algorithm of webpage information hiding based on attributes permutation. In *Proceedings of the Intelligent Information Hiding and Multimedia Signal Processing,* (pp. 257-260). IEEE.

Kahn, D. (1996). *The codebreaksers — The story of secret writing*. New York, NY: Scribner.

Khairullah, M. (2009). A novel text steganography system using font color of the invisible characters in microsoft word documents. In *Proceedings of the International Conference on Computer and Electrical Engineering,* (pp. 482-484). IEEE.

Khairullah, M. (2011). A novel text steganography system in cricket match scorecard. *International Journal of Computers and Applications*, *21*(9), 43–47. doi:10.5120/2537-3462

Lee, H., & Kaneko, K. (2008). New approaches for software watermarking by register allocation. In *Proceedings of the 2008 ACIS International Conference on Software Engineering, Artificial Intelligence, Networking, and Parallel/Distributed Computing,* (pp. 63-68). ACIS.

Lu, B., Liu, F., Ge, X., Liu, B., & Luo, X. (2007). A software birthmark based on dynamic opcode n-gram. In *Proceedings of the International Conference on Semantic Computing 2007*, (pp. 37-44). IEEE.

Monden, A., Iida, H., Matsumoto, K., Torii, K., & Inoue, K. (2000). A practical method for watermarking java programs. In *Proceedings of the Computer Software and Applications Conference*, (pp. 191-197). IEEE.

Myles, G., & Collberg, C. (2004). Detecting software theft via whole program path birthmarks. In *Proceedings of Information Security* (pp. 404–415). IEEE. doi:10.1007/978-3-540-30144-8_34

Myles, G., & Collberg, C. (2004). Software watermarking through register allocation: Implementation, analysis, and attacks. In *Proceedings of the Information Security and Cryptology — ICISC 2003*, (pp. 274-293). ICISC.

Myles, G., & Collberg, C. (2005). K-gram based software birthmarks. In *Proceedings of the 2005 ACM Symposium on Applied Computing*, (pp. 314-318). ACM Press.

Park, H., Lim, H.-I., Choi, S., & Han, T. (2011). Detecting common modules in java packages based on static object trace birthmark. *The Computer Journal*, *54*(1), 108–124. doi:10.1093/comjnl/bxp095

Ping, Z., Xi, C., & Xu-Guang, Y. (2010). The software watermarking for tamper resistant radix dynamic graph coding. *Information Technology Journal*, *9*(6), 1236–1240. doi:10.3923/itj.2010.1236.1240

Qu, G., & Potkonjak, M. (1998). Analysis of watermarking techniques for graph coloring problem. In *Proceedings of the 1998 IEEE/ACM International Conference on Computer-Aided Design*, (pp. 190-193). IEEE Press.

Shirali-Shahreza, M. (2008). Text steganography by changing words spelling. In *Proceedings of the 10th International Conference on Advanced Communication Technology,* (pp. 1912-1913). IEEE.

Shirali-Shahreza, M. H., & Shirali-Shahreza, M. (2008a). A new synonym text steganography. *Proceedings of the Intelligent Information Hiding and Multimedia Signal Processing, 2008*, 1524–1526. doi:10.1109/IIH-MSP.2008.6

Shirali-Shahreza, M. H., & Shirali-Shahreza, M. (2008b). Steganography in SMS by sudoku puzzle. In *Proceedings of the IEEE/ACS International Conference on Computer Systems and Applications 2008*, (pp. 844-847). IEEE Press.

Stern, J. P., Hachez, G., Koeune, F., & Quisquater, J.-J. (2000). *Robust* object watermarking: Application to code. In *Proceedings of Information Hiding,* (pp. 368-378). IEEE.

Sun, G. (2010). An algorithm of webpage information hiding based on class selectors. In *Proceedings of the Third International Symposium on Intelligent Information Technology and Security Informatics,* (pp. 691-694). IEEE.

Swaminathan, A., Mao, Y., Wu, M., & Kailas, K. (2005). Data hiding in compiled program binaries for enhancing computer system performance. In *Proceedings of Information Hiding* (pp. 357–371). IEEE. doi:10.1007/11558859_26

Topkara, M., Topkara, U., & Atallah, M. J. (2006). Words are not enough: Sentence level natural language watermarking. In *Proceedings of the ACM Workshop on Content Protection and Security,* (pp. 37-46). ACM Press.

Topkara, M., Topkara, U., & Atallah, M. J. (2007). Information hiding through errors: A confusing approach. In *Proceedings of the SPIE International Conference on Security, Steganography, and Watermarking of Multimedia Contents,* (pp. 65050V1-65050V12). IEEE.

Venkatesan, R., Vazirani, V., & Sinha, S. (2001). A graph theoretic approach to software watermarking. In *Proceedings of Information Hiding* (pp. 157–168). IEEE. doi:10.1007/3-540-45496-9_12

Watanabe, A., Katoh, T., Bista, B. B., & Takata, T. (2006). On a watermarking scheme for MusicXML. In *Proceedings of the 20th International Conference on Advanced Information Networking and Applications,* (pp. 894-898). IEEE.

Wayner, P. (2009). *Disappearing cryptography* (3rd ed.). Burlington, MA: Morgan Kaufmann Publishers.

Xu, J., & Zeng, G. (2010). A software watermarking algorithm based on stack-state transition graph. In *Proceedings of the 2010 4th International Conference on Network and System Security,* (pp. 83-88). IEEE.

Yang, J. (2010). Algorithm of XML document information hiding based on equal element. In *Proceedings of the International Conference on Computer Science and Information Technology,* (pp. 250-253). IEEE.

Zhu, J., Liu, Y., & Yin, K. (2009). A novel dynamic graph software watermark scheme. In *Proceedings of the 2009 First International Workshop on Education Technology and Computer Science,* (Vol. 3), (pp. 775-780). IEEE.

Zhu, W., & Thomborson, C. (2006). Algorithms to watermark software through register allocation. In *Proceedings of the Digital Rights Management: Technologies, Issues, Challenges and Systems,* (pp. 180-191). IEEE.

ADDITIONAL READING

Collberg, C., & Thomborson, C. (2002). Watermarking, tamper-proofing, and obfuscation—tools for software protection. *IEEE Transactions on Software Engineering, 28*(8), 735–746. doi:10.1109/TSE.2002.1027797

Hamilton, J., & Danicic, S. (2011). A survey of static software watermarking. In *Proceedings of the 2011 World Congress on Internet Security (WorldCIS),* (pp. 100-107). IEEE.

KEY TERMS AND DEFINITIONS

Bijection: A mapping $f : X \to Y$ is a bijection if and only if, for every element $y \in Y$, there is a unique element $x \in X$ such that $f(x) = y$.

Binary Data Hiding Method: This method takes a binary file (executable or library) as a cover object and embeds a message into the binary file. A binary file is then obtained where the message is hidden.

Embedding Capacity: In a data hiding method, the amount of data that can be embedded into a cover object by the method.

Permutation: A permutation of a set *X* is a bijection from *X* to *X* itself. If a set *X* consists of *n* elements, there are *n!* different permutations for *X*.

Software Watermarking: A type of binary data hiding method and is used for protecting software from piracy acts by embedding software's identifier.

Steganography: A type of data hiding method, which is used for concealing a secret message by embedding it into an apparently innocuous cover object.

Text Data Hiding Method: This method takes a text as a cover object and embeds a message into the text. A text is then obtained where the message is hidden.

Chapter 17
Data Embedding Methods Not Based on Content Modification

Hirohisa Hioki
Kyoto University, Japan

ABSTRACT

Creation of a stego object by embedding information in a cover object often distorts the cover object. As more information is embedded, more annoying noise is introduced in stego objects. Although reversible embedding methods enable us to restore the original cover object even after embedding, stego objects are not free from distortions. Embedding information does not, however, always result in damaging the contents of the cover object. This chapter introduces data embedding methods that are not based on modification of the contents of cover objects: permutation steganography, metadata steganography, and cover generation methods. This chapter focuses on elaborating the basic principles of these techniques.

INTRODUCTION

Steganographic methods aim to hide a secret message by embedding it unnoticeably into a cover object, such as an image, audio, text, or executable file. A stego object, which is obtained as a result of embedding, should be plausible.

Embedding is often performed by slightly modifying a cover object, which results in distortions in a stego object. As more information is embedded, more annoying noise is introduced in the stego object. Such distortions may become noticeable, and they can arouse the suspicion of third parties regarding information hidden within the stego object. Obvious distortions in a stego object defeat the purpose of trying to hide a secret message.

A steganographic method is said to be reversible if it enables us to restore the original cover object from a stego object (Tian, 2003; Tsai, Hu, & Yeh, 2009). In reversible methods, information needed to restore original content is kept in stego objects along with messages. Reversible methods are sometimes called distortion-free in the sense that the original cover object is restorable (Fridrich, Goljan, & Du, 2002). Such methods are, however, not distortion-free in the strict sense, because stego objects are not free from distortions.

Embedding information does not necessarily cause damage to the contents of cover objects.

DOI: 10.4018/978-1-4666-2217-3.ch017

This chapter first introduces steganographic methods that embed information without creating distortions in the contents of cover objects. These methods are called distortion-free (or distortion-less) steganographic methods that are useful when the quality of stego object matters crucially.

As a distortion-free method, permutation steganography is introduced first. This method embeds a secret message by rearranging the elements of a cover object without changing its content. The next method we look into is metadata steganography. A message is embedded into a set of metadata associated with cover files in a file system. The cover files are kept totally intact, i.e., each bit of every file is preserved, since the files are stored separately from the metadata in the file system.

In addition to distortion-free methods, this chapter also discusses cover generation methods in which a cover object is created so that it becomes a stego object. Instead of modifying an existing cover object, a secret message is hidden into an apparently innocuous object generated from scratch. In this chapter, a text-based method where stego texts are generated according to customized grammars is described first. Next, image-based methods are outlined. A stego object is constructed from a number of innocuous images.

PERMUTATION STEGANOGRAPHY

This section is devoted to the description of permutation steganography. Permutation steganography is an effective method for hiding messages provided that the contents of cover objects are not affected by the rearrangement of their elements. Even if rearrangement of the elements does affect the content, permutation steganography is useful if the original content can be restored by adjusting the cover object after rearrangement. Example of cover objects that can be used for permutation steganography include indexed color (palette) images (Kwan, 1998), polygonal meshes (Bogomjakov, Gotsman, & Isenburg, 2008), and HTML files (Huang, Zhong, & Sun, 2008).

In an indexed color image, color data are stored in a color map. Each color is associated with its index number in the color map, and the pixel data are specified by these color indices. The colors in the color map can be shuffled and the image appearance can be preserved if the pixel data are changed accordingly. A polygonal mesh is a geometric data set consisting of vertices and faces, both of which are indexed by numbers. The indices of vertices and faces are just arbitrary. We can change indices of vertices and faces while preserving the shape they represent. In HTML files, start-tags and empty-element tags can have attributes. The order of attribute specifications is insignificant. We can freely arrange attributes without affecting the result of rendering. These examples show that there are cover objects that can be described in more than one way while preserving their appearances completely. Permutation steganography exploits this kind of redundancy.

In this section, the permutation is introduced first. Next, the embedding principle based on the permutation is outlined. The embedding algorithm is then detailed. A variant of the standard permutation steganography is also presented, which runs more efficiently than the standard algorithm at a little expense of embedding capacity.

Permutation

A permutation σ of a set X is a bijection from X onto X itself. This section focuses on permutations of a totally ordered finite set $X = \{x_0, x_1, x_2, \dots x_{n-1}\}$ in which either $x_i < x_j$ or $x_j < x_i$ for every pair of elements x_i and x_j when $i \neq j$. Because such a set $X = \{x_0, x_1, x_2, \dots x_{n-1}\}$ can be naturally identified with the set of indices $\{0, 1, 2, \& , n-1\}$, it is enough to consider an index set instead of X.

Let $[a, b]$ be the set

$$[a,b] = \begin{cases} \{i \in Z \mid a \le i \le b\} & \text{if } a \le b \\ \varnothing & \text{otherwise} \end{cases} \quad (1)$$

Permutation σ of the set $[0, n-1]$ can be represented by the tuple $(\sigma(0), \sigma(1), \ldots, \sigma(n-1))$. For example, $(2,0,1,3)$ represents a permutation $\sigma(0)=2, \sigma(1)=0, \sigma(2)=1$, and $\sigma(3)=3$ (Figure 1). Hereafter, this permutation notation is called one-line representation.

Let S_n be the set of all permutations of set $[0,n\text{-}1]$. Because $n!$ different orderings of n elements exist, $|S_n| = n!$

We can now define a bijection $\varphi : S_n \to [0, n!-1]$ as

$$\varphi(\sigma) = \sum_{j=0}^{n-1} |C_j| \cdot (n-j-1)! \quad (2)$$

$$C_k = \{x \in \sigma([k+1, n-1]) \mid x < \sigma(k)\} \quad (3)$$

Note that

$$\sigma([k+1, n-1]) = \{\sigma(k+1), \sigma(k+2), \ldots, \sigma(n-1)\}$$

The bijection φ preserves the lexicographical order of the permutations. For two permutations $\sigma, \sigma' \in S_n$, $\varphi(\sigma) \le \varphi(\sigma')$ if $\sigma \le \sigma'$ in the lexicographical order of their one-line representations.

Figure 1. One-line representation of a permutation

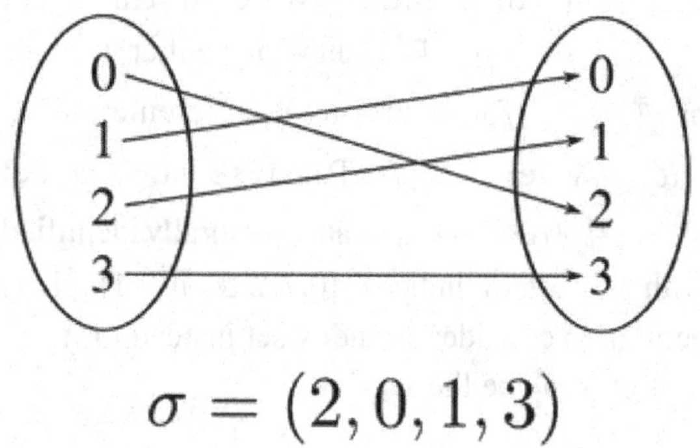

For example, the set $\{0,1,2,3\}$ has $4! = 24$ permutations. Table 1 shows each permutation σ and $\varphi(\sigma)$. For (1,3,2,0), we obtain the following:

$C_0 = \{0\}$
$C_1 = \{0,2\}$
$C_2 = \{0\}$
$C_3 = \varnothing$

The value of φ for $(1,3,2,0)$ is therefore

$$|C_0| \cdot 3! + |C_1| \cdot 2! + |C_2| \cdot 1! + |C_3| \cdot 0! = 11$$

Principle of Permutation Steganography

Permutations can be used to embed messages in cover objects in a distortion-free manner. The cover object can be a file, a component of a file, a set of files, or any data set where elements are different from each other and are totally ordered. A way to traverse the elements should also be defined.

Let $X = \{x_0, x_1, \ldots, x_{n-1}\}$ be a totally ordered set in a cover object and either $x_i < x_j$ or $x_j < x_i$ when $i \ne j$. An n-tuple $(x_0, x_1, \ldots, x_{n-1})$ is obtained after a traversal path is specified for the elements. A permutation σ can then be derived from the n-tuple based on a rank function

$$\rho(x_i) = |\{x \in X \mid x < x_i\}|$$

This function $\rho(x_i)$ specifies that x_i is at the $\rho(x_i)$-th position when all the elements $x_0, x_1, \ldots, x_{n-1}$ are ordered as $x_{k_0} < x_{k_1} < \ldots < x_{k_{n-1}}$. We can now find that the tuple $(\rho(x_0), \rho(x_1), \ldots, \rho(x_{n-1}))$ represents a one-line representation of a permutation.

Table 1. Permutations of the set {0,1,2,3} and values of φ

σ	$\varphi(\sigma)$	σ	$\varphi(\sigma)$	σ	$\varphi(\sigma)$	σ	$\varphi(\sigma)$
(0,1,2,3)	0	(1,0,2,3)	6	(2,0,1,3)	12	(3,0,1,2)	18
(0,1,3,2)	1	(1,0,3,2)	7	(2,0,3,1)	13	(3,0,2,1)	19
(0,2,1,3)	2	(1,2,0,3)	8	(2,1,0,3)	14	(3,1,0,2)	20
(0,2,3,1)	3	(1,2,3,0)	9	(2,1,3,0)	15	(3,1,2,0)	21
(0,3,1,2)	4	(1,3,0,2)	10	(2,3,0,1)	16	(3,2,0,1)	22
(0,3,2,1)	5	(1,3,2,0)	11	(2,3,1,0)	17	(3,2,1,0)	23

As an example, consider the colors in the color map of an indexed color image. A color map is a list of colors used in an image. A color is described by a vector $c=(r,g,b)$. The relation $c_i < c_j$ can be defined as

$$c_i < c_j \equiv (r_i < r_j) \vee (r_i = r_j \wedge g_i < g_j) \vee (r_i = r_j \wedge g_i = g_j \wedge b_i < b_j) \tag{4}$$

Because the colors are unique in the color map, they specify a permutation. Assume that there is a color map consisting of the following four colors:

$c_0 = (255, 0, 0)$,
$c_1 = (0, 0, 0)$,
$c_2 = (0, 255, 0)$,
$c_3 = (255, 255, 255)$.

Because $c_1 < c_2 < c_0 < c_3$ we find that $\rho(c_0) = 2, \rho(c_1) = 0, \rho(c_2) = 1$ and $\rho(c_3) = 3$. The permutation

$$(\rho(c_0), \rho(c_1), \rho(c_2), \rho(c_3)) = (2, 0, 1, 3)$$

can then be derived from the tuple (c_0, c_1, c_2, c_3) represented by the color map.

As we have seen so far, a permutation $\sigma \in S_n$ can be derived from an n-tuple of a cover object, and the bijection $\varphi : S_n \rightarrow [0, n! - 1]$ can be used to represent a number in set $[0, n! - 1]$ by a permutation. It follows that a message $x \in [0, n! - 1]$ can be embedded in the n elements by shuffling them to obtain another permutation σ' such that $x = \varphi(\sigma')$

Mere shuffling of the elements might corrupt the contents of the cover object; however, in such a case, other components of the cover object can be adjusted, and a stego object is obtained without any distortion.

Figure 2 depicts an example. The cover object is a 5x4 indexed color image. It has four colors, as shown in its color map. To embed a secret message, the colors in the color map of the cover image can be rearranged.

The color map of the cover image (c_0, c_1, c_2, c_3) results in the permutation $\sigma = (2, 0, 1, 3)$ because $c_1 < c_2 < c_0 < c_3$ from the order given by Equation 4. This permutation yields the bit string "1100" by $\varphi(\sigma) = 12$. Assume that the bit string 0100 (decimal number 4) is the message to be hidden. To embed this message, the colors (c_0, c_1, c_2, c_3) are rearranged as (c_0', c_1', c_2', c_3') in the stego image so that $c_0' < c_2' < c_3' < c_1'$. From this new color map, the permutation $\sigma' = (0, 3, 1, 2)$ is obtained, which gives $\varphi(\sigma') = 4$ as required.

In this case, the colors numbered 0, 1, 2, and 3 are renumbered as 3, 0, 2, and 1 respectively. The

Figure 2. Permutation steganography performed with an indexed color image

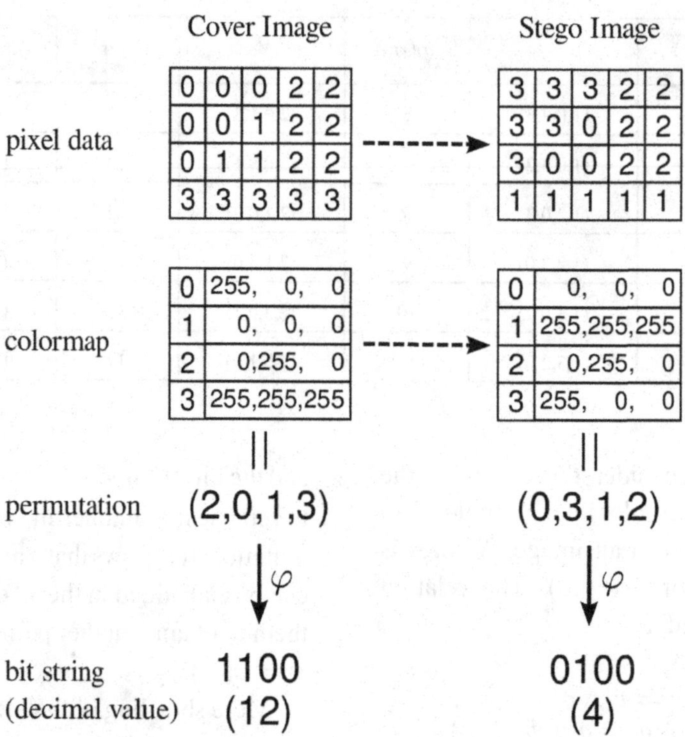

pixel data are adjusted accordingly to preserve the appearance of the image. As a result, a stego image is obtained.

As previously discussed, one of $n!$ different messages can be represented by the permutation of n elements. The embedding capacity of permutation steganography is thus

$$\log_2(n!) = \sum_{j=2}^{n} \log_2 j$$

Figure 3 shows the relationship between the number of elements in a permutation and the embedding capacity.

Message Embedding

To embed a message $x \in [0, n!-1]$, a permutation σ must be obtained, from which x is restored as $x = \varphi(\sigma)$. Let us find out here how to obtain the permutation σ for the message x.

For a totally ordered set $X = \{x_0, x_1, \ldots, x_{n-1}\}$ define $\xi(X,k)$ as follows:

$$\xi(X,k) = x_{j_k} \text{ s.t. } \rho(x_{j_k}, X) = k \tag{5}$$

$$\rho(x, X) = \left|\{x' \in X \mid x' < x\}\right| \tag{6}$$

Note that $\xi(X,k)$ gives the k-th smallest element in X.

Then $\sigma(0), \sigma(1), \ldots, \sigma(n-1)$ can be derived iteratively for x as follows:

$$\sigma(i) = \xi(R_i, q_{n-i-1}) \tag{7}$$

$$q_k = (x / k!) \bmod (k+1) \tag{8}$$

$$R_i = [0, n-1] \setminus \sigma([0, i-1]) \tag{9}$$

Figure 3. Embedding capacity of permutation steganography

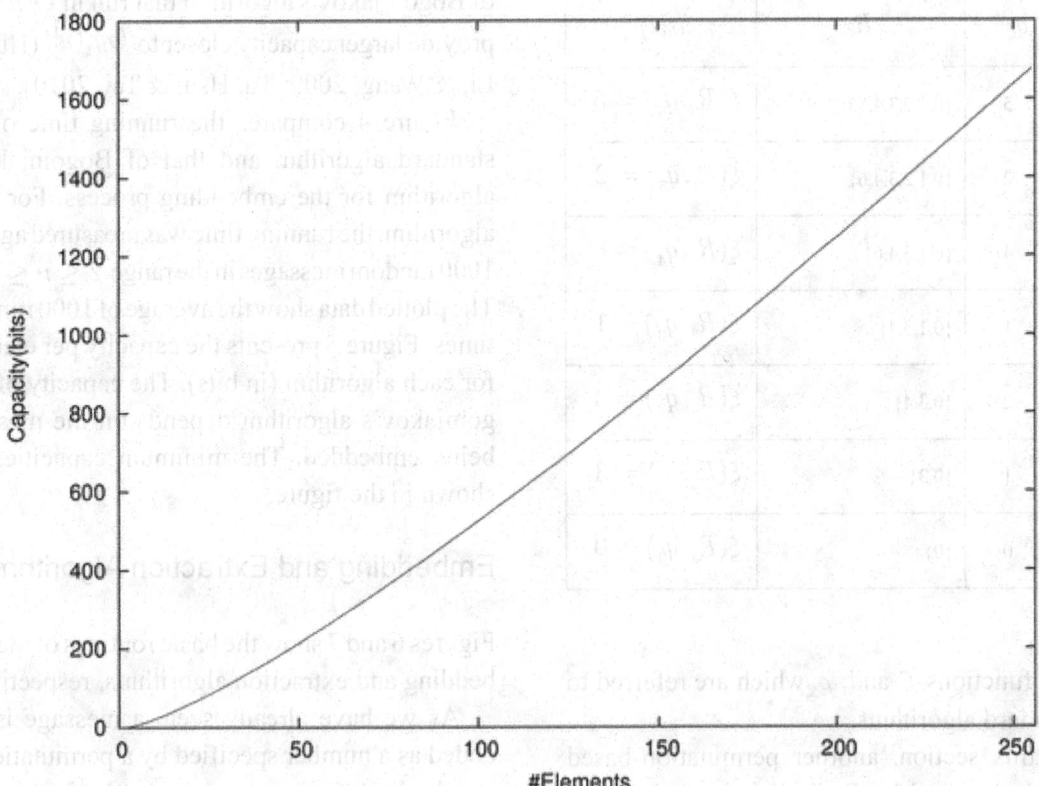

where $/$ is the quotient operator, mod is the modulo operator, and $A \setminus B = \{u \in A \mid u \notin B\}$. Note that $[a, b] = \varnothing$ when $a > b$ and $\sigma(\varnothing) = \varnothing$. In addition, note that the sequence $q_{n-1}q_{n-2}\cdots q_0$ is the factoradic representation of x as follows:

$$x = \sum_{j=0}^{n-1} q_j \cdot j!, \quad 0 \leq q_j \leq j \qquad (10)$$

For example, assume that $x = 3947$ is the message to be embedded; then, because $6! < 3947 < 7!$, seven elements are required. In this case, $\sigma = (5, 2, 6, 1, 4, 3, 0)$ is the required permutation. Table 2 provides details.

From the permutation $\sigma = (5, 2, 6, 1, 4, 3, 0)$ the message x=3947 is restored by φ as follows:

$$C_0 = \{0,1,2,3,4\}$$
$$C_1 = \{0,1\}$$
$$C_2 = \{0,1,3,4\}$$
$$C_3 = \{0\}$$
$$C_4 = \{0,3\}$$
$$C_5 = \{0\}$$
$$C_6 = \varnothing,$$
$$\varphi(\sigma) = \sum_{j=0}^{6} \left|C_j\right| \cdot (6-j)! = 3947$$

Bogomjakov's Method

The previous discussion dealt with the principle of permutation steganography and the algorithms for embedding and extracting information based

Table 2. Derivation of the permutation for 3947

i	q_{6-i}	R_i	$\sigma(i)$
0	5	{0,1,2,3,4,5,6}	$\xi(R_0, q_6) = 5$
1	2	{0,1,2,3,4,6}	$\xi(R_1, q_5) = 2$
2	4	{0,1,3,4,6}	$\xi(R_2, q_4) = 6$
3	1	{0,1,3,4}	$\xi(R_3, q_3) = 1$
4	2	{0,3,4}	$\xi(R_4, q_2) = 4$
5	1	{0,3}	$\xi(R_5, q_1) = 3$
6	0	{0}	$\xi(R_6, q_0) = 0$

on the functions ξ and φ which are referred to as standard algorithms.

In this section, another permutation-based method proposed by Bogomjakov et al. is described. Bogomjakov's algorithm (Bogomjakov, Gotsman, & Isenburg, 2008) runs more efficiently than the standard algorithm at a little expense of embedding capacity.

When n elements are provided for embedding, the time complexity of the standard algorithm is $\Omega(n^2 \log^2 n \operatorname{loglog} n)$, whereas the time complexity of Bogomjakov's algorithm is *O(n)*. Although the embedding capacity of Bogomjakov's algorithm is less than that of the standard algorithm $(\log_2(n!))$, the difference is less than one bit per element (Bogomjakov, Gotsman, & Isenburg, 2008). In the standard algorithm, a message should be given as an integer value in $[0, n! - 1]$ and is encoded as a permutation as a whole. The embedding process thus usually involves arithmetic of quite large integers. In contrast, in Bogomjakov's method, a message is regarded as a bit string and is encoded piece by piece by each element of a permutation. The embedding algorithm is skillfully designed and stays simple. There are variants of Bogomjakov's algorithm that run in $O(n)$ and provide larger capacity closer to $log_2(n!)$ (Huang, Li, & Wang, 2009; Tu, Hsu, & Tai, 2010).

Figure 4 compares the running time of the standard algorithm and that of Bogomjakov's algorithm for the embedding process. For each algorithm, the running time was measured against 1000 random messages in the range $2 \leq n \leq 255$. The plotted data show the average of 1000 running times. Figure 5 presents the capacity per element for each algorithm (in bits). The capacity of Bogomjakov's algorithm depends on the message being embedded. The minimum capacities are shown in the figure.

Embedding and Extraction Algorithms

Figures 6 and 7 show the basic routines of the embedding and extraction algorithms, respectively.

As we have already seen, a message is encoded as a number specified by a permutation in standard permutation steganography. In contrast, a message is encoded piece by piece by each element of a permutation in Bogomjakov's method.

In the embedding process of Bogomjakov's method, the array of all the cover elements (cover array) is prepared first, and the elements of the permutation are collected one by one from the cover array. The first i elements of the permutation are collected up to the i-th iteration, and the first $n - i$ elements of the cover array are available at that time. It is possible to encode $k = \lfloor \log_2(n - i) \rfloor$ or $k + 1$ bits of the message in the i-th iteration by selecting one of $n - i$ elements that remain available in the cover array. The element at the j-th position $\left(0 \leq j < 2^k\right)$ encodes k bits, whereas the element at the j'-th position $\left(2^k \leq j' < n - i\right)$ encodes $k + 1$ bits. Let b be the next $k + 1$ bits of the message. If $2^k \leq b < n - i$, $k + 1$ bits can be embedded;

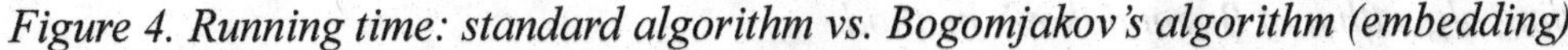

Figure 4. Running time: standard algorithm vs. Bogomjakov's algorithm (embedding)

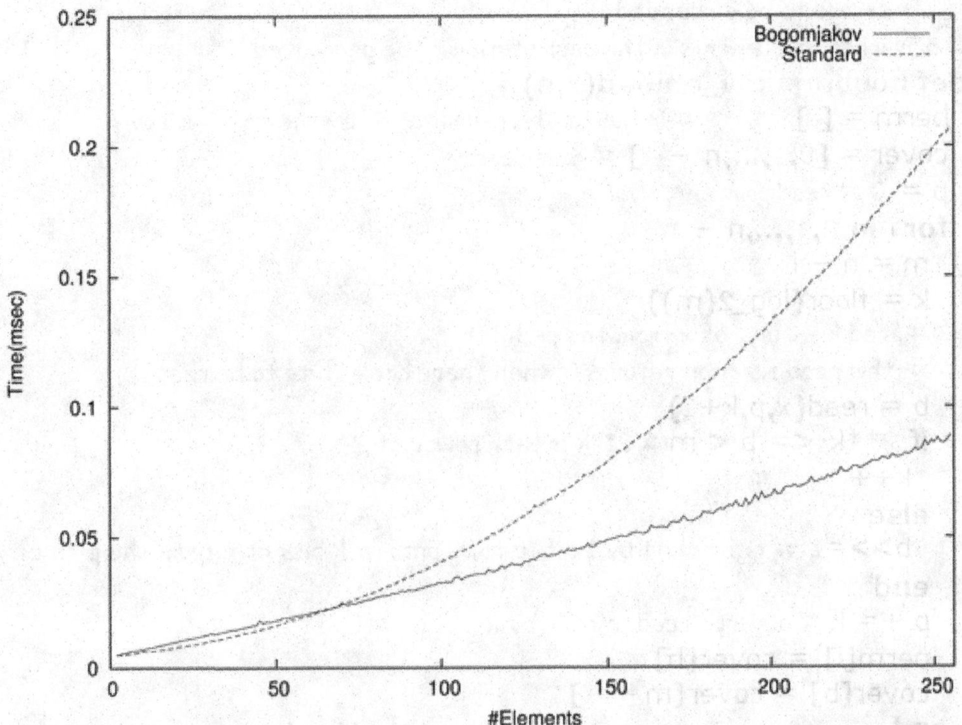

Figure 5. Capacity per element: standard algorithm vs. Bogomjakov's algorithm (minimum)

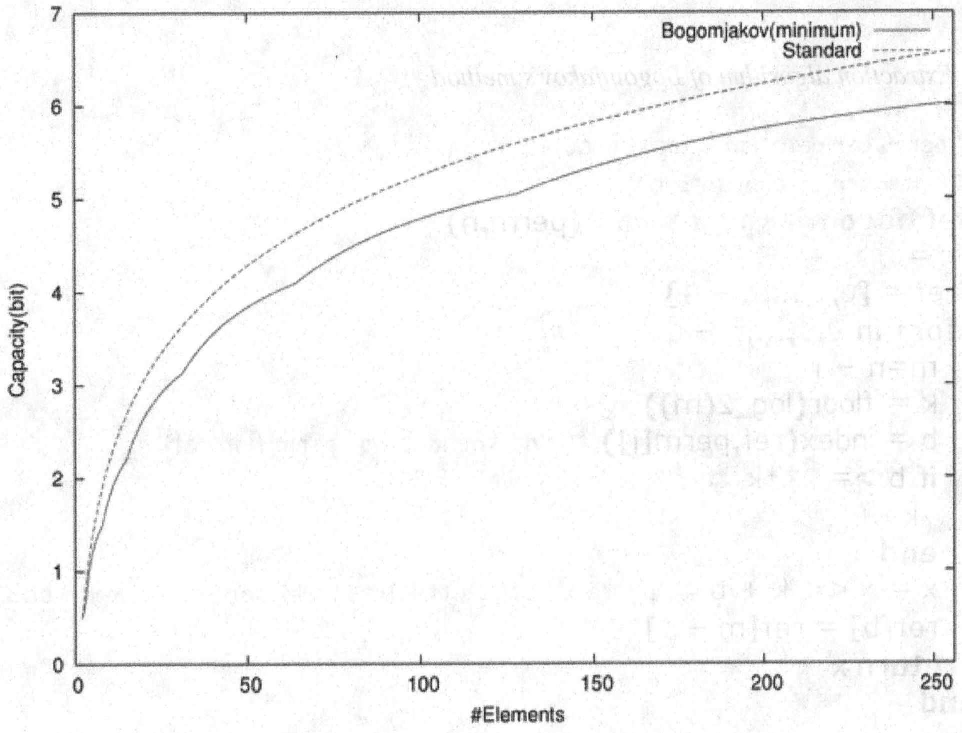

Figure 6. Embedding algorithm of Bogomjakov's method

```
# x: message to be embedded
# n: number of elements in the permutation to be generated
def bogomjakov_embed(x,n)
  perm = [ ]          # initialize the permutation by the empty array
  cover = [0,1,...,n - 1] # cover array
  p = 0 # read pointer
  for i in 0,1,...,n - 1
    m = n - i
    k = floor(log_2(m))
    # read k + 1 bits of x from the p-th bit
    # (this read function returns 0 when there are no bits to be read)
    b = read(x,p,k+1)
    if 2**k <= b < m # 2**k is k-th power of 2
      k++
    else
      b>>=1 # right shift by 1 bit (b now contains k bits of x from the p-th bit)
    end
    p += k # advance read pointer by k
    perm[i] = cover[b]
    cover[b] = cover[m - 1]
  end
  return perm
end
```

Figure 7. Extraction algorithm of Bogomjakov's method

```
# perm: permutation (stego object)
# n: number of elements in perm
def bogomjakov_extract(perm,n)
  x = 0
  ref = [0,1,...,n - 1]
  for i in 0,1,...,n - 1
    m=n - i
    k = floor(log_2(m))
    b = index(ref,perm[i]) # find the index of perm[i] in ref
    if b >= 2**k # 2**k is k-th power of 2
      k++
    end
    x = x << k + b # update x (left shift k bits and insert b into lower bits)
    ref[b] = ref[m - 1]
  return x
end
```

otherwise b is shifted to right by one bit, and k bits are embedded.

The b-th element of the cover array selected in the i-th iteration is collected as the i-th element of the permutation to be generated. The $(n-i)$-th element of the cover array—the last element available at this point—is then moved to the b-th position. This move operation is performed to collect the elements available at the head of the cover array, i.e., the operation keeps the first $n-i$ elements of the array available in the i-th iteration. The same move operations are performed during the extraction process to interpret each element of the permutation correctly. The time complexity of these move operations is $O(1)$

Table 3 shows an example of the embedding process. The first row of the table shows the initial states of the message x, the cover array *cover*, and the permutation *perm*. The bit string of the message x is 11100001101 (1805 in decimal). The states of *x*, *cover*, and *perm* at the end of each iteration are shown from the second row to bottom. In the i-th iteration, the k-bit string b is cut out from the head of the message *x*. The string b represents the position of the element of the cover array to be taken and collected as the i-th element of the permutation.

The following example shows this embedding process in detail. When *i*=1, the cover array has six elements [1,2,3,6,4,5] (as obtained at the end of the previous iteration) and the remaining message is 100001101. Because there are six elements in the cover array and $\lfloor \log_2(6) \rfloor = 2$ it is possible to embed two or three bits. The three-bit prefix of 100001101 is 100 (4 in decimal). This three-bit string can be embedded because $2^2 \leq 4 < 6$. As a result, *k*=3 and *b*=100. Next, *cover[b]* = *cover*[4] =4 is obtained from *cover* and is pushed into *perm*. The last element of *cover*, i.e., 5, is then moved to b-th (*b*=4) position. By repeating this process, the permutation [3,4,0,6,5,1,2] is obtained when embedding is completed.

The message 11100001101 can be restored from the permutation [3,4,0,6,5,1,2], as shown in Table 4. In the i-th iteration, the i-th element of the permutation $perm[i]$ is interpreted as the k-bit string b, which is derived from the position of *perm*[*i*] in the *ref* array. The array *ref* is equivalent to the cover array of the embedding process. This array is required to retrace the changes of the cover array during the embedding process.

Table 3. Embedding 11100001101 by Bogomjakov's algorithm

i	k	b	x	*cover*	*perm*
			11100001101	[0,1,2,3,4,5,6]	[]
0	2	11	100001101	[0,1,2,6,4,5]	[3]
1	3	100	001101	[0,1,2,6,5]	[3,4]
2	2	00	1101	[5,1,2,6]	[3,4,0]
3	2	11	01	[5,1,2]	[3,4,0,6]
4	1	0	1	[2,1]	[3,4,0,6,5]
5	1	1		[2]	[3,4,0,6,5,1]
6	0	0		[]	[3,4,0,6,5,1,2]

Table 4. Extracting a message from [3,4,0,6,5,1,2] by Bogomjakov's algorithm

i	k	$perm[i]$	b	*ref*	x
				[0,1,2,3,4,5,6]	
0	2	3	11	[0,1,2,6,4,5]	11
1	3	4	100	[0,1,2,6,5]	11100
2	2	0	00	[5,1,2,6]	1110000
3	2	6	11	[5,1,2]	111000011
4	1	5	0	[2,1]	1110000110
5	1	1	1	[2]	11100001101
6	0	2	0	[]	11100001101

As an example, let us examine the extraction process when i=3. The *ref* array at the end of the previous iteration is [5,1,2,6]. The element of *perm* to be checked is *perm*[i] = *perm*[3] =6. In the *ref* array, the index of the element 6 is 3; hence, the bit string 11 is extracted accordingly.

METADATA STEGANOGRAPHY

Permutation steganography is distortion-free because it generates a stego object that retains the representation of the content of the cover object. The cover and stego objects appear to be the same when they are presented.

The data of the cover object, however, must be modified to embed a message, which might be detected by an attacker trying to intercept or eliminate the message. An attacker might notice that steganography is being employed if he or she finds some unusual arrangements of data inside the stego object. For example, if the color map of an indexed color image is well organized and the colors present some smooth gradation throughout the map, the map could be considered as genuine. In contrast, a color map might appear to be strange if it reveals a randomized pattern of colors caused by the embedding process.

Data of cover objects do not have to be necessarily modified for embedding messages. Instead, embedding processes can modify the metadata of files such as the filename or timestamps. Because the metadata are stored separately from the files, the contents of cover files remain intact even when the metadata are modified.

In order to practically perform embedding by modifying the metadata, a critical problem must be resolved: the amount of metadata is quite small compared to contents of cover files. Hence, the amount of information that can be secretly embedded in the metadata of a single file is severely limited.

This section introduces a distortion-free steganographic method based on modification of the metadata. First, the topic of which type of metadata is suitable for embedding is discussed. Then, the issue of obtaining sufficient capacity by modification of the metadata is addressed.

Metadata Suitable for Embedding

Every file has its own metadata along with its data. Typical examples of metadata are as follows:

- Filename
- File size
- File type (e.g., regular file, directory, link, or device)
- Ownership information
- Access control information
- Timestamps (e.g., the time of last access or the time of last modification)

Because these metadata are associated with files and are used for managing them, not all of them are freely available for embedding. In order to find metadata suitable for embedding, the following aspects must be considered:

1. It should be possible to embed bit strings as valid metadata values.
2. The results of the embedding process should be plausible.
3. The modification of the metadata should not affect the system operations.
4. It should be possible to use normal operation to control metadata values.

Now let us consider which of the above metadata are suitable for embedding according to these conditions.

- **File Type:** The type of a file is constant as long as the file exists and cannot be modified.
- **File Size:** The size of a file represents the amount of data in the file, and it cannot be

modified freely without changing the contents of the file.

- **Ownership:** A user cannot change ownership information of files freely unless he or she is a system administrator. Although system administrators can change the ownership information, the changes might cause a system error or create security risks.
- **Access Control Information:** Access control information cannot be changed freely because such changes may cause security risks.
- **Filename:** A file can be named as we want if the name we use is not already assigned to another file and consists of valid characters available in the system. However, if filenames are used to hide messages without any restriction, the names would appear to be quite strange and arouse an attacker's suspicion.
- **Timestamps:** Often, by using a system call, timestamps are recorded for a file, for example, the time the file was last accessed or the time it was last modified. The timestamp of a user's file can be modified freely without resulting in serious problems, unless the modified value represents a time in the future or a time that is too far in the past.

The above discussion shows that timestamps are the most suitable metadata for embedding information. However, the message embedded in timestamps can corrupt easily because timestamps of a file are automatically updated each time a file is read or modified. Despite this difficulty, it is possible to preserve the embedded message if a dedicated tool that can adjust timestamps automatically as required is used. This tool functions as a wrapper for common file viewers or editors. When the tool is invoked with a viewer or an editor, it records the current timestamps first and then launches the viewer or editor. As soon as the launched program exits, the tool writes back the original timestamps.

Scraping Metadata and Obtaining Sufficient Capacity

A timestamp field is given by an integer that represents seconds since the beginning of the epoch. In general, an integer is recorded as a bit string of a fixed length of 32 or 64 bits. A single timestamp field can thus provide only a small amount of embedding capacity. Furthermore, it is almost impossible to use the entire timestamp field, because if all parts of the field are used in the modification, an odd timestamp value will be obtained. Hence, to obtain a plausible timestamp field, the timestamp cannot be modified by a large amount.

This restriction does not necessarily indicate that metadata-based embedding is not useful. If a set of files are organized in a particular manner and the metadata of the files are provided for embedding at the same time, a practical capacity can be obtained.

In one such method (Hioki, 2007), the metadata of regular files in a directory tree are scraped for embedding. A message is divided into pieces and embedded in the metadata of regular files by traversing each directory under the given directory tree. The directories are traversed in a depth-first manner, and the order of visiting child directories of a directory depends on a secret key. The same key is also used to sort the regular files in a directory. To embed a piece of a message in a directory, two methods are proposed in (Hioki, 2007): one based on the Least Significant Bits (LSB) and the other based on permutations.

In the LSB-based method, the lower e bits of the timestamp field of each file are sequentially replaced with e bits in the message. If this simple replacement yields a timestamp in the future, the value of the timestamp is decreased by 2^e. This adjustment is feasible if the value of the timestamp is not less than 2^e, which is true as long as 2^e is smaller than the integer value of the current time. The embedding capacity of a directory is en bits where n is the number of regular files stored in the directory.

In the permutation-based method, the timestamps of regular files in a directory are adjusted to obtain the permutation that represents a piece of a message, as already described in this chapter. Assume that a directory has n regular files and that timestamps of the files $t_0, t_1, \ldots, t_{n-1}$ are to be modified as $t'_0, t'_1, \ldots, t'_{n-1}$ such that $t'_{j_0} < t'_{j_1} < \cdots < t'_{j_{n-1}}$. The last entry $t'_{j_{n-1}}$ is set to the current time first. Now let $\tau_{n-1} = t'_{j_{n-1}}$ and D denote a small integer larger than two. For each k= n-2, n-3,...0, let $\tau_k = \tau_{k+1} - \delta_k$ where δ_k is a random value in [1,D-1]. The timestamp t'_{j_k} is then set to τ_k. The embedding capacity of the directory is $\log_2(n!)$. Figure 8 shows the embedding algorithm (The process concerning the secret key is not included for simplicity).

COVER GENERATION METHOD

To hide information, instead of modifying an existing cover object, a cover object that secretly represents the information can be created. This section introduces cover generation methods (Katzenbeisser & Petitcolas, 2000) in which a cover object is generated so that it becomes a stego object. Two types of cover generation methods are discussed. One is text-based, in which a stego text is generated according to customized grammars. The other is image-based, in which a stego object is assembled from innocuous images.

Text-Based Cover Generation Method

The text-based cover generation method is a linguistic-based steganographic method. Using this method, a message is hidden by generating syntactically legitimate sentences according to customized grammars. In what follows, a class of formal grammar called context-free grammar is introduced first. The principle of generating a sentence that encodes a secret message is then explained.

Context-Free Grammar

A context-free grammar describes the syntactic structure of a class of sentences. A context-free grammar G is defined by a quadruple tuple as follows:

$$G = (V_N, V_T, P, S) \tag{11}$$

where V_N, V_T, P, and S are a set of nonterminals, a set of terminals, a set of production rules, and a start symbol, respectively. The start symbol S is an element of V_N

The structure of a sentence is described by a tree called a parse tree. A parse tree contains start symbol S at the root node. Each leaf node has a terminal. A sentence is represented by the sequence of terminals in leaf nodes. The terminals in V_T are thus words and phrases. Every internal node has a nonterminal in V_N. The nonterminal of an internal node represents the syntactic structure corresponding to the subtree rooted at the node. A production rule in P denotes a relationship between a nonterminal and a sequence of terminals and/or nonterminals. This relationship appears as a parent–child structure at an internal node.

A production rule is written in a form like" A → B C which denotes that a syntactic structure "A" can be decomposed into a more detailed

Figure 8. Permutation-based metadata steganography (embedding)

```
# x: message
# root: root of the directory tree
def embed(x,root)
  embed_rec(x,0,root)
end

# x: message
# p: read pointer
# dir: current directory
def embed_rec(x,p,dir)
  for d in child_nodes(dir)
    p = embed_rec(x,p,d)
    return p if p >= |x| # |x| is the length of x
  end
  return embed_in_dir(x,p,dir)
end

# x: message
# p: read pointer
# dir: current directory
def embed_in_dir(x,p,dir)
   return p if p >= |x|
   f = regular_files(dir) # list of regular files
   n = |f|                # number of regular files
   # y is a substring of x starting from the p-th bit
   # perm is the permutation representing the string y
   y,perm = permutation(x,p,n)
   p += |y|
   j = index(perm,n - 1) # index such that perm[j]=n - 1
   t = get_current_time()
   set_time_stamp(f[j],t)
   for k in n - 2,n - 3,...,0
     # rand(m) returns a random integer in [0,m - 1]
     # DELTA is a constant
     t -= rand(DELTA)
     j = index(perm,k)
     set_time_stamp(f[j],t)
  end
  return p
end
```

structure described by the sequences "B" and "C." Production rules starting with the same nonterminal are often combined as one rule with alternatives. For example, two rules $\mathrm{A} \rightarrow \mathrm{B}$ and $\mathrm{A} \rightarrow \mathrm{C\ D\ E}$ can be combined into a single rule $\mathrm{A} \rightarrow \mathrm{B} \mid \mathrm{C\ D\ E}$, which denotes that the nonterminal "A" can be either rewritten as "B" or decomposed into "C D E." The parse tree of a sentence is thus derived according to production rules.

Consider a simple example of context-free grammar G_s as follows:

$$G_s = (V_N, V_T, P, S) \tag{12}$$

$$V_N = \{\textbf{subj}, \textbf{pred}, \textbf{verb}, \textbf{what}, \textbf{when}, S\} \tag{13}$$

$$V_T = \{\text{I}, \text{She}, \text{He}, \text{My father}, \text{read}, \text{found}, \text{a book}, \text{a magazine}, \text{yesterday}, \text{last Sunday}\} \tag{14}$$

$$\begin{aligned} P = \{\ & S \rightarrow \textbf{subj}\ \textbf{pred}, \\ & \textbf{subj} \rightarrow \text{I} \mid \text{She} \mid \text{He} \mid \text{My father}, \\ & \textbf{pred} \rightarrow \textbf{verb}\ \textbf{what}\ \textbf{when}, \\ & \textbf{verb} \rightarrow \text{read} \mid \text{bought}, \\ & \textbf{what} \rightarrow \text{a book} \mid \text{a magazine}, \\ & \textbf{when} \rightarrow \text{yesterday} \mid \text{last Sunday}\ \ \} \end{aligned} \tag{15}$$

We can derive many sentences according to the grammar G_s. Some examples are as follows:

a. She bought a book yesterday.
b. My father read a book last Sunday.

The parse trees of these two sentences are shown in Figure 9.

Let L_{G_s} represent the set of all sentences that can be derived according to grammar G_s. Each sentence in L_{G_s} can be generated from start symbol S by repeatedly applying production rules

Figure 9. Parse trees of sentences derived according to grammar G_s

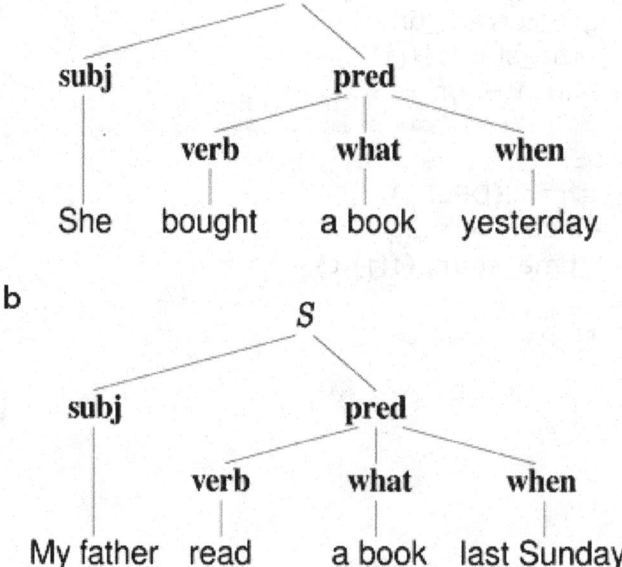

to nonterminals. The process of generating sentence (a) is shown in Table 5.

The parse tree of a sentence is obtained from such a generation process. When an appropriately composed grammar is used, a parse tree of a sentence can be reconstructed from the sentence by parsing it, i.e., by matching words and phrases against nonterminals and terminals according to the grammar.

A grammar is called context-free if each production rule is independently applicable to a nonterminal irrespective of its context, i.e., preceding and succeeding parts. When a grammar has production rules that depend on context, it is called context-sensitive.

Cover Generation Based on Context-Free Grammars

A cover generation method based on context-free grammars was proposed in Wayner (2009). In this method, secret messages can be retained as innocuous texts by generating sentences according to customized context-free grammars. Messages can be restored from sentences by parsing them and reconstructing parse trees if the grammars are composed appropriately. The basic strategy of the method is explained in what follows.

As previously mentioned, many sentences can be generated from a context-free grammar. During the generation of a sentence, it is usual that more than one production rule can be used for rewriting a certain nonterminal. Different sentences can be generated by applying different rules to such nonterminals. In case of grammar G_s introduced previously, the nonterminals **subj**, **verb**, **what**, and **when** have the following alternative rules:

subj $\rightarrow$ I | She | He | My father
verb $\rightarrow$ read | bought
what $\rightarrow$ a book | a magazine
when $\rightarrow$ yesterday | last Sunday.

Nonterminal **subj** has four rules; thus, **subj** can be written as "I," "She," "He," or "My father." The other nonterminals have two alternatives each.

Assume that there are 2^k production rules for a nonterminal. It is then possible to assign a k-bit string to each rule so that each rule corresponds to a different bit string. Hence, any k-bit string

Table 5. Sentence generating process

"She bought a book yesterday."	
S	$S \rightarrow$ **subj pred**
subj pred	**subj** $\rightarrow$ She
She **pred**	**pred** $\rightarrow$ **verb what when**
She **verb what when**	**verb** $\rightarrow$ bought
She bought **what when**	**what** $\rightarrow$ a book
She bought a book **when**	**when** $\rightarrow$ yesterday
She bought a book yesterday.	

x can be encoded by selecting the rule corresponding to the string x. An entire message can be hidden as a sequence of sentences. The message is encoded piece by piece using nonterminals that appear during the generation of each sentence. The message encoded by sentences obviously depends on how bit strings are assigned to rules for nonterminals. A stego sentence can be decoded by reconstructing the parse tree of the sentence and reading bits from the tree using the same assignment of bit strings to rules. The grammar employed specifies the length of the message that can be represented by a single sentence.

Note that decoding is successful only if a properly composed grammar is used. Not all grammars are suitable for this purpose. If a grammar has ambiguities, a sentence might have more than one possible parse tree. The result of decoding will be incorrect if the reconstructed parse tree is different from the one used for encoding. The details of this topic will be discussed later.

The following examples demonstrate sentences that encode messages using the sample grammar G_s. The sentences (a) and (b) encode five-bit strings, as shown in Table 6. The assignments below the sentences are used for encoding.

Similarly, other five-bit messages can be encoded by selecting words appropriately. Any sentence generated using grammar G_s can be properly decoded.

As previously stated, not all context-free grammars are acceptable. A sentence cannot necessarily be decoded correctly if the grammar is ambiguous and the sentence can be parsed in more than one way. For example, the following grammar G_a is ambiguous:

$$G_a = (V_N, V_T, P, S) \tag{16}$$

$$V_N = \{\mathrm{x}, \mathrm{y}, S\} \tag{17}$$

$$V_T = \{\mathrm{p}, \mathrm{v}\} \tag{18}$$

$$P = \{S \rightarrow \mathrm{x},\ \ \mathrm{x} \rightarrow \mathrm{y} \mid \mathrm{v},\ \ \mathrm{y} \rightarrow \mathrm{p\ x} \mid \mathrm{p\ x\ x}\} \tag{19}$$

The sentence "p p v v" can be parsed in two ways as shown in Figure 10. Hence, the sentence can be read as in two ways, e.g., either "111000" or "100110" under certain bit assignments.

In principle, any unambiguous grammar can be used to generate sentences that are uniquely decodable. The generated sentences, however, do

Table 6. Messages encoded by sentences

Sentence	Message
(a) She bought a book yesterday	01100
(b) My father read a book last Sunday	11001
Assignment:	
subj → I(00) | She(01) | He(10) | My father(11)	
verb → read(0) | bought(1)	
what → a book(0) | a magazine(1)	
when → yesterday(0) | last Sunday(1)	

Figure 10. Parse trees for the same sentence "p p v v" generated according to grammar G_a

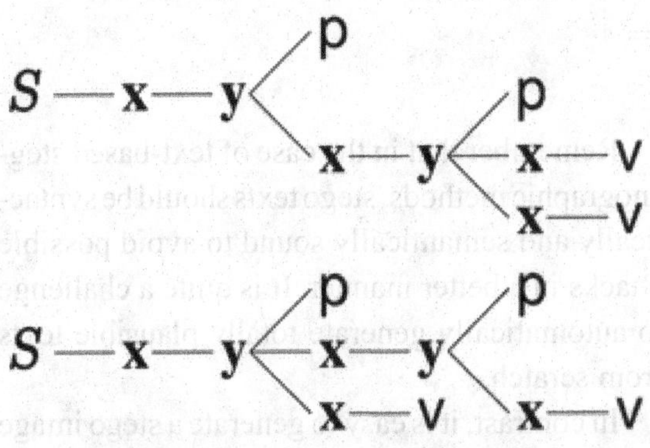

not necessarily appear innocuous. Sample grammar G_s shown above is too simple to be practically used. Because one sentence can represent only five bits, many sentences must be generated to hide a meaningful message. Furthermore, sentences that repeatedly discuss simple topics, such as who bought or read a book or magazine, are quite suspicious.

In order to generate fairly plausible sentences that encode a message, it is desirable to compose a rich grammar that does not narrate a story. Because sentences are generated in a sequence independently, it is quite unlikely that the entire text follows a consistent story. Although it is possible that a grammar will yield more than one sentence simultaneously as a unit, which allows a story to be created, it does not ensure continuity of the story between the units of the generated text. In addition, it is difficult to invent a grammar that yields a large amount of text as a unit.

Let us see now an example of a practical text-based cover generation method. Spammimic (2000) is a steganographic program that can be used to generate spam-like stego texts. A stego text generated by spammimic is shown in Figure 11. This text encodes the message "Steganography." The spammimic program is publicly available at the website http://spammimic.com/. Most e-mail users receive a lot of spams everyday, but e-mail applications usually simply filter them out automatically as junk messages and users do not care about them. Spam messages are not likely to attract attention and are therefore suitable as cover objects.

Figure 11. A stego text for "steganography" generated by spammimic

```
Dear Friend ; We know you are interested in receiving cutting-edge
announcement . If you are not interested
in our publications and wish to be removed from our
lists, simply do NOT respond and ignore this mail !
This mail is being sent in compliance with Senate bill
1627 ; Title 3 , Section 305 . This is NOT unsolicited
bulk mail . Why work for somebody else when you can
become rich within 14 days . Have you ever noticed
society seems to be moving faster and faster and most
everyone has a cellphone ! Well, now is your chance
to capitalize on this ! WE will help YOU decrease perceived waiting time
by 130% plus sell more . You can begin
at absolutely no cost to you ! But don't believe us
. Mr Jones who resides in Georgia tried us and says
"I was skeptical but it worked for me" . We are licensed
to operate in all states ! For God's sake, order now
! Sign up a friend and you'll get a discount of 90%. God Bless !
```

Image-Based Cover Generation Method

The basic idea of image-based cover generation method is to establish a map η between images and bit strings. Let U be a set of images available for embedding as follows:

$$U = \{I_0, I_1, \ldots, I_{N-1}\}. \quad (20)$$

Let

$$\eta(I_i) = w_i \in [0,1]^m \ (0 \le i < N)$$

where $[0,1]^m$ is the set of the m-bit strings. Define the set $U_w \subseteq U$ as

$$U_w = \{I \in U \mid \eta(I) = w\} \quad (21)$$

Let s be the mn-bit string to be hidden, and $s[i,k]$ be the k-bit substring of s starting from the i-th bit. Assume that

$$U_{s[m \cdot i, m]} \neq \varnothing (0 \le i < n)$$

Bit string s can then be represented by an image sequence as

$$I_{j_0}, I_{j_1}, \ldots, I_{j_{n-1}}, \quad (22)$$

where

$$I_{j_i} \in U_{s[m \cdot i, m]} (0 \le i < n)$$

Restoration of bit string s from this sequence is straightforward:

$$\eta(I_{j_0})\eta(I_{j_1}) \cdots \eta(I_{j_{n-1}})$$
$$= s[0,m]s[m,m] \cdots s[m \cdot (n-1), m]$$
$$= s$$

Remember that in the case of text-based steganographic methods, stego texts should be syntactically and semantically sound to avoid possible attacks in a better manner. It is quite a challenge to automatically generate totally plausible texts from scratch.

In contrast, it is easy to generate a stego image sequence that appears plausible, because an image sequence does not often have a rigid internal structure. For example, images of the same type, such as flowers, can be freely arranged without causing implausibility. Of course, not all image sequences are acceptable. For example, if images used to tell a story are not arranged according to the plot of the story, they would appear to be suspicious.

As is just mentioned, an image sequence should be constructed so that it is apparently innocuous to retain a message secretly. At the same time, the image sequence should be saved in a plausible form; otherwise the hidden message is easily discernable. For this purpose, in a previous study, a stego image sequence was saved as a picture gallery in the HTML format (Hioki, 2008). Figure 12 shows a steganographic image gallery. Each image in the gallery represents four bits, and this entire gallery represents a message of 10 bytes. Blundo and Galdi (2003) mimicked an image mosaic with a stego image sequence.

Another important issue in image-based cover generation methods is how to define map $\eta : U \to [0,1]^m$ which associates an image I with an m-bit string w as $w = \eta(I)$. Map η should be a surjection, i.e., $\eta(U) = [0,1]^m$ is required. If map η is not a surjection and $D = [0,1]^m \setminus \eta(U)$ is nonempty, then each bit string $w \in D$ cannot be represented by any image in U. It is therefore

Figure 12. A steganographic image gallery

required that map η be a surjection to ensure that any message can be represented by a stego image sequence. Note that this is just a necessary condition. In order to retain a secret message, the issue of plausibility must be considered.

In Blundo and Galdi (2003), a stego image sequence is composed as an image mosaic, as stated above. To generate a stego image mosaic, all the images are classified into groups. Each group consists of images that can be used as tiles of a certain color. Then, each image is numbered uniquely in each group in an arbitrary manner. The number of an image is interpreted as an m-bit string. To increase plausibility, the numbers assigned to images in a group are permuted. Thus, map η is different for each group and tile. Let $\{I_{i,0}, I_{i,1}, \&, I_{i,n_i-1}\}$ be the images in the i-th group. For the j-th tile of an image mosaic, map η_{ij} can be defined as

$$\eta_{ij}(I_{i,k}) = \sigma_{ij}(k)$$

where $k \in [0, n_i - 1]$ and σ_{ij} is a permutation. Note that it is impossible to restore the message represented by a stego image mosaic unless the images $I_{i,0}, I_{i,1}, \cdots, I_{i,n_i-1}$, their numbers and permutations are saved.

In Hioki (2008), map η is constructed on the basis of the average colors of images. For each image I_i in $\{I_0, I_1, \cdots, I_{N-1}\}$, the average color of the pixels $\bar{c}_i = (\bar{r}_i, \bar{g}_i, \bar{b}_i)$ is computed, where the average colors $\bar{c}_0, \bar{c}_1, \cdots, \bar{c}_{N-1}$ are regarded as points in the RGB color space. Those N points in the RGB color space are classified into 2^m groups, and each image is accordingly labeled as one of $0, 1, \ldots, 2^m - 1$ by finding the group to which its average color belongs. The label of an image can be interpreted as an m-bit string.

To obtain a nearly equal population in each group, the median-cut color reduction algorithm (Heckbert, 1982) is employed for grouping. In this algorithm, all the color points are first packed into a single group, and the bounding box of the color points is computed. The box is then cut into half at the median plane along its longest edge, creating two groups of color points. The bounding boxes are then computed for both groups. This median cut operation is repeatedly applied to the most populated group until the number of groups reaches a predefined value, in this case, 2^m.

When the algorithm is completed, a binary decision tree is obtained, through which an image can be classified into 2^m groups. Each leaf node of the tree represents one of the 2^m groups, and the internal nodes provide test predicates for classifying the images. The test predicate of a node is described using the median plane, and it shows to which subtree the group of a given image belongs. Figure 13 depicts an example of the binary decision tree for the gallery of Figure 12. Images are classified into 16 groups by test predicates of this tree. Each test predicate is of the form

$$c < v, \quad c \in \{R, G, B\}, v \in [0, 255] \tag{23}$$

The predicate denotes that "the c component of the average color is less than v." If the predicate of a node is true for a given image, the upper edge is selected; otherwise, the lower is selected.

Let us see here how an image is classified by an example. Assume that an image whose average

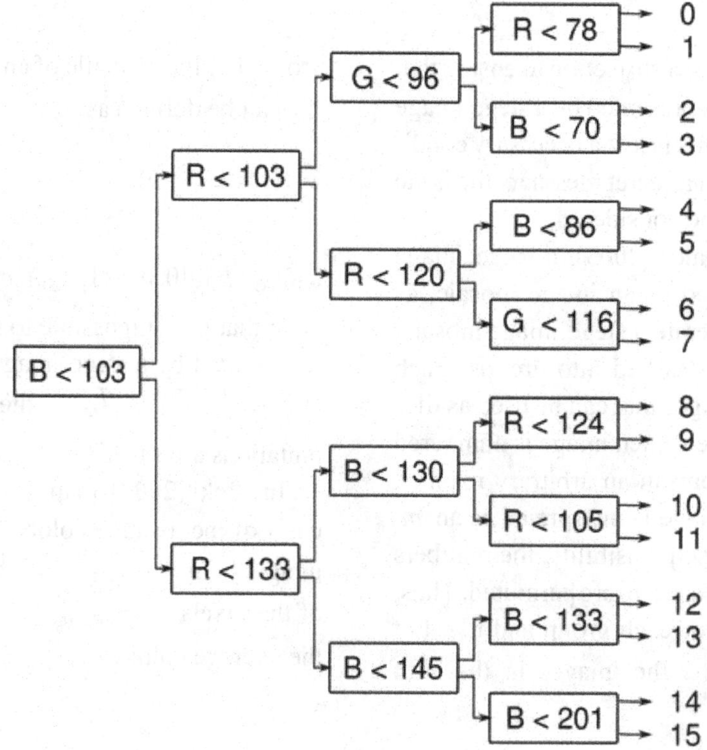

Figure 13. A binary decision tree for a steganographic image gallery

color is (132,97,82) is found in a steganographic image gallery. In this case, the predicates are evaluated in the following order:

$B < 103$ (true)
$R < 103$ (false)
$R < 120$ (false)
$G < 116$ (true)

As a result, the image is classified as belonging to group 6.

SUMMARY

This chapter introduced steganographic methods that are not based on modification of the contents of cover objects. Three different methods—permutation steganography, metadata steganography, and cover generation method—have been explored.

In permutation steganography, a secret message is embedded as a number corresponding to a permutation that is represented by a tuple of cover elements. Embedding is performed by shuffling cover elements appropriately. Even when the elements are shuffled, the content of a cover object is preserved if the rearrangement of its elements does not affect the content or the influence of rearrangement can be negated by adjusting other components of the cover. A variant of standard permutation steganography called Bogomjakov's method was also reviewed.

Metadata steganography does not modify data in cover objects. Instead, the metadata of the cover files are adjusted to represent a secret message. Because the embedding capacity of metadata of a single file is severely limited, the metadata of files in a directory tree are simultaneously used for embedding. Among various types of metadata, timestamp fields are found to be useful for embedding. To embed bits into timestamps in each directory under a certain directory tree, either the LSBs of the timestamps are directly used or timestamps are modified to represent a permutation.

In the cover generation method, a cover object is generated so that it becomes a stego object that encodes a message as it is. Text-based and image-based methods were described. The text-based method is based on a customized context-free grammar. In this method, a message is encoded into sentences using production rules of grammars. In image-based methods, an image is mapped to a bit string, and a message is encoded by a sequence of images to be saved as an image gallery or image mosaic.

REFERENCES

Blundo, C., & Galdi, C. (2003). Hiding information in image mosaics. *The Computer Journal*, *46*(2), 202–212. doi:10.1093/comjnl/46.2.202

Bogomjakov, A., Gotsman, C., & Isenburg, M. (2008). *Distortion-free steganography for polygonal meshes.* Paper presented at Eurographics 2008. Crete, Greece.

Fridrich, J., Goljan, M., & Du, R. (2002). Lossless data embedding: new paradigm in digital watermarking. *EURASIP Journal on Applied Signal Processing*, *1*, 185–196. doi:10.1155/S1110865702000537

Heckbert, P. (1982). Color image quantization for frame buffer display. *Proceedings of SIGGRAPH, 1982*, 297–307. doi:10.1145/965145.801294

Hioki, H. (2007). A steganographic method based on a file attribute. In *Proceedings of the Intelligent Information Hiding and Multimedia Signal Processing*, (Vol. 2), (pp. 441-444). IEEE.

Hioki, H. (2008). Steganogallery: Steganographic gallery. In *Proceedings of the IEEE 10th Workshop on Multimedia Signal Processing*, (pp. 719-724). IEEE Press.

Huang, H., Zhong, S., & Sun, X. (2008). An algorithm of webpage information hiding based on attributes permutation. In *Proceedings of the Intelligent Information Hiding and Multimedia Signal Processing*, (pp. 257-260). IEEE Press.

Huang, N.-C., Li, M.-T., & Wang, C.-M. (2009). Toward optimal embedding capacity for permutation steganography. *IEEE Signal Processing Letters*, *16*(9), 802–805. doi:10.1109/LSP.2009.2024794

Katzenbeisser, S., & Petitcolas, F. A. (2000). *Information hiding techniques for steganography and digital watermarking*. Norwood, MA: Artech House. doi:10.1201/1079/43263.28.6.20001201/30373.5

Kwan, M. (1998). *Gishuffle*. Retrieved from http://www.darkside.com.au/gifshuffle/

Spammimic. (2000). *Website*. Retrieved from http://spammimic.com/

Tian, J. (2003). High capacity reversible data embedding and content authentication. In *Proceedings of the International Conference on Acoustics, Speech, and Signal Processing*, (Vol. 3), (pp. 517-520). IEEE.

Tsai, P., Hu, Y.-C., & Yeh, H.-L. (2009). Reversible image hiding scheme using predictive coding and histogram shifting. *Signal Processing*, *89*(6), 1129–1143. doi:10.1016/j.sigpro.2008.12.017

Tu, S.-C., Hsu, H.-W., & Tai, W.-K. (2010). Permutation steganography for polygonal meshes based on coding tree. *The International Journal of Virtual Reality*, *9*(4), 55–60.

Wayner, P. (2009). *Disappearing cryptography* (3rd ed.). Burlington, MA: Morgan Kaufmann Publishers.

KEY TERMS AND DEFINITIONS

Bijection: A mapping $f: X \rightarrow Y$ is a bijection if and only if, for every element $y \in Y$ there is a unique element $x \in X$ such that $f(x) = y$.

Context-Free Grammar: A context-free grammar is defined by the quadruple tuple (V_N, V_T, P, S) where V_N is a set of nonterminals, V_T is a set of terminals, P is a set of production rules, and S is a special element in the set V_N called a start symbol. A nonterminal represents a syntactic structure. A terminal is either a word or a phrase. A production rule gives the transformation from a nonterminal to a sequence of nonterminals and/or terminals. According to the grammar, a sentence can be generated from start symbol S by repeatedly rewriting nonterminals via production rules until a sequence consisting of only terminals is obtained.

Distortion-Free/ Distortion-Less Steganographic Method: A steganographic method is said to be distortion-free or distortion-less if the method does not modify the contents of cover objects when a message is embedded.

Embedding Capacity: The embedding capacity of a data hiding method is the amount of data that can be embedded into a cover object by the method.

Metadata: Metadata describe properties of (another) data.

Permutation: A permutation of a set X is a bijection from X onto X itself. For a set consisting of n elements, there are $n!$ different permutations.

Steganography: Steganography is a type of data hiding method which is used for concealing a secret message by embedding it into an apparently innocuous cover object.

Surjection: A mapping $f: X \rightarrow Y$ is a surjection if, and only if, for every element $y \in Y$ there is at least one element $x \in X$ such that $f(x) = y$.

Section 4
New Directions in Multimedia Information Hiding

Chapter 18
Data-Embedding Pen

Seiichi Uchida
Kyushu University, Japan

Marcus Liwicki
German Research Center for Artificial Intelligence (DFKI), Germany

Masakazu Iwamura
Osaka Prefecture University, Japan

Shinichiro Omachi
Tohoku University, Japan

Koichi Kise
Osaka Prefecture University, Japan

ABSTRACT

In this chapter, the authors present a new writing device called data-embedding pen, where a single inkjet nozzle is attached to its pen tip. When writing a stroke, the nozzle produces an additional ink-dot sequence along the stroke. The ink-dot sequence can represent various meta-information, such as the writer's ID, the writing date, and a certain URL. Since the embedded meta-information is placed on the paper, it can be extracted by scanning or photographing the paper. Accordingly, by the data-embedding pen, a physical paper conveys any digital information. In other words, handwriting by the data-embedding pen can be a new medium connecting the physical and cyber worlds.

INTRODUCTION

Handwritings have been one of the most important media for human beings for thousands of years. One underlying reason is that we can create handwritings very easily. If we have a pen (or any writing tool) and paper (or any object surface), we can create arbitrary handwritings immediately. Even though we currently have various digital media, such as the keyboard and the mouse, we still use a pen and paper regularly and create handwritings.

The other reason is that handwritings can represent and transmit various pieces of information. For example, handwritings have been created as characters for transmitting linguistic information accurately to others or just for recording ideas.

DOI: 10.4018/978-1-4666-2217-3.ch018

Handwritings also have been created as line drawings, diagrams, graphics, cartoons, and signatures.

Handwritings, however, cannot transmit meta-information about themselves in any explicit way. In other words, a handwritten pattern on a physical paper is just an ink stroke and thus cannot provide any information but its shape. For example, it is impossible to retrieve who wrote this pattern, or when it was written, or any other context related to the handwriting.

Digital pens seem to be a possible choice to store and retrieve such meta-information; unfortunately, they cannot increase the value of handwriting on paper either. Nowadays, several digital pens to capture handwriting on normal paper have been developed and those pens can store the stroke sequences on a computer along with some meta-information, such as the writer's ID. However, the handwriting on the paper is still just an ink pattern without any meta-information.

In this chapter, we propose a new pen device to enrich the handwriting on the physical paper. The proposed pen device, called data-embedding pen, can embed arbitrary information by an additional ink-dot sequence along the ink stroke of the handwriting (Uchida, Tanaka, Iwamura, Omachi, & Kise, 2006; Liwicki, Uchida, Iwamura, Omachi, & Kise, 2010a; Liwicki, Uchida, Iwamura, Omachi, & Kise, 2010b; Liwicki, Yoshida, Uchida, Iwamura, Omachi, & Kise, 2011). Each ink-dot represents an information bit and thus an ink-dot sequence represents a bit-stream of the information to be embedded. The information can be retrieved by scanning or photographing the paper and decoding the ink-dot sequence.

The most important property of the data-embedding pen is the increased value of handwriting on the physical paper. If we embed the writer's ID, the handwriting on the physical paper itself stores this meta-information and identifies the writer without using an electronic memory. If we embed an URL into the handwriting, the handwriting becomes a link between the physical world (paper) and the cyber-space (the Internet). Furthermore, if we embed any temporal information or hints into the pattern, it is possible to convert the strokes into the online representation which is helpful to attain better handwriting recognition accuracy.

Another property is the omission of preparing any special paper or sensing device before writing. There is no need to take care where to write down a note or comment. Thus this device does not interrupt the thinking process, especially when something important pops into one's mind. This fact is also supported by the feature that a data-embedding pen is a pen-type device and thus can be simple and handy. While the current prototype is comprised of several devices for controlling several parameters, those devices can be removed or down-sized for a final version.

RELATED WORK

Data embedding into papers has been done statically by a printer. For example, XEROX DataGlyph (Hecht, 1994) is a kind of digital watermarks and information is printed and embedded as a fine texture into font images or photographs. Universal character pattern (Uchida, Iwamura, Omachi, & Kise, 2006; Omachi, Iwamura, Uchida, & Kise, 2006; Uchida, Sakai, Iwamura, Omachi, & Kise, 2007) is also printed character where class information is embedded in various ways.

Nowadays, the most famous digital pen may be Anoto[1]. Anoto reads the dot pattern printed on the paper surface from its pen-tip camera and detects its absolute position on the paper by interpreting the pattern. By continuously detecting the position during the pen movement, Anoto can acquire the online patterns. Many Anoto-based document managing systems, such as Guimbretière (2003) and Weibel, Ispas, Signer, and Norrie (2008), have been proposed Anoto and our data-embedding pen have very different purposes. The purpose of Anoto is to get the pen motion and to identify the absolute position on the paper. Thus, Anoto is considered as a kind of pen-tablet and the handwritten strokes on the paper have no additional value. In contrast, the purpose of the data-embedding pen is to enhance the value of the strokes on the paper.

THE DATA-EMBEDDING PEN

General Idea

The data-embedding pen is a device which comprises a normal ball-point pen and an ink-jet nozzle element. Figure 1, Figure 2, and Figure 3 show three versions of the data-embedding pen. All of these versions have almost the same structure. In all versions, during the writing, the nozzle produces small ink-dots alongside the handwritten stroke. The color of the ink-dots is different from the color of the stroke. In this chapter, yellow is used for the ink-dots. The number of the ink-dots and their timing are used to encode the desired information.

In order to extract the information, the image is first scanned or photographed. Then document analysis algorithms are applied for recovering the online stroke representation. Next, the sequence information of the ink-dots is determined by using the online stroke representation. Finally, the sequence is decoded. Since the ink-dots are small, a high resolution is required for capturing them in an image. Although in the following experiments a digital scanner has been used to capture them, even a recent small digital camera has enough resolution for capturing the ink-dots.

Hardware

As shown in Figure 1, Figure 2, and Figure 3, the data-embedding pen basically consists of a normal ball-point pen and an inking nozzle element. For example, in Figure 1, the right part is the pen and the left is the nozzle. In the current prototype, other three devices are used to control the nozzle element and its ink tank. The first device is an amplifier for

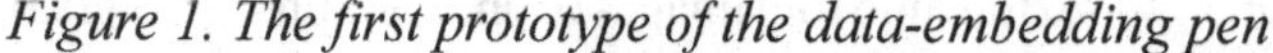
Figure 1. The first prototype of the data-embedding pen

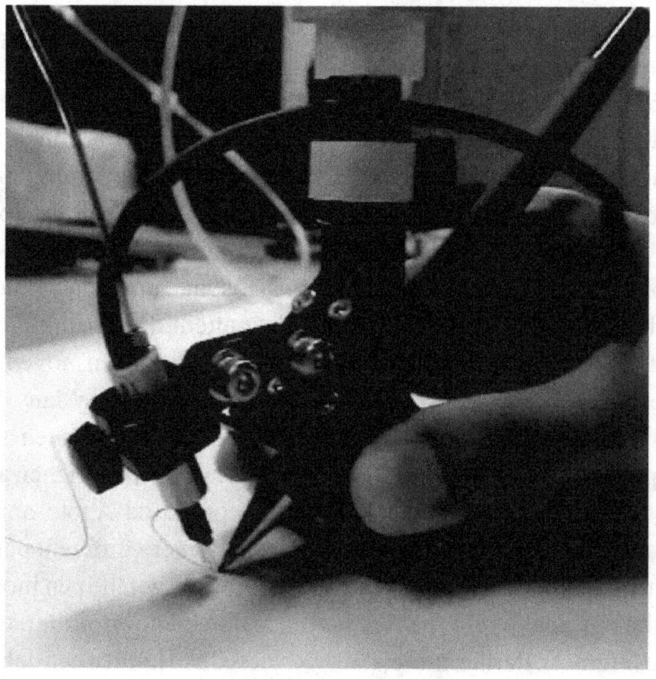

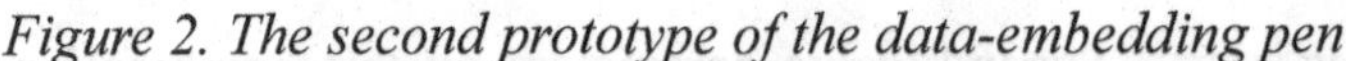

Figure 2. The second prototype of the data-embedding pen

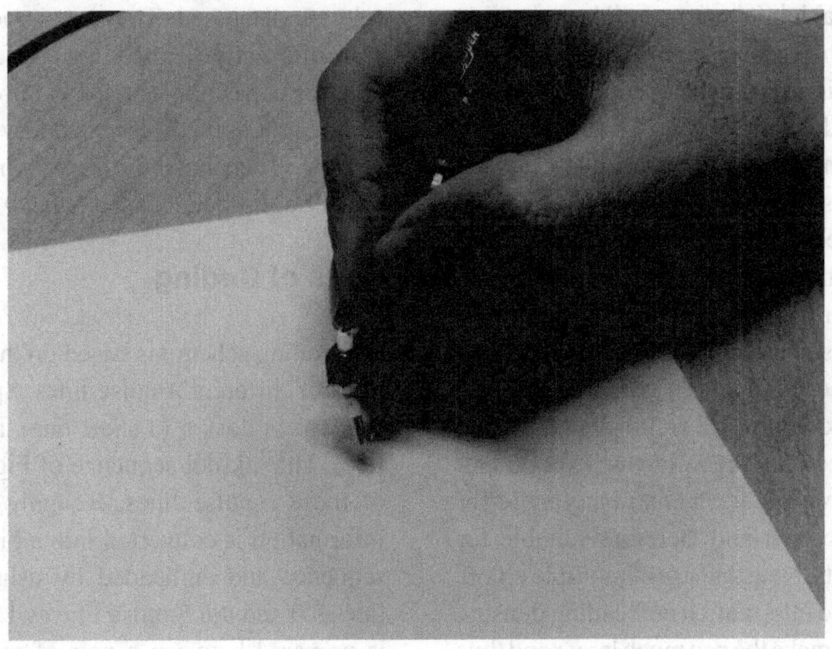

Figure 3. The third prototype of the data-embedding pen

activating the piezoelectric jet inside the nozzle. It is connected to the nozzle element by a cable. The second is a vacuum pump for controlling the pressure of the ink; it is connected to the ink tank to avoid the ink pressure from becoming too high (which would result in a blocking of the nozzle) and too low (which would restrain the ink flow). The third is a programmable D/A converter for providing triggers to the amplifier for controlling the timing of ink-dots. Although the current prototypes require such large devices, the authors believe that it is possible to make them more compact. For example, the vacuum pump will be unnecessary by giving negative and constant pressure in some way. The use of a sponge as is done in a normal ink-jet printer will be a possible alternative to the vacuum pump.

The nozzle is able to generate up to 2,000 ink-dots per second. Using this high frequency, it is possible to form a connected line by a sequence of several ink-dots. Hereafter, a line by n sequential ink-dots is called n-pulse line. If $n = 1$, the n-pulse line forms a single ink-dot. The line, of course, becomes longer by increasing n.

We now assume a single color for the ink-dots, due to the fact that the current prototype has a single inking nozzle. Yellow was assumed as the ink-dot color in the following experiment. Yellow is less visible for human but visible for cameras and scanner and therefore suitable for printing ink-dots. Note that use of multiple colors will increase the information embedding density, although it will make the pen much larger and thus be less feasible. Use of invisible ink has already been tested as a good alternative for the future.

INFORMATION EMBEDDING

This section provides the detail of the coding scheme. First, units of coding are described in detail. The smallest unit is an ink-dot representing, for example, a bit corresponding to 0. Several ink-dots are then combined to form a larger unit. Second, some parameters on this combination rule are discussed. They are important for reliable information embedding and recovery. Third, an error correction scheme is introduced for the coding scheme. This is mandatory because many errors will occur in the information recovery from the ink-dot sequence on a paper.

Units of Coding

Our coding scheme is based on the combination of three different n-pulse lines. Specifically, we use n=1 (a dot), 5 (a short line), and 20 (a long line). The ink-dot sequence of Figure 4 consists of these n-pulse lines. Roughly speaking, the information is converted into a binary (0 and 1) sequence and embedded by using the 1-pulse line as 0 and the 5-pulse line as 1. A short pause is prepared between a pair of consecutive bits (1-pulse or 5-pulse line) like in the Morse code. The 20-pulse line, hereafter called synchronization blob, is used as an anchor to make sure that a correct position is extracted. The leftmost dot in Figure 4 depicts such a synchronization blob.

Our coding scheme is defined by three units, called frame, block, and bit (these names are motivated by the terminology of network protocol design). The bit is the smallest unit and defined by a 1-pulse line or a 5-pulse line. Several consecutive bits comprise a block and several con-

Figure 4. Ink-dots nearby a handwriting stroke, from left to right: a synchronization blob, 0110-1010-1010-1010-0000-1100, and another synchronization blob

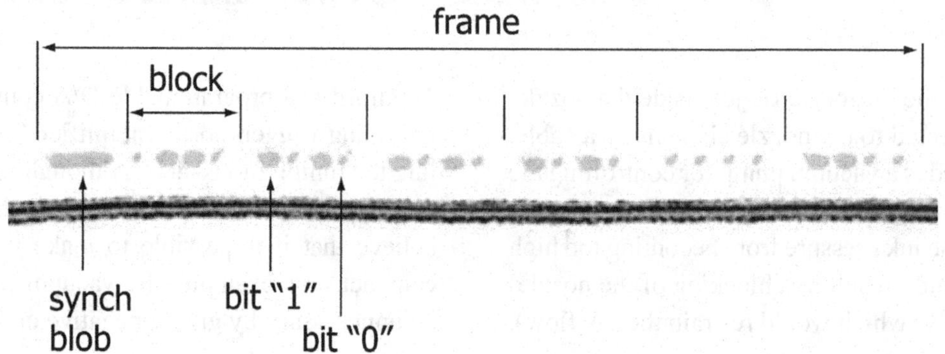

secutive blocks comprise a frame. A pause which is longer than the pause between bits is inserted between two consecutive blocks. Each frame begins (or, equivalently, ends) with a synchronization blob. Figure 4 is an example of a single frame. From left to right, the ink-dot sequence of the frame is comprised of a synchronization blob, and 6 blocks. Another synchronization blob will come as the next dot. In each block, 4 bits are encoded and thus in the frame 24 bits (0110-1010-1010-1010-0000-1100) are embedded.

Parameters

The main parameters of the coding scheme are the number of bits per block (*bB*) and the number of blocks per frame (*bF*). Accordingly, the number of bits per frame becomes $bF \times bB$. In the example of Figure 4, $bF = 6$ and $bB = 4$.

Another important parameter is the bit time (*bT*). It controls the time duration assigned for each bit. For example, if $bT = 20$, there would be a 19-pulse pause after a 1-pulse line and a 15-pulse pause after a 5-pulse line. Having a constant bit time increases the probability that the-pulse lines within a block have equal distance to each other, which is beneficial for the information recovery. After each block we make a pause of length *bT*, and before the start of a synchronization-pulse line, we make another pause of length *bT*. This results in a larger gap at the end of a frame, making it possible to recover the writing direction.

Error Correction

The process of embedding the ink next to the handwritten stroke is always accompanied with several errors. Figure 5 shows a pattern created by the data-embedding pen and its parts. First, the black ink sometimes overlaps with the information ink (b). Second, several ink-dots might overlap at turning points or stopping points (c). Finally, it is impossible to recover the correct information from double strokes (d), since it is not known which dot belongs to which direction. Consequently, in order to recover from the errors, some error correction scheme has to be introduced.

Simple and intuitive ideas would be to apply repetition and parity check (Liwicki, Uchida, Iwamura, Omachi, & Kise, 2010a). A possible realization of a parity check scheme is to use the last bits of each frame as parities. For example, in the frame in Figure 4, the last 8 bits can be considered as the parities for detecting and correcting the errors of the first 16 blocks. The parity check is done by a matrix; the first four blocks are aligned as a 4×4 matrix (each row corresponds to a block) and then the fifth block is used as parity bits for each column and the sixth block is used similarly for each row. Note that by introducing the parity check (2 blocks × 4 bits), the amount

Figure 5. (a) Example of a difficult pattern, (b)-(d) specific parts of the pattern

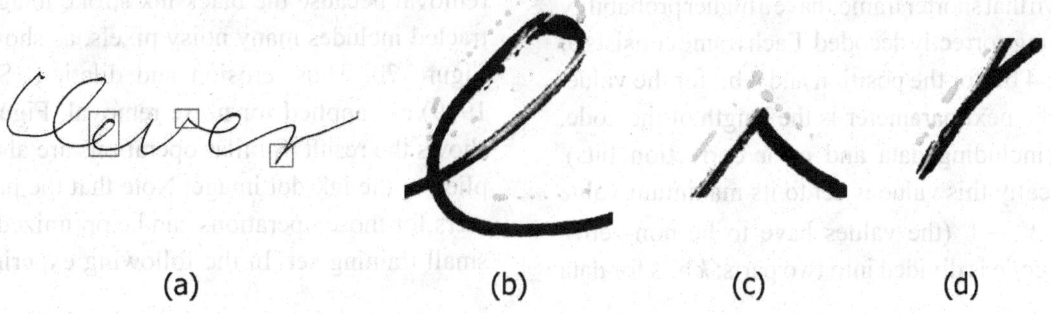

of encodeable data by a frame (24 bits) becomes 16 bits. In Liwicki, Uchida, Iwamura, Omachi, and Kise (2010a), the frame address, or the 2-bit serial number of the frame, was also used, and thus this amount becomes 14 bits. However, this simple parity check shows some limitations, especially when it comes to more complicated handwritten patterns like signatures or handwritten words with many crossings and double strokes.

A promising alternative for reliably recovering from the errors is Reed-Solomon error correction (Reed & Solomon, 1960; MacWilliams & Sloane, 1977). The idea is to oversample a polynomial

$$f\left(x\right) = a_1 + a_2x^1 + \ldots + a_kx^{k-1}$$

from the data with more points a_j than needed. This makes the polynomial over-determined. Therefore, it is not needed to recover all points correctly as long as enough points are present. One problem of this encoding is that the position *j* of each point a_j needs to be known for a reliable decoding. To solve this problem, we design each frame to be comprised of two blocks, the first block for the position of the point and the second block for its value. While the details of Reed-Solomon codes can be found in many references, only the important parameters and properties of this encoding scheme are given here.

The first parameter of Reed-Solomon encoding is the base *m* bits for the points. Here, we have set *m*=4. This choice of this value is based on the observation that previous experiments (Liwicki, Uchida, Iwamura, Omachi, & Kise, 2010a) have shown that shorter frames have a higher probability of being correctly decoded. Each frame consists of 8 bit; 4 bit for the position and 4 bit for the value.

The next parameter is the length of the code, n, (including data and error correction bits). Typically this value is set to its maximum value $n = 2^m - 1$ (the values have to be non-zero). This code is divided into two parts; *k* bits for data points (the data to be encoded) and *n-k* bits for error correction. Given the *k* data points $a_1, \ldots, a_k$ (a message to be encoded), the other values $a_{k+1}, \ldots, a_n$ of the polynomial are determined and all *n* points are encoded. Note that the determination of the values is based on the primitive element of the finite field α and finding a function *f(x)* for which $f\left(a^{i-1}\right) = a_i$ holds for *i*= 1,…,*k*,, and then applying *f(x)* to the remaining α^i, *i*=*k*, ...,*n*-1.

INFORMATION RECOVERY

This section provides the detail of recovery of information embedded as an ink-dot sequence on a paper. First, image processing steps for detecting ink dots on the paper are described. Second, the method to align the ink dots as a sequence is described. By this method, the embedded information is retrieved as a 0-1 bit sequence with gaps between blocks. Third, the decoding method with error correction is detailed.

Image Processing

Information recovery begins with image processing which extracts ink-dots and black ink strokes from a scanned image. As an example, a two-loop pattern of Figure 6 and its crossing part, i.e., Figure 7a, are employed here. Four steps of image processing are illustrated.

The first step of ink-dot extraction is a simple threshold operation to extract the black ink stroke and yellow ink-dots. The second step is noise removal because the black ink stroke image extracted includes many noisy pixels, as shown in Figure 7b. Thus, erosion and dilation (Soille, 1999) are applied for noise removal. Figure 7c shows the result. Similar operations are also applied to the ink-dot image. Note that the parameters for those operations can be optimized on a small training set. In the following experiment,

Figure 6. Two loops with ink-dots

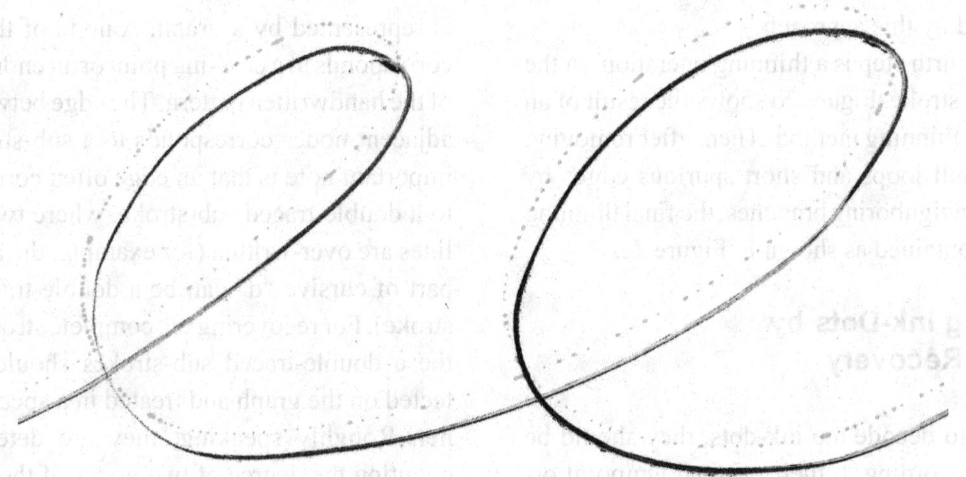

Figure 7. Image processing on an intersection part of Figure 6

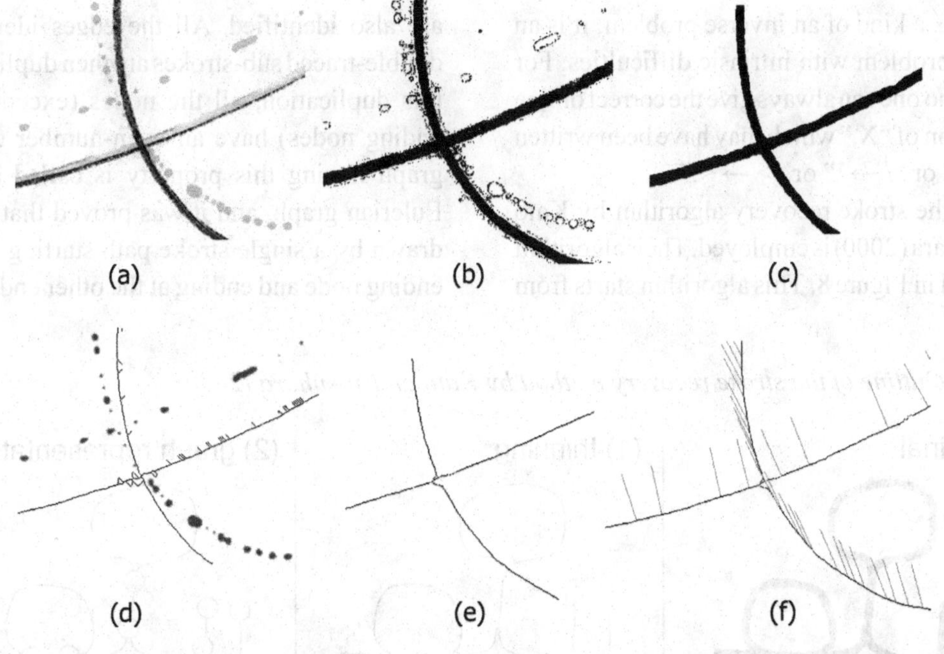

the structure element sizes on erosion for black and yellow inks were 5x5 and 3x3 respectively. The same sizes were applied on dilation.

The third step is a special treatment of ink-dots occluded by the black ink stroke. Fortunately, those yellow ink-dots are still visible on the stroke (they just appear to be a bit darker). Thus, after extracting the pixels of the black ink stroke, another threshold operation is performed on those pixels with a lower threshold to recover dark yellow ink-dots. In the following experiments, it turned out that about 50% of those dots could be recovered by this approach.

The fourth step is a thinning operation on the black ink stroke. Figure 7d shows the result of an orthodox thinning method. Then, after removing many small loops and short spurious edges by unifying neighboring branches, the final thinning result is obtained as shown in Figure 7e.

Aligning Ink-Dots by Stroke Recovery

In order to decode the ink-dots, they should be aligned according to their original temporal order. Since this order is lost in the scanned image, we must estimate it by using the result of stroke recovery (Doermann & Rosenfeld, 1995; Kato & Yasuhara, 2000; Nel, et al., 2005). Since stroke recovery is a kind of an inverse problem, it is an ill-posed problem with intrinsic difficulties. For example, no one can always give the correct online information of "X," which may have been written as "\ → /" or "/ → \" or "> → <."

Here, the stroke recovery algorithm by Kato and Yasuhara (2000) is employed. Their algorithm is outlined in Figure 8. This algorithm starts from a thinning process of the target handwritten pattern. Then the skeleton of the handwritten pattern is represented by a graph. A node of the graph corresponds to a crossing point or an ending point of the handwritten pattern. The edge between two adjacent nodes corresponds to a sub-stroke. An important note is that an edge often corresponds to a double-traced sub-stroke, where two stroke lines are over-written (for example, the ascender part of cursive "d" can be a double-traced sub-stroke). For recovering the complete stroke order, these double-traced sub-strokes should be detected on the graph and treated in a special manner. Roughly speaking, they are detected by counting the degree of two nodes of the edge. If one or both nodes have an odd-number degree, the edge will be a double-traced sub-stroke or an ending sub-stroke. Since the ending sub-stroke can be easily identified, double-traced sub-strokes are also identified. All the edges identified as double-traced sub-strokes are then duplicated. By this duplication, all the nodes (except for two ending nodes) have an even-number degree. A graph having this property is called a (semi-) Eulerian graph, and it was proved that it can be drawn by a single stroke path starting from one ending node and ending at the other ending node.

Figure 8. Outline of the stroke recovery method by Kato and Yasuhara (2000)

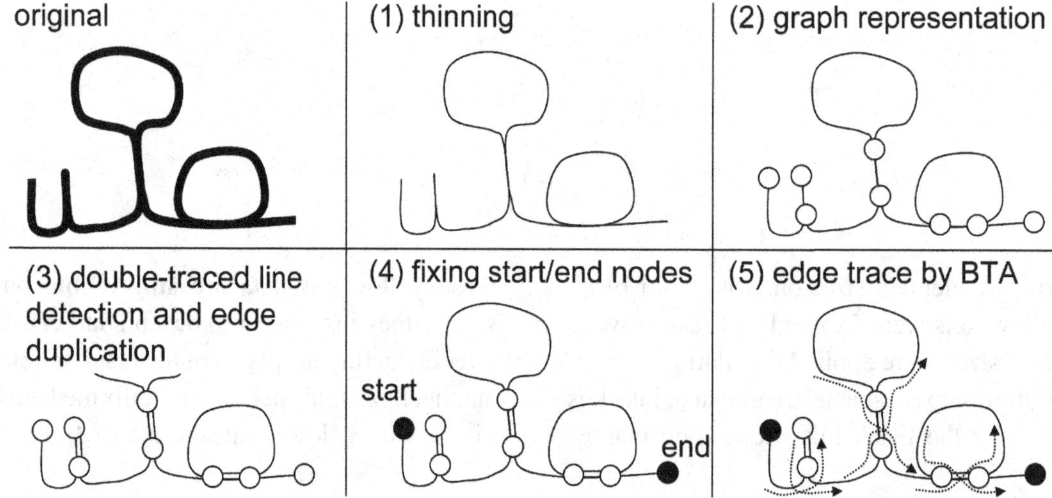

The final process is to find the optimal single stroke path. In Kato and Yasuhara (2000) this path is found by a simple strategy called Basic Trace Algorithm (BTA). According to the BTA, when we arrive at an intersection node (i.e., a node with degree 4), we will take the center path. For example, assume a pattern like "±" and that we start our tour from one ending point. We soon encounter an intersection point and there are three possibilities as the next direction. Using BTA, we take the path of the middle direction. Clearly soon we come back to the same node. By repeating BTA, we will finally arrive at the other ending point; that is, the stroke recovery is completed.

After recovering the writing order of the black ink stroke, we align the ink-dots by establishing the correspondence between the ink-dots and the stroke. The basic idea of this process is shown in Figure 7f. The idea is to find the closest point on the stroke for each ink-dot. A simple nearest neighbor, however, cannot always provide a correct result because a dot and its corresponding point might be a bit distant due to the pen tilt. Thus, at each ink-dot k of all K dots, we first calculate the minimum distance $d_{k,\theta}$ to the stroke for each θ of 36 directions (with 10° interval). Then, we select the direction $\overline{\theta}$ with minimum variance, i.e.:

$$\overline{\theta} = \arg\min_{\theta} \operatorname{Var}\left\{d_{1,\theta},\ldots,d_{K,\theta}\right\}$$

This direction is the most stable direction and thus represents the pen tilt. Finally, for each ink-dot, the corresponding point is determined as the closest point in the direction $\overline{\theta}$.

Data Decoding

For decoding, the bit information (i.e., 1-pulse and 5-pulse lines and synchronization blob) is first recovered at every ink-dot, just by checking its size. The sequence is separated into frames using the synchronization blobs. Larger gaps are detected within each frame and assumed as the gaps between block.

Next, a plausibility control is performed on the extracted data. For each block, the number of bits (*bB*) is confirmed. Sometimes a block has spurious bits, resulting from a wrong mapping or just from noise. In this case, these adjacent bits whose geometrical distance deviates too much from the mean distance are deleted. If the number of bits and blocks do not correspond to the values *bB* and *bF*, the frame is rejected.

If the parity check scheme is employed for detecting and correcting replacement errors (i.e., 1→0 or 0→1), checking the parity bit is performed within each frame. If there is a failure in only one parity bit, it can be ignored as the error of the parity bit. If there are two failures, one in a row and one in a column, the corresponding data bit is negated. In any other case, the frame is rejected because of uncertainty. Note that since we employ a repetitive code, the information of a rejected frame can be recovered by a frame with the same address at another repetition.

Otherwise, if the Reed-Solomon coding scheme is employed, the data decoding process is performed as follows. As an example, we assume that not all n points need to be correctly recovered and c points were correctly recovered, s points are missing (erasures) and e points are erroneous. According to the Reed-Solomon coding scheme, the code can still be correctly decoded if the following condition holds:

$$2e + s \leq n - k$$

This important property makes the Reed-Solomon codes very useful for applications where burst errors occur. In our case usually a whole block can be either recognized or not, i.e., it rarely occurs that just one bit is missing (even if only one bit is missing, we do not know the position of the bit).

Since we encode the positions of the points in the frame, the positions of the missing points are known before decoding. In the extreme case, up to *n-k* points can be missing and still it would be possible to decode the information correctly. In the other extreme case, i.e., if there is no missing point, up to *n-k*/2 errors are allowed to occur, which means for each erroneous point, one more correct point should be at hand.

EXPERIMENT ON SIMPLE HANDRWITINGS

Data

Two sets of data-embedded handwriting were collected using the current pen prototype.

Set 1: The first set contains 50 horizontal straight lines with a length of 20 cm. All lines have been drawn with approximately the same velocity

Set 2: The second set contains patterns which might appear in a real world scenario, i.e., 12 at-mark symbols, 12 checkmarks, 12 simulated signatures ("Meyer"), and 12 instances of the handwritten word "Clever." The former two symbols have sizes of 3×3 cm at maximum, and the latter symbols have a size of 4× 3 cm.

Note that the writing speed was about 20 cm for 1.5 seconds for the straight lines. That is, they were written in normal writing speed. Also for the other patterns, the writing speed was normal and not too slow

Reed-Solomon Encoding

In the following experiments, the Reed-Solomon encoding scheme was used. For its implementation, the Shifra Open Source error correcting code library (Available at http://www.schifra.com/) was used. We used a Galois field polynomial of the order 4. The code length was fixed to 15 points $\left(= 2^4 - 1\right)$, each point being a hexadecimal number (4 bit).

As mentioned above, a crucial parameter for Reed-Solomon Codes is *k*, i.e., the number of data points. A smaller value of *k* means less information stored in the same number of *n*=15 points (including the *n-k* points for error correction). Thus, we need to find a high value of *k* without losing the robustness of the correction. To achieve this goal, we would have to repeat the experiments 15 times, i.e., for each possible value of *k*. However, some Reed-Solomon code words have the property that for each k the remaining *n-k* values are the error correction points, e.g., the code word 1, 9, 13, 15, 14, 7, 10, 5, 11, 12, 6, 3, 8, 4, 2. We embed this code word just once and try decoding with each value of k. Thus we avoid producing 15 times the ink traces[2]. This makes the full use of all collected data, i.e., it is not needed to write down new patterns for each value of *k*. Note that using this strategy also eliminates side-effects like more noise in some patterns, because the same patterns are always used for the evaluation. The code was repeatedly embedded in the data.

Results for Straight Lines

In the experiments on Set1 we wanted to find out how much information can be embedded in straight lines. In this task, decoding errors occur on the frame level only rarely since there are no crossings. Figure 9 provides an example for the extraction result of a 5 cm long part of a straight line where no errors occurred. The only problem was some overlapping ink-dots if there was a slow pen-movement. This happened in about 10% of the frames. Note that these frames were rejected during the frame-decoding step, resulting in missing points for the Reed-Solomon error correction.

As stated above, the straight lines had a length of 20 cm. Since the code was repeated, no errors

Figure 9. Ink-dot extraction result from a 5 cm long line

occurred on these long lines. We decided to measure the results on shorter lines. Therefore we cut the line first into 10 cm parts and finally into 5 cm parts.

The results of the experiments on Set1 appear in Table 1. This table shows the percentage of samples where the information could be correctly recovered by using the Reed-Solomon error correction. Up to a number of k=8 data points the code word was always correctly recovered even for straight lines as short as 5 cm. For larger k value, the performance decreases, because only a limited number of frames appear in a 5 cm line. For the length 10 cm there were only problems if no error correction point appears, i.e., in 8 cases there was a missing point which could not be recovered.

The drawback of Reed-Solomon codes is that it loses all information if not enough data points are present, while with the previous method (Liwicki, Uchida, Iwamura, Omachi, & Kise, 2010a) still parts of the data could be correctly recovered.

Table 1. Percentage (%) of correctly recovered information for set 1

#data points (k)	#bits	5cm line (%)	10 cm line (%)
1	4	100	100
8	32	100	100
9	36	94	100
10	40	72	100
11	44	56	100
12	48	20	100
13	52	0	100
15	60	0	92

However, in practical applications, it is often important to recover all information.

This experiment proved that 32 bit (k=8) were correctly extracted from a line of 5cm length. If we embed writer's ID, 32 bit is enough to distinguish 2^{32} people (that is, more than half of world population). An idea for a company is that 16 bit is used for employee identification and the remaining 16 bit is used for written date and time.

Results for Various Patterns

As stated above, Set2 consists of patterns which might occur in practice. Examples for these patterns are shown in Figure 10. Table 2 presents the results of the experiments on Set 2. In all patterns, 32 bits could be correctly recovered. This proves that even on the more complicated patterns, correct information could be decoded.

The main reason for unsuccessful decoding are either missing points (for short sequences like the hook) or some errors, e.g., a 1-bit was interpreted as a 0-bit if it was partially occluded by black ink (first frame of Figure 5b).

APPLICATIONS

From the above experiments, it was proved that we can embed 32 bits into a small handwriting pattern. Using 32 bits, we can consider various applications. In this section, several possible applications are listed as follows.

As indicated before, meta-information about the handwriting is the most straightforward target to be embedded; for example, as shown in Figure

Figure 10. Patterns from set 2

Table 2. Percentage (%) of correctly recovered information for set 2

#data points (k)	#bits	check mark (%)	at mark (%)	Meyer (%)	Clever (%)
8	32	100	100	100	100
9	36	83	100	75	100
10	40	75	92	67	100
11	44	58	83	33	100
12	48	50	67	0	83
13	52	16	7	0	42
14	56	0	0	0	0

11a, time/date of writing, geo-location, writer ID, and pen ID. Of course, this meta-information is useful for signature verification and other forensic applications. In addition, if we know the author of a handwritten note, the recognition of the handwriting will become easier because we can apply some character recognition model tuned to the writer. Discrimination of multiple writers on a single document is also possible.

As shown in Figure 11b, embedding information on the paper opens up new possibilities for diaries and notebooks. The owner can always find out when and where the information has been written down. After recognizing and recovering all information, we can easily bridge to the digital world and fill Web 2.0 communication platforms with contents. For creating a blog of a journey, for example, you just need to write down short notes about the places where you are, the information where you have been and when the event took place would be automatically available.

As shown in Figure 11c, if we embed the price of a product onto its package by a handwritten checkmark, the checkmark can be considered as a "handwritten" bar-code. If we embed a URL onto a physical paper by a handwritten word (or phrase), the word becomes a link between physical world (paper) and a cyber-space (the Internet).

If we embed any temporal information (such as the writing direction) by an ink-dot sequence, it is possible to make the stroke recovery problem well posed. This implies that we can convert handwritten images into online patterns and thus apply online handwriting recognition, which is generally more accurate than offline recognition. More dreamy application is to embed the recognition result of the current handwritten word onto itself or the succeeding word. For this application, the handwriting pattern should be captured by a pen-tip camera or another sensor and recognized quickly.

CONCLUSION

In this chapter, we have presented a new device called, data-embedding pen. This pen makes it possible to augment handwritten patterns with meta-information like the writer ID, the writing date, and other application-dependent data. The main idea is to encode the desired information in an ink-dot sequence plotted nearby the writing

Figure 11. Applications of data-embedding pen

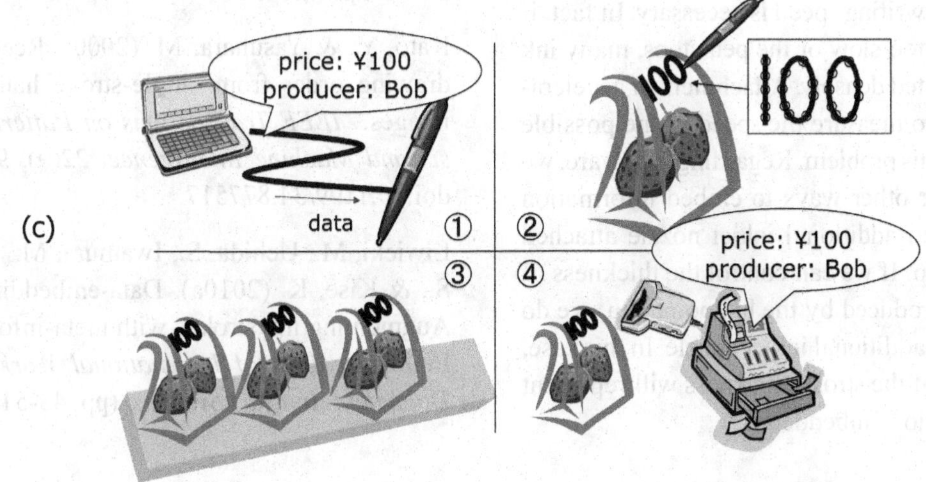

strokes. The hardware design as well as the methods for embedding and recovering information has been also described. Experimental evaluations have shown the following facts:

- It was possible to embed and retrieve 32 bit information from straight lines only 5cm long. From 10 cm straight lines, it was possible to embed and retrieve more than 50 bits.
- Even from more realistic handwriting patterns with double-traced strokes or crossings, it was possible to retrieve 32 bit information.

Using the data-embedding pen, it is possible to increase the value of handwriting on the physical paper. As shown in the applications above, the data-embedding pen has many possibilities by embedding the writer ID, the writing time, and other various kinds of information into handwriting patterns.

Since this chapter describes the result of just our first-stage feasible study, there are many future works to be tackled. Information retrieval from multiple-stroke patterns is the most important one. There is still room for improvement on the data encoding scheme. A deeper examination of the effect of writing speed is necessary. In fact, if the speed is too slow or the pen stops, many ink dots are created densely. Attachment of acceleration sensor to measure the speed is one possible solution of this problem. Regarding hardware, we can consider other ways to embed information than using an additional inkjet nozzle attached to the pen-tip. If we can control the thickness of the stroke produced by the ballpoint pen, we do not need the additional inkjet nozzle. In this case, the change of the stroke thickness will represent the information embedded.

ACKNOWLEDGMENT

The authors thank Mr. Y. Hori, Microjet Corp., Japan, for his kind support on customizing their inkjet nozzle technologies for our pen device. The authors also thank Mr. K. Tanaka and Mr. A. Yoshida for their experimental trials, in the Human interface laboratory at Kyushu University.

REFERENCES

Anoto. (2012). *Website.* Retrieved from http://www.anoto.com

Doermann, D., & Rosenfeld, A. (1995). Recovery of temporal information from static images of handwriting. *International Journal of Computer Vision, 15*(1-2), 143–164. doi:10.1007/BF01450853

Guimbretière, F. (2003). Paper augmented digital documents. In *Proceedings of the 16th Annual ACM Symposium on User Interface Software and Technology*, (pp. 51-60). ACM Press.

Hecht, D. L. (1994). Embedded data glyph technology for hardcopy digital documents: Color imaging: Devide-independent color. *Color Hardcopy and Graphic Arts III, 2171*, 341–352.

Kato, Y., & Yasuhara, M. (2000). Recovery of drawing order from single-stroke handwriting images. *IEEE Transactions on Pattern Analysis and Machine Intelligence, 22*(9), 938–949. doi:10.1109/34.877517

Liwicki, M., Uchida, S., Iwamura, M., Omachi, S., & Kise, K. (2010a). Data-embedding pen - Augmenting ink strokes with meta-information. In *Proceedings of International Workshop on Document Analysis Systems,* (pp. 43-51). IEEE.

Liwicki, M., Uchida, S., Iwamura, M., Omachi, S., & Kise, K. (2010b). Embedding meta-information in handwriting—Reed-Solomon for reliable error correction. In *Proceedings of International Conference on Frontiers in Handwriting Recognition*, (pp. 51-56). IEEE.

Liwicki, M., Yoshida, A., Uchida, S., Iwamura, M., Omachi, S., & Kise, K. (2011). Reliable online stroke recovery from offline data with the data-embedding pen. In *Proceedings of International Conference on Document Analysis and Recognition,* (pp. 1384-1388). IEEE.

MacWilliams, F. J., & Sloane, N. J. A. (1977). *The theory of error-correcting code*. New York, NY: North-Holland Publishing Company.

Nel, E.-M., du Preez, J. A., & Herbst, B. M. (2005). Estimating the pen trajectories of static signatures using hidden Markov models. *IEEE Transactions on Pattern Analysis and Machine Intelligence*, *27*(11), 1733–1746. doi:10.1109/TPAMI.2005.221

Omachi, S., Iwamura, M., Uchida, S., & Kise, K. (2006). Affine invariant information embedment for accurate camera-based character recognition. In *Proceedings of International Conference on Pattern Recognition, 2*, 1098-1101.

Reed, I. S., & Solomon, G. (1960). Polynomial codes over certain finite fields. *Journal of the Society for Industrial and Applied Mathematics*, *8*(2), 300–304. doi:10.1137/0108018

Soille, P. (1999). *Morphological image analysis: Principles and applications*. Berlin, Germany: Springer.

Uchida, S., Iwamura, M., Omachi, S., & Kise, K. (2006). OCR fonts revisited for camera-based character recognition. In *Proceedings of International Conference on Pattern Recognition, 2*, 1134-1137.

Uchida, S., Sakai, M., Iwamura, M., Omachi, S., & Kise, K. (2007). Extraction of embedded class information from universal character pattern. In *Proceedings of International Conference on Document Analysis and Recognition, 1*, 437-441.

Uchida, S., Tanaka, K., Iwamura, M., Omachi, S., & Kise, K. (2006). A data-embedding pen. In *Proceedings of International Workshop on Frontiers in Handwriting Recognition*. IEEE.

Weibel, N., Ispas, A., Signer, B., & Norrie, M. (2008). Paperproof: A paper-digital proof-editing system. In *Proceedings of ACM Conference on Human Factors in Computing Systems (CHI)*, (pp. 2349-2354). ACM Press.

KEY TERMS AND DEFINITIONS

Data Embedding: A method to embed binary or other information into some medium.

Data-Embedding Pen: A pen interface which can embed arbitrary information into handwriting patterns.

Handwriting: Patterns made by a pen.

Pen Interface: A pen-shaped device for inputting information into computer or paper through its pen tip.

Stroke Recovery: A method to estimate the writing order of the handwritten pattern.

ENDNOTES

1. See Anoto (2012).
2. The code word was generated by setting k=1 and calculating the remaining field values.

Chapter 19
Multimedia Copyright Protection Scheme Based on the Direct Feature-Based Method

Rimba Whidiana Ciptasari
Kyushu University, Japan & Telkom Institute of Technology, Indonesia

Kouichi Sakurai
Kyushu University, Japan

ABSTRACT

This chapter discusses the direct feature-based method as an alternative approach to digital watermarking. Fundamentally, the direct feature-based method is an extension of the digital signature scheme, which aims at multimedia authentication. The method covers several copyright protection properties, i.e. robustness to content manipulations and sensitivity to content modification. In addition, this method provides solutions to inherent problems that arise in traditional watermarking, such as quality degradation, the trade-off between data payload, and imperceptibility or robustness.

Researchers have devised the direct feature-based method to improve traditional digital watermarking whilst developing the copyright protection scheme. A discussion on various multimedia copyright protection schemes based on the direct feature-based method (e.g., image, audio, text document, geospatial data, and relational databases) follows. In conclusion, the authors show that a good copyright protection scheme should not only be robust enough to endure acceptable manipulations, but also secure enough to withstand malicious attacks. In addition, the direct feature-based method can be considered a viable solution to the trade-off between data payload, fidelity, and robustness.

DOI: 10.4018/978-1-4666-2217-3.ch019

INTRODUCTION

The art of data hiding, which is embedding data inside a host medium without substantially altering it, is used in copyright protection. In 2003, direct feature-based extraction was proposed as another approach in the field of multimedia copyright protection. The direct feature-based method, an extension of the digital signature scheme, was ostensibly intended for the purpose of multimedia authentication. The premise of this development accommodates the need for copyright protection, i.e. an ability to withstand content manipulations and sensitivity to content modification. Therefore, several researchers have incorporated these properties into copyright protection.

One branch of research has led to the development of a copyright protection scheme (based on the direct feature-based method) known as zero-watermarking, although this is not widely known to those unfamiliar with the scheme. However, this term is most commonly used when the host medium is not changed during the embedding process. Researchers with an interest in cryptography meanwhile, strenuously argue that zero-watermarking should not be considered as watermarking since the host medium is not affected. While such distinction may be valid, the schemes presented in this chapter mainly focus on the zero-watermarking scheme. However, to avoid misinterpretation, zero-watermarking is hereby termed "DeFeat-based method," which refers to the copyright protection scheme based on the direct feature-based method. Where necessary, the term zero-watermarking and DeFeat-based method may be used interchangeably for a particular purpose.

In summary, this chapter has several objectives: (1) to define the scope of the copyright protection scheme based on a DeFeat-based extraction; (2) to discuss briefly the fundamental knowledge used in the DeFeat-based extraction; (3) to describe state-of-the-art of multimedia copyright protection based on DeFeat-based extraction; (4) to provide a summary on the performance of the DeFeat-based method in terms of robustness and security.

BACKGROUND

Copyright protects the author's original work against plagiarism and the distribution, commercial or otherwise, of unauthorized reproductions. The use of the Internet has resulted in the ease of copying digital information without any loss of quality. This has a considerable impact on the originators and owners of intellectual property. To solve the problem of publishing digital multimedia, researchers have come up with digital image watermarking. This method allows the owner of an original image to add an invisible watermark to the digital image before publishing it. The watermark serves to enforce copyright on the image. The owner protects the watermark with a cryptographic secret key in order to prevent an unauthorized party from reading or even detecting the watermark. The watermark is also designed to be robust against image tampering. Therefore, anyone who wants to distribute the image further will also distribute the watermark with it, which implies that they will have violated the copyright of the image. If the copyright holder can detect the fraud, he/she can prove ownership by showing that the image contains his/her proper private watermark.

The protection of the creators' work encompasses many different aspects including copyright protection and moral rights protection. We examine three types of watermarking applications dealing with Intellectual Property Right (IPR) protection (Barni & Bartolini, 2004).

Rightful Ownership

The owner wishes to prove that he/she is the only legitimate owner of the work. To do so, as soon as he/she creates the work, he/she embeds a watermark identifying him/her unambiguously within it. Unfortunately, this simple scheme cannot provide a valid proof in front of a court of law, unless the non-invertibility (non-quasi-invertibility) of the watermarking algorithm is demonstrated. A common way to confer the watermark verification procedure a legal value is to introduce the presence of a Trusted Third Party (TTP) in the watermarking protocol. For example, the watermark identifying the author may be assigned to him/her by a trusted registration authority, thus preventing the possibility to use the SWICO attack (Single-Watermarked-Image-Counterfeit-Original) to fool the ownership verification procedure. Protecting rightful ownership is the main focus of this chapter. For the convenience, the general term "copyright protection" is used in the rest of the chapter instead of rightful ownership.

Fingerprinting

A second classical application of digital watermarking is copy protection. Two scenarios are possible here; according to the first one, a mechanism is envisaged to make it impossible, or at least very difficult, to make illegal copies of a protected work. In the second scenario, a so-called copy deterrence mechanism is adopted to discourage unauthorized duplication and distribution. Copy deterrence is usually achieved by providing a mechanism to trace unauthorized copies to the original owner of the work. In the most common case, distribution tracing is made possible by letting the seller (owner) inserting a distinct watermark, which in this case is called a fingerprint, identifying the buyer, or any other address of the work, within any copy of data which is distributed. If, later on, an unauthorized copy of the protected work is found, then its origin can be recovered by retrieving the unique watermark contained in it. As in the case of rightful ownership demonstration, a possible solution consists of resorting to a trusted third party. The protected work must be transmitted from the seller to the TTP and from the TTP to the customer, or, in an even worse case, from the TTP to the seller and from the seller to the customer, thus generating a very heavy traffic on the communication channel.

Copy Control

When copy deterrence is not sufficient to effectively protect legitimate right-owner, a true copy protection mechanism must be envisaged. The following is a brief mechanism for protection of DVD video. The DVD copy protection system outlined below is the result of the efforts of many important companies, including IBM, NEC, Sony, Hitachi, Pioneer, Signafy, Philips, Macrovision, and Digimarc. The mechanism employed to make illegal duplication and distribution difficult enough to keep losses caused by missed revenues sustainable, and relies on the distinction between Copyright Compliant Devices (CC-Devices) and Non-Compliant Devices (NC-Devices). In particular, the DVD copy protection system is designed in such a way that the CC world and the NC worldare kept as distinct as possible, for example, by allowing NC devices toplay only illegal disks and CC devices to play only legal disks. In this way, users must buy two series of devices, one for legal and one for illegal disks, in the hope that this will prevent massive, unauthorized, copying, as it happened in the case of audio.

Most of the conventional digital watermarking methods embed the watermark by changing components of the host data, such as modifying the Least Significant Bit (LSB), generating a pseudo-random noise pattern and integrating it into specific chrominance or luminance pixel values, or integrating a watermark into frequency components using discrete cosine, discrete Fourier, or wavelet transformation. Unfortunately, all these techniques lead to distortion of the host data, such as quality degradation. Barni and Bartolini (2004) stated that there is always a trade-off between capacity and other important properties, namely imperceptibility and robustness. A higher capacity is always obtained at the expense of either robustness or imperceptibility (or both) (Barni & Bartolini, 2004). To meet the requirements of capacity while keeping good property of imperceptibility, the direct feature-based method is proposed. A detailed description is given in the following section.

FUNDAMENTAL KNOWLEDGE

This section provides basic concepts dealing with copyright protection based on direct feature-based extraction. The reader is first introduced to the basic concept of a media signature scheme utilized as a fundamental scheme in the direct feature-based method. Visual cryptography is then described as an approach to enhance the security of a copyright protection scheme. The severity of the errors incurred in the copyright protection scheme is explained as well. The following is a description of the most common transform domains of multimedia data today.

Media Signature Scheme

Almost all proposed traditional watermarking methods cannot simultaneously fulfill all copyright protection properties, especially the trade-off between robustness, transparency, and the embedding capacity. In more recent works, Media Signature Scheme (MSS) has been used to improve the traditional watermarking scheme in terms of those trade-offs. In essence, MSS deals with content authentication which fulfills the requirement of robustness to incidental distortion whilst being sensitive to intentional distortion. In other words, the multimedia content is considered authentic as long as the meaning of the multimedia data remains unchanged (He & Sun, 2006).

The general scheme of MSS is depicted in Figure 1. MSS is essentially an extension of the Digital Signal Signature (DSS). The only difference between MSS and DSS is the input to the encryption block. In MSS, the input can either be a feature of multimedia data or a hash digest of the feature indicated by the symbol (1) and (2), respectively. In DSS, the input is the hash digest of the multimedia data. Since the DSS aims to perform complete authentication, the scheme is not robust to any distortions. To meet the requirement of robustness in content authentication while keeping good properties of DSS (integrity protection, source identification, and security), finding a set of features which are capable of representing the multimedia content is proposed in MSS (He & Sun, 2006).

According to the input of an encryption module, MSS can be classified into two categories: direct feature-based authentication and hash digest-based authentication. In direct feature-based authentication, a media signature is generated by signing features of the original image using the sender's private key. During verification, an original feature is obtained by decrypting the received signature using a public key and then compared to the extracted feature obtained from the received image to determine the authenticity. The received image can be considered authentic if it fulfills two conditions: the public key is permissible and the feature between original and extracted is matched. He and Sun (2006) described in detail how to decide whether the original and extracted features are matched. In hash digest-based authentication, there exists two types of hash functions: content-hash and crypto-hash.

With content-hash, the input of the one-way hash function is the image data. "To reduce the signature size, a content-hash digest is proposed to avoid directly using the extracted feature for generating the media signature" (He & Sun, 2006, pp. 124). Therefore, content-hash digests from visually similar images that are similar, while content-hash digests from visually different images that are different. The concept of a content-hash was first proposed by Fridrich and Goljan

Figure 1. Block diagram of media signature scheme. Note that the key sequences "1AFF12CF" and "1AFF12CF" employed in this figure are only examples

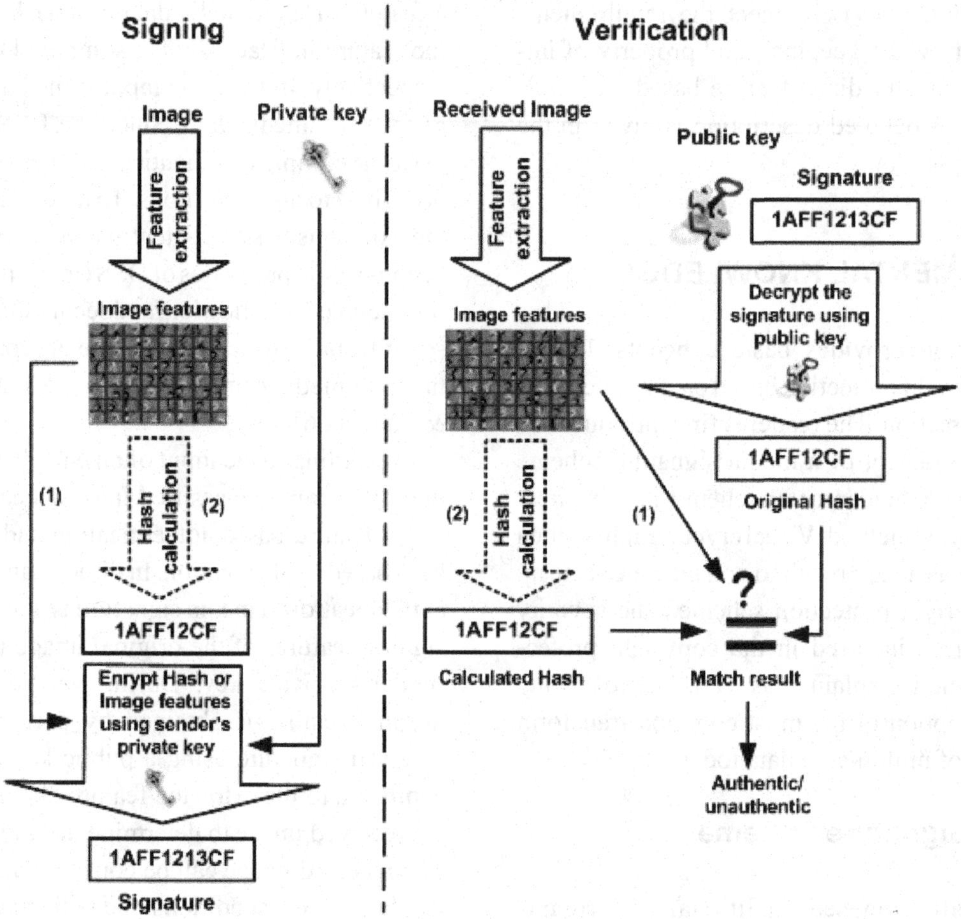

(2000). Unlike the content-hash function, with crypto-hash function the input of hash function are the features of an image instead of the image data. Hence, a one-bit difference in the input features will result in a totally different output. Those who intend to design a media signature due to its security and wide adoption in data authentication prefer to employ crypto-hash rather than content-hash function.

MSS properties are fundamentally similar to watermarking requirements. Therefore, people in the field of multimedia watermarking embrace the idea of MSS to improve their copyright protection scheme.

Visual Cryptography

Visual cryptography is a cryptographic paradigm introduced by Naor and Shamir (1995). They analyzed the case of a k out of n threshold visual cryptography scheme, in which the secret image is visible if and only if any k transparencies are stacked together. A visual cryptography scheme for a set P of n participants is a method to encode a secret image SI into n shadow images called shares, where each participant in P receives one share. Certain qualified subsets of participants can "visually" recover the secret image, but other, forbidden, sets of participants have no information (in an information-theoretic sense) on SI. A "visual" recovery for a set $X \subseteq P$ consists of copying the shares given to the participants in X onto transparencies, and then stacking them. The participants in a qualified set X will be able to see the secret image without any knowledge of cryptography and without performing any cryptographic computation. The general visual cryptography scheme is depicted in Figure 2. According to the concept of Naor and Shamir (1995) scheme, each pixel of an image is replaced by 2 x 2 pixels. Hence, a secret image with M by N pixels can be divided into two sharing images with $2M$ x $2N$ pixels. To enhance the security of copyright protection scheme, some researchers employ visual cryptography as well. It is used to generate image sharing of secret image watermark into several transparencies and register these transparencies to certification authority for further protection. Those who have no corresponding transparencies are unable to extract the watermark.

The main advantages of Naor and Shamir's scheme are low computation cost, fast decoding, and secure. Figure 3 shows that visual cryptography scheme eliminates complex computation problem in decryption process, and the secret images can be restored by stacking operation instead of decryption. In verification process, the stacking operation exploits the human visual system.

Figure 2. The general scheme of visual cryptography

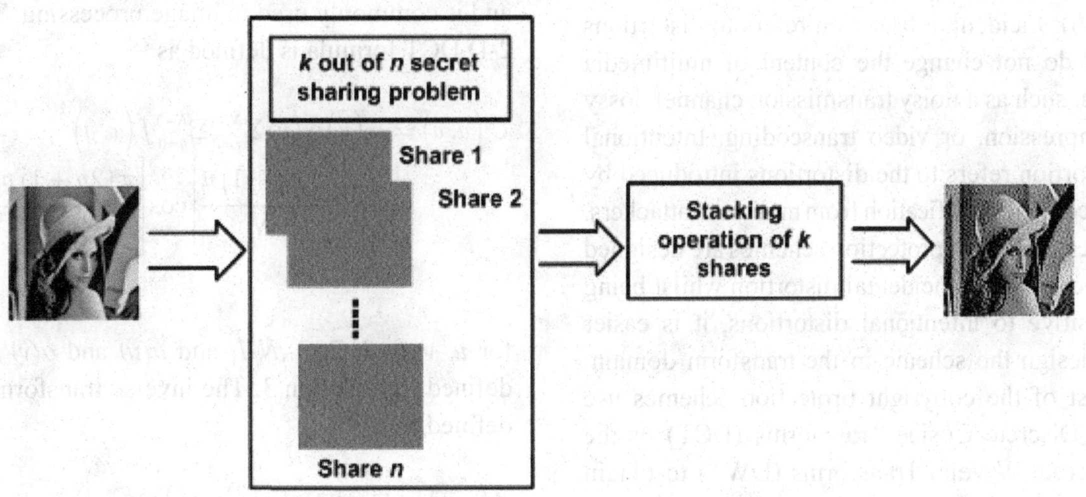

Figure 3. Association between classical and visual cryptography. Note that in decryption process, secret image is solely revealed by human visual system. The key advantage of visual cryptography compared with classical cryptography algorithms lies in that no computations or prior knowledge are required in secret image decryption.

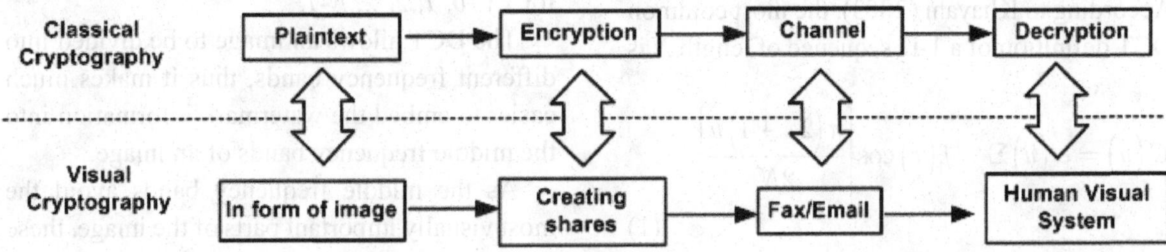

In the beginning, visual cryptography is intended for binary image. To meet the demand of today's multimedia information, several works have been proposed for gray and color image format as well (Revenkar, Anjum, & Gandhare, 2010). To construct image sharing, or shadow, in grayscale, the secret image is first converted to halftone image. Then, we can utilize the density of black dots to simulate the content of grayscale image. While in color image, CMY (Cyan, Magenta, Yellow) color model decomposition is accomplished to yield CMY halftone. The shadow is generated based on the halftone image.

Transform Domain

Distortion can be classified in two ways, namely incidental and intentional distortions (He & Sun, 2006). Incidental distortion refers to distortions that do not change the content of multimedia data, such as a noisy transmission channel, lossy compression, or video transcoding. Intentional distortion refers to the distortions introduced by the content modification from malicious attackers. Since copyright protection schemes are designed to be robust to incidental distortion whilst being sensitive to intentional distortions, it is easier to design the scheme in the transform domain. Most of the copyright protection schemes use the Discrete Cosine Transforms (DCT) or the Discrete Wavelet Transforms (DWT) to obtain the particular features from the image.

The DCT attempts to decorrelate the image data. After decorrelation each transform coefficient can be encoded independently without losing compression efficiency. At first, let us overview on 1-D DCT that is mostly exploited in audio signal. According to Khayam (2003), the most common DCT definition of a 1-D sequence of length N is

$$C(u) = \alpha(u)\Sigma_{x=0}^{N-1} f(x)\cos\left[\frac{\pi(2x+1)u}{2N}\right] \quad (1)$$

for $u=0, 1, 2, ..., N-1$. Similarly, the inverse transformation is defined as

$$f(x) = \Sigma_{u=0}^{N-1}\alpha(u)C(u)\cos\left[\frac{\pi(2x+1)u}{2N}\right] \quad (2)$$

for $u=0, 1, 2, ..., N-1$. In both Equations 1 and 2 $\alpha(u)$ is defined as

$$\alpha(u) = \begin{cases} \sqrt{\frac{1}{N}} & \text{for } u = 0 \\ \sqrt{\frac{1}{N}} & \text{for } u \neq 0 \end{cases} \quad (3)$$

The 2-D DCT is direct extension of 1-D DCT and is commonly used in image processing. The 2-D DCT formula is defined as

$$C(u,v) = \alpha(u)\alpha(v)\Sigma_{x=0}^{N-1}\Sigma_{y=0}^{N-1} f(x,y) \cos\left[\frac{\pi(2x+1)u}{2N}\right]\cos\left[\frac{\pi(2y+1)v}{2N}\right] \quad (4)$$

for $u, v=0, 1, 2, ..., N-1$, and $\alpha(u)$ and $\alpha(v)$ are defined in Equation 3. The inverse transform is defined as

$$f(x,y) = \Sigma_{u=0}^{N-1}\Sigma_{v=0}^{N-1}\alpha(u)\alpha(v)C(u,v) \cos\left[\frac{\pi(2x+1)u}{2N}\right]\cos\left[\frac{\pi(2y+1)v}{2N}\right] \quad (5)$$

for $x,y=0, 1, 2, ..., N-1$.

The DCT allows an image to be divided into different frequency bands, thus it makes much easier to embed the watermark information into the middle frequency bands of an image.

As the middle frequency bands avoid the most visually important parts of the image, these sub-bands are frequently selected for embedding process.

An alternative transformation is the DWT, which splits the signal into two parts: high frequency and low frequency parts. The signal is passed through a series of high pass filters to analyze the high frequency bands, and it is passed through a series of low pass filters to analyze the low frequency bands. Filters of different cut off frequencies are used to analyze the signal at different resolutions. Let us suppose that $x[n]$ is the original signal spanned by frequency bands from 0 to π rad/s. The original signal $x[n]$ is first passed through a half band high-pass filter $g[n]$ and a low-pass filter $h[n]$. After the filtering, half of the samples can be eliminated according to Nyquist's rule, thus the signal now has the highest frequency of $\pi/2$ rad/s instead of π. The signal can therefore be subsampled by 2, simply by discarding every second sample. This constitutes one level of decomposition and can mathematically be expressed as follows:

$$y_{high}\left[k\right] = \Sigma_n x\left[k\right] g\left[2k - n\right] \quad (6)$$

$$y_{low}\left[k\right] = \Sigma_n x\left[k\right] h\left[2k - n\right] \quad (7)$$

where $y_{high}[k]$ and $y_{low}[k]$ are the outputs of the high-pass and low-pass filters, respectively, after subsampling by 2. The above procedure can be repeated for further decompositions.

The reconstructed process is called Inverse Discrete Wavelet Transform (IDWT). The signals at every level are up-sampled by 2, passed through the synthesis filters $g'[n]$, and $h'[n]$ (high-pass and low-pass, respectively), and then added. The analysis and synthesis filters are identical to each other, except for a time reversal. Therefore, the reconstruction formula of each layer becomes

$$x\left[n\right] = \Sigma_n \left(y_{high}\left[k\right] g\left[-n + 2k\right] + y_{low}\left[k\right] h\left[-n + 2k\right] \right) \quad (8)$$

The DWT and IDWT for a two dimensional image $x[m,n]$ can be similarly defined by implementing DWT and IDWT for each dimension m and n separately, which is shown in Figure 4.

An image can be decomposed into a pyramidal structure, which is shown in Figure 5, with various band information: low-low frequency band *LL*, low-high frequency band *LH*, high-low frequency band *HL*, high-high frequency band *HH*.

Cox, Miller, & Bloom (2002) suggested that a watermark should be placed in perceptually significant regions of the host signal so that the scheme could achieve high robustness property. Wavelet decomposition is employed to obtain the

Figure 4. 2-Dimensional DWT

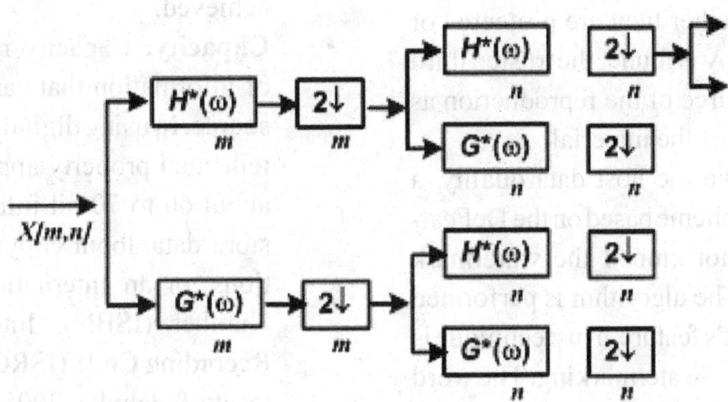

Figure 5. A pyramidal structure

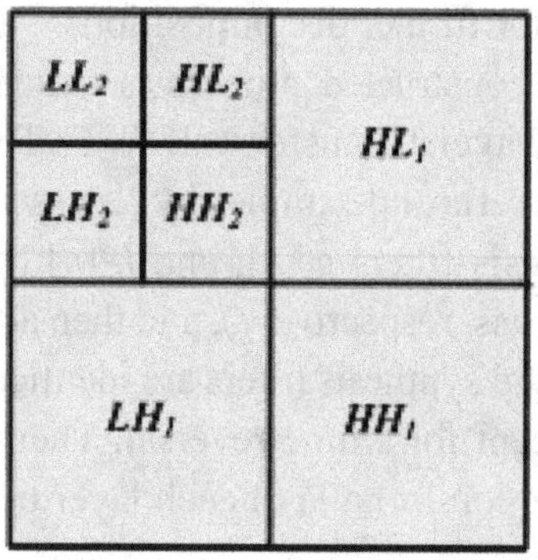

low-frequency sub-band of the host signal, which is considered as the perceptually significant region.

MULTIMEDIA COPYRIGHT PROTECTION

Copyright protection of digital images is defined as the process of proving the intellectual property rights to a court of law against the unauthorized reproduction, processing, transformation or broadcasting of a digital image (Herrigel, Ruanaidh, Petersen, Pereira, & Pun, 1998). Depending on the law in various countries, this process may be based on a prior registration of the copyright with a trusted third party. After successful registration, the copyright ownership is legally bound by a copyright notice, which is required to notify and prove copyright ownership (Herrigel, Ruanaidh, Petersen, Pereira, & Pun, 1998). If a copyright protection mechanism is used, the consumer can copy all material, whether they are protected or not, but if an illegal copy is found, the trusted third party can trace the source of the reproduction as well as the originator of the material.

In order to preserve the host data quality, a copyright protection scheme based on the DeFeat-based method does not embed the watermark within the host data. The algorithm is performed by extracting the cover's feature. This technique is also well known as zero-watermarking. The word "zero-watermarking" means that the watermark is constructed by extracting the feature of host data instead of embedding the watermark within the host data. The general copyright protection scheme based on the DeFeat-based method adapted from MSS is illustrated in Figure 6. Unlike MSS, this copyright protection scheme performs watermark generation and watermark extraction instead of encryption and decryption blocks. The input of these watermark generations and extractions is a feature of the host data. Note that watermark generation and watermark extraction may require the knowledge of a secret key. The only accepted way to protect intellectual property and offer indisputable proof of ownership is to entrust theimage registration to a trusted authority. Hence, all copyright protection schemes based on the DeFeat-based method introduce the presence of a Certification Authority (CA) to accomplish the verification process.

In order to achieve the purpose of copyright protection, a scheme should have the following properties:

- **Perceptual Transparency:** Watermarking processes should be performed without affecting the perceptual quality of the host signal. Fidelity of the watermarking algorithm is usually defined as a perceptual similarity between the original and the watermarked version of the host signal. By using the direct feature-based scheme, perceptual transparency can be perfectly achieved.
- **Capacity:** Capacity refers to the amount of information that can be stored in a data source. In using digital watermarking for intellectual property applications, it requires about 60 to 70 bit information capacity to store data about copyright, author, limitations, or an International Standard Book Number (ISBN), International Standard Recording Code (ISRC), or OEM numbers (Seitz & Jahnke, 2005).

Figure 6. Block diagram of copyright protection scheme based on direct feature-based method

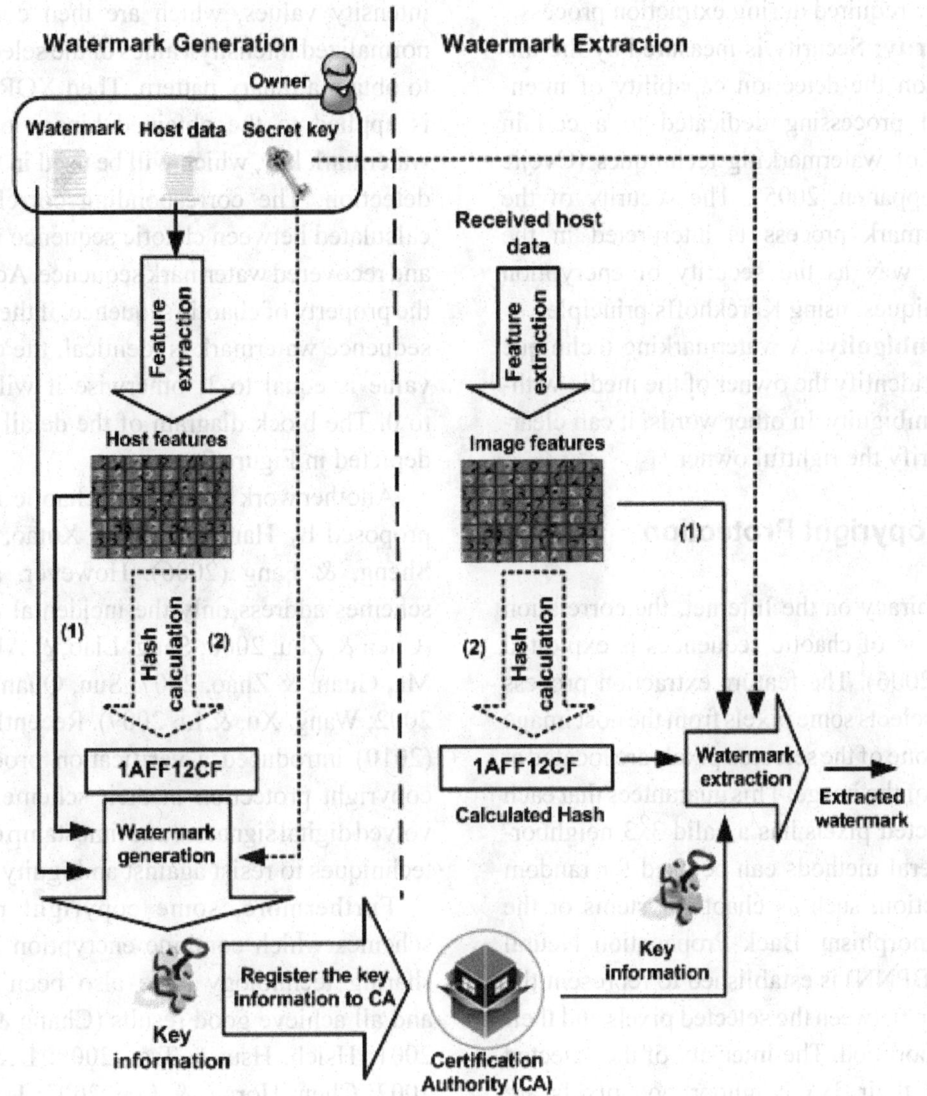

- **Robustness:** Referring to Cox *et al* (2002), robustness refers to the ability to detect the watermark after common signal processing operations. Examples of common operations on images include spatial filtering, lossy compression, printing and scanning, and geometric distortions (rotation, translation, scaling, and so on). Video watermarks may need to be robust to many of the same transformations, as well as to recording on video tape and changes in frame rate, among other influences. Audio watermarks may need to be robust to such processes as temporal filtering, recording on audiotape, and variations in playback speed that result in wow and flutter. Text watermarks may need to be robust against typical document distortions including printing, scanning, photocopying, and faxing.

- **Blindness:** The original host signal may not be required during extraction process.
- **Security:** Security is measured by the impact on the detection capability of intentional processing dedicated to a certain class of watermarking techniques (Cvejic & Seppänen, 2005). The security of the watermark process is interpreted in the same way as the security of encryption techniques, using Kerckhoffs principle.
- **Unambiguity:** A watermarking technique must identify the owner of the media without ambiguity. In other words, it can clearly verify the rightful owner.

Image Copyright Protection

To detect piracy on the Internet, the correlation characteristic of chaotic sequences is exploited by Sang (2006). The feature extraction process randomly selects some pixels from the host image such that none of the selected pixels are located at the border of the image. This guarantees that each of the selected pixels has a valid 3x3 neighborhood. Several methods can be used for random pixel selection, such as chaotic systems or the toral automorphism. Back Propagation Neural Network (BPNN) is established to represent the relationship between the selected pixels and their 3x3 neighborhood. The intensity of the selected pixels and their 3x3 neighborhood pixels are normalized to be used for inputs and outputs of the neural network. After selecting the pixels, the original normalized intensity values as well as the neural network output are obtained. A binary pattern is then generated by comparing those obtained values. Another key representing a discrete chaotic sequence is generated by a chaotic system. Watermark key is then generated by performing XOR operation between the binary pattern and chaotic sequence. At the detection part, specific pixels and their neighborhoods are selected by following the same procedure as in the feature extraction stage. Afterward, the neural network is applied to calculate the predicted normalized intensity values, which are then compared to normalized intensity values of the selected pixels to obtain a binary pattern. Then XOR operation is applied to the obtained binary pattern and watermark key, which will be used in watermark detection. The corresponding correlation was calculated between chaotic sequence watermark and recovered watermark sequence. According to the property of chaotic sequence, if the compared sequence watermark is identical, the correlation value is equal to 1; otherwise it will be close to 0. The block diagram of the detail process is depicted in Figure 7.

Another work based on the chaotic system was proposed by Hanqiang, Hua, Xutao, Li, Miao, Sheng, & Fang (2006). However, almost all schemes address only the incidental distortions (Chen & Zhu, 2008; Sang, Liao, & Alam, 2006; Ma, Guan, & Zhao, 2007; Sun, Quan, & Wang, 2002; Wang, Xu, & Li, 2009). Recently, Li *et al.* (2010) introduced a verification procedure for copyright protection in their scheme. They involved digital signature and timestamp encryption techniques to resist against ambiguity attacks.

Furthermore, some copyright protection schemes which combine encryption and secret sharing technology have also been proposed, and all achieve good results (Chang & Chuang, 2001; Hsieh, Hsu, & Tsai, 2005; Lee & Chen, 2002; Chen, Horng, & Lee, 2005; Lou, Tso, & Liu, 2006). Lou (2006) proposed the scheme that extracts the feature from the protected image by utilizing the secret key and the relation between the low and middle sub-band wavelet coefficients. The feature and watermark are used to generate a secret image by the codebook of visual cryptography technique. To provide further protection, the secret image is registered to CA, except the secret key and the codebook. In the verification procedure, a public image is first generated from the suspected image. The extracted watermark is obtained by performing an XOR operation between the secret and public image. The experi-

Figure 7. Block diagram of neural network-based

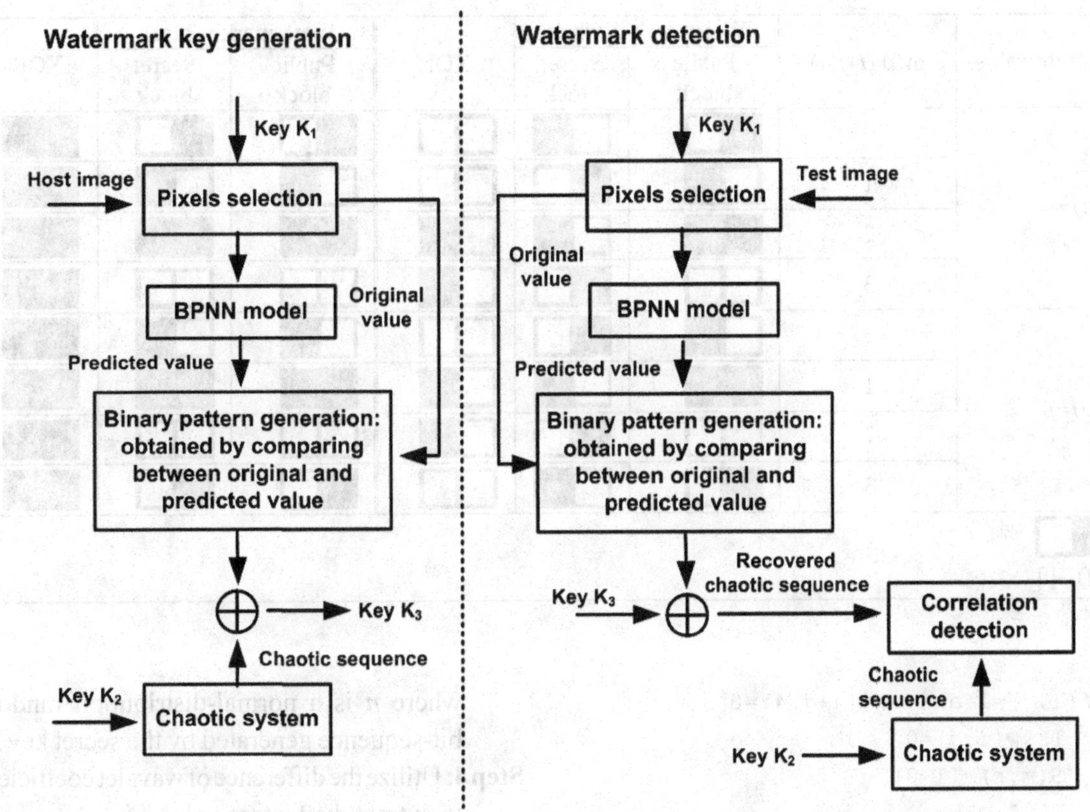

ment also shows that by using different images and a secret key, the extracted watermark appears like noise and is meaningless. It demonstrates that the scheme can clearly verify the copyright of the images. The detail procedures of both secret image generation and watermark extraction are described as follows.

Secret Image Generation Procedure

Input: A protected image *I*, a watermark *W*, a secret key *K*, and a codebook *C*.

Output: A secret image *S*.

Step 1: Decompose the protected image *I* into ten sub-bands by three-level DWT

Step 2: Extract low sub-band *L* and middle sub-band *M*.

Step 3: Compute new coefficients of low sub-band by the following equation:

$$L'(i,j) = L(i,j) + n \times \left(L(i,j) - M(i,j)\right) \quad (9)$$

where *n* is a normal-distribution random bit-sequence generated by a secret key *K*.

Step 4: Utilize the difference of wavelet coefficient to extract the feature value *F*:

$$f(i,j) = \begin{cases} 1 & \text{if } L(i,j) > L'(i,j) \\ 0 & \text{if } L(i,j) \le L'(i,j) \end{cases} \quad (10)$$

Step 5: Generate a secret image *S* by utilizing the codebook *C* as shown in Figure 8. For example:

Figure 8. Codebook used in the scheme by Lou et al (2006)

Feature value	mod (*i*+*j*,4)	Watermark is white			Watermark is black		
		Public block	Secret block	XOR	Public block	Secret block	XOR
f(i,j)=0	0	■□	□■	□□	■□	■□	■■
	1	□■	■□	□□	□■	□■	■■
	2	■■	□■	□■	■■	■■	■■
	3	□□	■□	□■	□□	□□	■■
f(i,j)=0	0	□■	■□	□□	□■	□■	■■
	1	■■	□■	□■	■■	■■	■■
	2	□□	■□	□■	□□	□□	■■
	3	■□	□■	□□	■□	■□	■■
■□ [0 1]							

```
IF f(i,j)=1 and mod(i+j,4)=0
      IF w(i,j)=0
      S(m,n)=[1 0]
      ELSE
      S(m,n)=[0 1]
      END
END
```

Step 6: Register to CA the secret image.

Watermark Extraction Procedure

Input: A suspected image I', a secret image S, a secret key K, and codebook C.
Output: A watermark $\widehat{W}$.
Step 1: Decompose the suspected image I' into ten sub-bands by three-level DWT.
Step 2: Extract low sub-band L' and middle sub-band M'.
Step 3: Compute new coefficients of low sub-band by the following equation:

$$L''(i,j) = L'(i,j) + n \times \left(L'(i,j) - M'(i,j)\right) \tag{11}$$

where n is a normal-distribution random bit-sequence generated by the secret key K.
Step 4: Utilize the difference of wavelet coefficient to extract the feature value F':

$$f'(i,j) = \begin{cases} 1 & \text{if } L'(i,j) > L'''(i,j) \\ 0 & \text{if } L'(i,j) \le L'''(i,j) \end{cases} \tag{12}$$

Step 5: Generate a public image P by utilizing the codebook C shown as Figure 8. For example:

```
IFf'(i,j)=1 and mod(i+j,4)=0
      P(m,n)=[1 0]
END
```

Step 6: Obtain the watermark W' as follows

$$W' = S \oplus P \tag{13}$$

where $\oplus$ denotes the XOR operation.
Step 7: Perform the reduction process to get reduced watermark $\widehat{W}$ by the following equation:

$$\hat{w}(i,j) = \begin{cases} 1 \ \text{if} \ \Sigma_m^m \Sigma_n^n w'(m,n) \geq 1 \\ 0 \ \text{if} \ \Sigma_m^m \Sigma_n^{n+1} w'(m,n) < 1 \end{cases} \quad (14)$$

To evaluate the robustness, several common attacks are exploited, such as JPEG compression, sharpening, blurring, and mixing attacks (blurring and sharpening, blurring and cropping). The Peak Signal to Noise Ratio (*PSNR*) is used to measure the image quality, which is defined as:

$$PSNR = 10\log_{10}\frac{255^2}{\text{MSE}}(dB) \quad (15)$$

$$MSE = \frac{1}{MN}\Sigma_{i=0}^{m-1}\Sigma_{j=0}^{n-1}\left(X_{ij} - X'_{ij}\right)^2 \quad (16)$$

where X_{ij} and X'_{ij} represent the pixel value of original image and an attacked image, respectively. The accuracy ratio (*AR*) is used to evaluate the similarity between the original watermark and the extracted one, and is defined as follows:

$$AR = \frac{CB}{NB} \quad (17)$$

where *NB* is the number of the original watermark bits, and *CB* is the number of correct bits between the original watermark and the extracted one. The *AR* value ranges from 0 to 1.

In JPEG compression experiment, the image is compressed by using quality factor 10 and then utilizes the step of watermarking extraction. Despite the compression ratio is extremely high, the extracted watermark remains good. Lou *et al.* (2006) use scaling, that is reduce image from 256×256 to 16×16 and then recover to original dimension, to test the effort of other attacks, and noise adding with variation 100 attacks to test the robustness. To investigate the ambiguity property, different images and secret key are applied in the experiments. Based on the results, the extracted watermark is somewhat meaningless and it is obvious that the scheme can be applied to the area of copyright protection.

To avoid malicious attacks, Chen et al. (2005) involved two cryptographic tools, a digital signature and a timestamp, to monitor and discover illegal object distribution. They exploited low-frequency components of the original image and permutated watermark logo *W* to compute a verification key *K*. The following is the detailed algorithm.

Certificate Generation Algorithm

Input: Original image *X* and watermark logo *W* are defined as

$$X = \left\{x_{ij} \middle| 0 \leq x_{ij} \leq 255, 0 \leq i < W_X, 0 \leq j < H_X\right\} \quad (18)$$

where W_X and H_X are the width and height of *X*, respectively.

$$W = \left\{w_{ij} \middle| w_{ij} \in \{0,1\}, 0 \leq i < W_{W,} 0 \leq j < H_W\right\} \quad (19)$$

where W_W and H_W are the width and height of *W*, respectively.

Step 1: Original image decomposition. An image *X* is decomposed by performing *t*-level wavelet transform to obtain subband LL_t denoted as *L*.

Step 2: Watermark logo permutation. The logo *W* is permutated based on a two-dimension pseudorandom permutation generated by seed *s*. The permutated logo *W'* is denoted as

$$W' = \left\{w'_{i'j'} \middle| w'_{i'j'} = PRP_s\left(w_{ij}\right), 0 \leq i', i < W_{W,} 0 \leq j', j < H_W\right\} \quad (20)$$

where $PRP_s(\bullet)$ represents the permutation function using seed s.

Step 3: Polarity table construction. At first, the average value P_{av} of all pixels in L is calculated. Then, the polarity table P is constructed and denoted as:

$$P = \left\{ p_{mn} \middle| p_{mn} \in \{0,1\}, 0 \le m < W_{W,} 0 \le N < H_W \right\} \tag{21}$$

where

$$p_{mn} = \begin{cases} 0, & \text{if } l_{mn} < P_{av} \\ 1, & \text{if } l_{mn} \ge P_{av} \end{cases}$$

Step 4: Verification key generation. Once the polarity table P is constructed, the verification key K is computed as follows:

$$K = P \text{XOR} W' \tag{22}$$

The security of their scheme lies on the parameters s and K.

Step 5: Signing and timestamping the parameters. The security parameters are signed by the owner using the digital signature technique.

$$DS = Sign_{OSK}(s, K, t, W_X, H_X) \tag{23}$$

where $Sign_{OSK}(\bullet)$ is a digital signature function using the owner's private key OSK. Afterwards, the owner sends the signature DS to CA and CA creates a timestamp TS as

$$TS = TS_{TPSK}(DS) \tag{24}$$

where $TS_{TPSK}(\bullet)$ is a timestamp function using CA's private key TPSK. Once the owner receives TS, TS and DS are incorporated with the original image X and can be used to verify the copyright logo when the dispute arises.

Logo Verification Algorithm

The verification steps are similar to the certificate generation steps and are described as follows.

Input: A test image

Step 1: A test image is decomposed by a t-level wavelet transformation to obtain the sub-band LL'_t

Step 2: A new polarity table P' is calculated from LL'_t.

Step 3: Watermark logo extraction. The logo W'' is obtained by performing XOR operation between a polarity table P' and verification key K.

Step 4: The retrieved logo $\hat{W}$ is obtained by inversing the permutation in Equation 20 based on the parameter s and is defined as follows:

$$\hat{W} = \left\{ \hat{w}_{ij} \middle| \begin{array}{l} \hat{w}_{ij} = PRP_s^{-1}\left(w''_{i'j'}\right), 0 \le i', \\ i < W_{W,} 0 \le j', j < H_W \end{array} \right\} \tag{25}$$

where $PRP^{-1}_s(\bullet)$ represents the inverse permutation function.

To test the robustness, several various attacks are applied including blurring, JPEG compression, noise adding, sharpening, rotation, cropping, print-photocopy-scan, StirMark, unZign, and blind pattern matching attacks. Generally, the scheme can withstand all of these attacks with the recovered correct bits achieving over 95%. Based on their experimental results in Chen, Horng, and Lee (2005), in case of extreme attacks, such as rotation, cropping, and cropping-scaling, the recovered correct bits still can attain up to 80.3%. Performance comparison of their scheme with several conventional watermarking schemes is shown in Table 1.

Table 1. Performance comparison between Chen's scheme and several conventional watermarking schemes (Chen, Horng, & Lee, 2005)

Property	Chen *et al.* (2005)	Cox *et al.* (1997)	Tsai *et al.* (2000)	Barni *et al.* (2001)
Blindness	Yes	No	Yes	Yes
Multiple logos	Yes	Yes	No	No
Publicly verifiable	Yes	No	No	No
Copy attack resistance	Yes	No	No	No
Counterfeit attack resistance	Timestamp	No	No	No
BPM attack resistance	Yes	No	No	No
StirMark attack resistance	Yes	No	No	No
Extraction/Detection	Extraction	Detection	Extraction	Detection
Visual recognizable logo	Yes	No	Yes	No
Robustness	Compression Blurring Sharpening Scaling Cropping Rotation Print-photocopy-scan StirMark unZign BPM attack	Compression Blurring Scaling Dithering Print-photocopy-scan Cropping	Compression	Compression Cropping Morphing

Audio Copyright Protection

Digital music is one of the digital properties that can be easily distributed over the Internet. The Secure Digital Music Initiative (SDMI) made watermarking a central component of their system for protecting music (Cox, Miller, & Bloom, 2002).

Several copyright protection schemes for audio based on direct feature-based extraction have been proposed in Chen and Zhu (2008) and Wang and Hu (2007). Most previous copyright protection schemes by the direct feature-based method were developed for images, as a result Chen and Zhu (2008) developed a novel robust zero-watermarking technique for audio signals. Three-level wavelet decomposition is applied to get the low-frequency subband of the host audio, which is the perceptually significant region of it. The decorrelation, energy compaction, separability, symmetry, and orthogonality properties of discrete cosine transform led to its widespread deployment in audio processing standards, for example, MPEG-1. To make the scheme resist lossy compression operations such as MP3 compression, Discrete Cosine Transform (DCT) is performed on the obtained low-frequency wavelet coefficients. In addition, considering the Gaussian signal suppression property of higher-order cumulants, the fourth-order cumulants of the obtained DWT-DCT coefficients are calculated to ensure the robustness of the scheme against various noise addition operations. Finally, the essential features extracted based on DWT, DCT, and higher-order cumulants are used for generating a binary pattern. Thus, any manipulations attempting to destroy the watermark will destroy the host audio signal first, so that the high robustness of the scheme is ensured. And since the essential features of different host audio signals are different, the detection reliability can also be achieved. The detail procedures of both watermark generation and extraction are given as follows.

Watermark Generation Procedure

Step 1: At first, **A** is segmented into L frames, denoted as $\mathbf{F} = \{\mathbf{f}_i | i = 0, ..., L-1, L > 2MN\}$, and each frame has L_f samples. Next, the energy value of each frame is calculated and all the frames are rearranged in order of decreasing energy value. Then, the first T frames are selected for watermark generation. And, the indices of the selected frames in **F**, denoted as $\mathbf{I}_1$,

$$I_1 = \left\{ i(k) \middle| i(k) \in \{0, \ldots, L-1\}, k = 0, \ldots, T-1 \right\} \tag{26}$$

are saved as the first secret key $\mathbf{K}_1$.

Step 2: H-level wavelet decomposition is performed on each selected frame $\mathbf{f}_{i(k)}$ to get its coarse signal $A^H_{i(k)}$ and detail signals

$$D^H_{i(k)}, D^{H-1}_{i(k)}, \ldots, D^1_{i(k)}$$

To take the advantage of low frequency coefficient which has a high-energy value and is robust against various signal processing manipulations the DCT is only performed on $A^H_{i(k)}$ as follows:

$$A^{HC}_{i(k)} = DCT\left(A^H_{i(k)}\right) = \left\{ a^{HC}_{i(k)}(n) \middle| n = 0, \ldots, \frac{L_f}{2^H} - 1 \right\} \tag{27}$$

Step 3: For each $A^{HC}_{i(k)}$, calculate its fourth-order cumulant, denoted as $\mathbf{C}_{i(k)}$,

$$C_{i(k)} = \left\{ c_{i(k)}(n) \middle| n = 0, \ldots, \frac{L_f}{2^{H-1}} \right\} \tag{28}$$

Then, the elements in $\mathbf{C}_{i(k)}$ are rearranged in order of decreasing absolute value and the first P ($P=(M\times N)/T$) elements are selected to generate a new sequence $\mathbf{D}_{i(k)}$ as follows:

$$D_{i(k)} = \left\{ d_{i(k)}(p) \middle| p = 0, \ldots, P-1 \right\} \tag{29}$$

where

$$P = \frac{MxN}{T}$$

The index of $d_{i(k)}(p)$ in $\mathbf{C}_{i(k)}$ denoted as I_2

$$I_2 = \left\{ i_{i(k)}(p) \middle| i_{i(k)}(p) \in \left\{0, \ldots, \frac{L_f}{2^{H-1}}\right\}, p = 0, \ldots, P-1 \right\} \tag{30}$$

is saved as the second secret key $\mathbf{K}_2$.

Step 4: A binary pattern, denoted as $\mathbf{B}_{i(k)}$,

$$B_{i(k)} = \left\{ b_{i(k)}(p) \middle| p = 0, \ldots, P-1 \right\} \tag{31}$$

is generated as follows:

$$B_{i(k)}(p) = \begin{cases} 1, & d_{i(k)}(p) \geq 0 \\ 0, & \text{otherwise} \end{cases} \tag{32}$$

The watermark detection key $\mathbf{K}_3 = \{K_{i(k)}(p) \mid k = 0, ..., T-1, p = 0, ..., P-1\}$ is obtained by performing XOR operation between $\mathbf{B}_{i(k)}$ and the binary watermark **W** as follows:

$$K_{i(k)}(p) = b_{i(k)}(p) \oplus w(i,j) \tag{33}$$

$$k = 0, \ldots, T-1, p = 0, \ldots, P-1 \tag{34}$$

$$i = floor\left(\frac{k \times P + p}{N}\right), j = mod\left(\frac{k \times P + p}{N}\right) \quad (35)$$

Watermark Extraction Procedure

Step 1: At first, the test audio signal **A'** = $\{a'(i) \mid i = 0, ..., L_A - 1\}$ is divided into L frames **F** = $\{\mathbf{f}_i \mid i = 0, ..., L-1\}$, from which T frames, denoted as $\mathbf{f}_{i(k)}$, $k = 0, ..., T - 1$, are selected with $\mathbf{K}_1$.

Step 2: Next, H-level wavelet decomposition is performed on each selected frame to get its coarse signal $A'^{H}_{i(k)}$ on which DCT is performed to obtain $A'^{HC}_{i(k)}$

Step 3: Next, for each $A'^{HC}_{i(k)}$ calculate its fourth-order cumulant $\mathbf{C'}_{i(k)}$, from which P elements are selected with secret key $\mathbf{K}_2$ to get a new sequence $\mathbf{D'}_{i(k)}$:

$$D'_{i(k)} = \left\{d'_{i(k)}(p) \middle| k = 0, ..., T-1, p = 0, ..., P-1\right\} \quad (36)$$

Step 4: Then, the estimated binary pattern $\mathbf{B'}_{i(k)}$

$$B'_{i(k)} = \left\{b'_{i(k)}(p) \middle| k = 0, ..., T-1, p = 0, ..., P-1\right\} \quad (37)$$

is generated as follows:

$$b'_{i(k)}(p) = \begin{cases} 1, & \text{if } d'_{i(k)}(p) \geq 0 \\ 0, & \text{otherwise} \end{cases} \quad (38)$$

Finally, XOR operation is performed between the estimated binary pattern and the watermark detection key $\mathbf{K}_3$ to obtain the estimated binary image watermark **W'**.

The experiments show that the scheme not only introduces no distortion into the host audio, but also achieves great robustness against various attacks such as MP3 compression, re-quantization, re-sampling, low-pass filtering, equalizing, amplifying, time delaying, echo-adding, and noise-adding. In addition, the scheme introduces the presence of authentication center for keeping the copyright information such as the secret keys, original host audio, and the corresponding digital timestamp, to be used in copyright demonstration. To investigate the effectiveness, comparison with conventional audio watermarking (Wang & Zhao, 2006) is conducted as well. Chen and Zhu's (2008) scheme outperforms conventional watermarking in many types of StirMark attacks, such as equalization, adding a white noise, amplify, and invert. The detail results are provided in the paper (Chen & Zhu, 2008).

Another feature of the audio copyright protection scheme by direct-feature based extraction was proposed by Wang and Hu (2007). The zero-watermark was created by selecting some large absolute values of low frequency wavelet coefficients of the original audio. The construction of the watermark is random by a chaotic sequence. After generating the watermark, the chaotic inverse search is adopted to get the initial value of the watermark sequence. The watermark extracting process is an inverse process and the initial value, instead of the original audio is required for recovering the embedded watermark. The ownership of the audio can be determined by computing normalized correlation coefficient between the original watermark and the extracted watermark. The experimental results prove that this method of watermarking attains a high quality of imperceptibility and robustness. The experiments for attacks, such as additive Gaussian noise, low-pass filtering, requantization, re-sampling, and MP3 compression, give strong evidences for the robustness of the approach.

Text Document Copyright Protection

Text watermarking began in 1993 and was proposed by Maxemchuk and Low (1997) as the initiators. The basic idea is to encode information by moving the objects by small amounts. For text marking we can move a paragraph vertically (or horizontally), move a text line vertically, move a block of words or a single word horizontally, or move a character horizontally. The movements can be nested or combined to encode more information. For instance, a line can be moved slightly up and down while words within that line can be moved slightly left or right (Maxemchuk & Low, 1997).

Since this development, a number of text watermarking techniques have been proposed. However, those developed algorithms embed a watermark in the host text document itself, and result in text quality, meaning and value degradation. Jalil *et al.* (Jalil, Mirza, & Sabir, 2010) proposed a watermarking approach in which the host text document is not altered during watermark generation. The algorithm utilizes the contents of text to protect it. A keyword from the text is selected based on the author's choice and a watermark is generated based on the length of the preceding and the following words adjacent to the keyword. The watermark is not embedded in the text itself, but it is generated using the characteristics of text. This scheme also adapts the MSS. The watermarking process consists of two parts: (1) watermark generation and (2) watermark extraction. Watermark generation is done by the original author and extraction is done later by a Certification Authority (CA) to prove the ownership. CA is an essential requirement in this scheme with which the original copyright owner registers his/her watermark. Whenever the content ownership is in question, this CA acts as a decision authority (Jalil, Mirza, & Sabir, 2010).

The watermark-embedding algorithm requires an original text file as input and a keyword is selected by the original author/copyright owner. The keyword should appear most frequently in the text. A watermark is generated as output by this algorithm. This watermark is then registered with the certifying authority along with the original text document, author name, keyword, current date and time. The watermark-embedding algorithm is described in Algorithm 1.

The original text (OT) is first obtained from the author and the frequency of each word within the text is analyzed. A keyword is selected by the author as described above. The frequency of the proceeding and following words are then analyzed and a numeric watermark is generated.

The extraction algorithm takes the plain text and keyword as input. The text may undergo some

Algorithm 1. Watermark-embedding

```
1. Read TO.
2. Count Occurrence of each word in TO.
3. Select KW based on occurrence frequency
4. KWCOUNT = Total occurrence count of KW intext TO
5. for i=1 to KWCOUNT, repeat step 6 to 8.
6. WM [j] = length (Pi)
7. WM [j+1] = length (Ni)
8. i=i+1 and j=j+1
9. Output WM
```

TO= Original text; KW=keyword; KWCOUNT= keyword count ; WM= Watermark; Pi= 'Proceeding word' of the ith occurrence of keyword (KW); Ni= 'Next word' of the ith occurrence of keyword (KW)

distortions including insertion, deletion, paraphrasing, or reordering of the words and sentences. The watermark is generated from the text by the extraction algorithm and is then, compared to the original watermark registered with the CA. The extraction algorithm is described in Algorithm 2.

In the experimental results, text samples collected from Reuters' corpus, e-books, and Web pages are used. Insertion and deletion of words and sentences was performed at multiple randomly selected locations in the sample text. Three different keywords "and," "of," and "in" are analyzed in the original and attacked text samples. These keywords are selected because of their occurrences in all text samples. The experiments show that the scheme can detect the tampered text even though there are only a few words or sentences that have been tampered.

The related work proposed by Jalil, Farooq, Sabir, Zafar, and Ashraf (2010) was a watermarking scheme resistant attack on preserving the meaning of content. The scheme utilizes the existence of non-vowel characters to watermark the text document. The text document is first analyzed and prepositions are identified. The occurrence of all prepositions is counted and the Average Frequency Preposition (AFP) is identified. This AFP is then used to create the partitions of text. After this, the occurrence count of all alphabetical characters in each partition is obtained and the most frequent non-vowel ASCII characters are identified and summarized as the MFNV list. This MFNV list is then used to generate an author's key based on the watermark provided by the owner. In order to protect the copyrights of the owner this author's key is registered to the CA. The original watermark and author's key are time stamped and set aside from the CA. This scheme is specifically for copyright protection of medium size documents such as emails, newspaper articles, and blogs. The experiments demonstrate that robustness is based on the watermark length. The longer the watermark used is, the more robust the copyright scheme is against such attacks.

Another development proposed by Jalil, Mirza, and Iqbal (2010) is an algorithm that uses an image watermark that can be a logo, fingerprint or digital signature taken from the original author. In this scheme, text partitions are formed by considering the preposition assigned by the user as the separator. These partitions are then combined together to form groups based on group size. Afterwards, for each group, the occurrence of the first letter in each double letter word is analyzed and the most frequent first letter of each group is identified to form a MFFL (Most Frequent First Letter) list.

Algorithm 2. Extraction algorithm

```
1. Read TO or TA, WM and KW.
2. Count frequency of KW in given text.
3. KWCOUNT = Total occurrence count of KW intext
4. for i=1 to KWCOUNT, repeat step 5 to 7.
5. EWM [ j ] = length (Pi)
6. EWM [j+1] = length (Ni)
7. i=i+1 and j=j+1
8. if (EWM not equals WM)
Tamper = YES
9. Output EWM.
```

TO= Original text; TA= Attacked text; KW=keyword;
KWCOUNT= keyword count ; EWM= Extracted Watermark;
Pi= 'Proceeding word' of the ith occurrence of keyword (KW);
Ni= 'Next word' of the ith occurrence of keyword (KW)

This MFFL list is used to generate a watermark key based on watermark. The possible attacks on this scheme can be random insertion, deletion, and re-ordering of words in the text.

ROBUSTNESS AND SECURITY

Robustness is an important property of a copyright protection scheme. It describes the capability of the hidden data to survive host signal manipulations, including both incidental and intentional distortions. To evaluate the robustness, incidental distortions are often applied to the copyright protection scheme. Then, the message error can be analyzed throughout the extraction process (Cox, Miller, & Bloom, 2002). Bit error rate, or *BER*, is a metric used for measuring the frequency of bit errors. In general, *BER* can be defined as follows:

$$BER = \frac{\text{the number of bit errors}}{\text{the total number of transferred bits}} 100\% \tag{39}$$

Security is another important property in the copyright protection scheme. Security issues are related to attacks that can benefit from the knowledge of the copyright protection scheme. There are three main categories of attacks dealing with copyright protection, including benchmark attacks, malicious attacks, and blind pattern matching attacks.

Benchmark Attacks

StirMark and UnZign are two examples of benchmark attacks that can remove copyright information from files. Like many other programs which break the established security mechanisms, these programs are intended to demonstrate the weaknesses in current algorithms so that companies will be motivated to develop more robust watermarking technologies. When the copyright protection scheme cannot resist StirMark and UnZign, it is considered broken (Chen, Horng, & Lee, 2005). Chen and Zhu (2008) have exploited StirMark for Audio v0.2 to evaluate their scheme against benchmark attacks.

Malicious Attacks

The aim of this attack is to remove or make the watermark unrecoverable. For copyright protection purposes, the scheme should withstand malicious attacks. According to Barni and Bartolini (2004), malicious attacks are classified into two ways: blind and informed.

An attack is said to be informed if an attempt is made to remove or make the watermark unrecoverable by exploiting the knowledge of the particular algorithm used for a watermarking asset. These attacks attempt to extract some secret information about the algorithm from publicly available data, and then, based on this information, attempt to nullify the effectiveness of the watermarking system (Barni & Bartolini, 2004). Counterfeit attacks fall into this category. In general, the aim of these attacks is to enable multiple claims to ownership of an intellectual property. These attacks are as follows:

1. **Single-Watermarked-Image-Counterfeit-Original (SWICO) Attack:** The counterfeiting is accomplished by inverting the encoding function of a watermark scheme, in order to "remove" a watermark rather than insert one (Craver, Memon, Yeo, & Yeung, 1997). Then, the inserted fake watermark onto the counterfeit original produces the same watermarked data.
2. **Twin-Watermarked-Image-Counterfeit-Original (TWICO) Attack:** The counterfeiting is exactly the same as SWICO attack. Unlike SWICO, the insertion of the watermark onto the counterfeit original produces additional watermarked data (Craver, Memon, Yeo, & Yeung, 1997).

Barni and Bartolini (2004) stated that in order to prevent the possibility of SWICO attacks, one common way is to introduce the presence of a Trusted Third Party in the watermarking protocol. In this way, the watermark verification procedure will have a legal value.

An attack is said to be blind if it tries to remove or make a watermark unrecoverable without any knowledge of the employed watermarking algorithm. Copy attack is one example of this type of attack. It estimates the watermark signal with the aim of adding it to another asset (Barni & Bartolini, 2004). Cox, Miller, and Bloom (2002) provided an example dealing with such an attack. Suppose Alice is an advertiser who intends to distribute her radio commercials to 600 radio stations. She embeds a watermark in each of her radio commercials before distributing them. Afterwards, she could identify any false charges by monitoring the radio stations with her watermark detector, logging the broadcast of her commercials and matching her logs with the 600 invoices she receives. On the other side, Bob operates one of these 600 radio stations and would like to air one of his commercials in place of Alice's commercials. Since he still wants to charge Alice for the airtime, he secretly embeds Alice's watermark into his advertisement and airs it in place of Alice's. Alice detects this watermark and without any doubt she fully believes that her advertisement was correctly broadcast.

Cox *et al.* (2002) described several methods of implementing copy attacks. One of them is conducted by reconstructing the original data. Given a legitimately watermarked data, c_{1w}, and the target data without a watermark, c_2, this method begins by applying a watermark removal attack to c_{1w} to obtain an approximation of the original, $\hat{c}_1$. Cox *et al.* (2002) proposed using a nonlinear noise-reduction filter. Then, the added watermark pattern is estimated by subtracting the predicted original from the watermarked one:

$$\hat{w}_a = c_{1w} - \hat{c}_1 \quad (40)$$

Finally, the estimated watermark pattern is added to the data without a watermark to obtain a watermarked version:

$$c_{2W} = c_2 + \hat{w}_a \quad (41)$$

Blind Pattern Matching (BPM) Attacks

The aim of this attack is to reduce the correlation of a watermarked signal with its watermark by replacing blocks of samples of the marked signal with perceptually similar blocks that are either not marked or that are marked with a different watermark (Petticolas & Kirovski, 2002). BPM is a new model of attack against generic watermarking system and it consists of three stages:

1. Partition the watermarked content into overlapping low-granularity signal blocks.
2. Identify the subsets of perceptually similar blocks and perform the similarity function.
3. Randomly permutate their locations in the signal.

Petticolas and Kirovski (2002) stated if the number of blocks that have perceptually similar counterparts within the media clip is small, to achieve a successful attack, the adversary can alternatively search replacement blocks in an external multimedia library. Thus finding perceptually similar blocks is a challenging task. The effectiveness of BPM attacks depends on two factors (Petticolas & Kirovski, 2002):

1. Block size is a variable with an important trade-off. Since it is difficult to find large similar blocks, the search obviously take advantage of small blocks. In contrast, it is difficult to estimate perceptual factors in

small blocks. Moreover, small blocks have a tendency to preserve high correlation between the original and the substitute. This situation reduces the impact of BPM on the reliability of the watermark detector. Small blocks increase the number of total blocks that need to be replaced, which significantly increases search run-time.

2. The content may have little redundancy regardless of block size and relative looseness of the upper bound on similarity. In this case, the adversary needs to search a larger database of content with expectation that similar sound (suppose it is in audio) can be found.

Chen *et al.* (2005) have involved this attack on their experiments. To survive against BPM attacks, Chen *et al.* (2005) introduced the usage of timestamp and digital signature scheme to generate the secret information.

DISCUSSION

In this section, we provide comparative discussion between conventional watermarking and direct feature-based method. Consider the general scheme of conventional watermarking as depicted in Figure 9.

The watermarked data A_w is generated by embedding the watermark w directly within the host data A. Note that embedding and watermark recovery may require the knowledge of a secret key K, and that recovery may benefit from the knowledge of the original host data A. The main concern of the embedding part of any data hiding system is to make the hidden data imperceptible as well as robust against various attacks. However, most conventional watermarking schemes affect the visual/audible quality of host data more or less, even though the strength of embedding algorithm is considered. In terms of copyright protection's attacks, Chen *et al.* (2005) has proven that most conventional watermarking schemes (Cox, et al., 1997; Tsai, et al., 2000; Barni, et al., 2001) cannot resist BPM attacks and benchmark attacks.

In contrast to conventional watermarking, direct feature-based method, as illustrated in Figure 6, extracts the features from the host data instead of embedding data directly within it. In this case, direct feature-based method eliminates the visual/audible quality degradation problem since the host data remains unaffected. All the experimental results discussed in preceding section show that the watermarked data is identical to original one.

Further, multiple claims' situation may occur due to the absence of embedded information. An adversary may embed his/her information into the host data and claim the copyright. In this case, both owner and adversary's information can be perfectly extracted. To overcome the dispute situation, the direct feature-based scheme must

Figure 9. General scheme of conventional watermarking adapted from Barni and Bartolini (2004)

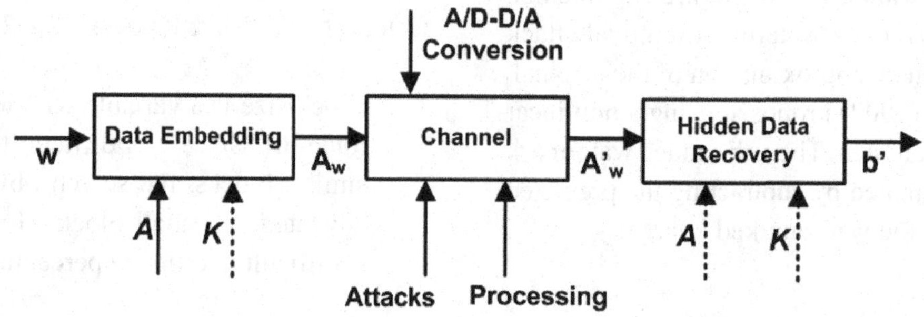

be registered or associated to an authentication center for copyright demonstration and then rightful ownership is verified by the CA based on the earlier registration.

Additional Topics

The issue on copyright protection makes significant sense to the construction of Geographic Information System (GIS), the copyright protection system for digital products, the legislation draft on copyright protection, national information security, as well as the development of GIS, electronic navigation, digital city and other geographic information industries (Li, Lin, Chen, & Lü, 2008). Li *et al.* (2008) had proposed copyright authentication of GIS vector data by using hash function. Hash function has the ability to convert multi-sizes of messages to fixed-size ones and it could be used for expressing the visual characters of GIS vector data. The following is performance demand of hash function of GIS vector data:

- **Robustness:** If data I1 and I2 have similar content, most part of H(I1) should be the same as H(I2). I1 and I2 refer to the GIS vector data, and H(I1) and H(I2) refer to hash function which is applied to I1and I2.
- **Collision:** If map I1 and I2 have different content, for most part of H(I1) should be different from H(I2).
- **Security:** If the key is unknown, the hash value could not be forged or estimated since it is generated using the key.
- **Complexity:** The algorithm of hash function should have low computational complexity.

GIS vector data might suffer coordinate transformation, projection transformation, data format transformation, data compression, and other operations. Although those operations changed the data information or structure, they do not influence the visual content of the map. Considering different render modes, it will lead to different visual domain information. As a result, the hash function is constructed by the topology relationship of data and the result is registered to CA for further protection. In the extraction stage, there is a possibility where the original data transferred by the network undergoes some normal operations, thus differences may appear between the extracted watermark and the registered one. The following formula is provided to measure the distance between extracted and registered watermark:

$$dis = norm\left(\frac{\left|hash_{new} - hash_{origin}\right|}{\sqrt{norm\left(hash_{new}\right) \cdot norm\left(hash_{origin}\right)}}\right) \tag{42}$$

where $hash_{new}$ is a hash value of test GIS vector data, $hash_{origin}$ is a hash value of original GIS vector data, and the norm refers to 2-norms. To determine the watermark authenticity, a threshold *T* is employed. Then, the authenticity is decided by

$$\begin{cases} dis \leq T & \text{Authentic} \\ dis > T & \text{Unauthentic} \end{cases} \tag{43}$$

An additional outstanding work was proposed by Hamadou, Sun, Gao, and Shah (2011) for protecting the integrity of relational databases. To enhance the security, a Message Authentication Code (MAC) was computed on a cryptographic hash function (e.g., SHA-1 or MD5) concatenated with the secret key in order to prevent unauthorized person to reproduce valid hash codes. The watermark was constructed based on the hash values of all attributes and was registered to CA for certification purpose. The result demonstrates that their scheme was effective in detecting malicious data alterations such as attribute value alteration, tuple insertion, and tuple deletion.

CONCLUSION AND FUTURE DIRECTIONS

In this chapter, we introduced a list of copyright protection schemes based on the direct feature-based method. In terms of copyright protection, employing the direct feature-based method could meet all the requirements such as transparency, robustness, unambiguity, security, and blindness. We then focused on the discussion of various multimedia copyright protection schemes based on the direct feature-based method, e.g., image, audio, text document, geospatial data, and relational databases. We argued that a good copyright protection scheme should be not only robust enough to acceptable manipulations, but also secure enough against malicious attacks. In addition, the direct feature-based method can be considered as a solution to trade-off problems between data payload and other two properties: fidelity and/or robustness. As a future research direction, it is reasonable to combine either visual secret sharing or encryption with the direct feature-based method in order to enhance its security against malicious attacks.

REFERENCES

Barni, M., & Bartolini, F. (2004). *Watermarking systems engineering: Enabling digital assets security and other applications*. New York, NY: Marcel Decker, Inc.

Barni, M., Bartolini, F., & Piva, A. (2001). Improved wavelet-based watermarking through pixel-wise masking. *IEEE Transactions on Image Processing, 10*(5), 783–791. doi:10.1109/83.918570

Chang, C. C., & Chuang, J. C. (2001). An image intellectual property protection scheme for gray-level images using visual secret sharing strategy. *Pattern Recognition Letters, 23*, 931–941. doi:10.1016/S0167-8655(02)00023-5

Chen, N., & Zhu, J. (2008). A robust zero-watermarking algorithm for audio. *EURASIP Journal on Advances in Signal Processing*. Retrieved from http://downloads.hindawi.com/journals/asp/2008/453580.pdf

Chen, T. H., Horng, G. B., & Lee, W. B. (2005). A publicly verifiable copyright-proving scheme resistant to malicious attacks. *IEEE Transactions on Industrial Electronics, 52*(1). doi:10.1109/TIE.2004.841083

Cox, I., & Miller, M. (2001). Electronic watermarking: The first 50 years. In *Proceedings of the IEEE Workshop on Multimedia Signal Processing*, (pp. 225–230). IEEE Press.

Cox, I. J., Kilian, J., Leighton, F. T., & Shamoon, T. (1997). Secure spread spectrum watermarking for multimedia. *IEEE Transactions on Image Processing, 6*(12), 1673–1687. doi:10.1109/83.650120

Cox, I. J., Miller, M. L., & Bloom, J. A. (2002). *Digital watermarking*. San Francisco, CA: Morgan Kauffman Publisher.

Craver, S., Memon, N., Yeo, B. L., & Yeung, M. M. (1997). On the invertibility of invisible watermarking techniques. In *Proceedings of IEEE International Conference on Image Processing (ICIP 1997)*. IEEE Press.

Cvejic, N., & Seppänen, T. (2005). Audio watermarking: Requirements, algorithms, and benchmarking . In Seitz, J. (Ed.), *Digital Watermarking for Digital Media* (pp. 135–181). Hershey, PA: IGI Global. doi:10.4018/978-1-59140-518-4.ch006

Fridrich, J., & Goljan, M. (2000). Robust hash functions for digital watermarking. In *Proceedings of the IEEE International Conference on Information Technology—Coding and Computing*, (pp. 178–183). IEEE Press.

Hamadou, A., Sun, X., Gao, L., & Shah, S. A. (2011). A fragile zero-watermarking technique for authentication of relational databases. *International Journal of Digital Content Technology and its Applications, 5*(5).

Hanqiang, C., & Hua, X. Xutao, Li., Miao, L., Sheng, Y., & Fang, W. (2006). A zero-watermarking algorithm based on DWT and chaotic modulation. In *Proceeding of SPIE*, (Vol. 6247). SPIE.

He, D., & Sun, Q. (2006). Multimedia authentication . In Zeng, W., Yu, H., & Lin, C. Y. (Eds.), *Multimedia Security Technologies for Digital Rights Management* (pp. 111–138). London, UK: Academic Press. doi:10.1016/B978-012369476-8/50007-5

Herrigel, A., Ruanaidh, J. O., Petersen, H., Pereira, S., & Pun, T. (1998). Secure copyright protection techniques for digital images. In *Proceedings of the Workshop on Information Hiding*. IEEE.

Hsieh, S. L., Hsu, L. Y., & Tsai, I. J. (2005). A copyright protection scheme for color images using secret sharing and wavelet transform . In *Proceedings of World Academy of Science, Engineering And Technology*. IEEE. doi:10.4304/jmm.3.4.42-49

Jalil, Z., Farooq, M., Zafar, H., Sabir, M., & Ashraf, E. (2010). Improved zero text watermarking algorithm against meaning preserving attacks. In *Proceedings of the World Academy of Science, Engineering and Technology*. IEEE.

Jalil, Z., Mirza, A. M., & Iqbal, T. (2010). A zero-watermarking algorithm for text documents based on structural components. In *Proceedings of the International Conference on Information and Emerging Technologies (ICIET)*. ICIET.

Jalil, Z., Mirza, A. M., & Sabir, M. (2010). Content based zero watermarking algorithm for authentication of text documents. *International Journal of Computer Science and Information Technology, 7*(2).

Khayam, S. A. (2003). *The discrete cosine transform (DCT): Theory and application*. East Lansing, MI: Michigan State University.

Lee, W. B., & Chen, T. H. (2002). A public verifiable copy protection technique for still images. *Journal of Systems and Software, 62*(3), 195–204. doi:10.1016/S0164-1212(01)00142-X

Li, A., Lin, B., Chen, Y., & Lü, G. (2008). Study on copyright authentication of GIS vector data based on zero-watermarking. *The International Archives of the Photogrammetry, Remote Sensing and Spatial Information Sciences, 37*(B4).

Li, F., Tiegang, G., & Qunting, Y. (2010). A novel zero-watermark copyright authentication scheme based on lifting wavelet and harris corner detection. *Wuhan University Journal of Natural Sciences, 15*(5).

Lou, D. C., Tso, H. K., & Liu, J. L. (2006). A copyright protection scheme for digital images using visual cryptography technique. *Journal of Computer Standards and Interfaces, 29*(1), 125–131. doi:10.1016/j.csi.2006.02.003

Ma, J. H., Guan, Y. J., & Zhao, Y. H. (2007). A method of zero-watermarking based on lifting wavelet. In *Proceeding of the 2007 International Conference on Wavelet Analysis and Pattern Recognition*. IEEE.

Maxemchuk, N. F., & Low, S. (1997). Marking text documents. In *Proceedings of the IEEE International Conference on Image Processing*, (pp. 13–16). IEEE Press.

Naor, N., & Shamir, A. (1995). Visual cryptography. *Proceedings of Advances in Cryptology: Eurocrypt, 1994*, 1–12.

Petitcolas, F. A., & Kirovski, D. (2002). The blind pattern matching attack on watermark systems. In *Proceedings of IEEE International Conference on Acoustics, Speech, and Signal Processing*, (vol. 4), (pp. 3740–3743). IEEE Press.

Revenkar, P. S., Anjum, A., & Gandhare, W. Z. (2010). Survey of visual cryptography schemes. *International Journal of Security and Its Applications*, *4*(2).

Sang, J., Liao, X., & Alam, M. S. (2006). Neural-network-based zero-watermark scheme for digital images. *Optical Engineering (Redondo Beach, Calif.)*, 45.

Seitz, J., & Jahnke, T. (2005). Digital watermarking: An introduction . In Seitz, J. (Ed.), *Digital Watermarking for Digital Media* (p. 13). Hershey, PA: IGI Global. doi:10.4018/978-1-59140-518-4.ch001

Sun, T., Quan, W., & Wang, S. (2002). Zero-watermark watermarking for image authentication. In *Proceeding of the Fourth IASTED International Conference Signal and Image Processing*. IASTED.

Tsai, M. J., Yu, K. Y., & Chen, Y. Z. (2000). Joint wavelet and spatial transformation for digital watermarking. *IEEE Transactions on Consumer Electronics*, *46*(1), 241–245.

Wang, R., & Hu, W. (2007). Robust audio zero-watermark based on LWT and chaotic modulation. In *Proceeding of International Workshop on Digital Watermarking (IWDW 2007)*, (pp. 373–381). IWDW.

Wang, W. X., Xu, H. L., & Li, S. (2009). Double zero-watermarking algorithm on hyperchaotic iteration. In *Proceedings of the Third International Symposium on Intelligent Information Technology Application*. IEEE.

Wang, X.-Y., & Zhao, H. (2006). A novel synchronization invariant audio watermarking scheme based on DWT and DCT. *IEEE Transactions on Signal Processing*, *54*(12), 4835–4840. doi:10.1109/TSP.2006.881258

ADDITIONAL READING

Chen, T. H., Chang, C. C., Wu, C. S., & Lou, D. C. (2009). On the security of a copyright protection scheme based on visual cryptography. *Computer Standards & Interfaces*, *31*, 1–5. doi:10.1016/j.csi.2007.09.001

Craver, S., Memon, N., Yeo, B. L., & Yeung, M. M. (1998). Resolving rightful ownerships with invisible watermarking techniques: Limitations, attacks, and implications. *IEEE Journal on Selected Areas in Communications*, *16*(4). doi:10.1109/49.668979

Jaseena, K. U., & John, A. (2011). An invisible zero watermarking algorithm using combined image and text for protecting text documents. *International Journal on Computer Science and Engineering (IJCSE)*, *3*(6).

Koval, O., Voloshynovskiy, S., Bas, P., & Cayre, F. (2009). On security threats for robust perceptual hashing. In *Proceedings of SPIE Media Forensics Security*, (vol. 7254), (pp. 72540H–72540H-13). SPIE.

Revenkar, P. S., Anisa Anjum, & Gandhare, W. Z. (2010). Survey of visual cryptography schemes. *International Journal of Security and Its Applications*, *4*(2).

KEY TERMS AND DEFINITIONS

Certification Authority: The trusted third party which aim at issuing a certificate to the owner. The certificate attaches an owner's identity and his/her secret information. Based on the certificate, anyone can ascertain that secret information belongs to a particular person.

Copyright Protection Scheme Based on Direct Feature-Based Method: It refers to zero watermarking or lossless watermarking. Most zero-watermarking algorithms adopt direct feature-based method and are intended to copyright protection.

Direct: Feature-Based: One of categories in media signature scheme. A media signature is generated by signing features of the original image using sender's private key.

Media Signature Scheme: Extension of digital signature scheme that incorporates feature extraction process prior to hash computation process.

Multimedia Copyright Protection: Mechanism to prevent or deter unauthorized copying of digital media.

Traditional Watermarking: Process of embedding information or watermark into digital signal in a way that is difficult to remove. Due to embedding process, it is expected to be difficult to distinguish between original signals and watermarked one for human visual system.

Zero-Watermarking: To solve an inherent problem in traditional watermarking such as quality degradation, and trade-off between robustness and imperceptibility, the watermark is not embedded into digital signal but is combined with extracted feature of digital signal to generate secret information. For further protection, the secret information is registered to trusted party.

Compilation of References

Aarts, R. M., Larsen, E., & Schobben, D. (2002). Improving perceived bass and reconstruction of high frequencies for band limited signals. In *Proceedings of IEEE Benelux Workshop on Model based Processing and Coding of Audio (MPCA-2002)*, (pp. 59-71). IEEE Press.

Agarwal, C., Mishra, A., & Sharma, A. (2011). Genetic algorithm-backpropagation network hybrid architecture for grayscale image watermarking in DCT domain. In *Proceedings of the 7th International Conference on Intelligent Information Hiding and Multimedia Signal Processing*, (pp. 177-180). Dalian, China: IEEE.

Aiba, E., & Tsuzaki, M. (2007). Perceptual judgement in synchronization of two complex tones: Relation to the cochlear delays. *Acoustical Science and Technology*, *28*(5), 357–359. doi:10.1250/ast.28.357

Aiba, E., Tsuzaki, M., Tanaka, S., & Unoki, M. (2008). Judgment of perceptual synchrony between two pulses and verification of its relation to cochlear delay by an auditory model. *The Japanese Psychological Research*, *50*(4), 204–213. doi:10.1111/j.1468-5884.2008.00376.x

Akagi, M., & Yasutake, K. (1998). *Perception of time-related information: Influence of phase variation on timbre. Technical report of IEICE*. IEICE.

Alattar, A. M. (2004). Reversible watermark using the difference expansion of a generalized integer transform. *IEEE Transactions on Image Processing*, *13*(8), 1147–1156. doi:10.1109/TIP.2004.828418

Anand, D., & Niranjan, U. C. (1998). Watermarking medical images with patient information. In *Proceedings of the 20th Annual International Conference of the IEEE Engineering in Medicine and Biology Society*, (pp. 703-706). Hong Kong, China: IEEE Press.

Anckaert, B., Sutter, B. D., Chanet, D., & Bosschere, K. D. (2005). Steganography for executables and code transformation signatures. In *Proceedings of the Information Security and Cryptology—ICISC 2004*, (pp. 7-10). ICISC.

Ando, K., Kobayashi, H., & Kiya, H. (2002). A method for embedding binary data into JPEG2000 bit streams based on the layer structure. In *Proceedings of 2002 EURASIP EUSIPCO*, (vol 3), (pp. 89–92). EURASIP.

Anoto. (2012). *Website*. Retrieved from http://www.anoto.com

Aoki, N. (2003). A packet loss concealment technique for VoIP using steganography. In *Proceedings of the IEEE 2003 International Symposium on Intelligent Signal Processing and Communication Systems (ISPACS 2003)*, (pp. 470-473). Awaji Island, Japan: IEEE Press.

Aoki, N. (2004). Modification of two-side pitch waveform replication technique for VoIP packet loss concealment using steganography. In *Proceedings of the IEICE and IEEK 2004 International Technical Conference on Circuits/Systems, Computers and Communications (ITC-CSCC 2004)*. Matsushima, Japan: IEICE/IEEK.

Aoki, N. (2004). VoIP packet loss concealment based on two-side pitch waveform replication technique using steganography. In *Proceedings of the IEEE Region 10 Conference TENCON*, (pp. 52-55). Chiang Mai, Thailand: IEEE Press.

Aoki, N. (2006). A band extension technique for G.711 speech using steganography. *IEICE Transactions on Communications*, *89*(B), 1896-1898.

Aoki, N. (2007). Potential of value-added speech communications by using steganography. In *Proceedings of the 3rd International Conference on Intelligent Information Hiding and Multimedia Signal Processing*, (pp. 251-254). IEEE.

Aoki, N. (2008). Improvement of band extension technique for G.711 telephony speech based on full wave rectification. In *Proceedings of the 11th International Conference on Digital Audio Effects (DAFx-08)*, (pp. 161-164). Espoo, Finland: DAFx.

Apple Inc. (2008). *iTunes*. Retrieved from http://www.apple.com/itunes/download

Arnold, M. (2000). *Audio watermarking: Features, applications, and algorithms.* Paper presented at the IEEE International Conference on Multimedia and Expo. New York, NY.

Artz, D. (2001). Digital steganography: Hiding data within data. *IEEE Internet Computing*, *5*(3), 75–80. doi:10.1109/4236.935180

ATR. (1997). *Speech dialogue database for spontaneous speech recognition.* ATR.

Babadi, B., Kalouptsidis, N., & Tarokh, V. (2010). SPARLS: The sparse RLS algorithm. *IEEE Transactions on Signal Processing*, *58*(8), 4013–4025. doi:10.1109/TSP.2010.2048103

Babaguchi, N. (2011). *Multimedia processing for rights protection*. Paper presented at the 1st Meeting of the IEICE Technical Group on Enriched Multimedia. Tokyo, Japan.

Baraniuk, R. G. (2007). Compressive sensing. *IEEE Signal Processing Magazine*, *24*(4), 118–121. doi:10.1109/MSP.2007.4286571

Barnett, R., & Pearson, D. E. (1998). Frequency mode LR attack operator for digitally watermarked images. *Electronics Letters*, *34*(19), 1837–1838. doi:10.1049/el:19981323

Barni, M., & Bartolini, F. (2004). *Watermarking systems engineering: Enabling digital assets security and other applications*. New York, NY: Marcel Decker, Inc.

Barni, M., Bartolini, F., Cappellini, V., & Piva, A. (1998). A DCT-domain system for robust image watermarking. *Signal Processing*, *66*(3), 357–372. doi:10.1016/S0165-1684(98)00015-2

Barni, M., Bartolini, F., & Piva, A. (2001). Improved wavelet-based watermarking through pixel-wise masking. *IEEE Transactions on Image Processing*, *10*(5), 783–791. doi:10.1109/83.918570

Barreto, P. S. L. M., Kim, H. Y., & Rijmen, V. (2002). Toward secure public-key blockwise fragile authentication watermarking. *IEEE Proceedings-Vision Image and Signal Processing*, *149*(2), 57-62.

Bassia, P., & Pitas, I. P. (1998). Robust audio watermarking in the time domain. In *Proceedings of EUSIPCO 1998, European Signal Processing Conference*, (pp. 25-28). EUSIPCO.

Bassia, P., & Pitas, I. (2001). Robust audio watermarking in the time domain. *IEEE Transactions on Multimedia*, *3*(2), 232–241. doi:10.1109/6046.923822

Beerends, J. G., Hekstra, A. P., Rix, A. W., & Hollier, M. P. (2002). Perceptual Evaluation of speech quality (PESQ): The new ITU standard for end-to-end speech quality assessment, part 2 – Psychoacoustic model. *Journal of the Audio Engineering Society. Audio Engineering Society*, *50*(10), 765–778.

Bender, W., Gruhl, D., Morimoto, N., & Lu, A. (1996). Techniques for data hiding. *IBM System Journey*, *35*(3), 313–336. doi:10.1147/sj.353.0313

Bennett, K. (2004). *Linguistic steganography: Survey, analysis, and robustness concerns for hiding information in text*. Lafayette, IN: Purdue University.

Bioucas, J., & Figueiredo, M. (2007). A new TwIST: Two-step iterative shrinkage/thresholding algorithms for image restoration. *IEEE Transactions on Image Processing*, *16*(12), 2992–3004. doi:10.1109/TIP.2007.909319

Blauert, J. (1983). *Spatial hearing: The psychophysics of human sound localization*. Cambridge, MA: MIT Press. doi:10.1121/1.392109

Blauert, J. (1997). *Spatial hearing*. Cambridge, MA: The MIT Press.

Bloom, J. A., Cox, I. J., Kalker, T., Linnartz, J. P. M. G., Miller, M. L., & Traw, C. B. S. (1999). Copy protection for DVD video. *Proceedings of the IEEE*, *87*(7), 1267–1276. doi:10.1109/5.771077

Blumensath, T., & Davies, M. E. (2008). Gradient pursuits. *IEEE Transactions on Signal Processing*, *56*(6), 2370–2382. doi:10.1109/TSP.2007.916124

Blundo, C., & Galdi, C. (2003). Hiding information in image mosaics. *The Computer Journal*, *46*(2), 202–212. doi:10.1093/comjnl/46.2.202

Bogomjakov, A., Gotsman, C., & Isenburg, M. (2008). *Distortion-free steganography for polygonal meshes*. Paper presented at Eurographics 2008. Crete, Greece.

Boney, L., Tewfik, A., & Hamdy, K. N. (1996). Digital watermarks for audio signals. In *Proceedings of the IEEE International Conference on Multimedia Computing and Systems*, (pp. 473-480). IEEE Press.

Braci, S., Boyer, R., & Delpha, C. (2010). Analysis of the resistance of the spread transform against temporal frame averaging attack. In *Proceedings of 2010 IEEE 17th International Conference on Image Processing*, (pp. 213-216). IEEE Press.

Brans, E., Brombach, B., Zeidler, T., & Bimber, O. (2007). Enabling mobile phones to support large-scale museum guidance. *Journal of IEEE Multimedia*, *14*(2), 16–25. doi:10.1109/MMUL.2007.33

Brassil, J. T., Low, S., Maxemchunk, N. F., & O'Gorman, L. (1995). Electronic marking and identification techniques to discourage document copying. *IEEE Journal on Selected Areas in Communications*, *13*(8), 1495–1504. doi:10.1109/49.464718

Breebaart, J., & Faller, C. (2007). *Spatial audio processing*. West Sussex, UK: John Wiley & Sons. doi:10.1002/9780470723494

Broom, S. R. (2006). VoIP quality assessment: Taking account of the edge-device. *IEEE Transactions on Audio. Speech & Language Processing*, *14*(6), 1977–1983. doi:10.1109/TASL.2006.883233

Burg, J. P. (1975). *Maximum entropy spectral analysis*. (Doctoral dissertation). Stanford University. Palo Alto, CA. Retrieved from http://sepwww.stanford.edu/theses/sep06/

Caldelli, R., Filippini, F., & Becarelli, R. (2010). Reversible watermarking techniques: An overview and a classification. *European Association for Signal Processing Journal on Information Security, 2*.

Candès, E. J., Romberg, J., & Tao, T. (2006). Robust uncertainty principles: exact signal reconstruction from highly incomplete frequency information. *IEEE Transactions on Information Theory*, *52*(2), 489–509. doi:10.1109/TIT.2005.862083

Cano, P., Batlle, E., Kalker, T., & Haitsma, J. (2002). A review of algorithms for audio fingerprinting. In *Proceedings of the 2002 IEEE Workshop on Multimedia Signal Processing*, (169-173). IEEE Press.

Caronni, G. (1995). *Reliable IT systems*. Wiesbaden, Germany: Vieweg Publishing Company.

Carroll, L. (1871). *Through the looking-glass, and what alice found there*. London, UK: Macmillan.

Celik, M., Sharma, G., & Tekalp, A. M. (2005). Pitch and duration modification for speech watermarking. In *Proceedings of IEEE International Conference on Acoustics, Speech, and Signal Processing*, (pp. 17-20). Philadelphia, PA: IEEE Press.

Celik, M. U., Sharma, G., Saber, E., & Tekalp, A. M. (2002). Hierarchical watermarking for secure image authentication with localization. *IEEE Transactions on Image Processing*, *11*(6), 585–595. doi:10.1109/TIP.2002.1014990

Celik, M. U., Sharma, G., Saber, E., & Tekalp, A. M. (2006). Lossless watermarking for image authentication: A new framework and an implementation. *Institute of Electrical and Electronics Engineers Transactions on Image Processing*, *15*(4), 1042–1049.

Chan, P., Hui, L., & Yiu, S.-M. (2011). Dynamic software birthmark for java based on heap memory analysis. In *Proceedings of the Communications and Multimedia Security*, (pp. 94-107). IEEE.

Chang, C.-Y., & Clark, S. (2010). Practical linguistic steganography using contextual synonym substitution and vertex colour coding. In *Proceedings of the 2010 Conference on Empirical Methods in Natural Language Processing*, (pp. 1194-1203). IEEE.

Chang, C. C., Chen, G. M., & Lin, M. H. (2004). Information hiding based on search-order coding for VQ indices. *Pattern Recognition Letters*, *25*(11), 1253–1261. doi:10.1016/j.patrec.2004.04.003

Chang, C. C., & Chuang, J. C. (2001). An image intellectual property protection scheme for gray-level images using visual secret sharing strategy. *Pattern Recognition Letters*, *23*, 931–941. doi:10.1016/S0167-8655(02)00023-5

Chang, C. C., Fan, Y. H., & Tai, W. L. (2008). Four-scanning attack on hierarchical digital watermarking method for image tamper detection and recovery. *Pattern Recognition*, *41*(2), 654–661. doi:10.1016/j.patcog.2007.06.003

Checkmark. (2001). *Checkmark*. Retrieved from http://cvml.unige.ch/ResearchProjects/Watermarking/Checkmark/

Chen, B., & Wornell, G. W. (1998). *Digital watermarking and information embedding using dither modulation*. Paper presented at the IEEE Second Workshop on Multimedia Signal Processing. Santa Clara, CA.

Chen, N., & Zhu, J. (2008). A robust zero-watermarking algorithm for audio. *EURASIP Journal on Advances in Signal Processing*. Retrieved from http://downloads.hindawi.com/journals/asp/2008/453580.pdf

Chen, B., & Wornell, G. W. (2001). Quantization index modulation: A class of provably good methods for digital watermarking and information embedding. *IEEE Transactions on Information Theory*, *47*(4), 1423–1443. doi:10.1109/18.923725

Cheng, Q., & Sorensen, J. (2001). Spread spectrum signaling for speech watermarking. In *Proceedings of IEEE International Conference on Acoustics, Speech, and Signal Processing*, (pp. 1337-1349). Salt Lake City, UT: IEEE Press.

Chen, G. R., Mao, Y. B., & Chui, C. K. (2004). A symmetric image encryption scheme based on 3D chaotic cat maps. *Chaos, Solitons, and Fractals*, *21*(3), 749–761. doi:10.1016/j.chaos.2003.12.022

Cheng, H., & Li, X. B. (2000). Partial encryption of compressed images and videos. *IEEE Transactions on Signal Processing*, *48*(8), 2439–2451. doi:10.1109/78.852023

Chen, T. H., Horng, G. B., & Lee, W. B. (2005). A publicly verifiable copyright-proving scheme resistant to malicious attacks. *IEEE Transactions on Industrial Electronics*, *52*(1). doi:10.1109/TIE.2004.841083

Chitprasert, B., & Rao, K. R. (1990). Human visual weighted progressive image transmission. *IEEE Transactions on Communications*, *38*, 1040–1044. doi:10.1109/26.57501

Choi, S., Park, H., Lim, H.-I., & Han, T. (2007). A static birthmark of binary executables based on API call structure. In *Proceedings of the Advances in Computer Science — ASIAN 2007*, (pp. 2-16). ASIAN.

Chou, L. D., Wu, C. H., Ho, S. P., Lee, C. C., & Chen, J. M. (2004). Requirement analysis and implementation of palm-based multimedia museum guide systems. In *Proceedings of IEEE 18th International Conference on Advanced Information Networking and Applications*, (Vol. 1), (pp. 352-357). IEEE Press.

Collberg, C., & Thomborson, C. (1999). Software watermarking: Models and dynamic embeddings. In *Proceedings of the 26th ACM SIGPLAN-SIGACT Symposium on Principles of Programming Languages*, (pp. 311-324). ACM Press.

Collberg, C., Kobourov, S., Carter, E., & Thomborson, C. (2003). Error-correcting graphs for software watermarking. In *Proceedings of the Graph-Theoretic Concepts in Computer Science*, (pp. 156-167). IEEE.

Collberg, C., Myles, G., & Huntwork, A. (2003). Sandmark — A tool for software protection research. *IEEE Security and Privacy*, *1*(4), 40–49. doi:10.1109/MSECP.2003.1219058

Connell, W., Tamir, D., & Guirguis, M. (2010). Prime-based mimic functions for the implementation of covert channels. In *Proceedings of the IEEE International Conference on Wireless Communications, Networking and Information Security 2010*, (pp. 538-543). IEEE Press.

Conotter, V., Boato, G., Carli, M., & Egiazarian, K. (2010). Near lossless reversible data hiding based on adaptive prediction. In *Proceedings of the International Conference on Image Processing of Institute of Electrical and Electronics Engineers*, (pp. 2585-2588). Hong Kong, China: IEEE.

Coppersmith, D., Mintzer, F. C., Tresser, C. P., Wu, C. W., & Yeung, M. M. (1999). Fragile imperceptible digital watermark with privacy control. In P. M. Wong (Ed.), *Conference on Security and Watermarking of Multimedia Contents,* (pp. 79-84). San Jose, CA: IEEE.

Cox, I. J. (1998). *Spread spectrum watermark for embedded signaling*. United States Patent 5,848,155. Washington, DC: US Patent Office.

Cox, I. J., & Miller, M. L. (1997). A review of watermarking and the importance of perceptual modeling. In *Proceedings of SPIE Conference of Human Vision and Electronic Imaging II*, (vol 3016), (pp. 92-99). San Jose, CA: SPIE.

Cox, I., & Miller, M. (2001). Electronic watermarking: The first 50 years. In *Proceedings of the IEEE Workshop on Multimedia Signal Processing,* (pp. 225-230). Cannes, France: IEEE Press.

Cox, I., Kilian, J., Leighton, T., & Shamoon, T. (1995). *Secure spread spectrum watermarking for multimedia.* Technical Report 95-10. Princeton, NJ: NEX Research Institute.

Cox, I. J., Kilian, J., Leighton, F. T., & Shanmoon, T. (1997). Secure spread spectrum watermarking for multimedia. *IEEE Transactions on Image Processing*, *6*(12), 1673–1687. doi:10.1109/83.650120

Cox, I. J., Miller, M. L., & Bloom, J. A. (2002). *Digital watermarking.* San Diego, CA: Academic Press.

Cox, I. J., Miller, M. L., Bloom, J. A., Fridrich, J., & Kalker, T. (2008). *Digital watermarking and steganography* (2nd ed.). Burlington, MA: Morgan Kaufmann.

Cox, I., Miller, M., Bloom, J., Fridrich, J., & Kalker, T. (2008). *Digital watermarking and steganography* (2nd ed.). San Francisco, CA: Morgan Kaufmann Publishers.

Craver, S., Memon, N., Yeo, B. L., & Yeung, M. M. (1997). On the invertibility of invisible watermarking techniques. In *Proceedings of IEEE International Conference on Image Processing (ICIP 1997).* IEEE Press.

Craver, S., Memon, N., Yeo, B. L., & Yeung, M. (1996). *Can invisible watermarking resolve rightful ownership? IBM Research Report*. Armonk, NY: IBM.

Craver, S., Memon, N., Yeo, B. L., & Yeung, M. (1998). Resolving rightful ownerships with invisible watermarking technique: Limitations, attacks, and implications. *IEEE Journal on Selected Areas in Communications*, *16*, 573–586. doi:10.1109/49.668979

Curran, D., Hurley, N. J., & Cinnéide, M. Ó. (2003). Securing java through software watermarking. In *Proceedings of the 2nd International Conference on Principles and Practice of Programming in Java,* (pp. 145-148). IEEE.

Cvejic, N., & Seppänen, T. (2001). *Improving audio watermarking scheme using psychoacoustic watermark filtering*. Paper presented at the 1st IEEE International Symposium on Signal Processing and Information Technology. Cairo, Egypt.

Cvejic, N., & Seppänen, T. (2003). *Robust audio watermarking in wavelet domain using frequency hopping and patchwork method.* Paper presented at the third International Symposium on Image and Signal Processing and Analysis. Rome, Italy.

Cvejic, N., & Seppänen, T. (2004). Spread spectrum audio watermarking using frequency hopping and attack characterization. *Signal Processing*, *84*, 207–213. doi:10.1016/j.sigpro.2003.10.016

Cvejic, N., & Seppänen, T. (2005). Audio watermarking: Requirements, algorithms, and benchmarking. In Seitz, J. (Ed.), *Digital Watermarking for Digital Media* (pp. 135–181). Hershey, PA: IGI Global. doi:10.4018/978-1-59140-518-4.ch006

Cvejic, N., & Seppänen, T. (2005). Increasing robustness of LSB audio steganography by reduced distortion LSD coding. *Journal of Universal Computer Science*, *11*(1), 56–65.

Cvejic, N., & Seppänen, T. (2008). Introduction to digital audio watermarking. In Cvejic, N., & Seppänen, T. (Eds.), *Digital Audio Watermarking Techniques and Technologies* (pp. 1–10). Hershey, PA: IGI Global.

Cvejic, N., & Seppänen, T. (Eds.). (2008). *Digital audio watermarking techniques and technologies*. Hershey, PA: IGI Global.

Dai, W., Yu, Y., & Deng, B. (2009). BinText steganography based on Markov state transferring probability. In *Proceedings of the 2nd International Conference on Interaction Sciences: Information Technology, Culture and Human,* (pp. 1306-1311). IEEE.

Dalkilic, O., Ekrem, E., Varlik, S. E., & Mihcak, M. K. (2010). A detection theoretic approach to digital fingerprinting with focused receivers under uniform linear averaging Gaussian attacks. *IEEE Transactions on Information Forensics and Security, 5*(4), 658–669. doi:10.1109/TIFS.2010.2078505

Dau, T., Wegner, O., Mallert, V., & Kollmeier, B. (2000). Auditory brainstem responses (ABR) with optimized chirp signals compensating basilar membrane dispersion. *The Journal of the Acoustical Society of America, 107,* 1530–1540. doi:10.1121/1.428438

de Boer, E. (1980). Auditory physics, physical principles in hearing theory I. *Physics Reports, 62,* 87–187. doi:10.1016/0370-1573(80)90100-3

de Boor, C. (1978). *A practical guide to splines.* New York, NY: Springer-Verlag. doi:10.1007/978-1-4612-6333-3

Deller, J. R. Jr, Hansen, J. H. L., & Proakis, J. G. (2000). *Discrete time processing of speech signals* (2nd ed.). New York, NY: IEEE Press.

Deshpande, A., & Prabhu, K. M. M. (2009). A substitution-by-interpolation algorithm for watermarking audio. *Signal Processing, 89,* 218–225. doi:10.1016/j.sigpro.2008.07.015

Desoky, A., Younis, M., & El-Sayed, H. (2008). Auto-summarization-based steganography. In *Proceedings of the International Conference on Innovations in Information Technology 2008,* (pp. 608-612). IEEE.

Desoky, A., & Younis, M. (2009). Chestega: Chess steganography methodology. *Security and Communication Networks, 2*(6), 555–566.

Dey, S., Al-Qaheri, H., & Sanyal, S. (2010). *Embedding secret data in HTML web page.* Retrieved from http://www.arxiv.org

Diehl, M. (2008). Secure covert channels in multiplayer games. In *Proceedings of the 10th ACM Workshop on Multimedia and Security,* (pp. 117-122). ACM Press.

Digital Signal Processing Committee. (1979). *Programs for digital signal processing.* Piscataway, NJ: IEEE Press.

Dittmann, J., Megias, D., Lang, A., & Herrera-Joancomarti, J. (2006). Theoretical framework for a practical evaluation and comparison of audio watermarking schemes in the triangle of robustness, transparency and capacity. *Lecture Notes in Computer Science, 4300,* 1–40. doi:10.1007/11926214_1

Doermann, D., & Rosenfeld, A. (1995). Recovery of temporal information from static images of handwriting. *International Journal of Computer Vision, 15*(1-2), 143–164. doi:10.1007/BF01450853

Doerr, G., & Dugelay, J. L. (2003). A guide tour of video watermarking. *Signal Processing Image Communication, 18*(4), 263–282. doi:10.1016/S0923-5965(02)00144-3

Donoho, D. L. (2006). Compressive sensing. *IEEE Transactions on Information Theory, 52*(4), 1289–1306. doi:10.1109/TIT.2006.871582

Dumitrescu, S., Wu, X., & Wang, Z. (2003). Detection of LSB steganography via sample pair analysis. *IEEE Transactions on Signal Processing, 51*(7), 1995–2007. doi:10.1109/TSP.2003.812753

Eggers, J. J., Bauml, R., & Girod, B. (2002). A communications approach to image steganography. *Proceedings of the Society for Photo-Instrumentation Engineers, 4675,* 26–37. doi:10.1117/12.465284

El-Khalil, R., & Keromytis, A. D. (2004). Hydan: Hiding information in program binaries. In *Proceedings of the International Conference on Information and Communications Security,* (pp. 187-199). IEEE.

Elliot, L. L. (1969). Masking of tones before, during, and after brief silent periods in noise. *The Journal of the Acoustical Society of America, 45,* 1277–1279. doi:10.1121/1.1911600

Epps, J., & Holmes, W. H. (1999). A new technique for wideband enhancement of coded narrowband speech. In *Proceedings of the IEEE Workshop on Speech Coding,* (pp. 174-176). IEEE Press.

Fallahpour, M., & Megias, D. (2009). High capacity audio watermarking using FFT amplitude interpolation. *IEICE Electronics Express, 6*(14), 1057–1063. doi:10.1587/elex.6.1057

Farid, H. (2002). Detecting hidden messages using higher-order statistical models. In *Proceedings of the International Conference on Image Processing 2002*, (vol 2), (pp. 905-908). IEEE.

Farid, H. (2009). Image forgery dection. *IEEE Signal Processing Magazine*, *26*(2), 16–25. doi:10.1109/MSP.2008.931079

Feng, B., Zhang, M., Xu, G., Niu, X., & Hu, Z. (2009). Dynamic data flow graph-based software watermarking. In *Proceedings of the International Conference on Network Infrastructure and Digital Content, 2009*, (pp. 1029-1033). IEEE.

Feng, H., Ling, H., Zou, F., Lu, Z., & Chen, J. (2009). A performance evaluation of collusion attacks in multimedia fingerprinting. In *Proceedings of the International Conference on Multimedia Information Networking and Security*, (pp. 530-534). IEEE.

Foo, S. W. (2008). Three techniques of digital audio watermarking. In Cvejic, N., & Seppanen, T. (Eds.), *Digital Audio Watermarking Techniques and Technologies* (pp. 104–122). Hershey, PA: IGI Global.

Foote, J., Adcock, J., & Girgensohn, A. (2003). Time base modulation: A new approach to watermarking audio. In *Proceedings of International Conference on Multimedia and Expo*, (pp. 221-224). Baltimore, MD: IEEE.

Fridrich, J., & Du, R. (1999). Steganographic methods for palette images. In *Proceedings of the Third International Workshop on Information Hiding*, (pp. 47–60). IEEE.

Fridrich, J., & Goljan, M. (1999). Images with self-correcting capabilities. In *Proceedings of the 1999 International Conference on Image Processing*, (pp. 792-796). Kobe, Japan: IEEE Press.

Fridrich, J., & Goljan, M. (2000). Robust hash functions for digital watermarking. In *Proceedings of the IEEE International Conference on Information Technology—Coding and Computing*, (pp. 178–183). IEEE Press.

Fridrich, J. (2009). Digital image forensics. *IEEE Signal Processing Magazine*, *26*(2), 26–37. doi:10.1109/MSP.2008.931078

Fridrich, J., Goljan, M., & Du, R. (2001). Invertible authentication. *Proceedings of the Society for Photo-Instrumentation Engineers*, *4314*, 197–208. doi:10.1117/12.435400

Fridrich, J., Goljan, M., & Du, R. (2001). Reliable detection of LSB steganography in color and grayscale images. *IEEE MultiMedia*, *8*, 22–28. doi:10.1109/93.959097

Fridrich, J., Goljan, M., & Du, R. (2002). Lossless data embedding: new paradigm in digital watermarking. *EURASIP Journal on Applied Signal Processing*, *1*, 185–196. doi:10.1155/S1110865702000537

Fridrich, J., Goljan, M., & Hogea, D. (2003). New methodology for breaking steganographic techniques for JPEGs. *Proceedings of the Society for Photo-Instrumentation Engineers*, *5020*, 143–155. doi:10.1117/12.473142

Fujii, Y., Nakano, K., Echizen, I., & Yoshiura, H. (2005). *Method of watermarking for binary images*. US Patent 2005 0 025 333. Washington, DC: US Patent Office.

Fujimoto, R., Iwaki, M., & Kiryu, T. (2006). A method of high bit-rate data hiding in music using spline interpolation. In *Proceedings of the 2006 International Conference on Intelligent Information Hiding and Multimedia*, (pp. 11-14). Pasadena, CA: IEEE.

Fujiyoshi, M., Sato, S., Jin, H., & Kiya, H. (2007). A location-map free reversible data hiding method using block-based single parameter. In *Proceedings of the International Conference on Image Processing of Institute of Electrical and Electronics Engineers*, (pp. 257-260). San Antonio, TX: IEEE.

Fujiyoshi, M., Tsuneyoshi, T., & Kiya, H. (2010). A parameter memorization-free lossless data hiding method with flexible payload size. *Institute of Electronics. Information and Communication Engineers Electronics Express*, *7*(23), 1702–1708.

Funk, W., & Schmucker, M. (2001). High capacity information hiding in music scores. In *Proceedings of the First International Conference on Web Delivering of Music*, (pp. 12-19). IEEE.

Geiger, R., Sporer, T., Koller, J., & Brandenburg, K. (2001). *Audio coding based on integer transforms*. Paper presented at the 111th Audio Engineering Society Convention. New York, NY.

Geiger, R., Yokotani, Y., & Schuller, G. (2006). *Audio data hiding with high data rates based on Int-MDCT*. Paper presented at IEEE International Conference on Acoustics, Speech and Signal Processing. Toulouse, France.

Geiser, B., & Vary, P. (2007). *Backwards compatible wideband telephony in mobile networks: CELP watermarking and bandwidth extension*. Paper presented at IEEE International Conference on Acoustics, Speech and Signal Processing. Honolulu, HI.

Gibson, J. D., Berger, T., Lookabaugh, T., Lindberg, D., & Baker, R. L. (1998). *Digital compression for multimedia*. San Francisco, CA: Morgan-Kaufmann.

Goljan, M., Fridrich, J., & Holotyak, T. (2006). New blind steganalysis and its implications. In *Proceedings of the SPIE, Electronic Imaging, Security, Steganography, and Watermarking of Multimedia Contents VIII*, (vol 6072), (pp. 1–13). SPIE.

Gordy, J. D., & Bruton, L. T. (2000). Performance evaluation of digital audio watermarking algorithms. In *Proceedings of IEEE Midwest Symposium on Circuits and Systems*, (pp. 456-459). IEEE Press.

Gorodnitsky, I. F., & Rao, B. D. (1997). Sparse signal reconstruction from limited data using FOCUSS: A re-weighted norm minimization algorithm. *IEEE Transactions on Signal Processing*, *45*(3), 600–616. doi:10.1109/78.558475

Goto, M., Hashiguchi, H., Nishimura, T., & Oka, R. (2003). *RWC music database: Music genre database and musical instrument sound database*. Paper presented at the 4th International Conference on Music Information Retrieval. Baltimore, MD.

Gross-Amblard, D., Rigaux, P., Abrouk, L., & Cullot, N. (2009). Fingering watermarking in symbolic digital scores. In *Proceedings of the 10th International Symposium on Music Information Retrieval*, (pp. 141-146). IEEE.

Grothoff, C., Grothoff, K., Alkhutova, L., Stutsman, R., & Atallah, M. (2005). Translation-based steganography. In *Proceedings of Information Hiding* (pp. 219–233). IEEE. doi:10.1007/11558859_17

Gruhl, D., Lu, A., & Bender, W. (1996). Echo hiding. In *Proceedings of Information Hiding 1st Workshop*, (pp. 295-315). IEEE.

Gruhl, D., Lu, A., & Bender, W. (1996). Echo hiding. *Lecture Notes in Computer Science*, *1174*, 295–315. doi:10.1007/3-540-61996-8_48

Guimbretière, F. (2003). Paper augmented digital documents. In *Proceedings of the 16th Annual ACM Symposium on User Interface Software and Technology*, (pp. 51-60). ACM Press.

Gurijala, A. R., & Deller, J. R., Jr. (2003). Speech watermarking by parametric embedding with an l_∞ fidelity criterion. In *Proceedings of EUROSPEECH-2003/INTERSPEECH-2003*, (pp. 2933-2936). Geneva, Switzerland: EUROSPEECH.

Hai Bin, H., Susanto, R., Rongshan, Y., & Xiao, L. (2004). *A fast algorithm of integer MDCT for lossless audio coding*. Paper presented at IEEE International Conference on Acoustics, Speech and Signal Processing. Quebec, Canada.

Hamadou, A., Sun, X., Gao, L., & Shah, S. A. (2011). A fragile zero-watermarking technique for authentication of relational databases. *International Journal of Digital Content Technology and its Applications, 5*(5).

Handa, H., Nishimura, R., Munekata, T., & Suzuki, Y. (2007). *Prototype of universal information system using audio watermarking*. Paper presented at the 2nd Meeting of the IEICE Technical Group on Multimedia Information Hiding. Miyagi Zao, Japan.

Hanqiang, C., & Hua, X. Xutao, Li., Miao, L., Sheng, Y., & Fang, W. (2006). A zero-watermarking algorithm based on DWT and chaotic modulation. In *Proceeding of SPIE*, (Vol. 6247). SPIE.

Han, S., Fujiyoshi, M., & Kiya, H. (2009). A reversible image authentication method without memorization of hiding parameters. *Institute of Electronics, Information and Communication Engineers Transactions on Fundamentals of Electronics. Communications and Computer Sciences*, *92*(10), 2572–2579.

Hartung, F., & Kutter, M. (1999). Multimedia watermarking techniques. *Proceedings of the IEEE*, *8*(7), 1709–1107.

He, X., Iliev, A. I., & Scordilis, M. S. (2004). *A High capacity watermarking technique for stereo audio*. Paper presented at the IEEE International Conference on Acoustics, Speech & Signal Processing. Montreal, Canada.

Hecht, D. L. (1994). Embedded data glyph technology for hardcopy digital documents: Color imaging: Devide-independent color. *Color Hardcopy and Graphic Arts III*, *2171*, 341–352.

Heckbert, P. (1982). Color image quantization for frame buffer display. *Proceedings of SIGGRAPH, 1982*, 297–307. doi:10.1145/965145.801294

He, D., & Sun, Q. (2006). Multimedia authentication. In Zeng, W., Yu, H., & Lin, C. Y. (Eds.), *Multimedia Security Technologies for Digital Rights Management* (pp. 111–138). London, UK: Academic Press. doi:10.1016/B978-012369476-8/50007-5

He, H. J., Zhang, J. S., & Chen, F. (2009). Adjacent-block based statistical detection method for self-embedding watermarking techniques. *Signal Processing, 89*(8), 1557–1566. doi:10.1016/j.sigpro.2009.02.009

He, H. J., Zhang, J. S., & Wang, H. X. (2006). Synchronous counterfeiting attacks on self-embedding watermarking schemes. *International Journal of Computer Science and Network Security*, *6*(1).

Hernandez-Castroa, J. C., Blasco-Lopezb, I., Estevez-Tapiadora, J. M., & Ribagorda-Garnachoa, A. (2006). Steganography in games: A general methodology and its application to the game of Go. *Computers & Security, 25*(1), 64–71. doi:10.1016/j.cose.2005.12.001

Herre, J., Brandenburg, K., & Lederer, D. (1994). *Intensity stereo coding.* Paper presented at the 96th AES Convention. Amsterdam, The Netherlands.

Herrigel, A., Ruanaidh, J. O., Petersen, H., Pereira, S., & Pun, T. (1998). Secure copyright protection techniques for digital images. In *Proceedings of the Workshop on Information Hiding*. IEEE.

He, X., & Scordilis, M. (2008). Spread spectrum for digital audio watermarking. In Cvejic, N., & Seppanen, T. (Eds.), *Digital Audio Watermarking Techniques and Technologies* (pp. 11–49). Hershey, PA: IGI Global.

Hioki, H. (2007). A steganographic method based on a file attribute. In *Proceedings of the Intelligent Information Hiding and Multimedia Signal Processing*, (Vol. 2), (pp. 441-444). IEEE.

Hioki, H. (2008). Steganogallery: Steganographic gallery. In *Proceedings of the IEEE 10th Workshop on Multimedia Signal Processing*, (pp. 719-724). IEEE Press.

Hiratsuka, K., Kondo, K., & Nakagawa, K. (2008). *On the accuracy of estimated synchronization positions for audio digital watermarks using the modified patchwork algorithm on analog channels.* Paper presented at the IEEE International Conference on Intelligent Information Hiding and Multimedia Signal Processing. Harbin, China.

Hiratsuka, K., Nakagawa, K., & Kondo, K. (2007). *The tolerance of digital watermarking using patchwork method on analog channels.* Paper presented at the 2nd Meeting of the IEICE Technical Group on Multimedia Information Hiding. Miyagi Zao, Japan.

Hiwasaki, Y., Mori, T., Sasaki, S., Ohmuro, H., & Kataoka, A. (2008). A wideband speech and audio coding candidate for ITU-T G.711 WBE standardization. In *Proceedings of the IEEE International Conference on Acoustics, Speech and Signal Processing,* (pp. 4017–4020). IEEE Press.

HoerTech. (2010). *Home page of PEMO-Q by HoerTech.* Retrieved from http://www.hoertech.de/web_en/produkte/pemo-q.shtml

Holland, K. R. (2001). Chapter in Borwick, J. (Ed.), *Loudspeaker and Headphone Handbook* (pp. 11–13). London, UK: Focal Press.

Holliman, M., & Memon, N. (2000). Counterfeiting attacks on oblivious block-wise independent invisible watermarking schemes. *IEEE Transactions on Image Processing, 9*(3). doi:10.1109/83.826780

Hong, J. K., Takahashi, J., Kusaba, M., Yamada, S., & Sugita, S. (1995). *Multimedia applications in the national museum of ethnology*. IPSJ SIG Technical Report, 1995-CH-026, 31-35. IPSJ.

Hsieh, S. L., Hsu, L. Y., & Tsai, I. J. (2005). A copyright protection scheme for color images using secret sharing and wavelet transform. In *Proceedings of World Academy of Science, Engineering And Technology*. IEEE. doi:10.4304/jmm.3.4.42-49

Huang, H., Zhong, S., & Sun, X. (2008). An algorithm of webpage information hiding based on attributes permutation. In *Proceedings of the Intelligent Information Hiding and Multimedia Signal Processing*, (pp. 257-260). IEEE Press.

Huang, X., Echizen, I., & Nishimura, A. (2010). *A new approach of reversible acoustic steganography for tamper-ing detection*. Paper presented at International Conference on Intelligent Information Hiding and Multimedia Signal Processing. Darmstadt, Germany.

Huang, N.-C., Li, M.-T., & Wang, C.-M. (2009). Toward optimal embedding capacity for permutation steganography. *IEEE Signal Processing Letters*, *16*(9), 802–805. doi:10.1109/LSP.2009.2024794

ISO/IEC JTC1/SC29 13818-7. (2006). *Generic coding of moving pictures and associated audio information – Part 7: Advanced audio coding (AAC)*. Retrieved from http://www.mp3-tech.org

ISO/IEC JTC1/SC29/WG11 11172-3. (1999). *Coding of moving pictures and associated audio for digital storage media up to about 1.5 Mbit/s – Part 3: Audio*. Retrieved from http://www.mp3-tech.org

Ito, A., & Makino, S. (2009). Data hiding is a better way for transmitting side information for MP3 bitstream. In *Proceedings of the 2009 Fifth International Conference on Intelligent Information Hiding and Multimedia Signal Processing (IIHMSP2009)*, (pp. 495-498). Kyoto, Japan: IIHMSP.

Ito, A., Handa, H., & Suzuki, Y. (2009). A band extension of G.711 speech with low computational cost for data hiding application. In *Proceedings of the 2009 Fifth International Conference on Intelligent Information Hiding and Multimedia Signal Processing (IIHMSP2009)*, (pp. 491-494). Kyoto, Japan: IIHMSP.

Ito, A., Konno, K., Ito, M., & Makino, S. (2010). Improvement of packet loss concealment for MP3 audio based on switching of concealment method and estimation of MDCT signs. In *Proceedings of the 2010 Sixth International Conference on Intelligent Information Hiding and Multimedia Signal Processing (IIHMSP2010)*, (pp. 518-521). Darmstadt, Germany: IIHMSP.

Ito, K., Soda, H., Ihara, F., Kimura, T., & Fuse, M. (2005). *Fuji Xerox technical report, No.15*, 32-41. IEICE Transactions.

ITU BS. 1534-1. (2003). *Method for the subjective assessment of intermediate quality level of coding systems*. Retrieved from http://www.itu.int

ITU. (1988). *G.711: Pulse code modulation (PCM) of voice frequencies*. Retrieved from http://www.itu.int

ITU. (1990). *G.726: 40, 32, 24, 16 kbit/s adaptive differential pulse code modulation (ADPCM)*. Retrieved from http://www.itu.int

ITU. (1992). *G.728: Coding of speech at 16 kbit/s using low-delay code excited linear prediction*. Retrieved from http://www.itu.int

ITU. (2001). *Perceptual evaluation of speech quality (PESQ): An objective method for end-to-end speech quality assessment of narrow-band telephone networks and speech codecs*. Retrieved from http://www.itu.int

ITU. (2003). *Mapping function for transforming of P.862 to MOS-LQO*. Retrieved from http://www.itu.int

ITU. (2005). *P.862.2 wideband extension to recommendation P.862 for the assessment of wideband telephone networks and speech codecs*. Retrieved from http://www.itu.int

ITU. (2006). *G.729.1: G.729 based embedded variable bit-rate coder: An 8-32 kbit/s scalable wideband coder bitstream interoperable with G.729*. Retrieved from http://www.itu.int

ITU-R BS. 1387-1. (2001). *Method for objective measurements of perceived audio quality*. Retrieved from http://www.itu.int

ITU-R Recommendation BS. 1534. (2001). *Method for the subjective assessment of intermediate quality level of coding systems*. Retrieved from http://www.itu.int

ITU-T P.862. (2001). *Perceptual evaluation of speech quality (PESQ): An objective method for end-to-end speech quality assessment of narrow-band telephone networks and speech codecs*. Retrieved from http://www.itu.int

ITU-T. (1988). *G.711: Pulse code modulation (PCM) of voice frequencies*. Retrieved from http://www.itu.int

ITU-T. (1996). *P.800: Methods for subjective determination of transmission quality*. Retrieved from http://www.itu.int

ITU-T. (1999). *G.711: Appendix 1: A high quality low-complexity algorithm for packet loss concealment with G.711*. Retrieved from http://www.itu.int

ITU-T. (2001). *P.862: Perceptual evaluation of speech quality (PESQ), an objective method for end-to-end speech quality assessment of narrow-band telephone networks and speech codecs*. Retrieved from http://www.itu.int

Iwakiri, N., & Matsui, K. (1997). Embedding a text into audo codes under ADPCM quantizer. *Journal Information Processing Society of Japan*, *38*(10), 2053–2061.

Jalil, Z., Farooq, M., Zafar, H., Sabir, M., & Ashraf, E. (2010). Improved zero text watermarking algorithm against meaning preserving attacks. In *Proceedings of the World Academy of Science, Engineering and Technology*. IEEE.

Jalil, Z., Mirza, A. M., & Iqbal, T. (2010). A zero-watermarking algorithm for text documents based on structural components. In *Proceedings of the International Conference on Information and Emerging Technologies (ICIET)*. ICIET.

Jalil, Z., Mirza, A. M., & Sabir, M. (2010). Content based zero watermarking algorithm for authentication of text documents. *International Journal of Computer Science and Information Technology*, *7*(2).

Jayanthi, V. E., Rajamani, V., & Karthikayen, P. (2011). Performance analysis for geometrical attack on digital image watermarking. *International Journal of Electronics*, *98*, 1565–1580. doi:10.1080/00207217.2011.601444

JEWELS. (2001). *Research report on watermarking*. Retrieved from http://home.jeita.or.jp/tech/oldfile/report/2001/01-jou-04.pdf

Jin, H., Choe, Y., & Kiya, H. (2010). Reversible data hiding based on adaptive modulation of statistics invertibility. *Institute of Electronics, Information and Communication Engineers Transactions on Fundamentals of Electronics. Communications and Computer Sciences*, *93*(2), 565–569.

Johnson, K. F., Duric, Z., & Jajodia, S. (2000). *Information hiding: Steganography and watermarking – Attacks and countermeasures*. Reading, MA: Kluwer Academic Publishers. doi:10.1007/978-1-4615-4375-6

Johnston, J. (1988). Transform coding of audio signals using perceptual noise criteria. *IEEE Journal on Selected Areas in Communications*, *6*, 314–323. doi:10.1109/49.608

Kabal, P. (2002). *An examination and interpretation of ITU-R BS.1387: Perceptual evaluation of audio quality*. TSP Lab Technical Report. Montreal, Canada: McGill University. Retieved from http://www-mmsp.ece.mcgill.ca/Documents/Reports/2002/KabalR2002v2.pdf

Kahn, D. (1996). *The codebreaksers — The story of secret writing*. New York, NY: Scribner.

Kalker, T., Depovere, G., Haitsma, J., & Maes, M. (1999). A video watermarking system for broadcast monitoring. *Proceedings of the Society for Photo-Instrumentation Engineers*, *3657*, 103–112. doi:10.1117/12.344661

Kamstra, L., & Heijmans, H. J. (2005). Reversible data embedding into images using wavelet techniques and sorting. *Institute of Electrical and Electronics Engineers Transactions on Image Processing*, *14*(12), 2082–2090.

Kaneda, K., Fujii, Y., Iwamura, K., & Hangai, S. (2010). An improvement of robustness against physical attacks and equipment independence in information hiding based on the artificial fiber pattern. In *Proceedings of WAIS-2010*. Krakow, Poland: WAIS.

Kaneda, K., Hirano, K., Iwamura, K., & Hangai, S. (2008). Information hiding method utilizing low visible natural fiber pattern for printed document. In *Proceedings of the 2008 International Conference on Intelligent Information Hiding and Multimedia Signal Processing, IIHMSP-2008-IS05-007*. IIHMSP.

Kaneda, K., Kito, Y., & Iwamura, K. (2011). Information hiding based on the artificial fiber pattern with improved robustness against foreground objects. In *Proceedings of the 2011 International Conference on Intelligent Information Hiding and Multimedia Signal Processing, IIH-MSP-2011-233*. IIHMSP.

Kaneda, K., Nagai, F., Iwamura, K., & Hangai, S. (2008). A study of information hiding performance using simple dot pattern with different tile sizes. In *Proceedings of the 2008 International Conference on Intelligent Information Hiding and Multimedia Signal Processing, IIHMSP-2008-IS05-008*. IIHMSP.

Kaneda, K., Tachibana, Y., & Iwamura, K. (2011). Information hiding based on a single dot pattern method with improved extraction and robustness against foreground objects. In *Proceedings of the 2011 International Conference on Intelligent Information Hiding and Multimedia Signal Processing, IIH-MSP-2011-238*. IIHMSP.

Kanetou, R., Nakashima, Y., & Babaguchi, N. (2009). Position estimation using detect strength of digital watermarking for audio signals. In *Proceedings of IEICE General Conference: DS-3-10,* (pp. S37-38). IEICE.

Kataoka, A., Mori, T., & Hayashi, S. (2008). Bandwidth extension of G.711 using side information. *IEICE Transactions on Information and Systems*, *91*(4), 1069–1081.

Kato, Y., & Yasuhara, M. (2000). Recovery of drawing order from single-stroke handwriting images. *IEEE Transactions on Pattern Analysis and Machine Intelligence*, *22*(9), 938–949. doi:10.1109/34.877517

Katzenbeisser, S., & Petitcolas, F. A. (2000). *Information hiding techniques for steganography and digital watermarking*. Norwood, MA: Artech House. doi:10.1201/1079/43263.28.6.20001201/30373.5

Khairullah, M. (2009). A novel text steganography system using font color of the invisible characters in microsoft word documents. In *Proceedings of the International Conference on Computer and Electrical Engineering*, (pp. 482-484). IEEE.

Khairullah, M. (2011). A novel text steganography system in cricket match scorecard. *International Journal of Computers and Applications*, *21*(9), 43–47. doi:10.5120/2537-3462

Khayam, S. A. (2003). *The discrete cosine transform (DCT): Theory and application*. East Lansing, MI: Michigan State University.

Kim, H., Sachnev, V., Shi, Y., Nam, J., & Choo, H.-G. (2008). A novel difference expansion transform for reversible data embedding. *Institute of Electrical and Electronics Engineers Transactions on Information Forensics and Security*, *3*(3), 456–465.

Kirovski, D., & Malvar, H. S. (2003). Spread-spectrum watermarking of audio signals. *IEEE Transactions on Signal Processing*, *51*(4), 1020–1033. doi:10.1109/TSP.2003.809384

Ko, B. S., Nishimura, R., & Suzuki, Y. (2005). Time-spread echo method for digital audio watermarking. *IEEE Transactions on Multimedia*, *7*(2), 212–221. doi:10.1109/TMM.2005.843366

Ko, B.-S., Nishimura, R., & Suzuki, Y. (2004). Robust watermarking based on time-spread echo method with subband decomposition. *IEICE Transactions on Fundamentals*, *87*, 1647–1650.

Komaki, N., Aoki, N., & Yamamoto, T. (2003). A packet loss concealment technique for VoIP using steganography. *IEICE Transactions on Fundamentals of Electronics, Communications and Computer Science*, *86*(8), 2069–2072.

Kondo, K. (2011). A data hiding method for stereo audio signals using interchannel decorrelator polarity inversion. *Journal of the Audio Engineering Society. Audio Engineering Society*, *59*(6), 379–395.

Kondo, K., & Nakagawa, K. (2010). A digital watermark for stereo audio signals using variable inter-channel delay in high-frequency bands and its evaluation. *International Journal of Innovative Computing, Information, & Control*, *6*(3B), 1209–1220.

Koukopoulos, D., & Stamatiou, Y. C. (2001). *A compressed-domain watermarking algorithm for mpeg layer 3*. Paper presented at the workshop on Multimedia and security: New Challenges. Ottawa, Canada.

Kuisa, A. (2007). *Host-cooperative metadata embedding framework*. Paper presented at International Conference on Intelligent Information Hiding and Multimedia Signal Processing. Kaohsiung, Taiwan.

Kuo, S. S., Johnston, J. D., Turin, W., & Quackenbush, S. R. (2002). *Covert audio watermarking using perceptually tuned signal independent multiband phase modulation.* Paper presented at the IEEE International Conference on Acoustics, Speech, and Signal Processing. Orlando, FL.

Kurematsu, A., Takeda, K., Sagisaka, Y., Katagiri, S., Kuwabara, H., & Shikano, K. (1990). ATR Japanese speech database as a tool of speech recognition and synthesis. *Speech Communication, 19*(4), 357–363. doi:10.1016/0167-6393(90)90011-W

Kurita, Y. (2000). *Minpaku denshi guide (electronic guide of the national museum of ethnology)*. Osaka, Japan: The Senri Foundation.

Kusunoki, F., Satoh, I., Mizoguchi, H., & Inagaki, S. (2008). SoundSpot: Location-bound audio guide system for exhibition supports in museums. *IEICE Transactions on Information and Systems, 91*(2), 229–237.

Kwan, M. (1998). *Gishuffle.* Retrieved from http://www.darkside.com.au/gifshuffle/

Kwon, O. H., & Park, R.-H. (2006). Computation of the watermark weighting factor in the DCT-based watermarking methods for the specified PSNR of the still image. In *Proceedings of 7th International Workshop Image Analysis for Multimedia Interactive Services*, (pp. 41-43). Incheon, Korea: IEEE.

Kwon, O. H., Kim, Y. S., & Park, R.-H. (1999). Watermarking for still images using the human visual system. In *Proceedings of IEEE International Symposium on Circuits and Systems,* (vol 4), (pp. 76-79). Orlando, FL: IEEE Press.

LAME Project. (2008). *LAME aint't an MP3 encoder.* Retrieved from http://lame.sourcforge.net

Larsen, E., & Aarts, R. M. (2004). *Audio bandwidth extension: Application of psychoacoustics, signal processing and loudspeaker design.* Hoboken, NJ: John Wiley & Sons, Inc.doi:10.1002/0470858710

Latzenbeisser, S. (2000). *Information hiding techniques for steganography and digital watermarking.* New York, NY: Artech House.

Lee, H., & Kaneko, K. (2008). New approaches for software watermarking by register allocation. In *Proceedings of the 2008 ACIS International Conference on Software Engineering, Artificial Intelligence, Networking, and Parallel/Distributed Computing,* (pp. 63-68). ACIS.

Lee, C. C., Wu, H. C., Tsai, C. S., & Chu, Y. P. (2008). Adaptive lossless steganographic scheme with centralized difference expansion. *Pattern Recognition, 41*(6), 2097–2106. doi:10.1016/j.patcog.2007.11.018

Lee, H. S., & Lee, W. S. (2005). Audio watermarking through modification of tonal maskers. *ETRI Journal, 27*(5), 608–616. doi:10.4218/etrij.05.0105.0037

Lee, T. Y., & Lin, S. D. (2008). Dual watermark for image tamper detection and recovery. *Pattern Recognition, 41*(11), 3497–3506. doi:10.1016/j.patcog.2008.05.003

Lee, W. B., & Chen, T. H. (2002). A public verifiable copy protection technique for still images. *Journal of Systems and Software, 62*(3), 195–204. doi:10.1016/S0164-1212(01)00142-X

Li, A., Lin, B., Chen, Y., & Lü, G. (2008). Study on copyright authentication of GIS vector data based on zero-watermarking. *The International Archives of the Photogrammetry, Remote Sensing and Spatial Information Sciences, 37*(B4).

Li, C. T. (2004). Digital fragile watermarking scheme for authentication of JPEG images. *IEEE Proceedings-Vision Image and Signal Processing, 151*(6), 460-466.

Li, F., Tiegang, G., & Qunting, Y. (2010). A novel zero-watermark copyright authentication scheme based on lifting wavelet and harris corner detection. *Wuhan University Journal of Natural Sciences, 15*(5).

Li, M., Jiao, Y., & Niu, X. (2008). *Reversible watermarking for compressed speech.* Paper presented at International Conference on Intelligent Information Hiding and Multimedia Signal Processing. Harbin, China.

Lin, C. Y., & Chang, S. F. (2000). Semi-fragile watermarking for authenticating JPEG visual content. *Security and Watermarking of Multimedia Contents II, 3971*, 140–151.

Linnartz, J. P. M. G., Kalker, A. C. C., & Depovere, G. F. (1998). Modelling the false-alarm and missed detection rate for electronic watermarks. In Aucsmith, L. D. (Ed.), *Notes in Computer Science* (*Vol. 1525*, pp. 329–343). Berlin, Germany: Springer-Verlag. doi:10.1007/3-540-49380-8_23

Lin, P. L., Hsieh, C. K., & Huang, P. W. (2005). A hierarchical digital watermarking method for image tamper detection and recovery. *Pattern Recognition*, *38*(12), 2519–2529. doi:10.1016/j.patcog.2005.02.007

Lin, Y., & Abdulla, W. H. (2008). Perceptual evaluation of audio watermarking using objective quality measure. *Proceedings of ICASSP*, *2008*, 1745–1748.

Lipshitz, S. P., Pocock, M., & Vanderkooy, J. (1982). On the audibility of midrange phase-distortion in audio systems. *Journal of the Audio Engineering Society. Audio Engineering Society*, *30*(9), 580–595.

Liu, Y. W., & Smith, J. O. (2003). Watermarking parametric representations for synthetic audio. In *Proceedings of IEEE International Conference on Acoustics Speech and Signal Processing*, (pp. 660-663). Hong Kong, China: IEEE Press.

Liu, Y. W., & Smith, J. O. (2004). Watermarking sinusoidal audio representations by quantization index modulation in multiple frequencies. In *Proceedings of IEEE International Conference on Acoustics, Speech, and Signal Processing*, (pp. 373-376). Montreal, Canada: IEEE Press.

Li, W., & Xue, X. (2004). Audio watermarking based on music content analysis: Robust against time scale modification. *Lecture Notes in Computer Science*, *2939*, 289–300. doi:10.1007/978-3-540-24624-4_22

Liwicki, M., Uchida, S., Iwamura, M., Omachi, S., & Kise, K. (2010). Data-embedding pen - Augmenting ink strokes with meta-information. In *Proceedings of International Workshop on Document Analysis Systems*, (pp. 43-51). IEEE.

Liwicki, M., Uchida, S., Iwamura, M., Omachi, S., & Kise, K. (2010). Embedding meta-information in handwriting — Reed-Solomon for reliable error correction. In *Proceedings of International Conference on Frontiers in Handwriting Recognition*, (pp. 51-56). IEEE.

Liwicki, M., Yoshida, A., Uchida, S., Iwamura, M., Omachi, S., & Kise, K. (2011). Reliable online stroke recovery from offline data with the data-embedding pen. In *Proceedings of International Conference on Document Analysis and Recognition,* (pp. 1384-1388). IEEE.

Lou, D. C., Tso, H. K., & Liu, J. L. (2006). A copyright protection scheme for digital images using visual cryptography technique. *Journal of Computer Standards and Interfaces*, *29*(1), 125–131. doi:10.1016/j.csi.2006.02.003

Louvre-DNP. (2009). *Augmented reality museum – YouTube, Metaio's cooperation with Japanese company DNP within the Louvre - DNP museum lab in Tokyo.* Retrieved August 22, 2011, from http://www.youtube.com/watch?v=lQfCndsnXUc

Löytynoja, N., Cvejic, N. E., Lähetkangas, E., & Seppänen, T. (2005). *Audio encryption using fragile watermarking.* Paper presented at the Fifth International Conference on Information, Communications and Signal Processing. Bangkok, Thailand.

Lu, B., Liu, F., Ge, X., Liu, B., & Luo, X. (2007). A software birthmark based on dynamic opcode n-gram. In *Proceedings of the International Conference on Semantic Computing 2007*, (pp. 37-44). IEEE.

Lukas, J., Fridrich, J., & Goljan, M. (2006). Digital camera identification from sensor pattern noise. *IEEE Transactions on Information Forensics and Security*, *1*(2), 205–214. doi:10.1109/TIFS.2006.873602

Lundberg, T., de Bruin, P., Bruhn, S., Hakansson, S., & Craig, S. (2005). Adaptive thresholds for AMR codec mode selection. In *Proceedings of the IEEE Vehicular Technology Conference,* (pp. 2325–2329). IEEE Press.

Luo, H., Chu, S. C., & Lu, Z. M. (2008). Self embedding watermarking using halftoning technique. *Circuits, Systems, and Signal Processing*, *27*(2), 155–170. doi:10.1007/s00034-008-9024-0

Ma, J. H., Guan, Y. J., & Zhao, Y. H. (2007). A method of zero-watermarking based on lifting wavelet. In *Proceeding of the 2007 International Conference on Wavelet Analysis and Pattern Recognition*. IEEE.

MacWilliams, F. J., & Sloane, N. J. A. (1977). *The theory of error-correcting code*. New York, NY: North-Holland Publishing Company.

Maeno, K., Sun, Q. B., Chang, S. F., & Suto, M. (2006). New semi-fragile image authentication watermarking techniques using random bias and nonuniform quantization. *IEEE Transactions on Multimedia*, *8*(1), 32–45. doi:10.1109/TMM.2005.861293

Mahdian, B., & Saic, S. (2010). A bibliography on blind methods for identifying image forgery. *Signal Processing Image Communication*, *25*(6), 389–399. doi:10.1016/j.image.2010.05.003

Makhoul, J., & Berouti, M. (1979). High frequency regeneration in speech coding systems. In *Proceedings of the International Conference on Acoustics, Speech, Signal Processing,* (pp. 428-431). IEEE.

Malik, H. M., Ansari, R., & Khokhar, A. A. (2007). Robust data hiding in audio using allpass filters. *IEEE Transactions on Audio, Speech, and Language Processing*, *15*(4), 1296–1304. doi:10.1109/TASL.2007.894509

Malik, H., Ansari, R., & Khokhar, A. (2008). Robust audio watermarking using frequency-selective spread spectrum. *IET Information Security*, *2*(4), 129–150. doi:10.1049/iet-ifs:20070145

Mario, G. L., Mariko, N. M., & Meana, H. M. P. (2006). Optimal detection system of digital watermarks in spatial domain. *Telecommunications and Radio Engineering*, *65*, 739–751. doi:10.1615/TelecomRadEng.v65.i8.60

Martin, V., Chabert, M., & Lacaze, B. (2008). An interpolation-based watermarking scheme. *Signal Processing*, *88*, 539–557. doi:10.1016/j.sigpro.2007.08.016

Marvel, L. M., Boncelet, C. G., & Retter, C. T. (1999). Spread spectrum image steganography. *IEEE Transactions on Image Processing*, *8*(8), 1075–1083. doi:10.1109/83.777088

Mason, M., Sridharan, S., & Prandolini, R. (1999). *Digital coding of covert audio for monitoring and storage*. Paper presented at the Fifth International Symposium on Signal Processing and its Applications. Queensland, Australia.

Matsuoka, H., Nakashima, Y., & Yoshimura, T. (2006). *Aerial acoustic communications in audible band-acoustic OFDM.* Technical Report of IEICE, EA2006-24, 106(125), 25-29. IEICE.

Maxemchuk, N. F., & Low, S. (1997). Marking text documents. In *Proceedings of the IEEE International Conference on Image Processing*, (pp. 13–16). IEEE Press.

Mazurczyk, W., & Lubacz, J. (2010). LACK—A VoIP steganographic method. *Telecommunication Systems*, *45*(2-3), 153–163. doi:10.1007/s11235-009-9245-y

Megias, D., Herrera-Joancomarti, J., & Minguillon, J. (2004). *An audio watermarking scheme robust against stereo attacks.* Paper presented at the ASM Multimedia and Security Workshop. Magdeburg, Germany.

Meltzer, S., & Moser, G. (2006). MPEG-4 HE-AAC v2 – Audio coding for today's digital media world. *EBU Technical Review*. Retrieved Sept. 2011 from http://tech.ebu.ch/docs/techreview/trev_305-moser.pdf

Miaou, S. G., Hsu, C. H., Tsai, Y. S., & Chao, H. M. (2000). A secure data hiding technique with heterogeneous data-combining capability for electronic patient records. In *Proceedings of the 22nd Annual International Conference of the IEEE Engineering in Medicine and Biology Society*, (pp. 280-283). Chicago, IL: IEEE Press.

Miller, M. L., & Bloom, M. A. (1999). Computing the probability of false watermark detection. In *Proceedings of the Third International Workshop on Information Hiding*, (pp. 146-158). Dresden, Germany: IEEE.

Modegi, T. (2006). *Nearly lossless audio watermark embedding techniques to be extracted contactlessly by cell phone*. Paper presented at the IEEE International Conference on Mobile Data Management. Nara, Japan.

Modegi, T. (2008). Prototyping of push-type information delivery system using audio watermark technology. In *Proceedings of IEICE General Conference,* (Vol. DS-4-5), (pp. S27-28). IEICE.

Modegi, T. (2009). Detection method of mobile terminal spatial location using audio watermark technique. In *Proceedings of ICROSS-SICE International Joint Conference,* (pp. 5479-5484). ICROSS-SICE.

Modegi, T. (2010). Evaluation method for quality losses generated by miscellaneous audio signal processing using MIDI encode tool auto-F. In *Proceedings of IEEE Region10 TENCON,* (pp. 2066-2071). IEEE Press.

Modegi, T. (2010). Robust audio watermark method resistant to room reverberation for realizing ubiquitous acoustic spaces. In *Proceedings of IEICE General Conference: DS-3-3*, (pp. S19-20). IEICE.

Modegi, T. (2006). Development of audio watermark technology to be extracted contactlessly by cell phone. *IEEJ Transactions on Electronics. Information Systems*, *126*(7), 825–831.

Modegi, T. (2007). Construction of ubiquitous acoustic spaces using audio watermark technology and mobile terminals. *IEEJ Transactions on Electrical and Electronic Engineering*, *2*(6), 608–619. doi:10.1002/tee.20216

Monden, A., Iida, H., Matsumoto, K., Torii, K., & Inoue, K. (2000). A practical method for watermarking java programs. In *Proceedings of the Computer Software and Applications Conference*, (pp. 191-197). IEEE.

Moore, J. C. B. (2003). *An introduction to the psychology of hearing* (5th ed.). New York, NY: Academic Press.

Motwani, R., Harris, F. C., & Bekris, K. (2010). A proposed digital rights management system for 3D graphics using biometric watermarks. In *Proceedings of International Conference on Signal Acquisition and Processing*, (pp. 125-129). Bangalore, India: IEEE.

Munekata, T., Yamaguchi, T., Nishimura, R., & Suzuki, Y. (2011). *Information hiding technologies for establishing a barrier-free environment in sound space.* Paper presented at the 12th Meeting of the IEICE Technical Group on Multimedia Information Hiding. Sendai, Japan.

Munekata, T., Yamaguchi, T., Handa, H., Nishimura, R., & Suzuki, Y. (2009). Portable acoustic caption decoder using IH techniques for enhancing lives of the people who are deaf or hard-of-hearing - System configuration and robustness for airborne sound. *International Journal of Innovative Computing, Information, & Control*, *5*(7), 1829–1836.

Myles, G., & Collberg, C. (2004). Software watermarking through register allocation: Implementation, analysis, and attacks. In *Proceedings of the Information Security and Cryptology — ICISC 2003*, (pp. 274-293). ICISC.

Myles, G., & Collberg, C. (2005). K-gram based software birthmarks. In *Proceedings of the 2005 ACM Symposium on Applied Computing*, (pp. 314-318). ACM Press.

Myles, G., & Collberg, C. (2004). Detecting software theft via whole program path birthmarks. In *Proceedings of Information Security* (pp. 404–415). IEEE. doi:10.1007/978-3-540-30144-8_34

Nakajima, Y. (2009). *Home page of Yoshitaka Nakajima Laboratory in Kyushu University*. Retrieved August 22, 2011, from http://www.design.kyushu-u.ac.jp/~ynhome/ENG/index.html

Nakashima, Y., Kaneto, R., Tachibana, R., & Babaguchi, N. (2007). *Maximum-likelihood estimation of recording position based on synchronization position of audio watermarking*. Paper presented at the 2nd Meeting of the IEICE Technical Group on Multimedia Information Hiding. Miyagi Zao, Japan.

Nakashima, Y., Tachibana, R., Nishimura, M., & Babaguchi, N. (2007). Determining recording location based on synchronization positions of audio watermarking. In *Proceedings of ICASSP2007*, (vol. 2), (pp. 253-256). ICASSP.

Nakashima, Y., Tachibana, R., & Babaguchi, N. (2009). Watermarked movie soundtrack finds the position of the camcorder in a theater. *IEEE Transactions on Multimedia*, *11*(3), 443–454. doi:10.1109/TMM.2009.2012938

Nakashima, Y., Tachibana, R., Nishimura, M., & Babaguchi, N. (2009). Watermarked movie soundtrack finds the position of the camcorder in a theater. *IEEE Transactions on Multimedia*, *11*(3), 443–454. doi:10.1109/TMM.2009.2012938

Nakata, K. (1995). *Speech*. New York, NY: Corona Publishing.

Naor, N., & Shamir, A. (1995). Visual cryptography. *Proceedings of Advances in Cryptology: Eurocrypt, 1994*, 1–12.

Nel, E.-M., du Preez, J. A., & Herbst, B. M. (2005). Estimating the pen trajectories of static signatures using hidden Markov models. *IEEE Transactions on Pattern Analysis and Machine Intelligence*, *27*(11), 1733–1746. doi:10.1109/TPAMI.2005.221

Niimi, M., Nakamura, T., & Noda, H. (2006). Application of complexity measure to reversible information hiding. In *Proceedings of the International Conference on Image Processing 2006*, (pp. 113–116). IEEE.

Niimi, M., Eason, R., Noda, H., & Kawaguchi, E. (2001). Intensity histogram steganalysis in BPCS-steganography. *Proceedings of the Society for Photo-Instrumentation Engineers*, *4314*, 555. doi:10.1117/12.435440

Niimi, M., Eason, R., Noda, H., & Kawaguchi, E. (2002). A method to apply BPCS-steganography to palette-based images using luminance quasi-preserving color quantization. *IEICE Transactions on Fundamentals of Electronics, Communications and Computer Science*, *85*(9), 2141–2148.

Niimi, M., Noda, H., & Kawaguchi, E. (1999). Steganography based on region segmentation with a complexity measure. *Systems and Computers in Japan*, *30*(3), 1–9. doi:10.1002/(SICI)1520-684X(199903)30:3<1::AID-SCJ1>3.0.CO;2-M

Nikolaidis, N., & Pitas, I. (1998). Robust image watermarking in the spatial domain. *Signal Processing*, *66*(3), 385–403. doi:10.1016/S0165-1684(98)00017-6

Nishimura, A. (2006). Audio watermarking based on sinusoidal amplitude modulation. In *Proceedings of IEEE International Conference on Acoustics, Speech and Signal Processing ICASSP2006,* (Vol. 4), (pp. 797-800). IEEE Press.

Nishimura, A. (2007). *Subjective and objective quality evaluation for audio watermarking based on sinusoidal amplitude modulation.* Paper presented at the 19th International Congress on Acoustics. Madrid, Spain.

Nishimura, A. (2007). *Robustness against speech codecs on an audio data hiding based on amplitude modulation.* Paper presented at the 2nd Meeting of the IEICE Technical Group on Multimedia Information Hiding. Miyagi Zao, Japan.

Nishimura, A. (2007). *Presentation of information synchronized with the audio signal reproduced by loudspeakers using an AM-based watermark.* Paper presented at the 3rd International Conference on Intelligent Information Hiding and Multimedia Signal Processing. Kaohsiung, Taiwan.

Nishimura, R., Suzuki, M., & Suzuki, Y. (2001). Detection threshold of a periodic phase shift in music sound. In *Proceedings of the 17th International Congress on Acoustics.* IEEE.

Nishimura, A. (2010). Audio data hiding that is robust with respect to aerial transmission and speech codecs. *International Journal of Innovative Computing, Information, & Control*, *6*(3B), 1389–1400.

Nishimura, A. (2010). Audio watermarking based on subband amplitude modulation. *Acoustical Science and Technology*, *31*(5), 328–336. doi:10.1250/ast.31.328

Nishimura, R., & Suzuki, Y. (2004). Audio watermark based on periodical phase shift. *Journal of Acoustical Society of Japan*, *60*(5), 269–272.

Nishimura, R., Suzuki, Y., & Ko, B. S. (2008). Advanced audio watermarking based on echo hiding: Time-spread echo hiding. In Cvejic, N., & Seppänen, T. (Eds.), *Digital Audio Watermarking Techniques and Technologies* (pp. 123–151). Hershey, PA: IGI Global.

Noda, H., Niimi, M., & Kawaguchi, E. (2006). High-performance JPEG steganography using quantization index modulation. *Pattern Recognition Letters*, *27*(5), 455–461. doi:10.1016/j.patrec.2005.09.008

Noda, H., Spaulding, J., Shirazi, M. N., & Kawaguchi, E. (2002). Application of bit-plane decomposition steganography to JPEG2000 encoded images. *IEEE Signal Processing Letters*, *9*(12), 410–413. doi:10.1109/LSP.2002.806056

Noda, H., Tsukamizu, Y., & Niimi, M. (2007). JPEG2000 steganography which preserves histograms of DWT coefficients. *IEICE Transactions on Information and Systems*, *90*(4), 783–786. doi:10.1093/ietisy/e90-d.4.783

NPO Japan Network Security Association. (2010). *2009 investigation report about a year information security incident.* Tokyo, Japan: NPO.

Ohyama, S., Nimi, M., & Noda, H. (2009). Lossless data hiding using bit-depth embedding for JPEG2000 compressed bit-stream. *Journal of Communication and Computer*, *6*(2), 35–39.

Omachi, S., Iwamura, M., Uchida, S., & Kise, K. (2006). Affine invariant information embedment for accurate camera-based character recognition. In *Proceedings of International Conference on Pattern Recognition, 2,* 1098-1101.

Ono, M., Han, S., Fujiyoshi, M., & Kiya, H. (2009). A location map-free reversible data hiding method for specific area embedding. *Institute of Electronics. Information and Communication Engineers Electronics Express*, *6*(8), 483–489.

Ono, T. (2001). Watermark embedded in sound. In *Watermark and Content Protection* (pp. 122–138). Tokyo, Japan: Ohm Publishing.

Optimark. (2002). *Optimark*. Retrieved from http://poseidon.csd.auth.gr/optimark/

Ozawa, K., Suzuki, Y., & Sone, T. (1993). Monaural phase effects on timbre of two-tone signals. *The Journal of the Acoustical Society of America*, *93*, 1007–1011. doi:10.1121/1.405548

Ozer, H., Sankur, B., & Memon, N. (2005). An SVD-based audio watermarking technique. In *Proceedings of the 7th Workshop on Multimedia and Security*, (pp. 51-56). New York, NY: IEEE.

Paliwal, K. K., & Alsteris, L. (2003). Usefulness of phase spectrum human speech perception. *Proceedings of Eurospeech*, *2003*, 2117–2120.

Palo Alto Research Center Incorporated. (2012). *Website*. Retrieved from http://www.microglyphs.com/english/html/dgtech.shtml

Park, H., Lim, H.-I., Choi, S., & Han, T. (2011). Detecting common modules in java packages based on static object trace birthmark. *The Computer Journal*, *54*(1), 108–124. doi:10.1093/comjnl/bxp095

Patra, J. C., Phua, J. E., & Bornand, C. (2010). A novel DCT domain CRT-based watermarking scheme for image authentication surviving JPEG compression. *Digital Signal Processing*, *20*, 1597–1611. doi:10.1016/j.dsp.2010.03.010

Pennebaker, W. B., & Mitchell, J. L. (1993). *JPEG: Still image data compression standard*. New York, NY: Springer.

Perkins, C., Hodson, O., & Hardman, V. (1998, September/October). A survey of packet loss recovery techniques for streaming audio. *IEEE Network Magazine*, 40-48.

Perkins, C., Hodson, O., & Hardman, V. (1998). A survey of packet loss recovery techniques for streaming audio. *IEEE Network*, *12*(5), 40–48. doi:10.1109/65.730750

Personal Media Corp. (2009). *Technical resources of UC (ubiquitous communicator)*. Retrieved August 22, 2011, from http://www.uid4u.com/products/uc.html

Petitcolas, F. A. P., Anderson, R. J., & Kuhn, M. G. (1998). Attacks on copyright marking systems. In *Proceedings of the Second International Workshop on Information Hiding*, (pp. 218-238). IEEE Press.

Petitcolas, F. A., & Kirovski, D. (2002). The blind pattern matching attack on watermark systems. In *Proceedings of IEEE International Conference on Acoustics, Speech, and Signal Processing*, (vol. 4), (pp. 3740–3743). IEEE Press.

Petitcolas, F. A. P., Anderson, R. J., & Kuhn, M. G. (1999). Information hiding -- A survey. *Proceedings of the IEEE*, *87*(7), 1062–1078. doi:10.1109/5.771065

Pickholtz, R. L., Schilling, D. L., & Milstein, L. B. (1982). Theory of spread-spectrum communications - A tutorial. *IEEE Transactions on Communications*, *30*, 855–884. doi:10.1109/TCOM.1982.1095533

Ping, Z., Xi, C., & Xu-Guang, Y. (2010). The software watermarking for tamper resistant radix dynamic graph coding. *Information Technology Journal*, *9*(6), 1236–1240. doi:10.3923/itj.2010.1236.1240

Pitas, I. (1998). A method for watermark casting on digital images. *IEEE Transactions on Circuits and Systems for Video Technology*, *8*, 775–780. doi:10.1109/76.728421

Piva, A., Barni, M., Bartolini, F., & Cappellini, V. (1997). DCT-based watermark recovering without resorting to the uncorrupted original images. In *Proceedings of IEEE International Conference on Image Processing*, (vol 1), (pp. 520-523). Santa Barbara, CA: IEEE Press.

Plack, C. J. (2005). *The sense of hearing*. London, UK: Lawrence Erlbaum Association.

Plack, C. J. (2010). *The Oxford handbook of auditory science*. Oxford, UK: Oxford University Press.

Popescu, A. C., & Farid, H. (2005). Exposing digital forgeries by detecting traces of resampling. *IEEE Transactions on Signal Processing*, *53*(2), 758–767. doi:10.1109/TSP.2004.839932

Provos, N. (2001). Defending against statistical steganalysis. In *Proceedings of the 10th USENIX Security Symposium*, (vol 10), (pp. 323–336). USENIX.

Qu, G., & Potkonjak, M. (1998). Analysis of watermarking techniques for graph coloring problem. In *Proceedings of the 1998 IEEE/ACM International Conference on Computer-Aided Design*, (pp. 190-193). IEEE Press.

Rabbani, M., & Joshi, R. (2002). An overview of JPEG 2000 still image compression standard. *Signal Processing Image Communication*, *17*, 3–48. doi:10.1016/S0923-5965(01)00024-8

Reed, I. S., & Solomon, G. (1960). Polynomial codes over certain finite fields. *Journal of the Society for Industrial and Applied Mathematics*, *8*(2), 300–304. doi:10.1137/0108018

Revenkar, P. S., Anjum, A., & Gandhare, W. Z. (2010). Survey of visual cryptography schemes. *International Journal of Security and Its Applications*, *4*(2).

Rey, C., & Dugelay, J.-L. (2002). A survey of watermarking algorithms for image authentication. *European Association for Signal Processing Journal on Applied Signal Processing*, *1*, 613–621. doi:10.1155/S1110865702204047

Ruiz, F. J., & Deller, J. R., Jr. (2000). Digital watermarking of speech signals for the national gallery of the spoken word. In *Proceedings. of IEEE International Conference on Acoustics, Speech, and Signal Processing*, (pp. 1499-1502). Istanbul, Turkey: IEEE Press.

Sang, J., Liao, X., & Alam, M. S. (2006). Neural-network-based zero-watermark scheme for digital images. *Optical Engineering (Redondo Beach, Calif.)*, 45.

Sasaki, Y., Hahm, S. J., & Ito, A. (2011). Manipulating vocal signal in mixed music sounds using small amount of side information. In *Proceedings of the 2011 Seventh International Conference on Intelligent Information Hiding and Multimedia Signal Processing (IIHMSP2011)*, (pp. 298-301). Dalian, China: IIHMSP.

Schneier, B. (1994). *Applied cryptography: Protocols, algorithms, and source code in C* (2nd ed.). New York, NY: John Wiley & Sons.

Schulzrinne, H., Casner, S., Frederick, R., & Jacobson, V. (2003). *RTP: A transport protocol for real-time applications, RFC 3550*. Retrieved from http://www.ietf.org

Schyndel, R. G., Tirkel, A. Z., & Osborne, C. F. (1994). A digital watermark. In *Proceedings of International Conference on Image Processing*, (vol 2), (pp. 86-90). Austin, TX: IEEE.

Seadle, M. S., Deller, J. R., Jr., & Gurijala, A. (2002). Why watermark? The copyright need for an engineering solution. In *Proceedings of the 2nd ACM/IEEE-CS Joint Conference on Digital Libraries*, (pp. 324-325). Portland, OR: ACM/IEEE.

Şehirli, M., Gűrgen, F., & Ikizoğlu, S. (2004). Performance evaluation of digital audio watermarking techniques designed in time, frequency and cepstrum domains. *Lecture Notes in Computer Science*, *3261*, 430–440. doi:10.1007/978-3-540-30198-1_44

Seitz, J., & Jahnke, T. (2005). Digital watermarking: An introduction. In Seitz, J. (Ed.), *Digital Watermarking for Digital Media* (p. 13). Hershey, PA: IGI Global. doi:10.4018/978-1-59140-518-4.ch001

Shirali-Shahreza, M. (2008). Text steganography by changing words spelling. In *Proceedings of the 10th International Conference on Advanced Communication Technology*, (pp. 1912-1913). IEEE.

Shirali-Shahreza, M. H., & Shirali-Shahreza, M. (2008). Steganography in SMS by sudoku puzzle. In *Proceedings of the IEEE/ACS International Conference on Computer Systems and Applications 2008*, (pp. 844-847). IEEE Press.

Shirali-Shahreza, M. H., & Shirali-Shahreza, M. (2008). A new synonym text steganography. *Proceedings of the Intelligent Information Hiding and Multimedia Signal Processing*, *2008*, 1524–1526. doi:10.1109/IIH-MSP.2008.6

Shrivastava, S., & Choubey, S. (2011). A secure image based watermark for 3D images. In *Proceedings of the 2011 International Conference on Communication Systems and Network Technologies*, (pp. 559-562). Katra, India: IEEE.

Singh, S. (2000). *The code book: The science of secrecy from ancient Egypt to quantum cryptography*. New York, NY: Anchor Books.

Smith, J. R., Jiang, B., Roy, S., Philipose, M., Sundara-Rajan, K., & Mamishev, A. (2005). ID modulation: Embedding sensor data in an RFID time series. *Lecture Notes in Computer Science*, *3727*, 234–246. doi:10.1007/11558859_18

Soille, P. (1999). *Morphological image analysis: Principles and applications*. Berlin, Germany: Springer.

Sonoda, K., Suzuki, J., & Takizawa, O. (2008). *Information hiding for moving public address audio signal.* Paper presented at the 5th Meeting of the IEICE Technical Group on Multimedia Information Hiding. Sendai, Japan.

Sonoda, K., Yoshioka, K., & Takizawa, O. (2007). *Information hiding for public address audio signals using FH/FSK spread-spectrum scheme.* Paper presented at the 3rd IEEE International Conference on Intelligent Information Hiding and Multimedia Signal Processing. Splendor Kaohsiung, Taiwan.

Sonoda, K., Nishimura, R., & Suzuki, Y. (2004). Blind detection of watermarks embedded by periodical phase shifts. *Acoustical Science and Technology*, *25*(1), 103–105. doi:10.1250/ast.25.103

Soong, F., & Juang, B. (1984). Line spectrum pair (LSP) and speech data compression. In *Proceedings of the IEEE International Conference on Acoustics, Speech and Signal Processing,* (pp. 37–40). IEEE Press.

Spammimic. (2000). *Website.* Retrieved from http://spammimic.com/

Speth, M. (1988). Optimum receiver design for wireless broadband systems using OFDM-part 1. *IEEE Transactions on Communications*, *47*, 1668–1677. doi:10.1109/26.803501

Steinebach, M., Petitcolas, F. A. P., Raynal, F., Dittmann, J., Fontaine, C., & Seibel, C. … Ferri, L. C. (2001). StirMark benchmark: Audio watermarking attacks. In *Proceedings of Coding and Computing 2001*, (pp. 49-54). IEEE.

STEP2001. (2001). News release: Final selection of technology toward the global spread of digital audio watermarks. *Japanese Society for Rights of Authors, Composers and Publishers*. Retrieved from http://www.jasrac.or.jp/ejhp/release/2001/0629.html

Stern, J. P., Hachez, G., Koeune, F., & Quisquater, J.-J. (2000). *Robust* object watermarking: Application to code. In *Proceedings of Information Hiding,* (pp. 368-378). IEEE.

Stirmark. (1998). *Stirmark benchmark 4.0.* Retrieved from http://www.petitcolas.net/fabien/watermarking/stirmark/

Sun, G. (2010). An algorithm of webpage information hiding based on class selectors. In *Proceedings of the Third International Symposium on Intelligent Information Technology and Security Informatics,* (pp. 691-694). IEEE.

Sun, T., Quan, W., & Wang, S. (2002). Zero-watermark watermarking for image authentication. In *Proceeding of the Fourth IASTED International Conference Signal and Image Processing.* IASTED.

Su, P. C., & Kuo, C. C. (2003). Steganography in JPEG2000 compressed images. *IEEE Transactions on Consumer Electronics*, *49*(4), 824–832. doi:10.1109/TCE.2003.1261161

Suzaki, M., & Sudo, M. (2005). A watermark embedding and extracting method for printed documents. *ECJC*, *88*(7), 43–51.

Swaminathan, A., Mao, Y., Wu, M., & Kailas, K. (2005). Data hiding in compiled program binaries for enhancing computer system performance. In *Proceedings of Information Hiding* (pp. 357–371). IEEE. doi:10.1007/11558859_26

Swanson, M., Zhu, B., & Tewfik, A. (1999). Current state-of-the-art, challenges and future directions for audio watermarking. In *Proceedings of the IEEE International Conference on Multimedia Computing and Systems,* (pp. 19-24). Florence, Italy: IEEE Press.

Tachibana, R., Shimizu, S., Kobayashi, S., & Nakamura, T. (2002). An audio watermarking method using a two-dimensional pseudo-random array. *Signal Processing*, *82*(10), 1455–1469. doi:10.1016/S0165-1684(02)00284-0

Tahara, Y., Sato, H., & Nishiwaki, S. (2005). A study on auditory integration characteristics based on critical time delay for distinct perception of echo. *Journal of the Acoustical Society of Japan*, *61*(11), 14–23.

Takahashi, A., Nishimura, R., & Suzuki, Y. (2005). Multiple watermarks for stereo audio signals using phase-modulation techniques. *IEEE Transactions on Signal Processing*, *53*(2), 806–815. doi:10.1109/TSP.2004.839901

Tanaka, S., Niimi, M., & Noda, H. (2007). A study on reversible information hiding using complexity measure for binary images. *IEEE Proceedings of the Intelligent Information Hiding and Multimedia Signal Processing*, *2007*, 29–32.

Tang, C. W., & Hang, H. M. (2003). A feature-based robust digital image watermarking scheme. *IEEE Transactions on Signal Processing*, *51*(4), 950–959. doi:10.1109/TSP.2003.809367

Thodi, D. M., & Rodriguez, J. J. (2007). Expansion embedding techniques for reversible watermarking. *IEEE Transactions on Image Processing*, *16*(3), 721–730. doi:10.1109/TIP.2006.891046

Tian, H., Zhou, K., Jiang, H., Liu, J., Huang, Y., & Feng, D. (2009). An m-sequence based steganography model for voice over IP. In *Proceedings of the International Conference on Communications*, (pp. 1-5). IEEE.

Tian, J. (2003). High capacity reversible data embedding and content authentication. In *Proceedings of the International Conference on Acoustics, Speech, and Signal Processing*, (Vol. 3), (pp. 517-520). IEEE.

Tian, J. (2003). Reversible data embedding using a difference expansion. *IEEE Transactions on Circuits and Systems for Video Technology*, *13*(8), 890–896. doi:10.1109/TCSVT.2003.815962

Topkara, M., Topkara, U., & Atallah, M. J. (2006). Words are not enough: Sentence level natural language watermarking. In *Proceedings of the ACM Workshop on Content Protection and Security*, (pp. 37-46). ACM Press.

Topkara, M., Topkara, U., & Atallah, M. J. (2007). Information hiding through errors: A confusing approach. In *Proceedings of the SPIE International Conference on Security, Steganography, and Watermarking of Multimedia Contents*, (pp. 65050V1-65050V12). IEEE.

Tow, R. F. (1994). *Methods and means for embedding machine readable digital data in halftone images*. US Patent 5 315 098. Washington, DC: US Patent Office.

Tropp, J. A., & Gilbert, A. C. (2007). Signal recovery from random measurements via orthogonal matching pursuit. *IEEE Transactions on Information Theory*, *53*(12), 4655–4666. doi:10.1109/TIT.2007.909108

Tsai, M. J., Yu, K. Y., & Chen, Y. Z. (2000). Joint wavelet and spatial transformation for digital watermarking. *IEEE Transactions on Consumer Electronics*, *46*(1), 241–245.

Tsai, P., Hu, Y. C., & Yeh, H. L. (2009). Reversible image hiding scheme using predictive coding and histogram shifting. *Signal Processing*, *89*(6), 1129–1143. doi:10.1016/j.sigpro.2008.12.017

Tu, S.-C., Hsu, H.-W., & Tai, W.-K. (2010). Permutation steganography for polygonal meshes based on coding tree. *The International Journal of Virtual Reality*, *9*(4), 55–60.

Uchida, S., Iwamura, M., Omachi, S., & Kise, K. (2006). OCR fonts revisited for camera-based character recognition. In *Proceedings of International Conference on Pattern Recognition*, *2*, 1134-1137.

Uchida, S., Sakai, M., Iwamura, M., Omachi, S., & Kise, K. (2007). Extraction of embedded class information from universal character pattern. In *Proceedings of International Conference on Document Analysis and Recognition*, *1*, 437-441.

Uchida, S., Tanaka, K., Iwamura, M., Omachi, S., & Kise, K. (2006). A data-embedding pen. In *Proceedings of International Workshop on Frontiers in Handwriting Recognition*. IEEE.

Upham, D. (1997). *Website*. Retrieved from http://ftp.funet.fi/pub/crypt/cypherpunks/steganography/jsteg/

Vahedi, E., Zoroofi, R. A., & Shiva, M. (2012). Toward a new wavelet-based watermarking approach for color images using bio-inspired optimization principles. *Digital Signal Processing*, *22*, 153–162. doi:10.1016/j.dsp.2011.08.006

Valin, J.-M., & Montgomery, C. (2006). Improved noise weighting in CELP coding of speech - Applying the vorbis psychoacoustic model to speex. In *Proceedings of the 120th AES Convention*. AES.

van der Veen, M., van Leest, A., & Bruekers, F. (2003). *Reversible audio watermarking*. Paper presented at the 114th Audio Engineering Society Convention. Amsterdam, The Netherlands.

Van Schyndel, R. G., & Osborne, C. F. (1994). A digital watermark. In *Proceedings of IEEE International Conference Image Processing*, (pp. 86-90). Austin, TX: IEEE Press.

Varshney, U., Snow, A., McGivern, M., & Howard, C. (2002). Voice over IP. *Communications of the ACM*, *45*(1), 89–96. doi:10.1145/502269.502271

Vary, P., & Geiser, B. (2007). Steganographic wideband telephony using narrowband speech codecs. In *Proceedings of the 41st Asilomer Conference on Signals, Systems and Computers,* (pp. 1475-1479). Asilomer.

Venkatesan, R., Vazirani, V., & Sinha, S. (2001). A graph theoretic approach to software watermarking. In *Proceedings of Information Hiding* (pp. 157–168). IEEE. doi:10.1007/3-540-45496-9_12

VLCC. (2007). *Home page of visible light communications consortium*. Retrieved August 22, 2011, from http://www.vlcc.net/?ml_lang=en

Voloshynovskiy, S., Pereira, S., Pun, T., Su, J. K., & Eggers, J. J. (2001). Attacks and benchmarking. *IEEE Communications Magazine*, *39*(8).

Wang, R., & Hu, W. (2007). Robust audio zero-watermark based on LWT and chaotic modulation. In *Proceeding of International Workshop on Digital Watermarking (IWDW 2007),* (pp. 373–381). IWDW.

Wang, W. X., Xu, H. L., & Li, S. (2009). Double zero-watermarking algorithm on hyperchaotic iteration. In *Proceedings of the Third International Symposium on Intelligent Information Technology Application*. IEEE.

Wang, W., Dong, J., & Tan, T. N. (2009). A survey of passive image tampering detection. In A. T. S. Ho (Ed.), *8th International Workshop on Digital Watermarking,* (pp. 308-322). Guildford, UK: University of Surrey.

Wang, S., Sekey, A., & Gersho, A. (1992). An objective measure for predicting subjective quality of speech coders. *IEEE Journal on Selected Areas in Communications*, *10*(5), 819–829. doi:10.1109/49.138987

Wang, X. Y., & Zhao, H. (2006). A novel synchronization invariant audio watermarking scheme based on DWT and DCT. *IEEE Transactions on Signal Processing*, *54*(12), 4835–4840. doi:10.1109/TSP.2006.881258

Watanabe, A., Katoh, T., Bista, B. B., & Takata, T. (2006). On a watermarking scheme for MusicXML. In *Proceedings of the 20th International Conference on Advanced Information Networking and Applications,* (pp. 894-898). IEEE.

Wayner, P. (2002). *Disappearing cryptography*. San Francisco, CA: Morgan Kaufmann Publishers.

Wayner, P. (2009). *Disappearing cryptography* (3rd ed.). Burlington, MA: Morgan Kaufmann Publishers.

Weibel, N., Ispas, A., Signer, B., & Norrie, M. (2008). Paperproof: A paper-digital proof-editing system. In *Proceedings of ACM Conference on Human Factors in Computing Systems (CHI)*, (pp. 2349-2354). ACM Press.

Weinstein, S. B., & Ebert, P. M. (1971). Data transmission by frequency-division multiplexing using the discrete fourier transform. *IEEE Transactions on Communications, 19*, 628–634. doi:10.1109/TCOM.1971.1090705

Westfeld, A. (2001). F5 - A steganographic algorithm: High capacity despite better steganalysis. *Lecture Notes in Computer Science, 2137*, 289–302. doi:10.1007/3-540-45496-9_21

Wong, P. W., & Memon, N. (2001). Secret an public key image watermarking schemes for image authentication and ownership verification. *IEEE Transactions on Image Processing, 10*(10), 1593–1601. doi:10.1109/83.951543

Wu, Z., & Yang, W. (2006). G.711-based adaptive speech information hiding approach. In *Proceedings of the International Conference of Intelligent Computing,* (pp. 1139-1144). IEEE.

Wu, C. P., & Kuo, C. C. J. (2005). Design of integrated multimedia compression and encryption systems. *IEEE Transactions on Multimedia*, *7*(5), 828–839. doi:10.1109/TMM.2005.854469

Wu, C. W. (2002). On the design of content-based multimedia authentication systems. *IEEE Transactions on Multimedia*, *4*(3), 385–393. doi:10.1109/TMM.2002.802018

Wu, C.-P., Su, P.-C., & Kuo, C.-C. J. (1999). Robust audio watermarking for copyright protection. *Proceedings of the Society for Photo-Instrumentation Engineers, 3807*, 387–397. doi:10.1117/12.367655

Wu, M., & Liu, B. (2003). *Multimedia data hiding*. New York, NY: Springer-Verlag.

Wu, M., & Liu, B. (2004). Data hiding in binary image for authentication and annotation. *IEEE Transactions on Multimedia*, *6*(4), 528–538. doi:10.1109/TMM.2004.830814

Wu, S. Q., Huang, J. W., Huang, D. R., & Shi, Y. Q. (2005). Efficiently self-synchronized audio watermarking for assured audio data transmission. *IEEE Transactions on Broadcasting*, *51*(1), 69–76. doi:10.1109/TBC.2004.838265

Wu, W. C., & Chen, O. (2008). Analysis-by-synthesis echo watermarking. In Cvejic, N., & Seppänen, T. (Eds.), *Digital Audio Watermarking Techniques and Technologies* (pp. 152–171). Hershey, PA: IGI Global.

Wu, Y. (2006). Nonlinear collusion attack on a watermarking scheme for buyer authentication. *IEEE Transactions on Multimedia*, *8*(3), 626–629. doi:10.1109/TMM.2006.870720

Xu, J., & Zeng, G. (2010). A software watermarking algorithm based on stack-state transition graph. In *Proceedings of the 2010 4th International Conference on Network and System Security,* (pp. 83-88). IEEE.

Yan, D., & Wang, R. (2008). *Reversible data hiding for audio based on prediction error expansion.* Paper presented at International Conference on Intelligent Information Hiding and Multimedia Signal Processing. Harbin, China.

Yang, J. (2010). Algorithm of XML document information hiding based on equal element. In *Proceedings of the International Conference on Computer Science and Information Technology*, (pp. 250-253). IEEE.

Yang, W.-J., Chung, K.-L., Yu, W.-K., & Liao, H.-Y. M. (2010). Edge-sensing prediction-based reversible data hiding. In *Proceedings of the Annual Summit and Conference of Asia-Pacific Signal and Information Processing Association*, (pp. 919-922). Biopolis, Singapore: IEEE.

Yang, C. W., & Shen, J. J. (2010). Recover the tampered image based on VQ indexing. *Signal Processing*, *90*(1), 331–343. doi:10.1016/j.sigpro.2009.07.007

Yang, M. (2004). Low bit rate speech coding. *IEEE Potentials*, *23*(4), 32–36. doi:10.1109/MP.2004.1343228

Yardimei, Y., Cetin, A. E., & Ansari, R. (1997). Data hiding in speech using phase coding. *Proceedings of EUROSPEECH*, *1997*, 1679–1682.

Yeo, I.-K., & Kim, H. J. (2001). *Modified patchwork algorithm: A novel audio watermarking scheme*. Paper presented at the International Conference on Information Technology: Coding and Computing. Las Vegas, NV.

Yilmaz, A., & Alatan, A. A. (2003). Error concealment of video sequences by data hiding. In *Proceedings of the International Conference on Image Processing,* (pp. 679–682). IEEE.

Yiqing, L., & Abdulla, M. H. (2008). *Perceptual evaluation of audio watermarking using objective quality measures*. Paper presented at IEEE International Conference on Acoustics, Speech and Signal Processing. Las Vegas, NV.

Yu, G., Zuo, J., & Cui, D. (2011). Performance evaluation of digital audio watermarking algorithm under low bits rates. *Lecture Notes in Computer Science*, *6987*, 336–343. doi:10.1007/978-3-642-23971-7_42

Yura, S., Fujimori, K., Mori, H., & Sakamura, K. (1998). A multimedia MUD (multi-user dungeon) system for the digital museum. In *Proceedings of IEEE 3rd Asia Pacific Computer Human Interaction* (pp. 32–37). IEEE Press.

Zhang, X. P., Qian, Z. X., Ren, Y. L., & Feng, G. R. (2011). Watermarking with flexible self-recovery quality based on compressive sensing and compositive reconstruction. *IEEE Transactions on Information Forensics and Security*, *6*(4), 1223–1232. doi:10.1109/TIFS.2011.2159208

Zhang, X. P., Wang, S. Z., Qian, Z. X., & Feng, G. R. (2011). Reference sharing mechanism for watermark self-embedding. *IEEE Transactions on Image Processing*, *20*(2), 485–495. doi:10.1109/TIP.2010.2066981

Zhu, J., Liu, Y., & Yin, K. (2009). A novel dynamic graph software watermark scheme. In *Proceedings of the 2009 First International Workshop on Education Technology and Computer Science,* (Vol. 3), (pp. 775-780). IEEE.

Zhu, W., & Thomborson, C. (2006). Algorithms to watermark software through register allocation. In *Proceedings of the Digital Rights Management: Technologies, Issues, Challenges and Systems*, (pp. 180-191). IEEE.

Zhu, X. Z., Ho, A. T. S., & Marziliano, P. (2007). A new semi-fragile image watermarking with robust tampering restoration using irregular sampling. *Signal Processing Image Communication*, *22*(5), 515–528. doi:10.1016/j.image.2007.03.004

Zurek, P. M. (1987). The precedence effect. In Yost, W. A., & Gourevitch, G. (Eds.), *Directional Hearing* (pp. 85–105). New York, NY: Springer-Verlag. doi:10.1007/978-1-4612-4738-8_4

Zwicker, E. (1982). *Psychoakustik*. Heidelberg, Germany: Springer-Verlag. doi:10.1007/978-3-642-68510-1

Zwicker, E., & Fastl, H. (1990). *Psychoacoustics facts and models*. Berlin, Germany: Springer-Verlag.

Zwicker, E., & Zwicker, U. T. (1991). Audio engineering and psychoacoustics: Matching signals to the final receiver, the human auditory system. *Journal of the Audio Engineering Society. Audio Engineering Society*, *39*, 115–126.

About the Contributors

Kazuhiro Kondo received the B.E., the M.E., and the Ph.D. degrees from Waseda University in 1982, 1984, and 1998, respectively. From 1984 to 1992, he was with the Central Research Laboratory, Hitachi Limited, Tokyo, Japan, where he was engaged in research on speech and video coding systems. From 1992 to 1995, he was with the Texas Instruments Tsukuba R & D Center, Tsukuba, Japan, and from 1995 to 1998, the DSP R & D Center, Texas Instruments Inc., Dallas, Texas, USA. During this time, he worked on speech recognition systems and multimedia signal processing. In 1999, he joined the Faculty of Engineering at Yamagata University, Yamagata, Japan. His current interests include broad aspects of speech and audio signal processing, multimedia signal processing, and speech and audio quality evaluation methods. Dr. Kondo is a senior member of the IEEE, and a member of the Audio Engineering Society, the Institute of Electronics, Information and Communication Engineers of Japan, and the Acoustical Society of Japan.

* * *

Naofumi Aoki graduated from the bachelor course at the Faculty of Engineering, Hokkaido University in 1995. He graduated from the master course at the Graduate School of Engineering, Hokkaido University in 1997. He received the Ph.D. degree from the Graduate School of Engineering, Hokkaido University in 2000. Currently, he is working at the Graduate School of Information Science and Technology, Hokkaido University, as an Assistant Professor. One of his research interests includes the study of information hiding techniques for enriched multimedia communications.

Masaaki Fujiyoshi is an Assistant Professor of the Department of Information and Communication Systems at Tokyo Metropolitan University (TMU), Japan. He received his B.Arts, M.Eng., and Ph.D. degrees from Saitama University, Japan, in 1995, 1997, and 2001, respectively. In 2001, he joined TMU as a Research Associate of the Department of Electrical Engineering. His research interests include image processing and secure communications, including data hiding for images. He received the IEICE Young Researcher's Award in 2001. He served as a Councilor of the IEICE and the IEICE Tokyo Section. He is a member of the IEEE, the APSIPA, the IEICE, and the ITE.

Hirohisa Hioki received his B.S, M.S, and D.Sc degrees in Computer Science from the University of Tokyo, Japan, in 1992, 1994, and 2000, respectively. In 1997, he started his career as a research associate at Kyoto University, Japan, where he subsequently became and is currently an Associate Professor, since 2003. His research interests include steganography, digital watermarking, augmented reality, and information visualization. He is a member of the IEEE, IPSJ (Information Processing Society of Japan), and the IEICE (Institute of Electronics, Information, and Communication Engineers). He is currently a member of the Editorial Committee of the *IEICE Transactions on Fundamentals of Electronics, Communications, and Computer Sciences* (Japanese Edition).

Rong Huang received the B.S. degree and completed the master course from East China University of Science and Technology, Shanghai, China, in 2008 and 2010, respectively. He is supported by China Scholarship Council (CSC) and currently pursuing the Ph.D. degree in Faculty of Information Science and Electrical Engineering, Kyushu University, Fukuoka, Japan. His research interests include image processing, multimedia security, and pattern recognition.

Akinori Ito was born in Yamagata, Japan, in 1963. He received the B.E., M.E., and Ph. D. degrees from Tohoku University, Sendai, Japan, in 1984, 1986, and 1992, respectively. He is now a Professor of Graduate School of Engineering, Tohoku University. He has engaged in spoken language processing, speech and audio coding, multimedia data processing, and music information processing. He is a member of the Acoustical Society of Japan, the Institute of Electronics, Information and Communication Engineers, the Information Processing Society of Japan, Human Interface Society, and the IEEE.

Mamoru Iwaki was born in Toyama, Japan, in 1966. He received the B.E., M.E., and Dr. Eng. degrees in Electronic and Information Engineering from the University of Tsukuba, Tsukuba, Ibaraki, Japan, in 1989, 1991, and 1994, respectively. He joined the School of Information Science, Japan Advanced Institute of Science and Technology, Hokuriku, Japan, as a Research Associate in April 1994. Since October 1998, he has been an Associate Professor in the Graduate School of Science and Technology, Niigata University, Niigata, Japan. His main research interests include digital signal processing for analysis, synthesis, and recognition of waveforms, especially speech signals, human auditory systems, and bio-signal interpretation. Dr. Iwaki is a member of the Institute of Electrical and Electronics Engineers (IEEE), the Institute of Electronics, Information and Communication Engineers (IEICE) of Japan, and the Acoustical Society of Japan (ASJ).

Keiichi Iwamura received the B.E. and M.E. degrees in Information Engineering from Kyushu University, Japan, in 1980 and 1982, respectively. He received the Ph.D. degree from the Institute of Industrial Science, the University of Tokyo, Japan, in 1994. He joined Canon Inc. in 1982 and resigned Canon in 2006 and moved to Tokyo University of Science. He is currently a Professor of the Department of Electrical Engineering. He received CSS Paper Award in 2003 and FIT Paper Award in 2011 from IPSJ. His research interests are information security, network communication, information theory, and image processing. He is a member of IPSJ, IEICE, and IEEE.

Masakazu Iwamura received his B.E., M.E., and Ph. D degrees in Engineering from Tohoku University, Japan, in 1998, 2000, and 2003, respectively. He is an Associate Professor of the Department of Computer Science and Intelligent Systems, Osaka Prefecture University, Japan. His research interests include scene text recognition, document image retrieval, and object recognition. He received the best paper award from IEICE in 2008, the IAPR/ICDAR best paper award of ICDAR2007, the IAPR Nakano award of DAS2010, the best paper awards of ICFHR2010. He is now the webmaster of IAPR TC11 (Reading Systems).

Kitahiro Kaneda received the B.E. and M.E. degrees in Mechanical Engineering from Waseda University, Japan, in 1984 and 1986, respectively. He received the M.E. degree in Electrical Engineering from Duke University, USA, in 1995. He received the Ph.D. degree in Electrical Engineering from Tokyo University of Science, Japan, in 2010. He has been working on a technology development related to printer and camera in Canon Inc. since 1986 and is currently a General Manager of Applied Software Technology Development Center. He received FIT Paper Award from IPSJ in 2011. His research interests are image and character recognition, image processing, and security. He is a member of IPSJ and IIEEJ.

Koichi Kise received the B.E., M.E., and Ph.D. degrees in Communication Engineering from Osaka University, Osaka, Japan, in 1986, 1988, and 1991, respectively. From 2000 to 2001, he was a visiting professor at German Research Center for Artificial Intelligence (DFKI), Germany. He is now a Professor of the Department of Computer Science and Intelligent Systems, Osaka Prefecture University, Japan. His research interests include object recognition, document analysis, and retrieval. He received the best paper award from IEICE in 2008, the IAPR/ICDAR best paper award of ICDAR2007, the IAPR Nakano award of DAS2010, the best paper awards of ICFHR2010 and ACPR2011. He is now the vice chair of IAPR TC11 (Reading Systems), and a member of IAPR Conference and Meetings Committee.

Hitoshi Kiya is a Professor of the Department of Information and Communication Systems and a Board Member of the Faculty of System Design at Tokyo Metropolitan University (TMU), Japan. He received his B.Eng. and M.Eng. degrees from Nagaoka University of Technology, Japan, in 1980 and 1982, respectively, and a Dr. Eng. degree from TMU in 1987. In 1982, he joined TMU where he became a Full Professor in 2000. His research interests are in the areas of multirate signal processing and image processing. In these areas, he has published over 300 refereed papers in leading international conferences and journals. He authored seven books and co-authored three books. He received the Telecommunications Advancement Foundation Award in 2011 and the IEICE Best Paper Award in 2008. He is a Fellow of the IEICE and the ITE, a senior member of the IEEE, and a member of the APSIPA and the EURASIP.

O-Hyung Kwon was born in Pusan, Korea, in 1958. He received the B.S., M.S., and PhD. degrees in Electronic Engineering from Sogang University, Seoul, Korea, in 1981, 1983, and 2004, respectively. Since 1983, he has worked at Broadcasting and Telecommunications Convergence Future Technology Research Department of Creative and Challenging Research Division of Electronics and Telecommunications Research Institute (ETRI) as a Managing Director. Since 2002, he is a Vice President of Korea Digital Cable Forum (KDCF). His research interests are in multimedia content protection and digital CATV transmission.

Marcus Liwicki received his M.S. degree in Computer Science from the Free University of Berlin, Germany, in 2004, and his PhD degree from the University of Bern, Switzerland, in 2007. Subsequently, he successfully finished his Habiliation and received the Postdoctoral Lecture Qualification from the Technical University of Kaiserslautern, Germany, in 2011. Currently, he is a Senior Researcher and Private Lecturer at the German Research Center for Artificial Intelligence (DFKI). His research interests include knowledge management, semantic desktop, electronic pen-input devices, on-line and off-line handwriting recognition, and document analysis. From October 2009 to March 2010, he visited Kyushu University (Fukuoka, Japan). He has more than 80 publications, including more than ten journal papers.

Hosei Matsuoka is a Research Engineer at NTT DOCOMO's Research Laboratories. His research interests are in multimedia signal processing and transport technology for future mobile communications. He has a BS and an MS in Information Science from the Tokyo Institute of Technology.

Ryota Miyauchi is an Assistant Professor of School of Information Science, Japan Advanced Institute of Science and Technology (JAIST). He received his Ph.D. (Design) from the Kyushu Institute of Design in 2005. His main research field is experimental psychology, in particular, psychoacoustics, temporal and spatial perception, and multimodal perception.

Toshio Modegi was born in Tokyo, 1959. He received the BE degree in Electronic Engineering from Chiba University, Japan in 1982. Since April 1982, he has been working with several fields of research laboratories of Dai Nippon Printing Co., Ltd., Tokyo, Japan. From October 1995 to March 1998, he also worked as a Visiting Researcher in the Communications Research Laboratory of the Ministry of Post and Telecommunications, Japan. Currently, he is a Senior Researcher in the Media Technology Research Center, Dai Nippon Printing Co., Ltd. Since April 2003, he has been also a part-time Lecturer in Shobi University, Saitama, Japan. Some of his research works showed in this book were awarded by the SICE Annual Conference 2005 of the Society of Instrument and Control Engineers, and the MBL Special Interest Group of Information Processing Society of Japan in 2008.

Michiharu Niimi received B.E. and M.E. degrees in Computer Engineering from Kyushu Institute of Technology, Japan, in 1992 and 1994, respectively. He then worked at Nagasaki Institute of Applied Science. He moved to Faculty of Engineering, Kyushu Institute of Technology, in 1996. He received Dr. Eng. from Kyushu Institute of Technology, Japan, in 2003. Since 2007, He has been an Associate Professor at Faculty of Computer Science and Systems Engineering, Kyushu Institute of Technology. His research interests include multimedia information processing, image processing, and media security.

Akira Nishimura was born in Kochi, Japan. He received B. Eng. and M. Eng. degrees in Acoustics from Kyushu Institute of Design in 1990 and 1992, respectively. He received his Ph.D. in Audio Information Hiding from Kyushu University in 2011. Since 1996, he is a faculty member of Tokyo University of Information Sciences. He is a Professor in the Department of Media and Cultural Studies. His current research interests are auditory modeling, audio information hiding, musical acoustics, and psychology of music. He is a member of Acoustical Society of Japan, Audio Engineering Society, IEEE, and Japanese Society of Music and Cognition. He was awarded the best paper award from the IEEE International Conference on Intelligent Information Hiding and Multimedia Signal Processing (IIH-MSP 2011) in 2011. He was also awarded the Sato Prize from Acoustical Society of Japan in 2012.

Hideki Noda received B.E. and M.E. from Kyushu University, Japan, in 1973 and 1975, respectively, and Dr. Eng. from Kyushu Institute of Technology, Japan, in 1993. He worked in the National Research Institute of Police Science, Japan National Police Agency, and then in Communications Research Laboratory, Japan Ministry of Posts and Telecommunications. In 1995, he moved to Kyushu Institute of Technology, where he is now a Professor. His research interests include speaker and speech recognition, image processing, and information security.

Shinichiro Omachi received his B.E., M.E., and Doctor of Engineering degrees in Information Engineering from Tohoku University, Japan, in 1988, 1990, and 1993, respectively. He is currently a professor of Graduate School of Engineering, Tohoku University. From 2000 to 2001, he was a Visiting Associate Professor at Brown University, USA. His research interests include pattern recognition, computer vision, image processing, and parallel processing. He received the IAPR/ICDAR Best Paper Award in 2007, Best Paper Method Award of 33rd Annual Conference of the GfKl in 2010, and the ICFHR Best Paper Award in 2010.

Rae-Hong Park was born in Seoul, Korea, in 1954. He received the B.S. and M.S. degrees in Electronics Engineering from Seoul National University, Seoul, Korea, in 1976 and 1979, respectively, and the M.S. and Ph.D. degrees in Electrical Engineering from Stanford University, CA, in 1981 and 1984, respectively. In 1984, he joined the faculty of the Department of Electronic Engineering, School of Engineering, Sogang University, Seoul, Korea, where he is currently a Professor. In 1990, he spent his sabbatical year as a Visiting Associate Professor with the Computer Vision Laboratory, University of Maryland at College Park. Dr. Park was the recipient of a 1990 Post-Doctoral Fellowship (KOSEF), the 1987 Academic Award (KITE), and the 2000 Haedong Paper Award (IEEK), the 1997 First Sogang Academic Award, and the 1999 Professor Achievement Excellence Award presented by Sogang University. He is a Senior Member of the IEEE. His current research interests are computer vision, video communication, and pattern recognition.

Kyung-Hyune Rhee received his M.S. and Ph.D. degrees from Korea Advanced Institute of Science and Technology (KAIST), Daejon Korea in 1985 and 1992, respectively. He worked as a Senior Researcher in Electronic and Telecommunications Research Institute (ETRI), Daejon, Korea, from 1985 to 1993. He also worked as a Visiting Scholar in the University of Adelaide in Australia, the University of Tokyo in Japan, the University of California at Irvine in USA, and Kyushu University in Japan. He has served as a Chairman of Technician Education in Manila, the Philippines. He is currently a Professor in the Department of IT Convergence and Application Engineering, Pukyong National University, Busan Korea. His research interests center on multimedia security and analysis, key management protocols, and mobile ad-hoc and VANET communication security.

Kouichi Sakurai received the B.S degree in Mathematics from the Faculty of Science, Kyushu University, and the M.S degree in Applied Science from the Faculty of Engineering, Kyushu University, in 1986 and 1988, respectively. He had been engaged in the research and development on the cryptography and information security at the Computer and Information Systems Laboratory at Mitsubishi Electric Corporation from 1988 to 1994. He received D.E. degree from the Faculty of Engineering, Kyushu University in 1993. Since 1994, he has been working for the Department of Computer Science of Kyushu University as Associate Professor, and now he is Full Professor from 2002. His current research interests are in cryptography and information security. Dr. Sakurai is a member of the Information Processing Society of Japan, the Mathematical Society of Japan, ACM, and the International Association for Cryptologic Research.

Yôiti Suzuki graduated from Tohoku University in 1976 and received his Ph. D. degree in Electrical and Communication Engineering in 1981. He is currently a Professor at the Research Institute of Electrical Communication, Tohoku University. His research interests include psychoacoustics, high-definition auditory display, and digital signal processing of acoustic signals. He received the Awaya Kiyoshi Award and Sato Prize from the Acoustical Society of Japan.

Seiichi Uchida received B.E., M.E., and Dr. Eng. degrees from Kyushu University in 1990, 1992, and 1999, respectively. From 1992 to 1996, he joined SECOM Co., Ltd., Tokyo, Japan, where he worked on speech processing. Currently, he is a Professor at Faculty of Information Science and Electrical Engineering, Kyushu University. His research interests include pattern recognition and image processing. He received 2007 IAPR/ICDAR Best Paper Award, 2009 IEICE Best Paper Award, and 2010 ICFHR Best Paper Award.

Masashi Unoki is an Associate Professor of School of Information Science, Japan Advanced Institute of Science and Technology (JAIST) since April 2005. He received his M.S. and Ph.D. (Information Science) from the JAIST in 1996 and 1999, respectively. His main research interests are auditory-motivated signal processing, the modeling of auditory systems, and digital-audio/speech information hiding techniques. He was a JSPS research fellow from 1998 to 2001. He was associated with the Advanced Telecommunications Research Institute (ATR) Human Information Processing Laboratories as a Visiting Researcher during 1999-2000, and from 2000 to 2001, he was a Visiting Research Associate at the Centre for the Neural Basis of Hearing (CNBH) in the Dept. of Physiology at the University of Cambridge. He has been on the faculty of the School of Information Science at JAIST since 2001, and he is now an Associate Professor.

Rimba Whidiana Ciptasari received the M.Eng degree in Software Engineering from Bandung Institute of Technology (ITB), Indonesia, in 2005. She is currently pursuing the Ph.D degree in Graduate School of Information Science and Electrical Engineering, Department of Informatics, Information Technology and Multimedia Security Laboratory, Kyushu University, under the supervision of Professor Kouichi Sakurai. Her master thesis is concerning text image watermarking, while her current research is in image forensic. Her research interest includes information hiding, image processing, and multimedia security. She is also a faculty member at Faculty of Informatics, Telkom Institute of Technology, Indonesia.

Index

D

E

F

G

H

I

J

L

M

N

O

P

Q

R

S

T

U

V

W

Y

Z